Image Processing, Analysis and Machine Vision

Image Processing, Analysis and Machine Vision

Milan Sonka PhD
University of Iowa
Iowa City, USA

Vaclav Hlavac PhD
Czech Technical University
Prague, Czech Republic

and

Roger Boyle DPhil, MBCS, CEng
University of Leeds
Leeds, UK

CHAPMAN & HALL COMPUTING
London · Glasgow · New York · Tokyo · Melbourne · Madras

Published by Chapman & Hall, 2–6 Boundary Row, London SE1 8HN

Chapman & Hall, 2–6 Boundary Row, London SE1 8HN, UK

Blackie Academic & Professional, Wester Cleddens Road, Bishopbriggs, Glasgow G64 2NZ, UK

Chapman & Hall Inc., 29 West 35th Street, New York NY10001, USA

Chapman & Hall Japan, Thomson Publishing Japan, Hirakawacho Nemoto Building, 6F, 1–7–11 Hirakawa-cho, Chiyoda-ku, Tokyo 102, Japan

Chapman & Hall Australia, Thomas Nelson Australia, 102 Dodds Street, South Melbourne, Victoria 3205, Australia

Chapman & Hall India, R. Seshadri, 32 Second Main Road, CIT East, Madras 600 035, India

First edition 1993

© 1993 Milan Sonka, Vaclav Hlavac and Roger Boyle

Printed in Great Britain at the University Press, Cambridge

ISBN 0 412 45570 6

Contents

FEB 15 1994

List of Algorithms

List of symbols and abbreviations

$\emptyset$	empty set
A^c	complement of the set A
$A \subset B,\ B \supset A$	set A is included in set B
$A \cap B$	intersection between sets A and B
$A \cup B$	union of sets A and B
$A \mid B$	difference between sets A and B
$\mid x \mid$	absolute value of a scalar
$\tilde{x}$	estimate of the value x
div	integer division
mod	remainder after integer division
$round(x)$	largest integer which is not bigger than $x + 0.5$
$\mathbf{x}$	(lower case bold) vectors
$\mathbf{A}$	(upper case bold) matrices
$\mid \mathbf{f} \mid$	magnitude (or modulus) of the vector $\mathbf{f}$
$\frac{\partial f}{\partial x}$	partial derivative of the function f with respect to x
$grad\,\mathbf{f},\ \nabla\,\mathbf{f}$	gradient of $\mathbf{f}$
$\nabla^2\,\mathbf{f}$	Laplace operator applied to $\mathbf{f}$
$\mathbf{f} \cdot \mathbf{g}$	scalar product between vectors $\mathbf{f}$ and $\mathbf{g}$
$\Delta\,x$	small finite interval of x, difference
$\delta(x)$	Dirac function
$f * g$	convolution between functions f and g
$\mathcal{E}$	mean value operator
$\mathcal{L}$	linear operator
$\mathcal{O}$	origin of the coordinate system
D_E	Euclidean distance (see section 2.3.1)
D_4	city block distance (see section 2.3.1)
D_8	chessboard distance (see section 2.3.1)
$F^\#$	complex conjugate of the complex function F
$\#$	number of (e.g. pixels)
T^*	transformation dual to transformation T

$\check{B}$	point set symmetrical to point set B
$\oplus$	morphological dilation
$\ominus$	morphological erosion
$\circ$	morphological opening
$\bullet$	morphological closing
$\otimes$	morphological hit or miss transformation
$\oslash$	morphological thinning
$\odot$	morphological thickening
arg(x,y)	angle (in radians) from x axis to the point (x, y)

1D	one dimension(al)
2D	two dimension(al)
3D	three dimension(al)
AI	artificial intelligence
B-rep	boundary representation
CAD	computer aided design
CCD	charge coupled device
CSG	constructive solid geometry
CT	computer tomography
ECG	electro-cardiogram
EEG	electro-encephalogram
FFT	fast Fourier transform
FOE	focus of expansion
GA	genetic algorithm
IHS	intensity, hue, saturation
JPEG	Joint Photographic Experts Group
MR	magnetic resonance
MRI	magnetic resonance imaging
OCR	optical character recognition
OS	order statistics
PET	positron emission tomography
PMF	Pollard-Mayhew-Frisby (correspondence algorithm)
RGB	red, green, blue
TV	television

Preface

Image Processing, Analysis and Machine Vision represent an exciting part of modern cognitive and computer science. Following an explosion of interest during the Seventies, the Eighties were characterized by the maturing of the field and the significant growth of active applications; Remote Sensing, Technical Diagnostics, Autonomous Vehicle Guidance and Medical Imaging are the most rapidly developing areas. This progress can be seen in an increasing number of software and hardware products on the market as well as in a number of digital image processing and machine vision courses offered at universities world-wide.

There are many texts available in the areas we cover – most (indeed, all of which we know) are referenced somewhere in this book. The subject suffers, however, from a shortage of texts at the 'elementary' level – that appropriate for undergraduates beginning or completing their studies of the topic, or for Master's students – and the very rapid developments that have taken and are still taking place, which quickly age some of the very good text books produced over the last decade or so. This book reflects the authors' experience in teaching one and two semester undergraduate and graduate courses in Digital Image Processing, Digital Image Analysis, Machine Vision, Pattern Recognition and Intelligent Robotics at their respective institutions. We hope that this combined experience will give a thorough grounding to the beginner and provide material that is advanced enough to allow the more mature student fully to understand the relevant areas of the subject. At the same time, we hope that the book is up to date in as many respects as possible, although we acknowledge that in a very short time the more active areas will have moved on.

This book could have been arranged in many ways. It begins with low-level processing and works its way up to higher levels of image interpretation; the authors have chosen this framework because they believe that image understanding originates from a common data base of information. The book is formally divided into fourteen chapters, beginning with low-level processing and working toward higher level image representation, although this structure will be less apparent after Chapter 9 when we present transforms, compression, morphology, texture, etc. which are very useful but often special purpose approaches that may not always be included in the processing chain. Decimal section numbering is used, and equations and figures are numbered within each chapter; further, each chapter is accompanied by an extensive list of references. A selection of algorithms is summarized formally in a manner that should aid implementation – we have not presented all the algorithms discussed in this way (an approach that would have perhaps doubled the length of the book) but have chosen what we regard as the key, or most useful or illustrative, examples for this treatment.

Each chapter presents material from an introductory level through to an overview of current work; as such, it is unlikely that the beginner will, at the first reading, expect to absorb all of a given topic. Often it has been necessary to make reference to material in later Chapters and Sections, but when this is done an understanding of material in hand will not depend on an understanding of that which comes later. It is expected that the more advanced student will use the book as a reference text and signpost to current activity in the field – we believe at the time of going to press that the reference list is full in its indication of current directions, but record here our apologies to any work we have overlooked. The serious reader will note that many references are very recent, and should be aware that before long more relevant work will have been published that is not listed here.

This is a long book and therefore contains material sufficient for much more than one course. Clearly, there are many ways of using it, but for guidance we suggest an ordering that would generate four distinct modules as follows;

Digital Image Processing. An undergraduate course, using Chapters and Sections 1, 2.1.1, 2.3.1, 2.3.2, 2.3.5, 3.1, 3.2.1, 3.2.2, 4.1, 4.2, 4.3.1, 4.3.2, 4.4.1, 4.4.2, 5.1.1, 5.1.2, 5.2.1, 5.2.3, 5.2.6 - 5.2.8, 5.3.1, 11 and 12. Suitable assignments might be chosen from among: Display images at different resolutions, or with different numbers of grey levels; compute and display an image histogram; conduct experiments with image acquisition (appropriate lighting, resolution, image acquisition for different processing goals, etc.); generate noisy images (additive and multiplicative noise); correct systematic errors of image acquisition caused by lighting and/or camera using pixel brightness corrections; compute and display images after grey scale transforms; compute and display histogram-equalized images; compute and display images after geometric transforms (size, rotation); reduce noise in noisy images using different image smoothing methods; compute edge images using different edge detectors; compute segmented images using interactive thresholding; compute segmented images as thresholded edge images; compute image Fourier frequency spectra; conduct low-pass and high-pass filtering in the frequency domain; filter images with periodic noise in the frequency domain; compare performance of several image compression methods; and reconstruct images after a known degradation.

Image Analysis. An undergraduate/graduate course, for which Digital Image Processing may be regarded as prerequisite, using Chapters and Sections 1, 2 (for review), 3, 4.3.3, 4.3.4, 4.3.8, 5.1, 5.2, 5.3, 6.1 6.2.1 - 6.2.6, 6.3, 7.1, 7.2, 10, 13.1 and 13.4. Suitable assignments might be chosen from among: Implement a zero crossing edge detector; apply a zero crossing edge detector at different scales, compare and discuss results; implement threshold segmentation with automatic threshold detection; implement threshold segmentation with variable local thresholds; implement threshold segmentation for multispectral images; implement basic mathematical morphology transformations; use mathematical morphology for noise removal from binary images; using mathematical morphology, compute skeletons of objects; for objects segmented from an image, compute their shape characteristics; implement a simple minimum distance statistical classifier; implement a simple cluster analysis method; implement an object recognition system that automatically recognizes simple objects in images (image acquisition, pre-processing, segmentation, object description, classifier training, classification); implement different texture description methods; and implement a texture recognition system and compare performance of different texture descriptors.

Computer Vision I. An undergraduate/graduate course, for which Digital Image Processing may be regarded as prerequisite, using Chapters and Sections 1, 2 (for review), 3, 4.3.3 - 4.3.6, 5.1 (for review), 5.2.2, 5.2.4 - 5.2.6, 5.3, 5.4, 6, 7.1 - 7.4, and 8.1. Suitable assignments might be chosen from among: Implement zero crossing edge detection; discuss the role of scale-space edge detection on particular examples; implement a simplified version of the Canny edge detector; implement graph search border detection algorithms (heuristic graph search, dynamic programming); implement a Hough transform for detection of lines, circles, ellipses, and general shapes in noisy images; implement an edge relaxation method and discuss the role of seeking a global image maximum – compare results after varying numbers of iterations; implement region growing segmentation methods using different region homogeneity criteria; implement region merging via boundary melting and discuss its strengths; implement image matching segmentation and apply appropriate matching strategies; for objects segmented from an image, compute their statistical shape description; for objects segmented from an image, compute their syntactic shape description; use a statistical classifier for object recognition; use neural networks for object recognition; and use a syntactic classifier for object recognition.

Computer Vision II. A graduate course, for which Computer Vision I may be regarded as prerequisite, using Chapters and Sections 7.5, 7.6, 8, 9, 13 and 14. Suitable assignments might be chosen from among: Implement a method for detection of graph isomorphism; implement a method for evaluation of graph similarity; implement a genetic algorithm optimization; implement a method for contextual image classification; implement a method for scene labelling and constraint propagation; implement a method for semantic region growing; implement a stereo correspondence algorithm; implement a method for syntactic texture description; implement a method for computation of optical flow; and based on an image motion sequence, determine the focus of expansion for a simple motion, determine possible collisions, and time to collision for two objects in simple motion.

What are, or are not, important parts of a course, and necessary prerequisites, will naturally be specified locally. Assignments should wherever possible make use of existing libraries and packages; it is our experience that courses of this nature should not be seen as 'programming courses', but it is the case that the more direct practical experience the students have of the material discussed, the better is their understanding.

The book has been prepared using the LaTeX text processing system. Its completion would have been impossible without extensive usage of the Internet computer network and electronic mail. We should like to acknowledge the Czech Technical University, the University of Iowa and the School of Computer Studies at Leeds University for providing the environment in which this book was prepared. In particular, the assistance of Leeds University in providing hard copy facilities was invaluable.

Milan Sonka was a faculty member of the Department of Control Engineering, Faculty of Electrical Engineering, Czech Technical University, Prague, Czech Republic for ten years, and now has a four-year visiting position at the Department of Electrical and Computer Engineering, University of Iowa, Iowa City, Iowa, USA. His research interests include medical image analysis, knowledge-based image analysis, and machine vision. Vaclav Hlavac is a faculty member at the Department of Control Engineering, Czech Technical University, Prague. His research interests are knowledge-based image analysis and 3D model-based vision. Roger Boyle lectures in the School of Computer Studies at the University of Leeds, England, where his research interests are in low-level vision and pattern recognition. The first two authors have worked together for some years, and we are grateful to the publisher for introducing the third to them.

The authors have spent many hours in discussions with their teachers, colleagues, and students from which many improvements to early drafts of this text resulted. Particular thanks are due to Václav Chalupa, Zdeněk Kotek, Radek Mařík, Michal Meloun, Jiří Matas, Mirko Navara, Miroslav Svoboda, and Jaroslav Woska at the Czech Technical University; Steve Collins, David Fisher, David Forsyth, and Joe Kearney at the University of Iowa; Jussi Parkkinen at the University of Kuopio, Finland; David Hogg and Richard

Thomas at the University of Leeds, and many others whose omission from this list does not diminish the value of their contribution. Future domestic life would be jeopardised if we did not also mention the continuous support and encouragement we received from our wives and families, for which we are very grateful (and to whom we promise that our next book will not be written outside standard office hours or during holidays).

Chapter 1 was written by Roger Boyle and Vaclav Hlavac. Chapters 2, 3, 4 (except Section 4.3.8), and 10 were written by Vaclav Hlavac. Chapters 5, 6, 7, 8, 11, 12, 13, 14, and Section 4.3.8 were written by Milan Sonka. Chapter 9 was written by Roger Boyle, who collated the text. However, any errors of fact are the joint responsibility of all the authors, while any errors of typography are the responsibility of Roger Boyle. Jointly, they will be glad to incorporate any corrections into future editions.

Milan Sonka (sonka@suzie.eng.uiowa.edu)
University of Iowa, Iowa City, Iowa, USA

Vaclav Hlavac (hlavac@vision.felk.cvut.cs)
Czech Technical University, Prague, Czech Republic

Roger Boyle (roger@scs.leeds.ac.uk)
University of Leeds, Leeds, England

1

Introduction

Vision allows humans to perceive and understand the world surrounding them. Computer vision aims to duplicate the effect of human vision by electronically perceiving and understanding an image. Giving computers the ability to see is not an easy task – we live in a three-dimensional (3D) world, and when computers try to analyse objects in 3D space, available visual sensors (e.g. TV cameras) usually give two-dimensional (2D) images, and this projection to a lower number of dimensions incurs an enormous loss of information. Dynamic scenes such as those to which we are accustomed, with moving objects or a moving camera, make computer vision even more complicated.

An image analysis problem will illustrate a few commonly encountered problems. Figure 1.1 shows the ozone layer hole over Antarctica, as captured

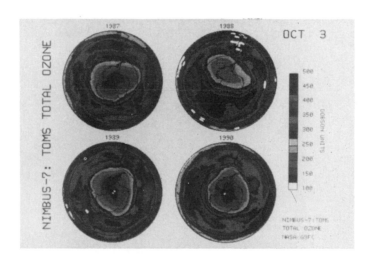

Figure 1.1 *The ozone layer hole. A colour version of this picture may be seen in the colour inset. Courtesy NASA, Goddard Space Flight Center, Greenbelt, Md.*

by apparatus on board NASA's Nimbus 7 satellite over a period of years: 'TOMS' here stands for Total Ozone Mapping Spectrometer, and Dobson

1

units are standard units (multiple of molecules per cubic centimetre) used in ozone mapping – the normal value is about 300 Dobson units and so depletion is obvious in these pictures. The ozone hole is observed to open each year between September and November; shortly after the last picture in this sequence was taken, the lowest ever level was recorded (110 Dobson units on 6th October 1991 [Appenzeller 91]).

It is natural to investigate ways in which pictures like these may be analysed automatically – the *qualitative* conclusion that there is a trend towards ozone depletion should be available from the changes in colours between the successive pictures, and we might also hope for some *quantitative* conclusions saying exactly how much change is occurring. In fact, though, these pictures contain formidable quantities of information that make them far from trivial to analyse. In the picture presented, a great deal of computer processing has already been applied in the form of intensity normalization, geometric transformation and a number of other filters which will be described in later chapters. Overlooking all the textual annotation, and concentrating on just the most recent shot, Figure 1.2 shows the result of some very early processing

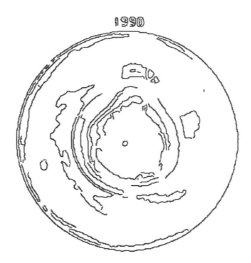

Figure 1.2 *Early processing of part of Figure 1.1.*

that we might perform in an attempt to process the information *beyond* requirements simply of display (that is, for human inspection) – this picture is the result of applying algorithms described fully in Chapter 4. The purpose of deriving this picture might be to delimit accurately the regions visible in the original, then to assign labels related to ozone concentration to each one, and then to draw conclusions about overall concentrations and trends. We see that, while some of the clear evidence in the original is still visible, not all of it is, and we would have a significant amount of further work to do on the early processing before being able to proceed. Several of the boundaries are incomplete, while some significant information has disappeared altogether. These are problems that will be discussed, and solutions presented, in later chapters. Following this stage would come higher level analysis in which numbers derived from the scale on the right of Figure 1.1 would be attached to the regions of Figure 1.2 – here we would make reference to the colours detected within the regions located, and would probably deploy high-level ('domain') knowledge, such as expecting ozone concentration to vary continuously across the surface of the globe. This sequence of operations – image capture, early processing, region extraction, region labelling, high-level identification, qualitative/quantitative conclusion – is characteristic of image understanding and computer vision problems.

This example is a relatively simple one, however many computer vision techniques use the results and methods of mathematics, pattern recognition, artificial intelligence (AI), psycho-physiology, computer science, electronics, and other scientific disciplines. In order to simplify the task of computer vision understanding, two levels are usually distinguished; *low-level* image processing and *high-level* image understanding.

Low-level methods usually use very little knowledge about the content of images. In the case of the computer knowing image content, it is usually provided by high-level algorithms or directly by a human who knows the problem domain. Low-level methods often include image compression, pre-processing methods for noise filtering, edge extraction and image sharpening, all of which we shall discuss in this book. Low-level image processing uses data which resemble the input image; for example, an input image captured by a TV camera is 2D in nature, being described by an image function whose value is usually brightness depending on two parameters, the co-ordinates of the location in the image. If the image is to be processed using a computer it will be digitized first, after which it may be represented by a rectangular matrix with elements corresponding to the brightness at appropriate image locations. Such matrices are the inputs and outputs of low-level image processing.

High-level processing is based on knowledge, goals, and plans of how to achieve those goals. Artificial intelligence (AI) methods are used in many cases. High-level computer vision tries to imitate human cognition and the ability to make decisions according to the information contained in the image. In the example described, high-level knowledge would be the continuity of the ozone concentration figures (that is, they do not change too sharply between closely neighbouring areas), and the fact that areas of similar concentration appear as (distorted) annuli centred at the polar area.

Computer vision is based on high-level processing and the cognition process is tightly bound to prior knowledge about image content (semantics). An image is mapped into a formalized model of the world, but this model does not remain unchanged. Although the initial model may consist of some general

a priori knowledge, high-level processing constantly extracts new information
from the images, and updates and clarifies the knowledge.

High-level vision begins with a formal model of the world and the 'reality'
perceived in the form of digitized images is compared to the model. When
differences between the model and perceived reality emerge, new partial goals
are made and the computer switches to low-level image processing to find
information needed to update the model. This process is then repeated iteratively, and 'understanding' an image thereby becomes more than merely a
bottom-up process. A feedback loop is introduced in which high-level partial
results create tasks for low-level image processing, and the iterative image
understanding process should eventually converge to the global goal.

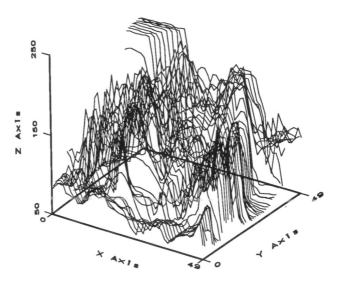

Figure 1.3 *An unusual image representation.*

Computer vision is expected to solve very complex tasks, the goal being
to obtain similar results to those provided by biological systems. To illustrate
the complexity of these tasks, consider Figure 1.3 in which a particular image
representation is presented – the value on the vertical axis gives the brightness
of its corresponding location in the image. Consider what this image might
be before looking at Figure 1.4 overleaf which is a rather more common representation of the same image. Both representations contain exactly the same
information[1], but for a human observer it is very difficult to find a correspon-

---

[1]This is not entirely true in this example – the plot (Figure 1.3) has had some information

dence between them, and without the second, it is unlikely that one would recognize the face of a child. The point is that a lot of a priori knowledge is used by humans to interpret the images; the machine only ever begins with an array of numbers and so will be attempting to make identifications and draw conclusions from data that to us is more like Figure 1.3 than Figure 1.4. Internal image representations are not directly understandable – while the computer is able to process local parts of the image, it is difficult for it to locate global knowledge. General knowledge, domain-specific knowledge and information extracted from the image will be essential in attempting to 'understand' these arrays of numbers.

Low-level computer vision techniques overlap almost completely with digital image processing, which has been practiced for decades. The following sequence of processing steps is commonly recognized: An image is captured by a sensor (such as a TV camera) and digitized; then the computer suppresses noise (image pre-processing) and maybe enhances some object features which are relevant to understanding the image. Edge extraction is an example of processing carried out at this stage.

Image segmentation is the next step, in which the computer tries to separate objects from the image background. Total and partial segmentation may be distinguished; total segmentation is possible only for very simple tasks, an example being the recognition of dark non-touching objects from a light background. In more complicated problems (the general case), low-level image processing techniques handle the partial segmentation tasks, in which only the cues which will aid further high-level processing are extracted. Often finding parts of object boundaries is an example of low-level partial segmentation.

Object description and classification in a totally segmented image is also understood as part of low-level image processing. Other low-level operations are image compression, and techniques to extract information from moving scenes.

Low-level image processing and high-level computer vision differ in the data used. Original images represented by matrices composed of brightness values comprise low-level data, while high-level data originates in images as well, but only those data which are relevant to high-level goals are extracted, reducing the data quantity considerably. High-level data represent knowledge about the image content – for example object size, shape, and mutual relations between objects in the image. High-level data are usually expressed in symbolic form.

Most current low-level image processing methods were proposed in the Seventies or earlier. Recent research is trying to find more efficient and more general algorithms and is implementing them on more technologically sophisticated equipment – in particular, parallel machines are being used to ease the enormous computational load of operations conducted on image data sets.

---

removed for the purpose of clarity of display.

A complicated and so far unsolved problem is how to order low-level steps to solve a specific task, and the aim of automating this problem has not yet been achieved. It is usually still a human operator who finds a sequence of relevant operations, and domain-specific knowledge and uncertainty cause much to depend on this operator's intuition and previous experience. It is not surprising that in the Eighties many projects focused on this problem using expert systems, but expert systems do not solve the problem by themselves. They only allow the use of conflicting opinions of experts in the field.

High-level vision tries to extract and order image processing steps using all available knowledge – image understanding is the heart of the method, in which feedback from high-level to low-level is used. Unsurprisingly this task is very complicated and compute intensive. David Marr's book [Marr 82] influenced computer vision considerably throughout the Eighties; it described a new methodology and computational theory inspired by biological vision systems.

Computer vision uses pattern recognition and AI techniques and terminology, and where necessary, concepts from these disciplines will be explained in the appropriate chapters of this book. However, it is important to explain a few of them here in order to have a common vocabulary for our basic ideas.

Figure 1.4 *Another representation of Figure 1.3.*

The first concept is that of a **heuristic**. In physics, engineering, and other exact sciences, a deterministic approach is common, where for example the acceleration of a mass can be expressed exactly by a mathematical function. However, knowledge need not be a set of defined assertions with precisely specified domains; it may be both empirical and very vague in nature, and artificial intelligence calls this vague knowledge heuristic. Problems with exponential complexity may often be solved using heuristics to reduce the solution search space. A heuristic solution might be found faster compared to precise and exhaustive methods. In contrast to exact knowledge, one often does not know under which conditions a heuristic is applicable. Heuristic methods are also used in the case when exact algorithms do not exist; also the heuristic domain is not precisely defined, so in some cases a solution may exist but a heuristic method may not find it.

A priori knowledge (information) is a second useful concept, this being knowledge available before the search for a problem solution starts. This concept is similar to a priori probability in probability theory. A priori knowledge – if available – may ease the image understanding task.

Thirdly there are **syntactic** and **semantic** concepts, which come from the theory of formal languages and logic [Fu 74, Fu 77, Gonzalez and Thomason 78, Fu 82]. Syntax and semantics allow us to study formal relationships between form and content: Syntax is defined as a set of rules that enable formulae to be created from symbols, and semantics is concerned with formulae interpretation, i.e. finding a mapping from formulae to some model. When we use the expression 'semantic information', we will be referring to the information originating from image content.

Many books discuss low-level image processing but fewer concern computer vision. A chronological list of basic monographs and textbooks is [Duda and Hart 73, Rosenfeld and Kak 76, Gonzalez and Wintz 77, Pavlidis 77, Hanson and Riseman 78, Pratt 78, Castleman 79, Hall 79, Rosenfeld 79, Nagao and Matsuyama 80, Duff and Levialdi 81, Ballard and Brown 82, Marr 82, Nilsson 82, Pavlidis 82, Rosenfeld and Kak 82, Serra 82, Ekstrom 84, Rosenfeld 84, Bates and McDonnell 86, Horn 86, Pentland 86, Dougherty and Giardina 87a, Dougherty and Giardina 87b, Gonzalez and Wintz 87, Aggarwal and Martin 88, Boyle and Thomas 88, Fairhurst 88, Giardina and Dougherty 88, Netravali 88, Aloimonos and Shulman 89, Horn and Brooks 89, Jain 89, Simon 89, Lim 90, Murray and Buxton 90, Niemann 90, Tomita and Tsuji 90, Wechsler 90, Kasturi and Jain 91, Prasanna Kumar 91, Low 91, Pratt 91, Rabbani 91, Gonzalez and Woods 92, Mundy and Zisserman 92, Zhou 92, Haralick and Shapiro 92, Haralick and Shapiro 93].

Another important source of information of particular importance in this fast moving science are the research journals; the major current ones are: Artificial Intelligence, Computer Vision, Graphics and Image Processing [CVGIP] (to 1990), CVGIP – Graphical Models and Image Processing (1991 onward), CVGIP – Image Understanding (1991 onward), IEE Proceedings, Part I: Communications, Speech and Vision, IEEE Transactions on Acoustics, Speech, and Signal Processing, IEEE Transactions on Medical Imaging, IEEE Transactions on Pattern Analysis and Machine Intelligence, IEEE Transactions on Remote Sensing, IEEE Transactions on Systems, Man and Cybernetics, Image and Vision Computing, Information Sciences, International Journal of Computer Vision, International Journal on Pattern Recognition and Artificial Intelligence, International Journal of Remote Sensing, International Journal of Robotics Research, Machine Vision and Applications, Neural Networks, Pattern Recognition, Pattern Recognition Letters, Perception, Radiology, Robotics, Signal Processing: Image Communication and Vision Research.

Recent developments and results are published in the proceedings of regularly held image processing and computer vision conferences. Each year an excellent survey of published material is given by Professor A. Rosenfeld of the University of Maryland in the May volume of CVGIP (Image Understanding). In addition, there is an increasing number of more popular magazines that cover some part of the subject, in particular the 'trade' and related journals that document commercially available hardware and software systems. We do not in this book attempt to present up-to-date hardware information since it would age so very quickly ... in common with many other areas of computer science, vision technology is improving rapidly and often dropping in price simultaneously.

This book is intended for those interested in computer vision and image processing; it may serve as an introductory textbook for university students and as a handbook for experts in the field. Knowledge of elementary calculus is assumed. The outline and content of the book is motivated by practical needs, and stress has been put on algorithms, but even so it is not a collection of algorithms usable in all cases. Algorithms should be studied, understood, and their range of applicability carefully taken into account before applying them to specific cases. The authors have tried to give the reader a key to easy access of the literature and have provided references to original papers, and later developments are referenced wherever possible. Both computer vision and image processing are rapidly expanding fields, with more than a thousand papers published each year – despite our best efforts, the reader engaged in research would always be well advised to search the recent literature.

References

[Aggarwal and Martin 88] J K Aggarwal and W Martin. *Motion Understanding*. Kluwer Academic Publishers, Boston, Ma, 1988.

[Aloimonos and Shulman 89] Y Aloimonos and D Shulman. *Integration of Visual Modules - An Extension of the Marr Paradigm*. Academic Press, New York, 1989.

[Appenzeller 91] T Appenzeller. Ozone loss hits us where we live. *Science*, 254:645, November 1991.

[Ballard and Brown 82] D H Ballard and C M Brown. *Computer Vision*. Prentice-Hall, Englewood Cliffs, NJ, 1982.

[Bates and McDonnell 86] R H T Bates and M J McDonnell. *Image Restoration and Reconstruction*. Clarendon Press, Oxford, England, 1986.

[Boyle and Thomas 88] R D Boyle and R C Thomas. *Computer Vision: A First Course*. Blackwell Scientific, 1988.

[Castleman 79] K R Castleman. *Digital Image Processing*. Prentice-Hall, Englewood Cliffs, NJ, 1979.

[Dougherty and Giardina 87a] E R Dougherty and C R Giardina. *Image Processing - Continuous to Discrete, Vol.1*. Prentice-Hall, Englewood Cliffs, NJ, 1987.

[Dougherty and Giardina 87b] E R Dougherty and C R Giardina. *Structured Image Processing*. Prentice-Hall, Englewood Cliffs, NJ, 1987.

[Duda and Hart 73] R O Duda and P E Hart. *Pattern Classification and Scene Analysis*. John Wiley and Sons, New York, 1973.

[Duff and Levialdi 81] M B J Duff and S Levialdi, editors. *Languages and Architectures for Image Procesing*. Academic Press, New York, 1981.

[Ekstrom 84] M P Ekstrom. *Digital Image Processing Techniques*. Academic Press, New York, 1984.

[Fairhurst 88] M C Fairhurst. *Computer Vision for Robotic Systems: An Introduction*. Prentice-Hall, Englewood Cliffs, NJ, 1988.

[Fu 74] K S Fu. *Syntactic Methods in Pattern Recognition*. Academic Press, New York, 1974.

[Fu 77] K S Fu. *Syntactic Pattern Recognition – Applications*. Springer Verlag, Berlin, 1977.

[Fu 82] K S Fu. *Syntactic Pattern Recognition and Applications*. Prentice-Hall, Englewood Cliffs, NJ, 1982.

[Giardina and Dougherty 88] C R Giardina and E R Dougherty. *Morphological Methods in Image and Signal Processing*. Prentice-Hall, Englewood Cliffs, NJ, 1988.

[Gonzalez and Thomason 78] R C Gonzalez and M G Thomason. *Syntactic Pattern Recognition: An Introduction*. Addison-Wesley, Reading, Ma, 1978.

[Gonzalez and Wintz 77] R C Gonzalez and P Wintz. *Digital Image Processing*. Addison-Wesley, Reading, Ma, 1977.

[Gonzalez and Wintz 87] R C Gonzalez and P Wintz. *Digital Image Processing*. Addison-Wesley, Reading, Ma, 2nd edition, 1987.

[Gonzalez and Woods 92] R C Gonzalez and R E Woods. *Digital Image Processing*. Addison-Wesley, Reading, Ma, 1992.

[Hall 79] E L Hall. *Computer Image Processing and Recognition*. Academic Press, San Diego-New York, 1979.

[Hanson and Riseman 78] A R Hanson and E M Riseman, editors. *Computer Vision Systems*. Academic Press, New York, 1978.

[Haralick and Shapiro 92] R M Haralick and L G Shapiro. *Computer and Robot Vision, Volume I*. Addison-Wesley, Reading, Ma, 1992.

[Haralick and Shapiro 93] R M Haralick and L G Shapiro. *Computer and Robot Vision, Volume II*. Addison-Wesley, Reading, Ma, 1993.

[Horn 86] B K P Horn. *Robot Vision*. MIT Press, Cambridge, Ma, 1986.

[Horn and Brooks 89] B K P Horn and M J Brooks, editors. *Shape from Shading*. MIT Press, Cambridge, Ma, 1989.

[Jain 89] A K Jain. *Fundamentals of Digital Image Processing*. Prentice-Hall, Englewood Cliffs, NJ, 1989.

[Kasturi and Jain 91] R Kasturi and R C Jain, editors. *Computer Vision*. IEEE Computer Press, Los Alamitos, Ca, 1991.

[Lim 90] J S Lim. *Two-Dimensional Signal and Image Processing*. Prentice-Hall, Englewood Cliffs, NJ, 1990.

[Low 91] A Low. *Introductory Computer Vision and Image Processing*. McGraw Hill, 1991.

[Marr 82] D Marr. *Vision – A Computational Investigation into the Human Representation and Processing of Visual Information*. W.H. Freeman and Co., San Francisco, 1982.

[Mundy and Zisserman 92] J L Mundy and A Zisserman. *Geometric Invariance in Computer Vision*. MIT Press, Cambridge, Ma; London, 1992.

[Murray and Buxton 90] D W Murray and B F Buxton. *Experiments in the Machine Interpretation of Visual Motion*. MIT Press, Cambridge, Ma, 1990.

[Nagao and Matsuyama 80] M Nagao and T Matsuyama. *A Structural Analysis of Complex Aerial Photographs*. Plenum Press, New York, 1980.

[Netravali 88] A N Netravali. *Digital Pictures: Representation and Compression.* Plenum Press, New York, 1988.

[Niemann 90] H Niemann. *Pattern Analysis and Understanding.* Springer Verlag, Berlin-New York-Tokyo, 2nd edition, 1990.

[Nilsson 82] N J Nilsson. *Principles of Artificial Intelligence.* Springer Verlag, Berlin, 1982.

[Pavlidis 77] T Pavlidis. *Structural Pattern Recognition.* Springer Verlag, Berlin, 1977.

[Pavlidis 82] T Pavlidis. *Algorithms for Graphics and Image Processing.* Computer Science Press, New York, 1982.

[Pentland 86] A P Pentland, editor. *From Pixels to Predicates.* Ablex Publishing Corporation, Norwood, NJ, 1986.

[Prasanna Kumar 91] V K Prasanna Kumar. *Parallel Architectures and Algorithms for Image Understanding.* Academic Press, Boston, Ma, 1991.

[Pratt 78] W K Pratt. *Digital Image Processing.* John Wiley and Sons, New York, 1978.

[Pratt 91] W K Pratt. *Digital Image Processing.* John Wiley and Sons, New York, 2nd edition, 1991.

[Rabbani 91] M Rabbani. *Digital Image Compression.* SPIE Optical Engineering Press, Bellingham, Wa, 1991.

[Rosenfeld 79] A Rosenfeld. *Picture Languages – Formal Models for Picture Recognition.* Academic Press, New York, 1979.

[Rosenfeld 84] A Rosenfeld, editor. *Multiresolution Image Processing and Analysis.* Springer Verlag, Berlin, 1984.

[Rosenfeld and Kak 76] A Rosenfeld and A C Kak. *Digital Picture Processing.* Academic Press, New York, 1st edition, 1976.

[Rosenfeld and Kak 82] A Rosenfeld and A C Kak. *Digital Picture Processing.* Academic Press, New York, 2nd edition, 1982.

[Serra 82] J Serra. *Image Analysis and Mathematical Morphology.* Academic Press, London, 1982.

[Simon 89] J C Simon, editor. *From Pixels to Features: Proceedings of a Workshop held at Bonas, France, 22-27 August, 1988.* Elsevier, 1989.

[Tomita and Tsuji 90] F Tomita and S Tsuji. *Computer Analysis of Visual Textures*. Kluwer Academic Publishers, Norwell, Ma, 1990.

[Wechsler 90] H Wechsler. *Computational Vision*. Academic Press, London – San Diego, 1990.

[Zhou 92] Y T Zhou. *Artificial Neural Networks for Computer Vision*. Springer Verlag, New York, 1992.

2

The digitized image and its properties

2.1 Basic concepts

In this chapter some useful concepts and mathematical tools will be introduced which will be used throughout the book. Some readers with a less mathematical background might find some parts difficult to follow; in this case, skip the mathematical details and concentrate on the intuitive meaning of the basic concepts, which are emphasised in the text. This approach will not affect an understanding of the book.

Mathematical models are often used to describe images and other signals. A signal is a function depending on some variable with physical meaning; signals can be one-dimensional (e.g. dependent on time), two-dimensional (e.g. images dependent on two co-ordinates in a plane), three-dimensional (e.g. describing an object in space), or higher-dimensional. A scalar function might be sufficient to describe a monochromatic image, while vector functions are used in image processing to represent, for example, colour images consisting of three component colours.

Functions we shall work with may be categorized as **continuous, discrete** or **digital**. A continuous function has continuous domain and range; if the domain set is discrete then we get a discrete function; if the range set is also discrete then we have a digital function.

2.1.1 Image functions

By **image**, we shall understand an intuitive meaning of image – an example might be the image on the human eye retina or the image captured by a TV camera. The image can be modelled by a continuous function of two or three variables; in the simple case arguments are co-ordinates (x, y) in a plane, while if images change in time a third variable t might be added.

The image function values correspond to the brightness at image points. The function value can express other physical quantities as well (temperature, pressure distribution, distance from the observer, etc.). The **brightness** integrates different optical quantities – using brightness as a basic quantity allows us to avoid the description of the very complicated process of image formation.

The image on the human eye retina or on a TV camera sensor is intrinsically two-dimensional (2D). We shall call such a 2D image bearing information about brightness points an **intensity image**.

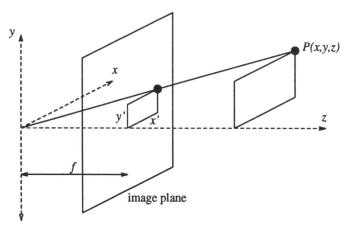

Figure 2.1 *Perspective projection geometry.*

The real world which surrounds us is intrinsically three-dimensional (3D). The 2D intensity image is the result of a **perspective projection** of the 3D scene, which is modelled by the image captured by a pin-hole camera, illustrated in Figure 2.1 – the image plane has been reflected with respect to the xy plane in order not to get a mirrored image with negative co-ordinates. The quantities x, y, and z are co-ordinates of the point P in a 3D scene in world co-ordinates, and f is the focal length. The projected point has co-ordinates (x', y') in the 2D image plane, where

$$x' = \frac{x\,f}{z} \qquad y' = \frac{y\,f}{z} \tag{2.1}$$

A nonlinear perspective projection is often approximated by linear **parallel** (or **orthographic**) **projection** where the focal length $f \to \infty$.

When 3D objects are mapped into the camera plane by perspective projection a lot of information disappears as such a transformation is not one-to-one. Recognizing or reconstructing objects in a 3D scene from one image is an ill-posed problem.

In due course, in Chapter 9, we shall consider more elaborate representations that attempt to recapture information about the 3D original scene that an image depicts. As may be expected, this is not a simple business and involves intermediate representations (in particular, the **2.5D sketch**) that try to establish the **depth** of points in the image. The aim here is to recover a full

3D representation such as may be used in computer graphics – that is, a representation that is independent of viewpoint, and expressed in the co-ordinate system of the object rather than of the viewer. If such a representation can be recovered, then any intensity image view of the object(s) may be synthesized by standard computer graphics techniques.

Recovering information lost by perspective projection is only one, mainly geometric, problem of computer vision – a second problem is how to understand image brightness. The only information available in an intensity image is the brightness of the appropriate pixel, which is dependent on a number of independent factors such as object surface reflectance properties (given by the surface material, microstructure and marking), illumination properties, and object surface orientation with respect to a viewer and light source. It is a non-trivial and again ill-posed problem to separate these components when one wants to recover the 3D geometry of an object from the intensity image.

Some scientific and technical disciplines work with 2D images directly; for example, an image of the flat specimen viewed by a microscope with transparent illumination, a character drawn on a sheet of paper, the image of a fingerprint, etc. Many basic and useful methods used in digital image analysis do not therefore depend on whether the object was originally 2D or 3D. Much of the material in this book restricts itself to the study of such methods – the problem of 3D understanding is addressed explicitly in Chapter 9.

The image formation process is described in [Horn 86]. Related disciplines are **photometry** which is concerned with brightness measurement, and **colorimetry**, which studies light reflectance or emission depending on wavelength. Both these topics are considered in the domain of image processing in [Pratt 78, Pratt 91].

A light source energy distribution $C(x, y, t, \lambda)$ depends in general on image co-ordinates (x, y), time t, and wavelength λ. For the human eye and most technical image sensors (e.g. TV cameras) the brightness f depends on the light source energy distribution C and the spectral sensitivity of the sensor, $S(\lambda)$ (dependent on the wavelength)

$$f(x, y, t) = \int_0^\infty C(x, y, t, \lambda) \, S(\lambda) \, d\lambda \qquad (2.2)$$

An image is then represented by a set of functions $f(x, y, t)$. A **monochromatic image** $f(x, y, t)$ provides the brightness distribution. In a **colour** or **multispectral** image the image is represented by a real vector function $\mathbf{f}$

$$\mathbf{f}(x, y, t) = (f_1(x, y, t), f_2(x, y, t), \ldots, f_n(x, y, t)) \qquad (2.3)$$

where, for example, there may be red, green and blue components.

Image processing often deals with **static** images, in which time t is constant. A monochromatic static image is represented by a continuous image function $f(x, y)$ whose arguments are two co-ordinates in the plane. Most images considered in this book will be monochromatic, static images, unless the contrary is explicitly stated.

Computerized image processing uses digital image functions which are usually represented by matrices, so co-ordinates are integer numbers. The domain of the image function is a region R in the plane

$$R = \{(x, y),\ 0 \leq x \leq x_m,\ 0 \leq y \leq y_n\} \tag{2.4}$$

where x_m, y_n represent maximal image co-ordinates. The image function has a limited domain – infinite summation or integration limits can be used as it is assumed that the image function value is zero outside the domain R. The customary orientation of co-ordinates in an image is in the normal Cartesian fashion (horizontal x axis, vertical y axis), although the (*row, column*) orientation used in matrices is also quite often used in digital image processing.

The range of image function values is also limited; by convention, in monochromatic images the lowest value corresponds to black and the highest to white. Brightness values bounded by these limits are **grey levels**.

The quality of a digital image grows in proportion to the spatial, spectral, radiometric, and time resolutions. The **spatial resolution** is given by the proximity of image samples in the image plane; **spectral resolution** is given by the bandwidth of the light frequencies captured by the sensor; **radiometric resolution** corresponds to the number of distinguishable grey levels; and **time resolution** is given by the interval between time samples at which images are captured. The question of time resolution is important in dynamic image analysis where time sequences of images are processed.

Images $f(x, y)$ can be treated as deterministic functions or as realizations of stochastic processes. Mathematical tools used in image description have roots in linear system theory, integral transformations, discrete mathematics and the theory of stochastic processes. In this section only an overview of mathematical tools used in later explanations is presented; precise descriptions of background mathematics can be found in supporting references given to individual problems. If the reader intends to study image processing mathematics the recommended books with which to start are [Pavlidis 82, Rosenfeld and Kak 82].

Mathematical transforms assume that the image function $f(x, y)$ is 'well-behaved', meaning that the function is integrable, has an invertible Fourier transform, etc. Existence problems of the Fourier transform of special signals (constant, impulses, non-periodical functions) [Papoulis 62] are not discussed; the Fourier transform always exists for discrete images.

2.1.2   The Dirac distribution and convolution

An ideal impulse is an important input signal that enables the use of linear mathematical theory in the domain of continuous image functions. The ideal impulse in the image plane is defined using the **Dirac distribution** $\delta(x, y)$

$$\int_{-\infty}^{\infty} \int_{-\infty}^{\infty} \delta(x, y) \, dx \, dy = 1 \qquad (2.5)$$

and $\delta(x, y) = 0$ for all $x, y \neq 0$.

The following equation (2.6) is called the 'sifting property' of the Dirac distribution; it provides the value of the function $f(x, y)$ at the point λ, μ;

$$\int_{-\infty}^{\infty} \int_{-\infty}^{\infty} f(x, y) \, \delta(x - \lambda, y - \mu) \, dx \, dy = f(\lambda, \mu) \qquad (2.6)$$

The sifting equation can be used to describe the sampling process of a continuous image function $f(x, y)$. We may express the image function as a linear combination of Dirac pulses located at the points a, b that cover the whole image plane; samples are weighted by the image function $f(x, y)$

$$\int_{-\infty}^{\infty} \int_{-\infty}^{\infty} f(a, b) \, \delta(a - x, b - y) \, da \, db = f(x, y) \qquad (2.7)$$

A **convolution** is an important operation in the linear approach to image analysis. The convolution g of two-dimensional functions f and h is defined by the integral

$$\begin{aligned}
g(x, y) &= \int_{-\infty}^{\infty} \int_{-\infty}^{\infty} f(a, b) \, h(x - a, y - b) \, da \, db \\
&= \int_{-\infty}^{\infty} \int_{-\infty}^{\infty} f(x - a, y - b) \, h(a, b) \, da \, db \\
&= f(*h)(x, y) = h(*f)(x, y) \qquad (2.8)
\end{aligned}$$

An asterisk $*$ denotes the convolution operator. Convolution is a very useful linear, translation-invariant operation. A digital image has a limited domain on the image plane, and so translational invariance is valid only for small translations – convolution is thus often used locally. The convolution expresses a linear filtering process using the filter h; linear filtering is often used in local image pre-processing and image restoration.

2.1.3 The Fourier transform

An image is a function of two parameters in a plane. One possible way to investigate its properties is to decompose the image function using a linear combination of orthonormal functions. A **Fourier** transform uses harmonic functions for the decomposition [Papoulis 62, Rosenfeld and Kak 82]. The two-dimensional Fourier transform is defined by the integral

$$F(u, v) = \int_{-\infty}^{\infty} \int_{-\infty}^{\infty} f(x, y) \, e^{-2\pi i(xu + yv)} \, dx \, dy \qquad (2.9)$$

The existence conditions of the Fourier transform can be found in [Papoulis 62], but for image processing purposes it is reasonable to assume that the Fourier transform of periodic functions always exists. An inverse Fourier transform is defined by

$$f(x,y) = \int_{-\infty}^{\infty} \int_{-\infty}^{\infty} F(u,v) \, e^{2\pi i(xu+yv)} \, du \, dv \qquad (2.10)$$

Parameters (x,y) denote image co-ordinates, and co-ordinates (u,v) are called **spatial frequencies**. The function $f(x,y)$ on the left hand side of equation (2.10) can be interpreted as a linear combination of simple periodic patterns $e^{2\pi i(xu+yv)}$. The real and imaginary component of the pattern are sine and cosine functions, and the function $F(u,v)$ is a weight function which represents the influence of the elementary patterns.

Denote the Fourier transform by an operator $\mathcal{F}$; then equation (2.9) can be abbreviated to

$$\mathcal{F}\{f(x,y)\} = F(u,v)$$

The following properties of the Fourier transform are interesting from the image processing point of view:

- Linearity

$$\mathcal{F}\{a\, f_1(x,y) + b\, f_2(x,y)\} = a\; F_1(u,v) + b\, F_2(u,v) \qquad (2.11)$$

- Shift of the origin in the image domain

$$\mathcal{F}\{f(x-a,\, y-b)\} = F(u,v)\, e^{-2\pi i(au+bv)} \qquad (2.12)$$

- Shift of the origin in the frequency domain

$$\mathcal{F}\{f(x,y)\, e^{2\pi i(u_0 x + v_0 y)}\} = F(u - u_0, v - v_0) \qquad (2.13)$$

- Symmetry: If $f(x,y)$ is real valued

$$F(-u,-v) = F^{\#}(u,v) \qquad (2.14)$$

where # denotes complex conjugate. An image function is always real valued and we can thus use the results of its Fourier transform in the first quadrant, i.e. $u \geq 0$, $v \geq 0$, without loss of generality. If in addition the image function is symmetrical, $f(x,y) = f(-x,-y)$, then the result of the Fourier transform $F(u,v)$ is a real function.

- Duality of the convolution: Convolution (equation (2.8)), and its Fourier transform are related by

$$\begin{aligned} \mathcal{F}\{(f * h)(x,y)\} &= F(u,v)\, H(u,v) \\ \mathcal{F}\{f(x,y)\, h(x,y)\} &= (F * H)(u,v) \end{aligned} \qquad (2.15)$$

This is the **Convolution theorem**.

These remarks about convolution and the Fourier transform in the continuous function domain are also valid for discrete functions (images). Integration is changed to summation in the respective equations.

2.1.4 Images as a stochastic process

Images are statistical in nature due to random changes and noise, and it is sometimes of advantage to treat image functions as realizations of a stochastic process [Papoulis 65, Rosenfeld and Kak 82].

Questions regarding image information content and redundancy might be answered using probability distributions and correlation functions. If a probability distribution is known we can measure image information content using **entropy** H – entropy is calculated for n values of a random variable with probability distribution p_k as

$$H = -\sum_{k=1}^{n} p_k \log_2(p_k) \tag{2.16}$$

The base of the logarithm in this formula determines the unit in which entropy is measured. If this base is two then the entropy is given in bits.

A **stochastic process** (random process, random field) is a generalization of the random variable concept. Denote a stochastic process by $f(x, y, \omega_i)$, where the event ω_i is an element from a set of all events $\Omega = \{\omega_1, \omega_2, \ldots, \omega_n\}$. In our case the event may represent an image picked from a given set of images. The probability distribution p_i corresponds to each event ω_i, and the function $f(x, y, \omega_i)$ is the random variable for fixed image co-ordinates (x, y). If an event is fixed then the function $f(x, y, \omega_i)$ is a deterministic function which is called a **realization** of the stochastic process.

A stochastic process f is entirely described by a collection of k-dimensional distribution functions P_k, $k = 1, 2, \ldots$. The distribution function of k arguments $z_1, \ldots, z_k$ is

$$P_k(z_1, \ldots, z_k; x_1, y_1, \ldots, x_k, y_k) =$$
$$\mathcal{P}\{f(x_1, y_1, \omega_{i_1}) < z_1, f(x_2, y_2, \omega_{i_2}) < z_2, \ldots, f(x_n, y_n, \omega_{i_k}) < z_k\} \tag{2.17}$$

where $\mathcal{P}$ denotes the probability of the conjunction of events listed in the brackets in equation (2.17).

The k-order probability density is defined by

$$p_k(z_1, \ldots, z_k; x_1, y_1, \omega_{i_1}, \ldots, x_k, y_k, \omega_{i_k}) =$$
$$\frac{\partial P_k(z_1, \ldots, z_n; x_1, y_1, \omega_{i_1}, \ldots, x_k, y_k, \omega_{i_k})}{\partial z_1 \ldots \partial z_n} \tag{2.18}$$

The k-order distribution function or k-order probability distribution is often not known in practice – it expresses a complex relation among many events. The second-order distribution function or second-order probability density is used to relate pairs of events. Even simpler is the first-order probability density $p_1(z; x, y)$, which can quite often be modelled if it is known how an image was obtained.

Simpler characteristics are used to describe the stochastic processes. The **mean** of the stochastic process f is defined using first-order probability density by the equation

$$\mu_f(x, y, \omega_i) = \mathcal{E}\{f(x, y, \omega_i)\} = \int_{-\infty}^{\infty} z \, p_1(z; x, y, \omega_i) \, dz \qquad (2.19)$$

The **autocorrelation** and **cross correlation** functions [Papoulis 65] are often used in searching for similarities in images or image parts. The autocorrelation function R_{ff} of the random process f is defined as a mean of the product of the random variables $f(x_1, y_1, \omega_i)$ and $f(x_2, y_2, \omega_i)$,

$$R_{ff}(x_1, y_1, \omega_i, x_2, y_2, \omega_i) = \mathcal{E}\{f(x_1, y_1, \omega_i) \, f(x_2, y_2, \omega_i)\} \qquad (2.20)$$

The **autocovariance** function C_{ff} is defined as

$$C_{ff}(x_1, y_1, \omega_i, x_2, y_2, \omega_i) =$$
$$R_{ff}(x_1, y_1, \omega_i, x_2, y_2, \omega_i) - \mu_f(x_1, y_1, \omega_i) \, \mu_f(x_2, y_2, \omega_i) \qquad (2.21)$$

The cross correlation function R_{fg} and **cross covariance** function C_{fg} use similar definitions to equations (2.20), and (2.21). The only difference is that a point from one image (process) $f(x_1, y_1, \omega_i)$ is related to a point from another image (process) $g(x_2, y_2, \omega_j)$. Two stochastic processes are **uncorrelated** if their cross covariance function equals zero for any two points (x_1, y_1, ω_i), (x_2, y_2, ω_j).

The **stationary process** is a special stochastic process. Its properties are independent of absolute position in the image plane. The mean μ_f of the stationary process is a constant.

The autocorrelation function R_{ff} of a stationary stochastic process is translation-invariant, and depends only on the difference between co-ordinates $a = x_1 - x_2; \, b = y_1 - y_2$

$$R_{ff}(x_1, y_1, \omega_i, x_2, y_2, \omega_i) = R_{ff}(a, b, \omega_i, 0, 0, \omega_i) \equiv R_{ff}(a, b, \omega_i)$$

$$R_{ff}(a, b, \omega_i) = \int_{-\infty}^{\infty} \int_{-\infty}^{\infty} f(x + a, y + b, \omega_i) \, f(x, y, \omega_i) \, dx \, dy \qquad (2.22)$$

Similarly, the cross correlation function between samples of processes $f(x_1, y_1, \omega_i)$ and $g(x_2, y_2, \omega_i)$ is defined as

$$R_{fg}(x_1, y_1, \omega_i, x_2, y_2, \omega_i) = R_{fg}(a, b, \omega_i, 0, 0, \omega_i) \equiv R_{fg}(a, b, \omega_i)$$

$$R_{fg}(a, b, \omega_i) = \int_{-\infty}^{\infty} \int_{-\infty}^{\infty} f(x + a, y + b, \omega_i) \, g(x, y, \omega_i) \, dx \, dy \qquad (2.23)$$

The properties of correlation functions are interesting after transformation into the frequency domain. The Fourier transform of the cross correlation function of the stationary stochastic process can be expressed as the product of the Fourier transforms of processes (images)

$$\mathcal{F}\{R_{fg}(a,b,\omega_i)\} = F^{\#}(u,v)\,G(u,v) \tag{2.24}$$

Similarly the autocorrelation function can be written

$$\mathcal{F}\{R_{ff}(a,b,\omega_i)\} = F^{\#}(u,v)\,F(u,v) = \mid F(u,v)\mid^2 \tag{2.25}$$

The Fourier transform of the autocorrelation function, equation (2.22), is given by the following expression – the result is called the **power spectrum**[1] or **spectral density**.

$$S_{ff}(u,v) = \int_{-\infty}^{\infty}\int_{-\infty}^{\infty} R_{ff}(a,b,\omega_i)\,e^{-2\pi i(au+bv)}\,da\,db \tag{2.26}$$

where u, v are spatial frequencies. Power spectral density communicates how much power the corresponding spatial frequency of the signal has.

Note that infinitely many functions have the same correlation function and therefore the same power spectrum as well. If an image is shifted its power spectrum remains unchanged.

Let $g(x,y)$ be the result of the convolution of the functions $f(x,y)$ and $h(x,y)$ (equation (2.8)). Assume that $f(x,y)$, $g(x,y)$ are stationary stochastic processes and S_{ff}, S_{gg} are their corresponding power spectral densities. If the mean of the process $f(x,y)$ is zero then

$$S_{gg}(u,v) = S_{ff}(u,v)\mid H(u,v)\mid^2, \tag{2.27}$$

where $H(u,v)$ is the Fourier transform of the function $h(x,y)$. Equation (2.27) is used to describe spectral properties of a linear image filter h.

A special class of stochastic processes are the **ergodic processes** [Rosenfeld and Kak 82]. This is a stationary process for which the mean calculated from realizations is equal to the mean computed according to spatial variables. The mean from realization is calculated according to equation (2.19), when there is not usually enough data to evaluate in the domain of real images. This calculation is often replaced by calculation of the mean in image spatial co-ordinates (x,y). Be aware that this replacement is valid from the theoretical point of view only for ergodic processes.

---

[1]The concept of power spectrum can also be defined for functions for which the Fourier transform is not defined.

2.1.5 Images as linear systems

Images and their processing can be modelled as a superposition of point spread functions which are represented by Dirac pulses δ (equation (2.5)). If this image representation is used, well-developed linear system theory can be employed.

A linear system is an operator $\mathcal{L}$ which maps two (or more) input functions into an output function according to the following rule

$$\mathcal{L}\{af_1 + bf_2\} = a\ \mathcal{L}\{f_1\} + b\,\mathcal{L}\{f_2\} \tag{2.28}$$

An image f can be expressed as the linear combination of point spread functions represented by Dirac pulses δ. Assume that the input image $f(x,y)$ is given by equation (2.7) and that the operation is translation invariant. The response $g(x,y)$ of the linear system $\mathcal{L}$ to the input image $f(x,y)$ is given by

$$
\begin{aligned}
g(x,y) &= \mathcal{L}\{f(x,y)\} \\
&= \int_{-\infty}^{\infty}\int_{-\infty}^{\infty} f(a,b)\,\mathcal{L}\{\delta(x-a, y-b)\}\ da\ db \\
&= \int_{-\infty}^{\infty}\int_{-\infty}^{\infty} f(a,b)\,h(x-a, y-b)\ da\ db \\
&= f(*h)(x,y) \tag{2.29}
\end{aligned}
$$

where $h(x,y)$ is the impulse response of the linear system $\mathcal{L}$. In other words the output of the linear system $\mathcal{L}$ is expressed as the convolution of the input image f with an impulse response h of the linear system $\mathcal{L}$. If the Fourier transform is applied to the equation (2.29) the following equation is obtained

$$G(u,v) = F(u,v)\,H(u,v) \tag{2.30}$$

Equation (2.30) is often used in image pre-processing to express the behaviour of smoothing or sharpening operations, and is considered further in Chapter 4.

One should remember that real images are not in fact linear – both the image co-ordinates and values of the image function (brightness) are limited. The real image always has limited size and the number of brightness levels is also finite. Nevertheless images can be approximated by linear systems in many cases.

2.2 Image digitization

An image to be processed by computer should be represented using an appropriate discrete data structure, for example, a matrix. An image captured by a sensor is expressed as a continuous function $f(x,y)$ of two co-ordinates in the plane. Image digitization means that the function $f(x,y)$ is **sampled** into a matrix with M rows and N columns. The image **quantization** assigns to each continuous sample an integer value. The continuous range of the image function $f(x,y)$ is split into K intervals. The finer the sampling (i.e. the larger M and N) and quantization (the larger K) the better the approximation of the continuous image function $f(x,y)$ achieved.

Two questions should be answered in connection with image function sampling: First, the sampling period should be determined – this is the distance between two neighbouring sampling points in the image. Second, the geometric arrangement of sampling points (sampling grid) should be set.

2.2.1 Sampling

A continuous image function $f(x,y)$ can be sampled using a discrete grid of sampling points in the plane. A second possibility is to expand the image function using some orthonormal function as a base – the Fourier transform is an example. The coefficients of this expansion then represent the digitized image. Here we consider only the first possibility, but a detailed description of both approaches can be found in [Rosenfeld and Kak 82].

The image is sampled at points $x = j\Delta x$, $y = k\Delta y$, for $j = 1\ldots M$, $k = 1\ldots N$. Two neighbouring sampling points are separated by distance Δx along the x axis and Δy along the y axis. Distances Δx and Δy arc called the **sampling interval** (on the x or y axis), and the matrix of samples $f(j\,\Delta x, k\,\Delta y)$ constitutes the discrete image. The ideal sampling $s(x,y)$ in the regular grid can be represented using a collection of Dirac distributions δ

$$s(x,y) = \sum_{j=1}^{M} \sum_{k=1}^{N} \delta(x - j\Delta x, y - k\Delta y) \tag{2.31}$$

The sampled image $f_s(x,y)$ is the product of the continuous image $f(x,y)$ and the sampling function $s(x,y)$

$$
\begin{aligned}
f_s(x,y) &= (f\,s)(x,y) \\
&= \sum_{j=1}^{M} \sum_{k=1}^{N} f(x,y)\,\delta(x - j\Delta x, y - k\Delta y) \\
&= f(x,y) \sum_{j=1}^{M} \sum_{k=1}^{N} \delta(x - j\Delta x, y - k\Delta y) \tag{2.32}
\end{aligned}
$$

The collection of Dirac distributions in equation (2.32) can be regarded as periodic with period Δx, Δy and expanded into a Fourier series. To fulfil the periodicity condition of the Fourier transform let us assume for a moment that the sampling grid covers the whole plane (infinite limits).

$$\mathcal{F}\{ \sum_{j=-\infty}^{\infty} \sum_{k=-\infty}^{\infty} \delta(x - j\Delta x, y - k\Delta y) \} = \sum_{m=-\infty}^{\infty} \sum_{n=-\infty}^{\infty} a_{mn}\, e^{2\pi i(\frac{mx}{\Delta x} + \frac{ny}{\Delta y})} \tag{2.33}$$

Coefficients of the Fourier expansion a_{mn} can be calculated as

$$a_{mn} = \frac{1}{\Delta x\,\Delta y} \int_{-\frac{\Delta x}{2}}^{\frac{\Delta x}{2}} \int_{-\frac{\Delta y}{2}}^{\frac{\Delta y}{2}} \sum_{j=-\infty}^{\infty} \sum_{k=-\infty}^{\infty} \delta(x - j\Delta x, y - k\Delta y)\, e^{-2\pi i\left(\frac{mx}{\Delta x} + \frac{ny}{\Delta y}\right)} dx\,dy$$

$$(2.34)$$

Then, noting that only the term for $j = 0$ and $k = 0$ in the sum is non-zero in the range of integration, we see

$$a_{mn} = \frac{1}{\Delta x\,\Delta y} \int_{-\frac{\Delta x}{2}}^{\frac{\Delta x}{2}} \int_{-\frac{\Delta y}{2}}^{\frac{\Delta y}{2}} \delta(x, y)\, e^{-2\pi i\left(\frac{mx}{\Delta x} + \frac{ny}{\Delta y}\right)} dx\,dy \qquad (2.35)$$

Noting that the integral in equation (2.35) is uniformly one [Rosenfeld and Kak 82], we see that coefficients a_{mn} can be expressed as

$$a_{mn} = \frac{1}{\Delta x\,\Delta y} \qquad (2.36)$$

Thus equation (2.32) can be rewritten using the derived value of the coefficients a_{mn}

$$f_s(x, y) = f(x, y)\,\frac{1}{\Delta x\,\Delta y} \sum_{m=-\infty}^{\infty} \sum_{n=-\infty}^{\infty} e^{2\pi i\left(\frac{mx}{\Delta x} + \frac{ny}{\Delta y}\right)} \qquad (2.37)$$

Equation (2.37) can be expressed in the frequency domain using equation (2.13)

$$F_s(u, v) = \frac{1}{\Delta x\,\Delta y} \sum_{j=-\infty}^{\infty} \sum_{k=-\infty}^{\infty} F\left(u - \frac{j}{\Delta x}, v - \frac{k}{\Delta y}\right) \qquad (2.38)$$

Thus the Fourier transform of the sampled image is the sum of periodically repeated Fourier transforms $F(u, v)$ of the image (see Figure 2.2).

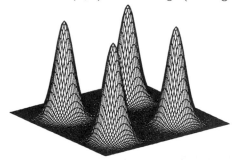

Figure 2.2 *2D spectrum of sampled image function.*

Periodic repetition of the Fourier transform result $F(u, v)$ may under certain conditions cause distortion of the image which is called **aliasing**; this happens when individual digitized components $F(u, v)$ overlap. The situation without spectra overlapping is shown in Figure 2.2, which assumes that the image function $f(x, y)$ has a **band-limited** spectrum, meaning that its Fourier transform $F(u, v)$ is equal to zero outside a certain interval of frequencies $\mid u \mid > U$, $\mid v \mid > V$.

Overlapping of the periodically repeated results of the Fourier transform $F(u, v)$ of an image with a band-limited spectrum can be prevented if the sampling interval is chosen such that

$$\Delta x \leq \frac{1}{2U}, \ \Delta y \leq \frac{1}{2V} \tag{2.39}$$

This is the **Shannon sampling theorem**, known from signal processing theory or control theory. The theorem has a simple physical interpretation in image analysis: The sampling interval should be chosen in size such that it is less than or equal to half of the smallest interesting detail in the image.

The sampling function is not the Dirac distribution in real digitizers – limited impulses (quite narrow ones with limited amplitude) are used instead. Assume a rectangular sampling grid which consists of $M \times N$ such equal and non-overlapping impulses $h_s(x, y)$ with sampling period Δx, Δy; this function simulates realistically the real image sensors. Out of the sensitive area of the sensor element $h_s(x, y) = 0$. Values of image samples are obtained by integration of the product $f(x, y) \ h_s(x, y)$ – in reality this integration is done on the surface of the sensor sensitive element. The sampled image is then given by the convolution computed in discrete co-ordinates $j\Delta x$, $k\Delta y$,

$$f_s(x, y) = \sum_{j=1}^{M} \sum_{k=1}^{N} f(x, y) \ h_s(x - j\Delta x, y - k\Delta y) \tag{2.40}$$

The sampled image f_s is distorted by the convolution of the original image f and the limited impulse h_s. The distortion of the frequency spectrum of the function F_s can be expressed using the Fourier transform

$$F_s(u, v) = \frac{1}{\Delta x \ \Delta y} \sum_{j=1}^{M} \sum_{k=1}^{N} F(u - \frac{j}{\Delta x}, v - \frac{k}{\Delta y}) \ H_s(u - \frac{j}{\Delta x}, v - \frac{k}{\Delta y}) \tag{2.41}$$

In real image digitizers, a sampling interval about ten times smaller than that indicated by the Shannon sampling theorem (equation 2.39) is used. The reason is that algorithms which reconstruct the continuous image on a display from the digitized image function use only a step function [Pavlidis 82], i.e. a line is created from pixels represented by individual squares.

A demonstration with an image of 256 grey levels will illustrate the effect of sparse sampling. Figure 2.3a shows a monochromatic image with 256×256 pixels; Figure 2.3b shows the same scene digitized into a reduced grid of 128×128 pixels, Figure 2.3c into 64×64 pixels, and Figure 2.3d into 32×32 pixels. Decline in image quality is clear from Figures 2.3a to 2.3d. Quality may be improved by viewing from a distance and with screwed up eyes, implying that the undersampled images still hold substantial information.

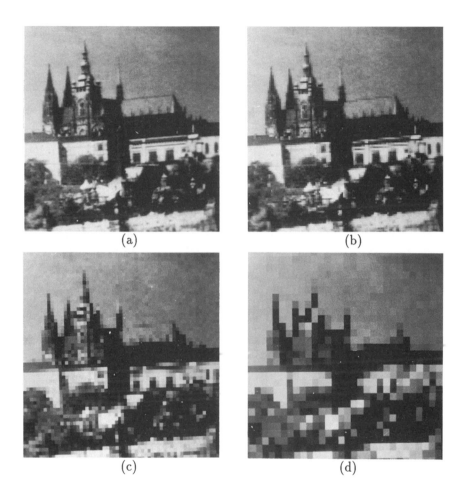

Figure 2.3 *Digitizing: (a) 256 × 256, (b) 128 × 128, (c) 64 × 64, (d) 32 × 32. Images have been enlarged to the same size to illustrate the loss of detail.*

This visual degradation is caused by aliasing in the reconstruction of the continuous image function for display. This display can be improved by the reconstruction algorithm interpolating brightness values in neighbouring pixels; this technique is called **antialiasing** and is often used in computer graphics [Rogers 85]. If antialiasing is used, the sampling interval can be brought near to the theoretical value of Shannon's theorem (equation 2.39). In real image processing devices, antialiasing is rarely used because of its computational requirements.

If quality comparable to an ordinary television image is required, sampling into a 512 × 512 grid is used; this is the reason most image frame grabbers use this (or higher) resolution.

A continuous image is digitized at **sampling points**. These sampling points are ordered in the plane and their geometric relation is called the **grid**. The digital image is then a data structure, usually a matrix. Grids used in practice are mainly square (Figure 2.4a) or hexagonal, (Figure 2.4b).

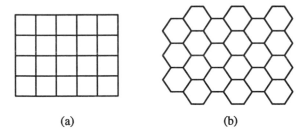

(a)   (b)

Figure 2.4 *(a) Square grid, (b) hexagonal grid.*

It is important to distinguish the grid from the raster; the **raster** is the grid on which a neighbourhood relation between points is defined[2].

One infinitely small sampling point in the grid corresponds to one picture element (**pixel**) in the digital image. The set of pixels together covers the entire image, however the pixel captured by a real digitization device has finite size since the sampling function is not a collection of ideal Dirac impulses but a collection of limited impulses (equation (2.40)). The pixel is a unit which is not further divisible[3] from the image analysis point of view. Keeping in mind its finite size, we shall call a pixel a 'point' as well.

---

[2]E.g., if 4-neighbourhoods are used on the square grid the square raster is obtained. Similarly, if 8-neighbourhoods are used on the the same square grid then the octagonal raster is obtained. These 4-neighbourhood and 8-neighbourhood concepts are introduced in Section 2.3.1.

[3]The properties of an image at subpixel resolution can be computed in some cases. This is achieved by approximating the image function by a continuous function.

2.2.2 Quantization

A magnitude of the sampled image $f_s(j\Delta x, k\Delta y)$ is expressed as a digital value in image processing. The transition between continuous values of the image function (brightness) and its digital equivalent is called **quantization**. The number of quantization levels should be high enough for human perception of fine shading details in the image.

Most digital image processing devices use quantization into k equal intervals. If b bits are used to express the values of the pixel brightness then the number of brightness levels is $k = 2^b$. Eight bits per pixel are commonly used, although some systems use six or four bits. A binary image, which contains only black and white, can be represented by one bit. Specialized measuring devices use twelve and more bits per pixel, although these are becoming more common.

The occurrence of false contours is the main problem in images which have been quantized with insufficient brightness levels. This effect arises when the number of brightness levels is lower than approximately fifty, which is the number which humans can distinguish. This problem can be reduced when quantization into intervals of unequal length is used; the size of intervals corresponding to non-probable brightnesses in the image is enlarged. These grey scale transformation techniques are considered in Section 4.1.2.

An efficient representation of brightness values in digital images requires that eight bits, four bits or one bit are used per pixel, meaning that one, four or eight pixel brightnesses can be stored in one byte of computer memory.

Figures 2.3a and 2.5a – 2.5d demonstrate the effect of reducing the number of brightness levels in an image. An original image with 256 brightness levels is in Figure 2.3a. If the number of brightness levels is reduced to 64 (Figure 2.5a) no degradation is perceived. Figure 2.5b uses 16 brightness levels and false contours begin to emerge, and this becomes clearer in Figure 2.5c with 4 brightnesses and in Figure 2.5d with only 2.

2.2.3 Colour images

A monochromatic image does not contain enough information for some applications for which we might want to use **colour** or **multispectral images**. Colour is a property connected with the ability of objects to reflect electromagnetic waves of different wavelengths. It is not possible to work with all wavelengths at the same time when capturing or processing images by computer and so the band of interesting frequencies is divided into several spectral bands. The image can be captured by several sensors each of which is sensitive to a rather narrow band of wavelengths. The image function at the sensor output is given by equation (2.2).

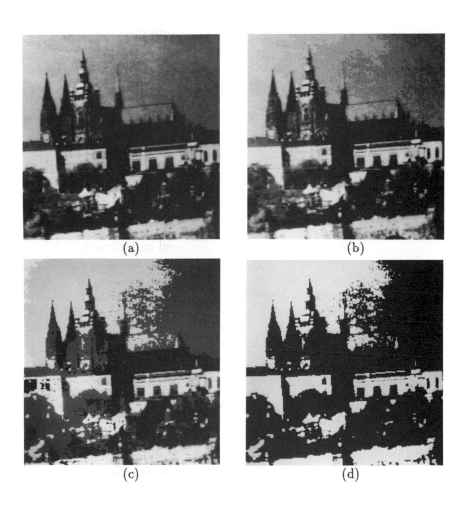

Figure 2.5 *Brightness levels: (a) 64, (b) 16, (c) 4, (d) 2.*

Each spectral band is digitized independently and is represented by an individual digital image function as if it were a monochromatic image. All that has been said about sampling and quantization is valid here as well. The choice of wavelength bands depends strongly on the desired application: Multispectral images captured from aircraft or satellites are often used in remote sensing. For instance, the LANDSAT 4 satellite transmits digitized images in five spectral bands from near ultraviolet to infrared.

Signals used in colour television consist of three spectral components (red 700 nm, green 546.1 nm, and blue 435.8 nm) [Pratt 78]. Blending of these three basic components provides the colour image.

Colour digital image processing systems process colour components independently and join them at the end for display purpose; the processing methods used are identical to those for monochromatic images. Two points specific to colour images are worth mentioning:

- More memory is required for storage; the requirement is the number of spectral components times larger than that for a monochromatic image.

- There is a strong interdependence between individual spectral components.

2.3   Digital image properties

A digital image has several properties, both metric and topological, which are somewhat different to those of continuous two-dimensional functions with which we are familiar from basic calculus. Another question is how humans perceive images, since judgement of image quality is also important.

2.3.1   Metric and topological properties of digital images

A digital image consists of picture elements with finite size – these pixels bear information about the brightness of a particular location in the image. Usually (and we assume this hereafter) pixels are arranged into a rectangular sampling grid. Such a digital image is represented by a two-dimensional matrix whose elements are integer numbers corresponding to the quantization levels in the brightness scale.

Some intuitively clear properties of continuous images have no straightforward analogy in the domain of digital images [Pavlidis 77, Ballard and Brown 82]. **Distance** is an important example. The distance between two pixels in a digital image is a significant quantitative measure. The distance between points with co-ordinates (i, j) and (h, k) may be defined in several different ways; the **Euclidean distance** D_E known from classical geometry and everyday experience is defined by

$$D_E((i,j),(h,k)) = \sqrt{(i-h)^2 + (j-k)^2} \qquad (2.42)$$

The advantage of the Euclidean distance is the fact that it is intuitively obvious. The disadvantages are costly calculation due to the square root, and its non-integer value.

The distance between two points can also be expressed as the minimum number of elementary steps in the digital grid which are needed to move from starting point to the end point. If only horizontal and vertical moves are allowed the distance D_4 is obtained – D_4 is also called 'city block' distance – there is an analogy with the distance between two locations in a city with a rectangular grid of streets and closed blocks of houses,

$$D_4((i,j),(h,k)) = \mid i - h \mid + \mid j - k \mid \tag{2.43}$$

If moves in diagonal directions are allowed in the digitization grid we obtain the distance D_8, often called 'chessboard' distance. The distance D_8 is equal to the number of moves of the king on the chessboard from one part to another,

$$D_8((i,j),(h,k)) = max\{\mid i - h \mid, \mid j - k \mid\} \tag{2.44}$$

Pixel **adjacency** is another important concept in digital images. Any two pixels are called **4-neighbours** if they have distance $D_4 = 1$ from each other. Analogously, **8-neighbours** are two pixels with $D_8 = 1$. The neighbourhood of a pixel is constituted by all its neighbours. 4-neighbours and 8-neighbours are illustrated in Figure 2.6.

Figure 2.6 *Pixel neighbourhoods.*

It will become necessary to consider important sets consisting of several adjacent pixels – **regions**. We define several intermediate concepts first (for those familiar with set theory, we can simply say that a region is a contiguous set).

A **path** from pixel P to pixel Q is a sequence of points $A_1, A_2, \ldots, A_n$ where $A_1 = P$, $A_n = Q$, and A_{i+1} is a neighbour of A_i, $i = 1, \ldots, n-1$.

A **simple path** is a path with no pixels repeated (except perhaps the first and last) in which no pixel has more than two neighbours.

A **closed path** is a simple path in which the first pixel is a neighbour of the last.

A **region** is a set of pixels in which there is a path between any pair of its pixels, all of whose pixels also belong to the set.

If there is a path between two pixels in the image these pixels are called **contiguous**. Alternatively we can say that a region is the set of pixels where each pair of pixels in the set is contiguous. The relation *to be contiguous* is reflexive, symmetric and transitive and therefore defines a decomposition of the set (in our case image) into equivalence classes (regions).

Assume that R_i are disjoint regions in the image which were created by the relation *to be contiguous*, and further assume, to avoid special cases, that these regions do not touch the image limits (meaning the rows or columns in the image matrix with minimum and maximum indices). Let region R be the union of all regions R_i; it then becomes sensible to define a set R^C which is the set complement of region R with respect to the image. The subset of R^C which is contiguous with the image limits is called **background**, and the rest of the complement R^C is called **holes**. If there are no holes in the region we call it a **simply contiguous** region. A region with holes is called **multiply contiguous**.

Note that the concept of *region* uses only the property *to be contiguous*. Secondary properties can be attached to regions which originate in image data interpretation. It is common to call some regions in the image **objects**; a process which says which regions in an image correspond to objects in the surrounding world is called image **segmentation** and is discussed in Chapter 5.

The brightness of a pixel is a very simple property which can be used to find objects in some images; if for example the pixel is darker than some predefined value (threshold) then it belongs to the object. All such points which are also contiguous constitute one object. A hole consists of points which do not belong to the object and are surrounded by the object, and all other points constitute the background.[4]

An example is the black printed text on this white sheet of paper, in which individual letters are objects. White areas surrounded by the letter are holes, for example the area inside a letter 'o'. Other white parts of the paper are background.

These neighbourhood and contiguity definitions on the square grid create some paradoxes. Figure 2.7 shows two digital line segments with 45° slope. If 4-neighbourhoods are used the lines are not contiguous at each of their points. An even worse conflict with intuitive understanding of line properties is also illustrated; two perpendicular lines do intersect in one case (upper right intersection) and do not intersect in another case (lower left) as they do not have any common point.

It is known from Euclidean geometry that each closed curve (e.g. a circle)

---

[4]Some image processing literature does not distinguish holes and background and calls both of them background.

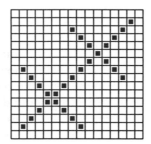

Figure 2.7 *Digital line.*

divides the plane into two non-contiguous regions. If images are digitized in a square grid using the 8-neighbourhood relation we can draw a line from the inner part of a closed curve into the outer part which does not intersect the curve (Figure 2.8). This implies that the inner and outer part of the curve constitute only one region because all pixels of the line belong to only one region. This is another paradox.

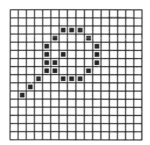

Figure 2.8 *Closed curve paradox.*

One possible solution to contiguity paradoxes is to treat objects using 4-neighbourhoods and background using 8-neighbourhoods (or vice versa). More exact treatment of digital images paradoxes and its solution for binary images and images with more brightness levels can be found in [Pavlidis 77, Horn 86].

These problems are typical on square grids – a hexagonal grid (see Figure 2.4), however, solves many of them. Any point in the hexagonal raster has the same distance to all its six neighbours. There are some problems peculiar to the hexagonal raster as well – for instance it is difficult to express a Fourier transform on it. Most digitizing devices use a square grid.

The **border** of a region is another important concept in image analysis. The border of region R is the set of pixels within the region that have one or more neighbours outside R. The definition corresponds to an intuitive understanding of the border as a set of points at the limit of the region. This definition of border is sometimes referred to as **inner border** to distinguish it from the **outer border** that is the border of the background (i.e. its complement) of the region.

An **edge** is a further concept. *Edge* is a local property of a pixel and its immediate neighbourhood – it is a vector given by a magnitude and direction. Images with many brightness levels are used for edge computation, and the gradient of the image function is used to compute edges. The edge direction is perpendicular to the gradient direction which points in the direction of image function growth. Edges are considered in detail in Section 4.3.2.

Note that there is a difference between *border* and *edge*. The border is a global concept related to a region, while *edge* expresses local properties of an image function. The border and edges are related as well. One possibility for finding boundaries is chaining the significant edges (points with high gradient of the image function). Methods of this kind are described in Section 5.2.

The edge property is attached to one pixel and its neighbourhood – sometimes it is of advantage to assess properties between pairs of neighbouring pixels and the concept of the **crack edge** comes from this idea. Four crack edges are attached to each pixel, which are defined by its relation to its 4-neighbours. The direction of the crack edge is that of increasing brightness, and is a multiple of $90°$, while its magnitude is the absolute difference between the brightness of the relevant pair of pixels. Crack edges are illustrated in Figure 2.9 and will be used later on in image segmentation, Chapter 5.

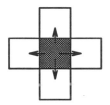

Figure 2.9 *Crack edges.*

Topological properties of images are invariant to *rubber sheet transformations*. Imagine a small rubber balloon with an object painted on it; topological properties of the object are those which are invariant to the arbitrary stretching of the rubber sheet. Stretching does not change contiguity of the object parts and does not change the number of holes in regions. One such image property is the **Euler–Poincaré characteristic**, defined as the difference between the number of regions and the number of holes in them. Further properties that are not *rubber sheet* invariant are described in Section 6.3.1.

A **convex hull** is a concept used to describe topological properties of objects. The convex hull is the smallest region which contains the object, such that any two points of the region can be connected by a straight line, all points of which belong to the region. For example, consider an object whose shape resembles a letter 'R' (see Figure 2.10a). Imagine a thin rubber band pulled around the object (Figure 2.10b). The shape of the rubber band provides the convex hull of the object. Calculation of the convex hull is described in Section 6.3.3.

Figure 2.10 *Description using topological components: (a) An 'R' object, (b) its convex hull, (c) lakes and bays.*

An object with non-regular shape can be represented by a collection of its topological components. The set inside the convex hull which does not belong to an object is called the **deficit of convexity**; this can be split into two subsets. Firstly, **lakes** (Figure 2.10c and hatched), are fully surrounded by the object and secondly, **bays** are contiguous with the border of convex hull.

The convex hull, lakes and bays are sometimes used for object description; these features are used in Chapter 6 (object description) and in Chapter 10 (mathematical morphology).

2.3.2 Histograms

The **brightness histogram** $h_f(z)$ of an image provides the frequency of the brightness value z in the image – the histogram of an image with L grey levels is represented by a one-dimensional array with L elements.

Algorithm 2.1: Computing the brightness histogram

---

1. Assign zero values to all elements of the array h_f.

2. For all pixels (x, y) of the image f, increment $h_f(f(x,y))$ by one.

An image can be analysed as the realization of a stochastic process; in this case we might want to find a first order density function $p_1(z, x, y)$ to indicate that pixel (x, y) has brightness z. If the position of the pixel is not of interest, we obtain a density function $p_1(z)$, and the brightness histogram is its estimate.

The histogram is often displayed as a bar graph. The histogram of the image from Figure 2.3 is given in Figure 2.11.

The histogram is usually the only global information about the image which is available. It is used when finding optimal illumination conditions for capturing an image, grey scale transformations, and image segmentation to

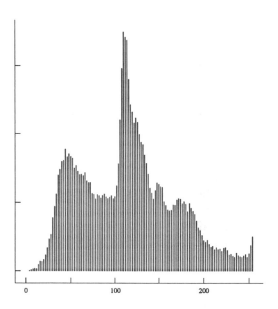

Figure 2.11 *A brightness histogram.*

objects and background. Note that one histogram may correspond to several images; for instance, change of object position on a constant background does not affect the histogram.

The histogram of a digital image typically has many local minima and maxima, which may complicate its further processing. This problem can be avoided by local smoothing of the histogram, for which local averaging of neighbouring histogram elements is the base. A new histogram $h'_f(z)$ is calculated according to

$$h'_f(z) = \frac{1}{2K+1} \sum_{i=-K}^{K} h_f(z+i) \qquad (2.45)$$

where K is a constant representing the size of the neighbourhood used for smoothing. Other techniques for smoothing exist, notably Gaussian blurring; in the case of a histogram, this would be a one-dimensional simplification of the 2D Gaussian blur, equation (4.50) which will be introduced in Section 4.3.3.

2.3.3 Visual perception of the image

Anyone who creates or uses algorithms or devices for digital image processing should take into account the principles of human image perception. If an image is to be analysed by a human the information should be expressed using such variables which are easy to perceive; these are psycho-physical parameters such as contrast, border, shape, texture, colour, etc. Humans will find objects in images only if they may be distinguished effortlessly from the background. A detailed description of the principles of human perception can be found in [Cornsweet 70, Winston 75, Marr 82, Levine 85]. Human perception of images provokes many illusions, the understanding of which provides valuable clues about visual mechanisms. Some of the better known illusions will be mentioned here – the topic is exhaustively covered from the point of view of computer vision in [Frisby 79].

The situation would be relatively easy if the human visual system had a linear response to composite input stimuli – i.e. a simple sum of individual stimuli. A decrease of some stimulus, e.g. area of the object in the image, could be compensated by its intensity, contrast or duration. In fact, the sensitivity of human senses is roughly logarithmically proportional to the intensity of an input signal. In this case after an initial logarithmic transformation, response to composite stimuli can be treated as linear.

Contrast

Contrast is the local change in brightness and is defined as the ratio between average brightness of an object and the background brightness. The human eye is logarithmically sensitive to brightness, implying that for the same perception, higher brightness requires higher contrast.

Apparent brightness depends very much on the brightness of the local background; this effect is called conditional contrast. Figure 2.12 illustrates this with two small squares of the same brightness on a dark and light background. Humans perceive the brightness of the small squares as different.

Acuity

Acuity is the the ability to detect details in the image. A human eye is less sensitive to slow and fast changes in brightness in the image plane but is more sensitive to intermediate changes. Acuity also decreases with increase in distance from the optical axis.

Resolution in an image is firmly bounded by the resolution ability of the human eye; there is no sense in representing visual information with higher resolution than that of the viewer. Resolution in optics is defined as the inverse value of a maximum viewing angle between the viewer and two proximate points which humans cannot distinguish, and so fuse together.

Human vision has the best resolution for objects which are at a distance of about 250 mm from an eye under illumination about 500 lux; this illumination is provided by a 60W bulb from a distance of 400 mm. Under these conditions the distance between two distinguishable points is approximately 0.16 mm.

Figure 2.12 *Conditional contrast.*

Object border

The object border carries a lot of information [Marr 82]. Boundaries of objects and simple patterns such as blobs or lines enable adaptation effects similar to conditional contrast, mentioned above. The Ebbinghaus illusion is a well known example – two circles of the same diameter in the centre of images appear to have different diameters (Figure 2.13).

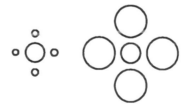

Figure 2.13 *The Ebbinghaus illusion.*

Colour

Colour is another image property which is very important for perception since the human eye is more sensitive to colour than to brightness under normal illumination conditions. Colour quantization and representation have been mentioned in Section 2.2.2; colour can be expressed as a combination of the three basic components red, green, and blue (RGB). Colour **perception** is better expressed in an alternative co-ordinate system, **intensity, hue** and

saturation (IHS). Intensity is the sum of R, G, and B components; hue is approximately proportional to the average wavelength in the appropriate spectrum; saturation measures the deficit of white colour. For instance, grass green or fire-engine red is saturated. Conversely, pink or light blue colours are not saturated.

Colour perception is burdened with similar adaptation illusions as other psycho-physical quantities.

2.3.4 Image quality

An image might be degraded during capture, transmission or processing. Measures of image quality can be used to assess the degree of degradation. The quality required naturally depends on the purpose for which an image is used.

Methods for assessing image quality can be divided into two categories: subjective and objective. Subjective methods are often used in television technology, where the ultimate criterion is the perception of a selected group of professional and lay viewers. They appraise an image according to a list of criteria and give appropriate marks. Details about subjective methods may be found in [Pratt 78].

Objective quantitative methods measuring image quality are more interesting for our purposes. Good assent to subjective criteria and an easy evaluation procedure are expected, then the quantitative image quality measure can be used as a criterion in parameter optimization. The quality of the image $f(x,y)$ is usually estimated by comparison with a known reference image $g(x,y)$ [Rosenfeld and Kak 82]. A synthesized image is often used for this purpose. One class of methods uses simple measures such as the mean quadratic difference $\int \int (g - f)^2 \, dx \, dy$. The problem here is that it is not possible to distinguish a few big differences from a lot of small differences. Instead of the mean quadratic difference, the mean absolute difference or simply maximal absolute difference may be used. Correlation between images f and g is another alternative.

Another class measures the resolution of small or proximate objects in the image. An image consisting of parallel black and white stripes is used for this purpose; then the number of black and white pairs per millimetre gives the resolution.

2.3.5 Noise in images

Real images are often degraded by some random errors – this degradation is usually called **noise**. Noise can occur during image capture, transmission or processing, and may be dependent on, or independent of, image content.

Noise is usually described by its probabilistic characteristics. Idealized noise, called **white noise**, which has constant power spectrum $S = const$

(see equation (2.26)), meaning that its intensity does not decrease with increasing frequency, is often used. White noise is frequently applied as the worst approximation of degradation, its advantage being that its use simplifies calculations. **Gaussian noise** is another popular noise approximation. A random variable with Gaussian (normal) distribution has its probability density given by the Gaussian curve. In the 1D case the density function is

$$p(x) = \frac{1}{\sigma\sqrt{2\pi}} e^{\frac{-(x-\mu)^2}{2\sigma^2}} \tag{2.46}$$

where μ is the mean and σ the standard deviation of the random variable. Gaussian noise is a very good approximation to noise that occurs in many practical cases.

When an image is transmitted through some channel, noise which is usually independent of the image signal occurs. Similar noise arises in a vidicon camera. This signal-independent degradation is called **additive noise** and can be described by the following model

$$f(x,y) = g(x,y) + \nu(x,y) \tag{2.47}$$

where the noise ν and the input image g are independent variables.

The noise magnitude depends in many cases on the signal magnitude itself. If the noise magnitude is much higher in comparison with the signal we can write

$$f = g + \nu g = g(1 + \nu) \approx g\nu \tag{2.48}$$

This model describes **multiplicative noise**. An example of multiplicative noise is television raster degradation which depends on TV lines; in the area of a line this noise is maximal, and between two lines it is minimal. Another example of multiplicative noise is the degradation of film material caused by the finite size of silver grains used in photosensitive emulsion.

Quantization noise occurs when insufficient quantization levels are used, for example, 50 levels for a monochromatic image. In this case false contours appear. Quantization noise can be eliminated simply, see Section 2.2.2.

Impulsive noise means that an image is corrupted with individual noisy pixels whose brightness significantly differs from the neighbourhood. The term **salt and pepper noise** is used to describe saturated impulsive noise – an image corrupted with white and/or black pixels is an example. Salt and pepper noise can corrupt binary images.

The problem of suppressing noise in images is addressed in Chapter 4. If nothing is known a priori about noise properties, local pre-processing methods are appropriate (Section 4.3). If the noise parameters are known in advance, image restoration techniques can be used (Section 4.4).

References

[Ballard and Brown 82] D H Ballard and C M Brown. *Computer Vision.* Prentice-Hall, Englewood Cliffs, NJ, 1982.

[Cornsweet 70] T N Cornsweet. *Visual Perception.* Academic Press, New York, 1970.

[Frisby 79] J P Frisby. *Seeing – Illusion, Brain and Mind.* Oxford University Press, Oxford, UK, 1979.

[Horn 86] B K P Horn. *Robot Vision.* MIT Press, Cambridge, Ma, 1986.

[Levine 85] M D Levine. *Vision in Man and Machine.* McGraw Hill, New York, 1985.

[Marr 82] D Marr. *Vision – A Computational Investigation into the Human Representation and Processing of Visual Information.* W.H. Freeman and Co., San Francisco, 1982.

[Papoulis 62] A Papoulis. *The Fourier Integral and Its Application.* McGraw Hill, New York, 1962.

[Papoulis 65] A Papoulis. *Probability, Random Variables, and Stochastic Processes.* McGraw Hill, New York, 1965.

[Pavlidis 77] T Pavlidis. *Structural Pattern Recognition.* Springer Verlag, Berlin, 1977.

[Pavlidis 82] T Pavlidis. *Algorithms for Graphics and Image Processing.* Computer Science Press, New York, 1982.

[Pratt 78] W K Pratt. *Digital Image Processing.* John Wiley and Sons, New York, 1978.

[Pratt 91] W K Pratt. *Digital Image Processing.* John Wiley and Sons, New York, 2nd edition, 1991.

[Rogers 85] D F Rogers. *Procedural Elements of Computer Graphics.* McGraw Hill, New York, 1985.

[Rosenfeld and Kak 82] A Rosenfeld and A C Kak. *Digital Picture Processing.* Academic Press, New York, 2nd edition, 1982.

[Winston 75] P H Winston, editor. *The Psychology of Computer Vision.* McGraw Hill, New York, 1975.

3

Data structures for image analysis

Data and an algorithm are the two basic parts of any program, and they are related to each other – data organization often considerably affect the simplicity of the selection and the implementation of an algorithm. The choice of data structures is therefore a fundamental question when writing a program [Wirth 76]. Information about the representation of image data, and the data which can be deduced from them, will here be introduced before explaining different image processing methods. Relations between different types of representations of image data will then be clearer.

First we shall deal with basic levels of representation of information in image analysis tasks; then with traditional data structures such as matrices, chains and relational structures. Lastly we consider hierarchical data structures such as pyramids and quadtrees.

3.1 Levels of image data representation

The aim of computer visual perception is to find a relation between an input image and models created of the real world. During the transition from the raw input image to the model, image information becomes denser and the semantic knowledge about the interpretation of image data is used more and more. Several levels of visual information representation are defined on the way between the input image and the model; computer vision then comprises a design of the;

- Intermediate representations (data structures)

- Algorithms used for the creation of representations and introduction of relations between them

The representations can be stratified in four levels [Ballard and Brown 82], however there are no strict borders between them and a more detailed classification of the representational levels is used in some applications. The proposed four representational levels are ordered from signals at a low level of abstraction to the description that a human can perceive. The information flow between the levels may be bi-directional. For some specific uses, some representations can be omitted.

The first, lowest representational level – **iconic images** – consists of images containing original data; integer matrices with data about pixel brightness. Images of this kind are also outputs of pre-processing operations (e.g. filtration or edge sharpening) used for highlighting some aspects of the image important for further treatment.

The second level of representation is **segmented images**. Parts of the image are joined into groups that probably belong to the same objects. For instance, the output of the segmentation of a scene with polyhedra is either line segments coinciding with borders or two-dimensional regions corresponding with faces of bodies. It is useful to know something about the application domain while doing image segmentation; it is then easier to deal with noise and other problems associated with erroneous image data.

The third representational level is **geometric representations** holding knowledge about 2D and 3D shapes. The quantification of a shape is very difficult but also very important. Geometric representations are useful while doing general and complex simulations of the influence of illumination and motion in real objects. We need them also for the transition between natural raster images (gained, for example, by a TV camera) and data used in computer graphics (CAD – computer aided design, DTP – desk top publishing).

The fourth level of representation of image data is **relational models**. They give us the ability to treat data more efficiently and at a higher level of abstraction. A priori knowledge about the case being solved is usually used in processing of this kind. AI techniques are often explored; the information gained from the image may be represented by semantic nets or frames [Nilsson 82].

An example will illustrate a priori knowledge. Imagine a satellite image of a piece of land, and the task of counting planes standing at an airport; the a priori knowledge is the position of the airport which can be deduced, for instance, from a map. Relations to other objects in the image may help as well, e.g. to roads, lakes, urban areas. Additional a priori knowledge is given by geometric models of planes for which we are searching.

3.2   Traditional image data structures

Traditional image data structures such as matrices, chains, graphs, lists of object properties, and relational databases are important not only for the direct representation of image information; they are also a basis of more complex hierarchical methods of image representation.

3.2.1 Matrices

A matrix is the most common data structure for low-level representation of an image. Elements of the matrix are integer numbers corresponding to brightness, or to another property of the corresponding pixel of the sampling grid. Image data of this kind are usually the direct output of the image capturing device, e.g. a scanner. Pixels of both rectangular and hexagonal sampling grids can be represented by a matrix. The correspondence between data and matrix elements is obvious for a rectangular grid; with a hexagonal grid every even row in the image is shifted half a pixel to the right.

Image information in the matrix is accessible through the co-ordinates of a pixel that correspond with row and column indices. The matrix is a full representation of the image independent of the contents of image data – it implicitly contains **spatial relations** among semantically important parts of the image. The space is two-dimensional in the case of an image – a plane. One very natural spatial relation is the **neighbourhood relation**. A representation of a segmented image by a matrix usually saves more memory than an explicit list of all spatial relations between all objects, however sometimes we need to record other relations between objects.

Some special images that are represented by matrices are:

- A **binary image** (an image with two brightness levels only) is represented by a matrix containing only zeros and ones.

- Several matrices can contain information about one **multispectral image**. Each of these matrices contains one image corresponding to one spectral band.

- Matrices of different resolution are used to obtain **hierarchical image data structures**. This hierarchical representation of the image can be very convenient for parallel computers with the 'processor array' architecture.

Most programming languages use a standard array data structure to represent a matrix, and most modern machines provide adequate physical memory to accommodate image data structures. If they do not, they are usually provided with virtual memory to make storage transparent. Historically, memory limitations were a significant obstacle to image applications, requiring individual image parts to be retrieved from disk independently.

There is much image data in the matrix so that processing takes a long time. Image algorithms can be speeded up if global information about the image is derived from the original image matrix first – global information is more concise and occupies less memory. We have already mentioned the most popular example of global information – the histogram – in Section 2.3.2. Looking at the image from a probabilistic point of view, the histogram is an estimate of the probability density of a phenomenon; that an image pixel has a certain brightness.

Another example of global information is the **co-occurrence matrix** [Pavlidis 82], which represents an estimate of the probability that a pixel (i_1, j_1) has intensity z and a pixel (i_2, j_2) has intensity y. Suppose that the probability depends only on a certain spatial relation r between a pixel of brightness z and a pixel of brightness y; then information about the relation r is recorded in the square co-occurrence matrix C_r, whose dimensions correspond to the number of brightness levels of the image. To reduce the number of matrices C_r, let us introduce some simplifying assumptions; firstly consider only direct neighbours, and then treat relations as symmetrical (without orientation). The following algorithm calculates the co-occurrence matrix C_r from the image $f(i, j)$.

Algorithm 3.1: Co-occurrence matrix $C_r(z, y)$ for the relation r

1. Assign $C_r(z, y) = 0$ for all $z, y \in [0, L]$, where L is the maximum brightness.

2. For all pixels (i_1, j_1) in the image, determine (i_2, j_2) which has the relation r with the pixel (i_1, j_1), and perform

$$C_r(f(i_1, j_1), f(i_2, j_2)) = C_r(f(i_1, j_1), f(i_2, j_2)) + 1$$

If the relation r is *to be a southern or eastern 4-neighbour of the pixel* (i_1, j_1), *or identity*[1] elements of the co-occurrence matrix have some interesting properties. Values of the elements at the diagonal of the co-occurrence matrix $C_r(k, k)$ are equal to the area of the regions in the image with the brightness k. Thus the diagonal elements correspond to the histogram. The values of elements off the diagonal of the matrix $C_r(k, j)$ are equal to the length of the border dividing regions with brightnesses k and j, $k \neq j$. For instance, in an image with low contrast the elements of the co-occurrence matrix that are far from the diagonal are equal to zero or are very small. For high contrast images the opposite is true.

The main reason for considering co-occurrence matrices is their ability to describe texture. This approach to texture analysis is introduced in Chapter 13.

---

[1] For the purpose of the co-occurrence matrix creation we need to consider the identity relation $(i_1, j_1) = (i_2, j_2)$ or individual pixels would not contribute into the histogram.

3.2.2 *Chains*

Chains are used for the description of object borders in computer vision. One element of the chain is a basic symbol; this approach permits the application of formal language theory for computer vision tasks. Chains are appropriate for data that can be arranged as a sequence of symbols, and the neighbouring symbols in a chain usually correspond to the neighbourhood of primitives in the image. The primitive is the basic descriptive element that is used in syntactic pattern recognition (see Chapter 7).

This rule of proximity (neighbourhood) of symbols and primitives has exceptions – for example, the first and the last symbol of the chain describing a closed border are not neighbours, but the corresponding primitives in the image are. Similar inconsistencies are typical of image description languages [Shaw 69], too. Chains are linear structures, which is why they cannot describe spatial relations in the image on the basis of neighbourhood or proximity.

Chain codes (and Freeman codes) [Freeman 61] are often used for the description of object borders, or other one-pixel wide lines in images. The border is defined by the co-ordinates of its reference pixel and the sequence of symbols corresponding to the line of the unit length in several predefined orientations. Notice that a chain code is of a relative nature; data are expressed relatively with respect to some reference point. An example of a chain code is shown in Figure 3.1, where 8-neighbourhoods were used. It is possible to define chain codes using 4-neighbourhoods as well. Chain codes and their properties are described in more detail in Chapter 6.

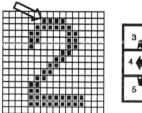

Figure 3.1 *An example chain code; the reference pixel is marked by an arrow:* *00007766555556600000006444444422211111122234445652211.*

If local information is needed from the chain code then it is necessary to search through the whole chain systematically. For instance if we want to know whether the border turns somewhere to the left by 90°, we must just find a sample pair of symbols in the chain – it is simple. On the other hand, a question about the shape of the border near the pixel (i_0, j_0) is not trivial. It is necessary to investigate all chains until the pixel (i_0, j_0) is found and only then we can start to analyse a short part of the border that is close to the pixel (i_0, j_0).

The description of an image by chains is appropriate for syntactic pattern recognition that is based on formal language theory methods. When working with real images, the problem of how to deal with uncertainty caused by noise arises, which is why several syntactic analysis techniques with deformation correction have arisen [Lu and Fu 78]. Another way to deal with noise is to smooth the border or to approximate it by another curve. This new border curve is then described by chain codes [Pavlidis 77].

Run length coding is quite often used to represent strings of symbols in an image matrix (for instance, FAX machines use run length coding). For simplicity, consider a binary image first. Run length coding records only areas that belong to the object in the image; the area is then represented as a list of lists. Each row of the image is described by a sublist, the first element of which is the row number. Subsequent terms are co-ordinate pairs; the first element of a pair is the beginning of a run and the second is the end. There can be several such sequences in the row. Run length coding is illustrated in Figure 3.2. The main advantage of run length coding is the existence of simple algorithms for intersections and unions of regions in the image.

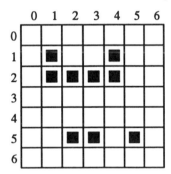

Figure 3.2 *Run length coding; the code is ((11144)(214)(52355)).*

Run length coding can be used for an image with multiple brightness levels as well – in this case sequences of neighbouring pixels in a row that has constant brightness are considered. In the sublist we must record not only the beginning and the end of the sequence, but its brightness, too.

From the implementational point of view chains can be represented using static data structures (e.g. 1D arrays); their size is the longest length of the chain expected. This might be too memory consuming, and so dynamic data structures are more advantageous. Lists from the LISP language are an example.

3.2.3 Topological data structures

Topological data structures describe the image as a set of elements and their relations. These relations are often represented using graphs. A **graph**

$G = (V, E)$ is an algebraic structure which consists of a set of nodes $V = \{v_1, v_2, \ldots, v_n\}$ and a set of arcs $E = \{e_1, e_2, \ldots, e_m\}$. Each arc e_k is incident to an unordered pair of nodes $\{v_i, v_j\}$ which are not necessarily distinct [Even 79]. The degree of the node is equal to the number of incident arcs of the node.

An **evaluated graph** is a graph in which values are assigned to arcs, to nodes or to both – these values may, for example, represent weights, or costs.

The **region adjacency graph** is typical of this class of data structures, in which nodes correspond to regions and neighbouring regions are connected by an arc. The segmented image, see Chapter 5, consists of regions with similar properties (brightness, texture, colour, ...) that correspond to some entities in the scene. The neighbourhood relation is fulfilled when the regions have some common border. An example of an image with areas labelled by numbers and the corresponding region adjacency graph is shown in Figure 3.3; the label zero denotes pixels out of the image. This value is used to indicate regions that touch borders of the image in the region adjacency graph.

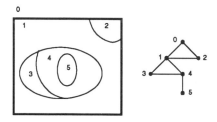

Figure 3.3 *An example region adjacency graph.*

The region adjacency graph has several attractive features. If a region encloses other regions, then the part of the graph corresponding with the areas inside can be separated by a cut in the graph. Nodes of degree one represent simple holes.

Arcs of the region adjacency graph can include a description of the relations between neighbouring regions – the relations *to be to the left* or *to be inside* are common. The region adjacency graph can be used for matching with a stored pattern for recognition purposes.

The region adjacency graph is usually created from the **region map**, which is a matrix of the same dimensions as the original image matrix whose elements are identification labels of the regions. To create the region adjacency graph, borders of all regions in the image are traced, and labels of all neighbouring regions are stored. The region adjacency graph can easily be created from an image represented by a quadtree as well (see Section 3.3.2).

The region adjacency graph stores information about the neighbours of all regions in the image explicitly. The region map contains this information as

No.	Object name	Colour	Min. row	Min. col.	Inside
1	sun	white	5	40	2
2	sky	blue	0	0	-
3	cloud	grey	20	180	2
4	tree trunk	brown	95	75	6
5	tree crown	green	53	63	-
6	hill	light green	97	0	-
7	pond	blue	100	160	6

Table 3.1 *Relational table*

well but it is much more difficult to recall from there. If we want to relate the region adjacency graph to the region map quickly, it is sufficient for a node in the region adjacency graph to be marked by the identification label of the region and some representative pixel (e.g. the top left pixel of the region).

3.2.4 Relational structures

Relational databases [Kunii et al. 74] can also be used for representation of information from an image; all the information is then concentrated in relations between semantically important parts of the image – objects – that are the result of segmentation (Chapter 5). Relations are recorded in the form of tables. An example of such a representation is shown in Figure 3.4 and Table 3.1, where individual objects are associated with their names and other features, e.g. the top-left pixel of the corresponding region in the image. Relations between objects are expressed in the relational table as well. In Figure 3.4 and Table 3.1, such a relation is *to be inside*; for example, the object 7 (pond) is situated inside the object 6 (hill).

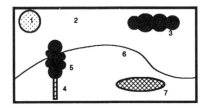

Figure 3.4 *Description of objects using relational structure.*

Description by means of relational structures is appropriate for higher levels of image understanding. In this case searches using keys, similar to database searches, can be used to speed up the whole process.

3.3   Hierarchical data structures

Computer vision is by its nature very computationally expensive, if for no other reason than the large amount of data to be processed. Systems which we might call sophisticated must process considerable quantities of image data – hundreds of kilobytes to tens of megabytes. Usually a very quick response is expected because the system should be interactive. One of the solutions is to use parallel computers (in other words brute force). Unfortunately there are many computer vision problems that are very difficult to divide among processors, or decompose in any way. Hierarchical data structures make it possible to use algorithms which decide a strategy for processing on the basis of relatively small quantities of data. They work at the finest resolution only with those parts of the image for which it is essential, using knowledge instead of brute force to ease and speed up the processing. We are going to introduce two typical structures, pyramids and quadtrees.

3.3.1   Pyramids

Pyramids are among the simplest hierarchical data structures. We distinguish between **M-pyramids** (matrix-pyramids) and **T-pyramids** (tree-pyramids).

A **Matrix-pyramid** (M-pyramid) is a sequence $\{M_L, M_{L-1}, \ldots, M_0\}$ of images, where M_L has the same dimensions and elements as the original image, and M_{i-1} is derived from the M_i by reducing the resolution by one half. When creating pyramids it is customary to work with square matrices having dimensions equal to powers of two – then M_0 corresponds to one pixel only.

M-pyramids are used when it is necessary to work with an image at different resolutions simultaneously. An image having one degree smaller resolution in a pyramid contains four times less data, so that it is processed approximately four times as quickly.

Often it is advantageous to use several resolutions simultaneously rather than to choose just one image from the M-pyramid. For such algorithms we prefer to use **tree-pyramids**, a tree structure. Let 2^L be the size of an original image (the highest resolution). A tree-pyramid (T-pyramid) is defined by:

1. A set of nodes $P = \{P = (k, i, j)$ such that level $k \in [0, L]; i, j \in [0, 2^k - 1]\}$.

2. A mapping F between subsequent nodes P_{k-1}, P_k of the pyramid,

$$F(k, i, j) = (k - 1, i \ div \ 2, j \ div \ 2)$$

where *div* denotes whole-number division.

3. A function V that maps a node of the pyramid P to Z, where Z is the subset of the whole numbers corresponding to the number of brightness levels, for example, $Z = \{0, 1, 2, \ldots, 255\}$.

Nodes of a T-pyramid correspond for a given k with image points of an M-pyramid; elements of the set of nodes $P = \{(k, i, j)\}$ correspond with individual matrices in the M-pyramid – k is called the level of the pyramid. An image $P = \{(k, i, j)\}$ for a specific k constitutes an image at the kth level of the pyramid. F is the so-called parent mapping, which is defined for all nodes P_k of the T-pyramid except its root $(0, 0, 0)$. Every node of the T-pyramid has four child nodes except leaf nodes, which are nodes of level L that correspond to the individual pixels in the image.

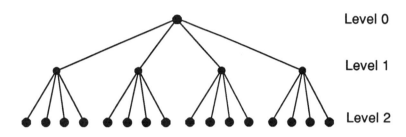

Level 0

Level 1

Level 2

Figure 3.5 *T-pyramid.*

Values of individual nodes of the T-pyramid are defined by the function V. Values of leaf nodes are the same as values of the image function (brightness) in the original image at the finest resolution; the image size is 2^{L-1}. Values of nodes in other levels of the tree are either an arithmetic mean of four child nodes or they are defined by coarser sampling, meaning that the value of one child (e.g. top left) is used. Figure 3.5 shows the structure of a simple T-pyramid.

The number of image pixels used by an M-pyramid for storing all matrices is given by

$$N^2 \left(1 + \frac{1}{4} + \frac{1}{16} + \ldots\right) \approx 1.33 \, N^2 \tag{3.1}$$

where N is the dimension of the original matrix (the image of finest resolution) – usually a power of two, 2^L.

The T-pyramid is represented in memory similarly. Arcs of the tree need not be recorded because addresses of the both child and parent nodes are easy to compute due to the regularity of the structure. An algorithm for the effective creation and storing of a T-pyramid is given in [Pavlidis 82].

3.3.2   Quadtrees

Quadtrees are modifications of T-pyramids. Every node of the tree except the leaves has four children (NW: north-western, NE: north-eastern, SW: south-western, SE: south-eastern). Similarly to T-pyramids, the image is divided into four quadrants at each hierarchical level, however it is not necessary to keep nodes at all levels. If a parent node has four children of the same value (e.g. brightness), it is not necessary to record them. This representation is less expensive for an image with large homogeneous regions; Figure 3.6 is an example of a simple quadtree.

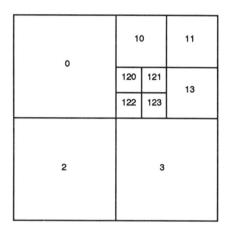 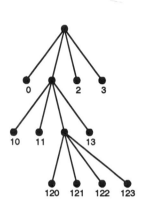

Figure 3.6 *Quadtree.*

An advantage of image representation by means of quadtrees is the existence of simple algorithms for addition of images, computing object areas and statistical moments. The main disadvantage of quadtrees and pyramid hierarchical representations is their dependence on the position, orientation and relative size of objects. Two similar images with just very small differences can have very different pyramid or quadtree representations. Even two images depicting the same, slightly shifted scene, can have entirely different representations.

These disadvantages can be overcome using a normalized shape of quadtree in which we do not create the quadtree for the whole image, but for its individual objects. Geometrical features of objects such as the centre of gravity and principal axis are used (see Chapter 6); the centre of gravity and principal axis of every object are derived first and then the smallest enclosing square centred at the centre of gravity having sides parallel with the principal axes is located. The square is then represented by a quadtree. An object described by a normalized quadtree and several additional items of data (co-ordinates of the centre of gravity, angle of main axes) is invariant to shifting, rotation and scale.

Node type
Pointer to the NW son
Pointer to the NE son
Pointer to the SW son
Pointer to the SE son
Pointer to the father
Other data

Figure 3.7 *Record describing a quadtree node.*

Quadtrees are usually represented by recording the whole tree as a list of its individual nodes, every node being a record with several items characterizing it. An example is given in Figure 3.7. In the item *Node type* there is information about whether the node is a leaf or inside the tree. Other data can be the level of the node in the tree, position in the picture, code of the node, etc. This kind of representation is expensive in memory. Its advantage is in easy access to any node thanks to pointers between parents and children.

It is possible to represent a quadtree with less demand on memory by means of a **leaf code**. Any point of the picture is coded by a sequence of digits reflecting successive divisions of the quadtree; zero means the NW (northwest) quadrant, and likewise for other quadrants: 1-NE, 2-SW, 3-SE. The most important digit of the code (on the left) corresponds to the division at the highest level, the least important one (on the right) with the last division. The number of digits in the code is the same as the number of levels of the quadtree. The whole tree is then described by a sequence of pairs – the leaf code and the brightness of the region. Programs creating quadtrees can use recursive procedures to advantage.

T-pyramids are very similar to quadtrees, but differ in two basic respects. A T-pyramid is a balanced structure, meaning that the corresponding tree divides the image regardless of the contents which is why it is regular and symmetric. A quadtree is not balanced. The other difference is in the interpretation of values of the individual nodes.

A modification of the pyramid structure is a pyramid having four parents and sixteen children. In [Burt et al. 81] this structure was used for hierarchical image segmentation. Using quadtrees, where every element of the kth level has exactly four children in the $(k + 1)^{th}$ level, corresponding areas always have a square shape, which is not the case in reality. For this reason, a more complicated data structure was proposed which is a pyramid, every element of which can belong to one of four potential parents and have as many as sixteen children. This type of structure removes inappropriate features – areas need not be square-shaped and approximate real objects better.

Some branches of the tree corresponding to hierarchical data structures have many levels while others, corresponding with homogeneous areas, have few of them. This feature results in poor balance which can be disadvantageous for access time and for its recording in computer memory. A similar problem had been met already in the field of database systems, and a solution found in B-trees (balanced-trees) [Comer 79]. The number of disk accesses necessary is lower for data files stored in an external memory and processing is quicker.

References

[Ballard and Brown 82] D H Ballard and C M Brown. *Computer Vision.* Prentice-Hall, Englewood Cliffs, NJ, 1982.

[Burt et al. 81] P Y Burt, T H Hong, and A Rosenfeld. Segmentation and estimation of image region properties through cooperative hierarchical computation. *IEEE Transactions on Systems, Man and Cybernetics*, 11(12):802–809, 1981.

[Comer 79] D Comer. The ubiquitous B–tree. *Computing Surveys*, 11(2):121–137, 1979.

[Even 79] S Even. *Graph Algorithms.* Computer Science Press, Rockville, Md, 1979.

[Freeman 61] H Freeman. On the enconding of arbitrary geometric configuration. *IRE Transactions on Electronic Computers*, EC–10(2):260–268, 1961.

[Kunii et al. 74] T L Kunii, S Weyl, and I M Tenenbaum. A relation database schema for describing complex scenes with color and texture. In *Proceedings of the 2nd International Joint Conference on Pattern Recognition*, pages 310–316, Copenhagen, Denmark, 1974.

[Lu and Fu 78] S Y Lu and K S Fu. A syntactic approach to texture analysis. *Computer Graphics and Image Processing*, 7:303–330, 1978.

[Nilsson 82] N J Nilsson. *Principles of Artificial Intelligence.* Springer Verlag, Berlin, 1982.

[Pavlidis 77] T Pavlidis. *Structural Pattern Recognition.* Springer Verlag, Berlin, 1977.

[Pavlidis 82] T Pavlidis. *Algorithms for Graphics and Image Processing.* Computer Science Press, New York, 1982.

[Shaw 69] A C Shaw. A formal picture description schema as a basis for picture processing systems. *Information and Control*, 14:9–52, 1969.

[Wirth 76] N Wirth. *Algorithms + Data Structures = Programs.* Prentice-Hall, Englewood Cliffs, NJ, 1976.

4

Image pre-processing

Pre-processing is a common name for operations with images at the lowest level of abstraction – both input and output are intensity images. These iconic images are of the same kind as the original data captured by the sensor, with an intensity image usually represented by a matrix of image function values (brightnesses). The aim of pre-processing is an improvement of the image data that suppresses unwilling distortions or enhances some image features important for further processing, although geometric transformations of images (e.g. rotation, scaling, translation) are classified among pre-processing methods here since similar techniques are used.

Image pre-processing methods are classified into four categories according to the size of the pixel neighbourhood that is used for the calculation of a new pixel brightness. Section 4.1 deals with pixel brightness transformations, Section 4.2 describes geometric transformations, Section 4.3 considers pre-processing methods that use a local neighbourhood of the processed pixel and Section 4.4 briefly characterizes image restoration that requires knowledge about the entire image.

Some authors [Moik 80, Rosenfeld and Kak 82] classify image pre-processing methods differently into **image enhancement**, covering pixel brightness transformations (local pre-processing in our sense), and **image restoration**.

Image pre-processing methods use the considerable redundancy in images. Neighbouring pixels corresponding to one object in real images have essentially the same or similar brightness value, so if a distorted pixel can be picked out from the image, it can usually be restored as an average value of neighbouring pixels.

If pre-processing aims to correct some degradation in the image, the nature of a priori information is important:

- A first group of methods uses no knowledge about the nature of the degradation; only very general properties of the degradation are assumed.

- A second group assumes knowledge about the properties of the image acquisition device, and the conditions under which the image was obtained. The nature of noise (usually its spectral characteristics) is sometimes known.

- A third approach uses knowledge about objects that are searched for in the image, which may simplify the pre-processing very considerably. If knowledge about objects is not available in advance it can be estimated during the processing. The following strategy is possible; first the image is coarsely processed to reduce data quantity and to find that which is needed to create a hypothesis. This hypothesis is then verified in the image at finer resolution. Such an iterative process can be repeated until the presence of knowledge is verified or rejected. This feedback may span not only pre-processing, since segmentation also yields semantic knowledge about objects – thus feedback can be initiated after the object segmentation.

4.1 Pixel brightness transformations

A brightness transformation modifies pixel brightness – the transformation depends on the properties of a pixel itself. There are two classes of pixel brightness transformations: **brightness corrections** and **grey scale transformations**. Brightness correction modifies the pixel brightness taking into account its original brightness and its position in the image. Grey scale transformations change brightness without regard to position in the image.

4.1.1 Position-dependent brightness correction

Ideally, the sensitivity of image acquisition and digitization devices should not depend on position in the image, but this assumption is not valid in many practical cases. The lens attenuates light more if it passes further from the optical axis, and the photosensitive part of the sensor (vacuum tube camera, CCD camera elements) is not of identical sensitivity. Uneven object illumination is also a source of degradation.

If degradation is of a systematic nature, it can be suppressed by brightness correction. A multiplicative error coefficient $e(i, j)$ describes the change from the ideal identity transfer function; assume that $g(i, j)$ is the original undegraded image (or desired or true image) and $f(i, j)$ is the image containing degradation. Then

$$f(i, j) = e(i, j) \, g(i, j) \qquad (4.1)$$

The error coefficient $e(i, j)$ can be obtained if a reference image $g(i, j)$ with known brightnesses is captured, the simplest being an image of constant brightness c. The degraded result is the image $f_c(i, j)$ – then systematic brightness errors can be suppressed by

$$g(i, j) = \frac{f(i, j)}{e(i, j)} = \frac{c \, f(i, j)}{f_c(i, j)} \qquad (4.2)$$

This method can be used only if the image degradation process is stable, and if we wish to suppress this kind of error in the image capturing process we should perhaps calibrate the device (find error coefficients $e(i, j)$) from time to time.

This method implicitly assumes linearity of the transformation, which is not true in reality as the brightness scale is limited to some interval. The calculation according to equation (4.1) can overflow, and the limits of the brightness scale are used instead, implying that the best reference image has brightness that is far enough from both limits. If the grey scale has 256 brightnesses the ideal image[1] has constant brightness value 128.

4.1.2 Grey scale transformation

Grey scale transformations do not depend on the position of the pixel in the image. A transformation T of the original brightness p from scale $[p_0, p_k]$ into brightness q from a new scale $[q_0, q_k]$ is given by

$$q = T(p) \tag{4.3}$$

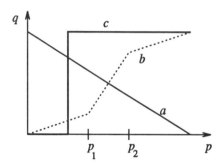

Figure 4.1 *Some grey scale transformations.*

The most common grey scale transformations are shown in Figure 4.1; the straight line a denotes the negative transformation; the piecewise linear function b enhances the image contrast between brightness values p_1 and p_2. The function c is called **brightness thresholding** and results in a black and white image.

Digital images have a very limited number of grey levels so grey scale transformations are easy to realise both in hardware and software. Often only 256 bytes of memory (called a **look-up table**) are needed. The original brightness is the index to the look-up, and the table content gives the new brightness. The image signal usually passes through a look-up table in image displays, enabling simple grey scale transformation in real time.

---

[1]Most TV cameras have automatic control of the gain which allows them to operate under changing illumination conditions. If systematic errors are suppressed using error coefficients this automatic gain control should be switched off first.

The same principle can be used for colour displays. A colour signal consists of three components – red, green, and blue; three look-up tables provide all possible colour scale transformations. These tables are called the **palette** in personal computer terminology.

Grey scale transformations are mainly used when an image is viewed by a human observer, and a transformed image might be more easily interpreted if the contrast is enhanced. For instance, an X-ray image can often be much clearer after transformation.

A grey scale transformation for contrast enhancement is usually found automatically using the **histogram equalization** technique. The aim is to get an image with equally distributed brightness levels over the whole brightness scale, see Figure 4.2. Histogram equalization enhances contrast for brightness values close to histogram maxima, and decreases contrast near minima.

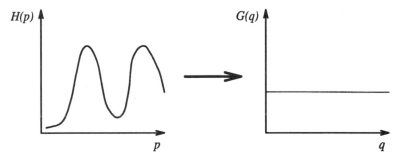

Figure 4.2 *Histogram equalization.*

Denote the input histogram by $H(p)$ and recall that the input grey scale is $[p_0, p_k]$. The intention is to find a monotonic pixel brightness transformation $q = T(p)$ such that the desired output histogram $G(q)$ is uniform over the whole whole output brightness scale $[q_0, q_k]$.

The histogram can be treated as a discrete probability density function. The monotonic property of the transform T implies

$$\sum_{i=0}^{k} G(q_i) = \sum_{i=0}^{k} H(p_i) \tag{4.4}$$

The sums in the equation (4.4) can be interpreted as the discrete distribution functions. Assume that the image has N rows and columns; then the equalized histogram $G(q)$ corresponds to the uniform probability density function f whose value is

$$f = \frac{N^2}{q_k - q_0} \tag{4.5}$$

The value from equation (4.5) replaces the left side of equation (4.4). The equalized histogram can be obtained precisely only for the 'idealized' continuous probability density, in which case equation (4.4) becomes

$$N^2 \int_{q_0}^{q} \frac{1}{q_k - q_0} \, ds = \frac{N^2(q - q_0)}{q_k - q_0} = \int_{p_0}^{p} H(s) \, ds \qquad (4.6)$$

The desired pixel brightness transformation $\mathcal{T}$ can then be derived as

$$q = \mathcal{T}(p) = \frac{q_k - q_0}{N^2} \int_{p_0}^{p} H(s) \, ds + q_0 \qquad (4.7)$$

The integral in equation (4.7) is called the **cumulative histogram**, which is approximated by a sum in digital images, and therefore the resulting histogram is not equalized ideally. The discrete approximation of the continuous pixel brightness transformation from equation (4.7) is

$$q = \mathcal{T}(p) = \frac{q_k - q_0}{N^2} \sum_{i=p_0}^{p} H(i) + q_0 \qquad (4.8)$$

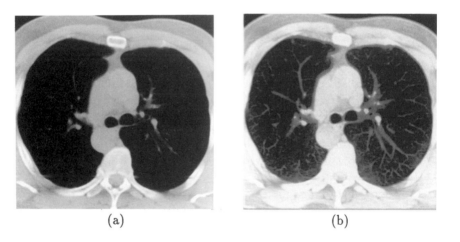

(a)   (b)

Figure 4.3 *Histogram equalization: (a) Original image, (b) equalized image.*

These results can be demonstrated on an image of a lung. An input image and its equalization are shown in Figure 4.3; their respective histograms are shown in Figure 4.4.

The **logarithmic** grey scale transformation function is another frequently used technique. It simulates the logarithmic sensitivity of the human eye to the light intensity.

Pseudocolour is another kind of grey scale transform. The individual brightnesses in the input monochromatic image are coded to some colour. Since the human eye is much more sensitive to change in colour than to change in brightness, one perceives much more detail in pseudocoloured images.

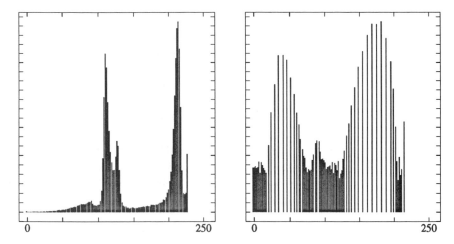

Figure 4.4 *Histogram equalization: Original and equalized histograms.*

4.2 Geometric transformations

Geometric transforms are common in computer graphics, and are often used in image analysis as well. Geometric transforms permit the elimination of the geometric distortion that occurs when an image is captured. If one attempts to match two different images of the same object, geometric transformation may be needed. We consider geometric transformations only in 2D, as this is sufficient for digital images. An example is an attempt to match remotely sensed images of the same area taken after one year, when the more recent image was probably not taken from precisely the same position. To inspect changes over the year, it is necessary first to execute a geometric transformation, and then subtract one image from the other.

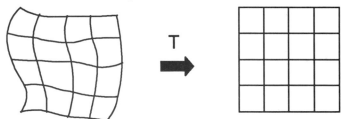

Figure 4.5 *Geometric transform on a plane.*

A geometric transform is a vector function **T** that maps the pixel (x, y) to a new position (x', y') – an illustration of the whole region transformed on a point-to-point basis is in Figure 4.5. **T** is defined by its two component equations

$$x' = T_x(x, y), \quad y' = T_y(x, y) \tag{4.9}$$

The transformation equations T_x and T_y are either known in advance, for example in the case of rotation, translation, scaling, or can be determined from known original and transformed images. Several pixels in both images with known correspondence are used to derive the unknown transformation.

A geometric transform consists of two basic steps: First is the **pixel co-ordinate transformation** which maps the co-ordinates of the input image pixel to the point in the output image. The output point co-ordinates should be computed as continuous values (real numbers) as the position does not necessarily match the digital grid after the transform. The second step is to find the point in the digital raster which matches the transformed point and determine its brightness value. The brightness is usually computed as an **interpolation** of the brightnesses of several points in the neighbourhood.

This idea enables the classification of geometric transforms among other pre-processing techniques, the criterion being that only the neighbourhood of a processed pixel is needed for the calculation. Geometric transforms are on the boundary between point and local operations.

4.2.1   Pixel co-ordinate transformations

Equation (4.9) shows the general case of finding the co-ordinates of a point in the output image after a geometric transform. It is usually approximated by a polynomial equation

$$x' = \sum_{r=0}^{m} \sum_{k=0}^{m-r} a_{rk}\, x^r\, y^k \qquad y' = \sum_{r=0}^{m} \sum_{k=0}^{m-r} b_{rk}\, x^r\, y^k \tag{4.10}$$

This transform is linear with respect to the coefficients a_{rk}, b_{rk} and so if pairs of corresponding points (x, y), (x', y') in both images are known, it is possible to determine a_{rk}, b_{rk} by solving a set of linear equations. More points than coefficients are usually used to provide robustness; the mean square method is often used.

In the case where the geometric transform does not change rapidly depending on position in the image, low-order approximating polynomials, $m = 2$ or $m = 3$, are used, needing at least 6 or 10 pairs of corresponding points. The corresponding points should be distributed in the image in a way that can express the geometric transformation – usually they are spread uniformly. In general, the higher the degree of the approximating polynomial, the more sensitive to the distribution of the pairs of corresponding points is the geometric transform.

Equation (4.9) is in practice approximated by a **bilinear transform** for which 4 pairs of corresponding points are sufficient to find transformation coefficients

$$x' = a_0 + a_1 x + a_2 y + a_3 xy$$
$$y' = b_0 + b_1 x + b_2 y + b_3 xy \tag{4.11}$$

Even simpler is the **affine transformation** for which three pairs of corresponding points are sufficient to find the coefficients

$$x' = a_0 + a_1 x + a_2 y$$
$$y' = b_0 + b_1 x + b_2 y \tag{4.12}$$

The affine transformation includes typical geometric transformations such as rotation, translation, scaling and skewing.

A geometric transform applied to the whole image may change the co-ordinate system, and a **Jacobean** J provides information about how the co-ordinate system changes

$$J = \left| \frac{\partial(x', y')}{\partial(x, y)} \right| = \begin{vmatrix} \frac{\partial x'}{\partial x} & \frac{\partial x'}{\partial y} \\ \frac{\partial y'}{\partial x} & \frac{\partial y'}{\partial y} \end{vmatrix} \tag{4.13}$$

If the transformation is singular (has no inverse) then $J = 0$. If the area of the image is invariant under the transformation then $J = 1$.

The Jacobean for the bilinear transform (4.11) is

$$J = a_1 b_2 - a_2 b_1 + (a_1 b_3 - a_3 b_1)x + (a_3 b_2 - a_2 b_3)y \tag{4.14}$$

and for the affine transformation (4.12) is

$$J = a_1 b_2 - a_2 b_1 \tag{4.15}$$

Some important geometric transformations are:

- **Rotation** by the angle ϕ about the origin

$$\begin{aligned} x' &= x \cos \phi + y \sin \phi \\ y' &= -x \sin \phi + y \cos \phi \\ J &= 1 \end{aligned} \tag{4.16}$$

- **Change of scale** a in the x axis and b in the y axis

$$\begin{aligned} x' &= ax \\ y' &= bx \\ J &= ab \end{aligned} \tag{4.17}$$

- **Skewing** by the angle ϕ is given by

$$\begin{aligned} x' &= x + y \tan \phi \\ y' &= y \\ J &= 1 \end{aligned} \tag{4.18}$$

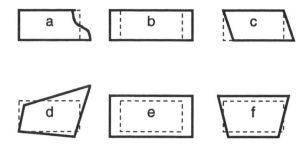

Figure 4.6 *Geometric distortion types.*

It is possible to approximate complex geometric transformations (distortion) by partitioning an image into smaller rectangular subimages; for each subimage, a simple geometric transformation, such as the affine, is estimated using pairs of corresponding pixels. The geometric transformation (distortion) is then repaired separately in each subimage.

There are some typical geometric distortions which have to be overcome in remote sensing. Errors may be caused by distortion of the optical systems, by the nonlinearities in row-by-row scanning and a non-constant sampling period. Wrong position or orientation of the sensor (or the satellite) with respect to the object is the main cause of rotation, skew, and line nonlinearity distortions. Panoramic distortion (Figure 4.6b) appears in line scanners with the mirror rotating at constant speed. Line nonlinearity distortion (Figure 4.6a) is caused by unequal distance of the object from the scanner mirror. The rotation of the Earth during image capture in a mechanical scanner generates skew distortion (Figure 4.6c). Change of distance from the sensor induces change-of-scale distortion (Figure 4.6e). Perspective projection causes perspective distortion (Figure 4.6f).

4.2.2 Brightness interpolation

Assume that the planar transformation given by equation (4.9) has been accomplished, and new point co-ordinates (x', y') obtained. The position of the point does not in general fit the discrete raster of the output image, and the collection of transformed points gives the samples of the output image with non-integer co-ordinates. Values on the integer grid are needed, and each pixel value in the output image raster can be obtained by **brightness interpolation** of some neighbouring non-integer samples [Moik 80].

Brightness interpolation influences image quality. The simpler the interpolation, the greater the loss in geometric and photometric accuracy, but the interpolation neighbourhood is often reasonably small due to computational load. The three most common interpolation methods are nearest neighbour, linear, and bicubic.

The brightness interpolation problem is usually expressed in a dual way by determining the brightness of the original point in the input image that corresponds to the point in the output image lying on the discrete raster. Assume that we wish to compute the brightness value of the pixel (x', y') in the output image where x' and y' lie on the discrete raster (integer numbers, illustrated by solid lines in Figures). The co-ordinates of the point (x, y) in the original image can be obtained by inverting the planar transformation in equation (4.9)

$$(x, y) = T^{-1}(x', y') \tag{4.19}$$

In general the real co-ordinates after inverse transformation (dashed lines in Figures) do not fit the input image discrete raster (solid lines), and so brightness is not known. The only information available about the originally continuous image function $f(x, y)$ is its sampled version $g_s(l\,\Delta x, k\,\Delta y)$. To get the brightness value of the point (x, y) the input image is resampled.

Denote the result of the brightness interpolation by $f_n(x, y)$, where n distinguishes different interpolation methods. The brightness can be expressed by the convolution equation

$$f_n(x, y) = \sum_{l=-\infty}^{\infty} \sum_{k=-\infty}^{\infty} g_s(l\,\Delta x,\ k\,\Delta y)\, h_n(x - l\,\Delta x,\ y - k\,\Delta y) \tag{4.20}$$

The function h_n is called the **interpolation kernel**. Usually, only a small neighbourhood is used, outside which h_n is zero. (The same idea was used in continuous image sampling – recall that in equation (2.40) the function h_s represented the limited impulse).

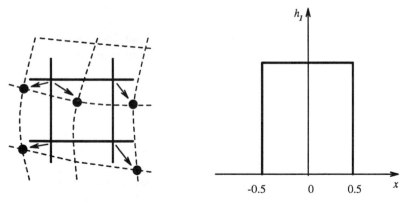

Figure 4.7 *Nearest neighbourhood interpolation.*

Nearest neighbourhood interpolation assigns to the point (x, y) the brightness value of the nearest point g in the discrete raster; this is demonstrated in Figure 4.7. On the left side is the interpolation kernel h_1 in the 1D case. The right side of Figure 4.7 shows how the new brightness is assigned. Dashed lines show how the inverse planar transformation maps the raster of the output image into the input image – full lines show the raster of the input image.

Let $r = round(x)$ denote the largest integer which is not bigger than $x + 0.5$. Nearest neighbourhood interpolation is given by

$$f_1(x, y) = g_s(round(x), round(y)) \tag{4.21}$$

The position error of the nearest neighbourhood interpolation is at most half a pixel. This error is perceptible on objects with straight line boundaries that may appear step-like after the transformation.

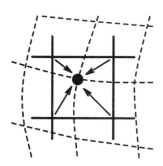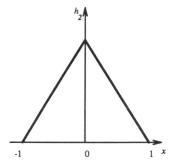

Figure 4.8 *Linear interpolation.*

Linear interpolation explores four points neighbouring the point (x, y), and assumes that the brightness function is linear in this neighbourhood. Linear interpolation is demonstrated in Figure 4.8, the left hand side of which shows which points are used for interpolation. Linear interpolation is given by the equation

$$
\begin{aligned}
f_2(x, y) = \ & (1 - a)(1 - b)\, g_s(l, k) \\
& + a(1 - b)\, g_s(l + 1, k) \\
& + b(1 - a)\, g_s(l, k + 1) \\
& + ab\, g_s(l + 1, k + 1)
\end{aligned}
\tag{4.22}
$$

$$
\begin{aligned}
l &= round(x), \quad a = x - l \\
k &= round(y), \quad b = y - k
\end{aligned}
$$

Linear interpolation can cause a small decrease in resolution, and blurring due to its averaging nature. The problem of step-like straight boundaries with the nearest neighbourhood interpolation is reduced.

Bicubic interpolation improves the model of the brightness function by approximating it locally by a bicubic polynomial surface; sixteen neighbouring

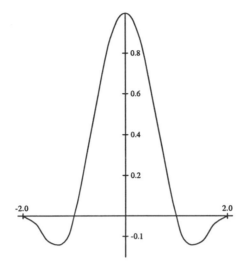

Figure 4.9 *Bicubic interpolation kernel.*

points are used for interpolation. The one-dimensional interpolation kernel ('Mexican hat') is shown in Figure 4.9 and is given by

$$h_3 = \begin{cases} 1 - 2|x|^2 + |x|^3 & \text{for } 0 < |x| < 1 \\ 4 - 8|x| + 5|x|^2 - |x|^3 & \text{for } 1 < |x| < 2 \\ 0 & \text{otherwise} \end{cases} \qquad (4.23)$$

Bicubic interpolation does not suffer from the step-like boundary problem of nearest neighbourhood interpolation, and copes with linear interpolation blurring as well. Bicubic interpolation is often used in raster displays that enable zooming with respect to an arbitrary point. If the nearest neighbourhood method were used, areas of the same brightness would increase. Bicubic interpolation preserves fine details in the image very well.

4.3 Local pre-processing

The object of interest in this section is pre-processing methods that use a small neighbourhood of a pixel in an input image to produce a new brightness value in the output image. Such pre-processing operations are called also **filtration** (or **filtering**) if signal processing terminology is used.

Local pre-processing methods can be divided into two groups according to the goal of the processing: First, **smoothing** aims to suppress noise or other small fluctuations in the image; it is equivalent to the suppression of high frequencies in the Fourier transform domain. Unfortunately, smoothing also blurs all sharp edges that bear important information about the image.

Second, **gradient operators** are based on local derivatives of the image function. Derivatives are bigger at locations of the image where the image function undergoes rapid changes, and the aim of gradient operators is to indicate such locations in the image. Gradient operators have a similar effect to suppressing low frequencies in the Fourier transform domain. Noise is often high frequency in nature; unfortunately, if a gradient operator is applied to an image the noise level increases simultaneously.

Clearly, smoothing and gradient operators have conflicting aims. Some pre-processing algorithms solve this problem and permit smoothing and edge enhancement simultaneously.

Another classification of local pre-processing methods is according to the transformation properties; **linear** and **nonlinear** transformations can be distinguished. Linear operations calculate the resulting value in the output image pixel $g(i, j)$ as a linear combination of brightnesses in a local neighbourhood $\mathcal{O}$ of the pixel $f(i, j)$ in the input image. The contribution of the pixels in the neighbourhood $\mathcal{O}$ is weighted by coefficients h

$$f(i,j) = \sum_{(m,n) \, \in \mathcal{O}} \sum h(i - m, \, j - n) \, g(m,n) \qquad (4.24)$$

Equation (4.24) is equivalent to discrete convolution with the kernel h, that is called a **convolution mask**. Rectangular neighbourhoods $\mathcal{O}$ are often used with an odd number of pixels in rows and columns, enabling the specification of the central pixel of the neighbourhood.

Local pre-processing methods typically use very little a priori knowledge about the image contents. It is very difficult to infer this knowledge while an image is processed as the known neighbourhood $\mathcal{O}$ of the processed pixel is small. Smoothing operations will benefit if some general knowledge about image degradation is available; this might, for instance, be statistical parameters of the noise.

The choice of the local transformation, size, and shape of the neighbourhood $\mathcal{O}$ depends strongly on the size of objects in the processed image. If objects are rather large an image can be enhanced by smoothing of small degradations.

Convolution-based operations (filters) can be used for smoothing, gradient operators and line detectors. There are methods that enable the speed up of calculations to ease implementation in hardware – examples are recursive filters or separable filters [Yaroslavskii 87].

4.3.1 Image smoothing

Image smoothing is the set of local pre-processing methods which has the aim of suppressing image noise – it uses redundancy in the image data. Calculation of the new value is based on the averaging of brightness values in some neighbourhood $\mathcal{O}$. Smoothing poses the problem of blurring sharp edges in the image, and so we shall concentrate on smoothing methods which are **edge preserving**. They are based on the general idea that the average is computed only from those points in the neighbourhood which have similar properties to the processed point.

Local image smoothing can effectively eliminate impulsive noise or degradations appearing as thin stripes, but does not work if degradations are large blobs or thick stripes. The solution for complicated degradations may be to use image restoration techniques, described in Section 4.4.

Averaging

Assume that the noise value ν at each pixel is an independent random variable with zero mean and standard deviation σ. We can obtain such an image by capturing the same static scene several times. The result of smoothing is an average of the same n points in these images $g_1, \ldots, g_n$ with noise values $\nu_1, \ldots, \nu_n$

$$\frac{g_1 + \ldots + g_n}{n} + \frac{\nu_1 + \ldots + \nu_n}{n} \tag{4.25}$$

The second term here describes the effect of the noise, which is again a random value with zero mean and standard deviation $\frac{\sigma}{\sqrt{n}}$; the standard deviation is decreased by a factor $\sqrt{n}$. Thus if n images of the same scene are available the smoothing can be accomplished without blurring the image by

$$f(i,j) = \frac{1}{n} \sum_{k=1}^{n} g_k(i,j) \tag{4.26}$$

In many cases only one image with noise is available, and averaging is then realized in a local neighbourhood. Results are acceptable if the noise is smaller in size than the smallest objects of interest in the image, but blurring of edges is a serious disadvantage. Averaging is a special case of discrete convolution (equation (4.24)). For a 3×3 neighbourhood the convolution mask h is

$$h = \frac{1}{9} \begin{bmatrix} 1 & 1 & 1 \\ 1 & 1 & 1 \\ 1 & 1 & 1 \end{bmatrix} \tag{4.27}$$

The significance of the pixel in the centre of the convolution mask h or its $4-$neighbours is sometimes increased, as it better approximates the properties of noise with a Gaussian probability distribution (Gaussian noise)

$$h = \frac{1}{10} \begin{bmatrix} 1 & 1 & 1 \\ 1 & 2 & 1 \\ 1 & 1 & 1 \end{bmatrix}, \quad h = \frac{1}{16} \begin{bmatrix} 1 & 2 & 1 \\ 2 & 4 & 2 \\ 1 & 2 & 1 \end{bmatrix} \tag{4.28}$$

Larger convolution masks for averaging are created analogously.

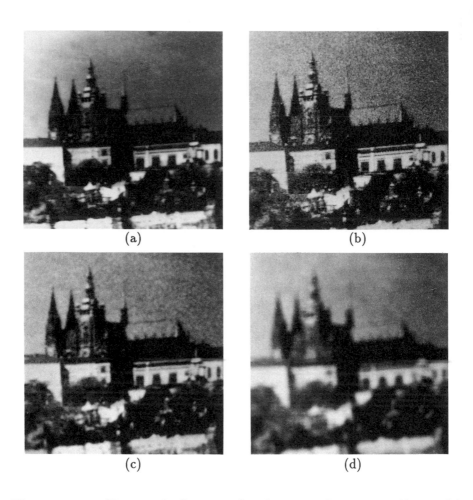

(a)   (b)

(c)   (d)

Figure 4.10 *Noise with Gaussian distribution and averaging filters: (a) Original image, (b) superimposed noise, (c) 3×3 averaging, (d) 7×7 averaging.*

An example will illustrate the effect of this noise suppression. Images with low resolution (256×256) were chosen deliberately to show the discrete nature of the process. Figure 4.10a shows an original image of Prague castle with 256 brightnesses; Figure 4.10b shows the same image with superimposed additive noise with Gaussian distribution; Figure 4.10c shows the result of averaging with a 3×3 convolution mask (4.28) – noise is significantly reduced and the image is slightly blurred. Averaging with a larger mask (7×7) is demonstrated in Figure 4.10d. The blurring is much more serious.

Alternative techniques attempt not to blur sharp edges. Such schemes tend to avoid averaging over edges, and most of them are nonlinear operations.

Averaging with limited data validity

Methods that average with limited data validity [McDonnell 81] try to avoid blurring by averaging only those pixels which satisfy some criterion, the aim being to prevent involving pixels that are part of a separate feature.

A very simple criterion is to use only pixels in the original image with brightness in a predefined interval $[min, max]$. Considering the point (m, n) in the image, the convolution mask is calculated in the neighbourhood $\mathcal{O}$ from the nonlinear formula

$$h(i, j) = \begin{cases} 1 & \text{for } g(m + i, n + j) \in [min, max] \\ 0 & \text{otherwise} \end{cases} \tag{4.29}$$

where (i, j) specify the mask element.

A second method performs the averaging only if the computed brightness change of a pixel is in some predefined interval. This method permits repair to large-area errors resulting from slowly changing brightness of the background without affecting the rest of the image.

A third method uses edge strength (i.e. magnitude of a gradient) as a criterion. The magnitude of some gradient operator (see Section 4.3.2) is first computed for the entire image, and only pixels in the input image with a gradient magnitude smaller than a predefined threshold are used in averaging. This method effectively rejects averaging at edges and therefore suppresses blurring, but automatic setting of the threshold is laborious.

Averaging according to inverse gradient

The convolution mask is calculated at each pixel according to the inverse gradient [Wang and Vagnucci 81], the idea being that the brightness change within a region is usually smaller than between neighbouring regions. Let (i, j) be the central pixel of a convolution mask with odd size; the inverse gradient δ at the point (m, n) with respect to (i, j) is then

$$\delta(i, j, m, n) = \frac{1}{|g(m, n) - g(i, j)|} \tag{4.30}$$

If $g(m,n) = g(i,j)$ then we define $\delta(i,j,m,n) = 2$; the inverse gradient δ is then in the interval $(0,2]$, and δ is smaller on the edge than in the interior of a homogeneous region. Weight coefficients in the convolution mask h are normalized by the inverse gradient, and the whole term is multiplied by 0.5 to keep brightness values in the original range. The constant 0.5 has the effect of assigning half the weight to the central pixel (i,j), and the other half to its neighbourhood

$$h(i,j,m,n) = 0.5 \frac{\delta(i,j,m,n)}{\sum_{(m,n)\in\mathcal{O}} \delta(i,j,m,n)} \tag{4.31}$$

The convolution mask coefficient corresponding to the central pixel is defined as $h(i,j) = 0.5$.

This method assumes sharp edges. When the convolution mask is close to an edge, pixels from the region have larger coefficients than pixels near the edge, and it is not blurred. Isolated noise points within homogeneous regions have small values of the inverse gradient; points from the neighbourhood take part in averaging and the noise is removed.

Averaging using a rotating mask

Averaging using a rotating mask is a method that avoids edge blurring by searching for the homogeneous part of the current pixel neighbourhood [Nagao and Matsuyama 80], and the resulting image is in fact sharpened. The brightness average is calculated only within this region; a brightness dispersion σ^2 is used as the region homogeneity measure. Let n be the number of pixels in a region R and $g(i,j)$ be the input image. Dispersion σ^2 is calculated as

$$\sigma^2 = \frac{1}{n}\left(\sum_{(i,j)\in R}\left(g(i,j) - \frac{1}{n}\sum_{(i,j)\in R} g(i,j)\right)^2\right) \tag{4.32}$$

The computational complexity (number of multiplications) of the dispersion calculation can be reduced if equation (4.32) is expressed another way;

$$\begin{aligned}
\sigma^2 &= \frac{1}{n}\sum_{(i,j)\in R}\left((g(i,j))^2 - 2g(i,j)\frac{\sum_{(i,j)\in R} g(i,j)}{n} + \left(\frac{\sum_{(i,j)\in R} g(i,j)}{n}\right)^2\right) \\
&= \frac{1}{n}\left(\sum_{(i,j)\in R}(g(i,j))^2 - 2\frac{\left(\sum_{(i,j)\in R} g(i,j)\right)^2}{n} + n\left(\frac{\sum_{(i,j)\in R} g(i,j)}{n}\right)^2\right) \\
&= \frac{1}{n}\left(\sum_{(i,j)\in R}(g(i,j))^2 - \frac{\left(\sum_{(i,j)\in R} g(i,j)\right)^2}{n}\right) \tag{4.33}
\end{aligned}$$

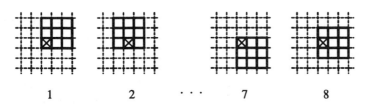

Figure 4.11 *8 possible rotated 3 × 3 masks.*

Having computed region homogeneity, we its consider shape and size. The eight possible 3 × 3 masks that cover a 5 × 5 neighbourhood of a current pixel (marked by the small cross) are shown in Figure 4.11. The ninth mask is the 3 × 3 neighbourhood of the current pixel itself. Other shapes of mask can also be used. Figure 4.12 shows another set of eight masks covering a 5 × 5 neighbourhood of the current pixel. Again the ninth mask is the 3 × 3 neighbourhood of the current pixel. Another possibility is to use small 2 × 1

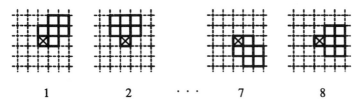

Figure 4.12 *Alternative shape of 8 possible rotated masks.*

masks covering the 3 × 3 neighbourhood of the current pixel.

Image smoothing using the rotating mask technique uses the following algorithm.

Algorithm 4.1: Rotated mask smoothing

---

1. Consider each image pixel (i, j).

2. Calculate dispersion in the mask for all possible mask rotations about pixel (i, j) according to equation (4.32).

3. Choose the mask with minimum dispersion.

4. Assign to the pixel $g(i, j)$ in the output image the average brightness in the chosen mask.

Algorithm 4.1 can be used iteratively; the iterative process converges quite quickly to the stable state (that is, the image does not change any more).

(a)   (b)

Figure 4.13 *Smoothing by the rotated mask technique: (a) One iteration, (b) two iterations.*

The size and shape of masks influence the convergence – the smaller the mask, the smaller are the changes and more iterations are needed. A larger mask suppresses noise faster and the sharpening effect is stronger. On the other hand information about details smaller than the mask may be lost. The number of iterations is also influenced by the shape of regions in the image and noise properties.

Smoothing and sharpening effects of the rotating mask technique are illustrated in two examples. An input image with superimposed noise was shown in Figure 4.10b; the result after one iteration with masks according to Figure 4.11 is shown in Figure 4.13a. Figure 4.13b shows the result of the second iteration.

Median smoothing

In a set of ordered values, the **median**[2] is the central value.

Median filtering is a smoothing method that reduces the blurring of edges [Tyan 81]. The idea is to replace the current point in the image by the median of the brightnesses in its neighbourhood. The median of the brightnesses in the neighbourhood is not affected by individual noise spikes and so median smoothing eliminates impulsive noise quite well. Further, as median filtering does not blur edges much, it can be applied iteratively.

The main disadvantage of median filtering in a rectangular neighbourhood

---

[2]The median is defined in probability theory. For a random variable x, the median M is the value for which the probability of the outcome $x < M$ is 0.5.

is its damaging of thin lines and sharp corners in the image – this can be avoided if another shape of neighbourhood is used. For instance, if horizontal/vertical lines need preserving a neighbourhood such as that in Figure 4.14 can be used.

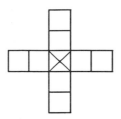

Figure 4.14 *Horizontal/vertical line-preserving neighbourhood for median filtering.*

Median smoothing is a special instance of more general **rank filtering** techniques [Rosenfeld and Kak 82, Yaroslavskii 87], the idea of which is to order pixels in some neighbourhood into sequence. The results of pre-processing are some statistics over this sequence, of which the median is one possibility. Another variant is the maximum or the minimum values of the sequence. This defines generalizations of dilation and erosion operators (Chapter 10) in images with more brightness values.

Figure 4.15 *Median smoothing.*

A similar generalization of median techniques is given in [Borik et al. 83] where it is called **Order Statistics (OS)** filtering. Values in the neighbourhood are again ordered into sequence, and a new value is given as a linear combination of the values of this sequence. Median smoothing, and minimum or maximum filters are a special case of OS filtering.

The effect of median filtering is shown in Figure 4.15, which is a median filter of an original image with superimposed noise, Figure 4.10b.

Nonlinear mean filter

The nonlinear mean filter is another generalization of averaging techniques [Pitas and Venetsanopulos 86]; it is defined by

$$f(m,n) = u^{-1} \left(\frac{\sum_{(i,j)\in\mathcal{O}} a(i,j)\, u(g(i,j))}{\sum_{(i,j)\in\mathcal{O}} a(i,j)} \right) \tag{4.34}$$

where $f(m,n)$ is the result of the filtering, $g(i,j)$ is the pixel in the input image, and $\mathcal{O}$ is a local neighbourhood of the current pixel (m,n). The function u of one variable has an inverse function u^{-1} and $a(i,j)$ are weight coefficients.

If the weights $a(i,j)$ are constant the filter is called **homomorphic**. Some homomorphic filters used in image processing are:

- Arithmetic mean, $u(g) = g$

- Harmonic mean, $u(g) = 1/g$

- Geometric mean, $u(g) = \log g$

4.3.2   Edge detectors

Edge detectors form a collection of very important local image pre-processing methods used to locate sharp changes in the intensity function; edges are pixels where this function (brightness) changes abruptly.

Calculus describes changes of continuous functions using derivatives; an image function depends on two variables – co-ordinates in the image plane – and so operators describing edges are expressed using partial derivatives. A change of the image function can be described by a gradient that points in the direction of the largest growth of the image function.

An edge is a property attached to an individual pixel and is calculated from the image function behaviour in a neighbourhood of the pixel. It is a **vector variable** that has two components, the **magnitude** and the **direction**. The edge magnitude is the magnitude of the gradient, and the edge direction ϕ is rotated with respect to the gradient direction ψ by $-90°$. The gradient direction gives the direction of maximum growth of the function, e.g. from black $(f(i,j) = 0)$ to white $(f(i,j) = 255)$. This is illustrated in Figure 4.16; closed lines are lines of the same brightness. The orientation $0°$ points East.

Edges are often used in image analysis for finding region boundaries. Provided that the region has homogeneous brightness its boundary is at the pixels

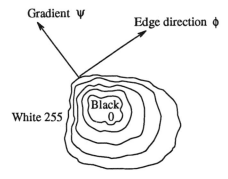

Figure 4.16 *Gradient direction and edge direction.*

where the image function varies, and so in the ideal case without noise consists of pixels with high edge magnitude. It can be seen that the boundary and its parts (edges) are perpendicular to the direction of the gradient.

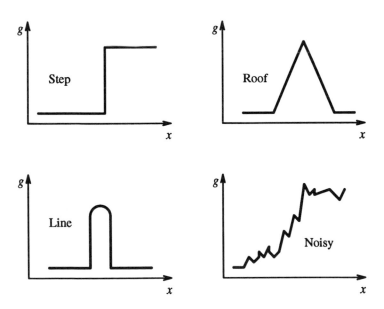

Figure 4.17 *Typical edge profiles.*

The edge profile in the gradient direction (perpendicular to the edge direction) is typical for edges, and Figure 4.17 shows examples of several standard edge profiles. Roof edges are typical for objects corresponding to thin lines in the image. Edge detectors are usually tuned for some type of edge profile.

The gradient magnitude $|grad\ g(x,y)|$ and gradient direction ψ are continuous image functions calculated as

$$|grad\ g(x,y)| = \sqrt{\left(\frac{\partial g}{\partial x}\right)^2 + \left(\frac{\partial g}{\partial y}\right)^2} \qquad (4.35)$$

$$\psi = arg(\frac{\partial g}{\partial x}, \frac{\partial g}{\partial y}) \qquad (4.36)$$

where $arg(x,y)$ is the angle (in radians) from the x-axis to the point (x,y).

Sometimes we are interested only in edge magnitudes without regard to their orientations – a linear differential operator, called the **Laplacian** is then may be used. The Laplacian has the same properties in all directions and is therefore invariant to rotation in the image. It is defined as

$$\nabla^2(x,y) = \frac{\partial^2 g(x,y)}{\partial x^2} + \frac{\partial^2 g(x,y)}{\partial y^2} \qquad (4.37)$$

Image **sharpening** [Rosenfeld and Kak 82] has the objective of making edges steeper – the sharpened image is intended to be observed by a human. The sharpened output image f is obtained from the input image g as

$$f(i,j) = g(i,j) - C\ S(i,j) \qquad (4.38)$$

where C is a positive coefficient which gives the strength of sharpening and $S(i,j)$ is a measure of the image function sheerness that is calculated using a gradient operator. The Laplacian is very often used for this purpose.

Image sharpening can be interpreted in the frequency domain as well. We already know that the result of the Fourier transform is a combination of harmonic functions. The derivative of the harmonic function $\sin(nx)$ is $n\cos(nx)$; thus the higher the frequency, the higher the magnitude of its derivative. This is another explanation of why gradient operators enhance edges.

A similar image sharpening technique to that given in equation (4.38) called **unsharp masking** is often used in printing industry applications [Jain 89]. A signal proportional to an unsharp image (e.g. blurred by a smoothing operator) is subtracted from the original image.

A digital image is discrete in nature and so equations (4.35) and (4.36) containing derivatives must be approximated by **differences**. The first differences of the image g in the vertical direction (for fixed i) and in the horizontal direction (for fixed j) are given by

$$\begin{aligned}
\Delta_i\, g(i,j) &= g(i,j) - g(i-n,j) \\
\Delta_j\, g(i,j) &= g(i,j) - g(i,j-n)
\end{aligned} \qquad (4.39)$$

where n is a small integer, usually 1. The value n should be chosen small enough to provide a good approximation to the derivative, but large enough to neglect unimportant changes in the image function. Symmetric expressions for the difference

$$\Delta_i g(i,j) = g(i+n,j) - g(i-n,j)$$
$$\Delta_j g(i,j) = g(i,j+n) - g(i,j-n) \tag{4.40}$$

are not usually used because they neglect the impact of the pixel (i,j) itself.

Gradient operators as a measure of edge sheerness can be divided into three categories.

1. Operators approximating derivatives of the image function using differences. Some of them are rotationally invariant (e.g. Laplacian) and thus are computed from one convolution mask only. Others, that approximate first derivatives, use several masks. The orientation is estimated on the basis of the best matching of several simple patterns.

2. Operators based on the zero crossings of the image function second derivative (e.g. Marr-Hildreth or Canny edge detector).

3. Operators which attempt to match an image function to a parametric model of edges.

The remainder of this section will consider some of the many operators which fall into the first category, and the next section will consider the second. The last category is not considered here; parametric models describe edges more precisely than simple edge magnitude and direction and are much more computationally intensive. Hueckel's model [Nevatia 77] is the best known.

Individual gradient operators that examine small local neighbourhoods are in fact convolutions (c.f. equation (4.24)), and can be expressed by convolution masks. Operators which are able to detect edge direction as well are represented by a collection of masks, each corresponding to a certain direction.

Roberts operator

The Roberts operator is one of the oldest [Roberts 65] operators. It is very easy to compute as it uses only a 2×2 neighbourhood of the current pixel. Its convolution masks are

$$h_1 = \begin{bmatrix} 1 & 0 \\ 0 & -1 \end{bmatrix} \quad h_2 = \begin{bmatrix} 0 & 1 \\ -1 & 0 \end{bmatrix} \tag{4.41}$$

so the magnitude of the edge is computed as

$$|g(i,j) - g(i+1,j+1)| + |g(i,j+1) - g(i+1,j)| \tag{4.42}$$

The primary disadvantage of the Roberts operator is its high sensitivity to noise, because very few pixels are used to approximate the gradient.

Laplace operator

The Laplace operator ∇^2 is a very popular operator approximating the second
derivative which gives the gradient magnitude only. The Laplacian, equation
(4.37), is approximated in digital images by a convolution sum. A 3×3 mask
h is often used; for 4-neighbourhoods and 8-neighbourhoods it is defined as

$$h = \begin{bmatrix} 0 & 1 & 0 \\ 1 & -4 & 1 \\ 0 & 1 & 0 \end{bmatrix} \qquad h = \begin{bmatrix} 1 & 1 & 1 \\ 1 & -8 & 1 \\ 1 & 1 & 1 \end{bmatrix} \qquad (4.43)$$

A Laplacian operator with stressed significance of the central pixel or its
neighbourhood is sometimes used. In this approximation it loses invariance
to rotation

$$h = \begin{bmatrix} 2 & -1 & 2 \\ -1 & -4 & -1 \\ 2 & -1 & 2 \end{bmatrix} \qquad h = \begin{bmatrix} -1 & 2 & -1 \\ 2 & -4 & 2 \\ -1 & 2 & -1 \end{bmatrix} \qquad (4.44)$$

The Laplacian operator has a disadvantage – it responds doubly to some edges
in the image.

Prewitt operator

The Prewitt operator, similarly to the Sobel, Kirsch, Robinson (as discussed
later) and some other operators, approximates the first derivative. The gradient is estimated in eight (for a 3×3 convolution mask) possible directions, and
the convolution result of greatest magnitude indicates the gradient direction.
Larger masks are possible.

Operators approximating the first derivative of an image function are sometimes called compass operators because of the ability to determine gradient
direction.

We present only the first three 3×3 masks for each operator; the others
can be created by simple rotation.

$$h_1 = \begin{bmatrix} 1 & 1 & 1 \\ 0 & 0 & 0 \\ -1 & -1 & -1 \end{bmatrix} \quad h_2 = \begin{bmatrix} 0 & 1 & 1 \\ -1 & 0 & 1 \\ -1 & -1 & 0 \end{bmatrix} \quad h_3 = \begin{bmatrix} -1 & 0 & 1 \\ -1 & 0 & 1 \\ -1 & 0 & 1 \end{bmatrix} \quad (4.45)$$

The direction of the gradient is given by the mask giving maximal response.
This is valid for all the following operators approximating the first derivative.

Sobel operator

$$h_1 = \begin{bmatrix} 1 & 2 & 1 \\ 0 & 0 & 0 \\ -1 & -2 & -1 \end{bmatrix} \quad h_2 = \begin{bmatrix} 0 & 1 & 2 \\ -1 & 0 & 1 \\ -2 & -1 & 0 \end{bmatrix} \quad h_3 = \begin{bmatrix} -1 & 0 & 1 \\ -2 & 0 & 2 \\ -1 & 0 & 1 \end{bmatrix} \quad (4.46)$$

The Sobel operator is often used as a simple detector of horizontality and verticality of edges in which case only masks h_1 and h_3 are used. If the h_1 response is y and the h_3 response x, we might then derive edge strength (magnitude) as

$$\sqrt{x^2 + y^2} \quad or \quad |x| + |y| \tag{4.47}$$

and direction as $tan^{-1}(y/x)$.

Robinson operator

$$h_1 = \begin{bmatrix} 1 & 1 & 1 \\ 1 & -2 & 1 \\ -1 & -1 & -1 \end{bmatrix} \quad h_2 = \begin{bmatrix} 1 & 1 & 1 \\ -1 & -2 & 1 \\ -1 & -1 & 1 \end{bmatrix} \quad h_3 = \begin{bmatrix} -1 & 1 & 1 \\ -1 & -2 & 1 \\ -1 & 1 & 1 \end{bmatrix} \tag{4.48}$$

Kirsch operator

$$h_1 = \begin{bmatrix} 3 & 3 & 3 \\ 3 & 0 & 3 \\ -5 & -5 & -5 \end{bmatrix} \quad h_2 = \begin{bmatrix} 3 & 3 & 3 \\ -5 & 0 & 3 \\ -5 & -5 & 3 \end{bmatrix} \quad h_3 = \begin{bmatrix} -5 & 3 & 3 \\ -5 & 0 & 3 \\ -5 & 3 & 3 \end{bmatrix} \tag{4.49}$$

(a)   (b)

Figure 4.18 *(a) Laplace gradient operator, (b) sharpening using the Laplace operator.*

To illustrate the application of gradient operators on real images consider again the original image of Prague castle (Figure 4.10a). The Laplace gradient is shown in Figure 4.18; the value of the operator was multiplied by ten to enhance its visibility. Figure 4.18 shows the result of image sharpening. An edge sharpening can be seen there, but unfortunately noise was strengthened as well.

   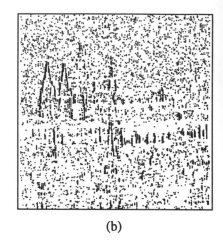

(a)   (b)

Figure 4.19 *(a) 1ˢᵗ derivative approximated by the Kirsch operator (negated for the benefit of display), (b) north direction obtained by the Kirsch operator (negated for the benefit of display).*

The properties of an operator approximating the first derivative are demonstrated using the Kirsch operator – results of others are similar. The original image is again Figure 4.10a; the Kirsch approximation to the gradient is in Figure 4.19a. It is hard to show all eight directions in a monochromatic image, and for this reason directions pointing to the North only (pointing up) are displayed in Figure 4.19b.

4.3.3 Zero crossings of the second derivative

In the seventies, Marr's theory (see Chapter 9) concluded from neurophysiological experiments that object boundaries are the most important cues that link an intensity image with its interpretation. Edge detection techniques existing at that time (e.g. the Kirsch, Sobel and Pratt operators) were based on convolution in very small neighbourhoods and worked well for specific images only. The main disadvantage of these edge detectors is their dependence on the size of the object and sensitivity to noise.

An edge detection technique, based on the **zero crossings** of the second derivative (in its original form, the **Marr-Hildreth** edge detector [Marr and Hildreth 80] or the same paper in a more recent collection [Marr and Hildreth 91]) explores the fact that a step edge corresponds to an abrupt change in the image function. The first derivative of the image function should have an extremum at the position corresponding to the edge in the image, and so the second derivative should be zero at the same position, however, it is much easier and more precise to find a zero crossing position than an extremum. In Figure 4.20 this principle is illustrated in 1D for the sake of simplicity.

Figure 4.20a shows step edge profiles of the original image function with two different slopes, Figure 4.20b depicts the first derivative of the image function, and Figure 4.20c illustrates the second derivative; notice that this crosses the zero level at the same position as the edge.   Considering a step-like edge

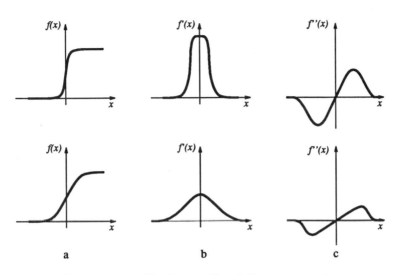

Figure 4.20 *1D edge profile of the zero crossing.*

in 2D, the 1D profile of Figure 4.20a corresponds to a cross-section through the 2D step. The steepness of the profile will change if the orientation of the cutting plane changes – the maximum steepness is observed when the plane is perpendicular to the edge direction.

The crucial question is how to compute the second derivative robustly. One possibility is to smooth an image first (to reduce noise) and then compute second derivatives. When choosing a smoothing filter, there are two criteria that should be fulfilled [Marr and Hildreth 80]. First, the filter should be smooth and roughly band-limited in the frequency domain to reduce the possible number of frequencies at which function changes can take place. Secondly, the constraint of spatial localization requires the response of a filter to be from nearby points in the image. These two criteria are conflicting, and the distribution that simultaneously optimizes them is called a Gaussian. In practise one has to be more precise about what is meant by the localization performance of an operator, and the Gaussian may turn out to be sub-optimal. We shall consider this in the next section.

The 2D Gaussian smoothing operator $G(x, y)$ (called also a Gaussian filter or simply a Gaussian) is given as[3]

$$G(x,y) = e^{-\frac{x^2+y^2}{2\sigma^2}} \tag{4.50}$$

where x, y are the image co-ordinates and σ is a standard deviation of the associated probability distribution. The standard deviation σ is the only parameter of the Gaussian filter – it is proportional to the size of neighbourhood on which the filter operates. Pixels more distant from the centre of the operator have smaller influence, and pixels further than 3σ from the centre have negligible influence.

Our goal is to obtain a second derivative of a smoothed 2D function $f(x,y)$. We have already seen that the Laplacian operator ∇^2 gives the second derivative, and is moreover non-directional (isotropic). Consider then the Laplacian of an image $f(x,y)$ smoothed by a Gaussian (expressed using a convolution $*$). The operation is abbreviated by some authors as **LoG** from **Laplacian of Gaussian**.

$$\nabla^2(G(x,y,\sigma) * f(x,y)) \tag{4.51}$$

The order of performing differentiation and convolution can be interchanged due to the linearity of the operators involved;

$$(\nabla^2 G(x,y,\sigma)) * f(x,y) \tag{4.52}$$

Since it is independent of the image under consideration, the derivative of the Gaussian filter $\nabla^2 G$ can be pre-computed analytically reducing the complexity of the composite operation. For simplicity, use the substitution $r^2 = x^2 + y^2$, where r measures distance from the origin; this is reasonable as the Gaussian is circularly symmetric. This substitution converts our 2D Gaussian (equation 4.50) into a 1D function that is easier to differentiate

$$G(r) = e^{-\frac{r^2}{2\sigma^2}} \tag{4.53}$$

The first derivative $G'(r)$ is then

$$G'(r) = -\frac{1}{\sigma^2}\, r\, e^{-\frac{r^2}{2\sigma^2}} \tag{4.54}$$

and the second derivative $G''(r)$, the Laplacian of a Gaussian, is

$$G''(r) = \frac{1}{\sigma^2}\left(\frac{r^2}{\sigma^2} - 1\right) e^{-\frac{r^2}{2\sigma^2}} \tag{4.55}$$

---

[3]Some authors define a Gaussian using different normalization factors, i.e.

$$G(x,y) = \frac{1}{2\pi\sigma^2}e^{-(x^2+y^2)/2\sigma^2}$$

or

$$G(x,y) = \frac{1}{\sqrt{2\pi}\sigma}e^{-(x^2+y^2)/2\sigma^2}$$

After returning to the original co-ordinates x, y and introducing a normalizing multiplicative coefficient c we get a convolution mask of a zero crossing detector

$$h(x,y) = c\left(\frac{x^2 + y^2}{\sigma^2} - 1\right) e^{-\frac{x^2+y^2}{2\sigma^2}} \qquad (4.56)$$

where c normalizes the sum of mask elements to unity.

Finding second derivatives in this way is very robust. Gaussian smoothing effectively suppresses the influence of the pixels that are up to a distance 3σ from the current pixel; then the Laplace operator $\nabla^2 G$ is an efficient and stable measure of changes in the image.

The location in the $\nabla^2 G$ image where the zero level is crossed corresponds to the position of the edges. The advantage of this approach compared to classical edge operators of small size is that a larger area surrounding the current pixel is taken into account; the influence of more distant points decreases according to the σ of the Gaussian. The σ variation does not affect the location of the zero crossings.

Convolution masks become large for larger σ; for example, $\sigma = 4$ needs a mask about 40 pixels wide. Fortunately there is a separable decomposition of the $\nabla^2 G$ operator [Huertas and Medion 86] that can speed up computation considerably.

Neurophysiological experiments [Marr 82, Ullman 81] provide evidence that the human eye retina in the form of the **ganglion cells** performs operations very similar to the $\nabla^2 G$ operations. Each such cell responds to light stimuli in a local neighbourhood called the **receptive field** which has a centre surround organization of two complementary types; off-centre and on-centre. When a light stimulus occurs, activity of on-centre cells increases and that of off-centre cells is inhibited. The retinal operation on the image can be described analytically as the convolution of the image with the $\nabla^2 G$ operator.

The practical implication of Gaussian smoothing is that edges are found reliably. If only globally significant edges are required, the standard deviation σ of the Gaussian smoothing filter may be increased, having the effect of suppressing less significant evidence.

The $\nabla^2 G$ operator can be very effectively approximated by convolution with a mask that is the difference of two Gaussian averaging masks with substantially different σ – this method is called the **Difference of Gaussians**, abbreviated as **DoG**. The correct ratio of the standard deviations σ of the Gaussian filters is discussed in [Marr 82].

Even coarser approximations to $\nabla^2 G$ are sometimes used – the image is filtered twice by an averaging operator with smoothing masks of different size.

The traditional zero crossing of second derivatives technique has disadvantages as well. Firstly, it smoothes the shape too much; for example sharp corners are lost. Secondly, it tends to create closed loops of edges (nicknamed the 'plate of spaghetti' effect). Although this property was highlighted as an advantage in original papers it has been seen as a drawback in many applications.

4.3.4 Scale in image processing

Many image processing techniques work locally, theoretically at the level of individual pixels – edge detection methods are an example. The essential problem in such computation is **scale**. Edges correspond to the gradient of the image function that is computed as a difference between pixels in some neighbourhood. There is seldom a sound reason for choosing a particular size of neighbourhood: The right size depends on the size of the objects under investigation. To know what the objects are assumes that it is clear how to interpret an image, and this is not in general known at the pre-processing stage.

The solution to the problem formulated above is a special case of a general paradigm called the **system approach**. This methodology is common in cybernetics or general system theory that aim to study complex phenomena.

The phenomenon under investigation is expressed at different resolutions of the description, and a formal model is created at each resolution. Then the qualitative behaviour of the model is studied under changing resolution of the description. Such a methodology enables the deduction of metaknowledge about the phenomena that is not seen at the individual description level.

Different description levels are easily interpreted as different scales in the domain of digital images. An idea of scale is fundamental to Marr's edge detection technique introduced in Section 4.3.3 where different scales were introduced by different sizes of Gaussian filter masks. The aim was not only to eliminate fine scale noise but also to separate events at different scales arising from distinct physical processes [Marr 82].

Assume that a signal has been smoothed with several masks of variable size; every setting of the scale parameters implies a different description, but it is not known which is the correct one. No one scale is categorically correct for many tasks. If the ambiguity introduced by the scale is inescapable, the goal of scale-independent description is to reduce this ambiguity as much as possible.

Many publications tackle scale-space problems, e.g. [Hummel and Moniot 89, Perona and Malik 90, Williams and Shah 90]. A symbolic approach to constructing a multiscale primitive shape description to 2D binary (contour) shape images is presented in [Saund 90], and the use of a scale-space approach for object recognition is in [Topkar et al. 90]. Here, we shall consider just three examples of how the problem of multiple scale description was solved in image analysis.

The first approach [Lowe 89] aims to process planar noisy curves at a range of scales – the segment of curve that represents the underlying structure of the scene needs to be found. The problem is illustrated by an example of two noisy curves, see Figure 4.21. One of these may be interpreted as a closed (perhaps circular) curve, while the other could be described by two intersecting straight lines. Local tangent direction and curvature of the curve are significant only

Figure 4.21 *Curves analysed at multiple scale.*

with some idea of scale. The curve is smoothed by the Gaussian filter with varying standard deviations and the shrinkage of the curve that depends on local curvature compensated.

Once the curve smoothed with masks of different sizes is available, the significant segments of the original curve can be found. The task is formulated as an optimization problem in which two criteria are used simultaneously. First, the longer the curve segment the better, and second, the change of curvature (proportional to the third derivative) should be minimal.

A second approach [Witkin 83], called scale-space filtering, tries to describe signals qualitatively with respect to scale. The problem was formulated for the 1D signal $f(x)$ but it can easily be generalized for 2D functions as images. The original 1D signal $f(x)$ is smoothed by convolution with a 1D Gaussian

$$G(x,\sigma) = e^{-\frac{x^2}{\sigma^2}} \qquad (4.57)$$

If the standard deviation σ is slowly changed the function

$$F(x,\sigma) = f(x) * G(x,\sigma) \qquad (4.58)$$

represents a surface on the (x,σ) plane that is called the **scale–space image**. Inflection points of the curve $F(x,\sigma_0)$ for a distinct value σ_0

$$\frac{\partial^2 F(x,\sigma_0)}{\partial x^2} = 0 \ , \quad \frac{\partial^3 F(x,\sigma_0)}{\partial x^3} \neq 0 \qquad (4.59)$$

describe the curve $f(x)$ qualitatively. The positions of inflection points can be drawn as a set of curves in (x,σ) co-ordinates. Coarse to fine analysis of the curves corresponding to inflection points, i.e. in the direction of the decreasing value of the σ, localizes large–scale events.

The qualitative information contained in the scale–space image can be transformed into a simple **interval tree** that expresses the structure of the signal $f(x)$ over all observed scales. The interval tree is built from the root that corresponds to the largest scale (σ_{max}). Then the scale–space image is searched in the direction of decreasing σ. The interval tree branches at those points where new curves corresponding to inflection points appear (see Chapter 6 and Section 6.2.4).

The third example of the application of scale is that used by the popular **Canny edge detector**. As the Canny edge detector is a significant and widely used contribution to edge detection techniques we shall explain its principles in detail here.

4.3.5 Canny edge detection

Canny proposed a new approach to edge detection [Canny 83, Brady 84, Canny 86] which is optimal for step edges corrupted by white noise. The optimality of the detector is related to three criteria.

- The **detection** criterion expresses the fact that important edges should not be missed and that there should be no spurious responses.

- The **localization** criterion says that the distance between the actual and located position of the edge should be minimal.

- The **one response** criterion minimizes multiple responses to a single edge. This is partly covered by the first criterion since when there are two responses to a single edge one of them should be considered as false. This third criterion solves the problem of an edge corrupted by noise and works against non-smooth edge operators [Rosenfeld and Thurston 71].

Canny's derivation of a new edge detector is based on several ideas:

1. The edge detector was expressed for a 1D signal and the first two optimality criteria. A closed form solution was found using the calculus of variations.

2. If the third criterion (multiple responses) is added, the best solution may be found by numerical optimization. The resulting filter can be approximated effectively with error less than 20% by the first derivative of a Gaussian smoothing filter with standard deviation σ [Canny 86]; the reason for doing this is the existence of an effective implementation. There is a strong similarity here to the Marr-Hildreth edge detector [Marr and Hildreth 80] which is based on the Laplacian of a Gaussian, see Section 4.3.3.

3. The detector is then generalized to two dimensions. A step edge is given by its position, orientation, and possibly magnitude (strength). It can be shown that convolving an image with a symmetric 2D Gaussian and then differentiating in the direction of the gradient (perpendicular to the edge direction) forms a simple and effective directional operator (recall that the Marr-Hildreth zero crossing operator does not give information about edge direction as it uses Laplacian filter).

Suppose G is a 2D Gaussian (equation (4.50)) and assume we wish to convolve the image with an operator G_n which is a first derivative of G in the direction $\mathbf{n}$.

$$G_n = \frac{\partial G}{\partial \mathbf{n}} = \mathbf{n} \cdot \nabla G \tag{4.60}$$

The direction $\mathbf{n}$ should be oriented perpendicular to the edge. Although this direction is not known in advance, a robust estimate of it based on the smoothed gradient direction is available. If g is the image, the normal to the edge $\mathbf{n}$ is estimated as

$$\mathbf{n} = \frac{\nabla(G * g)}{|\nabla(G * g)|} \tag{4.61}$$

The edge location is then at the local maximum in the direction $\mathbf{n}$ of the operator G_n convolved with the image g

$$\frac{\partial}{\partial \mathbf{n}} G_n * g = 0 \tag{4.62}$$

Substituting in equation (4.62) for G_n from equation (4.60) we get

$$\frac{\partial^2}{\partial \mathbf{n}^2} G * g = 0 \tag{4.63}$$

This equation (4.63) shows how to find local maxima in the direction perpendicular to the edge; this operation is often referred to as **non-maximal suppression**.

As the convolution and derivative are associative operations in equation (4.63) we can first convolve an image g with a symmetric Gaussian G and then compute the directional second derivative using an estimate of the direction $\mathbf{n}$ computed according to equation (4.61). The strength of the edge (magnitude of the gradient of the image intensity function g) is measured as

$$|G_n * g| = |\nabla(G * g)| \tag{4.64}$$

A different generalization of this optimal detector into two dimensions was proposed by Spacek [Spacek 86], and the problem of edge localization is revisited in [Tagare and deFigueiredo 90].

4. Spurious responses to the single edge caused by noise usually create a so called 'streaking' problem that is very common in edge detection in general. The output of an edge detector is usually thresholded to decide which edges are significant, and streaking means the breaking up of the edge contour caused by the operator fluctuating above and below the threshold. Streaking can be eliminated by **thresholding with hysteresis**. If any edge response is above a *high threshold*, those pixels constitute definite output of the edge detector for a particular scale. Individual weak responses usually correspond to noise, but if these points are connected to any of the pixels with strong responses they are more likely to be actual edges in the image. Such connected pixels are treated as edge pixels if their response is above a *low threshold*. The low and high threshold are set according to an estimated signal to noise ratio [Canny 86].

5. The correct scale for the operator depends on the objects contained in the image. The solution to this unknown is to use multiple scales and aggregate information from them. Different scales for the Canny detector are represented by different standard deviations σ of the Gaussians. There may be several scales of operators that give significant responses to edges (i.e. signal to noise ratio above the threshold); in this case the operator with the smallest scale is chosen as it gives the best localization of the edge.

   Canny proposed a **feature synthesis** approach. All significant edges from the operator with the smallest scale are marked first, and the edges of a hypothetical operator with larger σ are synthesized from them (i.e. a prediction is made of how the large σ should perform on the evidence gleaned from the smaller σ). Then the synthesized edge response is compared with the actual edge response for larger σ. Additional edges are marked only if they have a significantly stronger response than that predicted from synthetic output.

   This procedure may be repeated for a sequence of scales, a cumulative edge map being built by adding those edges that were not identified at smaller scales.

Algorithm 4.2: Canny edge detector

1. Repeat steps (2) till (6) for ascending values of the standard deviation σ.

2. Convolve an image g with a Gaussian of scale σ.

 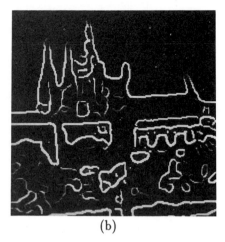

(a)   (b)

Figure 4.22 *Canny edge detector: (a) σ=1.0, (b) σ=2.8.*

3. Estimate local edge normal directions **n** using equation (4.61) for each pixel in the image.

4. Find the location of the edges using equation (4.63) (non-maximal suppression).

5. Compute the magnitude of the edge using equation (4.64).

6. Threshold edges in the image with hysteresis to eliminate spurious responses.

7. Aggregate the final information about edges at multiple scale using the 'feature synthesis' approach.

Figure 4.22a shows the edges of Figure 4.10a detected by a Canny operator with $\sigma = 1.0$. Figure 4.22b shows the edge detector response for $\sigma = 2.8$ (feature synthesis has not been applied here).

Canny's detector represents a complicated but major contribution to edge detection. Its full implementation is unusual, it being common to find implementations that omit feature synthesis – that is, just steps 2–6 of Algorithm 4.2.

4.3.6 Edges in multispectral images

One pixel in a multispectral image is described by an n-dimensional vector, and brightness values in n spectral bands are the vector components.

There are several possibilities for the detection of edges in multispectral images. The first is to detect edges separately in individual image spectral components using the ordinary local gradient operators mentioned in Section 4.3.2. Individual images of edges can be combined to get the resulting image with the value corresponding to edge magnitude and direction being the maximal edge value from all spectral components. A linear combination of edge spectral components can also be used, and other combination techniques are possible [Nagao and Matsuyama 80].

A second possibility is to use the brightness difference of the same pixel in two different spectral components. This is a very informative feature for classification based on properties of the individual pixel. The ratio instead of the difference can be used as well [Pratt 78], although it is necessary to assume that pixel values are not zero in this case.

A third possibility is to create a multispectral edge detector which uses brightness information from all n spectral bands; an edge detector of this kind is proposed in [Cervenka and Charvat 87]. The neighbourhood used has size $2 \times 2 \times n$ pixels, where the 2×2 neighbourhood is similar to that of the Roberts gradient, equation (4.41). The coefficient weighting the influence of the component pixels is similar to the correlation coefficients. Let $\overline{g}(i,j)$ denote the arithmetic mean of the brightnesses corresponding to the pixels with the same co-ordinates (i,j) in all n spectral component images, and g_r be the brightness of the r-th spectral component. The edge detector result in pixel (i,j) is given as the minimum of the following expressions

$$\frac{\sum_{r=1}^{n}(g_r(i,j) - \overline{g}(i,j))\,(g_r(i+1,j+1) - \overline{g}(i+1,j+1))}{\sqrt{\sum_{r=1}^{n}(g_r(i,j) - \overline{g}(i,j))^2\ \sum_{r=1}^{n}(g_r(i+1,j+1) - \overline{g}(i+1,j+1))^2}}$$

$$\frac{\sum_{r=1}^{n}(g_r(i+1,j) - \overline{g}(i+1,j))\,(g_r(i,j+1) - \overline{g}(i,j+1))}{\sqrt{\sum_{r=1}^{n}(g_r(i+1,j) - \overline{g}(i+1,j))^2\ \sum_{r=1}^{n}(g_r(i,j+1) - \overline{g}(i,j+1))^2}} \qquad (4.65)$$

This multispectral edge detector gives very good results on remotely sensed images.

4.3.7 Other local pre-processing operators

Several other local operations exist which do not belong to the taxonomy given in Section 4.3 as they are used for different purposes. Line finding, line thinning, line filling, and interest point operators are among them. Another class of local operators, mathematical morphology techniques, is mentioned in Chapter 10.

Line finding operators aim to find very thin curves in the image; it is assumed that curves do not bend sharply. Such curves and straight lines are called **lines** for the purpose of describing this technique. If a cross-section perpendicular in direction to the tangent of a line is examined we get a roof profile, seen in Figure 4.17 when examining edges. We assume that the width of the lines is approximately one or two pixels; such lines may correspond, for example, to roads in satellite images or to dimension lines in engineering drawings.

Lines in the image can be detected [Cervenka and Charvat 87] by a number of local convolution operators h_k. The output value of the line finding detector in pixel (i, j) is given by

$$f(i, j) = max[0, max_k(g * h_k)] \qquad (4.66)$$

where $g * h_k$ denotes convolution of the k-th mask with the neighbourhood of a pixel (i, j) in the input image g.

One possibility is a convolution mask of size 5×5. There are fourteen possible orientations of the line finding convolution mask of this size; we shall show only the first eight of them as the others are obvious by rotation

$$
h_1 = \begin{bmatrix} 0 & 0 & 0 & 0 & 0 \\ 0 & -1 & 2 & -1 & 0 \\ 0 & -1 & 2 & -1 & 0 \\ 0 & -1 & 2 & -1 & 0 \\ 0 & 0 & 0 & 0 & 0 \end{bmatrix}
\qquad
h_2 = \begin{bmatrix} 0 & 0 & 0 & 0 & 0 \\ 0 & 0 & -1 & 2 & -1 \\ 0 & -1 & 2 & -1 & 0 \\ 0 & -1 & 2 & -1 & 0 \\ 0 & 0 & 0 & 0 & 0 \end{bmatrix}
$$

$$
h_3 = \begin{bmatrix} 0 & 0 & 0 & 0 & 0 \\ 0 & 0 & -1 & 2 & -1 \\ 0 & -1 & 2 & -1 & 0 \\ -1 & 2 & -1 & 0 & 0 \\ 0 & 0 & 0 & 0 & 0 \end{bmatrix}
\qquad
h_4 = \begin{bmatrix} 0 & 0 & 0 & 0 & 0 \\ 0 & -1 & 2 & -1 & 0 \\ 0 & -1 & 2 & -1 & 0 \\ -1 & 2 & -1 & 0 & 0 \\ 0 & 0 & 0 & 0 & 0 \end{bmatrix}
$$

$$
h_5 = \begin{bmatrix} 0 & 0 & 0 & 0 & 0 \\ -1 & 2 & -1 & 0 & 0 \\ 0 & -1 & 2 & -1 & 0 \\ 0 & -1 & 2 & -1 & 0 \\ 0 & 0 & 0 & 0 & 0 \end{bmatrix}
\qquad
h_6 = \begin{bmatrix} 0 & 0 & 0 & 0 & 0 \\ 0 & -1 & 2 & -1 & 0 \\ 0 & -1 & 2 & -1 & 0 \\ 0 & 0 & -1 & 2 & -1 \\ 0 & 0 & 0 & 0 & 0 \end{bmatrix}
$$

$$
h_7 = \begin{bmatrix} 0 & 0 & 0 & 0 & 0 \\ -1 & 2 & -1 & 0 & 0 \\ 0 & -1 & 2 & -1 & 0 \\ 0 & 0 & -1 & 2 & -1 \\ 0 & 0 & 0 & 0 & 0 \end{bmatrix}
\qquad
h_8 = \begin{bmatrix} 0 & 0 & 0 & 0 & 0 \\ 0 & -1 & -1 & -1 & 0 \\ 0 & 2 & 2 & 2 & 0 \\ 0 & -1 & -1 & -1 & 0 \\ 0 & 0 & 0 & 0 & 0 \end{bmatrix} \quad (4.67)
$$

The line detector of equation (4.66) with masks similar to (4.67) sometimes produces more lines than needed. Some other nonlinear constraints may be added to reduce this number.

Local information about edges is the basis of a class of image segmentation techniques that are discussed in Chapter 5. Edges which are likely to

belong to object boundaries are usually found by simple thresholding of the
edge magnitude – such edge thresholding does not provide ideal contiguous
boundaries that are one pixel wide. Sophisticated segmentation techniques
that are dealt with in the next chapter serve this purpose. Here much simpler
edge thinning and filling methods are described. These techniques are based
on knowledge of small local neighbourhoods and are very similar to other local
pre-processing techniques.

Thresholded edges are usually wider than one pixel, and **line thinning**
techniques may give a better result. One line thinning method uses knowledge
about edge orientation and in this case edges are thinned before thresholding.
Edge magnitudes and directions provided by some gradient operator are used
as input, and the edge magnitude of two neighbouring pixels perpendicular
to the edge direction are examined for each pixel in the image. If at least
one of these pixels has edge magnitude higher than the edge magnitude of
the examined pixel then the edge magnitude of the examined pixel is assigned
a zero value. This technique is called **non-maximal suppression** and is
similar to the idea mentioned in conjunction with the Canny edge detector.

A second line thinning method [Cervenka and Charvat 87] does not explore
information about edge orientation. A binary image with edges that have
magnitude higher than a specified threshold is used as input; ones denote
edge pixels and zeros the rest of the image. Such edges are then thinned by
the local operator. Example 3×3 masks are shown in (4.68) where the letter
x denotes an arbitrary value (i.e. 0 or 1). The match of each mask at each
position of the image is checked and if the mask matches, the edge is thinned
by replacing the one in the centre of the mask by zero.

$$
\begin{bmatrix} 1 & x & 0 \\ 1 & 1 & 0 \\ x & 0 & 0 \end{bmatrix}
\begin{bmatrix} x & 1 & 1 \\ 0 & 1 & x \\ 0 & 0 & 0 \end{bmatrix}
\begin{bmatrix} x & 1 & x \\ 1 & 1 & x \\ x & x & 0 \end{bmatrix}
\begin{bmatrix} x & 1 & x \\ x & 1 & 0 \\ 0 & x & 0 \end{bmatrix}
$$

$$
\begin{bmatrix} 0 & 0 & 0 \\ x & 1 & 0 \\ 1 & 1 & x \end{bmatrix}
\begin{bmatrix} 0 & 0 & x \\ 0 & 1 & 1 \\ 0 & x & 1 \end{bmatrix}
\begin{bmatrix} x & x & 0 \\ 1 & 1 & x \\ x & 1 & x \end{bmatrix}
\begin{bmatrix} 0 & x & x \\ x & 1 & 1 \\ x & 1 & x \end{bmatrix}
\qquad (4.68)
$$

Another procedure permits a more reliable extraction of a set of edge points.
Edge points after thresholding do not create contiguous boundaries and the
edge-filling method tries to recover edge pixels on the potential object boundary which are missing. We present here a very simple local edge-filling technique, but more complicated methods based on edge relaxation are mentioned
in Chapter 5.

The local edge-filling procedure [Cervenka and Charvat 87] checks whether
the 3×3 neighbourhood of the current pixel matches one of the following

situations

$$
\begin{bmatrix} 0 & 1 & 0 \\ 0 & 0 & 0 \\ 0 & 1 & 0 \end{bmatrix}
\begin{bmatrix} 0 & 0 & 0 \\ 1 & 0 & 1 \\ 0 & 0 & 0 \end{bmatrix}
\begin{bmatrix} 1 & 0 & 0 \\ 0 & 0 & 0 \\ 0 & 1 & 0 \end{bmatrix}
\begin{bmatrix} 0 & 0 & 1 \\ 1 & 0 & 0 \\ 0 & 0 & 0 \end{bmatrix}
$$

$$
\begin{bmatrix} 0 & 1 & 0 \\ 0 & 0 & 0 \\ 0 & 0 & 1 \end{bmatrix}
\begin{bmatrix} 0 & 0 & 0 \\ 0 & 0 & 1 \\ 1 & 0 & 0 \end{bmatrix}
\begin{bmatrix} 1 & 0 & 0 \\ 0 & 0 & 0 \\ 0 & 0 & 1 \end{bmatrix}
\begin{bmatrix} 0 & 0 & 1 \\ 0 & 0 & 0 \\ 1 & 0 & 0 \end{bmatrix}
\tag{4.69}
$$

If so the central pixel of the mask is changed from zero to one.

These methods for edge thinning and filling do not guarantee that the width of the lines will be equal to one, and the contiguity of the lines is not certain either. Note that local thinning and filling operators can be treated as special cases of mathematical morphology operators which are described in Chapter 10.

In many cases it is of advantage to find pairs of corresponding points in two similar images; we came across this fact in Section 4.2 when considering geometric transforms. Knowing the position of corresponding points enables the estimation of mathematical formulae describing geometric transforms from live data. The same transformation usually holds for all pixels of the image. The number of corresponding pairs of points necessary is usually rather small and is equal to the number of parameters of the transform. We shall see later on that finding corresponding points is also a core problem in the analysis of moving images (Chapter 14), and for recovering depth information from pairs of stereo images (Chapter 9). In general, all possible pairs of points should be examined to solve this **correspondence problem,** and this is very computationally expensive. If two images have n pixels each the complexity is $\mathcal{O}(n^2)$. This process might be simplified if the correspondence is examined among a much smaller number of points, called **interest points.** An interest point should have some typical local property [Ballard and Brown 82]. For example, if square objects are present in the image then **corners** are very good interest points.

Corners in images can be located using local detectors; input to the corner detector is the grey level image, and output is the image $f(i,j)$ in which values are proportional to the likelihood that the pixel is a corner. The simplest corner detector is the **Moravec detector** [Moravec 77] that is maximal in pixels with high contrast. These points are on corners and sharp edges. The Moravec operator MO is given by

$$
MO(i,j) = \frac{1}{8} \sum_{k=i-1}^{i+1} \sum_{l=j-1}^{j+1} |g(k,l) - g(i,j)|
\tag{4.70}
$$

Better results are produced by computationally more expensive corner operators such as that proposed by Zuniga-Haralick or Kitchen-Rosenfeld [Huang

83]. The image function g is approximated in the neighbourhood of the pixel (i, j) by a cubic polynomial with coefficients c_k

$$g(i,j) = c_1 + c_2 x + c_3 y + c_4 x^2 + c_5 xy + c_6 y^2 + c_7 x^3 + c_8 x^2 y + c_9 xy^2 + c_{10} y^3 \quad (4.71)$$

The Zuniga-Haralick operator ZH is given by

$$ZH(i,j) = \frac{-2\left(c_2^2 c_6 - c_2 c_3 c_5 - c_3^2 c_4\right)}{\left(c_2^2 + c_3^2\right)^{\frac{3}{2}}} \quad (4.72)$$

The Kitchen–Rosenfeld operator has the same numerator as Equation (4.72) but the denominator is $(c_2^2 + c_3^2)$.

Interest points are obtained by thresholding the result of the corner detector.

A corner detection technique that defines a corner as two half edges and uses a more recent edge detection approach based on derivatives of Gaussian smoothing operators is given in [Mehrotra and Nichani 90].

4.3.8 Adaptive neighbourhood pre-processing

The importance of scale has been presented in Section 4.3.4 together with possible solutions. Nevertheless, the majority of pre-processing operators work in neighbourhoods of fixed sizes in the whole image of which square windows (3×3, 5×5, or 7×7) are most common. Further, pre-processing operators of variable sizes and shapes exist and bring improved pre-processing results. Often, they are based on detection of the most homogeneous neighbourhood of each pixel. However, they are not widely used, mostly because of computational demands and the nonexistence of a unifying approach.

A novel approach to image pre-processing introduces the concept of an adaptive neighbourhood which is determined for each image pixel [Gordon and Rangayyan 84, Morrow and Rangayyan 90, Morrow et al. 92]. The neighbourhood size and shape are dependent on characteristics of image data and on parameters, which define measures of homogeneity of a pixel neighbourhood. Therefore, a significant property of the neighbourhood for each pixel is the ability of self-tuning to contextual details in the image.

Neighbourhood

An adaptive neighbourhood is constructed for each pixel, this pixel being called a **seed pixel** of the neighbourhood. The adaptive neighbourhood consists of all the 8-connected pixels which satisfy a property of similarity with the seed pixel. The pixel property may represent a grey level, or some more complex image properties like texture, local motion parameters, etc. Consider grey level as a basic pixel property – the adaptive neighbourhood for grey level image pre-processing is based on an additive or multiplicative tolerance interval; all the pixels which are 8-connected with the seed pixel and which have their grey levels in a tolerance interval become members of the adaptive neighbourhood. Specifically, let $f(i,j)$ represent the seed pixel, and $f(k,l)$ represent pixels 8-connected to the seed pixel. Then, the adaptive neighbourhood of the pixel $f(i,j)$ is defined as a set of pixels $f(k,l)$ 8-connected to the seed pixel and either satisfying the additive tolerance property

$$|f(k,l) - f(i,j)| \leq T_1 \tag{4.73}$$

or satisfying a multiplicative property

$$\frac{|f(k,l) - f(i,j)|}{f(i,j)} \leq T_2 \tag{4.74}$$

where T_1, T_2 are parameters of the adaptive neighbourhood and represent the maximum allowed dissimilarity of a neighbourhood pixel from the seed pixel. Note that each pixel is assigned one adaptive neighbourhood, and therefore adaptive neighbourhoods may overlap. This specification defines the first layer of the adaptive neighbourhood (called the foreground layer) which is used in all adaptive neighbourhood pre-processing operations. Sometimes not only the foreground layer, but also a background layer must be used to represent more diverse contextual information. The second (background) layer is moulded to the outline of the first layer and has a thickness of s pixels, s being a parameter of the adaptive neighbourhood.

The foreground layer has grey levels similar to the grey level of the seed pixel, but the background layer values are quite different from the seed pixel. The adaptive neighbourhood definition may result in a neighbourhood with many interior holes, and these holes or parts thereof may represent a portion of the background layer. The foreground layer may be constructed using a region growing approach (see Section 5.3), and the background layer may result from a dilation-like operation applied to the foreground layer (see Section 10.1.2), the number of dilation steps being specified by the parameter s.

Although a neighbourhood is constructed for each pixel, all pixels in the given foreground layer that have the same grey level as the seed pixel construct the same adaptive neighbourhood. These pixels are called **redundant seed pixels**. Using redundant seed pixels significantly decreases the complexity of adaptive neighbourhood construction in the image (see Figure 4.23).

Many fixed neighbourhood pre-processing techniques may be implemented applying the adaptive neighbourhood concept. We shall demonstrate the power of adaptive neighbourhood pre-processing in noise suppression, histogram modification, and contrast enhancement [Paranjape et al. 92b, Paranjape et al. 92a].

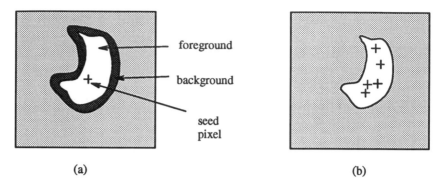

(a)   (b)

Figure 4.23 *Adaptive neighbourhood: (a) Construction, (b) redundant seed pixels – 8-connected seed pixels of the same grey level construct the same adaptive neighbourhood.*

Noise suppression

The adaptive neighbourhood is not formed across region boundaries; therefore, noise suppression will not blur image edges as often happens with other techniques. If noise suppression is the goal, only the foreground neighbourhood layer is used. Having constructed the adaptive neighbourhood for each pixel, the rest is straightforward: Each seed pixel is assigned a new value computed as a mean, median, etc. of all the pixels in the adaptive neighbourhood. If the noise is additive, the additive criterion for neighbourhood construction should be applied; if the noise is multiplicative, the multiplicative tolerance criterion is appropriate. Adaptive neighbourhood noise suppression may be applied several times in a sequence with good results, and the edges will not be blurred. If the median is used to compute a new seed pixel value, the operation does not destroy corners and thin lines as is typical in fixed-size neighbourhoods (see Section 4.3.1). Adaptive neighbourhood smoothing does not work well for impulse noise, because large grey level differences between the noise pixel and other pixels in the neighbourhood cause the adaptive neighbourhood to consist of only the noise pixel. A solution may be to apply a fixed-size averaging pre-processing step prior to the adaptive neighbourhood operations (a small size of fixed neighbourhood should be used in order not to blur the edges too much). Examples of adaptive neighbourhood noise suppression are given in Figure 4.24.

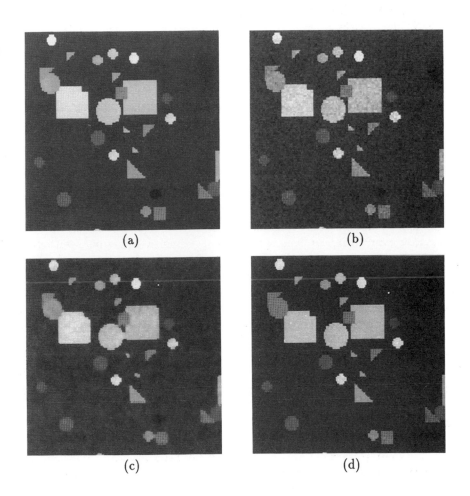

(a)   (b)

(c)   (d)

Figure 4.24 *Adaptive neighbourhood noise suppression: (a) Original image (b) noisy image (superimposed noise), (c) fixed neighbourhood median filter 3×3, (d) adaptive neighbourhood median filter, $T_1 = 16$. Compare corners, thin lines, and thin gaps. Courtesy R. Paranjape, R. Rangayyan, University of Calgary.*

Histogram modification

Full-frame histogram equalization was discussed in Section 4.1.2; its main disadvantage is that the global image properties may not be appropriate under a local context. Local area histogram equalization computes a new grey level for each pixel based on the equalization of a histogram acquired in a local fixed-size neighbourhood [Pizer et al. 87]. Adaptive neighbourhood histogram modification is based on the same principle – the local histogram is computed from a neighbourhood which reflects local contextual image properties.

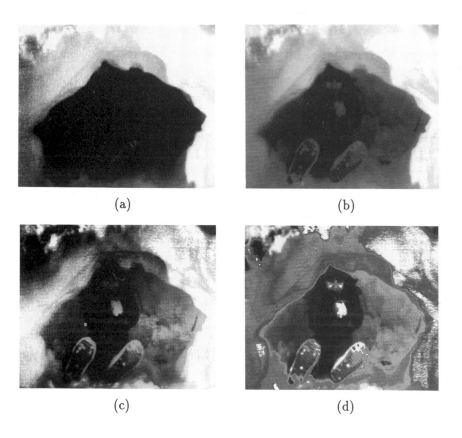

(a)   (b)

(c)   (d)

Figure 4.25 *Adaptive neighbourhood histogram modification: (a) Original image, (b) full-frame histogram equalization, (c) fixed neighbourhood adaptive histogram equalization, (d) adaptive neighbourhood histogram equalization, Courtesy R. Paranjape, R. Rangayyan, University of Calgary.*

The adaptive neighbourhood consists of both foreground and background layers in this application. The foreground variance is based on the additive criterion and the parameter T_1 should be chosen relatively large. The background portion of the adaptive neighbourhood provides a mechanism for mediating the introduced grey level change. Very good results from this method can be seen in Figure 4.25.

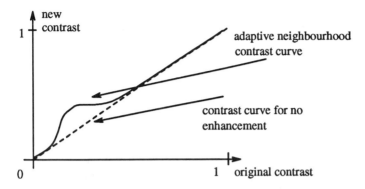

Figure 4.26 *Adaptive neighbourhood contrast curves*

Contrast enhancement

Contrast is a property based on human perception abilities. An approximate definition of contrast is [Gordon and Rangayyan 84]

$$c = \frac{F - B}{F + B} \tag{4.75}$$

where F and B are the mean grey levels of two regions whose contrast is evaluated. Standard contrast enhancement techniques like sharpening (Section 4.3.2) do not enhance the contrast of regions, only local edge perception. Moreover, the larger the contrast between image parts, the larger the enhancement. In other words, the most serious enhancement is achieved where the contrast is sufficient anyway. Conversely, the adaptive neighbourhood is associated with objects, and therefore it is feasible to enhance contrast in regions by modifying grey levels in regions and not only along their borders. Further, the contrast enhancement may be nonlinear: No enhancement for very small grey level differences between neighbourhoods (caused probably by quantization noise or very small grey level variance); moderate to strong enhancement applied if the contrast between regions is small but outside the range of quantization contrast; and no contrast enhancement is applied if the contrast is already sufficient. The contrast modification curve is shown in Figure 4.26. For contrast enhancement, both foreground and background adaptive neighbourhood layers are used, the background size being comparable in size with the foreground size. For each seed pixel and corresponding adaptive neighbourhood, the original contrast c is computed using equation (4.75). The new desired contrast c' is obtained from the applied contrast curve (Figure 4.26). The new grey value $f'(i, j)$ to be assigned to the seed pixel (i, j) is computed

$$f'(i,j) = \frac{B(1 + c')}{1 - c'} \tag{4.76}$$

where B is the original mean grey level of the background adaptive neighbourhood layer. Note that, in addition to the contrast enhancement, the grey level variations inside regions decrease. The multiplicative neighbourhood construction criterion should be used to avoid dependence of the resulting contrast on the mean grey level of the neighbourhood. The adaptive contrast enhancement results may be compared with the fixed-size neighbourhood contrast enhancement in Figure 4.27, and the contrast improvement is clearly visible.

The principle of adaptive neighbourhood pre-processing gives significantly better results in many images but large computational load is the price to pay for this improvement. Nevertheless, taking advantage of redundant seed pixels decreases the computational demands; also, feasibility of implementing these methods in parallel may soon make these methods as standard as fixed neighbourhood methods are today.

4.4   Image restoration

4.4.1   *Image restoration as inverse convolution of the whole image*

Pre-processing methods that aim to suppress degradation using knowledge about its nature are called **image restoration**. Most image restoration methods are based on convolution applied globally to the whole image.

Degradation of images can have many causes: defects of optical lenses, non-linearity of the electro–optical sensor, graininess of the film material, relative motion between an object and camera, wrong focus, atmospheric turbulence in remote sensing or astronomy, etc. The objective of image restoration is to reconstruct the original image from its degraded version.

Image restoration techniques can be classified into two groups: deterministic and stochastic. **Deterministic** methods are applicable to images with little noise and a known degradation function. The original image is obtained from the degraded one by a transformation inverse to the degradation. **Stochastic** techniques try to find the best restoration according to a particular stochastic criterion, e.g. a least squares method. In some cases the degradation transformation must be estimated first.

It is advantageous to know the degradation function explicitly. The better this knowledge is, the better are the results of the restoration. There are three typical degradations with a simple function: Relative constant speed movement of the object with respect to the camera, wrong lens focus, and atmospheric turbulence.

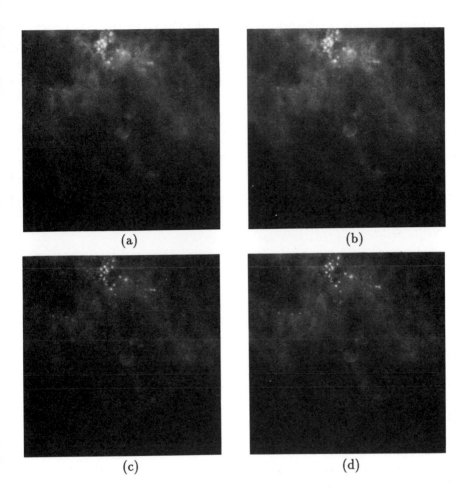

(a)   (b)

(c)   (d)

Figure 4.27 *Adaptive neighbourhood contrast enhancement: (a) Original mammogram image, (b) unsharp masking 3×3, (c) adaptive contrast enhancement, $T_2 = 0.03, s = 3$, (d) adaptive contrast enhancement, $T_2 = 0.05, s = 3$. Courtesy R. Paranjape, R. Rangayyan, University of Calgary.*

In most practical cases, there is insufficient knowledge about the degradation, and it must be estimated and modelled. The estimation can be classified into two groups according to the information available: a priori and a posteriori.

A priori knowledge about degradation is either known in advance or can be obtained before restoration. If it is clear in advance that the image was degraded by relative motion of an object with respect to the sensor then the modelling only determines the speed and direction of the motion. An example of the second case is an attempt to estimate parameters of a capturing device such as a TV camera or digitizer whose degradation can be modelled by studying a known sample image and its degraded version.

A posteriori knowledge is that obtained by analyzing the degraded image. A typical example is to find some interest points in the image (e.g. corners, straight lines) and guess how they looked before degradation. Another possibility is to use spectral characteristics of the regions in the image that are relatively homogeneous.

Image restoration is treated in more detail in [Pratt 78, Rosenfeld and Kak 82, Bates and McDonnell 86] and only the basic principle of the restoration and three typical degradations are considered here.

A degraded image g can arise from the original image f by a process which can be expressed as

$$g(i,j) = s \left(\int \int_{(a,b) \in \mathcal{O}} f(a,b)\, h(a,b,i,j)\, da\, db \right) + \nu(i,j) \qquad (4.77)$$

where s is some nonlinear function and ν describes the noise. The degradation is very often simplified by neglecting the nonlinearity and by assuming that the function h is invariant with respect to position in the image. Degradation can be than expressed as convolution

$$g(i,j) = (f * h)(i,j) + \nu(i,j) \qquad (4.78)$$

If the degradation is given by equation (4.78) and the noise is not significant then image restoration equates to inverse convolution (also called deconvolution). If noise is not negligible then the inverse convolution is solved as an overdetermined system of linear equations. Methods based on minimization of the least square error such as Wiener filtering (off-line) or Kalman filtering (recursive, on–line) are examples [Bates and McDonnell 86].

4.4.2 Degradations that are easy to restore

We mentioned that there are three types of degradations that can be easily expressed mathematically and also restored simply in images. These degradations can be expressed by convolution, equation (4.78); the Fourier transform H of the convolution function is used.

Relative motion of the camera and object

Assume an image is acquired with a camera with a mechanical shutter. Relative motion of the camera and the photographed object during the shutter open time T causes smoothing of the object in the image. Suppose V is the constant speed in the direction of the x axis; the Fourier transform $H(u, v)$ of the degradation caused in time T is given by [Rosenfeld and Kak 82]

$$H(u, v) = \frac{\sin(\pi V T u)}{\pi V u} \tag{4.79}$$

Wrong lens focus

Image smoothing caused by imperfect focus of a thin lens can be described by the following function [Born and Wolf 69]

$$H(u, v) = \frac{J_1(a\, r)}{a\, r} \tag{4.80}$$

where J_1 is the Bessel function of the first order, $r^2 = u^2 + v^2$, and a is the displacement.

Atmospheric turbulence

Atmospheric turbulence is degradation that needs to be restored in remote sensing and astronomy. It is caused by temperature non-homogeneity in the atmosphere that deviates passing light rays. The mathematical model is derived in [Hufnagel and Stanley 64] and is expressed as

$$H(u, v) = e^{-c(u^2 + v^2)^{\frac{5}{6}}} \tag{4.81}$$

where c is a constant that depends on the type of turbulence which is usually found experimentally. The power $\frac{5}{6}$ is sometimes replaced by 1.

4.4.3 Inverse filtration

Inverse filtration [Andrews and Hunt 77, Rosenfeld and Kak 82] is based on the assumption that degradation was caused by a linear function $h(i, j)$ (c.f. equation (4.78)), and the additive noise ν is another source of degradation. It is further assumed that ν is independent of the signal. After applying the Fourier transform to equation (4.78) we get

$$G(u, v) = F(u, v)\, H(u, v) + N(u, v) \tag{4.82}$$

The degradation can be eliminated if the restoration filter has a transfer function that is inverse to the degradation h. The Fourier transform of the inverse filter is then expressed as $H^{-1}(u, v)$.

We derive the original undegraded image F (after Fourier transform) from its degraded version G, cf. equation (4.82).

$$F(u,v) = G(u,v) \, H^{-1}(u,v) - N(u,v) \, H^{-1}(u,v) \qquad (4.83)$$

This equation shows that inverse filtration works well for images that are not corrupted by noise. If noise is present and additive error occurs, its influence is significant for frequencies where $H(u,v)$ has small magnitude. These usually correspond to high frequencies u,v and thus fine details are blurred in the image. The changing level of noise may cause problems as well because small magnitudes of $H(u,v)$ can cause large changes in the result. Inverse filter values should not be of zero value so as to avoid a zero denominator in equation (4.83).

4.4.4   Wiener filtration

It is no surprise that inverse filtration gives poor results in pixels suffering from noise since the noise is not taken into account. Wiener filtration [Rosenfeld and Kak 82] explores a priori knowledge about the noise.

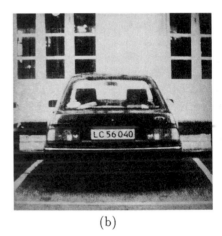

(a)   (b)

Figure 4.28 *Restoration of motion blur using Wiener filtration. Courtesy P. Kohout, Criminalistic Institute, Prague.*

Restoration by the Wiener filter gives an estimate of the original uncorrupted image $\hat{f}$ with minimal mean square error e^2 (recall that $\mathcal{E}$ denotes the mean operator);

$$e^2 = \mathcal{E}\left\{(f(i,j) - \hat{f}(i,j))^2\right\} \qquad (4.84)$$

If no constraints are applied to the solution of equation (4.84) then an optimal estimate $\hat{f}$ is the conditional mean value of the ideal image f under the

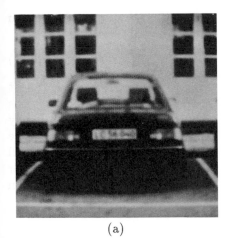 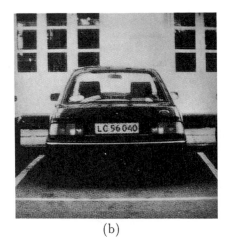

(a)   (b)

Figure 4.29 *Restoration of wrong focus blur using Wiener filtration. Courtesy P. Kohout, Criminalistic Institute, Prague.*

condition g. This approach is complicated from the computational point of view. Moreover the conditional probability density between the optimal image f and the corrupted image g is not usually known. The optimal estimate is in general a nonlinear function of the image g.

Minimization of equation (4.84) is easy if the estimate $\hat{f}$ is a linear combination of the values in the image g; the estimate $\hat{f}$ is then only close to the theoretical optimum. The estimate is equal to the theoretical optimum only if the stochastic processes describing images f, g, and the noise ν are homogeneous, and their probability density is Gaussian [Andrews and Hunt 77]. These conditions are not usually fulfilled for typical images.

Denote the Fourier transform of the Wiener filter H_W; the Fourier transform of the original image F can be estimated as

$$\hat{F}(u,v) = H_W(u,v)\, G(u,v) \tag{4.85}$$

We do not derive the function H_W of the Wiener filter here, which can be found elsewhere [Papoulis 65, Rosenfeld and Kak 82, Bates and McDonnell 86]. The result is

$$H_W(u,v) = \frac{H^{\#}(u,v)}{|H(u,v)|^2 + \frac{S_{\nu\nu}(u,v)}{S_{gg}(u,v)}} \tag{4.86}$$

where H is the transform function of the degradation, $\#$ denotes complex conjugate, $S_{\nu\nu}$ is the spectral density of the noise, and S_{gg} is the spectral density of the degraded image.

If Wiener filtration is used the nature of degradation H and statistical parameters of the noise need to be known. Wiener filtration theory solves the problem of a posteriori linear mean square estimate – all statistics (e.g. power spectrum) should be available in advance.

Note that the inverse filter is a special case of the Wiener filter where noise is absent i.e. $S_{\nu\nu} = 0$.

Restoration is illustrated in Figures 4.28 and 4.29. Figure 4.28a shows an image that was degraded by 5 pixels motion in the direction of the x axis. Figure 4.28b shows the result of restoration where Wiener filtration was used. Figure 4.29a shows an image degraded by the wrong focus and Figure 4.29b is the result of restoration using Wiener filtration.

References

[Andrews and Hunt 77] H C Andrews and B R Hunt. *Digital Image Restoration*. Prentice-Hall, Englewood Cliffs, NJ, 1977.

[Ballard and Brown 82] D H Ballard and C M Brown. *Computer Vision*. Prentice-Hall, Englewood Cliffs, NJ, 1982.

[Bates and McDonnell 86] R H T Bates and M J McDonnell. *Image Restoration and Reconstruction*. Clarendon Press, Oxford, England, 1986.

[Borik et al. 83] A C Borik, T S Huang, and D C Munson. A generalization of median filtering using combination of order statistics. *IEEE Proceedings*, 71(31):1342–1350, 1983.

[Born and Wolf 69] M Born and E Wolf. *Principles of Optics*. Pergamon Press, New York, 1969.

[Brady 84] M Brady. Representing shape. In M Brady, L A Gerhardt, and H F Davidson, editors, *Robotics and Artificial Intelligence*, pages 279–300. Springer + NATO, Berlin, 1984.

[Canny 83] J F Canny. Finding edges and lines in images. Technical Report AI-TR-720, MIT, Artificial Intelligence Lab., Cambridge, Ma, 1983.

[Canny 86] J F Canny. A computational approach to edge detection. *IEEE Transactions on Pattern Analysis and Machine Intelligence*, 8(6):679–698, 1986.

[Cervenka and Charvat 87] V Cervenka and K Charvat. Survey of the image processing research applicable to the thematic mapping based on aerocosmic data (in Czech). Technical Report A 12–346–811, Geodetic and Carthographic Institute, Prague, Czechoslovakia, 1987.

[Gordon and Rangayyan 84] R Gordon and R M Rangayyan. Feature enhancement of film mammograms using fixed and adaptive neighborhoods. *Applied Optics*, 23:560–564, 1984.

[Huang 83] T S Huang, editor. *Image Sequence Processing and Dynamic Scene Analysis*. Springer Verlag, Berlin, 1983.

[Huertas and Medion 86] A Huertas and G Medion. Detection of intensity changes with subpixel accuracy using Laplacian-Gaussian masks. *IEEE Transactions on Pattern Analysis and Machine Intelligence*, 8:651–664, 1986.

[Hufnagel and Stanley 64] R E Hufnagel and N R Stanley. Modulation transfer function associated with image transmission through turbulent media. *Journal of the Optical Society of America*, 54:52–61, 1964.

[Hummel and Moniot 89] R Hummel and R Moniot. Reconstructions from zero crossings in scale space. *IEEE Transactions on Acoustics, Speech and Signal Processing*, 37(12):2111–2130, 1989.

[Jain 89] A K Jain. *Fundamentals of Digital Image Processing*. Prentice-Hall, Englewood Cliffs, NJ, 1989.

[Lowe 89] D G Lowe. Organization of smooth image curves at multiple scales. *International Journal of Computer Vision*, 1:119–130, 1989.

[Marr 82] D Marr. *Vision – A Computational Investigation into the Human Representation and Processing of Visual Information*. W.H. Freeman and Co., San Francisco, 1982.

[Marr and Hildreth 80] D Marr and E Hildreth. Theory of edge detection. *Proceedings of the Royal Society*, B 207:187–217, 1980.

[Marr and Hildreth 91] D Marr and E Hildreth. Theory of edge detection. In R Kasturi and R C Jain, editors, *Computer Vision*, pages 77–107. IEEE, Los Alamitos, Ca, 1991.

[McDonnell 81] M J McDonnell. Box filtering techniques. *Computer Graphics and Image Processing*, 17(3):65–70, 1981.

[Mehrotra and Nichani 90] R Mehrotra and S Nichani. Corner detection. *Pattern Recognition Letters*, 23(11):1223–1233, 1990.

[Moik 80] J G Moik. *Digital Processing of Remotely Sensed Images*. NASA SP–431, Washington DC, 1980.

[Moravec 77] H P Moravec. Towards automatic visual obstacle avoidance. In *Proceedings of the 5th International Joint Conference on Artificial Intelligence*, August 1977.

[Morrow and Rangayyan 90] W M Morrow and R M Rangayyan. Feature-adaptive enhancement and analysis of high-resolution digitized mammograms. In *Proceedings of 12th IEEE Engineering in Medicine and Biology Conference*, pages 165–166, IEEE, Piscataway, NJ, 1990.

[Morrow et al. 92] W M Morrow, R B Paranjape, R M Rangayyan, and J E L Desautels. Region-based contrast enhancement of mammograms. *IEEE Transactions on Medical Imaging*, 11(3):392–406, 1992.

[Nagao and Matsuyama 80] M Nagao and T Matsuyama. *A Structural Analysis of Complex Aerial Photographs*. Plenum Press, New York, 1980.

[Nevatia 77] R Nevatia. Evaluation of simplified Hueckel edge-line detector. *Computer Graphics and Image Processing*, 6(6):582–588, 1977.

[Papoulis 65] A Papoulis. *Probability, Random Variables, and Stochastic Processes*. McGraw Hill, New York, 1965.

[Paranjape et al. 92a] R B Paranjape, R N Rangayyan, Morrow W M, and H N Nguyen. Adaptive neighborhood image processing. In *Proceedings of Visual Communications and Image Processing, Boston, Ma*, pages 198–207, SPIE, Bellingham, Wa, 1992.

[Paranjape et al. 92b] R B Paranjape, R N Rangayyan, W M Morrow, and H N Nguyen. Adaptive neighborhood image processing. *CVGIP – Graphical Models and Image Processing*, 54(3):259–267, 1992.

[Perona and Malik 90] P Perona and J Malik. Scale-space and edge detection using anisotropic diffusion. *IEEE Transactions on Pattern Analysis and Machine Intelligence*, 12(7):629–639, 1990.

[Pitas and Venetsanopulos 86] I Pitas and A N Venetsanopulos. Nonlinear order statistic filters for image filtering and edge detection. *Signal Processing*, 10(10):573–584, 1986.

[Pizer et al. 87] S M Pizer, E P Amburn, J D Austin, R Cromartie, A Geselowitz, T Greer, B Haar-Romeny, J B Zimmerman, and K Zuiderveld. Adaptive histogram equalization and its variations. *Computer Vision, Graphics, and Image Processing*, 39:355–368, 1987.

[Pratt 78] W K Pratt. *Digital Image Processing*. John Wiley and Sons, New York, 1978.

[Roberts 65] L G Roberts. Machine perception of three-dimensional solids. In J T Tippett, editor, *Optical and Electro-Optical Information Processing*, pages 159–197. MIT Press, Cambridge, Ma, 1965.

[Rosenfeld and Kak 82] A Rosenfeld and A C Kak. *Digital Picture Processing*. Academic Press, New York, 2nd edition, 1982.

[Rosenfeld and Thurston 71] A Rosenfeld and M Thurston. Edge and curve detection for visual scene analysis. *IEEE Transactions on Computers*, 20(5):562–569, 1971.

[Saund 90] E Saund. Symbolic construction of a 2D scale-space image. *IEEE Transactions on Pattern Analysis and Machine Intelligence*, 12:817–830, 1990.

[Spacek 86] L Spacek. Edge detection and motion detection. *Image and Vision Computing*, pages 43–52, 1986.

[Tagare and deFigueiredo 90] H D Tagare and R J P deFigueiredo. On the localization performance measure and optimal edge detection. *IEEE Transactions on Pattern Analysis and Machine Intelligence*, 12(12):1186–1190, 1990.

[Topkar et al. 90] V Topkar, B Kjell, and A Sood. Object detection using scale-space. In *Proceedings of the Applications of Artificial Intelligence VIII Conference, The International Society for Optical Engineering*, pages 2–13, Orlando, Fl, April 1990.

[Tyan 81] S G Tyan. Median filtering, deterministic properties. In T S Huang, editor, *Two–Dimensional Digital Signal Processing*, volume II. Springer Verlag, Berlin, 1981.

[Ullman 81] S Ullman. Analysis of visual motion by biological and computer systems. *IEEE Computer*, 14(8):57–69, August 1981.

[Wang and Vagnucci 81] D C C Wang and A H Vagnucci. Gradient inverse weighting smoothing schema and the evaluation of its performace. *Computer Graphics and Image Processing*, 15, 1981.

[Williams and Shah 90] D J Williams and M Shah. Edge contours using multiple scales. *Computer Vision, Graphics, and Image Processing*, 51:256–274, September 1990.

[Witkin 83] A P Witkin. Scale–space filtering. In *Proceedings of the 8th Joint Conference on Artificial Intelligence*, pages 1019–1022, Karlsruhe, Germany, 1983.

[Yaroslavskii 87] L P Yaroslavskii. *Digital Signal Processing in Optics and Holography (in Russian)*. Radio i svjaz, Moscow, USSR, 1987.

5

Segmentation

Image segmentation is one of the most important steps leading to the analysis of processed image data – its main goal is to divide an image into parts that have a strong correlation with objects or areas of the real world contained in the image. We may aim for **complete segmentation**, which results in a set of disjoint regions uniquely corresponding with objects in the input image, or for **partial segmentation**, in which regions do not correspond directly with image objects. To achieve a complete segmentation, cooperation with higher processing levels which use specific knowledge of the problem domain is necessary. However, there is a whole class of segmentation problems that can be successfully solved using lower level processing only. In this case, the image commonly consists of contrasted objects located on a uniform background – simple assembly tasks, blood cells, printed characters, etc. Here, a simple global approach can be used and the complete segmentation of an image into objects and background can be obtained. Such processing is context independent; no object-related model is used, and no knowledge about expected segmentation results contributes to the final segmentation.

If partial segmentation is the goal, an image is divided into separate regions that are homogeneous with respect to a chosen property such as brightness, colour, reflectivity, context, etc. If an image of a complex scene is processed, for example, an aerial photograph of an urban scene, a set of possibly overlapping homogeneous regions may result. The partially segmented image must then be subjected to further processing, and the final image segmentation may be found with the help of higher level information.

Totally correct and complete segmentation of complex scenes usually cannot be achieved in this processing phase, although an immediate gain is substantial reduction in data volume. A reasonable aim is to use partial segmentation as an input to higher level processing.

Image data ambiguity is one of the main segmentation problems, often accompanied by information noise. Segmentation methods can be divided into three groups according to the dominant features they employ: Firstly, **global knowledge** about an image or its part; the knowledge is usually represented by a histogram of image features. **Edge-based** segmentations form the second group, and **region-based** segmentations the third – many different characteristics may be used in edge detection or region growing, for example,

112

brightness, context, velocity field, etc. The second and the third groups solve a dual problem. Each region can be represented by its closed boundary, and each closed boundary describes a region. Because of the different natures of the various edge- and region-based algorithms, they may be expected to give somewhat different results and consequently different information. The segmentation results of these two approaches can therefore be combined in a single description structure. A common example of this is a relational graph, in which regions are represented by nodes and graph arcs represent adjacency relations based on detected region borders.

5.1 Thresholding

Grey level thresholding is the simplest segmentation process. This is because many objects or image regions are characterized by constant reflectivity or light absorption of their surfaces. A brightness constant or **threshold** can be determined to segment objects and background. Thresholding is computationally cheap and fast – it is the oldest segmentation method and is still widely used in simple applications. Thresholding can easily be done in real time using specialized hardware.

Complete segmentation can result from thresholding in simple scenes. Let us define some basic terms; a complete segmentation of an image R is a finite set of regions $R_1, \ldots, R_S$

$$R = \bigcup_{i=1}^{S} R_i \qquad R_i \cap R_j = \emptyset \qquad i \neq j \tag{5.1}$$

Thresholding is the transformation of an input image f to an output (segmented) binary image g as follows:

$$\begin{aligned} g(i,j) &= 1 \quad \text{for } f(i,j) \geq T \\ &= 0 \quad \text{for } f(i,j) < T \end{aligned} \tag{5.2}$$

where T is the threshold, $g(i,j) = 1$ for image elements of objects, and $g(i,j) = 0$ for image elements of the background (or vice versa).

Algorithm 5.1: Thresholding

---

1. Search all the pixels $f(i,j)$ of the image f. An image element $g(i,j)$ of the segmented image is an object pixel if $f(i,j) \geq T$, and is a background pixel otherwise.

If objects do not touch each other, and if their grey levels are clearly distinct from background grey levels, thresholding is a suitable segmentation method.

Such an example is found in Figure 5.1a, the threshold segmentation result for which is shown in Figure 5.1b. Figures 5.1c and 5.1d show segmentation results for different threshold values.

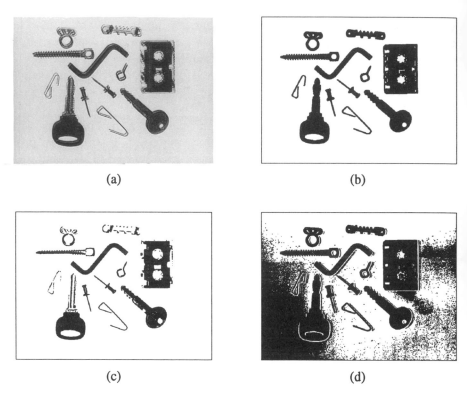

(a)   (b)

(c)   (d)

Figure 5.1 *Image thresholding: (a) Original image, (b) threshold segmentation, (c) threshold too low, (d) threshold too high.*

Correct threshold selection is crucial for successful threshold segmentation; this selection can be determined interactively or it can be the result of some threshold detection method that will be discussed in the next section. Only under very unusual circumstances can thresholding be successful using a single threshold for the whole image (global thresholding) since even in very simple images there are likely to be grey level variations in objects and background; this variation may be due to non-uniform lighting, non-uniform input device parameters or a number of other factors. Segmentation using variable thresholds, in which the threshold value varies over the image as a function of local image characteristics, can produce the solution in these cases.

A global threshold is determined from the whole image f

$$T = T(f) \tag{5.3}$$

On the other hand, local thresholds are position dependent

$$T = T(f, f_c) \tag{5.4}$$

where f_c is that image part in which the threshold is determined. One option is to divide the image f into subimages f_c and determine a threshold independently in each subimage; if then a threshold cannot be determined in some subimage, it can be interpolated from thresholds determined in neighbouring subimages. Each subimage is then processed with respect to its local threshold.

Basic thresholding as defined by equation 5.2 has many modifications. One possibility is to segment an image into regions of pixels with grey levels from a set D and into background otherwise (band-thresholding).

$$\begin{aligned} g(i,j) &= 1 \quad \text{for } f(i,j) \in D \\ &= 0 \quad \text{otherwise} \end{aligned} \tag{5.5}$$

This thresholding can be useful, for instance, in microscopic blood cell segmentations where a particular grey level interval represents cytoplasma, the background is lighter, and the cell kernel darker. This thresholding definition can serve as a border detector as well; assuming dark objects on a light background, some grey levels between those of objects and background can be found only in the object borders. If the grey level set D is chosen to contain just these object-border grey levels, and if thresholding according to equation 5.5 is used, object borders result as shown in Figure 5.2. Isolines of grey can be found using this appropriate grey level set D.

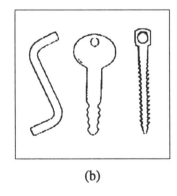

(a)   (b)

Figure 5.2 *Image thresholding modification: (a) Original image, (b) border detection using band-thresholding.*

There are many modifications that use multiple thresholds, after which the resulting image is no longer binary, but rather an image consisting of a very limited set of grey levels

$$
\begin{aligned}
g(i,j) \ &= 1 && \text{for } f(i,j) \in D_1 \\
&= 2 && \text{for } f(i,j) \in D_2 \\
&= 3 && \text{for } f(i,j) \in D_3 \\
&= 4 && \text{for } f(i,j) \in D_4 \\
&\cdots \\
&= n && \text{for } f(i,j) \in D_n \\
&= 0 && \text{otherwise}
\end{aligned} \tag{5.6}
$$

where each D_i is a specified subset of grey levels.

Another special choice of grey level subset D_i defines **semithresholding** that is sometimes used to make human assisted analysis easier

$$
\begin{aligned}
g(i,j) \ &= f(i,j) && \text{for } f(i,j) \geq T \\
&= 0 && \text{for } f(i,j) < T
\end{aligned} \tag{5.7}
$$

This process aims to mask out the image background leaving grey level information present in the objects.

Thresholding has been presented relying only on grey level image properties. Note that this is just one of many possibilities; thresholding can be applied if the values $f(i,j)$ do not represent grey levels, but instead represent gradient, a local context property (Chapter 13), or the value of any other image decomposition criterion.

5.1.1 Threshold detection methods

If some property of an image is known after segmentation the task of threshold selection is simplified, since the threshold is chosen to ensure this property is true. A printed text sheet may be an example if we know that characters of the text cover $1/p$ of the sheet area – using this prior information about the ratio between the sheet area and character area, it is very easy to choose a threshold T (based on the image histogram) such that $1/p$ of the image area has grey values less than T and the rest has grey values larger than T. This method is called **p-tile thresholding**. Unfortunately, we do not usually have such definite prior information about area ratios. This information can sometimes be substituted by knowledge of another property, for example the average width of lines in drawings, etc. The threshold can be determined to provide the required line width in the segmented image.

More complex methods of threshold detection are based on histogram shape analysis. If an image consists of objects of approximately the same grey level that differs from the grey level of the background, the resulting histogram is bimodal. Pixels of objects form one of its peaks, while pixels of the background form the second peak – Figure 5.3 shows a typical example. The histogram shape illustrates the fact that the grey values between the two

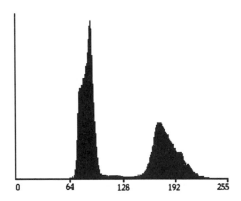

Figure 5.3 *A bimodal histogram.*

peaks are not common in the image, and probably result from border pixels between objects and background. The determined threshold must meet minimum segmentation error requirements; it makes intuitive sense to determine the threshold as the grey level that has a minimum histogram value between the two mentioned maxima, see Figure 5.3. If the histogram is multimodal, more thresholds may be determined as minima between any two maxima. Each threshold gives different segmentation results, of course. Multithresholding as given in equation 5.6 is another option.

To decide if a histogram is bimodal or multimodal may not be so simple in reality, it often being impossible to interpret the significance of local histogram maxima [Rosenfeld and de la Torre 83]. Bimodal histogram threshold detection algorithms usually find the highest local maxima first and detect the threshold as a minimum between them; this technique is called the **mode method**. To avoid detection of two local maxima belonging to the same global maximum, a minimum distance in grey levels between these maxima is usually required or techniques to smooth histograms (see Section 2.3.2) are applied. Note that histogram bimodality itself does not guarantee correct threshold segmentation – even if the histogram is bimodal, correct segmentation may not occur with objects located on a background of different grey levels. A two-part image with one half white and the second half black actually has the same histogram as an image with randomly spread white and black pixels (i.e. a random impulse noise image). This is one example showing the need to check threshold segmentation results whenever the threshold has been determined from a histogram only, using no other image characteristics.

A more general approach takes grey level occurrences inside a local neighbourhood into consideration when constructing a grey level histogram, the goal being to build a histogram with a better peak-to-valley ratio. One option is to weight histogram contributions to suppress the influence of pixels with a high image gradient. This means that a histogram will consist mostly of the grey values of objects and background, and that border grey levels (with higher gradient) will not contribute. This will produce a deeper histogram valley and allow an easier determination of the threshold. A different method uses only high gradient pixels to form the grey level histogram, meaning that the histogram will consist mostly of border grey levels and should be unimodal in which the peak corresponds to the grey level of borders between objects and background. The segmentation threshold can be determined as the grey value of this peak, or as a mean of a substantial part of the peak. Many modifications of **histogram transformation** methods can be found in [Weszka et al. 76, Weszka and Rosenfeld 79, Herman and Liu 78, Nagao and Matsuyama 80]

Methods based on approximation of the histogram of an image using a weighted sum of two or more probability densities with normal distribution represent a different approach called **optimal thresholding**. The threshold is set as the closest grey level corresponding to the minimum probability between the maxima of two or more normal distributions, which results in minimum error segmentation (the smallest number of pixels is mis-segmented) [Chow and Kaneko 72, Rosenfeld and Kak 82, Gonzalez and Wintz 87], see Figure 5.4 (and compare maximum likelihood classification methods, Section 7.2.2). The difficulty with these methods is in estimating normal distribution parameters together with the uncertainty that the distribution may be considered normal. These difficulties may be overcome if an optimal threshold is sought that maximizes grey level variance between objects and background. Note that this approach can be applied even if more than one threshold is needed [Otsu 79, Reddi et al. 84, Kittler and Illingworth 86, Mardia and Hainsworth 88, Cho et al. 89].

The following algorithm represents a simpler version that shows a rationale for this approach [Ridler and Calvard 78] and works well even if the image histogram is not bimodal. This method assumes that regions of two main grey levels are present in the image, thresholding of printed text being an example. The algorithm is iterative, four to ten iterations usually being sufficient.

Algorithm 5.2: Iterative (optimal) threshold selection

---

1. Assuming no knowledge about the exact location of objects, consider as a first approximation that the four corners of the image contain background pixels only and the remainder contains object pixels.

2. At step t, compute μ_B^t and μ_O^t as the mean background and object grey level respectively, where segmentation into background and objects at step t is defined by the threshold value T^t determined in the previous

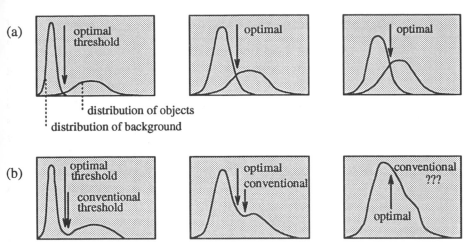

Figure 5.4 *Grey level histograms approximated by two normal distributions; the threshold is set to give minimum probability of segmentation error: (a) Probability distributions of background and objects, (b) corresponding histograms and optimal threshold.*

step (equation 5.9);

$$\mu_B^t = \frac{\sum_{(i,j)\in background} f(i,j)}{\#background\_pixels} \qquad \mu_O^t = \frac{\sum_{(i,j)\in objects} f(i,j)}{\#object\_pixels} \qquad (5.8)$$

3. Set

$$T^{(t+1)} = \frac{\mu_B^t + \mu_O^t}{2} \qquad (5.9)$$

$T^{(t+1)}$ now provides an updated background/object distinction.

4. If $T^{(t+1)} = T^{(t)}$, halt; otherwise return to (2).

The method performs well under a large variety of image contrast conditions.

Thresholding is a very popular tool in image segmentation, and a large variety of threshold detection techniques exist in addition to the main techniques which have been discussed. The survey [Sahoo et al. 88] gives a good overview of existing methods: **histogram concavity analysis, entropic** methods, **relaxation** methods, **multithresholding** methods, and others can be found there together with an extensive list of references. High processing speed has always been typical for threshold segmentations and images can easily be thresholded in real time. Real-time threshold detection is a current research effort [Hassan 89, Lavagetto 90].

5.1.2 Multispectral thresholding

Many practical segmentation problems need more information than is contained in one spectral band. Colour images are a natural example, in which information is coded in three spectral bands, red, green, and blue; multispectral remote sensing images or meteorological satellite images are similar. One segmentation approach determines thresholds independently in each spectral band and combines them into a single segmented image.

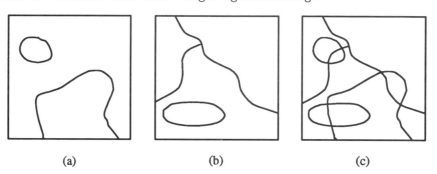

(a)   (b)   (c)

Figure 5.5 *Recursive multispectral thresholding: (a) Band 1 thresholding, (b) band 2 thresholding, (c) multispectral segmentation.*

Algorithm 5.3: Recursive multispectral thresholding

---

1. Initialize the whole image as a single region.

2. Compute a smoothed histogram (see Section 2.3.2) for each spectral band. Find the most significant peak in each histogram and determine two thresholds as local minima on either side of this maximum. Segment each region in each spectral band into subregions according to these determined thresholds. Each segmentation in each spectral band is projected into a multispectral segmentation – see Figure 5.5. Regions for the next processing steps are those in the multispectral image.

3. Repeat step (2) for each region of the image until each region's histogram contains only one significant peak.

Region shapes can be adjusted during recursive pre-processing – for instance boundary stretching, etc. (see Section 5.2.7). Better segmentation results can be achieved by analysing multi-dimensional histograms [Hanson and Riseman 78b] instead of histograms for each spectral band in step (2) of the previous algorithm.

Multispectral segmentations are often based on n-dimensional vectors of grey levels in n spectral bands for each pixel or small pixel neighbourhood. This segmentation approach, widely used in remote sensing, results from a classification process which is applied to these n-dimensional vectors. Generally speaking, regions are formed from pixels with similar properties in all spectral bands, with similar n-dimensional description vectors; see Chapter 7 and [Narendra and Goldberg 77, Ohta et al. 80, Kittler and Illingworth 85]. Segmentation and region labelling based on supervised, unsupervised and contextual classification is discussed in more detail in Section 8.3.

5.1.3   *Thresholding in hierarchical data structures*

The general idea of thresholding in hierarchical data structures is based on local thresholding methods (equation 5.4), the aim being to detect the presence of a region in a low-resolution image, and to give the region more precision in images of higher to full resolution. Certain methods work in pre-computed pyramid data structures (Chapter 3), where low-resolution images are computed from higher resolution images using averaging of grey values. The simplest method starts in the lowest resolution image (the highest pyramid level), applying any of the segmentation methods discussed so far. The next step yields better segmentation precision – pixels close to boundaries are re-segmented either into object or background regions (Figure 5.6). This increase in precision is repeated for each pair of pyramid levels up to the full resolution level at which the final segmentation is obtained. A big advantage of this method is the significantly lower influence of image noise on the segmentation results since segmentations at the lower resolution are based on smoothed image data, in which noise is suppressed. The imprecise borders that result from segmenting smoothed data are corrected by re-segmentation in areas close to borders using one step higher resolution data [Tanimoto and Pavlidis 75, Tanimoto 78, Hartley 82, Rosenfeld 84, Baugher and Rosenfeld 86, Gross and Rosenfeld 87, Song et al. 90].

Another approach looks for a significant pixel in image data and segments an image into regions of any appropriate size. The pyramid data structure is used again – either 2×2 or 4×4 averaging is applied to construct the pyramid. If 4×4 averaging is used, the construction tiles overlap in the pyramid levels. A significant pixel detector is applied to all pixels of a pyramid level – this detector is based on 3×3 detection which responds if the centre pixel of a 3×3 neighbourhood differs in grey level from most other pixels in the neighbourhood. It is assumed that the existence of this 'significant' pixel is caused by the existence of a different grey level region in the full-resolution image. The corresponding part of the full-resolution image is then thresholded (that is, the part which corresponds to the size of a 3×3 neighbourhood in the pyramid level where a significant pixel was found). The segmentation threshold is set to be between the grey level of the detected significant pixel (which represents

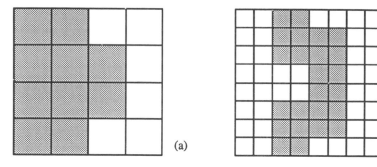

Figure 5.6 *Hierarchical thresholding: (a) Pyramid level n, segmentation to objects and background, (b) pyramid level n−1, showing where the thresholding must be repeated for better precision.*

the average grey level of the predicted region) and the average of the remaining 8-neighbours of the neighbourhood (which represent the average of grey levels of the predicted background).

Algorithm 5.4: Hierarchical thresholding

---

1. Represent the image as a pyramid data structure.

2. Search sequentially for significant pixels in all pixels of all pyramid levels starting in the uppermost level. If a significant pixel is detected, set a threshold T

$$T = \frac{c + \frac{1}{8}\sum_i n_i}{2} \qquad (5.10)$$

where c is the grey value of the significant pixel, and n_i are grey values of its 3×3 neighbours at the searched pyramid level. Apply the threshold to the corresponding part of the image at full resolution.

3. Continue the pyramid search as described in step (2).

5.2   Edge-based segmentation

Historically the first group of segmentation methods, which remains very important, is the large group based on information about edges in the image. Edge-based segmentations rely on edges found in an image by edge detecting operators – these edges mark image locations of discontinuities in grey level, colour, context, etc. A variety of edge detecting operators was described in Section 4.3.2, but the image resulting from edge detection cannot be used as a segmentation result. Other processing steps must follow to combine edges into edge chains that correspond better with borders in the image. The final aim is to reach at least a partial segmentation – that is, to group local edges into an image where only edge chains with a correspondence to existing objects or image parts are present.

We will discuss some different edge-based segmentation methods which differ in strategies leading to final border construction, and also differ in the amount of prior information that can be incorporated into the method. The more prior information that is available to the segmentation process, the better the segmentation results that can be obtained. Prior knowledge can be included in the confidence evaluation of the resulting segmentation as well. Prior information affects segmentation algorithms; if a large amount of prior information about the desired result is available, the boundary shape and relations with other image structures are specified very strictly and the segmentation must satisfy all these specifications. If little information about the boundary is known, the segmentation method must take more local information about the image into consideration and combine it with specific knowledge that is general for an application area. If little prior information is available, prior knowledge cannot be used to evaluate the confidence of segmentation results, and therefore no basis for feedback corrections of segmentation results is available.

The most common problems of edge-based segmentation, caused by image noise or unsuitable information in an image, are an edge presence in locations where there is no border, and no edge presence where a real border exists. Clearly both these cases have a negative influence on segmentation results.

Firstly, we will discuss simple edge-based methods requiring minimum prior information, and the necessity for prior knowledge will increase during the section. Construction of regions from edge-based partial segmentations is discussed at the end of the section.

5.2.1 Edge image thresholding

Almost no zero-value pixels are present in an edge image, but small edge values correspond to non-significant grey level changes resulting from quantization noise, small lighting irregularities, etc. Simple thresholding of an edge image can be applied to remove these small values. The approach is based on an image of edge magnitudes [Kundu and Mitra 87] processed by an appropriate threshold. Figure 5.7a shows an original image, an edge image is in Figure 5.7b, and the thresholded edge image in Figure 5.7c – if a larger threshold were to be applied, only more significant edges would appear in the resulting image. P-tile thresholding can be applied to define a threshold. A more exact approach using orthogonal basis functions is described in [Flynn 72]; if the original data has good contrast and is not noisy, this method gives good results. It may be advantageous to apply some form of post-processing, for example, to remove all border segments with length less than a specified value.

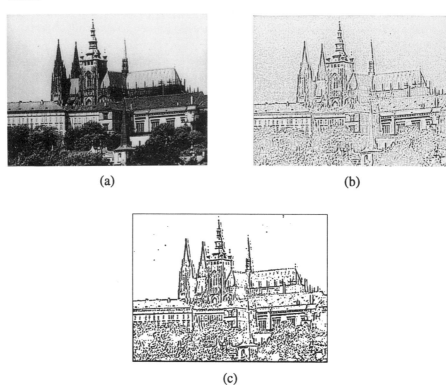

(a)   (b)

(c)

Figure 5.7 *Edge image thresholding: (a) Original image, (b) edge image, (c) thresholded edge image.*

5.2.2 Edge relaxation

Borders resulting from the previous method are strongly affected by image noise, often with important parts missing. Considering edge properties in the context of their mutual neighbours can increase the quality of the resulting image. All the image properties, including those of further edge existence, are iteratively evaluated with more precision until the edge context is totally clear. Based on the strength of edges in a specified local neighbourhood, the confidence of each edge is either increased or decreased [Rosenfeld et al. 76, Zucker 76, Riseman and Arbib 77, Hancock and Kittler 90]. A weak edge positioned between two strong edges provides an example of context; it is highly probable that this inter-positioned weak edge should be a part of a resulting boundary. If, on the other hand, an edge (even a strong one) is positioned by itself with no supporting context, it is probably not a part of any border.

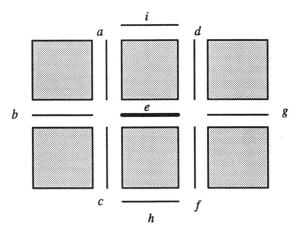

Figure 5.8 *Crack edges surrounding central edge e.*

A method we are going to discuss here [Hanson and Riseman 78b, Hanson and Riseman 78a, Prager 80] is a classical example of edge context evaluation. This method uses crack edges (edges located between pixels) which produce some favourable properties (see Section 2.3), although the method can work with other edge representations as well. Edge context is considered at both ends of an edge, giving the minimal edge neighbourhood shown in Figure 5.8. All three possible edge positions at the end of the edge e must be included to cover all the possible ways the border can continue from both ends of e. Furthermore, two edge positions parallel with the edge e can be included in the local neighbourhood – these parallel positions compete with the edge e in the placement of the border. Edge relaxation aims for continuous border construction so we discuss the edge patterns that can be found in the local neighbourhood. The central edge e has a vertex at each of its ends and three

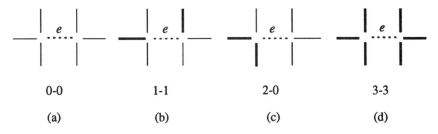

Figure 5.9 *Edge patterns and corresponding edge types.*

possible border continuations can be found from both of these vertices. Let each vertex be evaluated according to the number of edges emanating from the vertex, not counting the edge e; call this number the vertex type. The type of edge e can then be represented using a number pair $i - j$ describing edge patterns at each vertex, where i and j are the vertex types of the edge e. For example, it assigns type $0 - 0$ for the edges shown in Figure 5.9a, type $3 - 3$ in for Figure 5.9d, etc. By symmetry, we need only consider the cases where $i \leq j$. The following context situations are possible:

- **0-0** isolated edge – negative influence on the edge confidence

- **0-2, 0-3** dead end – negative influence on edge confidence

- **0-1** uncertain – weak positive, or no influence on edge confidence

- **1-1** continuation – strong positive influence on edge confidence

- **1-2, 1-3** continuation to border intersection – medium positive influence on edge confidence

- **2-2, 2-3, 3-3** bridge between borders – not necessary for segmentation, no influence on edge confidence

An edge relaxation can be defined from the given context rules that may be considered as a production system [Nilsson 82], Section 7.1. Edge relaxation is an iterative method, with edge confidences converging either to zero (edge termination) or one (the edge forms a border). The confidence $c^{(1)}(e)$ of each edge e in the first iteration can be defined as a normalized magnitude of the crack edge, with normalization based on either the global maximum of crack edges in the whole image, or on a local maximum in some large neighbourhood of the edge, thereby decreasing the influence of a few very high values of edge magnitude in the image.

Algorithm 5.5: Edge relaxation

---

1. Evaluate a confidence $c^{(1)}(e)$ for all crack edges e in the image.

2. Find the edge type of each edge based on edge confidences in its neighbourhood.

3. Update the confidence $c^{(k+1)}(e)$ of each edge e according to its type and its previous confidence $c^{(k)}(e)$.

4. Stop if all edge confidences have converged either to 0 or 1. Repeat steps (2) and (3) otherwise.

The main steps of Algorithm 5.5 are evaluation of vertex types followed by evaluation of edge types, and the manner in which the edge confidences are modified. A vertex is considered to be of type i if

$$type(i) = \max_k(type(k)), \qquad k = 0, 1, 2, 3 \qquad (5.11)$$

$$type(0) = (m - a)(m - b)(m - c)$$
$$type(1) = a(m - b)(m - c)$$
$$type(2) = ab(m - c)$$
$$type(3) = abc$$

where a, b, c are the normalized values of the other incident crack edges, and without loss of generality we can assume $a \geq b \geq c$. q is a constant, for which a value of approximately 0.1 seems to be appropriate, and $m = \max(a, b, c, q)$ [Ballard and Brown 82]. Note that the introduction of the quantity q ensures that $type(0)$ is non-zero for small values of a.

For example, choosing $q = 0.1$, a vertex $(a, b, c) = (0.5, 0.05, 0.05)$ is a type 1 vertex, while a vertex $(0.3, 0.2, 0.2)$ is a type 3 vertex. Similar results can be obtained by simply counting the number of edges emanating from the vertex above a threshold value. Edge type is found as a simple concatenation of vertex types, and edge confidences are modified as follows:

$$\text{confidence increase:} \qquad c^{(k+1)}(e) = \min(1, c^{(k)}(e) + \delta) \qquad (5.12)$$

$$\text{confidence decrease:} \qquad c^{(k+1)}(e) = \max(0, c^{(k)}(e) - \delta) \qquad (5.13)$$

where δ is an appropriate constant, usually in the range 0.1 to 0.3.

Edge confidence modification rules can be simplified and just one value of δ can be used, not including the weak, moderate, or strong confidence increase/decrease options. Further, vertex types 2 and 3 can be considered the same in implementation because they result in the same production rules.

Edge relaxation, as described above, rapidly improves the initial edge labelling in the first few iterations. Unfortunately, it slowly drifts giving worse results than expected after larger numbers of iterations. A theoretical explanation, convergence proof, and practical solutions are given in [Levy 88]. The reason for this strange behaviour is in searching for the global maximum of the edge consistency criterion over all the image, which may not give locally optimal results. A solution is found in setting edge confidences to zero under a certain threshold, and to one over another threshold which increases the influence of original image data. Therefore, one additional step must be added to the edge confidence computation (equations 5.12 and 5.13)

$$\text{if} \quad c^{(k+1)}(e) > T_1 \quad \text{then assign} \quad c^{(k+1)}(e) = 1 \qquad (5.14)$$

$$\text{if} \quad c^{(k+1)}(e) < T_2 \quad \text{then assign} \quad c^{(k+1)}(e) = 0 \qquad (5.15)$$

where T_1 and T_2 are parameters controlling the edge relaxation convergence speed and resulting border accuracy. Moreover, this method makes multiple labellings possible; the existence of two edges at different directions in one pixel may occur in corners, crosses, etc.

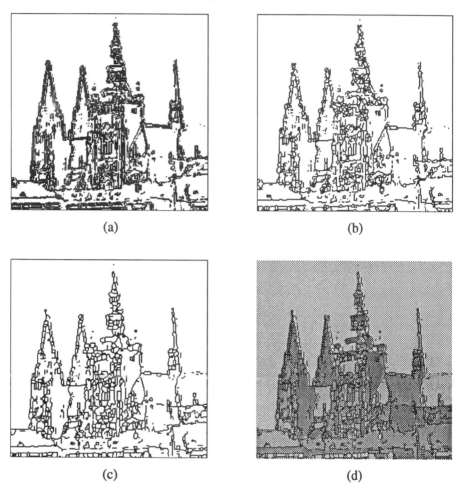

(a)   (b)

(c)   (d)

Figure 5.10 *Edge relaxation, see Figure 5.7a for original: (a) Resulting borders after 10 iterations, (b) borders after thinning, (c) borders after 100 iterations, thinned (d) borders after 100 iterations overlaid over original.*

Edge relaxation results are shown in Figure 5.10 where edges parallel with the central edge were not considered in the relaxation process. This result can be compared with the edge thresholding method applied to the same data shown in Figure 5.7c. The relaxation method can easily be implemented in parallel with a surprisingly good speed-up. Implementation on a 16-processor hypercube showed almost linear speed-up if 2, 4, 8, or 16 processors were used; in other words using 16 processors the processing was almost 16 times faster than using one processor (note that linear speed-up is uncommon in parallel implementations). All figures presented in this section were obtained running the parallel version of the algorithm [Clark 91].

5.2.3 Border tracing

If a region border is not known but regions have been defined in the image, borders can be uniquely detected. First, let us assume that the image with regions is either binary or that regions have been labelled (see Section 6.1). The first goal is to determine **inner** region borders. As defined earlier, an inner region border is a subset of a region – conversely, the **outer** border is not a subset of a region. The following algorithm covers inner boundary tracing in both 4-connectivity and 8-connectivity.

Algorithm 5.6: Inner boundary tracing

---

1. Search the image from top left until a pixel of a new region is found; this pixel P_0 then has the minimum column value of all pixels of that region having the minimum row value. Pixel P_0 is a starting pixel of the region border. Define a variable *dir* which stores the direction of the previous move along the border from the previous border element to the current border element. Assign

   (a) $dir = 3$ if the border is detected in 4-connectivity (Figure 5.11a)

   (b) $dir = 7$ if the border is detected in 8-connectivity (Figure 5.11b)

2. Search the 3×3 neighbourhood of the current pixel in an anti-clockwise direction, beginning the neighbourhood search in the pixel positioned in the direction

   (a) $(dir + 3)$ *mod* 4 (Figure 5.11c)

   (b) $(dir + 7)$ *mod* 8 if *dir* is *even* (Figure 5.11d)
   $(dir + 6)$ *mod* 8 if *dir* is *odd* (Figure 5.11e)

   The first pixel found with the same value as the current pixel is a new boundary element P_n. Update the *dir* value.

3. If the current boundary element P_n is equal to the second border element P_1, and if the previous border element P_{n-1} is equal to P_0, stop. Otherwise repeat step (2).

4. The detected inner border is represented by pixels $P_0 \ldots P_{n-2}$.

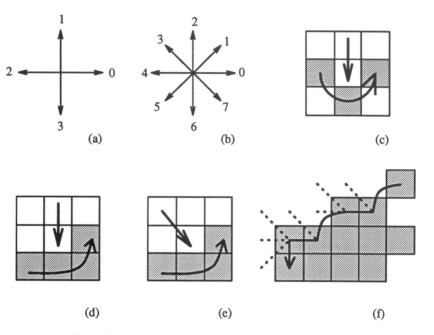

Figure 5.11 *Inner boundary tracing: (a) Direction notation, 4-connectivity, (b) 8-connectivity, (c) pixel neighbourhood search sequence in 4-connectivity, (d),(e) search sequence in 8-connectivity, (f) boundary tracing in 8-connectivity (dashed lines show pixels tested during the border tracing).*

Algorithm 5.6 works for all regions larger than one pixel (looking for the border of a single-pixel region is a trivial problem). This algorithm is able to find region borders but does not find borders of region holes. To search for hole borders as well, the border must be traced starting in each region or hole border element if this element has never been a member of any previously traced border. The search for border elements always starts after a currently traced border is closed, and the search for 'unused' border elements can continue in the same way as the search for the first border element was done. Note that if objects are of unit width, more conditions must be added.

If the goal is to detect an outer region border, the given algorithm may still be used based on 4-connectivity.

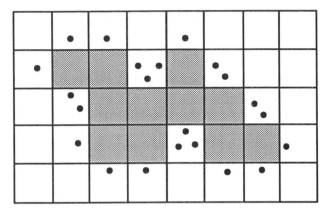

Figure 5.12 *Outer boundary tracing;* • *denotes outer border elements. Note that some pixels may be listed several times.*

Algorithm 5.7: Outer boundary tracing

---

1. Trace the inner region boundary in 4-connectivity until done.

2. The outer boundary consists of all non-region pixels that were tested during the search process; if some pixels were tested more than once, they are listed more than once in the outer boundary list.

Note that some outer border elements may be repeated in the border up to three times – see Figure 5.12. The outer region border is useful for deriving properties such as perimeter, compactness, etc., and is consequently often used – see Chapter 6.

The inner border is always part of a region but the outer border never is. Therefore, if two regions are adjacent, they never have a common border, which causes difficulties in higher processing levels with region description, region merging, etc. The inter-pixel boundary extracted for instance from crack edges is common to adjacent borders, nevertheless, its position cannot be specified in pixel co-ordinates (compare the supergrid data structure in Figure 5.37). Boundary properties better than those of outer borders may be found in extended borders [Pavlidis 77]. The main advantage of the extended boundary definition is that it defines a single common border between adjacent regions, and it may be specified using standard pixel co-ordinates (see Figure 5.13). All the useful properties of the outer border still remain; in addition, the boundary shape is exactly equal to the inter-pixel shape but is shifted one half-pixel down and one half-pixel right. The existence of a common border between regions makes it possible to incorporate into the boundary tracing a boundary description process. An evaluated graph consisting of border segments and vertices may result directly from the boundary tracing process; also, the border between adjacent regions may be traced only once and not twice as in conventional approaches.

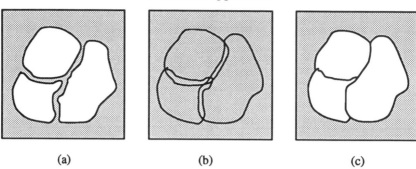

(a)   (b)   (c)

Figure 5.13 *Boundary locations for inner, outer, and extended boundary definition: (a) Inner, (b) outer, (c) extended.*

The extended boundary is defined using 8-neighbourhoods, and the pixels are coded according to Figure 5.14a (e.g. $P_4(P)$ denotes the pixel immediately to the left of pixel P). Four kinds of inner boundary pixels of a region R are defined; if Q denotes pixels outside the region R, then

a pixel $P \in R$ is a LEFT pixel of R if $P_4(P) \in Q$
a pixel $P \in R$ is a RIGHT pixel of R if $P_0(P) \in Q$
a pixel $P \in R$ is an UPPER pixel of R if $P_2(P) \in Q$
a pixel $P \in R$ is a LOWER pixel of R if $P_6(P) \in Q$

Let LEFT(R), RIGHT(R), UPPER(R), LOWER(R) represent the corresponding subsets of R. The extended boundary EB is defined as a set of points P, P_0, P_6, P_7 satisfying the following conditions [Pavlidis 77, Liow 91]:

$$EB = \{P : P \in \text{LEFT}(R)\} \cup \{P : P \in \text{UPPER}(R)\} \cup$$
$$\{P_6(P) : P \in \text{LOWER}(R)\} \cup \{P_6(P) : P \in \text{LEFT}(R)\} \cup \quad (5.16)$$
$$\{P_0(P) : P \in \text{RIGHT}(R)\} \cup \{P_7(P) : P \in \text{RIGHT}(R)\}$$

Figure 5.14 illustrates the definition.

The extended boundary can easily be constructed from the outer boundary. Using an intuitive definition of RIGHT, LEFT, UPPER, and LOWER outer boundary points, the extended boundary may be obtained by shifting all the UPPER outer boundary points one pixel down and right, shifting all the LEFT outer boundary points one pixel to the right, and shifting all the RIGHT outer boundary points one pixel down. The LOWER outer boundary point positions remain unchanged, see Figure 5.15.

A more sophisticated method for extended boundary tracing was introduced together with an efficient algorithm in [Liow 91]. The approach is based

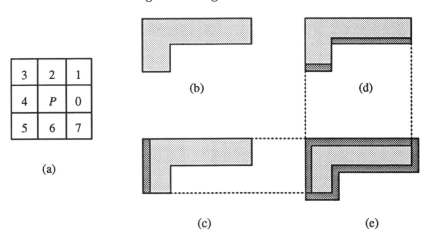

Figure 5.14 *Extended boundary definition: (a) Pixel coding scheme, (b) region R, (c) LEFT(R), (d) LOWER(R), (e) extended boundary.*

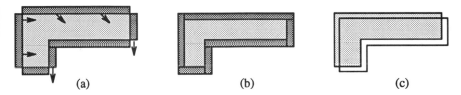

Figure 5.15 *Constructing the extended boundary from outer boundary: (a) Outer boundary, (b) extended boundary construction, (c) extended boundary has the same shape and size as the natural object boundary.*

on detecting common boundary segments between adjacent regions and vertex points in boundary segment connections. The detection process is based on a look-up table, which defines all 12 possible situations of the local configuration of 2×2 pixel windows, depending on the previous direction of detected boundary, and on the status of window pixels which can be inside or outside a region.

Algorithm 5.8: Extended boundary tracing

---

1. Define a starting pixel of an extended boundary in a standard way (the first region pixel found in a left-to-right and top-to-bottom line-by-line image search).

2. The first move along the traced boundary from the starting pixel is in direction $dir = 6$ (down), corresponding to the situation (i) in Figure 5.16.

3. Trace the extended boundary using the look-up table in Figure 5.16 until a closed extended border results.

Note that there is no hole-border tracing included in the algorithm. The holes are considered separate regions and therefore the borders between the region and its hole are traced as a border of the hole.

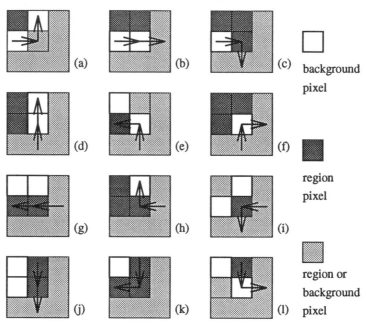

Figure 5.16 *Look-up table defining all 12 possible situations that can appear during extended border tracing. Current position is in the central pixel. The direction of the next move depends on the local configuration of background and region points, and on the direction of approach to the current pixel. Adapted from [Liow 91].*

The look-up table approach makes the tracing more efficient than conventional methods and makes parallel implementation possible. A pseudocode description of algorithmic details is given in [Liow 91], where a solution to the problems of tracing all the borders in an image in an efficient way is given. In addition to extended boundary tracing, it provides a description of each boundary segment in chain code form together with information about vertices. This method is very suitable for representing borders in higher level segmentation approaches including methods that integrate edge-based and region-based segmentation results. Moreover, in the conventional approaches, each border between two regions must be traced twice. The algorithm can trace each boundary segment only once storing the information about what has already been done in double-linked lists.

A more difficult situation is encountered if the borders are traced in grey level images where regions have not yet been defined [Dudani 76]. Therefore, the border is represented by a *simple path* of high-gradient pixels in the image (see Section 2.3.1). Border tracing should be started in a pixel with a high probability of being a border element, and then border construction is based on the idea of adding the next elements which are in the most probable direction. To find the following border elements, edge gradient magnitudes and directions are usually computed in pixels of probable border continuation [Ballard and Brown 82].

Algorithm 5.9: Border tracing in grey level images

---

1. Let the border be determined up to the border element x_i. An element x_j is defined as a pixel adjacent to x_i in the direction $\phi(x_i)$. If the gradient magnitude in x_j is larger than the preset threshold, x_j is considered a border element and step (1) is repeated. Otherwise proceed to step (2).

2. Compute the average grey level value in the 3×3 neighbourhood of the pixel x_j. Compare the result with some preset grey level value and decide if x_j is positioned inside or outside the region. Proceed to step (3).

3. Try to continue the border tracing in pixel x_k which is adjacent to x_i in direction $(\phi(x_i) \pm \pi/4)$, the sign being determined according to the result of step (2). If a border continuation was found, x_k is a new border element, and return to step (1). If x_k is not a border element, start the border tracing at another promising pixel.

This algorithm can be applied to multispectral or dynamic images as well, based on multi-dimensional gradients. Further details can be found for example in [Liu 77, Herman and Liu 78].

5.2.4 Edge following as graph searching

Whenever additional knowledge is available for boundary detection, it should be used. One example of prior knowledge is a known starting point and a known ending point of the border, even if the precise border location is not known. Even some relatively weak additional requirements such as smoothness, low curvature, etc. may be included as prior knowledge. If this kind of supporting information is available in the border detection task, general problem-solving methods widely used in AI can be applied [Nilsson 82].

A graph is a general structure consisting of a set of nodes n_i and arcs between the nodes $[n_i, n_j]$ (see Section 3.2.3). We consider oriented and numerically weighted arcs, these weights being called **costs**. The border detection process is transformed into a search for the optimal path in the weighted graph, the aim being to find the best path that connects two specified nodes, the starting and ending nodes.

Assume that both edge magnitude $s(\mathbf{x})$ and edge direction $\phi(\mathbf{x})$ information is available in an edge image. Each image pixel corresponds to a graph node weighted by a $s(\mathbf{x})$ value. Two nodes n_i and n_j corresponding to two 8-connected adjacent pixels $\mathbf{x}_i$ and $\mathbf{x}_j$ are connected by an arc if the edge directions $\phi(\mathbf{x}_i)$ and $\phi(\mathbf{x}_j)$ match the local border direction. We can apply the following rules to construct the graph: To connect a node n_i representing the pixel $\mathbf{x}_i$ with a node n_j representing the pixel $\mathbf{x}_j$, pixel $\mathbf{x}_j$ must be one of three existing neighbours of $\mathbf{x}_i$ in the direction $d \in [\phi(\mathbf{x}_i) - \pi/4, \phi(\mathbf{x}_j) + \pi/4]$. Further, $s(\mathbf{x}_i)$ and $s(\mathbf{x}_j)$ must be greater than T, where T is some preset threshold of edge significance. Another common requirement is to connect two nodes only if the difference of their edge directions is less then $\pi/2$.

These conditions can be modified in specific edge detection problems. Figure 5.17a shows an image of edge directions, with only significant edges according to their magnitudes listed. Figure 5.17b shows an oriented graph constructed in accordance with the presented principles.

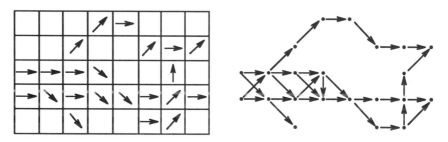

Figure 5.17 *Graph representation of an edge image: (a) Edge directions, (b) corresponding graph.*

The application of graph search to edge detection was first published in [Martelli 72] in which Nilsson's A-algorithm [Nilsson 82] applies. Let $\mathbf{x}_A$ be the starting border element, and $\mathbf{x}_B$ be the end border element. To use graph search for region border detection, a method of oriented weighted-graph expansion must first be defined (one possible method was described earlier). A cost function $f(\mathbf{x}_i)$ must also be defined that is a cost estimate of the path between nodes n_A and n_B (pixels $\mathbf{x}_A$ and $\mathbf{x}_B$) which goes through an intermediate node n_i (pixel $\mathbf{x}_i$). The cost function $f(\mathbf{x}_i)$ typically consists of two components; an estimate $\tilde{g}(\mathbf{x}_i)$ of the path cost between the starting border element $\mathbf{x}_A$ and $\mathbf{x}_i$, and an estimate $\tilde{h}(\mathbf{x}_i)$ of the path cost between $\mathbf{x}_i$ and the end border element $\mathbf{x}_B$. The cost $\tilde{g}(\mathbf{x}_i)$ of the path from the starting point to the node n_i is usually a sum of costs associated with the arcs or nodes that are in the path. The cost function must be separable and monotonic with respect to the path length, and therefore the local costs associated with arcs are required to be non-negative. A simple example of $\tilde{g}(\mathbf{x}_i)$ satisfying the given conditions is to consider the path length from $\mathbf{x}_A$ to $\mathbf{x}_i$. An estimate $\tilde{h}(\mathbf{x}_i)$ may be the length of the border from $\mathbf{x}_i$ to $\mathbf{x}_B$, it making sense to prefer shorter borders between $\mathbf{x}_A$ and $\mathbf{x}_B$ as the path with lower cost. This implies that the following heuristic search algorithm (Nilsson's A-algorithm) can be applied to the border detection.

Algorithm 5.10: Heuristic graph search

1. Expand the starting node n_A and put all its successors into an OPEN list with pointers back to the starting node n_A. Evaluate the cost function f for each expanded node.

2. If the OPEN list is empty, fail.
   Determine the node n_i from the OPEN list with the lowest associated cost $f(n_i)$ and remove it. If $n_i = n_B$, then trace back through the pointers to find the optimum path and stop.

3. If the option to stop was not taken in step (2), expand the specified node n_i, and put its successors on the OPEN list with pointers back to n_i. Compute their costs f. Go to step (2).

If no additional requirements are set on the graph construction and search, this process can easily result in an infinite loop (see Figure 5.18). To prevent

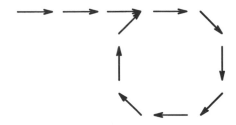

Figure 5.18 *Example of following a closed loop in image data.*

this behaviour, no node expansion is allowed that puts a node on the OPEN list if this node has already been visited, and put on the OPEN list in the past. A simple solution to the *loop* problem is not to allow searching in a backward direction. This approach can be used if a priori information about the boundary location and its local direction is available. In this case, it may be possible to straighten the processed image (and the corresponding graph) as shown in Figure 5.19. The edge image is geometrically warped by resampling the image along profile lines perpendicular to the approximate position of the searched border. The pre-processing step that straightens the image data provides a substantial computational convenience. No backward searches may be allowed to trace boundaries represented this way. This approach can be extremely useful if the borders of thin elongated objects like roads, rivers, vessels, etc. are to be detected [Collins and Skorton 86, Fleagle et al. 89].

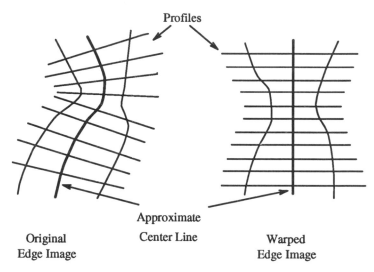

Figure 5.19 *Geometric warping produces a straightened image: The graph constructed requires (and allows) searches in one main direction only (e.g. top-down). Adapted from [Fleagle et al. 89].*

The estimate of the cost of the path from the current node n_i to the end node n_B has a substantial influence on the search behaviour. If this estimate $\tilde{h}(n_i)$ of the true cost $h(n_i)$ is not considered, so $(\tilde{h}(n_i) = 0)$, no heuristic is included in the algorithm and a breadth-first search is done. Because of this, the detected path will always be optimal according to the criterion used, and thus the minimum cost path will always be found. Applying heuristics, the detected cost does not always have to be optimal but the search can often be much faster.

Given natural conditions for estimates $\tilde{g}$, the minimum cost path result can be guaranteed if $\tilde{h}(n_i) \leq h(n_i)$ and if the real cost of any part of the path $c(n_p, n_q)$ is larger than the estimated cost of this part $\tilde{c}(n_p, n_q)$. The closer the estimate $\tilde{h}(n_i)$ is to $h(n_i)$, the lower the number of nodes expanded in the search. The problem is that the exact cost of the path from the node n_i to the end node n_B is not known beforehand. In some applications, it may be more important to get the solution quickly than to get an optimal result. Choosing $\tilde{h}(n_i) > h(n_i)$, optimality is not guaranteed but the number of expanded nodes will typically be smaller because the search can be stopped before the optimum is found.

A comparison of optimal and heuristic graph search border detection is given in Figure 5.20. The raw cost function (an inverted edge image) can be seen in Figure 5.20a; Figure 5.20b shows the optimal borders resulting from the graph search when $\tilde{h}(n_i) = 0$; 38% of nodes were expanded during the search, and expanded nodes are shown as white regions. When a heuristic search was applied ($\tilde{h}(n_i)$ was about 20% overestimated), only 2% of graph nodes were expanded during the search and the border detection was fifteen times faster (Figure 5.20c). Comparing resulting borders in Figures b and c, it can be seen that despite a very substantial speedup, the resulting borders do not differ significantly [Tadikonda et al. 92].

We can summarize:

- If $\tilde{h}(n_i) = 0$, the algorithm produces a minimum-cost search.

- If $\tilde{h}(n_i) > h(n_i)$, the algorithm may run faster, but the minimum-cost result is not guaranteed.

- If $\tilde{h}(n_i) \leq h(n_i)$, the search will produce the minimum-cost path if and only if

$$c(n_p, n_q) \geq \tilde{h}(n_p) - \tilde{h}(n_q)$$

for any p, q, where $c(n_p, n_q)$ is the real minimum cost of getting from n_i to n_j, which is not easy to fulfil for a specific $f(x)$.

- If $h(n_i) = \tilde{h}(n_i)$, the search will always produce the minimum-cost path with a minimum number of expanded nodes.

- The better the estimate of $h(n)$ is, the smaller the number of nodes that must be expanded.

In image segmentation applications, the existence of a path between a starting pixel x_A and an ending pixel x_B is not guaranteed due to possible discontinuities in the edge image and so more heuristics must often be applied to overcome these problems. For example, if there is no node in the OPEN list which can be expanded, it may be possible to expand nodes with non-significant edge-valued successors – this can build a bridge to pass these small discontinuities in border representations.

A crucial question is how to choose the evaluation cost functions for graph-search border detection. A good cost function should have elements common to most edge detection problems and also specific terms related to the particular application. Some generally applicable cost functions are;

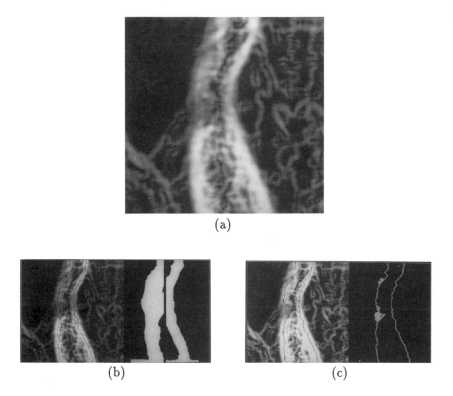

(a)

(b)   (c)

Figure 5.20 *Comparison of optimal and heuristic graph search performance: (a) Raw cost function (inverted edge image of a vessel), (b) optimal graph search, resulting vessel borders are shown adjacent to the cost function, expanded nodes shown (38%), (c) heuristic graph search, resulting borders and expanded nodes (2%).*

- Strength of edges forming a border: The heuristic 'the stronger the edges that form the border, the higher the probability of the border' is very natural and almost always gives good results. Note that if a border consists of strong edges, the cost of that border is small. The cost of adding another node to the border will be

$$\left(\max_{image} s(\mathbf{x}_k) \right) - s(\mathbf{x}_i) \tag{5.17}$$

where the maximum edge strength is obtained from all pixels in the image.

- Border curvature: Sometimes, borders with a small curvature are preferred. If this is the case, the total border curvature can be evaluated as a monotonic function of local curvature increments:

$$DIF(\phi(\mathbf{x}_i) - \phi(\mathbf{x}_j)) \tag{5.18}$$

where DIF is some suitable function evaluating the difference in edge directions in two consecutive border elements.

- Proximity to an approximate border location: If an approximate boundary location is known, it is natural to support the paths that are closer to the known approximation than others. When included into the border, a border element value can be weighted by the distance $dist$ from the approximate boundary, the distance having either additive or multiplicative influence on the cost:

$$dist(\mathbf{x}_i, approximate\_boundary) \tag{5.19}$$

- Estimates of the distance to the goal (end-point): If a border is reasonably straight, it is natural to support expansion of those nodes that are located closer to the goal node than other nodes:

$$\tilde{h}(\mathbf{x}_i) = dist(\mathbf{x}_i, \mathbf{x}_B) \tag{5.20}$$

Graph-based border detection methods very often suffer from extremely large numbers of expanded nodes stored in the OPEN list, these nodes with pointers back to their predecessors representing the searched part of the graph. The cost associated with each node in the OPEN list is a result of all the cost increases on the path from the starting node to that node. This implies that even a good path can generate a higher cost in the current node than costs of the nodes on worse paths which did not get so far from the starting node. This results in expansion of these 'bad' nodes representing shorter paths with lower total costs, even with the general view that their probabilities are low. An excellent way to solve this problem is to incorporate a heuristic estimate $\tilde{h}(\mathbf{x}_i)$ into the cost evaluation, but unfortunately, a good estimate of the path cost from the current node to the goal is not usually available. Some modifications which make the method more practically useful, even if some of them no longer guarantee the minimum-cost path, are available.

- Tree pruning the solution tree: The set of nodes in the OPEN list can be reduced during the search. Deleting those paths that have high average cost per unit length, or deleting paths that are too short whenever the total number of nodes in the OPEN list exceeds a defined limit, usually gives good results (see also Section 7.4.2).

- Least maximum cost: The strength of a chain may be given by the strength of the weakest element – this idea is included in cost function computations. The cost of the current path is then set as the cost of the most expensive arc in the path from the starting node to the current node [Lester 78], whatever the sum of costs along the path. The path cost does not therefore necessarily grow with each step, and this is what favours expansion of good paths for a longer time.

- Branch and bound: This modification is based on maximum allowed cost of a path, no path being allowed to exceed this cost [Chien and Fu 74]. This maximum path cost is either known beforehand or it is computed and updated during the graph search. All the paths that exceed the allowed maximum path cost are deleted from the OPEN list.

- Lower bound: Another way to increase the search speed is to reduce the number of poor edge candidate expansions. Poor edge candidates are always expanded if the cost of the best current path exceeds that of any worse but shorter path in the graph. If the cost of the best successor is set to zero, the total cost of the path does not grow after the node expansion and the good path will be expanded again. The method developed by Collins et al. [Collins et al. 91, Sonka et al. 93] assumes that the path is searched in a straightened graph resulting from a warped image as discussed earlier. The cost of the minimum-cost node on each profile is subtracted from each node on the profile (lower bound). In effect, this shifts the range of costs from

$$\min(profile\_node\_costs) \leq node\_cost \leq \max(profile\_node\_costs)$$

to

$$
\begin{aligned}
0 \;\leq\; & new\_node\_cost \\
\leq\; & [\max(profile\_node\_costs) - \min(profile\_node\_cost)]
\end{aligned}
$$

Note that the range of the costs on a given profile remains the same, but the range is translated such that at least one node for each profile is assigned a zero cost. Because the costs of the nodes for each profile are translated by different amounts, the graph is expanded in an order that supports expansion of good paths. For graph searching in the straightened image, the lower bound can be considered heuristic information when expanding nodes and assigning costs to subpaths in the graph. By summing the minimum value for each profile, the total is an estimate of the minimum-cost path through the graph. Obviously, the minimum cost nodes for each profile may not form a valid path, i.e. they may not be neighbours as required. However, the total cost will be the lower limit of the cost of any path through the graph. This result allows the heuristic to be admissible, thus guaranteeing the success of the algorithm in finding the optimal path. The assignment of a heuristic cost for a given node is implemented in a pre-processing step through the use of the lower bound.

- Multi-resolution processing: The number of expanded nodes can be decreased if a sequence of two graph search processes is applied. The first search is done in lower resolution, therefore a smaller number of graph nodes is involved in the search and a smaller number is expanded, compared to full resolution. The low-resolution search detects an approximate boundary. The second search is done in full resolution using the low-resolution results as a model, and the full-resolution costs are weighted by a factor representing the distance from the approximate boundary acquired in low resolution (equation 5.19). The weighting function should increase with the distance in a nonlinear way. This approach assumes that the approximate boundary location can be detected from the low-resolution image [Sonka et al. 93, Sonka and Collins 93].

- Incorporation of higher level knowledge: Including higher level knowledge into the graph search may significantly decrease the number of expanded nodes. The search may be directly guided by a priori knowledge of approximate boundary position. Another possibility is to incorporate a boundary shape model into the cost function computation. Both these approaches together with additional specific knowledge and the multi-resolution approach applied to coronary border detection are discussed in detail in Chapter 8 (see Figure 5.21 and Section 8.1.5).

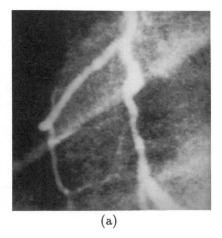 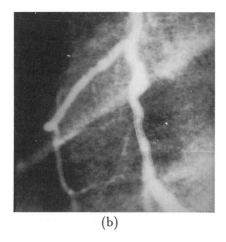

(a) (b)

Figure 5.21 *Graph search applied to the coronary vessel border detection: (a) Original image, (b) determined vessel borders.*

Graph searching techniques offer a convenient way to ensure global optimality of the detected contour. This technique has often been applied to the detection of approximately straight contours [Wang and Howarth 87, Wang and Howarth 89, Fleagle et al. 89]. The detection of closed structure contours would involve geometrically transforming the image using a polar to rectangular co-ordinate transformation in order to 'straighten' the contour, however this may prevent the algorithm from detecting the non-convex parts of the contour. To overcome this problem, the image may be divided into two segments and separate, simultaneous searches can be conducted in each segment [Philip et al. 90]. The searches are independent and proceed in opposite directions from a start point until they meet at the dividing line between the two image segments.

The approaches discussed above search for optimal borders between two specific image points. Searching for all the borders in the image without knowledge of the start and end-points is more complex. In an approach based on magnitudes and directions of edges in the image, edges are merged into edge chains (i.e. partial borders) [Ramer 75]. Edge chains are constructed by applying a bidirectional heuristic search in which half of each 8-neighbourhood expanded node is considered as lying in front of the edge, the second half as lying behind the edge (see Figure 5.22). Partial borders are grouped together using other heuristics which are similar to the approach previously described in edge relaxation (Section 5.2.2), and final region borders result. The following algorithm describes the ideas above in more detail and is an example of applying a bottom-up control strategy (see Chapter 8).

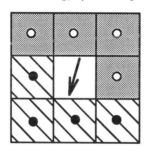

Figure 5.22 *Bidirectional heuristic search: Edge predecessors (marked o) and successors (marked •).*

Algorithm 5.11: Heuristic search for image borders

---

1. Search for the strongest edge in the image, not considering edges previously marked or edges that already are part of located borders. Mark the located edge. If the edge magnitude is less than the preset threshold or if no image edge was found, go to step (5).

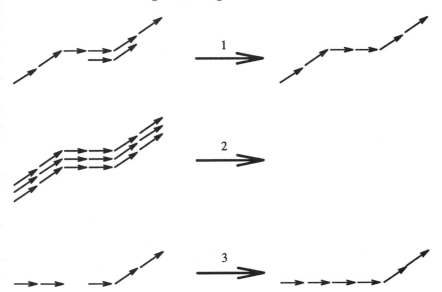

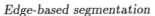

Figure 5.23 *Rules for edge chain modification; note that edge responses resulting from continuous changes of illumination are removed (case 2).*

2. Expand all the image edges positioned in front of the specified starting edge until new successors can be found.

3. Expand all the image edges positioned behind the specified starting edge until new predecessors can be found. In steps (2) and (3) do not include edges that are already part of any existing edge chain.

4. If the resulting edge chain consists of at least 3 edges, it is stored in the chain list, otherwise it is deleted. Proceed to step (1).

5. Modify edge chains according to the rules given in Figure 5.23.

6. Repeat step (5) until the resulting borders do not change substantially from step to step.

The rules given in Figure 5.23 (used in step (5) of Algorithm 5.11) solve three standard situations. First, thinner edge responses to a single border are obtained. Second, edge responses resulting from changes of lighting, where no real border exists, are removed. Third, small gaps in boundary element chains are bridged. Detailed behaviour given by these general rules can be modified according to the particular problem.

5.2.5 Edge following as dynamic programming

Boundary tracing as a graph searching technique using the A-algorithm requires knowledge of the first and the last boundary points. The dynamic programming approach may be applied even if this information is not available and the boundary may start and end in one of several points. Dynamic programming is an optimization method based on the **principle of optimality** [Bellmann 57, Pontriagin 62, Pontriagin 90]. It searches for optima of functions in which not all variables are simultaneously interrelated.

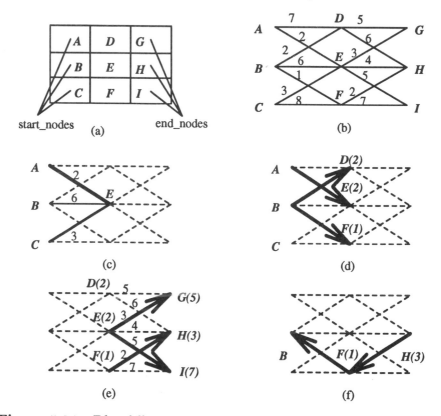

Figure 5.24 *Edge following as dynamic programming: (a) Edge image, (b) corresponding graph, partial costs assigned, (c) possible paths from any starting point to E, A − E is optimal, (d) optimal partial paths to nodes D, E, F, (e) optimal partial paths to nodes G, H, I, (f) backtracking from H defines the optimal boundary.*

Consider the following simple boundary tracing problem. The aim is to find the best path (minimum cost) between one of the possible starting points A, B, C and one of the possible ending points G, H, I. The boundary must be contiguous in 8-connectivity. The graph representing the problem together with assigned partial costs is shown in Figure 5.24a and b. As can be seen, there are 3 ways to get to the node E. Connecting A-E gives the cost $g(A, E) = 2$; connecting B-E, cost $g(B, E) = 6$; connecting C-E, cost $g(C, E) = 3$.

The **main idea** of the principle of optimality is: *whatever the path to the node E was, there exists an optimal path between E and the end_point. In other words, if the optimal path start_point – end_point goes through E then both its parts start_point – E and E – end_point are also optimal.*

In our case, the optimal path between *start_point* and E is the partial path A-E (see Figure 5.24c). Only the following information need be stored for future use; to get to E, the optimal path is A-E, cost $C(E) = 2$. Using the same approach, to get to D the optimal path is B-D, cost $C(D) = 2$; the best path to F is B-F, cost $C(F) = 1$ (see Figure 5.24d). The path may get to node G from either D or E. The cost of the path through the node D is a sum of the cumulative cost $C(D)$ of the node D and the partial path cost $g(D, G)$. This cost $C(G_D) = 7$ represents the path B-D-G because the best path to D is from B. The cost to get to G from E is $C(G_E) = 5$ representing the path A-E-G. It is obvious that the path going through the node E is better, the optimal path to G is the path A-E-G with cost $C(G) = 5$ (see Figure 5.24e). Similarly, cost $C(H) = 3$ (B-F-H) and cost $C(I) = 7$ (A-E-I). Now, the *end_point* with the minimum path cost represents the optimum path; node H is therefore the optimal boundary *end_point*, and the optimal boundary is B-F-H (see Figure 5.24f).

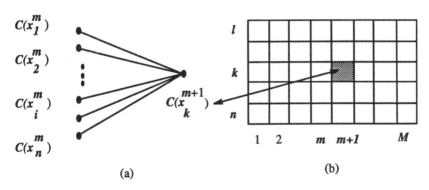

Figure 5.25 *Dynamic programming: (a) One step of the cost calculation, (b) graph layers, node notation.*

If the graph has more layers (in Figure 5.24 just 3 layers were present), the process is repeated until one of the *end_points* is reached. Each repetition consists of a simpler optimization as shown in Figure 5.25a

$$C(x_k^{m+1}) = \min_i (C(x_i^m) + g^m(i, k)) \qquad (5.21)$$

where $C(x_k^{m+1})$ is the new cost assigned to the node x_k^{m+1}, and $g^m(i,k)$ is the partial path cost between nodes x_i^m and x_k^{m+1}. It holds for the complete optimization problem that

$$\min(C(x^1, x^2, ..., x^M)) = \min_{k=1,...,n}(C(x_k^M)) \qquad (5.22)$$

where x_k^M are the *end-point* nodes, M is the number of graph layers between *start-points* and *end-points* (see Figure 5.25b) and $C(x^1, x^2, ..., x^M)$ denotes the cost of a path between the first and the last (M^{th}) graph layer. Requiring an 8-connected border and assuming n nodes x_i^m in each graph layer m, $3n$ cost combinations must be computed for each layer, $3n(M-1) + n$ being the total number of cost combination computations. Compared to the brute force enumerative search where $n(3^{M-1})$ combinations must be computed, the improvement is obvious. The final optimal path results from backtracking through the searched graph. Note that the number of neighbours depends on the definition of contiguity and definition of the searched graph, and is not limited to three.

The complete graph must be constructed to apply dynamic programming, and this may follow general rules given in the previous section. The objective function must be separable and monotonic (as for the A-algorithm); evaluation functions presented in the previous section may also be appropriate for dynamic programming.

Algorithm 5.12: Boundary tracing as dynamic programming

1. Specify initial costs $C(x_i^1)$ of all nodes in the first graph layer, $i = 1, ..., n$ and partial path costs $g^m(i,k)$, $m = 1, ..., M-1$.

2. Repeat step (3) for all $m = 1, ..., M-1$.

3. Repeat step (4) for all nodes $k = 1, ..., n$ in the graph layer m.

4. Let

$$C(x_k^{m+1}) = \min_{i=-1,0,1}(C(x_{k+i}^m) + g^m(i,k)) \qquad (5.23)$$

Set pointer from node x_k^{m+1} back to node x_i^{m*}; where $*$ denotes the optimal predecessor.

5. Find an optimal node x_k^{M*} in the last graph layer M and obtain an optimal path by backtracking through the pointers from x_k^{M*} to x_i^{1*}.

It has been shown that heuristic search may be more efficient than dynamic programming for finding a path between two nodes in a graph [Martelli 76].

Further, an A-algorithm based graph search does not require explicit definition of the graph. However, dynamic programming presents an efficient way of simultaneously searching for optimal paths from multiple starting and ending points. If these points are not known, dynamic programming is probably a better choice, especially if computation of the partial costs $g^m(i, k)$ is simple. Nevertheless, which approach is more efficient for a particular problem depends on evaluation functions and on the quality of heuristics for an A-algorithm. A comparison between dynamic programming and heuristic search efficiency can be found in [Ney 92]; dynamic programming was found to be faster and less memory demanding for a word recognition problem.

Dynamic programming was found to be more computationally efficient than edge relaxation (Section 5.2.2), [Bruel 88]. Another comparison [Wood 85] found dynamic programming more flexible and less restrictive than the Hough transform (Section 5.2.6), and it is a powerful tool in the presence of noise and in textured images [Furst 86, Derin and Elliot 87, Gerbrands 88, Cristi 88]. To increase processing speed, parallel implementations of dynamic programming are studied [Ducksbury 90]. Tracing borders of elongated objects like roads and rivers in aerial photographs, and vessels in medical images represent typical applications of dynamic programming in image segmentation [Pope et al. 85, Derin and Elliot 87, Degunst 90].

5.2.6 Hough transforms

If an image consists of objects with known shape and size, segmentation can be viewed as a problem of finding this object within an image. Typical tasks are to locate circular pads in printed circuit boards, or to find objects of specific shapes in aerial or satellite data, etc. One of many possible ways to solve these problems is to move a mask with an appropriate shape and size of the desired object along the image and look for correlation between the image and the mask, as discussed in Section 5.4. Unfortunately, the specified mask often differs too much from the object's representation in the processed data because of shape distortions, rotation, zoom, etc. One very effective method that can solve this problem is the **Hough transform** which can even be used successfully in segmentation of overlapping or semi-occluded objects.

The original Hough transform was designed to detect straight lines and curves [Hough 62], and this original method can be used if analytic equations of object borderlines are known – no prior knowledge of region position is necessary. Nevertheless, it is often impossible to get analytic expressions describing borders, and a generalized Hough transform that can find objects even if an analytic expression of the border is not known will be described later. A big advantage of this approach is robustness of segmentation results; that is, segmentation is not too sensitive to imperfect data or noise.

The basic idea of the method can be seen from the simple problem of detecting a straight line in an image [Duda and Hart 72, Duda and Hart 73].

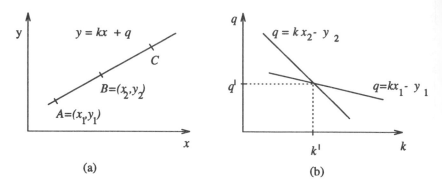

Figure 5.26 *Hough transform principles: (a) Image space, (b) k, q parameter space.*

A straight line is defined by two points $A = (x_1, y_1)$ and $B = (x_2, y_2)$ (shown in Figure 5.26a). All straight lines going through the point A are given by the expression $y_1 = kx_1 + q$ for some values of k and q. This means that the same equation can be interpreted as an equation in the parameter space k, q; all the straight lines going through the point A are then represented by the equation $q = x_1 k - y_1$ (see Figure 5.26b). Straight lines going through the point B can likewise be represented as $q = x_2 k - y_2$. The only common point of both straight lines in the k, q parameter space is the point which in the original image space represents the only existing straight line connecting points A and B.

This means that any straight line in the image is represented by a single point in the k, q parameter space and any part of this straight line is transformed into the same point. The main idea of line detection is to determine all the possible line pixels in the image, to transform all lines that can go through these pixels into corresponding points in the parameter space, and to detect the points (a, b) in the parameter space that frequently resulted from the Hough transform of lines $y = ax + b$ in the image.

These main steps will be described in more detail. Detection of all possible line pixels in the image may be achieved by applying an edge detector to the image; then, all pixels with edge magnitude exceeding some threshold can be considered possible line pixels (referred to as edge pixels below). In the most general case, nothing is known about lines in the image, and therefore lines of any direction may go through any of the edge pixels. In reality, the number of these lines is infinite, however, for practical purposes, only a limited number of line directions may be considered. The possible directions of lines define a discretization of the parameter k. Similarly, the parameter q is sampled into a limited number of values. The parameter space is not continuous any more, but rather is represented by a rectangular structure of cells. This array of cells is called the **accumulator array** A, whose elements are **accumulator cells**

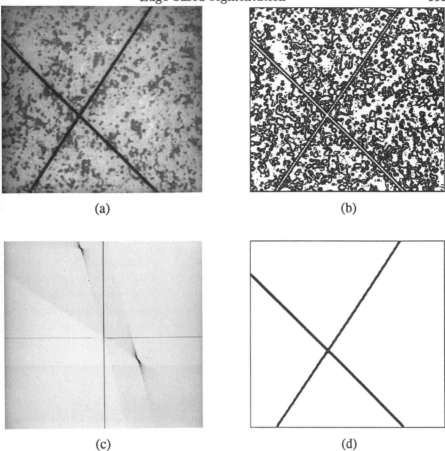

Figure 5.27 *Hough transform – line detection: (a) Original image, (b) edge image (note many edges, which do not belong to the line), (c) parameter space, (d) detected lines.*

$A(k, q)$. For each edge pixel, parameters k, q are determined, which represent lines of allowed directions going through this pixel. For each such line, the values of line parameters k, q are used to increase the value of the accumulator cell $A(k, q)$. Clearly, if a line represented by an equation $y = ax + b$ is present in the image, the value of the accumulator cell $A(a, b)$ will be increased many times – as many times as the line $y = ax + b$ is detected as a line possibly going through any of the edge pixels. For any pixel P, lines going through it may have any direction k (from the set of allowed directions), but the second parameter q is constrained by the image co-ordinates of the pixel P and the direction k. Therefore, lines existing in the image will cause large values of the appropriate accumulator cells in the image, while other lines possibly going through edge pixels, which do not correspond to lines existing in the image, have different k, q parameters for each edge pixel, and therefore the corresponding accumulator cells are increased only rarely. In other words, lines existing in the image may be detected as high-valued accumulator cells in the accumulator array, and the parameters of the detected line are specified by the accumulator array co-ordinates. As a result, line detection in the image is transformed to detection of local maxima in the accumulator space.

As already mentioned, an important property of the Hough transform is its insensitivity to missing parts of lines, to image noise, and to other non-line structures co-existing in the image. Insensitivity to data imprecision and noise can be seen in Figure 5.27. This is caused by the robustness of transformation from the image space into the accumulator space – a missing part of the line will only cause a lower local maximum because a smaller number of edge pixels contributes to the corresponding accumulator cell. A noisy or only approximately straight line will not be transformed into a point in the parameter space, but rather will result in a cluster of points, and the cluster centre of gravity can be considered the straight line representation. Note that the parametric equation of the line $y = kx + q$ is appropriate only for explanation of the Hough transform principles – it causes difficulties in vertical line detection $(k \to \infty)$ and in nonlinear discretization of the parameter k. If a line is represented as

$$s = x \cos \theta + y \sin \theta \qquad (5.24)$$

the Hough transform does not suffer from these limitations. Again, the straight line is transformed to a single point (see Figure 5.28). A practical example showing the segmentation of an MR image of the brain into the left and right hemispheres is given in Figure 5.29.

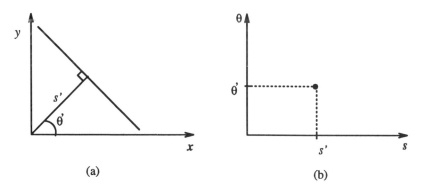

(a)   (b)

Figure 5.28 *Hough transform in s, θ space: (a) Straight line in image space, (b) s, θ parameter space.*

Discretization of the parameter space is an important part of this approach [Yuen and Hlavac 91]; also, detecting the local maxima in the accumulator array is a non-trivial problem. In reality, the resulting discrete parameter space

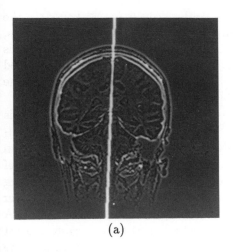
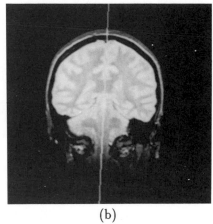

(a)   (b)

Figure 5.29 *Hough transform line detection used for MRI brain segmentation to the left and right hemispheres. (a) Edge image, detected midline, (b) segmentation line in original image data.*

usually has more than one local maximum per line existing in the image, and smoothing the discrete parameter space may be a solution. All these remarks remain valid if more complex curves are searched in the image using the Hough transform, the only difference being the dimensionality of the accumulator array.

Generalization to more complex curves that can be described by an analytic equation is straightforward. Consider an arbitrary curve represented by an equation $f(\mathbf{x}, \mathbf{a}) = 0$, where $\mathbf{a}$ is the vector of curve parameters.

Algorithm 5.13: Curve detection using the Hough transform.

---

1. Quantize parameter space within the limits of parameters $\mathbf{a}$. The dimensionality n of the parameter space is given by the number of parameters of the vector $\mathbf{a}$.

2. Form an n-dimensional accumulator array $A(\mathbf{a})$ with structure matching the quantization of parameter space; set all elements to zero.

3. For each image point (x_1, x_2) in the appropriately thresholded gradient image, increase all accumulator cells $A(\mathbf{a})$ if $f(\mathbf{x}, \mathbf{a}) = 0$

$$A(\mathbf{a}) = A(\mathbf{a}) + \Delta A$$

for all $\mathbf{a}$ inside the limits used in step (1).

4. Local maxima in the A-array correspond to realizations of curves $f(\mathbf{x}, \mathbf{a})$ that are present in the original image.

If we are looking for circles, the analytic expression $f(\mathbf{x}, \mathbf{a})$ of the desired curve is

$$(x_1 - a)^2 + (x_2 - b)^2 = r^2 \qquad (5.25)$$

where the circle has centre (a, b) and radius r. Therefore, the accumulator data structure must be three-dimensional. For each pixel $\mathbf{x}$ whose edge magnitude exceeds a given threshold, all accumulator cells corresponding to potential circle centres (a, b) are incremented in step (3) of the given algorithm. The accumulator cell $A(a, b, r)$ is incremented if the point (a,b) is at distance r from point $\mathbf{x}$, and this condition is valid for all triplets (a, b, r) satisfying equation 5.25. If some potential centre (a, b) of a circle of radius r is frequently found in the parameter space, it is highly probable that a circle with radius r and centre (a, b) really exists in the processed data.

The processing results in a set of parameters of desired curves $f(\mathbf{x}, \mathbf{a}) = 0$ that correspond to local maxima of accumulator cells in the parameter space; these maxima best match the desired curves and processed data. Parameters may represent infinite analytic curves (e.g. line, ellipse, parabola, etc.), but to look for finite parts of these curves, the end-points must be explicitly defined and other conditions must be incorporated into the algorithm. Even though the Hough transform is a very powerful technique for curve detection, exponential growth of the accumulator data structure with the increase of the number of curve parameters restricts its practical usability to curves with few parameters.

If prior information about edge directions is used, computational demands can be decreased significantly. Consider the case of searching the circular boundary of a dark region, letting the circle have a constant radius $r = R$ for simplicity. Without using edge direction information, all accumulator cells $A(a, b)$ are incremented in the parameter space if the corresponding point (a, b) is on a circle with centre $\mathbf{x}$. With knowledge of direction, only a small number of the accumulator cells need be incremented. For example, if edge directions are quantized into 8 possible values, only one eighth of the circle need take part in accumulator cell incrementing. Of course, estimates of edge direction are unlikely to be precise – if we anticipate edge direction errors of $\pi/4$, three eighths of the circle will require accumulator cell incrementing. Using edge directions, candidates for parameters a and b can be identified from the following formulae:

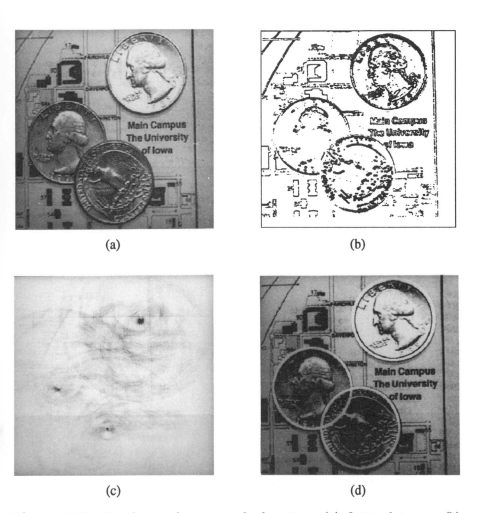

(a)   (b)

(c)   (d)

Figure 5.30 *Hough transform – circle detection: (a) Original image, (b) edge image (note that the edge information is far from perfect), (c) parameter space, (d) detected circles.*

$$a = x_1 - R\cos(\psi(\mathbf{x}))$$
$$b = x_2 - R\sin(\psi(\mathbf{x})) \tag{5.26}$$
$$\psi(\mathbf{x}) \in [\phi(\mathbf{x}) - \Delta\phi, \; \phi(\mathbf{x}) + \Delta\phi]$$

where $\phi(\mathbf{x})$ refers to the edge direction in pixel $\mathbf{x}$ and $\Delta\phi$ is the maximum anticipated edge direction error. Accumulator cells in the parameter space are then incremented only if (a, b) satisfy equation 5.26. Another heuristic that has a beneficial influence on the curve search is to weight the contributions to accumulator cells $A(\mathbf{a})$ by the edge magnitude in pixel $\mathbf{x}$; thus the increment ΔA in step (3) of Algorithm 5.13 ($A(\mathbf{a}) = A(\mathbf{a}) + \Delta A$) will be greater if it results from the processing of a pixel with larger edge magnitude. Figure 5.30 demonstrates circle detection when circular objects of known radius overlap and the image contains many additional structures causing the edge image to be very noisy. Note the parameter space with three local maxima corresponding to centres of three circular objects.

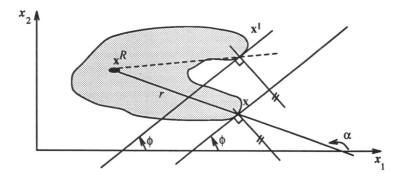

Figure 5.31 *Principles of the generalized Hough transform: Geometry of R-table construction.*

If the parametric representations of the desired curves or region borders are known, this method works very well, but unfortunately this is not often the case. The desired region borders can rarely be described using a parametric boundary curve with a small number of parameters; in this case, a generalized Hough transform [Ballard 81, Davis 82, Illingworth and Kittler 87] can offer the solution. This method constructs a parametric curve (region border) description based on sample situations detected in the learning stage. Assume that shape, size and rotation of the desired region are known. A reference point $\mathbf{x}^R$ is chosen at any location inside the sample region, then an arbitrary line can be constructed starting at this reference point aiming in the direction of the region border (see Figure 5.31). The border direction (edge direction) is found at the intersection of the line and the region border. A reference table (referred to as the R-table in [Ballard 81]) is constructed, and intersection parameters are stored as a function of the border direction at the intersection point; using different lines aimed from the reference point, all the distances of the reference point to region borders and the border directions at the intersections can be found. The resulting table can be ordered according to the border directions at the intersection points. As Figure 5.31 makes clear, different points $\mathbf{x}$ of the region border can have the same border direction, $\phi(\mathbf{x}) = \phi(\mathbf{x}')$. This implies that there may be more than one (r, α) pair for each ϕ that can determine the co-ordinates of a potential reference point. An example of an R-table is given in Table 5.1. Assuming no rotation and known size, remaining description parameters required are the co-ordinates of the reference point (x_1^R, x_2^R). If size and rotation of the region may vary, the number of parameters increases to four. Each pixel $\mathbf{x}$ with a significant edge in the direction $\phi(\mathbf{x})$ has co-ordinates of potential reference points $(x_1 + r(\phi)\cos(\alpha(\phi)), x_2 + r(\phi)\sin(\alpha(\phi)))$. These must be computed for all possible values of r and α according to the border direction $\phi(\mathbf{x})$ given in the R-table. The following algorithm presents the generalized Hough trans-

$$
\begin{array}{ll}
\phi_1 & (r_1^1, \alpha_1^1), (r_1^2, \alpha_1^2), \ldots, (r_1^{n_1}, \alpha_1^{n_1}) \\
\phi_2 & (r_2^1, \alpha_2^1), (r_2^2, \alpha_2^2), \ldots, (r_2^{n_2}, \alpha_2^{n_2}) \\
\phi_3 & (r_3^1, \alpha_3^1), (r_3^2, \alpha_3^2), \ldots, (r_3^{n_3}, \alpha_3^{n_3}) \\
\cdots & \cdots \\
\phi_k & (r_k^1, \alpha_k^1), (r_k^2, \alpha_k^2), \ldots, (r_k^{n_k}, \alpha_k^{n_k})
\end{array}
$$

Table 5.1 *R-table*

form in the most general of cases in which rotation (τ) and size (S) may both change. If either there is no change in rotation $(\tau = 0)$, or there is no size change $(S = 1)$, the resulting accumulator data structure A is simpler.

Algorithm 5.14: Generalized Hough transform

---

1. Construct an R-table description of the desired object.

2. Form a data structure A that represents the potential reference points

$$
A(x_1, x_2, \tau)
$$

Set all accumulator cell values $A(x_1, x_2, \tau)$ to zero.

3. For each pixel (x_1, x_2) in a thresholded gradient image determine the edge direction $\Phi(\mathbf{x})$; find all potential reference points $\mathbf{x}^R$ and increase all $A(\mathbf{x}^R, \tau)$

$$
A(\mathbf{x}^R, \tau) = A(\mathbf{x}^R, \tau) + \Delta A
$$

for all possible values of rotation and size change

$$x_1^R = x_1 + r(\phi)S\cos(\alpha(\phi) + \tau)$$

$$x_2^R = x_2 + r(\phi)S\sin(\alpha(\phi) + \tau)$$

4. The desired region location is given by local maxima in the A data structure.

The Hough transform was initially developed to detect analytically defined shapes, such as lines, circles or ellipses in general images, and the generalized Hough transform can be used to detect arbitrary shapes. However, even the generalized Hough transform requires the complete specification of the exact shape of the target object to achieve precise segmentation. Therefore, it allows detection of objects with complex, but pre-determined, shapes. The **fuzzy Hough transform** [Philip 91] allows detection of objects whose exact shape is unknown – there is often enough a priori knowledge to form an approximate model of the object. It requires only an approximate model of the target object and then identifies the object that most closely approximates the model. After detecting an approximate position of the model using the generalized Hough transform, elements of the true contour are recovered by choosing the point with the maximum weighted edge strength along each radial line (clearly, stronger edges represent more probable border location). The weighting factor also represents the distance from the approximate contour acquired in the generalized Hough transform step. The approximate model position guides the more precise border detection (see Figure 5.32). Since edge information is never perfect, there may be parts of a contour that are misplaced or missing, and it is recommended not to mark any border point if its confidence is below some threshold and to determine this border point position using, for instance, cubic B-splines (Section 6.2.5). To obtain even more reliable results, the border may be detected optimally all over the contour using a graph-search technique (Section 5.2.4).

Borders of the left and right ventricles obtained by applying the fuzzy Hough transform to CT (Computer Tomography) images of the canine thorax may be found in Figure 5.33.

The Hough transform has many desirable features [Illingworth and Kittler 88]. It recognizes partial or slightly deformed shapes, therefore behaving extremely well in recognition of occluded objects. It may be also used to measure similarity between a model and detected object on the basis of size and spatial location of peaks in the parameter space. The Hough transform is very robust in the presence of additional structures in the image (other lines, curves, or objects) as well as being insensitive to image noise. Moreover, it may search for several occurrences of the searched shape during the same processing pass.

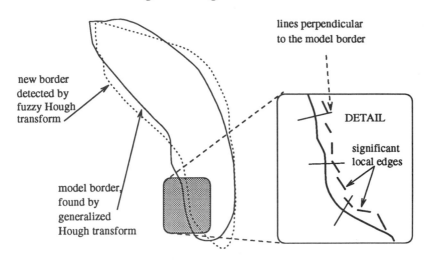

Figure 5.32 *Principles of the fuzzy Hough transform.*

Unfortunately, the conventional sequential approach requires a lot of storage and extensive computation. However, its naturally parallel character gives the potential for real-time implementations.

Many serious implementational problems were only touched upon here (shape parameterization, accumulation in parameter space, peak detection in parameter space, etc.). Details are discussed in surveys [Evans 85, Illingworth and Kittler 88] where an extensive list of references may also be found. Because of the large time requirements in the sequential version, effort has been devoted to hierarchical approaches [Neveu 86, Princen et al. 89]; methods combining the Hough transform and line tracing were studied [Wang and Howarth 89, Lerner and Morelli 90], and many parallel implementations were tested [Oyster 87, Kannan and Chuang 88, Chandran and Davis 89, Hsu and Huang 90, Shankar and Asokan 90]. The unique properties of the Hough transform also provoke more and more applications [Kashyap and Koch 84, McDonnel et al. 87, Illingworth and Kittler 88, McKenzie and Protheroe 90, Fetterer et al. 90, Brummer 91].

5.2.7 Border detection using border location information

If any information about boundary location or shape is known, it is of benefit to use it. The information may for instance be based on some higher level knowledge, or can result from segmentation applied to a lower resolution image.

One possibility is to determine a boundary in an image as the location of significant edges positioned close to an assumed border if the edge directions of these significant edges match the assumed boundary direction. The new

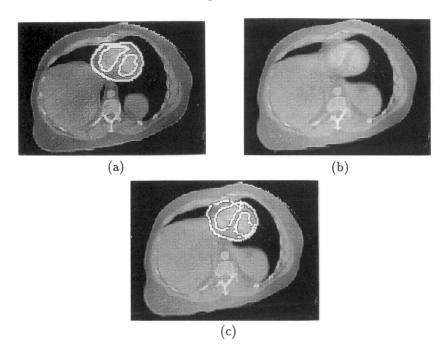

(a)   (b)

(c)

Figure 5.33 *Borders of left and right ventricles of dog heart detected from CT scanned images using the fuzzy Hough transform: (a) Contour model acquired in an adjacent slice, (b) original image of the processed slice, (c) contour resulting from fuzzy Hough transform (courtesy K. Philip, E. Dove, K. Chandran, University of Iowa).*

border pixels are searched in directions perpendicular to the assumed border (see Figure 5.34). If a large number of border elements satisfying the given conditions are found, an approximate curve is computed based on these pixels, and a new, more accurate, border results.

Another possibility is based on prior knowledge of end-points – this approach assumes low image noise and relatively straight boundaries. The process iteratively partitions the border and searches for the strongest edge located on perpendiculars to the line connecting end-points of each partition; perpendiculars are located at the centre of the connecting straight line, see Figure 5.35. The strongest significant edge is located on the perpendicular that is close to the straight line connecting the end-points of the current partition is accepted as a new border element. The iteration process is then repeated.

A recent approach to contour detection has been introduced [Kass et al. 87] in which active contour models (snakes) start their search for a contour taking advantage of user-provided knowledge about approximate position and

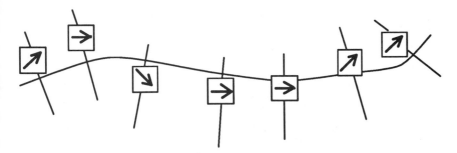

Figure 5.34 *A priori information about boundary location.*

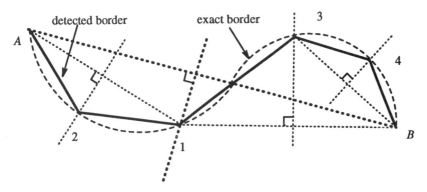

Figure 5.35 *Divide-and-conquer iterative border detection; numbers show the sequence of division steps.*

shape of the required contour. An optimization method refines the starting contour estimate and matches the desired contour. This approach is discussed in Section 8.2.

5.2.8 Region construction from borders

All methods considered hitherto have focused on the detection of borders that partially or completely segmented the processed image. If a complete segmentation is achieved the detected borders segment an image into regions, but if only a partial segmentation results, regions are not defined uniquely and region determination from borders may be a very complex task requiring cooperation with higher level knowledge. However, methods exist that are able to construct regions from partial borders which do not form closed boundaries. These methods do not always find acceptable regions but they are useful in many practical situations.

One of them is the **superslice** method [Milgram 79], which is applicable if regions have dominant grey level properties. The approach assumes that some border-part locations are known in the image; the image data is then thresholded using different thresholds. Regions resulting from the thresholding for which the detected boundaries best coincide with assumed boundary segments are then accepted as correct.

Better results can be obtained by applying a method described in [Hong et al. 80] based on the existence of partial borders in the processed image. Region construction is based on probabilities that pixels are inside a region closed by partial borders. The border pixels are described by their positions and by pixel edge directions $\phi(\mathbf{x})$. The closest 'opposite' edge pixel is searched for along a perpendicular to each significant image edge, and then closed borders are constructed from pairs of opposite edge pixels. A pixel is a potential region member if it is on a straight line connecting two opposite edge pixels. The final decision on which of the potential region pixels will form a region is probabilistic.

Algorithm 5.15: Region forming from partial borders

---

1. For each border pixel $\mathbf{x}$ search for an opposite edge pixel within a distance not exceeding a given maximum M. If an opposite edge pixel is not found, process the next border pixel in the image. If an opposite edge pixel is found, mark each pixel on the connecting straight line as a potential region member.

2. Compute the number of markers for each pixel in the image (the number of markers tells how often a pixel was on a connecting line between opposite edge pixels). Let $b(\mathbf{x})$ be the number of markers for the pixel $\mathbf{x}$.

3. The weighted number of markers $B(\mathbf{x})$ is then determined as follows:

$$
\begin{aligned}
B(\mathbf{x}) &= 0.0 &\quad \text{for} \quad & b(\mathbf{x}) = 0 \\
&= 0.1 &\quad \text{for} \quad & b(\mathbf{x}) = 1 \\
&= 0.1 &\quad \text{for} \quad & b(\mathbf{x}) = 1 \\
&= 0.2 &\quad \text{for} \quad & b(\mathbf{x}) = 2 \\
&= 0.5 &\quad \text{for} \quad & b(\mathbf{x}) = 3 \\
&= 1.0 &\quad \text{for} \quad & b(\mathbf{x}) > 3
\end{aligned}
\tag{5.27}
$$

The confidence that a pixel $\mathbf{x}$ is a member of a region is given as the sum $\sum_i B(\mathbf{x_i})$ in a 3×3 neighbourhood of the pixel $\mathbf{x}$. If the confidence that a pixel $\mathbf{x}$ is a region member is one or larger, then pixel $\mathbf{x}$ is marked as a region pixel, otherwise it is marked as a background pixel.

Note that this method allows the construction of bright regions on dark backgrounds as well as dark regions on a bright background by taking either of the two options in the search for opposite edge pixels – step (1). Search orientation depends on whether relatively dark or bright regions are constructed. If $\phi(\mathbf{x})$ and $\phi(\mathbf{y})$ are directions of edges, the condition which must be satisfied for $\mathbf{x}$ and $\mathbf{y}$ to be opposite is

$$\frac{\pi}{2} \; < \; |(\phi(\mathbf{x}) - \phi(\mathbf{y})) \bmod (2\pi)| \; < \; \frac{3\pi}{2} \tag{5.28}$$

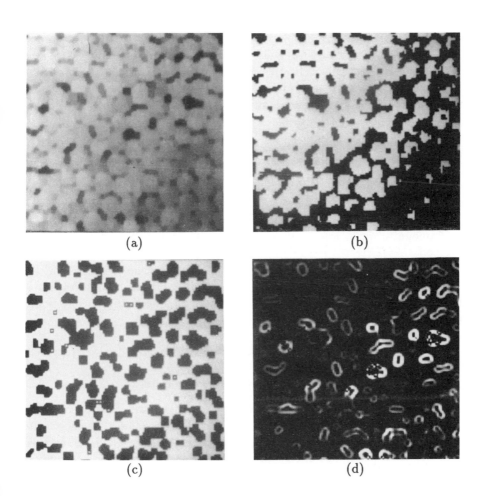

(a)

(b)

(c)

(d)

Figure 5.36 *Region forming from partial borders: (a) Original image, (b) thresholding, (c) regions formed from partial borders, (d) edge image.*

Note that it is possible to take advantage of prior knowledge of maximum region sizes – this information defines the value of M in step (1) of the algorithm, the maximum search length for the opposite edge pixel.

This method was applied to form texture primitives (Chapter 13, [Hong et al. 80, Sonka 86]) as shown in Figure 5.36. The differences between the results of this region detection method and those obtained by thresholding applied to the same data are clearly visible if Figures 5.36b and 5.36c are compared.

5.3   Region growing segmentation

The aim of the segmentation methods described in the previous section was to find borders between regions; the following methods construct regions directly. It is easy to construct regions from their borders and it is easy to detect borders of existing regions. However, segmentations resulting from edge-based methods and region growing methods are not usually exactly the same and a combination of results may often be a good idea. Region growing techniques are generally better in noisy images where edges are extremely difficult to detect. Homogeneity is an important property of regions and is used as the main segmentation criterion in region growing, whose basic idea is to divide an image into zones of maximum homogeneity. The criteria for homogeneity can be based on grey level, texture, model (using semantic information), etc. [Haralick and Shapiro 85, Zamperoni 86, Grimson and Lozano-Perez 87, Pal and Pal 87]. Properties chosen to describe regions influence the form, complexity, and amount of prior information in the specific region growing segmentation method.

Regions have already been defined in Chapter 2 and discussed in Section 5.1, where equation 5.1 stated the basic requirements of segmentation into regions. Further assumptions needed in this section are that regions must satisfy the following conditions:

$$H(R_i) = TRUE \qquad i = 1, 2, ..., S \qquad (5.29)$$

$$H(R_i \cup R_j) = FALSE \quad i \neq j, \quad R_i \ adjacent \ to \ R_j \qquad (5.30)$$

where S is the total number of regions in an image and $H(R_i)$ is a binary homogeneity evaluation of the region R_i. Resulting regions of the segmented image must be both homogeneous and maximal where by 'maximal' we mean that the homogeneity criterion would not be true after merging a region with any adjacent region.

We will discuss simpler versions of region growing first; that is, the merging, splitting, and split-and-merge approaches, and will discuss the possible gains from using semantic information later in Chapter 8. Of especial interest are the homogeneity criteria, whose choice is the most important factor affecting the methods mentioned; general and special heuristics may also be incorporated.

The simplest homogeneity criterion uses an average grey level of the region, simple context properties, or an m-dimensional vector of average grey values for multispectral images.

5.3.1 Region merging

The most natural method of region growing is to begin the growth in the raw image data, each pixel representing a single region. These regions almost certainly do not satisfy the condition of equation 5.30, and so regions will be merged as long as equation 5.29 remains satisfied.

Algorithm 5.16: Region merging (outline)

---

1. Define some starting method to segment the image into many small regions satisfying condition 5.29.

2. Define a criterion for merging two adjacent regions.

3. Merge all adjacent regions satisfying the merging criterion. If no two regions can be merged maintaining condition 5.29, stop.

This algorithm is a general approach to region merging segmentation. Specific methods differ in the definition of the starting segmentation and in the criterion for merging. In the descriptions that follow, regions are those parts of the image that can be sequentially merged into larger regions satisfying equations 5.29 and 5.30. The result of region merging usually depends on the order in which regions are merged, meaning that segmentation results will probably differ if segmentation begins, for instance, in the upper left or lower right corners. This is because the merging order can cause two similar adjacent regions R_1 and R_2 not to be merged since an earlier merge used R_1 and its new characteristics no longer allow it to be merged with region R_2. If the merging process used a different order, this merge may have been realized.

The simplest methods begin merging by starting the segmentation using regions of 2×2, 4×4 or 8×8 pixels. Region descriptions are then based on their statistical grey level properties – a regional grey level histogram is a good example. A region description is compared with the description of an adjacent region; if they match, they are merged into a larger region and a new region description is computed. Otherwise regions are marked as non-matching. Merging of adjacent regions continues between all neighbours, including newly formed ones. If a region cannot be merged with any of its neighbours, it is marked 'final' and the merging process stops when all image regions are so marked.

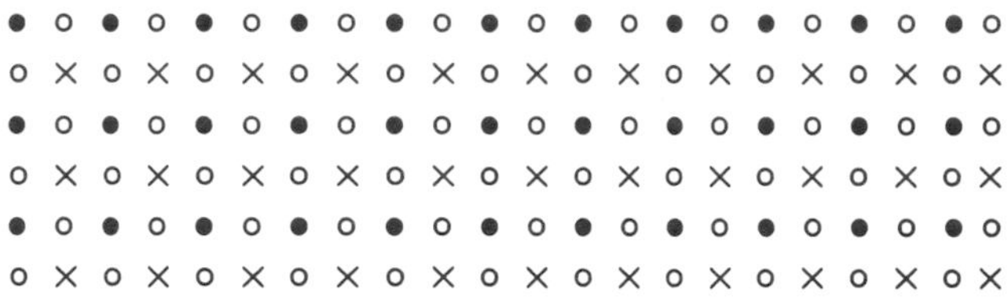

```
● o ● o ● o ● o ● o ● o ● o ● o ● o ● o ● o ● o ● o
o × o × o × o × o × o × o × o × o × o × o × o × o ×
● o ● o ● o ● o ● o ● o ● o ● o ● o ● o ● o ● o ● o
o × o × o × o × o × o × o × o × o × o × o × o × o ×
● o ● o ● o ● o ● o ● o ● o ● o ● o ● o ● o ● o ● o
o × o × o × o × o × o × o × o × o × o × o × o × o ×
```

Figure 5.37 *Supergrid data structure:* × - *image data,* o - *crack edges,* ● - *unused.*

State space search is one of the essential principles of problem solving in AI [Nilsson 82] whose application to image segmentation was first published in [Brice and Fennema 70]. According to this approach, pixels of the raw image are considered the starting state, each pixel being a separate region. A change of state can result from the merging of two regions or the splitting of a region into subregions. The problem can be described as looking for allowed changes of state while producing the best image segmentation. This state space approach brings two advantages; first, well known methods of state space search can be applied which also include heuristic knowledge; second, higher level data structures can be used which allow the possibility of working directly with regions and their borders, and no longer require the marking of each image element according to its region marking. Starting regions are formed by pixels of the same grey level – these starting regions are small in real images. The first state changes are based on crack edge computations (Section 2.3.1) where local boundaries between regions are evaluated by the strength of crack edges along their common border. The data structure used in this approach (the so called **supergrid**) carries all the necessary information (see Figure 5.37); this allows for easy region merging in 4-adjacency when crack edge values are stored in the 'o' elements. Region merging uses the following two heuristics:

- Two adjacent regions are merged if a significant part of their common boundary consists of weak edges (*significance* can be based on the region with the shorter perimeter; the ratio of the number of *weak* common edges to the total length of the region perimeter may be used).

- Two adjacent regions are also merged if a significant part of their common boundary consists of weak edges, but in this case not considering the total length of the region borders.

Of the two given heuristics, the first is more general and the second cannot be used alone because it does not consider the influence of different region sizes.

Edge significance can be evaluated according to the formula

$$v_{ij} = 0 \quad \text{if} \quad s_{ij} < T_1$$
$$= 1 \quad \text{otherwise} \tag{5.31}$$

where $v_{ij} = 1$ indicates a significant edge, $v_{ij} = 0$ a weak edge, T_1 is a preset threshold, and s_{ij} is the crack edge value ($s_{ij} = |f(\mathbf{x_i}) - f(\mathbf{x_j})|$).

Algorithm 5.17: Region merging via boundary melting

1. Define a starting image segmentation into regions of constant grey level. Construct a supergrid edge data structure in which to store the crack edge information.

2. Remove all weak crack edges from the edge data structure (using equation 5.31 and threshold T_1).

3. Recursively remove common boundaries of adjacent regions R_i, R_j, if

$$\frac{W}{\min(l_i, l_j)} \geq T_2$$

where W is the number of weak edges on the common boundary and l_i, l_j are the perimeter lengths of regions R_i, R_j, and T_2 is another preset threshold.

4. Recursively remove common boundaries of adjacent regions R_i, R_j if

$$\frac{W}{l} \geq T_3 \tag{5.32}$$

or, using a weaker criterion [Ballard and Brown 82]

$$W \geq T_3 \tag{5.33}$$

where l is the length of the common boundary and T_3 is a third threshold.

Note that even if we have described a region growing method, the merging criterion is based on border properties and so the merging does not necessarily keep condition 5.29 true. The supergrid data structure allows precise work with edges and borders but a big disadvantage of this data structure is that it is not suitable for the representation of regions – it is necessary to refer to each region as a part of the image, especially if semantic information about regions and neighbouring regions is included. This problem can be solved by the construction and updating of a data structure describing region adjacencies and their boundaries and for this purpose a good data structure to use can be a planar region adjacency graph and a dual region boundary graph [Pavlidis 77], (Section 8.5).

Figure 5.38 gives a comparison of region merging methods. An original image and its pseudocolour representation (to see the small grey level differences) are given in Figure 5.38a and b. The original image cannot be segmented by thresholding because of the significant and continuous grey level gradient in all regions. Results of a recursive region merging method, which uses a simple merging criterion (equation 4.73) are shown in Figure 5.38c, note the resulting horizontally elongated regions corresponding to vertical changes of image grey levels. If region merging via boundary melting is applied, the segmentation results improve dramatically, see Figure 5.38d, [Marik and Matas 89].

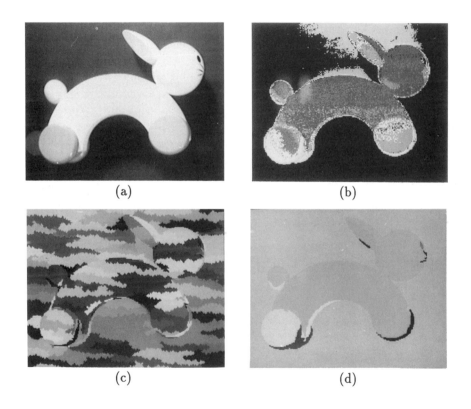

(a)   (b)

(c)   (d)

Figure 5.38 *Region merging segmentation: (a) Original image, (b) pseudocolour representation of the original image, (c) recursive region merging, (d) region merging via boundary melting. Colour versions of b, c and d may be seen in the colour inset. Courtesy R. Marik, Czech Technical University, Prague.*

5.3.2 Region splitting

Region splitting is the opposite of region merging. Region splitting begins with the whole image represented as a single region which does not usually satisfy condition 5.29. Therefore, the existing image regions are sequentially split to satisfy 5.1, 5.29 and 5.30. Even if this approach seems to be dual to region merging, region splitting does not result in the same segmentation even if the same homogeneity criteria are used. Some regions may be homogeneous during the splitting process and therefore are not split any more, while considering the homogeneous regions created by region merging procedures, some may not be constructed because of the impossibility of merging smaller subregions earlier in the process. A fine black and white chessboard is an example: Let average grey level be a homogeneity criterion – if the segmentation process is based on region splitting, it is probable that the image will not be split into subregions because these subregions would have the same value of the homogeneity measure as the starting region consisting of the whole image. The region merging approach, on the other hand, begins with merging single pixel regions into larger regions, and this process will stop when regions match the chessboard squares. Thus if splitting is applied, the whole image will be considered one region, whereas if merging is applied, a chessboard will be segmented into squares as shown in Figure 5.39. In this particular case, adding grey level variance as a measure of region homogeneity would also solve the problem. However, region merging and region splitting are not dual.

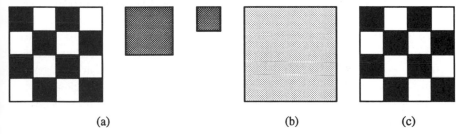

(a)   (b)   (c)

Figure 5.39 *Different segmentations may result from region splitting and region merging approaches: (a) Chessboard image, corresponding pyramid, (b) region splitting segmentation (upper pyramid level is homogeneous, no splitting possible), (c) region merging segmentation (lowest pyramid level consists of regions that are unhomogeneous and cannot be merged).*

Region splitting methods generally use similar criteria of homogeneity as region merging methods, and only differ in the direction of their application. The multispectral segmentation discussed in considering thresholding (Section 5.1.2) can be seen as an example of a region splitting method. As mentioned there, other criteria can be used to split regions (e.g. cluster analysis, pixel classification, etc.).

5.3.3 Splitting and merging

A combination of splitting and merging may result in a method with the
advantages of both approaches [Horowitz and Pavlidis 74, Pavlidis 77]. Split-
and-merge approaches work using pyramid image representations; regions are
square-shaped and correspond to elements of the appropriate pyramid level.

Figure 5.40 *Split-and-merge in a hierarchical data structure.*

If any region in any pyramid level is not homogeneous (excluding the lowest
level), it is split into four subregions – these are elements of higher resolution at
the level below. If four regions exist at any pyramid level with approximately
the same value of homogeneity measure, they are merged into a single region
in an upper pyramid level (see Figure 5.40). The segmentation process can
be understood as the construction of a segmentation quadtree where each leaf
node represents a homogeneous region – that is, an element of some pyramid
level. Splitting and merging corresponds to removing or building parts of the
segmentation quadtree – the number of leaf nodes of the tree corresponds to
the number of segmented regions after the segmentation process is over. These
approaches are sometimes called split-and-link methods if they use segmentation trees for storing information about adjacent regions. Split-and-merge
methods usually store the adjacency information in region adjacency graphs
(or similar data structures). Using segmentation trees, in which regions do not
have to be contiguous, is both implementationally and computationally easier.
An unpleasant drawback of segmentation quadtrees is the square region shape
assumption (see Figure 5.41), and it is therefore advantageous to add more
processing steps that permit the merging of regions which are not part of the
same branch of the segmentation tree. Starting image regions can either be
chosen arbitrarily, or can be based on prior knowledge. Because both split-
and-merge processing options are available, the starting segmentation does
not have to satisfy either condition 5.29 or 5.30.

The homogeneity criterion plays a major role in split-and-merge algorithms, just as it does in all other region growing methods. See [Chen et
al. 91] for an adaptive split-and-merge algorithm and a review of region homogeneity analysis. If the processed image is reasonably simple, a split-and-
merge approach can be based on local image properties. If the image is very
complex, even elaborate criteria including semantic information may not give
acceptable results.

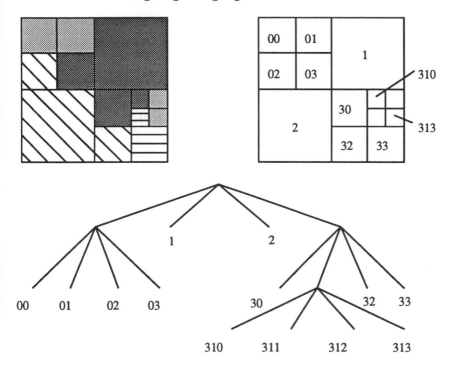

Figure 5.41 *Segmentation quadtree.*

Algorithm 5.18: Split and merge

---

1. Define an initial segmentation into regions, a homogeneity criterion, and a pyramid data structure.

2. If any region R in the pyramid data structure is not homogeneous ($H(R) = FALSE$), split it into 4 child-regions; if any 4 regions with the same parent can be merged into a single homogeneous region, merge them. If no region can be split or merged, go to step (3).

3. If there are any two adjacent regions R_i, R_j (even if they are in different pyramid levels or do not have the same parent) that can be merged into a homogeneous region, merge them.

4. Merge small regions with the most similar adjacent region if it is necessary to remove small-size regions.

A pyramid data structure with overlapping regions (Chapter 4) is an interesting modification of this method [Pietikainen and Rosenfeld 81, Hong

82, Pietikainen and Rosenfeld 82, Pietikainen et al. 82]. In this data structure, each region has four potential parent elements in the upper pyramid level and sixteen possible child elements in the lower pyramid level. Segmentation tree generation begins in the lowest pyramid level. Properties of each region are compared with properties of each of its potential parents and the segmentation branch is linked to the most similar of them. After construction of the tree is complete, all the homogeneity values of all the elements in the pyramid data structure are recomputed to be based on child-region properties only. This recomputed pyramid data structure is used to generate a new segmentation tree, beginning again at the lowest level. The pyramid updating process and new segmentation tree generation is repeated until no significant segmentation changes can be detected between steps. Assume that the segmented image has a maximum of 2^n (non-contiguous) regions. Any of these regions must link to at least one element in the highest allowed pyramid level – let this pyramid level consist of 2^n elements. Each element of the highest pyramid level corresponds to one branch of the segmentation tree and all the leaf nodes of this branch construct one region of the segmented image. The highest level of the segmentation tree must correspond to the expected number of image regions and the pyramid height defines the maximum number of segmentation branches. If the number of regions in an image is less than 2^n, some regions can be represented by more than one element in the highest pyramid level. If this is the case, some specific processing steps can either allow merging of some elements in the highest pyramid level, or restrict some of these elements to be segmentation branch roots. If the number of image regions is larger than 2^n, the most similar regions will be merged into a single tree branch, and the method will not be able to give acceptable results.

Algorithm 5.19: Split and link to the segmentation tree

---

1. Define a pyramid data structure with overlapping regions. Evaluate the starting region description.

2. Build a segmentation tree starting with leaves. Link each node of the tree to that one of the four possible parents to which it has the most similar region properties. Build the whole segmentation tree. If there is no link to an element in the higher pyramid level, assign the value zero to this element.

3. Update the pyramid data structure; each element must be assigned the average of the values of all its existing children.

4. Repeat steps (2) and (3) until no significant segmentation changes appear between iterations (a small number of iterations is usually sufficient).

The split-and-merge segmentation methods presented here are relatively memory demanding. Note that to segment a 512×512 image may require up to 1.5 Mwords of memory to store the data structures in the worst possible case [Browning and Tanimoto 82].

Considerably lower memory requirements can be found in a single-pass split-and-merge segmentation. A local 'splitting pattern' is detected in each 2×2 pixel image block and regions are merged in overlapping blocks of the same size [Suk and Chung 83]. In contrast to previous approaches, a single pass is sufficient here, although a second pass may be necessary for region identification (see Section 6.1). The computation is more efficient and the data structure implemented is very simple; the twelve possible splitting patterns for a 2×2 block are given in a list, starting with a homogeneous block up to a block consisting of 4 different pixels (see Figure 5.42). Pixel similarity can be evaluated adaptively according to the mean and variance of grey levels of blocks throughout the image.

Algorithm 5.20: Single-pass split-and-merge

1. Search an entire image line by line except the last column and last line. Perform the following steps for each pixel.

2. Find a splitting pattern for a 2×2 pixel block.

3. If a mismatch between assigned labels and splitting patterns in overlapping blocks is found, try to change the assigned labels of these blocks to remove the mismatch (discussed below).

4. Assign labels to unassigned pixels to match a splitting pattern of the block.

5. Remove small regions if necessary.

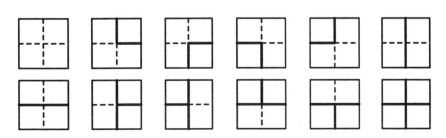

Figure 5.42 *Splitting of 2×2 image blocks, all 12 possible cases.*

The image blocks overlap during the image search. Except for locations at the image borders, three of the four pixels have been assigned a label in previous search locations, but these labels do not necessarily match the splitting pattern found in the processed block. If a mismatch is detected in step 3 of the algorithm, it is necessary to resolve possibilities of merging regions that were considered separate so far – to assign the same label to two regions previously labelled differently. Two regions R_1 and R_2 are merged into a region R_3 if

$$H(R_1 \cup R_2) = TRUE \qquad (5.34)$$

$$|m_1 - m_2| < T \qquad (5.35)$$

where m_1 and m_2 are the mean grey level values in regions R_1 and R_2, and T is some appropriate threshold. If region merging is not allowed, regions keep their previous labels. To get a final segmentation, information about region merging must be stored and the merged-region characteristics must be updated after each merging operation. The assignment of labels to non-labelled pixels in the processed block is based on the block splitting pattern and on the labels of adjacent regions (step 4). If a match between a splitting pattern and the assigned labels was found in step 3, then it is easy to assign a label to the remaining pixel(s) to keep the label assignment and splitting pattern matched. Conversely, if a match was not found in step 3, an unassigned pixel is either merged with an adjacent region (the same label is assigned) or a new region is started. If a 2×2 block size is used, the only applicable pixel property is grey level. If larger blocks are used, more complex image properties can be included in the homogeneity criteria (even if these larger blocks are divided into 2×2 sub-blocks to determine the splitting pattern).

Many other modifications exist, most of them trying to overcome the segmentation sensitivity to the order in which portions of the image are processed. The ideal solution would be to merge only the single most similar pair of adjacent regions in each iteration which would result in very slow processing. A method performing the best merge within each of sets of local subimages (possibly overlapping) is described in [Tilton 89]. Another approach insensitive to scanning order is suggested in [Pramotepipop and Cheevasuvit 88].

Hierarchical merging where different criteria are employed at different stages of the segmentation process is discussed in [Goldberg and Zhang 87]. More and more information is incorporated into the merging criteria in later segmentation phases. A modified split-and-merge algorithm where splitting steps are performed with respect to the edge information and merging is based on grey-value statistics of merged regions is introduced in [Cornelis et al. 92, Becker et al. 92]. As splitting is not required to follow a quadtree segmentation pattern, segmentation borders are more natural than borders after the application of standard split-and-merge techniques. Another group of powerful segmentation approaches utilizes mathematical morphology based watershed transformations to perform a region growing process [Digabel and

Lantuejoul 78, Beucher 82]. An efficient algorithm and overview of watershed segmentation principles is given in [Vincent and Soille 91].

Images segmented by region growing methods often contain either too many regions (undergrowing) or too few regions (overgrowing) as a result of non-optimal parameter setting. To improve the classification results, a variety of post-processors has been developed. Some of them combine segmentation information obtained from region growing and edge-based segmentation. An approach introduced in [Liow and Pavlidis 88, Pavlidis and Liow 90] solves several quadtree-related region growing problems and incorporates two post-processing steps. First, boundary elimination removes some borders between adjacent regions according to their contrast properties and direction changes along the border, taking resulting topology into consideration. Second, contours from the previous step are modified to be located precisely on appropriate image edges. Post-processing contour relaxation is suggested in [Aach et al. 89]. A combination of independent region growing and edge-based detected borders is described in [Koivunen and Pietikainen 90].

Simpler post-processors are based on general heuristics and decrease the number of small regions in the segmented image that cannot be merged with any adjacent region according to the originally applied homogeneity criteria. These small regions are usually not significant in further processing and can be considered as segmentation noise. It is possible to remove them from the image as follows:

Algorithm 5.21: Removal of small image regions

1. Search for the smallest image region R_{min}.

2. Find the region R most similar to R_{min}, according to the homogeneity criteria used. Merge R and R_{min}.

3. Repeat steps (1) and (2) until all regions smaller than a preselected size are removed from the image.

This algorithm will execute much faster if all regions smaller than a preselected size are merged with their neighbours without having to order them by size.

Parallel implementations become more and more affordable, and parallel region growing algorithms may be found in [Mukund and Gonzalez 89, Celenk and Lakshman 89, Willebeek-Lemair and Reeves 90]. Examples of region growing segmentations are given in [Cheevasuvit et al. 86, Cross 88, Laprade 88]. Additional sections describing more sophisticated methods of semantic region growing segmentation can be found in Chapter 8.

5.4 Matching

Matching is another basic approach to segmentation. It can be used to locate known objects in an image, to search for specific patterns, etc. Figure 5.43 shows an example of a desired pattern and its location found in the image. Matching is widely applicable; it can be used to determine stereoscopic scene properties if more than one image of the same scene taken from different locations is available. Matching in dynamic images (e.g. moving cars, clouds, etc.) is another application area. Generally speaking, one image can be used to extract objects or patterns, and directed search is used to look for the same (or similar) patterns in the remaining images. The best match is based on some criterion of optimality which depends on object properties and object relations.

Figure 5.43 *Segmentation by matching; matched pattern and location of the best match.*

Matched patterns can be very small, or they can represent whole objects of interest. Criteria of optimality can compute anything from simple correlations up to complex approaches of graph matching [Rosenfeld and Kak 82, Ballard and Brown 82].

5.4.1 Matching criteria

Match-based segmentation would be extremely easy if an exact copy of the pattern of interest could be expected in the processed image, however some part of the pattern is usually corrupted in real images by noise, geometric distortion, occlusion, etc. Therefore, it is not possible to look for an absolute match, and a search for locations of maximum match is more appropriate.

Algorithm 5.22: Match-based segmentation

1. Evaluate a match criterion for each location and rotation of the pattern in the image.

2. Local maxima of this criterion exceeding a preset threshold represent pattern locations in the image.

Matching criteria can be defined in many ways; in particular, correlation between a pattern and the searched image data is a general matching criterion (see Section 2.1.2). Let f be a processed image, h be a pattern for which to search, and V be the set of all image pixels in the processed image. The following formulae represent good matching optimality criteria describing a match between f and h located at a position (u, v).

$$C_1(u, v) = \frac{1}{\max_{(i,j) \in V} |f(i + u, j + v) - h(i, j)|} \tag{5.36}$$

$$C_2(u, v) = \frac{1}{\sum_{(i,j) \in V} |f(i + u, j + v) - h(i, j)|} \tag{5.37}$$

$$C_3(u, v) = \frac{1}{\sum_{(i,j) \in V} [f(i + u, j + v) - h(i, j)]^2} \tag{5.38}$$

It depends on the implementation whether only those pattern positions entirely within the image are considered, or if partial pattern positions, crossing the image borders, are considered as well. A simple example of the C_3 optimality criterion values is given in Figure 5.44 for varying pattern locations – the best matched position is in in the upper left corner. An X-shaped correlation mask was used to detect positions of magnetic resonance markers in [Fisher et al. 91]; the original image and the correlation image are shown in Figure 5.45. The detected markers are further used in heart motion analysis (see Section 14.3.2).

If a fast, effective Fourier transform algorithm is available, the convolution theorem can be used to evaluate matching. The correlation between a pattern h and image f can be determined by first taking the product of the corresponding Fourier transforms F and H and then applying the inverse transform (Chapter 11). Note that this approach considers an image to be periodic and therefore a target pattern is allowed to be positioned partially outside an image. To compute the product of Fourier transforms, F and H must be of the same size; if a pattern size is smaller, zero-valued lines and columns can be added to inflate it to the appropriate size. Sometimes, it may be better to add non-zero numbers, for example, the average grey level of processed images can serve the purpose well.

$$\begin{vmatrix} 1 & 1 & 0 & 0 & 0 \\ 1 & 1 & 1 & 0 & 0 \\ 1 & 0 & 1 & 0 & 0 \\ 0 & 0 & 0 & 0 & 0 \\ 0 & 0 & 0 & 0 & 8 \end{vmatrix} \qquad \begin{vmatrix} 1 & 1 & 1 \\ 1 & 1 & 1 \\ 1 & 1 & 1 \end{vmatrix} \qquad \begin{vmatrix} \underline{1/2} & 1/5 & 1/7 & \times & \times \\ 1/4 & 1/6 & 1/7 & \times & \times \\ 1/7 & 1/8 & 1/56 & \times & \times \\ \times & \times & \times & \times & \times \\ \times & \times & \times & \times & \times \end{vmatrix}$$

(a)   (b)   (c)

Figure 5.44 *Optimality matching criterion evaluation: (a) Image data, (b) matched pattern, (c) optimality criterion values, the best match underlined.*

5.4.2   Control strategies of matching

Match-based segmentation localizes all image positions at which close copies of the searched pattern are located. These copies must match the pattern in size and rotation, and the geometric distortion must be small. To adapt the match-based methods to detect patterns that are rotated, enlarged, and/or reduced, it would be necessary to consider patterns of all possible sizes and rotations. Another option is to use just one pattern and match an image with all possible geometric transforms of this pattern, and this may work well if some information about the probable geometric distortion is available. Note that there is no difference in principle between these approaches.

However, matching can be used even if an infinite number of transformations are allowed. Let us suppose a pattern consists of parts, these parts being connected by rubber bands. Even if a complete match of the whole pattern within an image may be impossible, good matches can often be found between pattern parts and image parts. Good matching locations may not be found in the correct relative positions, and to achieve a better match, the rubber connections between pattern parts must be either pushed or pulled. The final goal can be described as the search for good partial matches of pattern parts in locations that cause minimum force in rubber band connections between these parts. A good strategy is to look for the best partial matches first, followed by a heuristic graph construction of the best combination of these partial matches in which graph nodes represent pattern parts.

Match-based segmentation is time consuming even in the simplest cases with no geometric transformations, but the process can be made faster if a good operation sequence is found. The sequence of match tests must be data driven. Fast testing of image locations with a high probability of match may be the first step, then it is not necessary to test all possible pattern locations. Another speed improvement can be realized if a mismatch can be detected before all the corresponding pixels have been tested.

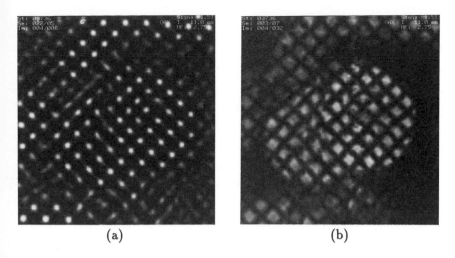

(a)   (b)

Figure 5.45 *X-shaped mask matching: (a) Original image, (b) correlation image; the better local correlation with the X-shaped mask, the brighter the correlation image. Courtesy D. Fisher, S. Collins, University of Iowa.*

If a pattern is highly correlated with image data in some specific image location, then typically the correlation of the pattern with image data in some neighbourhood of this specific location is good. In other words, the correlation changes slowly around the best matching location. If this is the case, matching can be tested at lower resolution first, looking for an exact match in the neighbourhood of good low-resolution matches only.

The mismatch must be detected as soon as possible since mismatches are found much more often than matches. Considering formulae 5.36 – 5.38, testing in a specified position must stop when the value in the denominator (measure of mismatch) exceeds some preset threshold. That implies that it is better to begin the correlation test in pixels with a high probability of mismatch in order to get a steep growth in the mismatch criterion. This criterion growth will be faster than that produced by an arbitrary pixel order computation.

References

[Aach et al. 89] T Aach, U Franke, and R Mester. Top-down image segmentation using object detection and contour relaxation. In *Proceedings - ICASSP, IEEE International Conference on Acoustics, Speech and Signal Processing, Glasgow, Scotland*, volume III, pages 1703–1706, IEEE, Piscataway, NJ, 1989.

[Ballard 81] D H Ballard. Generalizing the Hough transform to detect arbitrary shapes. *Pattern Recognition*, 13:111–122, 1981.

[Ballard and Brown 82] D H Ballard and C M Brown. *Computer Vision.* Prentice-Hall, Englewood Cliffs, NJ, 1982.

[Baugher and Rosenfeld 86] E S Baugher and A Rosenfeld. Boundary localization in an image pyramid. *Pattern Recognition*, 19(5):373–396, 1986.

[Becker et al. 92] J De Becker, M Bister, N Langloh, C Vanhove, G Demonceau, and J Cornelis. A split-and-merge algorithm for the segmentation of 2-d, 3-d, 4-d cardiac images. In *Proceedings of the IEEE Satellite Symposium on 3D Advanced Image Processing in Medicine, Rennes, France*, pages 185–189. IEEE, 1992.

[Bellmann 57] R Bellmann. *Dynamic Programming.* Princeton University Press, Princeton, NJ, 1957.

[Beucher 82] S Beucher. Watersheds of functions and picture segmentation. In *Proceedings IEEE International Conference Accoustics, Speech, and Signal Processing, Paris, France*, pages 1928–1931. IEEE, 1982.

[Brice and Fennema 70] C R Brice and C L Fennema. Scene analysis using regions. *Artificial Intelligence*, 1:205–226, 1970.

[Browning and Tanimoto 82] J D Browning and S L Tanimoto. Segmentation of pictures into regions with a tile–by–tile method. *Pattern Recognition*, 15(1):1–10, 1982.

[Bruel 88] E Bruel. *Precision of Line Following in Digital Images.* PhD thesis, ETN-89-93329, Technische Univ., Delft, Netherlands, 1988.

[Brummer 91] M E Brummer. Hough transform detection of the longitudinal fissure in tomographic head images. *IEEE Transactions on Medical Imaging*, 10(1):74–81, 1991.

[Celenk and Lakshman 89] M Celenk and P Lakshman. Parallel implementation of the split and merge algorithm on hypercube processors for object detection and recognition. In *Applications of Artificial Intelligence VII; Proceedings of the Meeting, Orlando, Fl*, pages 251–262, Society of Photo-Optical Instrumentation Engineers,, Bellingham, Wa, 1989.

[Chandran and Davis 89] S Chandran and L S Davis. Parallel vision algorithms - an approach. In *Parallel Processing for Scientific Computing; Proceedings of the Third SIAM Conference, Los Angeles, Ca*, pages 235–249, Society for Industrial and Applied Mathematics, Philadelphia, Pa, 1989.

[Cheevasuvit et al. 86] F Cheevasuvit, H Maitre, and D Vidal-Madjar. A robust method for picture segmentation based on a split-and-merge procedure. *Computer Vision, Graphics, and Image Processing*, 34:268–281, 1986.

[Chen et al. 91] S Y Chen, W C Lin, and C T Chen. Split-and-merge image segmentation based on localized feature analysis and statistical tests. *CVGIP – Graphical Models and Image Processing*, 53(5):457–475, 1991.

[Chien and Fu 74] Y P Chien and K S Fu. A decision function method for boundary detection. *Computer Graphics and Image Processing*, 2:125–140, 1974.

[Cho et al. 89] S Cho, R Haralick, and S Yi. Improvement of Kittler and Illingworth's minimum error thresholding. *Pattern Recognition*, 22(5):609–617, 1989.

[Chow and Kaneko 72] C K Chow and T Kaneko. Automatic boundary detection of the left ventricle from the cineangiograms. *Computers in Biomedical Research*, 5:388–410, 1972.

[Clark 91] D Clark. Image edge relaxation on a hypercube. Technical Report Project 55:295, University of Iowa, 1991.

[Collins and Skorton 86] S M Collins and D J Skorton. *Cardiac Imaging and Image Processing*. McGraw Hill, New York, 1986.

[Collins et al. 91] S M Collins, C J Wilbricht, S R Fleagle, S. Tadikonda, and M D Winniford. An automated method for simultaneous detection of left and right coronary borders. In *Computers in Cardiology 1990, Chicago, Il*, page 7, IEEE, Los Alamitos, Ca, 1991.

[Cornelis et al. 92] J Cornelis, J De Becker, M Bister, C Vanhove, G Demonceau, and A Cornelis. Techniques for cardiac image segmentation. In *Proceedings of the 14th IEEE EMBS Conference, Vol. 14, Paris, France*, pages 1906–1908, IEEE, Piscataway, NJ, 1992.

[Cristi 88] R Cristi. Application of Markov random fields to smoothing and segmentation of noisy pictures. In *Proceedings - ICASSP, IEEE International Conference on Acoustics, Speech and Signal Processing 1988, New York, NY*, pages 1144–1147, IEEE, New York, 1988.

[Cross 88] A M Cross. Segmentation of remotely-sensed images by a split-and-merge process. *International Journal of Remote Sensing*, 9:1329–1345, 1988.

[Davis 82] L S Davis. Hierarchical generalized Hough transforms and line segment based generalized Hough transforms. *Pattern Recognition*, 15(4):277–285, 1982.

[Degunst 90] M E Degunst. *Automatic Extraction of Roads from SPOT Images*. PhD thesis, ETN-91-99417, Technische Univ., Delft, Netherlands, 1990.

[Derin and Elliot 87] H Derin and H Elliot. Modelling and segmentation of noisy and textured images using Gibbs random fields. *IEEE Transactions on Pattern Analysis and Machine Intelligence*, 9(1):39–55, 1987.

[Digabel and Lantuejoul 78] H Digabel and C Lantuejoul. Iterative algorithms. In J L Chermant, editor, *Proceedings of 2nd European Symposium Quantitative Analysis of Microstructures in Material Science, Biology, and Medicine, Caen, France, 1977*, pages 85–99, Riederer Verlag, Stuttgart, Germany, 1978.

[Ducksbury 90] P G Ducksbury. Parallelisation of a dynamic programming algorithm suitable for feature detection. Technical report, RSRE-MEMO-4349; BR113300; ETN-90-97521, Royal Signals and Radar Establishment, Malvern, England, 1990.

[Duda and Hart 72] R O Duda and P E Hart. Using the Hough transforms to detect lines and curves in pictures. *Communications of the ACM*, 15(1):11–15, 1972.

[Duda and Hart 73] R O Duda and P E Hart. *Pattern Classification and Scene Analysis*. John Wiley and Sons, New York, 1973.

[Dudani 76] S A Dudani. Region extraction using boundary following. In C H Chen, editor, *Pattern Recognition and Artificial Intelligence*, pages 216–232. Academic Press, New York, 1976.

[Evans 85] F Evans. Survey and comparison of the Hough transform. In *IEEE Computer Society Workshop on Computer Architecture for Pattern Analysis and Image Database Management 1985, Miami Beach, Fl*, pages 378–380, IEEE, New York, 1985.

[Fetterer et al. 90] F M Fetterer, A E Pressman, and R L Crout. Sea ice lead statistics from satellite imagery of the Lincoln Sea during the iceshelf acoustic exercise. Technical report, AD-A228735; NOARL-TN-50, Naval Oceanographic and Atmospheric Research Lab., Bay Saint Louis, Ms, Spring 1990.

[Fisher et al. 91] D J Fisher, J C Ehrhardt, and S M Collins. Automated detection of noninvasive magnetic resonance markers. In *Computers in Cardiology, Chicago, Il*, pages 493–496, IEEE, Los Alamitos, Ca, 1991.

[Fleagle et al. 89] S R Fleagle, M R Johnson, C J Wilbricht, D J Skorton, R F Wilson, C W White, M L Marcus, and S M Collins. Automated analysis of coronary arterial morphology in cineangiograms: Geometric and physiologic validation in humans. *IEEE Transactions on Medical Imaging*, 8(4):387–400, 1989.

[Flynn 72] M J Flynn. Some computer organizations and their effectivness. *IEEE Transactions on Computers*, 21(9):948–960, 1972.

[Furst 86] M A Furst. Edge detection with image enhancement via dynamic programming. *Computer Vision, Graphics, and Image Processing*, 33:263–279, 1986.

[Gerbrands 88] J J Gerbrands. *Segmentation of Noisy Images*. PhD thesis, ETN-89-95461, Technische Univ., Delft, Netherlands, 1988.

[Goldberg and Zhang 87] M Goldberg and J Zhang. Hierarchical segmentation using a composite criterion for remotely sensed imagery. *Photogrammetria*, 42:87–96, 1987.

[Gonzalez and Wintz 87] R C Gonzalez and P Wintz. *Digital Image Processing*. Addison-Wesley, Reading, Ma, 2nd edition, 1987.

[Grimson and Lozano-Perez 87] W E L Grimson and T Lozano-Perez. Localizing overlapping parts by searching the interpretation tree. *IEEE Transactions on Pattern Analysis and Machine Intelligence*, 9(4):469–482, 1987.

[Gross and Rosenfeld 87] A D Gross and A Rosenfeld. Multiresolution object detection and delineation. *Computer Vision, Graphics, and Image Processing*, 39:102–115, 1987.

[Hancock and Kittler 90] E R Hancock and J Kittler. Edge-labeling using dictionary-based relaxation. *IEEE Transactions on Pattern Analysis and Machine Intelligence*, 12(2):165–181, 1990.

[Hanson and Riseman 78a] A R Hanson and E M Riseman, editors. *Computer Vision Systems*. Academic Press, New York, 1978.

[Hanson and Riseman 78b] A R Hanson and E M Riseman. Segmentation of natural scenes. In A R Hanson and E M Riseman, editors, *Computer Vision Systems*, pages 129–164. Academic Press, New York, 1978.

[Haralick and Shapiro 85] R M Haralick and L G Shapiro. Image segmentation techniques. *Computer Vision, Graphics, and Image Processing*, 29:100–132, 1985.

[Hartley 82] R L Hartley. Segmentation of images FLIR – a comparative study. *IEEE Transactions on Systems, Man and Cybernetics*, 12(4):553–566, 1982.

[Hassan 89] M H Hassan. A class of iterative thresholding algorithms for real-time image segmentation. In *Intelligent Robots and Computer Vision; Proceedings of the Seventh Meeting, Cambridge, Ma*, pages 182–193, Society of Photo-Optical Instrumentation Engineers, Bellingham, Wa, 1989.

[Herman and Liu 78] G T Herman and H K Liu. Dynamic boundary surface detection. *Computer Graphics and Image Processing*, 7:130–138, 1978.

[Hong 82] T H Hong. Image smoothing and segmentation by multiresolution pixel linking further experiments. *IEEE Transactions on Systems, Man and Cybernetics*, 12(5):611–622, 1982.

[Hong et al. 80] T H Hong, C R Dyer, and A Rosenfeld. Texture primitive extraction using an edge–based approach. *IEEE Transactions on Systems, Man and Cybernetics*, 10(10):659– 675, 1980.

[Horowitz and Pavlidis 74] S L Horowitz and T Pavlidis. Picture segmentation by a directed split–and–merge procedure. In *Proceedings of the 2nd Int. Joint Conference on Pattern Recognition*, pages 424–433, Copenhagen, Denmark, 1974.

[Hough 62] P V C Hough. *A Method and Means for Recognizing Complex Patterns*. U.S., Patent 3,069,654, 1962.

[Hsu and Huang 90] C C Hsu and J S Huang. Partitioned Hough transform for ellipsoid detection. *Pattern Recognition*, 23(3-4):275–282, 1990.

[Illingworth and Kittler 87] J Illingworth and J Kittler. The adaptive Hough transform. *IEEE Transactions on Pattern Analysis and Machine Intelligence*, 9(5):690–698, 1987.

[Illingworth and Kittler 88] J Illingworth and J Kittler. Survey of the Hough transform. *Computer Vision, Graphics, and Image Processing*, 44(1):87–116, 1988.

[Kannan and Chuang 88] C S Kannan and Y H Chuang. Fast Hough transform on a mesh connected processor array. In *Intelligent Robots and Computer Vision; Proceedings of the Meeting, Cambridge, Ma,* pages 581–585, Society of Photo-Optical Instrumentation Engineers, Bellingham, Wa, 1988.

[Kashyap and Koch 84] R L Kashyap and Mark W Koch. Computer vision algorithms used in recognition of occluded objects. In *First Conference on Artificial Intelligence Applications, Denver, Co,* pages 150–155, IEEE, New York, 1984.

[Kass et al. 87] M Kass, A Witkin, and D Terzopoulos. Snakes: Active contour models. In *Proceedings, First International Conference on Computer Vision, London, England,* pages 259–268, IEEE, Piscataway, NJ, 1987.

[Kittler and Illingworth 85] J Kittler and J Illingworth. On threshold selection using clustering criteria. *IEEE Transactions on Systems, Man and Cybernetics,* 15(5):652–655, 1985.

[Kittler and Illingworth 86] J Kittler and J Illingworth. Minimum error thresholding. *Pattern Recognition,* 19:41–47, 1986.

[Koivunen and Pietikainen 90] V Koivunen and M Pietikainen. Combined edge and region-based method for range image segmentation. In *Proceedings of SPIE - The International Society for Optical Engineering,* volume 1381, pages 501–512, Society for Optical Engineering, Bellingham, Wa, 1990.

[Kundu and Mitra 87] A Kundu and S K Mitra. A new algorithm for image edge extraction using a statistical classifier approach. *IEEE Transactions on Pattern Analysis and Machine Intelligence,* 9(4):569–577, 1987.

[Laprade 88] R H Laprade. Split-and-merge segmentation of aerial photographs. *Computer Vision, Graphics, and Image Processing,* 44(1):77–86, 1988.

[Lavagetto 90] F Lavagetto. Infrared image segmentation through iterative thresholding. In *Real-Time Image Processing II, Orlando, Fl,,* pages 29–38, The International Society for Optical Engineering v 1295, Bellingham, Wa, 1990.

[Lerner and Morelli 90] B T Lerner and M V Morelli. Extensions of algebraic image operators: An approach to model-based vision. In *Third Annual Workshop on Space Operations Automation and Robotics (SOAR 1989),* pages 687–695, NASA, Lyndon B. Johnson Space Center, 1990.

[Lester 78] J M Lester. Two graph searching techniques for boundary finding in white blood cell images. *Computers in Biology and Medicine*, 8:193–308, 1978.

[Levy 88] M Levy. New theoretical approach to relaxation, application to edge detection. In *Proceedings - 9th International Conference on Pattern Recognition, Rome, Italy*, pages 208–212, IEEE, New York, 1988.

[Liow 91] Y T Liow. A contour tracing algorithm that preserves common boundaries between regions. *CVGIP – Image Understanding*, 53(3):313–321, 1991.

[Liow and Pavlidis 88] Y Liow and T Pavlidis. Enhancements of the split-and-merge algorithm for image segmentation. In *1988 IEEE International Conference on Robotics and Automation, Philadelphia, Pa*, pages 1567–1572, Computer Society Press, Washington, DC, 1988.

[Liu 77] H K Liu. Two- and three-dimensional boundary detection. *Computer Graphics and Image Processing*, 6:123–134, 1977.

[Mardia and Hainsworth 88] K V Mardia and T J Hainsworth. A spatial thresholding method for image segmentation. *IEEE Transactions on Pattern Analysis and Machine Intelligence*, 10:919–927, 1988.

[Marik and Matas 89] R Marik and J Matas. Membrane method for graph construction. In *Computer Analysis of Images and Patterns. Third International Conference on Automatic Image Processing, Leipzig, Germany*, 1989.

[Martelli 72] A Martelli. Edge detection using heuristic search methods. *Computer Graphics and Image Processing*, 1:169–182, 1972.

[Martelli 76] A Martelli. An application of heuristic search methods to edge and contour detection. *Communications of the ACM*, 19(2):73–83, 1976.

[McDonnel et al. 87] M M McDonnel, M Lew, and T S Huang. Finding wheels of vehicles in stereo images. Technical report, AD-A194372; ETL-R-141, Army Engineer Topographic Labs., Fort Belvoir, Va, 1987.

[McKenzie and Protheroe 90] D S McKenzie and S R Protheroe. Curve description using the inverse Hough transform. *Pattern Recognition*, 23(3-4):283–290, 1990.

[Milgram 79] D L Milgram. Region extraction using convergent evidence. *Computer Graphics and Image Processing*, 11:1–12, 1979.

[Mukund and Gonzalez 89] P R Mukund and R C Gonzalez. Generalized approach to split and merge segmentation on parallel architectures. In *Proceedings of SPIE - The International Society for Optical Engineering V 1197*, pages 254–264, Society for Optical Engineering, Bellingham, Wa, 1989.

[Nagao and Matsuyama 80] M Nagao and T Matsuyama. *A Structural Analysis of Complex Aerial Photographs*. Plenum Press, New York, 1980.

[Narendra and Goldberg 77] P M Narendra and M Goldberg. A nonparametric clustering scheme for Landsat. *Pattern Recognition*, 9:207–215, 1977.

[Neveu 86] C F Neveu. Two-dimensional object recognition using multiresolution models. *Computer Vision, Graphics, and Image Processing*, 34(1):52–65, 1986.

[Ney 92] H Ney. A comparative study of two search strategies for connected word recognition: Dynamic programming and heuristic search. *IEEE Transactions on Pattern Analysis and Machine Intelligence*, 14(5):586–595, 1992.

[Nilsson 82] N J Nilsson. *Principles of Artificial Intelligence*. Springer Verlag, Berlin, 1982.

[Ohta et al. 80] Y I Ohta, T Kanade, and T Sakai. Color information for region segmentation. *Computer Graphics and Image Processing*, 13:222–241, 1980.

[Otsu 79] N Otsu. A threshold selection method from gray–level histograms. *IEEE Transactions on Systems, Man and Cybernetics*, 9(1):62–66, 1979.

[Oyster 87] J M Oyster. Associative network applications to low-level machine vision. *Applied Optics*, 26:1919–1926, 1987.

[Pal and Pal 87] N R Pal and S K Pal. Segmentation based on contrast homogeneity measure and region size. *IEEE Transactions on Systems, Man and Cybernetics*, 17(5):857–868, 1987.

[Pavlidis 77] T Pavlidis. *Structural Pattern Recognition*. Springer Verlag, Berlin, 1977.

[Pavlidis and Liow 90] T Pavlidis and Y Liow. Integrating region growing and edge detection. *IEEE Transactions on Pattern Analysis and Machine Intelligence*, 12(3):225–233, 1990.

[Philip 91] K P Philip. *Automatic Detection of Myocardial Contours in Cine Computed Tomographic Images.* PhD thesis, University of Iowa, 1991.

[Philip et al. 90] K P Philip, E L Dove, and K B Chandran. A graph search based algorithm for detection of closed contours in images. In *Proceedings: Annual International Conference IEEE - Engineering in Medicine and Biology Society*, IEEE, Philadelphia, Pa, 1990.

[Pietikainen and Rosenfeld 81] M Pietikainen and A Rosenfeld. Image segmentation by texture using pyramid node linking. *IEEE Transactions on Systems, Man and Cybernetics*, 11(12):822–825, 1981.

[Pietikainen and Rosenfeld 82] M Pietikainen and A Rosenfeld. Gray level pyramid linking as an aid in texture analysis. *IEEE Transactions on Systems, Man and Cybernetics*, 12(3):422–429, 1982.

[Pietikainen et al. 82] M Pietikainen, A Rosenfeld, and I Walter. Split–and–link algorithms for image segmentation. *Pattern Recognition*, 15(4):287–298, 1982.

[Pontriagin 62] L S Pontriagin. *The Mathematical Theory of Optimal Processes.* Interscience, New York, 1962.

[Pontriagin 90] L S Pontriagin. *Optimal Control and Differential Games: Collection of Papers.* American Mathematical Society, Providence, RI, 1990.

[Pope et al. 85] D L Pope, D L Parker, P D Clayton, and D E Gustafson. Left ventricular border detection using a dynamic search algorithm. *Radiology*, 155:513–518, 1985.

[Prager 80] J M Prager. Extracting and labeling boundary segments in natural scenes. *IEEE Transactions on Pattern Analysis and Machine Intelligence*, 2(1):16–27, 1980.

[Pramotepipop and Cheevasuvit 88] Y Pramotepipop and F Cheevasuvit. Modification of split-and-merge algorithm for image segmentation. In *Asian Conference on Remote Sensing, 9th, Bangkok, Thailand*, pages Q–26–1 – Q–26–6, Asian Association on Remote Sensing, Tokyo, 1988.

[Princen et al. 89] J Princen, J Illingworth, and J Kittler. Hierarchical approach to line extraction. In *Proceedings: IEEE Computer Society Conference on Computer Vision and Pattern Recognition, Rosemont, Il*, pages 92–97, IEEE, Piscataway, NJ, 1989.

[Ramer 75] U Ramer. Extraction of line structures from photographs of curved objects. *Computer Graphics and Image Processing*, 4:425–446, 1975.

[Reddi et al. 84] S S Reddi, S F Rudin, and H R Keshavan. An optimal multiple threshold scheme for image segmentation. *IEEE Transactions on Systems, Man and Cybernetics*, 14:661–665, 1984.

[Ridler and Calvard 78] T W Ridler and S Calvard. Picture thresholding using an iterative selection method. *IEEE Transactions on Systems, Man and Cybernetics*, 8(8):630–632, 1978.

[Riseman and Arbib 77] E M Riseman and M A Arbib. Computational techniques in the visual segmentation of static scenes. *Computer Graphics and Image Processing*, 6:221–276, 1977.

[Rosenfeld 84] A Rosenfeld, editor. *Multiresolution Image Processing and Analysis*. Springer Verlag, Berlin, 1984.

[Rosenfeld and de la Torre 83] A Rosenfeld and P de la Torre. Histogram concavity analysis as an aid in threshold selection. *IEEE Transactions on Systems, Man and Cybernetics*, 13(3):231–235, 1983.

[Rosenfeld and Kak 82] A Rosenfeld and A C Kak. *Digital Picture Processing*. Academic Press, New York, 2nd edition, 1982.

[Rosenfeld et al. 76] A Rosenfeld, R A Hummel, and S W Zucker. Scene labelling by relaxation operations. *IEEE Transactions on Systems, Man and Cybernetics*, 6:420–433, 1976.

[Sahoo et al. 88] P K Sahoo, S Soltani, A K C Wong, and Y C Chen. Survey of thresholding techniques. *Computer Vision, Graphics, and Image Processing*, 41(2):233–260, 1988.

[Shankar and Asokan 90] R V Shankar and N Asokan. A parallel implementation of the Hough transform method to detect lines and curves in pictures. In *Proceedings of the 32nd Midwest Symposium on Circuits and Systems, Champaign, Il*, pages 321–324, IEEE, Piscataway, NJ, 1990.

[Song et al. 90] S Song, M Liao, and J Qin. Multiresolution image dynamic thresholding. *Machine Vision and Applications*, 3(1):13–16, 1990.

[Sonka 86] M Sonka. A new texture recognition method. *Computers and Artificial Intelligence*, 5(4):357–364, 1986.

[Sonka and Collins 93] M Sonka and S M Collins. Robust detection of lumen centerlines in complex coronary angiograms. In *Biomedical Image Processing IV, San Jose, Ca*, SPIE, Bellingham, Wa, 1993. in print.

[Sonka et al. 93] M Sonka, C J Wilbricht, S R Fleagle, S K Tadikonda, M D Winniford, and S M Collins. Simultaneous detection of both coronary borders. *IEEE Transactions on Medical Imaging*, 12(3), 1993.

[Suk and Chung 83] M Suk and S M Chung. A new image segmentation technique based on partition mode test. *Pattern Recognition*, 16(5):469–480, 1983.

[Tadikonda et al. 92] S K Tadikonda, M Sonka, and S M Collins. Efficient coronary border detection using heuristic graph searching. In *Proceedings of the Annual International Conference of the IEEE EMBS, Paris, France*, volume 14, pages 1897–1899. IEEE, 1992.

[Tanimoto 78] S Tanimoto. Regular hierarchical image and processing structures in machine vision. In A R Hanson and E M Riseman, editors, *Computer Vision Systems*, pages 165–174. Academic Press, New York, 1978.

[Tanimoto and Pavlidis 75] S Tanimoto and T Pavlidis. A hierarchical data structure for picture processing. *Computer Graphics and Image Processing*, 4:104–119, 1975.

[Tilton 89] J C Tilton. Image segmentation by iterative parallel region growing and splitting. In *Quantitative Remote Sensing: An Economic Tool for the Nineties; Proceedings of IGARSS '89 and Canadian Symposium on Remote Sensing, 12th, Vancouver, Canada*, pages 2420–2423, IEEE, New York, 1989.

[Vincent and Soille 91] L Vincent and P Soille. Watersheds in digital spaces: An efficient algorithm based on immersion simulations. *IEEEPAMI*, 13(6):583–598, 1991.

[Wang and Howarth 87] J F Wang and P J Howarth. Automated road network extraction from Landsat TM imagery. In *American Society for Photogrammetry and Remote Sensing and ACSM, Annual Convention, Baltimore, Md*, pages 429–438, American Society for Photogrammetry and Remote Sensing and ACSM, Falls Church, Va, 1987.

[Wang and Howarth 89] J F Wang and P J Howarth. Edge following as graph searching and Hough transform algorithms for lineament detection. In *Proceedings of IGARSS '89 and Canadian Symposium on Remote*

Sensing, 12th, Vancouver, Canada, pages 93–96, IEEE, New York, 1989.

[Weszka and Rosenfeld 79] J S Weszka and A Rosenfeld. Histogram modification for threshold selection. *IEEE Transactions on Systems, Man and Cybernetics*, 9(1):38–52, 1979.

[Weszka et al. 76] J S Weszka, C Dyer, and A Rosenfeld. A comparative study of texture measures for terrain classification. *IEEE Transactions on Systems, Man and Cybernetics*, 6(4):269–285, 1976.

[Willebeek-Lemair and Reeves 90] M Willebeek-Lemair and A Reeves. Solving nonuniform problems on SIMD computers - case study on region growing. *Journal of Parallel and Distributed Computing*, 8:135–149, 1990.

[Wood 85] J W Wood. Line finding algorithms for SAR. Technical report, AD-A162024; RSRE-MEMO-3841; BR97301, Royal Signals and Radar Establishment, Malvern, England, 1985.

[Yuen and Hlavac 91] S Y K Yuen and V Hlavac. An approach to quantization of the Hough space. In *Proceedings of the 7th Scandinavian Conference on Image Analysis*, pages 733–740, Aalborg, Denmark, August 1991.

[Zamperoni 86] P Zamperoni. Analysis of some region growing operators for image segmentation. In V Cappelini and R Marconi, editors, *Advances in Image Processing and Pattern Recognition*, pages 204–208. North Holland, Amsterdam, 1986.

[Zucker 76] S W Zucker. Relaxation labelling, local ambiguity, and low-level vision. In C H Chen, editor, *Pattern Recognition and Artificial Intelligence*, pages 593–616, Academic Press, New York, 1976.

6

Shape representation and description

The last chapter was devoted to image segmentation methods which showed how to construct homogeneous regions of images and/or their boundaries. Recognition of image regions is one of the most important steps on the way to understanding image data, and requires an exact region description in a form suitable for a classifier (Chapter 7). This description step should generate a numeric feature vector, or a non-numeric syntactic description word, which characterizes properties (for example, shape) of the described region. Region description is the third of the four levels given in Chapter 3, implying that the description already comprises some abstraction – for example, 3D real objects can be represented in a 2D plane. Nevertheless, shape properties used for object description are usually computed in two dimensions. If we are interested in a 3D object description, we have to process at least two images of the same object taken from different viewpoints (stereo vision), or derive the 3D shape from a sequence of images if the object is in motion. A 2D shape representation is sufficient in the majority of practical applications, but if 3D information is necessary – if, say, a 3D object reconstruction is the processing goal, or the 3D characteristics bear the important information – the object description task is much more difficult; these topics are introduced in Chapter 9. In the following sections we will limit our discussion to 2D shape features and proceed under the assumption that described objects result from the image segmentation process.

Defining the shape of an object can prove to be very difficult. Shape is usually represented verbally or in figures and to do this, people use terms like *elongated, rounded, with sharp edges*, etc. The computer era has introduced the necessity to describe even very complicated shapes precisely, and while many practical shape description methods exist, there is no generally accepted methodology of shape description. Further, it is not known what in shape is important. Current approaches have both positive and negative attributes; computer graphics [Woodwark 86] or mathematics [Lord and Wilson 84] use effective shape representations which are unusable in shape recognition [Juday 88] and vice versa. In spite of this, it is possible to find features common to most shape description approaches. Location and description of substantial variations in the first derivative of object boundaries often yields suitable information. Examples of this can be found in alphanumeric character description, technical drawings, ECG curve characterization, etc.

Shape is an object property which has been carefully investigated in recent years and many papers may be found dealing with numerous applications - character recognition, ECG analysis, EEG analysis, cell classification, chromosome recognition, automatic inspection, technical diagnostics, etc. Despite this variety, most approaches are basically the same with existing differences limited mostly to terminology. These common methods can be characterized from different points of view [Pavlidis 78, Pavlidis 80, Ballard and Brown 82, Brady 84, Marshall 89b].

- Input representation form: Object description can be based on boundaries (contour-based, external) or on more complex knowledge of whole regions (region-based, internal).

- Object reconstruction ability: That is, whether an object's shape can or cannot be reconstructed from the description. Many varieties of shape-preserving methods exist. They differ in the degree of precision with respect to object reconstruction.

- Incomplete shape recognition ability: That is, to what extent an object's shape can be recognized from the description if objects are occluded and only partial shape information is available.

- Mathematical and heuristic techniques: A typical mathematical technique is a Fourier transform. A representative heuristic method may be elongatedness.

- Statistical or syntactic object description (Chapter 7).

- A description robustness to translation, rotation, and scale transformations: Shape description properties in different resolutions.

The role of different description methods in image analysis and image understanding is illustrated by the flowchart shown in Figure 6.1.

Problems of scale (resolution) are common in digital images. The sensitivity to scale is even more serious if a shape description is derived, because shape may change substantially with image resolution. Contour detection may be affected by noise in high resolution, and small details may disappear in low resolution (see Figure 6.2). Therefore, shape has been studied in multiple resolutions which again causes difficulties with matching corresponding shape representations from different resolutions. Moreover, the conventional shape descriptions change discontinuously. A **scale-space** approach has been introduced in recent years [Babaud et al. 86, Witkin 86, Yuille and Poggio 86, Maragos 89] that aims to obtain continuous shape descriptions if the

Object representation and shape description methods discussed in the following sections are not an exhaustive list – we will try to introduce generally applicable methods. It is necessary to apply a problem-oriented approach to the solution of specific problems of description and recognition. This means that the following methods are appropriate for a large variety of descriptive tasks and the following ideas may be used to build a specialized, highly efficient method suitable for a particular problem description. Such a method will no longer be general since it will take advantage of all a priori knowledge about the problem. This is the way human beings can solve their vision and recognition problems, by using highly specialized knowledge.

It should be understood that despite the fact that we are dealing with two-dimensional shape and its description, our world is three-dimensional and the same objects, if seen from different angles (or changing position/orientation in space), may form very different 2D projections (see Chapter 9). The ideal case would be to have a universal shape descriptor capable of overcoming these changes – to design projection-invariant descriptors. Consider an object with planar faces and imagine how many very different 2D shapes may result from a given face if the position and 3D orientation of this simple object changes with respect to an observer. In some special cases, like circles which transform to ellipses, or planar polygons, projectively invariant features (called **invariants**) can be found. Unfortunately, no existing shape descriptor is perfect; in fact, they are all far from being perfect. Therefore, a very careful choice of descriptors resulting from detailed analysis of the shape recognition problem must precede any implementation, and whether or not a 2D representation is capable of describing a 3D shape must also be considered. For some 3D shapes, their 2D projection may bear enough information for recognition – aircraft contours may be taken as an example; successful recognition of aeroplanes from projections are known even if they change their position and orientation in space. In many other cases, objects must be seen from a specific direction to get enough descriptive information – human faces are such a case.

Object occlusion is another hard problem in shape recognition. However, the situation is easier here (if pure occlusion is considered, not combined with orientation variations yielding changes in 2D projections as discussed above), since visible parts of objects may be used for description. Here, the shape descriptor choice must be based on its ability to describe local object properties – if the descriptor only gives a global object description (e.g. object size, average boundary curvature, perimeter), such a description is useless if only a part of an object is visible. If a local descriptor is applied (e.g. description of local boundary changes), this information may be used to compare the visible part of the object to all objects which may appear in the image. Clearly, if object occlusion is the case, the local or global character of the shape descriptor must be considered first.

In Sections 6.2 and 6.3, descriptors are sorted according to whether they are based on object boundary information (contour-based, external description) or whether the information from object regions is used (region-based, internal description). This classification of shape description methods corresponds to previously described boundary-based and region-based segmentation methods. However, both contour-based and region-based shape descriptors may be local or global and differ in sensitivity to translation, rotation, scaling, etc.

6.1 Region identification

Region identification is necessary for region description. One of the many methods of region identification is to label each region (or each boundary) with a unique (integer) number; such identification is called **labelling** or **colouring**, and the largest integer label usually gives the number of regions in the image. Another method is to use a smaller number of labels (four is theoretically sufficient [Appel and Haken 77, Saaty and Kainen 77, Nishizeki and Chiba 88, Wilson and Nelson 90]), and ensure that no two neighbouring regions have the same label; then information about some region pixel must be added to the description to provide full region reference. This information is usually stored in a separate data structure.

Assume that the segmented image R consists of m disjoint regions R_i (as in equation (5.1)). The image R often consists of objects and a background

$$\bigcup_{i=1,i\neq b}^{m} R_i = R_b^C$$

where R^C is the set complement, R_b is considered background, and other regions are considered objects. Input to a labelling algorithm is usually either a binary or multi-level image, where background is represented by zero pixels, and objects by non-zero values. A multi-level image is often used to represent the labelling result, background being represented by zero values, and regions represented by their non-zero labels. Algorithm 6.1 presents a sequential approach to labelling a segmented image.

Algorithm 6.1: 4-neighbourhood and 8-neighbourhood region identification

---

1. First pass: Search the entire image R row by row and assign a non-zero value v to each non-zero pixel $R(i, j)$. The value v is chosen according to the labels of the pixel's neighbours where the property *neighbouring* is defined by Figure 6.3. ('neighbours' outside the image R are not considered),

   - If all the neighbours are background pixels (with pixel value zero), $R(i, j)$ is assigned a new (and as yet) unused label.

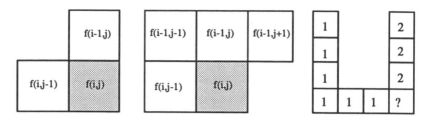

Figure 6.3 *Masks for region identification: (a) In 4-connectivity, (b) in 8-connectivity, (c) label collision.*

- If there is just one neighbouring pixel with a non-zero label, assign this label to the pixel $R(i,j)$.

- If there is more than one non-zero pixel among the neighbours, assign the label of any one to the labelled pixel. If the labels of any of the neighbours differ (*label collision*) store the label pair as being equivalent. Equivalence pairs are stored in a separate data structure – an equivalence table.

2. Second pass: All of the region-pixels were labelled during the first pass but some regions have pixels with different labels (due to label collisions). The whole image is scanned again, and pixels re-labelled using the equivalence table information (for example, with the lowest value in an equivalence class).

Label collision is a very common occurrence – examples of image shapes experiencing this are U-shaped objects, mirror E objects, etc. (see Figure 6.3c). The equivalence table is a list of all label pairs present in an image; all equivalent labels are replaced by a unique label in the second step. Since the number of label collisions is usually not known beforehand, it is necessary to allocate sufficient memory to store the equivalence table in an array. A dynamically allocated data structure is recommended. Further, if pointers are used for label specification, scanning the image for the second time is not necessary (the second pass of the algorithm) and only rewriting labels to which these pointers are pointing is much faster.

The algorithm is basically the same in 4-connectivity and 8-connectivity, the only difference being in the neighbourhood mask shape (Figure 6.3b). It is useful to assign the region labels incrementally to permit the regions to be counted easily in the second pass. An example of partial results is given in Figure 6.4.

Region identification can be performed on images that are not represented as straightforward matrices; the following algorithm [Rosenfeld and Kak 82] may be applied to images that are run-length encoded (see Chapter 3).

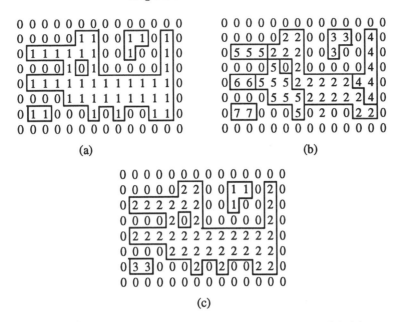

Figure 6.4 *Object identification in 8-connectivity: (a),(b),(c) Algorithm steps. Equivalence table after step (b): 2-5, 5-6, 2-4.*

Algorithm 6.2: Region identification in run-length encoded data

---

1. First pass: Use a new label for each continuous run in the first image row that is not part of the background.

2. For the second and subsequent rows, compare positions of runs. If a run in a row does not neighbour (in the 4- or 8- sense) any run in the previous row, assign a new label. If a run neighbours precisely one run in the previous row, assign its label to the new run. If the new run neighbours more than one run in the previous row, a label collision has occurred. Collision information is stored in an equivalence table, and the new run is labelled using the label of any one of its neighbours.

3. Second pass: Search the image row by row and re-label the image according to the equivalence table information.

If the segmented image is represented by a quadtree data structure, the following algorithm may be applied:

Algorithm 6.3: Quadtree region identification

---

1. First pass: Search quadtree nodes in a given order – e.g. beginning from the root and in NW, NE, SW, SE directions. Whenever an unlabelled non-zero leaf node is entered, a new label is assigned to it. Then search for neighbouring leaf nodes in the E and S directions (plus SE in 8-connectivity). If those leaves are non-zero and have not yet been labelled, assign the label of the node from which the search started. If the neighbouring leaf node has already been labelled, store the collision information in an equivalence table.

2. Repeat step (1) until the whole tree has been searched.

3. Second pass: Re-label the leaf nodes of the quadtree according to the equivalence table.

Algorithmic details and the procedure for looking for neighbouring leaf nodes can be found in [Rosenfeld and Kak 82, Samet 84].

The **region counting** task is closely related to the region identification problem. Object counting can be an intermediate result of region identification as we have seen. If it is only necessary to count regions with no need to identify them, a one-pass algorithm is sufficient [Rosenfeld and Kak 82, Atkinson et al. 85].

6.2   Contour-based shape representation and description

Region borders must be expressed in some mathematical form. The **rectangular** representation of x_n pixel co-ordinates as a function of the path length n is most common. Other useful representations use **polar** and **tangential** co-ordinates, see Figure 6.5. Border elements are represented as pairs of angle ϕ and distance r in the polar representation. The tangential representation of a curve codes the tangential directions $\theta(x_n)$ of curve points as a function of path length n.

6.2.1   Chain codes

Chain codes describe an object by a sequence of unit-size line segments with a given orientation (see Section 3.2.2). The first element of such a sequence must bear information about its position to permit the region to be reconstructed. The process results in a sequence of numbers (see Figure 6.6); to exploit the position invariance of chain codes the first element, which contains the position information, is omitted. This definition of the chain code is known as **Freeman's** code [Freeman 61].

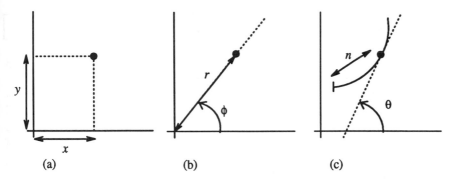

Figure 6.5 *Co-ordinate systems: (a) Rectangular (Cartesian), (b) polar, (c) tangential.*

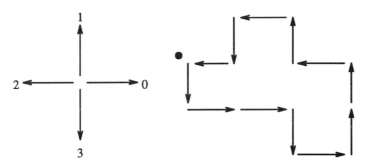

Figure 6.6 *Chain code in 4-connectivity, and its derivative. Code: 3, 0, 0, 3, 0, 1, 1, 2, 1, 2, 3, 2, derivative: 1, 0, 3, 1, 1, 0, 1, 3, 1, 1, 3, 1.*

If the chain code is used for matching it must be independent of the choice of the first border pixel in the sequence. One possibility for normalizing the chain code is to find the pixel in the border sequence which results in the minimum integer number if the description chain is interpreted as a base four number – that pixel is then used as the starting pixel. Such a chain-number is the minimum possible number which can result from the boundary sequence [Tsai and Yu 85]. A *mod 4* or *mod 8* difference code is another numbered sequence that represents relative directions of region boundary elements, measured as 90° or 45° direction changes. A chain code is very sensitive to noise, and arbitrary changes in scale and rotation may cause problems if used for recognition. The smoothed version of the chain code (averaged directions along a specified path length) is less noise sensitive [Li and Zhiying 88].

6.2.2 Simple geometric border representation

The following descriptors are mostly based on geometric properties of described regions. Because of the discrete character of digital images, all of them are sensitive to image resolution.

Boundary length

This is an elementary region property, simply derived from the chain code representation. Vertical and horizontal steps have unit length, and the length of diagonal steps in 8-connectivity is $\sqrt{2}$. It can be shown that the boundary is longer in 4-connectivity where a diagonal step consists of two rectangular steps with a total length of two. A closed-boundary length (**perimeter**) can also easily be evaluated from run length [Rosenfeld and Kak 82] or quadtree representations [Samet 81, Crowley 84] as well. Boundary length increases as the image raster resolution increases; on the other hand, region area is not affected by higher resolution and converges to some limit. To provide continuous-space perimeter properties (area computation from the boundary length, shape features, etc.), it is better to define the region border as being the outer or extended border (see Section 5.2.3). If inner borders are used, some properties are not satisfied – e.g. the perimeter of a one-pixel region is four if the outer boundary is used, and one using the inner.

Curvature

In the continuous case, curvature is defined as the rate of change of slope. In discrete space, the curvature description must be slightly modified to overcome difficulties resulting from violation of curve smoothness. The curvature scalar descriptor (also called boundary straightness) finds the ratio between the total number of boundary pixels (length) and the number of boundary pixels where the boundary direction changes significantly. The smaller the number of direction changes, the straighter the boundary. The evaluation algorithm is based on the detection of angles between line segments positioned b boundary pixels from the evaluated boundary pixel in both directions. The angle need not be represented numerically; rather, relative position of line segments can be used as a property. The parameter b determines sensitivity to local changes of the boundary direction (Figure 6.7). Curvature computed from the chain code can be found in [Rosenfeld 74]. Note that the tangential border representation is also suitable for curvature computation. Values of the curvature at all boundary pixels can be represented by a histogram; relative numbers then provide information on how common specific boundary direction changes are. Histograms of boundary angles, such as the β angle in Figure 6.7, can be built in a similar way– such histograms can be used for region description.

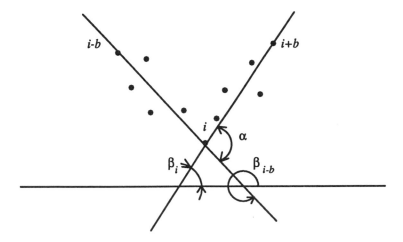

Figure 6.7 *Curvature.*

Bending energy

The bending energy of a border (curve) may be understood as the energy necessary to bend a rod to the desired shape, and can be computed as a sum of squares of the border curvature $c(k)$ over the border length L.

$$BE = \frac{1}{L} \sum_{k=1}^{L} c^2(k) \qquad (6.1)$$

Bending energy can easily be computed from Fourier descriptors using Parseval's theorem [Oppenheim et al. 83, Papoulis 91]. To represent the border, Freeman's chain code or its smoothed version may be used [Smeulders et al. 80], see Figure 6.8. Bending energy does not permit shape reconstruction.

Signature

The signature of a region may be obtained as a sequence of normal contour distances. The normal contour distance is calculated for each boundary element as a function of the path length. For each border point A the distance of an opposite border point B is sought in a direction perpendicular to the border tangent at point A, see Figure 6.9. Note that *being opposite* is not a symmetric relation (compare Algorithm 5.15). Signatures are noise sensitive, and using smoothed signatures or signatures of smoothed contours reduces noise sensitivity. Signatures may be applied to the recognition of overlapping objects or whenever only partial contours are available [Vernon 87]. Position, rotation, and scale-invariant modifications based on gradient-perimeter and angle-perimeter plots are discussed in [Safaee-Rad et al. 89].

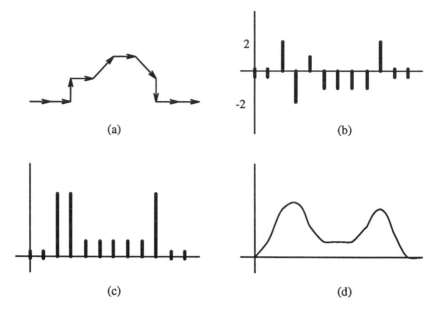

Figure 6.8 *Bending energy: (a) Chain code 0, 0, 2, 0, 1, 0, 7, 6, 0, 0, (b) curvature 0, 2, -2, 1, -1, -1, -1, 2, 0, (c) sum of squares gives the bending energy, (d) smoothed version.*

Chord distribution.

A line joining any two points of the region boundary is a chord, and the distribution of lengths and angles of all chords on a contour may be used for shape description. Let $b(x, y) = 1$ represent the contour points, and $b(x, y) = 0$ represent all other points. The chord distribution can be computed (see Figure 6.10a) as

$$h(\Delta x, \Delta y) = \int \int b(x, y)b(x + \Delta x, y + \Delta y)dxdy \qquad (6.2)$$

or in digital images as

$$h(\Delta x, \Delta y) = \sum_i \sum_j b(i, j)b(i + \Delta x, j + \Delta y) \qquad (6.3)$$

To obtain the rotation-independent radial distribution $h_r(r)$, the integral over all angles is computed (Figure 6.10b).

$$h_r(r) = \int_{-\pi/2}^{\pi/2} h(\Delta x, \Delta y)rd\theta \qquad (6.4)$$

where $r = \sqrt{\Delta x^2 + \Delta y^2}$, $\theta = \arcsin(\Delta y/r)$. The distribution $h_r(r)$ varies linearly with scale. The angular distribution $h_a(\theta)$ is independent of scale,

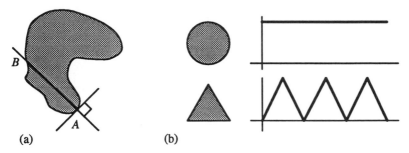

(a) (b)

Figure 6.9 *Signature: (a) Construction, (b) signatures for a circle and a triangle.*

while rotation causes a proportional offset

$$h_a(\theta) = \int_0^{\max(r)} h(\Delta x, \Delta y)dr \tag{6.5}$$

Combination of both distributions gives a robust shape descriptor [Smith and Jain 82, Cootes et al. 92].

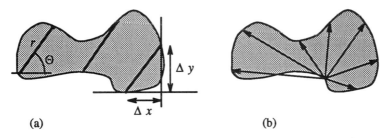

(a) (b)

Figure 6.10 *Chord distribution.*

6.2.3 Fourier transforms of boundaries

Suppose C is a closed curve (boundary) in the complex plane (Figure 6.11a). Travelling anti-clockwise along this curve keeping constant speed, a complex function $z(t)$ is obtained, where t is a time variable. The speed should be chosen such that one circumnavigation of the boundary takes time 2π; then a periodic function with period 2π is obtained after multiple passes around the curve. This permits a Fourier representation of $z(t)$ (see Section 2.1.3);

$$z(t) = \sum_n T_n e^{int} \tag{6.6}$$

The coefficients T_n of the series are called the **Fourier descriptors** of the curve C. It is more useful to consider the curve distance s in comparison to time

$$t = 2\pi s/L, \tag{6.7}$$

where L is the curve length. The Fourier descriptors T_n are given by

$$T_n = \frac{1}{L} \int_0^L z(s)e^{-i(2\pi/L)ns} ds \qquad (6.8)$$

The descriptors are influenced by the curve shape and by the initial point of the curve. Working with digital image data, boundary co-ordinates are discrete and the function $z(s)$ is not continuous. Assume that $z(k)$ is a discrete version of $z(s)$, where 4-connectivity is used to get a constant sampling interval. The descriptors T_n can be computed from the discrete Fourier transform (DFT, Section 11.2) of $z(k)$;

$$z(k) \longleftarrow DFT \longrightarrow T_n \qquad (6.9)$$

The Fourier descriptors can be invariant to translation and rotation if the co-ordinate system is appropriately chosen [Pavlidis 77, Persoon and Fu 77, Wallace and Wintz 80, Grimmins 82, Lin and Chellappa 87]. They have been used for handwritten alphanumeric character description in [Shridhar and Badreldin 84]; the character boundary in this description was represented by co-ordinate pairs (x_m, y_m) in 4-connectivity, $(x_1, y_1) = (x_L, y_L)$. Then

$$a_n = \frac{1}{L-1} \sum_{m=1}^{L-1} x_m e^{-i(2\pi/(L-1))nm} \qquad (6.10)$$

$$b_n = \frac{1}{L-1} \sum_{m=1}^{L-1} y_m e^{-i(2\pi/(L-1))nm} \qquad (6.11)$$

The coefficients a_n, b_n are not invariant, but after the transform

$$r_n = (\mid a_n \mid^2 + \mid b_n \mid^2)^{1/2}, \qquad (6.12)$$

r_n are translation and rotation invariant. To achieve a magnification invariance the descriptors w_n are used:

$$w_n = r_n/r_1 \qquad (6.13)$$

The first 10 – 15 descriptors w_n are found to be sufficient for character description.

A closed boundary can be represented as a function of angle tangents versus the distance between the boundary points from which the angles were determined (Figure 6.11b). Let φ_k be the angle measured at the kth boundary point, and let l_k be the distance between the boundary starting point and the kth boundary point. A periodic function can be defined

$$a(l_k) = \varphi_k + u_k, \qquad (6.14)$$

$$u_k = 2\pi l_k/L \qquad (6.15)$$

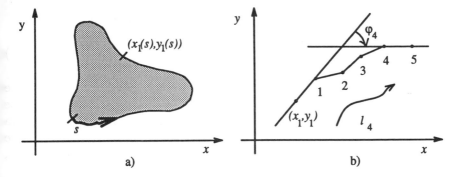

Figure 6.11 *Fourier description of boundaries: (a) Descriptors T_n, (b) descriptors S_n.*

The descriptor set is then

$$S_n = \frac{1}{2\pi} \int_0^{2\pi} a(u)e^{-inu}du \qquad (6.16)$$

The Discrete Fourier Transform is used in all practical applications [Pavlidis 77].

The high quality boundary shape representation obtained using only a few lower order coefficients is a favourable property common to Fourier descriptors. We can compare the results of using the S_n and T_n descriptors: The S_n descriptors have more high frequency components present in the boundary function due to more significant changes of tangent angles, and as a result, they do not decrease as fast as the T_n descriptors. In addition the S_n descriptors are not suitable for boundary reconstruction since they often result in a non-closed boundary. A method for obtaining a closed boundary using S_n descriptors is given in [Strackee and Nagelkerke 83]. The T_n descriptor values decrease quickly for higher frequencies and their reconstruction always results in a closed boundary. Moreover, the S_n descriptors cannot be applied for squares, equilateral triangles, etc. [Wallace 81] unless the solution methods introduced in [Wallace and Wintz 80] are applied.

Fourier descriptors can also be used for calculation of region area, location of centroid, and computation of second-order moments [Kiryati and Maydan 89]. Fourier descriptors are a general technique, but problems with describing local information exist. A modified technique using a combined frequency-position space that deals better with local curve properties is described in [Eichmann et al. 90], and another modification invariant under rotation, translation, scale, mirror reflection, and shifts in starting points is discussed in [Krzyzak et al. 89]. Conventional Fourier descriptors cannot be used for recognition of occluded objects. Nevertheless, classification of partial shapes using Fourier descriptors is introduced in [Lin and Chellappa 87].

Boundary detection and description using elliptic Fourier decomposition of the boundary is described in [Staib and Duncan 92].

6.2.4 Boundary description using a segment sequence; polygonal representation

Representation of a boundary using **segments** with specified properties is another option for boundary (and curve) description. If the segment type is known for all segments, the boundary can be described as a chain of segment types, a code-word consisting of representatives of a type alphabet. An example is given in Figure 6.14 which will be discussed later in more detail. This sort of description is suitable for syntactic recognition (see Section 7.4). A trivial segment chain is used to obtain the Freeman code description discussed in Section 6.2.1.

A **polygonal representation** approximates a region by a polygon, the region being represented using its vertices. Polygonal representations are obtained as a result of a simple boundary segmentation. The boundary can be approximated with varying precision; if a more precise description is necessary, a larger number of line segments may be employed. Any two boundary points x_1, x_2 define a line segment and a sequence of points x_1, x_2, x_3 represents a chain of line segments – from the point x_1 to the point x_2, and from x_2 to x_3. If $x_1=x_3$, a closed boundary results. There are many types of straight segment boundary representations [Pavlidis 77, Koch and Kashyap 87]; the problem lies in determining the location of boundary vertices, one solution to which is to apply a split-and-merge algorithm. The merging step consists of going through a set of boundary points and adding them to a straight segment as long as a segment straightness criterion is satisfied. If the straightness characteristic of the segment is lost, the last connected point is marked as a vertex and construction of a new straight segment begins. This general approach has many variations, some of which are described in [Pavlidis 77].

Boundary vertices can be detected as boundary points with a significant change of boundary direction using the curvature (boundary straightness) criterion (see Section 6.2.2). This approach works well for boundaries with rectilinear boundary segments.

Another method for determining the boundary vertices is a **tolerance interval approach** based on setting a maximum allowed difference e. Assume that point x_1 is the end-point of a previous segment and so by definition the first point of a new segment. Define points x_2, x_3 positioned a distance e from the point x_1 to be rectilinear – x_1, x_2, x_3 are positioned on a straight line – see Figure 6.12. The next step is to locate a segment which can fit between parallels directed from points x_2 and x_3. Resulting segments are sub-optimal, although optimality can be achieved with a substantial increase in computational effort [Tomek 74].

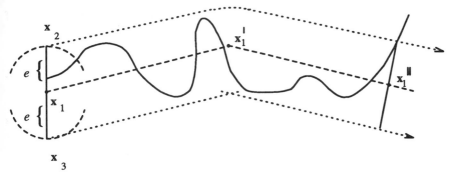

Figure 6.12 *Tolerance interval.*

The methods introduced above represent single-pass algorithms of boundary segmentation using a segment-growing approach. Often they do not result in the best possible boundary segmentation because the located vertex often indicates that the real vertex should have been located a few steps back. The splitting approach of segmenting boundaries into smaller segments can sometimes help and the best results can be anticipated using a combination of both methods. If the splitting approach is used, segments are usually divided into two new smaller segments until the new segments meet the final requirements [Duda and Hart 73, Pavlidis 77]. A simple procedure for splitting begins from end-points x_1 and x_2 of a curve; these end-points are connected by a line segment. The next step searches all the curve points for the curve point x_3 with the largest distance from the line segment. If the located point is within a preset distance between itself and the line segment, the segment x_1-x_2 is an end segment and all curve vertices are found, the curve being polygonally represented by vertices x_1 and x_2. Otherwise the point x_3 is set as a new vertex and the process is recursively applied to both resulting segments x_1-x_3 and x_3-x_2 (see Figure 6.13 and Section 5.2.7).

Boundary segmentation into segments of **constant curvature** is another possibility for boundary representation. The boundary may also be split into segments which can be represented by polynomials, usually of the second order, such as circular, elliptic, or parabolic segments [Costabile et al. 85, Wuescher and Boyer 91]. Curve segmentation into circular arcs and straight lines is presented in [Rosin and West 89]. Segments are considered as primitives for syntactic shape recognition procedures – a typical example is the syntactic description and recognition of chromosomes [Fu 74], where boundary segments are classified as convex segments of large curvature, concave segments of large curvature, straight segments, etc. as illustrated in Figure 6.14.

Other syntactic object recognition methods based on a contour partitioning into primitives from a specified set are described in [Jakubowski 85,

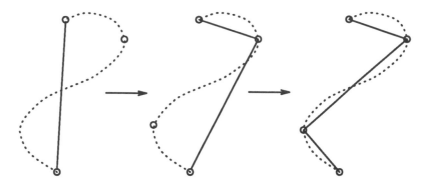

Figure 6.13 *Recursive boundary splitting.*

Jakubowski 90, Tampi and Sridhar 90]. Partitioning of the contour using location of points with high positive curvatures (corners) is described in [Chien and Aggarwal 89] together with applications to occluded contours. A discrete curvature function based on a chain code representation of a boundary is used with a morphological approach to obtain segments of constant curvature in [Leymarie and Levine 89]. Different contour partitioning using segments of constant intensity is suggested in [Marshall 89a]. Polygonal representation used in a *hypothesize and verify* approach to recognition of occluded objects may be found in [Koch and Kashyap 87].

Sensitivity of shape descriptors to scale (image resolution) has already been mentioned as an undesirable feature of a majority of descriptors. In other words, shape description varies with scale, and different results are achieved at different resolutions. This problem is no less important if a curve is to be divided into segments; some curve segmentation points exist in one resolution and disappear in others without any direct correspondence. Considering this, a **scale-space** approach to curve segmentation that guarantees a continuously changing position of segmentation points is a significant achievement [Babaud et al. 86, Witkin 86, Yuille and Poggio 86, Maragos 89, Florack et al. 92, Griffin et al. 92]. In this approach, only new segmentation points can appear at higher resolutions, and no existing segmentation points can disappear. This is in agreement with our understanding of varying resolutions; finer details can be detected in higher resolution but significant details should not disappear if the resolution increases. This technique is based on application of a unique Gaussian smoothing kernel to a one-dimensional signal (e.g. a curvature function) over a range of sizes and the result is differentiated twice. To determine the peaks of curvature, the zero crossing of the second derivative is detected, the positions of zero crossings give the position of curve segmentation points. Different locations of segmentation points are obtained at varying resolution (different Gaussian kernel size). An important property of the Gaussian kernel is that the location of segmentation points changes

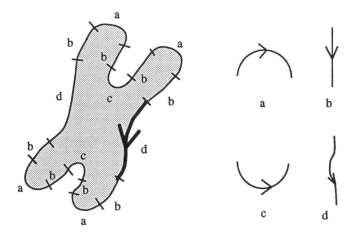

Figure 6.14 *Structural description of chromosomes by a chain of boundary segments, code word: d, b, a, b, c, b, a, b, d, b, a, b, c, b, a, b (adapted from [Fu 74]).*

continuously with resolution which can be seen in the **scale-space image** of the curve, Figure 6.15a. Fine details of the curve disappear in pairs with increasing size of the Gaussian smoothing kernel, and two segmentation points always merge to form a closed contour showing that any segmentation point existing in coarse resolution must also exist in finer resolution. Moreover, the position of a segmentation point is most accurate in finest resolution and this position can be traced from coarse to fine resolution using the scale-space image. A multiscale curve description can be represented by an **interval tree,** Figure 6.15b. Each pair of zero crossings is represented by a rectangle, its position corresponding with segmentation point locations on the curve, its height showing the lowest resolution at which the segmentation point can be detected. Interval trees can be used for curve decomposition in different scales keeping the possibility of segment description using higher resolution features.

Another scale-space approach to curve decomposition is the **curvature primal sketch** [Asada and Brady 86], (compare Section 9.1.1). A set of primitive curvature discontinuities is defined and convolved with first and second derivatives of a Gaussian in multiple resolutions. The curvature primal sketch is computed by matching the multiscale convolutions of a shape. The curvature primal sketch then serves as a shape representation; shape reconstruction may be based on polygons or splines. Another multiscale border-primitive detection technique that aggregates curve primitives at one scale into curve primitives at a coarser scale is described in [Saund 90]. A robust approach to multiscale curve corner detection that uses additional information extracted from corner behaviour in the whole multi-resolution pyramid

Increasing scale

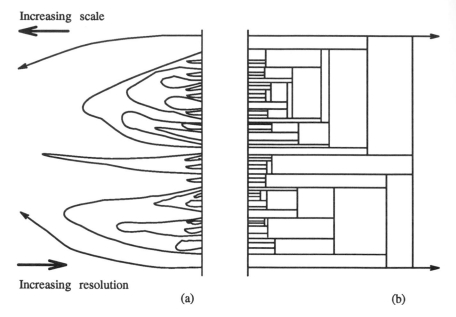

Increasing resolution

(a)   (b)

Figure 6.15 *Scale-space image: (a) Varying number and locations of curve segmentation points as a function of scale, (b) curve representation by an interval tree.*

is given in [Fermuller and Kropatsch 92].

6.2.5   B-spline representation

Representation of curves using piecewise polynomial interpolation to obtain smooth curves is widely used in computer graphics. B-splines are piecewise polynomial curves whose shape is closely related to their control polygon – a chain of vertices giving a polygonal representation of a curve. B-splines of the third-order are most common because this is the lowest order which includes the change of curvature. Splines have very good representation properties and are easy to compute: Firstly they change their shape less then their control polygon, and do not oscillate between sampling points as many other representations do. Furthermore, a spline curve is always positioned inside a convex $n + 1$-polygon for a B-spline of the nth order – Figure 6.16. Secondly, the interpolation is local in character. If a control polygon vertex changes its position, a resulting change of the spline curve will occur only in a small neighbourhood of that vertex. Thirdly, methods of matching region boundaries represented by splines to image data are based on a direct search of original image data. These methods are similar to the segmentation methods described in Section 5.2.6. A spline direction can be derived directly from its parameters.

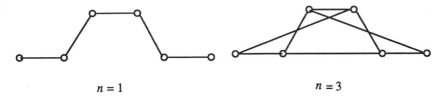

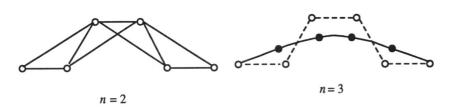

Figure 6.16 *Splines of order n.*

Let x_i, $i = 1, ..., n$ be points of a B-spline interpolation curve; call this interpolation curve $x(s)$. The s parameter changes linearly between points x_i – that is, $x_i = x(i)$. Each part of a cubic B-spline curve is a third-order polynomial meaning that it and its first and second derivatives are continuous. B-splines are given by

$$x(s) = \sum_{i=0}^{n+1} v_i B_i(s), \qquad (6.17)$$

where v_i are coefficients representing a spline curve, and $B_i(s)$ are base functions whose shape is given by the spline order. The coefficients v_i bear information dual to information about the spline curve points x_i – the values v_i can be derived from x_i values and vice versa. The coefficients v_i represent vertices of the control polygon and if there are n points x_i, there must be $n+2$ points v_i. The two end-points v_0, v_{n+1} are specified by binding conditions. If the curvature of a B-spline curvature is to be zero at the curve beginning and end, then

$$v_0 = 2v_1 - v_2$$

$$v_{n+1} = 2v_n - v_{n-1} \qquad (6.18)$$

If the curve is closed then $v_0 = v_n$ and $v_{n+1} = v_1$.

The base functions are non-negative and are of local importance only. Each base function $B_i(s)$ is non-zero only for $s \in (i-2, i+2)$ meaning that for any $s \in (i, i+1)$, there are only four non-zero base functions for any i : $B_{i-1}(s)$, $B_i(s)$, $B_{i+1}(s)$, and $B_{i+2}(s)$. If the distance between the x_i points is constant (e.g. unit distances), all the base functions are of the same form and consist of four parts $C_j(t)$, $j = 0, ..., 3$.

$$C_0(t) = \frac{t^3}{6}$$

$$C_1(t) = \frac{-3t^3 + 3t^2 + 3t + 1}{6}$$

$$C_2(t) = \frac{3t^3 - 6t^2 + 4}{6}$$ (6.19)

$$C_3(t) = \frac{-t^3 + 3t^2 - 3t + 1}{6}$$

Because of equation 6.17 and zero-equal base functions for $s \notin (i - 2, i + 2)$, $\mathbf{x}(s)$ can be computed from the addition of only four terms for any s.

$$\mathbf{x}(s) = C_{i-1,3}(s)\mathbf{v}_{i-1} + C_{i,2}(s)\mathbf{v}_i + C_{i+1,1}(s)\mathbf{v}_{i+1} + C_{i+2,0}(s)\mathbf{v}_{i+2}$$ (6.20)

Here, $C_{i,j}(s)$ means that we use j^{th} part of the base function B_i (see Figure 6.17). Note that

$$C_{i,j}(s) = C_j(s - i),$$ (6.21)

$$i = 0, ..., n + 1; \qquad j = 0, 1, 2, 3.$$

To work with values inside the interval $[i, i + 1)$, the interpolation curve $\mathbf{x}(s)$ can be computed as

$$\mathbf{x}(s) = C_3(s - i)\mathbf{v}_{i-1} + C_2(s - i)\mathbf{v}_i + C_1(s - i)\mathbf{v}_{i+1} + C_0\mathbf{v}_{i+2}$$ (6.22)

Specifically if $s = 5$, s is positioned at the beginning of the interval $[i, i + 1)$, therefore $i = 5$ and

$$\mathbf{x}(5) = C_3(0)\mathbf{v}_4 + C_2(0)\mathbf{v}_5 + C_1(0)\mathbf{v}_6 = \frac{1}{6}\mathbf{v}_4 + \frac{4}{6}\mathbf{v}_5 + \frac{1}{6}\mathbf{v}_6$$ (6.23)

or if $s = 7.7$ then $i = 7$ and

$$\mathbf{x}(5) = C_3(0.7)\mathbf{v}_6 + C_2(0.7)\mathbf{v}_7 + C_1(0.7)\mathbf{v}_8 + C_0(0.7)\mathbf{v}_9$$ (6.24)

Other useful formulae can be found in [DeBoor 78, Ballard and Brown 82, Ikebe and Miyamoto 82].

Splines generate curves which are usually considered pleasing. They allow a good curve approximation, and can easily be used for image analysis curve representation problems. A technique transforming curve samples to B-spline control polygon vertices is described in [Paglieroni and Jain 88] together with a method of efficient computation of boundary curvature, shape moments, and projections from control polygon vertices. Splines differ in their complexity; one of the simplest applies the B-spline formula for curve modelling as well as for curve extraction from image data [DeBoor 78]. Splines are used in computer vision to form exact and flexible inner model representations of complex shapes which are necessary in model-driven segmentation and in complex image understanding tasks. On the other hand, splines are highly sensitive to change in scale.

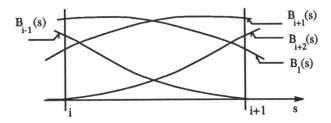

Figure 6.17 *The only four non-zero base functions for $s \in (i, i+1)$.*

6.2.6 Other contour-based shape description approaches

Many other methods and approaches can be used to describe two-dimensional curves and contours.

The **Hough transform** has excellent shape description abilities and is discussed in detail in the image segmentation context in Section 5.2.6 (see also [McKenzie and Protheroe 90]). Region-based shape description using **statistical moments** is covered in Section 6.3.2 where a technique of contour-based moments computation from region borders is also included. Further, it is necessary to mention the **fractal** approach to shape [Mandelbrot 83, Barnsley 88, Falconer 90] that is gaining growing attention in image shape description [Frisch et al. 87, Chang and Chatterjee 89].

Mathematical morphology can be used for shape description, typically in connection with region skeleton construction (see Section 6.3.4). A different approach is introduced in [Loui et al. 90] where a **geometrical correlation function** represents two-dimensional continuous or discrete curves. This function is translation, rotation, and scale invariant and may be used to compute basic geometrical properties.

Neural networks (Section 7.3) can be used to recognize shapes in raw boundary representations directly. Contour sequences of noiseless reference shapes are used for training, and noisy data are used in later training stages to increase robustness; effective representations of closed planar shapes result [Gupta et al. 90]. Another neural network shape representation system uses a modified Walsh-Hadamard transform (Chapter 11) to achieve position-invariant shape representation [Minnix et al. 90].

6.2.7 Shape invariants

Shape invariants represent a very active current research area in machine vision. Although the importance of shape invariance has been known for a long time, the first machine-vision related paper about shape invariants [Weiss 88] appeared in 1988 followed by a book of Kanatani [Kanatani 90] in 1990. The following section gives a brief overview of this topic and is mostly based on the paper [Forsyth et al. 91] and on the book [Mundy and Zisserman 92] in which additional details can be found. The book [Mundy and Zisserman 92] gives an overview of this topic in its Introduction and its Appendix presents an excellent and detailed survey of projective geometry for machine vision. Even if shape invariance is a novel approach in machine vision, invariant theory is not new and many of its principles were introduced in the nineteenth century.

As has been mentioned many times, object description is necessary for object recognition. Unfortunately, all the shape descriptors discussed so far depend on viewpoint, meaning that object recognition may often be impossible as a result of changed object or observer position, as illustrated in Figure 6.18. The role of shape description invariance is obvious – shape invariants represent properties of such geometric configurations which remain unchanged under an appropriate class of transforms [Mundy and Zisserman 92]. Machine vision is especially concerned with the class of projective transforms.

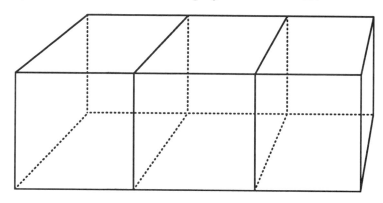

Figure 6.18 *Change of shape caused by a projective transform. The same rectangular cross-section is represented by different polygons in the image plane.*

Collinearity is the simplest example of a projectively invariant image feature. Any straight line is projected as a straight line under any projective transform. Similarly, the basic idea of the projection-invariant shape description is to find such shape features that are unaffected by the transform between the object and the image plane.

A standard technique of projection-invariant description is to hypothesize the pose (position and orientation) of an object and transform this object into a specific co-ordinate system; then shape characteristics measured in this co-ordinate system yield an invariant description. However, the pose must be hypothesized for each object and each image which makes this approach difficult and unreliable.

Application of **invariant theory** where invariant descriptors can be computed directly from image data without the need for a particular co-ordinate system represents another approach. In addition, invariant theory can determine the total number of functionally independent invariants for a given situation therefore showing completeness of the description invariant set. Invariant theory is based on a collection of transforms that can be composed and inverted. In vision, the **plane-projective group** of transforms is considered which contains all the perspectives as a subset. The **group approach** provides a mathematical tool for generating invariants; if the transform is not a group, this machinery is not available [Mundy and Zisserman 92]. Therefore, the change of co-ordinates due to the plane-projective transform is generalized as a **group action. Lie group** theory is especially useful in designing new invariants.

Let corresponding entities in two different co-ordinate systems be distinguished by large and small letters. An invariant of a linear transformation is defined in [Mundy and Zisserman 92] as follows:

> An invariant, $I(\mathbf{P})$, of a geometric structure described by a parameter vector $\mathbf{P}$, subject to a linear transformation $\mathbf{T}$ of the co-ordinates $\mathbf{x} = \mathbf{TX}$, is transformed according to $I(\mathbf{p}) = I(\mathbf{P})|\mathbf{T}|^w$. Here $I(\mathbf{p})$ is the function of the parameters after the linear transformation, and $|\mathbf{T}|$ is the determinant of the matrix $\mathbf{T}$.

In this definition, w is referred to as the weight of the invariant. If $w = 0$, the invariants are called **scalar invariants**, which are considered below. Invariant descriptors are unaffected by object pose, by perspective projection, and by the intrinsic parameters of the camera.

Several examples of invariants are now given.

1. **Cross ratio:** The cross ratio represents a classic invariant of a projective line. As mentioned earlier, a straight line is always projected as a straight line. Any four colinear points A, B, C, D may be described by the cross-ratio invariant

$$I = \frac{(A - C)(B - D)}{(A - D)(B - C)} \tag{6.25}$$

   where $(A - C)$ represents the distance between points A and C (see Figure 6.19). Note that the cross ratio depends on the order in which the four colinear points are labelled.

2. **Systems of lines or points:** A system of four coplanar concurrent lines (meeting at the same point) is dual to a system of four colinear points and the cross ratio is its invariant, see Figure 6.19.

   A system of five general coplanar lines forms two invariants

$$I_1 = \frac{|\mathbf{M}_{431}||\mathbf{M}_{521}|}{|\mathbf{M}_{421}||\mathbf{M}_{531}|} \qquad I_2 = \frac{|\mathbf{M}_{421}||\mathbf{M}_{532}|}{|\mathbf{M}_{432}||\mathbf{M}_{521}|} \tag{6.26}$$

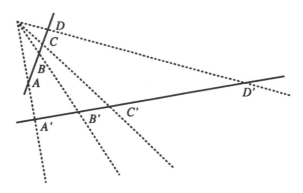

Figure 6.19 *Cross ratio; four colinear points form a projective invariant.*

where $M_{ijk} = (l_i, l_j, l_k)$. $l_i = (l_i^1, l_i^2, l_i^3)^T$ is a representation of a line $l_i^1 x + l_i^2 y + l_i^3 = 0$, where $i \in [1, 5]$, and $|M|$ is the determinant of M. If the three lines forming the matrix M_{ijk} are concurrent, the matrix becomes singular and the invariant is undefined.

A system of five coplanar points is dual to a system of five lines and the same two invariants are formed. These two functional invariants can also be formed as two cross ratios of two coplanar concurrent line quadruples, see Figure 6.20. Note that even combinations other than those given in Figure 6.20 may be formed, only the two presented functionally independent invariants exist.

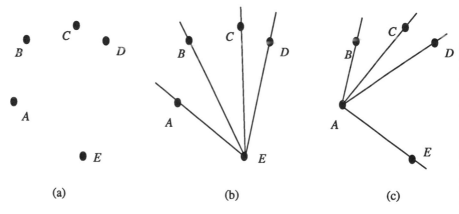

(a)   (b)   (c)

Figure 6.20 *Five coplanar points form two cross-ratio invariants: (a) Coplanar points, (b) five points form a system of four concurrent lines, (c) the same five points form another system of four coplanar lines.*

3. **Plane conics:** A plane conic may be represented by an equation

$$ax^2 + bxy + cy^2 + dx + ey + f = 0 \qquad (6.27)$$

for $\mathbf{x} = (x, y, 1)^T$. Then the conic may also be defined by a matrix $\mathbf{C}$

$$\mathbf{C} = \begin{vmatrix} a & b/2 & d/2 \\ b/2 & c & e/2 \\ d/2 & e/2 & f \end{vmatrix}$$

and

$$\mathbf{x}^T \mathbf{C} \, \mathbf{x} = 0 \qquad (6.28)$$

For any conic represented by a matrix $\mathbf{C}$, and any two coplanar lines not tangent to the conic, one invariant may be defined

$$I = \frac{(\mathbf{l}_1^T \mathbf{C}^{-1} \mathbf{l}_2)^2}{(\mathbf{l}_1^T \mathbf{C}^{-1} \mathbf{l}_1)(\mathbf{l}_2^T \mathbf{C}^{-1} \mathbf{l}_2)} \qquad (6.29)$$

The same invariant can be formed for a conic and two coplanar points.

Two invariants can be determined for a pair of conics represented by their respective matrices $\mathbf{C}_1, \mathbf{C}_2$ normalized so that $|\mathbf{C}_i| = 1$

$$I_1 = \text{Trace}[\mathbf{C}_1^{-1}\mathbf{C}_2] \qquad I_2 = \text{Trace}[\mathbf{C}_2^{-1}\mathbf{C}_1] \qquad (6.30)$$

For non-normalized conics, the invariants of associated quadratic forms are

$$I_1 = \text{Trace}[\mathbf{C}_1^{-1}\mathbf{C}_2] \left(\frac{|\mathbf{C}_1|}{|\mathbf{C}_2|}\right)^{\frac{1}{3}} \qquad I_2 = \text{Trace}[\mathbf{C}_2^{-1}\mathbf{C}_1] \left(\frac{|\mathbf{C}_2|}{|\mathbf{C}_1|}\right)^{\frac{1}{3}} \qquad (6.31)$$

and two true invariants of the conics are [Quan et al. 92]

$$I_1 = \frac{\text{Trace}[\mathbf{C}_1^{-1}\mathbf{C}_2]}{(\text{Trace}[\mathbf{C}_2^{-1}\mathbf{C}_1])^2} \frac{|\mathbf{C}_1|}{|\mathbf{C}_2|} \qquad I_2 = \frac{\text{Trace}[\mathbf{C}_2^{-1}\mathbf{C}_1]}{(\text{Trace}[\mathbf{C}_1^{-1}\mathbf{C}_2])^2} \frac{|\mathbf{C}_2|}{|\mathbf{C}_1|} \qquad (6.32)$$

An interpretation of these invariants is given in [Maybank 92]. Two plane conics uniquely determine four points of intersection, and any point that is not an intersection point may be chosen to form a five-point system together with the four intersection points. Therefore, two invariants exist for the pair of conics, as for the five-point system.

Many man-made objects consist of a combination of straight lines and conics, and these invariants may be used for their description. However, if the object has a contour which cannot be represented by an algebraic curve, the situation is much more difficult. **Differential invariants** can be formed (e.g. curvature, torsion, Gaussian curvature) which are not affected by projective transforms. These invariants are local – that is, the invariants are found for each point on the curve, which may be quite general. Unfortunately, these invariants are extremely large and complex polynomials requiring seventh derivatives of the curve, which makes them practically unusable due to image noise and acquisition errors, although noise-resistant local invariants are beginning to appear [Weiss 92]. However, if additional information is available, higher derivatives may be avoided. In [Brill et al. 92, Van Gool et al. 92], higher derivatives are traded for extra reference points which can be detected on curves in different projections although the necessity of matching reference points in different projections brings other difficulties.

Designing new invariants is an important part of invariant theory in its application to machine vision. The easiest way is to combine primitive invariants forming new ones from these combinations. Nevertheless, no new information is obtained from these combinations. Further, complete tables of invariants for systems of vectors under the action of the rotation group, the affine transform group, and the general linear transform group may be found in [Weyl 46]. To obtain new sets of functional invariants, several methods (eliminating transform parameters, the infinitesimal method, the symbolic method) can be found in [Forsyth et al. 91, Mundy and Zisserman 92].

Stability of invariants is another crucial property which affects their applicability. The robustness of invariants to image noise and errors introduced by image sensors is of prime importance, although not much is known about this. Results of plane-projective invariant stability testing (cross ratio, five coplanar points, two coplanar conics) can be found in [Forsyth et al. 91, Hopcroft et al. 92]. Further, different invariants have different stabilities and distinguishing powers. It was found, for example [Rothwell et al. 92a], that measuring a single conic and two lines in a scene is too computationally expensive to be worthwhile. It is recommended to combine different invariants to enable fast object recognition.

An example of recognition of man-made objects using invariant description of four coplanar lines, a conic and two lines, and a pair of coplanar conics is given in [Rothwell et al. 92a]. The recognition system is based on a model library containing over thirty object models – significantly more than that reported for other recognition systems. Moreover, the construction of the model library is extremely easy; no special measurements are needed, the object is digitized in a standard way and the projectively invariant description is stored as a model [Rothwell et al. 92b]. Further, there is no need for camera calibration. The recognition accuracy is 100% for occluded objects viewed from different viewpoints if the objects are not severely disrupted by shadows and specularities. An example of the object recognition is given in Figure 6.21.

6.3 Region-based shape representation and description

We can use boundary information to describe a region, and shape can be described from the region itself. A large group of shape description techniques is

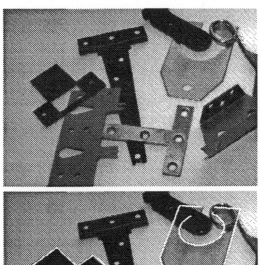

Figure 6.21 *Object recognition based on shape invariants: (a) Original image of overlapping objects taken from an arbitrary viewpoint, (b) object recognition based on line and conic invariants. Courtesy D. Forsyth, University of Iowa; C. Rothwell, A. Zisserman, University of Oxford; J. Mundy, General Electric Corporate Research and Development, Schenectady, NY.*

represented by heuristic approaches which yield acceptable results in description of simple shapes. Region area, rectangularity, elongatedness, direction, compactness, etc. are examples of these methods. Unfortunately, they cannot be used for region reconstruction and do not work for more complex shapes. Other procedures based on region decomposition into smaller and simpler subregions must be applied to describe more complicated regions, then subregions can be described separately using heuristic approaches. Objects are represented by a planar graph with nodes representing subregions resulting from region decomposition, and region shape is then described by the graph properties [Rosenfeld 79, Bhanu and Faugeras 84, Turney et al. 85]. There are two general approaches to acquiring a graph of subregions: The first one is region thinning leading to the **region skeleton**, which can be described by a graph. The second option starts with the **region decomposition** into subregions, which are then represented by nodes while arcs represent neighbourhood relations of subregions. It is common to stipulate that subregions be convex.

Graphical representation of regions has many advantages; the resulting graphs

- are translation and rotation invariant; position and rotation can be included in the graph description

- are insensitive to small changes in shape

- are highly invariant with respect to region magnitude

- generate a representation which is understandable

- can easily be used to obtain the information-bearing features of the graph

- are suitable for syntactic recognition

On the other hand, the shape representation can be difficult to obtain and the classifier-learning stage is not easy either (see Chapter 7). Nevertheless, if we are to get closer to the reality of computer vision, and to understand complex images, there is no alternative.

6.3.1 Simple scalar region descriptors

A number of simple heuristic shape descriptors exist which relate to statistical feature description. These methods are basic and are used for description of subregions in complex regions, and may then be used to define graph node classification [Bribiesca and Guzman 80].

Area

The simplest and most natural property of a region is its area, given by the number of pixels of which the region consists. The *real* area of each pixel may be taken into consideration to get the *real size* of a region, noting that in many cases, especially in satellite imagery, pixels in different positions correspond to different areas in the real world. If an image is represented as a rectangular raster, simple counting of region pixels will provide its area. If the image is represented by a quadtree, however, it may be a little bit more difficult to find the region area. Assuming that regions have been identified by labelling, the following algorithm may be used.

Algorithm 6.4: Calculating area in quadtrees

1. Set all region area variables to zero, and determine the global quadtree depth H; for example, the global quadtree depth is $H = 8$ for a 256×256 image.

2. Search the tree in a systematic way. If a leaf node at a depth h has a non-zero label, proceed to step (3).

3. Compute:

$$area[region\_label] = area[region\_label] + 4^{(H-h)}$$

4. The region areas are stored in variables $area[region\_label]$.

The region can be represented by n polygon vertices (i_k, j_k), and $(i_0, j_0) = (i_n, j_n)$. The area is given by

$$area = \frac{1}{2} | \sum_{k=0}^{n-1} (i_k j_{k+1} - i_{k+1} j_k)| \tag{6.33}$$

– the sign of the sum represents the polygon orientation. If a smoothed boundary is used to overcome noise sensitivity problems, the region area value resulting from equation 6.33 is usually somewhat reduced. Various smoothing methods and accurate area-recovering techniques are given in [Koenderink and van Doorn 86].

  If the region is represented by the (anti-clockwise) Freeman chain code the following algorithm provides the area;

Algorithm 6.5: Region area calculation from Freeman 4-connectivity chain code representation

1. Set the region *area* to zero. Assign the value of the starting point i co-ordinate to the variable *vertical_position*.

2. For each element of the chain code (values 0, 1, 2, 3) do

```
switch(code) {
    case 0:
        area := area - vertical_position;
        break;
    case 1:
        vertical_position := vertical_position + 1;
```

```
        break;
    case 2:
        area := area + vertical_position;
        break;
    case 3:
        vertical_position := vertical_position - 1;
        break;
}
```

3. If all boundary chain elements have been processed, the region area is stored in the variable *area*.

Euler's number

Euler's number ϑ (sometimes called **Genus** or the **Euler-Poincaré characteristic**) describes a simple topologically invariant property of the object. It is based on S, the number of contiguous parts of an object and N, the number of holes in the object (an object can consist of more than one region, otherwise the number of contiguous parts is equal to one (see Section 2.3.1)). Then

$$\vartheta = S - N \tag{6.34}$$

Special procedures to compute Euler's number can be found in [Dyer 80, Rosenfeld and Kak 82, Pratt 91], and in Chapter 10.

Projections, height, width

Horizontal and vertical region projections $p_h(i)$ and $p_v(j)$ are defined as

$$p_h(i) = \sum_j f(i,j), \qquad\qquad p_v(j) = \sum_i f(i,j). \tag{6.35}$$

Region description by projections is usually connected to binary image processing. The width (height) of a region is defined as the maximum value of the horizontal (vertical) projection of a binary image of the region. These definitions are illustrated in Figure 6.22. Note that projections can be defined in any direction.

Eccentricity

The simplest eccentricity characteristic is the ratio of the length of the maximum chord A to the maximum chord B which is perpendicular to A (the ratio of major and minor axes of an object) – see Figure 6.23. Another approximate eccentricity measure is based on a ratio of main region axes of inertia [Ballard and Brown 82, Jain 89].

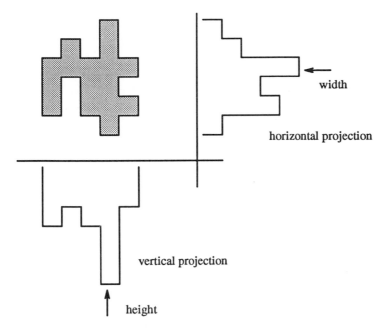

Figure 6.22 *Projections.*

Elongatedness

Elongatedness is a ratio between the length and width of the region bounding rectangle – the bounding rectangle is turned in discrete steps, and a minimum located (see Figure 6.24a). The rectangle considered is that of minimum area. This criterion cannot succeed in curved regions (see Figure 6.24b), for which the evaluation of elongatedness must be based on maximum region thickness. Elongatedness can be evaluated as a ratio of the region area and the square of its thickness. The maximum region thickness (holes must be filled if present) can be determined as the number of erosion steps that may be applied before the region totally disappears. If the number of erosion steps is d, elongatedness is then

$$elongatedness = \frac{area}{(2d)^2} \tag{6.36}$$

Another method based on longest central line detection is described in [Nagao and Matsuyama 80]; representation and recognition of elongated regions is also discussed in [Lipari and Harlow 88].

Note that the bounding rectangle can be computed efficiently from boundary points, if its direction θ is known. Defining

$$\alpha(x, y) = x \cos \theta + y \sin \theta, \quad \beta(x, y) = -x \sin \theta + y \cos \theta \tag{6.37}$$

search for the minimum and maximum of α and β over all boundary points

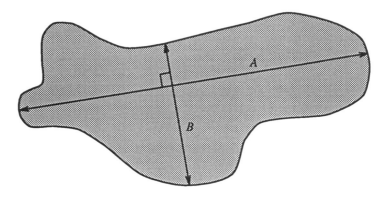

Figure 6.23 *Eccentricity.*

(x, y). The values of $\alpha_{min}, \alpha_{max}, \beta_{min}, \beta_{max}$ then define the bounding rectangle, and $l_1 = (\alpha_{max} - \alpha_{min})$ and $l_2 = (\beta_{max} - \beta_{min})$ are its length and width.

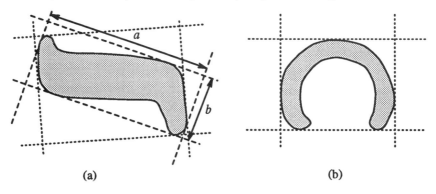

      (a)   (b)

Figure 6.24 *Elongatedness: (a) Bounding rectangle gives acceptable results, (b) bounding rectangle cannot represent elongatedness.*

Rectangularity

Let F_k be the ratio of region area and the area of a bounding rectangle, the rectangle having the direction k. The rectangle direction is turned in discrete steps as before, and **rectangularity** measured as a maximum of this ratio F_k;

$$rectangularity = \max_k(F_k) \qquad (6.38)$$

The direction need only be turned through one quadrant. Rectangularity assumes values from the interval $(0, 1]$, with 1 representing a perfectly rectangular region. Sometimes, it may be more natural to draw a bounding triangle; a method for similarity evaluation between two triangles called **sphericity** is presented in [Ansari and Delp 90].

Direction

Direction is a property which makes sense in elongated regions only. If the region is elongated, **direction** is the direction of the longer side of a minimum bounding rectangle. If the shape moments are known (Section 6.3.2), the direction θ can be computed as

$$\theta = \frac{1}{2} tan^{-1}(\frac{2\mu_{11}}{\mu_{20} - \mu_{02}}) \tag{6.39}$$

It should be noted that elongatedness and rectangularity are independent of linear transformations – translation, rotation, and scaling. Direction is independent on all linear transformations which do not include rotation. Mutual direction of two rotating objects is rotation invariant.

Compactness

Compactness is a popular shape description characteristic independent of linear transformations given by

$$compactness = \frac{(region\_border\_length)^2}{area} \tag{6.40}$$

The most compact region in a Euclidean space is a circle. Compactness assumes values in the interval $[1, \infty)$ in digital images if the boundary is defined as an inner boundary (see Section 5.2.3), while using the outer boundary, compactness assumes values in the interval $[16, \infty)$. Independence from linear transformations is gained only if an outer boundary representation is used. Examples of a compact and a non-compact region are shown in Figure 6.25.

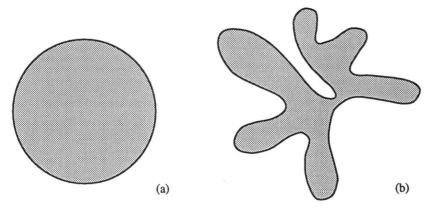

(a) (b)

Figure 6.25 *Compactness: (a) Compact, (b) non-compact.*

6.3.2 Moments

Region moment representations interpret a normalized grey level image function as a probability density of a 2D random variable. Properties of this random variable can be described using statistical characteristics – **moments** [Papoulis 91]. Moments can be used for binary or grey level region description. A moment of order $(p+q)$ is dependent on scaling, translation, rotation, and even on grey level transformations and is given by

$$m_{pq} = \int_{-\infty}^{\infty} \int_{-\infty}^{\infty} x^p y^q f(x,y) \, dx \, dy \qquad (6.41)$$

In digitized images we evaluate sums

$$m_{pq} = \sum_{i=-\infty}^{\infty} \sum_{j=-\infty}^{\infty} i^p j^q f(i,j) \qquad (6.42)$$

where x, y, i, j are the region point co-ordinates (pixel co-ordinates in digitized images). Translation invariance can be achieved if we use the central moments

$$\mu_{pq} = \int_{-\infty}^{\infty} \int_{-\infty}^{\infty} (x - x_c)^p (y - y_c)^q f(x,y) \, dx \, dy \qquad (6.43)$$

or in digitized images

$$\mu_{pq} = \sum_{i=-\infty}^{\infty} \sum_{j=-\infty}^{\infty} (i - x_c)^p (j - y_c)^q f(i,j) \qquad (6.44)$$

where x_c, y_c are the co-ordinates of the region's centre of gravity (centroid) which can be obtained using the following relationships

$$x_c = \frac{m_{10}}{m_{00}} \qquad (6.45)$$

$$y_c = \frac{m_{01}}{m_{00}}$$

In the binary case, m_{00} represents the region area (see equations (6.41) and (6.42)). Scale invariant features can also be found in scaled central moments η_{pq} (scale change $x' = \alpha x, y' = \alpha y$),

$$\eta_{pq} = \frac{\mu'_{pq}}{(\mu'_{00})^\gamma} \qquad (6.46)$$

$$\gamma = \frac{p+q}{2} + 1$$

$$\mu'_{pq} = \frac{\mu_{pq}}{\alpha^{(p+q+2)}}$$

and normalized unscaled central moments ϑ_{pq}

$$\vartheta_{pq} = \frac{\mu_{pq}}{(\mu_{00})^{\gamma}} \qquad (6.47)$$

Rotation invariance can be achieved if the co-ordinate system is chosen such that $\mu_{11} = 0$ [Cash and Hatamian 87]. Many aspects of moment properties, normalization, descriptive power, sensitivity to noise, and computational cost are discussed in [Savini 88]. A less general form of invariance was given in [Hu 62] and is discussed in [Maitra 79, Jain 89, Pratt 91], in which seven rotation, translation, and scale invariant moment characteristics were used.

$$\varphi_1 = \vartheta_{20} + \vartheta_{02} \qquad (6.48)$$

$$\varphi_2 = (\vartheta_{20} - \vartheta_{02})^2 + 4\vartheta_{11}^2 \qquad (6.49)$$

$$\varphi_3 = (\vartheta_{30} - 3\vartheta_{12})^2 + (3\vartheta_{21} - \vartheta_{03})^2 \qquad (6.50)$$

$$\varphi_4 = (\vartheta_{30} + \vartheta_{12})^2 + (\vartheta_{21} + \vartheta_{03})^2 \qquad (6.51)$$

$$\varphi_5 = (\vartheta_{30} - 3\vartheta_{12})(\vartheta_{30} + \vartheta_{12})[(\vartheta_{30} + \vartheta_{12})^2 - 3(\vartheta_{21} + \vartheta_{03})^2] + \\ (3\vartheta_{21} - \vartheta_{03})(\vartheta_{21} + \vartheta_{03})[3(\vartheta_{30} + \vartheta_{12})^2 - (\vartheta_{21} + \vartheta_{03})^2] \qquad (6.52)$$

$$\varphi_6 = (\vartheta_{20} - \vartheta_{02})[(\vartheta_{30} + \vartheta_{12})^2 - (\vartheta_{21} + \vartheta_{03})^2] + 4\vartheta_{11}(\vartheta_{30} + \vartheta_{12})(\vartheta_{21} + \vartheta_{03}) \qquad (6.53)$$

$$\varphi_7 = (3\vartheta_{21} - \vartheta_{03})(\vartheta_{30} + \vartheta_{12})[(\vartheta_{30} + \vartheta_{12})^2 - 3(\vartheta_{21} + \vartheta_{03})^2] - \\ (\vartheta_{30} - 3\vartheta_{12})(\vartheta_{21} + \vartheta_{03})[3(\vartheta_{30} + \vartheta_{12})^2 - (\vartheta_{21} + \vartheta_{03})^2] \qquad (6.54)$$

where the ϑ_{pq} values can be computed from equation (6.47).

All moment characteristics are dependent on the linear grey level transformations of regions; to describe region shape properties, we work with binary image data $(f(i, j) = 1$ in region pixels) and dependence on the linear grey level transform disappears.

Moment characteristics can be used in shape description even if the region is represented by its boundary. A closed boundary is characterized by an ordered sequence $z(i)$ that represents the Euclidean distance between the centroid and all N boundary pixels of the digitized shape. No extra processing is required for shapes having spiral or concave contours. Translation, rotation, and scale invariant one-dimensional normalized contour sequence moments $\overline{m}_r, \overline{\mu}_r$ are defined in [Gupta and Srinath 87]. The rth contour sequence moment m_r and the rth central moment μ_r can be estimated as

$$m_r = \frac{1}{N} \sum_{i=1}^{N} [z(i)]^r \qquad (6.55)$$

$$\mu_r = \frac{1}{N} \sum_{i=1}^{N} [z(i) - m_1]^r \tag{6.56}$$

The rth normalized contour sequence moment $\overline{m}_r$ and normalized central contour sequence moment $\overline{\mu}_r$ are defined as

$$\overline{m}_r = \frac{m_r}{(\mu_2)^{r/2}} = \frac{\frac{1}{N} \sum_{i=1}^{N} [z(i)]^r}{[\frac{1}{N} \sum_{i=1}^{N} [z(i) - m_1]^2]^{r/2}} \tag{6.57}$$

$$\overline{\mu}_r = \frac{\mu_r}{(\mu_2)^{r/2}} = \frac{\frac{1}{N} \sum_{i=1}^{N} [z(i) - m_1]^r}{[\frac{1}{N} \sum_{i=1}^{N} [z(i) - m_1]^2]^{r/2}} \tag{6.58}$$

While the set of invariant moments $\overline{m}_r, \overline{\mu}_r$ can be directly used for shape representation, less noise-sensitive results can be obtained from the following shape descriptors [Gupta and Srinath 87]

$$F_1 = \frac{(\mu_2)^{1/2}}{m_1} = \frac{[\frac{1}{N} \sum_{i=1}^{N} [z(i) - m_1]^2]^{1/2}}{\frac{1}{N} \sum_{i=1}^{N} z(i)} \tag{6.59}$$

$$F_2 = \frac{\mu_3}{(\mu_2)^{3/2}} = \frac{\frac{1}{N} \sum_{i=1}^{N} [z(i) - m_1]^3}{[\frac{1}{N} \sum_{i=1}^{N} [z(i) - m_1]^2]^{3/2}} \tag{6.60}$$

$$F_3 = \frac{\mu_4}{(\mu_2)^2} = \frac{\frac{1}{N} \sum_{i=1}^{N} [z(i) - m_1]^4}{[\frac{1}{N} \sum_{i=1}^{N} [z(i) - m_1]^2]^2} \tag{6.61}$$

$$F_4 = \overline{\mu}_5 \tag{6.62}$$

Lower probabilities of error classification were obtained using contour sequence moments than area based moments (equation 6.48 – 6.54) in a shape recognition test; also, contour sequence moments are less computationally demanding.

6.3.3 Convex hull

A region R is convex if and only if for any two points $x_1, x_2 \in R$, the whole line segment $x_1 x_2$ defined by its end-points x_1, x_2 is inside the region R. The convex hull of a region is the smallest convex region H which satisfies the condition $R \subset H$ – see Figure 6.26. The convex hull has some special properties in digital data which do not exist in the continuous case. For instance, concave parts can appear and disappear in digital data due to rotation, and therefore the convex hull is not rotation invariant in digital space. The convex hull can be used to describe region shape properties and can be used to build a tree structure of region concavity.

A discrete convex hull can be defined by the following algorithm which may also be used for convex hull construction. This algorithm has complexity $\mathcal{O}(n^2)$ and is presented here as an intuitive way of detecting the convex hull. A more efficient algorithm is given below.

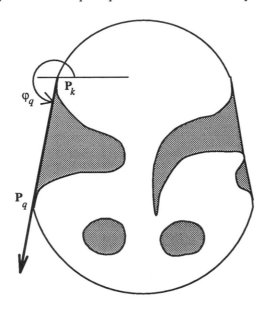

Figure 6.26 *Convex hull.*

Algorithm 6.6: Region convex hull construction

---

1. Find all pixels of a region R with the minimum row co-ordinate; among them, find the pixel P_1 with the minimum column co-ordinate.
   Assign $\mathbf{P}_k = \mathbf{P}_1$, $\mathbf{v} = (0, -1)$; the vector $\mathbf{v}$ represents the direction of the previous line segment of the convex hull.

2. Search the region boundary in an anti-clockwise direction (Algorithm 5.6) and compute the angle orientation φ_n for every boundary point $\mathbf{P}_n$ which lies after the point $\mathbf{P}_1$ (in the direction of boundary search – see Figure 6.26). The angle orientation φ_n is the angle of vector $\mathbf{P}_k\mathbf{P}_n$. The point $\mathbf{P}_q$ satisfying the condition $\varphi_q = \min_n \varphi_n$ is an element (vertex) of the region convex hull.

3. Assign $\mathbf{v} = \mathbf{P}_k\mathbf{P}_q$, $\mathbf{P}_k = \mathbf{P}_q$

4. Repeat steps (2) and (3) until $\mathbf{P}_k = \mathbf{P}_1$.

The first point $\mathbf{P}_1$ need not be chosen as described in the given algorithm, but it must be an element of a convex segment of the inner region boundary.

As has been mentioned, more efficient algorithms exist, especially if the object is defined by an ordered sequence $P = \{\mathbf{v}_1, \mathbf{v}_2, \ldots, \mathbf{v}_n\}$ of n vertices

v_i representing a polygonal boundary of the object. Many algorithms [Toussaint 85] exist for detection of the convex hull with computational complexity $\mathcal{O}(n \log n)$ in the worst case; these algorithms and their implementations vary in speed and memory requirements. As discussed in [Toussaint 91], the code of [Bhattacharya and Toussaint 83] (in which a Fortran listing appears) seems to be the fastest to date using only $5n$ storage space.

If the polygon P is a simple polygon (self-non-intersecting polygon) which is always the case in a polygonal representation of object borders, the convex hull may be found in linear time $\mathcal{O}(n)$. In the past two decades, many linear-time convex hull detection algorithms have been published, however more than half of them were later discovered to be incorrect [Toussaint 85, Toussaint 91], with counter-examples published. The algorithm of [McCallum and Avis 79] was the first correct linear-time one. The simplest correct convex hull algorithm was given in [Melkman 87] and was based on previous work [Lee 83, Bhattacharya and Gindy 84, Graham and Yao 84]. Melkman's convex hull detection algorithm is now discussed further.

Let the polygon for which the convex hull is to be determined be a simple polygon $P = \{v_1, v_2, \ldots, v_n\}$ and let the vertices be processed in this order. For any three vertices x,y,z in an ordered sequence, a directional function δ may be evaluated (Figure 6.27)

$$\begin{aligned} \delta(\mathbf{x}, \mathbf{y}, \mathbf{z}) &= 1 && \text{if } \mathbf{z} \text{ is to the right of the directed line } \mathbf{xy} \\ &= 0 && \text{if } \mathbf{z} \text{ is collinear with the directed line } \mathbf{xy} \\ &= -1 && \text{if } \mathbf{z} \text{ is to the left of the directed line } \mathbf{xy} \end{aligned}$$

The main data structure H is a list of vertices (deque) of polygonal vertices

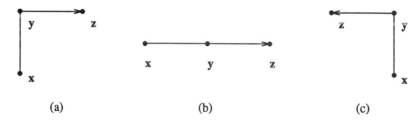

(a)   (b)   (c)

Figure 6.27 *Directional function δ: (a) $\delta(\mathbf{x}, \mathbf{y}, \mathbf{z}) = 1$, (b) $\delta(\mathbf{x}, \mathbf{y}, \mathbf{z}) = 0$, (c) $\delta(\mathbf{x}, \mathbf{y}, \mathbf{z}) = -1$.*

already processed. The current contents of H represents the convex hull of the currently processed part of the polygon, and after the detection is completed, the convex hull is stored in this data structure. Therefore, H always represents a closed polygonal curve, $H = \{d_b, \ldots, d_t\}$ where d_b points to the bottom of the list (deque) and d_t points to its top. Note that d_b and d_t always refer to the same vertex simultaneously representing the first and the last vertex of the closed polygon.

Here are the main ideas of the algorithm. The first three vertices A, B, C from the sequence P form a triangle (if not collinear) and this triangle represents a convex hull of the first three vertices – Figure 6.28a. The next vertex D in the sequence is then tested for being located inside or outside the current convex hull. If D is located inside, the current convex hull does not change – Figure 6.28b. If D is outside of the current convex hull, it must become a new convex hull vertex (Figure 6.28c) and based on the current convex hull shape, either none, one, or several vertices must be removed from the current convex hull – Figure 6.28c,d. This process is repeated for all remaining vertices in the sequence P.

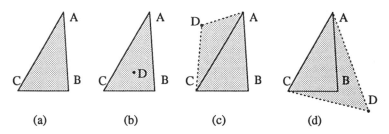

(a) (b) (c) (d)

Figure 6.28 *Convex hull detection: (a) First three vertices A, B, C form a triangle, (b) if the next vertex D is positioned inside the current convex hull ABC, current convex hull does not change, (c) if the next vertex D is outside of the current convex hull, it becomes a new vertex of the new current convex hull $ABCDA$, (d) in this case, vertex B must be removed from the current convex hull and the new current convex hull is $ADCA$.*

Following the terminology used in [Melkman 87], the variable $\mathbf{v}$ refers to the input vertex under consideration, and the following operations are defined:

```
push v      :  t := t + 1;   d_t → v
pop d_t     :  t := t - 1
insert v    :  b := b - 1;   d_b → v
remove d_b  :  b := b + 1
input v     :  next vertex is entered from sequence P, if P is empty, stop.
```

where $\rightarrow$ means 'points to'. The algorithm is then;

Algorithm 6.7: Simple polygon convex hull detection

---

1. Initialize;
   - $t := -1$;
   - $b := 0$;
   - input $\mathbf{v_1}$; input $\mathbf{v_2}$; input $\mathbf{v_3}$;
   - if ($\delta(\mathbf{v_1}, \mathbf{v_2}, \mathbf{v_3}) > 0$)

```
   .              { push v₁; push v₂; }
   .          else
   .              { push v₂; push v₁; }
   .          push v₃;
   .          insert v₃;
```

2. If the next vertex v is inside the current convex hull H, enter and check a new vertex; otherwise process steps (3) and (4);

```
   .          input v;
   .          while ( δ(v, d_b, d_{b+1}) ≥ 0    AND    δ(d_{t-1}, d_t, v) ≥ 0 )
   .          input v;
```

3. Rearrange vertices in H, top of the list.

```
   .          while ( δ(d_{t-1}, d_t, v) ≤ 0 )
   .              pop d_t;
   .          push v;
```

4. Rearrange vertices in H, bottom of the list.

```
   .          while ( δ(v, d_b, d_{b+1}) ≤ 0 )
   .              remove d_b;
   .          insert v;
   .          go to step (2);
```

The algorithm as presented may be difficult to follow, however, a less formal version would be impossible to implement; a formal proof is given in [Melkman 87]. The following example makes the algorithm more understandable.

Let $P = \{A, B, C, D, E\}$ as shown in Figure 6.29a. The data structure H is created in the first step;

$$
\begin{array}{ccccccc}
t, b \ldots & & -1 & 0 & 1 & 2 \\
H & = & C & A & B & C \\
& & d_b & & & d_t
\end{array}
$$

In the second step, vertex D is entered (Figure 6.29b);

$$
\begin{array}{rcccc}
\delta(D, d_b, d_{b+1}) & = & \delta(D, C, A) & = & 1 & > 0 \\
\delta(d_{t-1}, d_t, D) & = & \delta(B, C, D) & = & -1 & < 0
\end{array}
$$

Based on the values of the directional function δ, in this case, no other vertex is entered during this step. Step (3) results in the following current convex hull H;

$$
\delta(B, C, D) = -1 \longrightarrow \text{pop } d_t \longrightarrow
$$

$$
\begin{array}{ccccccc}
t, b \ldots & & -1 & 0 & 1 & 2 \\
H & = & C & A & B & C \\
& & d_b & & d_t
\end{array}
$$

$$\delta(A, B, D) = -1 \longrightarrow \text{pop } d_t \longrightarrow$$

$$
\begin{array}{lccccc}
t, b\ldots & & -1 & 0 & 1 & 2 \\
H & = & C & A & B & C \\
& & d_b & d_t & &
\end{array}
$$

$$\delta(C, A, D) = 1 \longrightarrow \text{push } D \longrightarrow$$

$$
\begin{array}{lccccc}
t, b\ldots & & -1 & 0 & 1 & 2 \\
H & = & C & A & D & C \\
& & d_b & & d_t &
\end{array}
$$

In step (4) – Figure 6.29c;

$$\delta(D, C, A) = 1 \longrightarrow \text{insert } D \longrightarrow$$

$$
\begin{array}{lcccccc}
t, b\ldots & & -2 & -1 & 0 & 1 & 2 \\
H & = & D & C & A & D & C \\
& & d_b & & & d_t &
\end{array}
$$

Go to step (2); vertex E is entered – Figure 6.29d;

$$
\begin{array}{lcccc}
\delta(E, D, C) & = & 1 & > & 0 \\
\delta(A, D, E) & = & 1 & > & 0
\end{array}
$$

A new vertex should be entered from P, however there is no unprocessed vertex in the sequence P and the convex hull generating process stops. The resulting convex hull is defined by the sequence $H = \{d_b, \ldots, d_t\} = \{D, C, A, D\}$ which represents a polygon $DCAD$, always in the clockwise direction – Figure 6.29e.

A **region concavity tree** is another shape representation option [Sklansky 72]. A tree is generated recursively during the construction of a convex hull. A convex hull of the whole region is constructed first, and convex hulls of concave residua are found next. The resulting convex hulls of concave residua of the regions from previous steps are searched until no concave residuum exists. The resulting tree is a shape representation of the region. Concavity tree construction can be seen in Figure 6.30.

6.3.4 Graph representation based on region skeleton

This method corresponds significantly curving points of a region boundary to graph nodes. The main disadvantage of boundary-based description methods is that geometrically close points can be far away from one another when the boundary is described – graphical representation methods overcome this disadvantage. Shape properties are then derived from the graph properties.

The region graph is based on the region skeleton, and the first step is the skeleton construction using thinning algorithms. Most thinning procedures

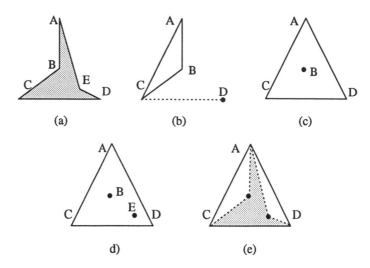

Figure 6.29 *Example of convex hull detection: (a) The processed object – polygon ABCDEA, (b) vertex D is entered and processed, (c) vertex D becomes a new vertex of the current convex hull ADC, (d) vertex E is entered and processed, E does not become a new vertex of the current convex hull, (e) the resulting convex hull DCAD.*

repeatedly remove boundary elements until a pixel set with maximum thickness of one or two is found. The following algorithm constructs a skeleton of maximum thickness two.

Algorithm 6.8: Skeleton by thinning

---

1. Let R be the set of region pixels and let $H_i(R)$ define its inner boundary, and $H_o(R)$ define its outer boundary. Let $S(R)$ be a set of pixels from the region R which have all their neighbours in 8-connectivity either from the inner boundary $H_i(R)$ or from the background – from the residuum of R. Assign $R_{old} = R$.

2. Construct a region R_{new} which is a result of one-step thinning as follows

$$R_{new} = S(R_{old}) \cup [R_{old} - H_i(R_{old})] \cup [H_o(S(R_{old})) \cap R_{old}]$$

3. If $R_{new} = R_{old}$, terminate the iteration and proceed to step (4). Otherwise assign $R_{old} = R_{new}$ and repeat step (2).

4. R_{new} is a set of skeleton pixels, the skeleton of the region R.

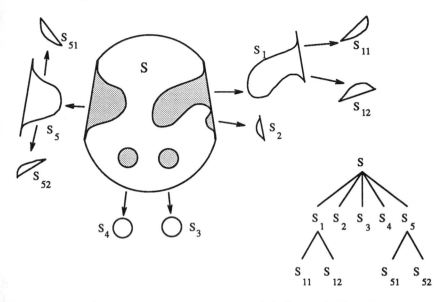

Figure 6.30 *Concavity tree construction: (a) Convex hull and concave residua, (b) concavity tree.*

Steps of this algorithm are illustrated in Figure 6.31. If there are skeleton segments which have a thickness of two in the skeleton, one extra step can be added to reduce those to a thickness of one, although care must be taken not to break the skeleton connectivity.

A large number of thinning algorithms can be found in image processing literature. If special prior conditions apply, these algorithms can be much simpler. Thinning is generally a time-consuming process, although sometimes it is not necessary to look for a skeleton, and one side of a parallel boundary can be used for skeleton-like region representation. Mathematical morphology is a powerful tool used to find the region skeleton, and thinning algorithms which use mathematical morphology are given in Chapter 10; see also [Maragos and Schafer 86] where the morphological approach is shown to unify many other approaches to skeletonization.

Thinning procedures often use a medial axis transform to construct a region skeleton [Pavlidis 77, Samet 85, Arcelli and Sanniti di Baja 86, Pizer et al. 87, Lam et al. 92]. Under the medial axis definition, the skeleton is the set of all region points which have the same minimum distance from the region boundary for at least two separate boundary points. Examples of skeletons resulting from this condition are shown in Figures 6.32 and 6.33. Every skeleton element can be accompanied by information about its distance from the boundary – this gives the potential to reconstruct a region as an envelope curve of circles with centre points at skeleton elements and radii

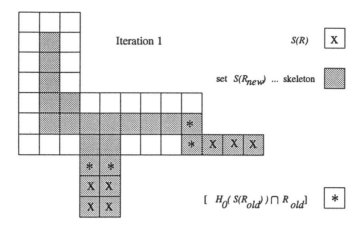

Figure 6.31 *Skeleton by thinning (Algorithm 6.8).*

corresponding to the stored distance values. Shape descriptions, as discussed in Section 6.3.1 can be derived from this skeleton but, with the exception of elongatedness, the evaluation can be difficult. In addition, this skeleton construction is time-consuming and a resulting skeleton is highly sensitive to boundary noise and errors. Small changes in the boundary may cause serious changes in the skeleton – see Figure 6.32. This sensitivity can be removed by first representing the region as a polygon, then constructing the skeleton. Boundary noise removal can be absorbed into the polygon construction. A multi-resolution (scale-space) approach to skeleton construction may also result in decreased sensitivity to boundary noise [Pizer et al. 87, Maragos 89].

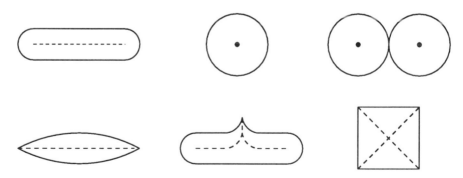

Figure 6.32 *Region skeletons; small changes in border can have a significant effect on the skeleton.*

A method of skeleton construction based on the Fourier coefficients of a boundary T_n and S_n (see Section 6.2.3) is given in [Persoon and Fu 77]. Neural networks [Krishnapuram and Chen 91] and a Voronoi diagram approach

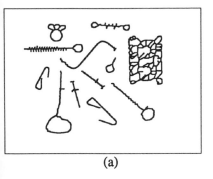 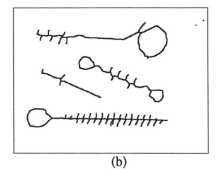

| (a) | (b) |

Figure 6.33 *Region skeletons, see Figures 5.1a and 6.2a for original images; thickened for visibility.*

[Brandt and Algazi 92, Ogniewicz and Ilg 92] can also be applied to find the skeleton. Fast parallel algorithms for thinning are given in [Guo and Hall 92].

Thinning algorithms do not result in graphs but the transformation from skeletons to graphs is relatively straightforward. Consider first the medial axis skeleton, and assume that a minimum radius circle has been drawn from each point of the skeleton which has at least one point common with a region boundary. Let *contact* be each contiguous subset of the circle which is common to the circle and to the boundary. If a circle drawn from its centre A has one contact only, A is a skeleton end-point. If the point A has two contacts, it is a normal skeleton point. If A has three or more contacts, the point A is a skeleton node-point.

Algorithm 6.9: Region graph construction from skeleton

1. Assign a point description to all skeleton points – end-point, node-point, normal-point.

2. Let graph node-points be all end-points and node-points. Connect any two graph nodes by a graph edge if they are connected by a sequence of normal-points in the region skeleton.

It can be seen that boundary points of high curvature have the main influence on the graph. They are represented by graph nodes, and therefore influence the graph structure.

If other than medial axis skeletons are used for graph construction, end-points can be defined as skeleton points having just one skeleton neighbour, normal-points as having two skeleton neighbours, and node-points as having at least three skeleton neighbours. It is no longer true that node-points are never neighbours and additional conditions must be used to decide when node-points should be represented as nodes in a graph and when they should not.

6.3.5 Region decomposition

The decomposition approach is based on the idea that shape recognition is a hierarchical process. Shape **primitives** are defined at the lower level, primitives being the simplest elements which form the region. A graph is constructed at the higher level – nodes result from primitives, arcs describe the mutual primitive relations. Convex sets of pixels are one example of simple shape primitives.

Figure 6.34 *Region decomposition: (a) Region, (b) primary regions, (c) primary subregions and kernels, (d) decomposition graph.*

The solution to the decomposition problem consists of two main steps: The first step is to segment a region into simpler subregions (primitives) and the second is the analysis of primitives. Primitives are simple enough to be successfully described using simple scalar shape properties (see Section 6.3.1). A detailed description of how to segment a region into primary convex subregions, methods of decomposition to concave vertices and graph construction resulting from a polygonal description of subregions are given in [Pavlidis 77]. The general idea of decomposition is shown in Figure 6.34 where the original region, one possible decomposition, and the resulting graph are presented. Primary convex subregions are labelled as primary subregions or kernels. Kernels (shown striped in Figure 6.34c) are subregions which belong to several primary convex subregions. If subregions are represented by polygons, graph nodes bear the following information;

1. Node type representing primary subregion or kernel.

2. Number of vertices of the subregion represented by the node.

3. Area of the subregion represented by the node.

4. Main axis direction of the subregion represented by the node.

5. Centre of gravity of the subregion represented by the node.

If a graph is derived using attributes 1-4, the final description is translation invariant. A graph derived from attributes 1-3 is translation and rotation invariant. Derivation using the first two attributes results in a description which is size invariant in addition to possessing translation and rotation invariance.

A decomposition of a region uses its structural properties, and a syntactic graph description is the result. Problems of how to decompose a region and how to construct the description graph are still open; an overview of some investigated techniques can be found in [Feng and Pavlidis 75, Moayer and Fu 75, Pavlidis 77, Stallings 76, Shapiro 80]. Shape decomposition into a complete set of convex parts ordered by size is described in [Cortopassi and Rearick 88], and a morphological approach to skeleton decomposition is used to decompose complex shapes into simple components in [Zhou and Venetsanopoulos 89, Pitas and Venetsanopoulos 90]; the decomposition is shown to be invariant to translation, rotation, and scaling. Recursive subdivision of shape based on second central moments is another translation, rotation, scaling, and intensity shift invariant decomposition technique [Zhu and Poh 88]. Hierarchical decomposition and shape description that uses region and contour information, addresses issues of local versus global information, scale, shape parts, and axial symmetry is given in [Rom and Medioni 92].

6.3.6   Region neighbourhood graphs

Any time a region decomposition into subregions or an image decomposition into regions is available, the region or image can be represented by a region neighbourhood graph (the region adjacency graph described in Section 3.2.3 being a special case). This graph represents every region as a graph node, and nodes of neighbouring regions are connected by edges. A region neighbourhood graph can be constructed from a quadtree image representation, from run-length encoded image data, etc. Binary tree shape representation is described in [Leu 89] where merging of boundary segments results in shape decomposition into triangles, their relations being represented by the binary tree.

Very often, the relative position of two regions can be used in the description process – for example, a region A may be positioned to the *left of* a region B, or *above B*, or *close to B*, or a region C may lie *between* regions A and B, etc. We know the meaning of all of the given relations if A, B, C are points, but, with the exception of the relation *to be close*, they can become ambiguous if A, B, C are regions. For instance (see Figure 6.35), the relation *to be left of* can be defined in many different ways;

- All pixels of A must be positioned to the left of all pixels of B.

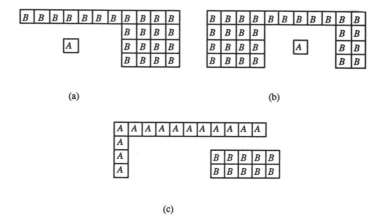

(a)

(b)

(c)

Figure 6.35 *Binary relation* to be left of; *see text.*

- At least one pixel of A must be positioned to the left of some pixel of B.

- The centre of gravity of A must be to the left of the centre of gravity of B.

All of these definitions seem to be satisfactory in many cases but they can sometimes be unacceptable because they do not meet the usual meaning of *being left of*. Human observers are generally satisfied with the definition:

- The centre of gravity of A must be positioned to the left of the leftmost point of B and (logical AND) the rightmost pixel of A must be left of the rightmost pixel of B [Winston 75].

Many other inter-regional relations are defined in [Winston 75] where relational descriptions are studied in detail.

An example of applying geometrical relations between simply shaped primitives to shape representation and recognition may be found in [Shariat 90], where recognition is based on a **hypothesize and verify** control strategy. Shapes are represented by region neighbourhood graphs that describe geometrical relations among primitive shapes. The model-based approach increases the shape recognition accuracy and makes partially occluded object recognition possible. Recognition of any new object is based on a definition of a new shape model.

References

[Ansari and Delp 90] N Ansari and E J Delp. Distribution of a deforming triangle. *Pattern Recognition*, 23(12):1333–1341, 1990.

[Appel and Haken 77] K Appel and W Haken. Every planar map is four colourable: Part I: discharging. *Illinois Journal of Mathematics*, 21:429–490, 1977.

[Arcelli and Sanniti di Baja 86] C Arcelli and G Sanniti di Baja. Endoskeleton and exoskeleton of digital figures, an effective procedure. In V Cappellini and R Marconi, editors, *Advances in Image Processing and Pattern Recognition*, pages 224–228, North Holland, Amsterdam, 1986.

[Asada and Brady 86] H Asada and M Brady. The curvature primal sketch. *IEEE Transactions on Pattern Analysis and Machine Intelligence*, 8(1):2–14, 1986.

[Atkinson et al. 85] H H Atkinson, Gargantini, I, and T R S Walsh. Counting regions, holes and their nesting level in time proportional to the border. *Computer Vision, Graphics, and Image Processing*, 29:196–215, 1985.

[Babaud et al. 86] J Babaud, A P Witkin, M Baudin, and R O Duda. Uniqueness of the Gaussian kernel for scale-space filtering. *IEEE Transactions on Pattern Analysis and Machine Intelligence*, 8(1):26–33, 1986.

[Ballard and Brown 82] D H Ballard and C M Brown. *Computer Vision*. Prentice-Hall, Englewood Cliffs, NJ, 1982.

[Barnsley 88] M F Barnsley. *Fractals Everywhere*. Academic Press, Boston, Ma, 1988.

[Bhanu and Faugeras 84] B Bhanu and O D Faugeras. Shape matching of two–dimensional objects. *IEEE Transactions on Pattern Analysis and Machine Intelligence*, 6(2):137–155, 1984.

[Bhattacharya and Gindy 84] B K Bhattacharya and H E Gindy. A new linear convex hull algorithm for simple polygons. *IEEE Transactions on Information Theory*, 30:85–88, 1984.

[Bhattacharya and Toussaint 83] B K Bhattacharya and G T Toussaint. Time-and-storage-efficient implementation of an optimal planar convex hull algorithm. *Image and Vision Computing*, 1(3):140–144, 1983.

[Brady 84] M Brady. Representing shape. In M Brady, L A Gerhardt, and H F Davidson, editors, *Robotics and Artificial Intelligence*, pages 279–300. Springer + NATO, Berlin, 1984.

[Brandt and Algazi 92] J W Brandt and V R Algazi. Continuous skeleton computation by Voronoi diagram. *CVGIP - Image Understanding*, 55(3), 1992.

[Bribiesca and Guzman 80] E Bribiesca and A Guzman. How to describe pure form and how to measure differences in shapes using shape numbers. *Pattern Recognition*, 12(2):101–112, 1980.

[Brill et al. 92] M H Brill, E B Barrett, and P M Payton. Projective invariants for curves in two and three dimensions. In J L Mundy and A Zisserman, editors, *Geometric Invariance in Computer Vision*. MIT Press, Cambridge, Ma; London, 1992.

[Cash and Hatamian 87] G L Cash and M Hatamian. Optical character recognition by the method of moments. *Computer Vision, Graphics, and Image Processing*, 39:291–310, 1987.

[Chang and Chatterjee 89] C Chang and S Chatterjee. Fractal based approach to shape description, reconstruction and classification. In *Twenty-Third Annual Asilomar Conference on Signals, Systems and Computers, Pacific Grove, Ca*, pages 172–176, IEEE, Los Alamitos, Ca, 1989.

[Chien and Aggarwal 89] C H Chien and J K Aggarwal. Model construction and shape recognition from occluding contours. *IEEE Transactions on Pattern Analysis and Machine Intelligence*, 11(4):372–389, 1989.

[Cootes et al. 92] T F Cootes, D H Cooper, C J Taylor, and J Graham. Trainable method of parametric shape description. *Image and Vision Computing*, 10(5), 1992.

[Cortopassi and Rearick 88] P P Cortopassi and T C Rearick. Computationally efficient algorithm for shape decomposition. In *Proceedings - CVPR '88: Computer Society Conference on Computer Vision and Pattern Recognition, Ann Arbor, Mi*, pages 597–601, IEEE, Los Alamitos, Ca, 1988.

[Costabile et al. 85] M F Costabile, C Guerra, and G G Pieroni. Matching shapes: A case study in time–varying images. *Computer Vision, Graphics, and Image Processing*, 29:296–310, 1985.

[Crowley 84] J L Crowley. A multiresolution representation for shape. In A Rosenfeld, editor, *Multiresolution Image Processing and Analysis*, pages 169–189. Springer Verlag, Berlin, 1984.

[DeBoor 78] C A DeBoor. *A Practical Guide to Splines*. Springer Verlag, New York, 1978.

[Duda and Hart 73] R O Duda and P E Hart. *Pattern Classification and Scene Analysis*. John Wiley and Sons, New York, 1973.

[Dyer 80] C R Dyer. Computing the Euler number of an image from its quadtree. *Computer Graphics and Image Processing*, 13:270–276, 1980.

[Eichmann et al. 90] G Eichmann, C Lu, M Jankowski, and R Tolimeiri. Shape representation by Gabor expansion. In *Hybrid Image and Signal Processing II, Orlando, Fl*, pages 86–94, Society for Optical Engineering, Bellingham, Wa, 1990.

[Falconer 90] K Falconer. *Fractal Geometry: Mathematical Foundations and Applications*. Wiley, Chichester, New York, 1990.

[Feng and Pavlidis 75] H Y Feng and T Pavlidis. Decomposition of polygons into simpler components. *IEEE Transactions on Computers*, 24:636–650, 1975.

[Fermuller and Kropatsch 92] C Fermuller and W Kropatsch. Multi-resolution shape description by corners. In *Proceedings, 1992 Computer Vision and Pattern Recognition, Champaign, Il*, pages 271–276, IEEE, Los Alamitos, Ca, 1992.

[Florack et al. 92] L M J Florack, B M Haar-Romeny, J J Koenderink, and M A Viergever. Scale and the differential structure of images. *Image and Vision Computing*, 10(6):376–388, 1992.

[Forsyth et al. 91] D Forsyth, J L Mundy, A Zisserman, C. Coelho, A. Heller, and C. Rothwell. Invariant descriptors for 3D object recognition and pose. *IEEE Transactions on Pattern Analysis and Machine Intelligence*, 13(10):971–991, 1991.

[Freeman 61] H Freeman. On the enconding of arbitrary geometric configuration. *IRE Transactions on Electronic Computers*, EC–10(2):260–268, 1961.

[Frisch et al. 87] A A Frisch, D A Evans, J P Hudson, and J Boon. Shape discrimination of sand samples using the fractal dimension. In *Coastal Sediments '87, Proceedings of a Specialty Conference on Advances in Understanding of Coastal Sediment Processes, New Orleans, LA*, pages 138–153, ASCE, Dallas, Tx, 1987.

[Fu 74] K S Fu. *Syntactic Methods in Pattern Recognition*. Academic Press, New York, 1974.

[Graham and Yao 84] R L Graham and F F Yao. Finding the convex hull of a simple polygon. *Journal of Algorithms*, 4:324–331, 1984.

[Griffin et al. 92] L D Griffin, A C F Colchester, and G P Robinson. Scale and segmentation of grey-level images using maximum gradient paths. *Image and Vision Computing*, 10(6):389–402, 1992.

[Grimmins 82] T R Grimmins. A complete set of Fourier descriptors for two–dimensional shapes. *IEEE Transactions on Systems, Man and Cybernetics*, 12(6):923–927, 1982.

[Guo and Hall 92] Z Guo and R W Hall. Fast fully parallel thinning algorithms. *CVGIP – Image Understanding*, 55(3):317–328, 1992.

[Gupta and Srinath 87] L Gupta and M D Srinath. Contour sequence moments for the classification of closed planar shapes. *Pattern Recognition*, 20(3):267–272, 1987.

[Gupta et al. 90] L Gupta, M R Sayeh, and R Tammana. Neural network approach to robust shape classification. *Pattern Recognition*, 23(6):563–568, 1990.

[Hopcroft et al. 92] J E Hopcroft, D P Huttenlocher, and P C Wayner. Affine invariants for model-based recognition. In J L Mundy and A Zisserman, editors, *Geometric Invariance in Computer Vision*. MIT Press, Cambridge, Ma; London, 1992.

[Hu 62] M K Hu. Visual pattern recognition by moment invariants. *IRE Transactions Information Theory*, 8(2):179–187, 1962.

[Ikebe and Miyamoto 82] Y Ikebe and S Miyamoto. Shape design, representation, and restoration with splines. In K S Fu and H Kunii, editors, *Picture Engineering*. Springer Verlag, Berlin, 1982.

[Jain 89] A K Jain. *Fundamentals of Digital Image Processing*. Prentice-Hall, Englewood Cliffs, NJ, 1989.

[Jakubowski 85] R Jakubowski. Extraction of shape features for syntactic recognition of mechanical parts. *IEEE Transactions on Systems, Man and Cybernetics*, 15(5):642–651, 1985.

[Jakubowski 90] R Jakubowski. Decomposition of complex shapes for their structural recognition. *Information Sciences*, 50(1):35–71, 1990.

[Juday 88] R D Juday, editor. *Digital and Optical Shape Representation and Pattern Recognition, Orlando, Fl*, Bellingham, Wa, 1988. SPIE.

[Kanatani 90] K Kanatani. *Group-Theoretical Methods in Image Understanding*. Springer Verlag, Berlin, 1990.

[Kiryati and Maydan 89] N Kiryati and D Maydan. Calculating geometric properties from Foutier representation. *Pattern Recognition*, 22(5):469–475, 1989.

[Koch and Kashyap 87] M W Koch and R L Kashyap. Using polygons to recognize and locate partially occluded objects. *IEEE Transactions on Pattern Analysis and Machine Intelligence*, 9(4):483–494, 1987.

[Koenderink and van Doorn 86] J J Koenderink and A J van Doorn. Dynamic shape. Technical report, Dept. Medical and Physiological Physics, State University, Utrecht, The Netherlands, 1986.

[Krishnapuram and Chen 91] R Krishnapuram and L F Chen. Iterative neural networks for skeletonization and thinning. In *Intelligent Robots and Computer Vision IX: Neural, Biological, and 3D Methods, Boston, Ma*, pages 271–281, Soc for Optical Engineering, Bellingham, Wa, 1991.

[Krzyzak et al. 89] A Krzyzak, S Y Leung, and C Y Suen. Reconstruction of two-dimensional patterns from Fourier descriptors. *Machine Vision and Applications*, 2(3):123–140, 1989.

[Lam et al. 92] L Lam, S W Lee, and C Y Suen. Thinning methodologies - a comprehensive survey. *IEEE Transactions on Pattern Analysis and Machine Intelligence*, 14(9):869–885, 1992.

[Lee 83] D T Lec. On finding the convex hull of a simple polygon. *International Journal of Computer and Information Sciences*, 12:87–98, 1983.

[Leu 89] J G Leu. View-independent shape representation and matching. In *IEEE International Conference on Systems Engineering, Fairborn, Oh*, pages 601–604, IEEE, Piscataway, NJ, 1989.

[Leymarie and Levine 89] F Leymarie and M D Levine. Shape features using curvature morphology. In *Visual Communications and Image Processing IV, Philadelphia, Pa*, pages 390–401, SPIE, Bellingham, Wa, 1989.

[Li and Zhiying 88] X Li and Z Zhiying. Group direction difference chain codes for the representation of the border. In *Digital and Optical Shape Representation and Pattern Recognition, Orlando, Fl*, pages 372–376, SPIE, Bellingham, Wa, 1988.

[Lin and Chellappa 87] C C Lin and R Chellappa. Classification of partial 2D shapes using Fourier descriptors. *IEEE Transactions on Pattern Analysis and Machine Intelligence*, 9(5):686–690, 1987.

[Lipari and Harlow 88] C Lipari and C A Harlow. Representation and recognition of elongated regions in aerial images. In *Applications of Artificial Intelligence VI, Orlando, Fl*, pages 557–567, SPIE, Bellingham, Wa, 1988.

[Lord and Wilson 84] E A Lord and C B Wilson. *The Mathematical Description of Shape and Form*. Halsted Press, Chichester, UK, 1984.

[Loui et al. 90] A C P Loui, A N Venetsanopoulos, and K C Smith. Two-dimensional shape representation using morphological correlation functions. In *Proceedings of the 1990 International Conference on Acoustics, Speech, and Signal Processing - ICASSP 90, Albuquerque, NM*, pages 2165–2168, IEEE, Piscataway, NJ, 1990.

[Maitra 79] S Maitra. Moment invariants. *Proceedings IEEE*, 67(4):697–699, 1979.

[Mandelbrot 83] B B Mandelbrot. *The Fractal Geometry of Nature*. Freeman, New York, 1983.

[Maragos 89] P Maragos. Pattern spectrum and multiscale shape representation. *IEEE Transactions on Pattern Analysis and Machine Intelligence*, 11:701–716, 1989.

[Maragos and Schafer 86] P A Maragos and R W Schafer. Morphological skeleton representation and coding of binary images. *IEEE Transactions on Acoustics, Speech and Signal Processing*, 34(5):1228–1244, 1986.

[Marshall 89a] S Marshall. Application of image contours to three aspects of image processing; compression, shape recognition and stereopsis. In *Third International Conference on Image Processing and its Applications, Coventry, England*, pages 604–608, IEE, Michael Faraday House, Stevenage, England, 1989.

[Marshall 89b] S Marshall. Review of shape coding techniques. *Image and Vision Computing*, 7(4):281–194, 1989.

[Maybank 92] S J Maybank. The projection of two non-coplanar conics. In J L Mundy and A Zisserman, editors, *Geometric Invariance in Computer Vision*. MIT Press, Cambridge, Ma; London, 1992.

[McCallum and Avis 79] D McCallum and D Avis. A linear algorithm for finding the convex hull of a simple polygon. *Information Processing Letters*, 9:201–206, 1979.

[McKenzie and Protheroe 90] D S McKenzie and S R Protheroe. Curve description using the inverse Hough transform. *Pattern Recognition*, 23(3-4):283–290, 1990.

[Melkman 87] A V Melkman. On-line construction of the convex hull of a simple polyline. *Information Processing Letters*, 25(1):11–12, 1987.

[Minnix et al. 90] J I Minnix, E S McVey, and R M Inigo. Multistaged neural network architecture for position invariant shape recognition. In *Visual Communications and Image Processing '90, Lausanne, Switzerland*, pages 58–68, SPIE, Bellingham, Wa, 1990.

[Moayer and Fu 75] B Moayer and K S Fu. A tree system approach for fingerprint pattern recognition. *IEEE Transactions on Computers*, 24(4):436–450, 1975.

[Mundy and Zisserman 92] J L Mundy and A Zisserman. *Geometric Invariance in Computer Vision*. MIT Press, Cambridge, Ma; London, 1992.

[Nagao and Matsuyama 80] M Nagao and T Matsuyama. *A Structural Analysis of Complex Aerial Photographs*. Plenum Press, New York, 1980.

[Nishizeki and Chiba 88] T Nishizeki and N Chiba. *Planar Graphs: Theory and Algorithms*. North Holland, Amsterdam-New York-Tokyo, 1988.

[Ogniewicz and Ilg 92] R Ogniewicz and M Ilg. Voronoi skeletons: Theory and applications. In *Proceedings, 1992 Computer Vision and Pattern Recognition, Champaign, Il*, pages 63–69, IEEE, Los Alamitos, Ca, 1992.

[Oppenheim et al. 83] A V Oppenheim, A S Willsky, and I T Young. *Signals and Systems*. Prentice-Hall, Englewood Cliffs, NJ, 1983.

[Paglieroni and Jain 88] D W Paglieroni and A K Jain. Control point transforms for shape representation and measurement. *Computer Vision, Graphics, and Image Processing*, 42(1):87–111, 1988.

[Papoulis 91] A Papoulis. *Probability, Random Variables, and Stochastic Processes*. McGraw Hill, New York, 3rd edition, 1991.

[Pavlidis 77] T Pavlidis. *Structural Pattern Recognition*. Springer Verlag, Berlin, 1977.

[Pavlidis 78] T Pavlidis. A review of algorithms for shape analysis. *Computer Graphics and Image Processing*, 7:243–258, 1978.

[Pavlidis 80] T Pavlidis. Algorithms for shape analysis of contours and waveforms. *IEEE Transactions on Pattern Analysis and Machine Intelligence*, 2(4):301–312, 1980.

[Persoon and Fu 77] E Persoon and K S Fu. Shape discrimination using Fourier descriptors. *IEEE Transactions on Systems, Man and Cybernetics*, 7:170–179, 1977.

[Pitas and Venetsanopoulos 90] I Pitas and A N Venetsanopoulos. Morphological shape decomposition. *IEEE Transactions on Pattern Analysis and Machine Intelligence*, 12(1):38–45, 1990.

[Pizer et al. 87] S M Pizer, W R Oliver, and S H Bloomberg. Hierarchical shape description via the multiresolution symmetric axis transform. *IEEE Transactions on Pattern Analysis and Machine Intelligence*, 9(4):505–511, 1987.

[Pratt 91] W K Pratt. *Digital Image Processing*. John Wiley and Sons, New York, 2nd edition, 1991.

[Quan et al. 92] L Quan, P Gros, and R Mohr. Invariants of a pair of conics revisited. *Image and Vision Computing*, 10(5):319–323, 1992.

[Rom and Medioni 92] H Rom and G Medioni. Hierarchical decomposition and axial shape description. In *Proceedings, 1992 Computer Vision and Pattern Recognition, Champaign, Il*, pages 49–55, IEEE, Los Alamitos, Ca, 1992.

[Rosenfeld 74] A Rosenfeld. Digital straight line segments. *IEEE Transactions on Computers*, 23:1264–1269, 1974.

[Rosenfeld 79] A Rosenfeld. *Picture Languages – Formal Models for Picture Recognition*. Academic Press, New York, 1979.

[Rosenfeld and Kak 82] A Rosenfeld and A C Kak. *Digital Picture Processing*. Academic Press, New York, 2nd edition, 1982.

[Rosin and West 89] P L Rosin and G A W West. Segmentation of edges into lines and arcs. *Image and Vision Computing*, 7(2):109–114, 1989.

[Rothwell et al. 92a] C A Rothwell, A Zisserman, D A Forsyth, and J L Mundy. Fast recognition using algebraic invariants. In J L Mundy and A Zisserman, editors, *Geometric Invariance in Computer Vision*. MIT Press, Cambridge, Ma; London, 1992.

[Rothwell et al. 92b] C A Rothwell, A Zisserman, J L Mundy, and D A Forsyth. Efficient model library access by projectively invariant indexing functions. In *Proceedings, 1992 Computer Vision and Pattern Recognition, Champaign, Il*, pages 109–114, IEEE, Los Alamitos, Ca, 1992.

[Saaty and Kainen 77] T L Saaty and P C Kainen. *The Four Colour Problem.* McGraw Hill, New York, 1977.

[Safaee-Rad et al. 89] R Safaee-Rad, B Benhabib, K C Smith, and K M Ty. Position, rotation, and scale-invariant recognition of 2 dimensional objects using a gradient coding scheme. In *IEEE Pacific RIM Conference on Communications, Computers and Signal Processing, Victoria, BC, Canada*, pages 306–311, IEEE, Piscataway, NJ, 1989.

[Samet 81] H Samet. Computing perimeters of images represented by quadtrees. *IEEE Transactions on Pattern Analysis and Machine Intelligence*, 3:683–687, 1981.

[Samet 84] H Samet. A tutorial on quadtree research. In A Rosenfeld, editor, *Multiresolution Image Processing and Analysis*, pages 212–223. Springer Verlag, Berlin, 1984.

[Samet 85] H Samet. Reconstruction of quadtree medial axis transforms. *Computer Vision, Graphics, and Image Processing*, 29:311–328, 1985.

[Saund 90] E Saund. Symbolic construction of a 2D scale-space image. *IEEE Transactions on Pattern Analysis and Machine Intelligence*, 12:817–830, 1990.

[Savini 88] M Savini. Moments in image analysis. *Alta Frequenza*, 57(2):145–152, 1988.

[Shapiro 80] L Shapiro. A structural model of shape. *IEEE Transactions on Pattern Analysis and Machine Intelligence*, 2(2):111–126, 1980.

[Shariat 90] H Shariat. A model-based method for object recognition. In *IEEE International Conference on Robotics and Automation, Cincinnati, Oh*, pages 1846–1851, IEEE, Los Alamitos, Ca, 1990.

[Shridhar and Badreldin 84] M Shridhar and A Badreldin. High accuracy character recognition algorithms using Fourier and topological descriptors. *Pattern Recognition*, 17(5):515–524, 1984.

[Sklansky 72] J Sklansky. Measuring concavity on a rectangular mosaic. *IEEE Transactions on Computers*, 21(12):1355–1364, 1972.

[Smeulders et al. 80] A W M Smeulders, A M Vossepoel, J Vrolijk, J S Ploem, and C J Cornelisse. Some shape parameters for cell recognition. In *Proceedings of Pattern Recognition in Practice*, pages 131–142, North Holland, Amsterdam, 1980.

[Smith and Jain 82] S Smith and A Jain. Cord distribution for shape matching. *Computer Graphics and Image Processing*, 20:259–265, 1982.

[Staib and Duncan 92] L H Staib and J S Duncan. Boundary finding with parametrically deformable models. *IEEE Transactions on Pattern Analysis and Machine Intelligence*, 14(11):1061–1075, 1992.

[Stallings 76] W Stallings. Approaches to Chinese character recognition. *Pattern Recognition*, 8(1):87–98, 1976.

[Strackee and Nagelkerke 83] J Strackee and N J D Nagelkerke. On closing the Fourier descriptor presentation. *IEEE Transactions on Pattern Analysis and Machine Intelligence*, 5(6):660–661, 1983.

[Tampi and Sridhar 90] K R Tampi and C S Sridhar. Shape detection using word like image description. In *Proceedings of the 1990 International Conference on Acoustics, Speech, and Signal Processing - ICASSP 90 Albuquerque, NM*, pages 2041–2043, IEEE, Piscataway, NJ, 1990.

[Tomek 74] I Tomek. Two algorithms for piecewise linear continuous approximation of functions of one variable. *IEEE Transactions on Computers*, 23(4):445–448, 1974.

[Toussaint 85] G Toussaint. A historical note on convex hull finding algorithms. *Pattern Recognition Letters*, 3(1):21–28, 1985.

[Toussaint 91] G Toussaint. A counter-example to a convex hull algorithm for polygons. *Pattern Recognition*, 24(2):183–184, 1991.

[Tsai and Yu 85] W H Tsai and S S Yu. Attributed string matching with merging for shape recognition. *IEEE Transactions on Pattern Analysis and Machine Intelligence*, 7(4):453–462, 1985.

[Turney et al. 85] J L Turney, T N Mudge, and R A Volz. Recognizing partially occluded parts. *IEEE Transactions on Pattern Analysis and Machine Intelligence*, 7(4):410–421, 1985.

[Van Gool et al. 92] L J Van Gool, T Moons, E. Pauwels, and A. Oosterlinck. Semi-differential invariants. In J L Mundy and A Zisserman, editors, *Geometric Invariance in Computer Vision*. MIT Press, Cambridge, Ma; London, 1992.

[Vernon 87] D Vernon. Two-dimensional object recognition using partial contours. *Image and Vision Computing*, 5(1):21–27, 1987.

[Wallace 81] T P Wallace. Comments on algorithms for shape analysis of contours and waveforms. *IEEE Transactions on Pattern Analysis and Machine Intelligence*, 3(5), 1981.

[Wallace and Wintz 80] T P Wallace and P A Wintz. An efficient three-dimensional aircraft recognition algorithm using normalized Fourier descriptors. *Computer Graphics and Image Processing*, 13:99–126, 1980.

[Weiss 88] I Weiss. Projective invariants of shapes. In *Proceedings of Image Understanding Workshop*, volume 2, pages 1125–1134, Cambridge, Ma, 1988.

[Weiss 92] I Weiss. Noise resistant projective and affine invariants. In *Proceedings, 1992 Computer Vision and Pattern Recognition, Champaign, Il*, pages 115–121, IEEE, Los Alamitos, Ca, 1992.

[Weyl 46] H Weyl. *The Classical Groups and Their Invariants*. Princeton University Press, Princeton, NJ, 1946.

[Wilson and Nelson 90] R Wilson and R Nelson. *Graph Colourings*. Longman Scientific and Technical; Wiley, Essex, England and New York, 1990.

[Winston 75] P H Winston, editor. *The Psychology of Computer Vision*. McGraw Hill, New York, 1975.

[Witkin 86] A P Witkin. Scale space filtering. In A P Pentland, editor, *From Pixels to Predicates*, pages 5–19. Ablex Publishing Corporation, Norwood, NJ, 1986.

[Woodwark 86] J Woodwark. *Computing Shape: An Introduction to the Representation of Component and Assembly Geometry for Computer-Aided Engineering*. Butterworths, London-Boston, 1986.

[Wuescher and Boyer 91] D M Wuescher and K L Boyer. Robust contour decomposition using a constant curvature criterion. *IEEE Transactions on Pattern Analysis and Machine Intelligence*, 13(10):41–51, 1991.

[Yuille and Poggio 86] A L Yuille and T A Poggio. Scaling theorems for zero-crossings. *IEEE Transactions on Pattern Analysis and Machine Intelligence*, 8(1):15–25, 1986.

[Zhou and Venetsanopoulos 89] Z Zhou and A N Venetsanopoulos. Generic ribbons: A morphological approach towards natural shape decomposition. In *Visual Communications and Image Processing IV, Philadelphia, Pa*, pages 170–180, Soc for Optical Engineering, Bellingham, Wa, 1989.

[Zhu and Poh 88] Q Zhu and L Poh. Transformation-invariant recursive subdivision method for shape analysis. In *9th International Conference on Pattern Recognition, Rome, Italy*, pages 833–835, IEEE, New York, 1988.

7

Object recognition

Even the simplest machine vision tasks cannot be solved without the help of recognition. Pattern recognition is used for region and object classification, and basic methods of pattern recognition must be understood in order to study more complex machine vision processes.

It has been mentioned several times that objects or regions are classified; recognition is then the last step of the bottom-up image processing approach. It is also often used in other control strategies for image understanding. Almost always when information about an object or region class is available, some pattern recognition method is used.

Consider a simple recognition problem. Two different parties take place at the same hotel at the same time – the first is a celebration of a successful basketball season, and the second a yearly meeting of jockeys. The doorman is giving directions to guests, asking which party they are to attend. After a while the doorman discovers that no questions are necessary and he directs the guests to the right places, noticing that instead of questions, he can just use the obvious physical features of basketball players and jockeys. Maybe he uses two features to make a decision, the weight and the height of the guests. All small and light men are directed to the jockey party, all tall and heavier guests are sent to the basketball party. Representing this example in terms of recognition theory, the early guests answered the doorman's question as to which party they are going to visit. This information, together with characteristic features of these guests, resulted in the ability of the doorman to classify them based only on their features. Plotting the guests' height and weight in a two-dimensional space (see Figure 7.1), it is clearly visible that jockeys and basketball players form two easily separable classes and that this recognition task is extremely simple. Although real object recognition problems are often more difficult, and the classes do not differ so substantially, the main principles remain the same.

The theory of pattern recognition is fully discussed in several references [Fu 82, Devijver and Kittler 82, Oja 83, Devijver and Kittler 86, Patrick and Fattu 86, Pavel 89, Fukunaga 90, Dasarathy 91], and here only a brief introduction will be given. In addition, we will introduce some other related techniques: graph matching, neural nets, genetic algorithms, and simulated annealing.

No recognition is possible without knowledge. Decisions about classes or

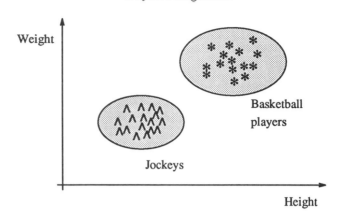

Figure 7.1 *Recognition of basketball players and jockeys; features are weight and height.*

groups into which recognized objects are classified are based on such knowledge – knowledge about objects and their classes gives the necessary information for object classification. Both specific knowledge about the processed objects and hierarchically higher and more general knowledge about object classes is required. First, common knowledge representation techniques will be introduced because the concept of knowledge representation in suitable form for a computer may not be straightforward.

7.1 Knowledge representation

Knowledge as well as knowledge representation problems are studied in AI, and computer vision takes advantage of these results. Use of AI methods is very common in higher processing levels and a study of AI is necessary for a full appreciation of computer vision and image understanding. Here we present a short outline of common techniques as they are used in AI, and an overview of some basic knowledge representations. More detailed coverage of knowledge representation can be found in [Michalski et al. 83, Winston 84, Simons 84, Devijver and Kittler 86, Wechsler 90, Reichgelt 91].

Experience shows that a good knowledge representation design is the most important part of solving the understanding problem. Moreover, a small number of relatively simple control strategies is often sufficient for AI systems to show complex behaviour, assuming an appropriately complex knowledge base is available. In other words, a high degree of control sophistication is not required for intelligent behaviour, but a rich, well structured representation of a large set of a priori data and hypotheses is needed [Schutzer 87].

Other terms of which regular use will be made are **syntax** and **semantics** [Winston 84].

- The **syntax** of a representation specifies the symbols that may be used and the ways that they may be arranged.

- The **semantics** of a representation specifies how meaning is embodied in the symbols and the symbol arrangement allowed by the syntax.

- A **representation** is a set of syntactic and semantic conventions that make it possible to describe things.

The main knowledge representation techniques used in AI are: Formal grammars and languages, predicate logic, production rules, semantic nets and frames. Even if features and descriptions are not usually considered knowledge representations, they are added for practical reasons; these low-level forms of knowledge representation will be mentioned many times throughout the coming sections.

Note that knowledge representation data structures are mostly extensions of conventional data structures like lists, trees, graphs, tables, hierarchies, sets, rings, nets and matrices.

Descriptions, features

Descriptions and features cannot be considered pure knowledge representations. Nevertheless, they can be used for representing knowledge as a part of a more complex representation structure.

Descriptions usually represent some scalar properties of objects, and are called features. Typically, a single description is insufficient for object representation, therefore the descriptions are combined into **feature vectors**. Numerical feature vectors are inputs for statistical pattern recognition techniques (see Section 7.2).

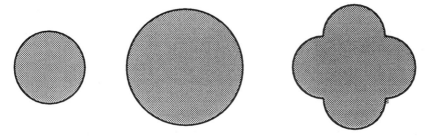

Figure 7.2 *Feature description of simple objects.*

A simple example of feature description of objects is shown in Figure 7.2. The *size* feature can be used to represent an area property and the *compactness* feature describes circularity (see Section 6.3.1). Then the feature vector $\mathbf{x} = (size, compactness)$ can be used for object classification into the following classes of objects: small, large, circular, noncircular, small and circular, small and noncircular, etc. assuming information about what is considered small/large and circular/noncircular is available.

Grammars, languages

If an object's structure needs to be described, feature description is not appropriate. A structural description is formed from existing primitives and the relations between them.

Primitives are represented by information about their types. The simplest form of structure representations are chains, trees and general graphs. Structural description of chromosomes using border segments as primitives is a classic example of structural object description [Fu 82] (see Figure 6.14), where borders are represented by a chain of symbols, the symbols representing specific types of border primitives. Hierarchical structures can be represented by trees – the concavity tree of Figure 6.30 serves as an example. A more general graph representation is used in Chapter 13 where a graph grammar (Figure 13.6) is used for texture description. Many examples of syntactic object description may be found in [Fu 74, Fu 77, Fu 80, Fu 82].

One object can be described by a chain, a tree, a graph, etc. of symbols. Nevertheless, the whole class of objects cannot be described by a single chain, a single tree, etc., but a class of structurally described objects can be represented by **grammars** and **languages**. Grammars and languages (similar to natural languages) provide rules defining how the chains, trees or graphs can be constructed from a set of symbols (primitives). A more specific description of grammars and languages is given in Section 7.4.

Predicate logic

Predicate logic plays a very important role in knowledge representation – it introduces a mathematical formalism to derive new knowledge from old knowledge by applying mathematical deduction. Predicate logic works with combinations of logic variables, quantifiers ($\exists, \forall$), and logic operators (*and, or, not, implies, equivalent*). The logic variables are binary (*true, false*). The idea of proof and rules of inference such as **modus ponens** and **resolution** are the main building blocks of predicate logic [Pospesel 76].

Predicate logic forms the essence of the programming language PROLOG that is widely used if objects are described by logic variables. Requirements of 'pure truth' represent the main weakness of predicate logic in knowledge representation since it does not allow work with uncertain or incomplete information. Predicate logic incorporates logic conditions and constraints into knowledge processing (see Section 8.4), [Hayes 77, Kowalski 79, Clocksin and Mellish 81].

Production rules

Production rules represent a wide variety of knowledge representations that are based on **condition-action** pairs. The essential model of behaviour of a system based on production rules (a production system) can be described as follows:

if condition X holds *then* action Y is appropriate

It can be seen that information about what action is appropriate at what time represents knowledge. The procedural character of knowledge represented by production rules is another important property – not all the information about objects must be listed as an object property. Consider a simple knowledge base where the following knowledge is present

$$if \quad \text{ball} \quad then \quad \text{circular} \tag{7.1}$$

Let the knowledge base also include the statements

$$
\begin{array}{lll}
\text{object A} & is\_a & \text{ball} \\
\text{object B} & is\_a & \text{ball} \\
\text{object C} & is\_a & \text{shoe} \\
& \text{etc.} &
\end{array} \tag{7.2}
$$

To answer the question *how many objects are circular?*, if enumerative knowledge representation is used, the knowledge must be listed as

object A *is_a* (ball, circular)
object B *is_a* (ball, circular)
etc.

If procedural knowledge is used, the knowledge base (7.2) together with the knowledge (7.1) gives the same information in a significantly more efficient manner.

Both production rule knowledge representation and production systems appear frequently in computer vision and image understanding problems. Furthermore, production systems together with a mechanism for handling uncertainty information, form a basis of expert systems.

Semantic nets

Semantic nets are a special variation of relational data structures (see Chapter 3). The semantics distinguish them from general nets – semantic nets consist of objects, their description, and a description of relations between objects (often just relations between neighbours). Logical forms of knowledge can be included in semantic nets, and predicate logic can be used to represent and/or evaluate the local information and local knowledge. Semantic nets can also represent common sense knowledge that is often imprecise and needs to be treated in a probabilistic way. Semantic nets have a hierarchical structure; complex representations consist of less complex representations, which can in turn be divided into simpler ones, etc. Relations between partial representations are described at all appropriate hierarchical levels.

Evaluated graphs are used as a semantic net data structure; nodes represent objects and arcs represent relations between objects. The following definition of a human face is an example of a simple semantic net:

- A *face* is a part of the human body that consists of two eyes, one nose, and one mouth.

- One eye is positioned left of the other eye.

- The nose is between and below the eyes.

- The mouth is below the nose.

- An eye is approximately circular.

- The nose is vertically elongated.

- The mouth is horizontally elongated.

The semantic net representing this knowledge is shown in Figure 7.3.

It is clear that the descriptive structures found in real images match the knowledge represented by a semantic net with varying degrees of closeness. The question of whether the described structure is similar to that represented by the semantic net is discussed in Section 7.5 and in Chapter 8.

A detailed discussion of semantic nets related to image information can be found in [Niemann 90], and more general properties of semantic nets are described in [Michalski et al. 83, Sharples et al. 89].

Frames, scripts

Frames provide a very general method for knowledge representation which may contain all the knowledge representation principles discussed so far. They are sometimes called **scripts** because of their similarity to film scripts. Frames are suitable for representing common sense knowledge under specific circumstances. Consider a frame called *plane_start*; this frame may consist of the following sequence of actions:

1. Start the engines

2. Taxi to the runway

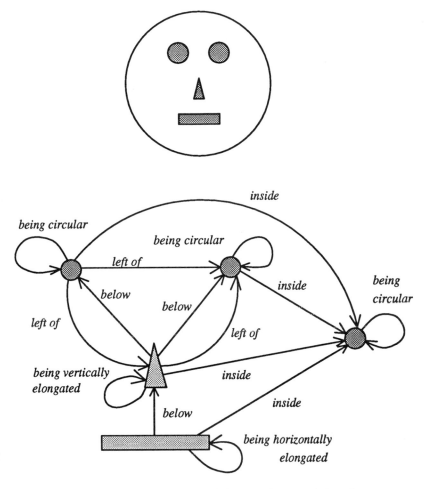

Figure 7.3 *Semantic nets: A human face model and its net.*

3. Increase RPMs of engines to maximum

4. Travel along runway increasing speed

5. Fly

Assuming this frame represents knowledge of how planes *usually* start, the situation of a plane standing on a runway with engines running causes the prediction that the plane will start in a short time. The frame can be used as a substitute for missing information which may be extremely important in vision-related problems.

Assuming that one part of the runway is not visible from the observation point, using the *plane_start* frame, a computer vision system can overcome the lack of continuous information between the plane moving at the beginning of the runway and flying when it next appears. If it is a passenger plane, the frame may have additional items like *time of departure, time of arrival, departure city, arrival city, airline, flight number, etc.* because in a majority of cases it makes sense to be interested in this information if we identify a starting passenger plane.

From a formal point of view, a frame is represented by a general semantic net accompanied by a list of relevant variables, concepts, and concatenation of situations. No standard form of frame exists. Frames represent a tool for organizing knowledge in prototypical objects, and for description of mutual influences of objects using stereotypes of behaviour in specific situations. Examples of frames can be found elsewhere [Michalski et al. 83, Winston 84, Schutzer 87, Sharples et al. 89]. Frames are considered high-level knowledge representations.

7.2 Statistical pattern recognition

An object is a physical unit, usually represented in an segmented image by a region in image analysis and computer vision. The set of objects can be divided into disjoint subsets, that, from the classification point of view, have some common features and are called **classes**. The definition of how the objects are divided into classes is ambiguous and depends on the classification goal.

Object recognition is based on assigning classes to objects and the device that does these assignments is called the **classifier**. The number of classes is usually known beforehand, and typically can be derived from the problem specification. Nevertheless, there are approaches in which the number of classes may not be known (see Section 7.2.4).

The classifier (similarly to a human) does not decide about the class from the object itself – rather, sensed object properties are used to serve this purpose. For example, to distinguish steel from sandstone, we do not have to determine their molecular structures, although this would describe these materials well. Properties like texture, specific weight, hardness, etc. are used instead. This sensed object is called the **pattern**, and the classifier does not actually recognize objects, but recognizes their patterns. Object recognition and pattern recognition are considered synonymous.

The main pattern recognition steps are shown in Figure 7.4. The block 'Construction of formal description' cannot be formally described as this stage of the recognition system design is based on the experience and intuition of the designer. A set of elementary properties is chosen which describe some characteristics of the object; these properties are measured in an appropriate way, and form the description pattern of the object. These properties can be either quantitative or qualitative in character and their form can vary (numerical vectors, chains, etc.). The theory of recognition deals with the problem of designing the classifier for the specific (chosen) set of elementary object descriptions.

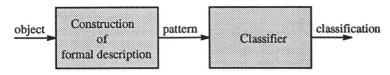

Figure 7.4 *Main pattern recognition steps.*

Statistical object description uses elementary numerical descriptions called **features**, $x_1, x_2, \ldots, x_n$; in image analysis, the features result from object description as discussed in Chapter 6. The pattern (also referred to as pattern vector, or feature vector) $\mathbf{x} = (x_1, x_2, \ldots, x_n)$ that describes an object is a vector of elementary descriptions, and the set of all possible patterns forms the **pattern space** X (also called **feature space**). If the elementary descriptions were appropriately chosen, similarity of objects in each class results in the proximity of their patterns in pattern space. The classes form clusters in the feature space, which can be separated by a discrimination curve (or hypersurface in a multi-dimensional feature space) – see Figure 7.5.

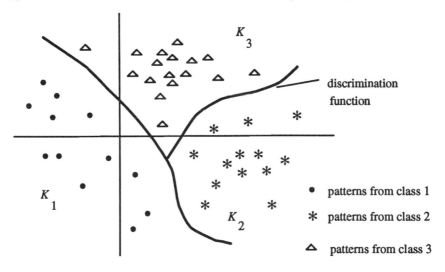

Figure 7.5 *General discrimination functions.*

If a discrimination hypersurface exists which separates the feature space such that only objects from one class are in each separated region, the problem is called a recognition task with **separable classes**. If the discrimination hypersurfaces are hyperplanes, it is called a **linearly separable** task. If the task has separable classes, each pattern will represent only objects from one class. Intuitively, we may expect that separable classes can be recognized without errors.

The majority of object recognition problems do not have separable classes in which case the locations of the discrimination hypersurfaces in the feature space can never separate the classes correctly and some objects will always be misclassified.

7.2.1   Classification principles

A statistical classifier is a device with n inputs and 1 output. Each input is used to enter the information about one of n features $x_1, x_2, \ldots, x_n$ that are measured from a classified object. An R class classifier will generate one of R symbols $\omega_1, \omega_2, \ldots, \omega_R$ as an output, and the user interprets this output as a decision about the class of the processed object. The generated symbols ω_r are the **class identifiers**.

The function $d(\mathbf{x}) = \omega_r$ describes relations between the classifier inputs and the output; this function is called the **decision rule**. The decision rule divides the feature space into R disjoint subsets K_r, $r = 1, \ldots, R$ each of which includes all the feature representation vectors $\mathbf{x}$ of objects for which the $d(\mathbf{x}) = \omega_r$. The borders between subsets K_r, $r = 1, \ldots, R$ form the discrimination hypersurfaces mentioned earlier. The determination of discrimination hypersurfaces (or definition of the decision rule) is the goal of classifier design.

The discrimination hypersurfaces can be defined by R scalar functions $g_1(\mathbf{x})$, $g_2(\mathbf{x})$, $\ldots$, $g_R(\mathbf{x})$ called **discrimination functions**. The design of discrimination functions must satisfy the following formula for all $\mathbf{x} \in K_r$ and for any $s \in [1, R]$, $s \neq r$

$$g_r(\mathbf{x}) \geq g_s(\mathbf{x}) \tag{7.3}$$

Therefore, the discrimination hypersurface between class regions K_r and K_s is defined by

$$g_r(\mathbf{x}) - g_s(\mathbf{x}) = 0 \tag{7.4}$$

The decision rule results from this definition. The object pattern $\mathbf{x}$ will be classified into the class whose discrimination function gives a maximum of all the discrimination functions:

$$d(\mathbf{x}) = \omega_r \iff g_r(\mathbf{x}) = \max_{s=1,..,R} g_s(\mathbf{x}) \tag{7.5}$$

Linear discrimination functions are the simplest and are widely used. Their general form is

$$g_r(\mathbf{x}) = q_{r0} + q_{r1}x_1 + \ldots + q_{rn}x_n \tag{7.6}$$

for all $r = 1, \ldots, R$. If all the discrimination functions of the classifier are linear, it is called a **linear classifier**.

Another possibility is to construct classifiers based on the **minimum distance** principle. The resulting classifier is just a special case of classifiers with discrimination functions, however they have computational advantages and may easily be implemented on digital computers.

Assume that R points are defined in the feature space, $v_1, v_2, \ldots, v_R$ that represent **exemplars** (sample patterns) of classes $\omega_1, \omega_2, \ldots, \omega_R$. A minimum distance classifier classifies a pattern x into the class to whose exemplar it is closest.

$$d(\mathbf{x}) = \omega_r \quad \Longleftrightarrow \quad |v_r - \mathbf{x}| = \min_{s=1,\ldots,R} |v_s - \mathbf{x}| \tag{7.7}$$

Each discrimination hyperplane is perpendicular to the line segment $v_s v_r$ and bisects it (Figure 7.6).

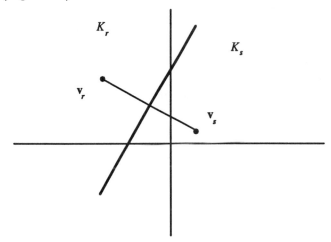

Figure 7.6 *Minimum distance discrimination functions.*

If each class is represented by just one exemplar, a linear classifier results. If more than one exemplar represents some class, the classifier results in piecewise linear discrimination hyperplanes. An algorithm for learning and classification using a minimum distance classifier can be found in Section 7.2.3, Algorithm 7.2.

Nonlinear classifiers usually transform the original feature space X^n into a new feature space X^m applying some appropriate nonlinear function Φ where the superscripts n, m refer to the space dimensionality. After the nonlinear transformation, a linear classifier is applied in the new feature space – the role of the function Φ is to 'straighten' the nonlinear discrimination hypersurfaces of the original feature space into hyperplanes in the transformed feature space. This approach to feature space transformation is called a **Φ-classifier**.

The discrimination functions of a Φ-classifier are

$$g_r(\mathbf{x}) = q_{r0} + q_{r1}\phi_1(\mathbf{x}) + \ldots + q_{rm}\phi_m(\mathbf{x}) \tag{7.8}$$

where $r = 1, \ldots, R$. We may rewrite the formula in vector representation

$$g_r(\mathbf{x}) = \mathbf{q}_r \cdot \mathbf{\Phi}(\mathbf{x}) \tag{7.9}$$

where $\mathbf{q}_r$, $\mathbf{\Phi}(\mathbf{x})$ are vectors consisting of $q_{r0}, \ldots, q_{rm}$ and $\phi_0(\mathbf{x}), \ldots, \phi_m(\mathbf{x})$, respectively, $\phi_0(\mathbf{x}) \equiv 1$. Nonlinear classifiers are described in detail in [Sklansky 81, Devijver and Kittler 82].

7.2.2 Classifier setting

A classifier based on discrimination functions is a deterministic machine – one pattern $\mathbf{x}$ will always be classified into the same class. Note that the pattern $\mathbf{x}$ may represent objects from different classes, meaning that the classifier decision may be correct for some objects and incorrect for others. Therefore, setting of the optimal classifier must be probabilistic. Incorrect classifier decisions cause some losses to the user, and according to the definition of loss, different criteria for optimal classifier settings will be obtained. Discussing these optimality criteria from the mathematical point of view, criteria represent the value of the mean loss caused by classification.

Let the classifier be considered a universal machine that can be set to represent any decision rule from the rule set D. The set D may be ordered by a parameter vector $\mathbf{q}$ that refers to particular discrimination rules. The value of the mean loss $J(\mathbf{q})$ depends on the applied decision rule $\omega = d(\mathbf{x}, \mathbf{q})$. In comparison with the definition of decision rule used in the previous section, the parameter vector $\mathbf{q}$ has been added to represent the specific decision rule used by the classifier. The decision rule

$$\omega = d(\mathbf{x}, \mathbf{q}^*) \tag{7.10}$$

that gives the minimum mean loss $J(\mathbf{q})$ is called the optimum decision rule, and $\mathbf{q}^*$ is called the vector of optimal parameters

$$J(\mathbf{q}^*) = \min_{\mathbf{q}} J(\mathbf{q}), \qquad d(\mathbf{x}, \mathbf{q}) \in D \tag{7.11}$$

The **minimum error criterion** (Bayes criterion, maximum likelihood) uses loss functions of the form $\lambda(\omega_r | \omega_s)$, where $\lambda(.)$ is the number that describes quantitatively the loss incurred if a pattern $\mathbf{x}$ which should be classified into the class ω_s is incorrectly classified into the class ω_r

$$\omega_r = d(\mathbf{x}, \mathbf{q}) \tag{7.12}$$

The mean loss is

$$J(\mathbf{q}) = \int_X \sum_{s=1}^{R} \lambda(d(\mathbf{x}, \mathbf{q}) | \omega_s) p(\mathbf{x} | \omega_s) P(\omega_s) d\mathbf{x} \tag{7.13}$$

where $P(\omega_s)$, $s = 1, \ldots, R$ are the a priori probabilities of classes, and $p(\mathbf{x} | \omega_s)$, $s = 1, \ldots, R$ are the conditional probability densities of objects $\mathbf{x}$ in the class ω_s.

A classifier that has been set according to the minimum loss optimality criterion is easy to construct using discrimination functions; usually, unit loss functions are considered

$$\begin{aligned} \lambda(\omega_r|\omega_s) &= 0 \text{ for } r = s \\ &= 1 \text{ for } r \neq s \end{aligned} \tag{7.14}$$

and the discrimination functions are

$$g_r(\mathbf{x}) = p(\mathbf{x}|\omega_r)P(\omega_r), \qquad r = 1, \ldots, R \tag{7.15}$$

where $g_r(\mathbf{x})$ corresponds (up to a multiplicative constant) to the value of the a posteriori probability $P(\omega_r|\mathbf{x})$.

This probability describes how often a pattern $\mathbf{x}$ is from the class ω_r. Clearly, the optimal decision is to classify a pattern $\mathbf{x}$ to a class ω_r if the a posteriori probability $P(\omega_r|\mathbf{x})$ is the highest of all possible a posteriori probabilities

$$P(\omega_r|\mathbf{x}) = \max_{s=1,\ldots,R} P(\omega_s|\mathbf{x}) \tag{7.16}$$

A posteriori probability may be computed from a priori probabilities using the Bayes formula

$$P(\omega_s|\mathbf{x}) = \frac{p(\mathbf{x}|\omega_s)P(\omega_s)}{p(\mathbf{x})} \tag{7.17}$$

where $p(\mathbf{x})$ is the mixture density. The mean loss is equal to the probability of an incorrect decision and represents a theoretical optimum – no other classifier setting can give a lower probability of the decision loss. Plots of a posteriori probabilities are shown in Figure 7.7, and corresponding discrimination hypersurfaces can be seen in Figure 7.8.

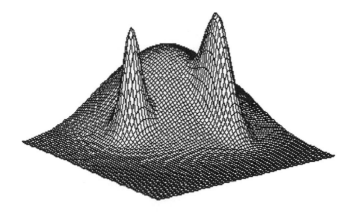

Figure 7.7 *Minimum error classifier: A posteriori probabilities.*

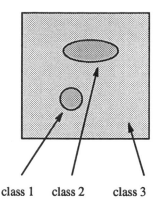

class 1   class 2   class 3

Figure 7.8 *Minimum error classifier: Discrimination hypersurfaces and resulting classes.*

Another criterion is the **best approximation criterion** which is based on the best approximation of discrimination functions by linear combinations of predetermined functions $\phi_i(\mathbf{x})$, $i = 1, \ldots, n$. The classifier is then constructed as a Φ-classifier.

Analytic minimization of the extrema problem (7.10) is in many practical cases impossible because the multi-dimensional probability densities are not available. Criteria for loss function evaluation can be found in [Sklansky 81, Devijver and Kittler 82]. The requirements for classification correctness, and the set of objects accompanied by information about their classes are usually available in practical applications – very often this is all the information that can be used for the classifier design and setting.

The ability to set classification parameters from a set of examples is very important and is called **classifier learning**. The classifier setting is based on a set of presented objects (represented by their feature vectors), each object being accompanied by information about its proper classification – this set of patterns and their classes is called the **training set**. Clearly, the quality of the classifier setting depends on the quality and size of the training set, which is always finite. Therefore, to design and set a classifier, it is not possible to use all the objects which will later need classifying; that is, the patterns that were not used for classifier design and setting will also enter the classifier, not merely the patterns contained in the training set. The classifier setting methods must be **inductive** in the sense that the information obtained from the elements of the training set must be generalized to cover the whole feature space, implying that the classifier setting should be (near) optimal for all feasible patterns, not only for those patterns that were present in the training set. In other words, the classifier should be able to recognize even those objects that it had never 'seen' before.

It may be that a solution for a given problem does not exist. If the require-

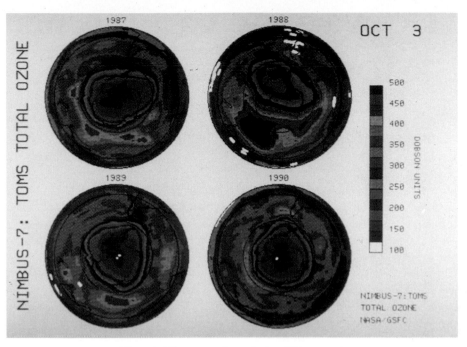

Plate 1 The ozone layer hole. (Figure 1.1)

Plate 2 Pseudocolour representation of the original image. (Figure 5.38(b))

Plate 3 Recursive region merging. (Figure 5.38(c))

Plate 4 Region merging via boundary melting. (Figure 5.38(d))

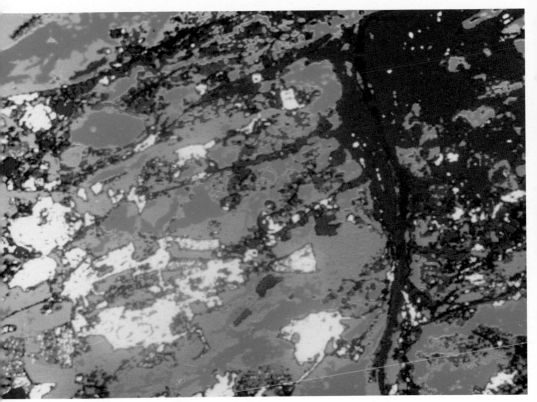

Plate 5 Remotely sensed data of Prague, Landsat Thematic Mapper. Unsupervised classification, post-processing filter applied: White – no vegetation, green – vegetation types, red – urban areas. (Figure 8.13)

Plate 6 Meteotrend: Cloud motion analysis in horizontal and vertical directions, vertical speed coded in colour. (Figure 14.14(a))

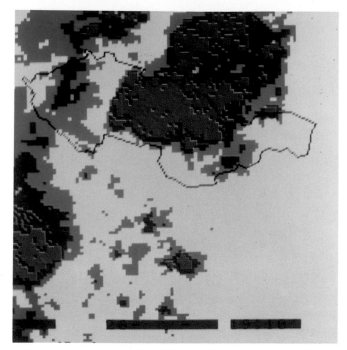

Plate 7 Meteotrend: Cloud type classification. (Figure 14.14(b))

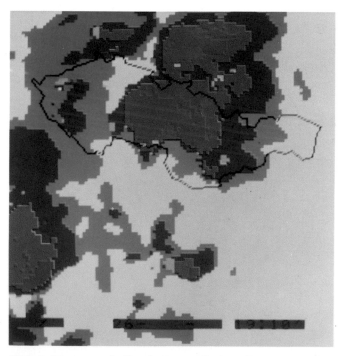

Plate 8 Meteotrend: Cloud type prediction. (Figure 14.14(d))

nents for classification correctness together with the set of training examples are given, it may be impossible to give an immediate answer as to whether the assignment can be fulfilled. The larger the training set, the better the guarantee that the classifier may be set correctly – classification correctness and the size of the training set are closely related. If the statistical properties of patterns are known, the necessary sizes of the training sets can be estimated, but the problem is that in reality they are not usually known. The training set is actually supposed to substitute this missing statistical information. Only after processing of the training set can the designer know whether it was sufficient, and whether an increase in the training set size is necessary.

The training set size will typically be increased several times until the correct classification setting is achieved. The problem, which originally could not be solved, uses more and more information as the training set size increases until the problem specifications can be met.

The general idea of sequential increase in training set size can be understood as presenting small portions of a large training set to the classifier whose performance is checked after each portion. The smallest portion size is one element of the training set. Sequential processing of information (which cannot be avoided in principle) has some substantial consequences in the classifier setting process.

All the properties of the classifier setting methods given have analogies in the learning process of living organisms. The basic properties of learning can be listed as;

- **Learning** is the process of automated system optimization based on the sequential presentation of examples.

- The **goal of learning** is to minimize the optimality criterion. The criterion may be represented by the mean loss caused by incorrect decisions.

- The finite size of the training set requires the **inductive** character of learning. The goal of learning must be achieved by generalizing the information from examples, before all feasible examples have been presented. The examples may be chosen at random.

- The unavoidable requirements of sequential information presentation and the finite size of system memory necessitate the **sequential character of learning**. Therefore, learning is not a one step process, but rather a step by step process of improvement.

The learning process searches out the optimal classifier setting from examples. The classifier system is constructed as a universal machine that becomes optimal after processing the training set examples (supervised learning), meaning that it is not necessary to repeat the difficult optimal system design if a new application appears. Learning methods do not depend on the application; the same learning algorithm can be applied if a medical diagnostics classifier is set just as if an object recognition classifier for a robot is set.

The quality of classifier decisions is closely related to the quality and amount of information that is available. From this point of view, the patterns should represent as complex a description as possible. On the other hand, a large number of description features would result. Therefore, the object description is always a trade-off between the permissible classification error, the complexity of the classifier construction and the time required for classification. This results in a question of how to choose the best features from a set of available features, and how to detect the features with the highest contribution to the recognition success. Methods of determination of **informativity** and **discriminativity** of measured features can be found in [Fu 68, Young and Calvert 74, Devijver and Kittler 82].

7.2.3 Classifier learning

Two common learning strategies will be presented in this section:

- **Probability density estimation** estimates the probability densities $p(\mathbf{x}|\omega_r)$ and probabilities $P(\omega_r)$, $r = 1, \ldots, R$. The discrimination functions are computed according to the minimum error criterion (equation 7.15).

- **Direct loss minimization** finds the decision rule $\omega = d(\mathbf{x}, \mathbf{q}^*)$ by direct minimization of losses $J(\mathbf{q})$ without estimation of probability densities and probabilities. The criterion of the best approximation is applied.

Probability density estimation methods differ in computational difficulty according to the amount of prior information available about them. If some prior information is available, it usually describes the shape of probability density functions $p(\mathbf{x}|\omega_r)$. The parameters describing the distribution are not usually known, and learning must find the estimate of these parameters. Therefore, this class of learning methods is sometimes called **parametric learning**.

Assume the patterns in the r-th class can be described by a normal distribution. The probability density for the normal distribution $N(\boldsymbol{\mu}_r, \boldsymbol{\Psi}_r)$ can be computed for patterns from the class ω_r

$$p(\mathbf{x}|\omega_r) = \frac{1}{(2\pi)^{\frac{n}{2}} \sqrt{(det\ \boldsymbol{\Psi}_r)}} \exp\left[-\frac{1}{2}(\mathbf{x} - \boldsymbol{\mu}_r)^T \boldsymbol{\Psi}_r^{-1}(\mathbf{x} - \boldsymbol{\mu}_r)\right] \qquad (7.18)$$

where $\boldsymbol{\Psi}_r$ is the dispersion matrix (and we recall that $\mathbf{x}$, $\boldsymbol{\mu}_i$ are column vectors). Details about multivariate probability density function estimation may be found in [Rao 65, Johnson and Wichern 90]. The computation process depends on additional information about the vector of values $\boldsymbol{\mu}_r$ and $\boldsymbol{\Psi}_r$; three cases can be distinguished:

1. The dispersion matrix $\boldsymbol{\Psi}_r$ is known, but the mean value vector $\boldsymbol{\mu}_r$ is unknown. One of the feasible estimates of the mean value may be the average

$$\tilde{\boldsymbol{\mu}}_r = \overline{\mathbf{x}} \qquad (7.19)$$

which can be computed recursively

$$\overline{\mathbf{x}}(k+1) = \frac{1}{k+1}(k\ \overline{\mathbf{x}}(k) + \mathbf{x}_{k+1}) \qquad (7.20)$$

where $\overline{\mathbf{x}}(k)$ is the average computed from k samples, and $\mathbf{x}_{k+1}$ is the $(k+1)$-st pattern from the class r from the training set. This estimate is unbiased, consistent, efficient, and linear.

2. The dispersion matrix $\boldsymbol{\Psi}_r$ is unknown, but the mean value vector $\boldsymbol{\mu}_r$ is known. The estimate of the dispersion matrix $\boldsymbol{\Psi}_r$ if the mean value $\boldsymbol{\mu}_r$ is known is usually taken as

$$\tilde{\boldsymbol{\Psi}}_r = \frac{1}{K}\sum_{k=1}^{K}(\mathbf{x}_k - \boldsymbol{\mu}_r)\ (\mathbf{x}_k - \boldsymbol{\mu}_r)^T \qquad (7.21)$$

or in recursive form

$$\tilde{\boldsymbol{\Psi}}_r(k+1) = \frac{1}{k+1}[k\ \tilde{\boldsymbol{\Psi}}_r(k) + (\mathbf{x}_{k+1} - \boldsymbol{\mu}_r)\ (\mathbf{x}_{k+1} - \boldsymbol{\mu}_r)^T] \qquad (7.22)$$

This estimate is unbiased and consistent.

3. Both the dispersion matrix $\boldsymbol{\Psi}_r$ and the mean value vector $\boldsymbol{\mu}_r$ are unknown. The following estimates can be used

$$\tilde{\boldsymbol{\mu}}_r = \overline{\mathbf{x}} \qquad (7.23)$$

$$\tilde{\boldsymbol{\Psi}}_r = \mathbf{S} = \frac{1}{K-1}\sum_{k=1}^{K}(\mathbf{x}_k - \overline{\mathbf{x}})\ (\mathbf{x}_k - \overline{\mathbf{x}})^T \qquad (7.24)$$

or in the recursive form

$$\begin{aligned}\mathbf{S}(k+1) = \ &\tfrac{1}{k}[(k-1)\mathbf{S}(k) \\ &+ (\mathbf{x}_{k+1} - \overline{\mathbf{x}}(k+1))\ (\mathbf{x}_{k+1} - \overline{\mathbf{x}}(k+1))^T \\ &+ k(\overline{\mathbf{x}}(k) - \overline{\mathbf{x}}(k+1))(\overline{\mathbf{x}}(k) - \overline{\mathbf{x}}(k+1))^T] \qquad (7.25)\end{aligned}$$

The a priori probabilities of classes $P(\omega_r)$ are estimated as relative frequencies

$$P(\omega_r) = \frac{K_r}{K} \qquad (7.26)$$

where K is the total number of objects in the training set; K_r is the number of objects from the class r in the training set.

Algorithm 7.1: Learning and classification based on estimates of probability densities assuming the normal distribution

---

1. Learning: Compute the estimates of the mean value vector μ_r and the dispersion matrix Ψ_r, equations (7.20) and/or (7.22), (7.25).

2. Compute the estimates of the a priori probability densities $p(x|\omega_r)$, equation (7.18).

3. Compute the estimates of the a priori probabilities of classes, equation (7.26).

4. Classification: Classify all patterns into the class r if

$$\omega_r = \max_{i=1,...,s} \left(p(x|\omega_i) P(\omega_i) \right)$$

(equations (7.15) and (7.5)).

If no prior information is available (i.e. even the distribution type is not known), the computation is more complex. In such cases, if it is not necessary to use the minimum error criterion, it is advantageous to use a direct loss minimization method.

No probability densities or probabilities are estimated in the second group of methods based on direct minimization of losses. The minimization process can be compared to gradient optimization methods, however pure gradient methods cannot be used because of unknown probability densities, so the gradient cannot be evaluated. Nevertheless, the minimum can be found using methods of **stochastic approximations** that are discussed in [Sklansky 81]. The most important conclusion is that the learning algorithms can be represented by recursive formulae in both groups of learning methods and it is easy to implement them.

We have noted that the most common and easily implementable classifier is the minimum distance classifier. Its learning and classification algorithm is;

Algorithm 7.2: Minimum distance classifier learning and classification

---

1. Learning: For all classes, compute class exemplars v_i based on the training set

$$v_i(k_i + 1) = \frac{1}{k_i + 1}(k_i v_i(k_i) + x_i(k_i + 1)) \tag{7.27}$$

where $x_i(k_i + 1)$ are objects from the class i and k_i denotes the number of objects from class i used thus far for learning.

2. Classification: For an object description vector $\mathbf{x}$ determine the distance of $\mathbf{x}$ from the class exemplars $\mathbf{v}_i$. Classify the object into the class j if the distance of $\mathbf{x}$ from $\mathbf{v}_j$ is the minimum such (equation 7.7).

7.2.4 Cluster analysis

We noted earlier that classification methods exist which do not need training sets for learning. In particular, they do not need information about the class of objects in the learning stage, but learn them without a teacher (unsupervised learning). One such group of classification methods is called **cluster analysis**. Cluster analysis can be applied in classification if for any reason the training set cannot be prepared, or if examples with known class evaluation are not available.

Cluster analysis methods divide the set of processed patterns into subsets (clusters) based on the mutual similarity of subset elements. Each cluster contains patterns representing objects that are similar according to the selected object description and similarity criteria. Objects that are not similar reside in different clusters.

There are two main groups of cluster analysis methods – the first is hierarchical and the second non-hierarchical. Hierarchical methods construct a clustering tree; the set of patterns is divided into the two most dissimilar subsets, and each subset is divided into other different subsets, etc. Non-hierarchical methods sequentially assign each pattern to one cluster. Methods and algorithms for cluster analysis can be found in [Duda and Hart 73, Devijver and Kittler 82, Romesburg 84, McQuitty 87, Kaufman and Rousseeuw 90].

A popular and simple non-hierarchical cluster analysis method will demonstrate its principles; this is the **MacQueen k-means** method [MacQueen 67]. Assume that the number of clusters k is known. If the number of classes (clusters) is not known beforehand, it can be determined as the number of classes that gives the maximum confidence in results, or some more complex clustering method can be applied that does not need this information. The starting cluster points are constructed in the first step, represented by k points in the n-dimensional feature space. These points can either be selected at random from the clustered set of patterns, or the first k patterns from the set can be chosen. If there are exemplars of clusters available, even if these exemplars are unreliable, it is worthwhile using them as the starting cluster points. The method has two main stages; patterns are allocated to one of the existing clusters in the first stage according to their distance from the cluster exemplars, choosing the closest. Then the exemplar is recomputed as the centre of gravity of all patterns in that cluster. If all the patterns from the set have been processed, the current exemplars of clusters are considered final; all the patterns are assigned to one of the clusters, represented by the exemplars determined in the first stage. Then the patterns are (re-)assigned to clusters according to their distance from the exemplars, patterns being assigned to the closest cluster. The exemplars are not recomputed in the second stage. It should be clear that elements that were used for the starting cluster point definitions need not be members of the same clusters at the end.

Algorithm 7.3: MacQueen cluster analysis

1. Define the number of clusters.

2. Initialize the cluster starting points (exemplars). Usually some patterns are chosen to serve as cluster starting points, perhaps chosen at random.

3. First Pass: Decide to which cluster each pattern belongs, choosing the closest (do not process those patterns that were used to initialize clusters). Recompute the relevant exemplar after an object is added to a cluster.

4. Second Pass: Let the final exemplars be exemplars of resulting clusters. Classify all objects (including those used to form starting exemplars) using the final exemplars from the first pass. Use the minimum distance criterion.

Because of its simplicity, the MacQueen method has its limitations. There are many variations on this algorithm; one is to repeat the second stage until convergence. The ISODATA cluster analysis method [Kaufman and Rousseeuw 90] may solve a complex clustering problem better. ISODATA uses two parameter sets, one which does not change during the clustering, and another which can be interactively adjusted until an acceptable clustering result is obtained. ISODATA represents a set of non-hierarchical cluster analysis methods from which the best can be picked.

How to determine the number of clusters has not been mentioned; for example, what metric is the most suitable in n-dimensional space, etc. Answers to these and many other questions can be found in [Romesburg 84, McQuitty 87, Kaufman and Rousseeuw 90].

Note that statistical pattern recognition and cluster analysis can be combined. For instance, the minimum distance classifier can be taught using cluster analysis methods, cluster exemplars can be considered class exemplars, these exemplars can be assigned appropriate names and other patterns can be recognized using the resulting classifier [Sonka 86].

7.3 Neural nets

Pattern recognition methods have been closely influenced by studies of the behaviour of biological neurons; **perceptrons** [Rosenblatt 62, Minsky 88] were an early such study. Perceptrons can be represented by a linear discrimination function (equation (7.6)) – a single perceptron is equivalent to a linear classifier that classifies patterns into two classes. A perceptron input is a feature vector x and its output is a scalar

$$y = f(\sum_{i=1}^{n}(w_i x_i + w_0))) \qquad (7.28)$$

where w consists of weights defining the discrimination hyperplane and f is a nonlinear function of which a threshold or sigmoid are the most common (see Figure 7.9).

The following algorithm [Rogers and Kabrisky 91] is one of several modifications of the Rosenblatt's original algorithm for perceptron learning;

Algorithm 7.4: Perceptron learning

1. Assign small random numbers to the weight vector w.

2. Repeat steps 3–5 for all patterns from the training set.

3. Input the feature vector x(k) from the training set together with the class information $\omega(k)$.

4. Evaluate the perceptron output

$$y(k) = f(\sum_{i}(w_i(k)x_i(k) + w_0(k))) \qquad (7.29)$$

   where k represents the training step number.

5. Learning: If $y(k) \neq \omega(k)$, adjust the weights

$$w_i(k+1) = w_i(k) + \alpha(\omega(k) - y(k))x_i(k) \qquad (7.30)$$

   where $\alpha \in (0, 1)$.

Neural nets (specifically multi-layered perceptrons) are developments of simple perceptrons. A neural net consists of a set of nodes (generally single perceptrons) and of interconnections between them.

The net properties are determined by its architecture, by the node behaviour, the inter-node weights w, the thresholds w_0, and the nonlinear function f. Note that only some of the nodes are directly connected with the

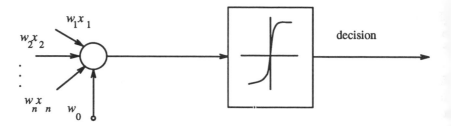

Figure 7.9 *Perceptron.*

input or output, and there may be nodes with no direct connection to input or output (interlayer, hidden nodes).

From the architectural point of view, neural nets can be divided into two main groups; recurrent nets and feed-forward nets.

- **Recurrent** nets are mostly used in optimization problems. Interconnecting weights are fixed and do not change during the iteration process. When used for pattern recognition, a pattern **x** is input into the net as an initial condition and the neural net converges to the closest exemplar that is stored in its memory.

- **Feed-forward** nets resemble conventional methods of statistical pattern recognition much more closely. The net consists of an input node layer, output layer, and zero or more hidden layers. There are interconnections between nodes in adjacent layers. These **synaptic** connections start with random weights that are changed during an iterative process of neural net learning which may be supervised or unsupervised. In the classification stage an unknown pattern **x** is input to the neural net and the output **y** indicates to which class it belongs.

Note that many varieties exist, some of them not in agreement with this categorization.

7.3.1 Feed-forward nets

A single layer of nodes cannot recognize objects if the classification problem is not linearly separable [Minsky 88]. As an example, the classification of patterns shown in Figure 7.10 cannot be done with a single layer net.

It has been shown that three layers are sufficient to determine any arbitrary discrimination functions, assuming that the net consists of a sufficient number of nodes. An example three-layered neural net is shown in Figure 7.11. Note that a multi-layer neural net can be compared with a Φ-classifier; the lower layer of the net transforms the feature space into a feature space of higher dimensionality where the discrimination functions may be easier to find. Feed-forward network learning is based on the **back-propagation** algorithm

Rumelhart and McClelland 86, Grossberg 70, Grossberg 91] that calculates a set of weights w_{ij} from a training set of examples, where the weight w_{ij} represents an interconnection between node i and node j in the next layer.

Patterns from the training set enter the net input, the information is fed forward through the layers and the output $\mathbf{y}$ is generated at the output layer. The back-propagation principle compares the acquired output $\mathbf{y}$ with the required classification ω and the weights w_{ij} are recomputed by back-propagation of the comparison result. The goal of back-propagation learning is to adapt the weights to minimize errors of classification by locating a minmum of the error measure.

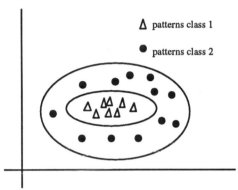

Figure 7.10 *Patterns in feature space – nonlinear discrimination functions are necessary.*

Algorithm 7.5: Back-propagation learning

1. Assign small random numbers to the weights w_{ij}.

2. For all patterns from the training set: input the feature vector $\mathbf{x}(k)$, enter the required output $\boldsymbol{\omega}(k)$.

3. Evaluate the neural net output $\mathbf{y}$.

4. Learning: If $\mathbf{y}$ does not match the required output vector $\boldsymbol{\omega}(k)$, the weights must be adjusted

$$w_{ij}(k+1) = w_{ij}(k) + \alpha \delta_j z_i(k) + \eta(w_{ij}(k) - w_{ij}(k-1)) \qquad (7.31)$$

where η, α are learning constants, $z_i(k)$ is the output of the node i, k is the iteration number, δ_j is an error associated with the node j in the adjacent upper level

$$\delta_j = \begin{cases} y_j(1 - y_j)(\omega_j - y_j) & \text{for output node } j \\ z_j(1 - z_j)(\sum_l \delta_l w_{jl}) & \text{for hidden node } j \end{cases} \qquad (7.32)$$

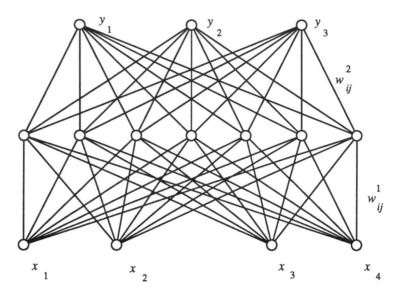

Figure 7.11 *A three-layered neural net structure.*

The learning process should be repeated until convergence, however the convergence process is very slow and weaker criteria like a requirement of small differences between the desired output vector $\omega(k)$ and the neural net output $\mathbf{y}$ are used to stop the learning process. Note also that the training set is not processed just once as was typical of the methods of the previous section. The number of iterations through the set is usually several thousand.

The number of nodes that are necessary in a neural net for an errorless classification of the training set is not known beforehand; also, existing learning algorithms do not guarantee the solution if the smallest necessary number of nodes is used. Therefore, neural nets usually consist of a larger number of nodes than is necessary during the learning stage. After the learning stage is over, nodes which have associated weights very similar to some other node of the net can be deleted, and such reduction in nodes is achieved without significant loss of classification accuracy.

The number of feature vectors required in the training set is a common question. It has been shown [Foley 72] that the training set must contain at least three times as many feature vectors for each class as the number of features.

Details of the back-propagation learning algorithm can be found in the appendix of [Rogers and Kabrisky 91], and an overview of several other methods is given in [Carpenter 89, Carpenter 91].

7.3.2 *Kohonen feature maps*

'ohonen self-organizing feature maps [Kohonen 89] represent unsupervised eed-forward learning. The goal of the self-organization is similar to that presented in cluster analysis – to achieve the same neural net output as a response to input of similar patterns. During the self-organizing process feature vectors enter the net with no information about the desired classification 'learning without a teacher). The architecture of a Kohonen neural net is a .hree-layer feed-forward net in which the internal nodes may be organized in natrix form for an easier definition of inter-node distance (Figure 7.12).

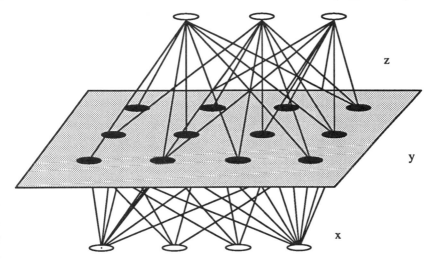

Figure 7.12 *Kohonen self-organizing neural net.*

The basic idea of Kohonen self-organization is to achieve in at least one node of the net weights **w** that are as close as possible to the values of the input feature vector **x**. After the learning process is over, one of the internal nodes has weights closest to the weights of the classified feature vector; that node is said to **fire**. Similar input vectors cause nodes from a local neighbourhood always to fire as a response to the patterns from one class (Figure 7.13). The third layer maps the final response of the neural net to give the same net output **y** if any of the nodes from the same cluster fire.

Algorithm 7.6: Unsupervised learning of the Kohonen feature map

1. Assign random numbers with a small variance around the average values of the input feature vector elements to the weights w_{ij}.

2. Repeat the next steps for patterns from the set to be analysed; input the feature vector $\mathbf{x}(k)$, calculate the distance d_j of the input vector

elements to the weights of each node j in the hidden layer

$$d_j = \sum_i (x_i - w_{ij}(k))^2 \qquad (7.33)$$

Find the node j with closest distance d_j.

3. Update all the weights w_{ij} of the selected node j and all its neighbours

$$w_{ij}(k+1) = w_{ij}(k) + \alpha(x_i - w_{ij}(k)) \qquad (7.34)$$

where k is the iteration number.

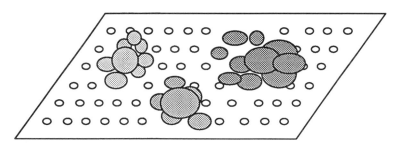

Figure 7.13 *Clusters in the hidden layer of a Kohonen feature map in which 3 clusters were found in the analysed data set. The size of the circle around the node represents the frequency with which the node fires (how often its weights were the closest to the values of the input vector).*

The value of the constant α decreases in later iterations steps, as does the size of the neighbourhood in which weights are updated.

7.3.3   Hybrid neural nets

Hybrid neural nets combine the ideas of supervised and unsupervised learning. Again, the three-layered net is common, the lower layer being set without a teacher, while the upper layer learns with a teacher applying the back-propagation learning algorithm. Behaviour is again similar to that of a Φ-classifier; the Kohonen clustering algorithm of the lower layer is supposed to transform the complex feature space to a simpler one (Figure 7.14). Great potential for good results from hybrid neural nets was documented in [Rogers and Kabrisky 91]. Better classification correctness was achieved, and a smaller number of iteration steps was necessary.

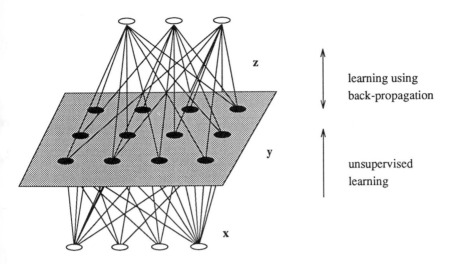

Figure 7.14 *Hybrid neural net; the lower layer consists of the Kohonen feature map, the upper level is a conventional feed-forward net layer with feedback learning.*

7.3.4 Hopfield neural nets

Hopfield nets are mostly used in optimization problems [Hopfield and Tank 85, Hopfield and Tank 86]; however it is possible to represent recognition as an optimization task: Find the maximum similarity between the pattern **x** and one of the existing exemplars **v**.

In the Hopfield model, interconnection weights T_{ij} do not change during the iteration process. These weights are computed from a set of known exemplars during initialization

$$T_{ij} = \sum_r (v_i^r v_j^r) \quad (i \neq j) \tag{7.35}$$

where T_{ij} is the interconnection weight between nodes i and j; and v_i^r is the ith element of the rth exemplar. $T_{ii} = 0$ for any i.

The Hopfield net acts as an associative memory where the exemplars are stored; its architecture is shown in Figure 7.15. If associative memory is used for recognition, the classified feature vector enters the net in the form of initial values of node outputs. The Hopfield neural net recurrently iterates using existing interconnections with fixed weights until a stable state is found. It can be shown that these networks always converge if the interconnection matrix is symmetric, and if the net is updated asynchronously. The resulting stable state should be equal to the values of the exemplar that is closest to the processed feature vector in the Hamming metric sense. Supposing these class exemplars $\mathbf{v}^r$ are assumed to be known, the recognition algorithm is:

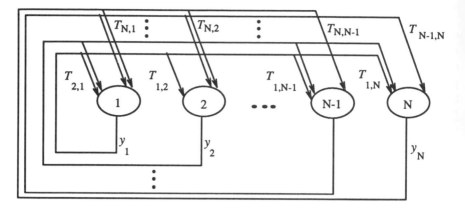

Figure 7.15 *Hopfield recurrent neural net.*

Algorithm 7.7: Recognition using a Hopfield net

---

1. Based on existing exemplars $\mathbf{v}^r$ of r classes compute the interconnection weights T_{ij} (equation 7.35).

2. Apply the feature vector $\mathbf{x}$ as initial outputs $\mathbf{y}(0)$ of the net.

3. Iterate until the net converges (output $\mathbf{y}$ does not change):

$$y_j(k+1) = f(\sum_{i=1}^{N}(T_{ij}y_i(k)))$$ (7.36)

The final output vector $\mathbf{y}$ represents the exemplar of the class into which the processed feature vector $\mathbf{x}$ is classified. In other words, a Hopfield neural net transforms a non-ideal representation of an object (fuzzy, noisy, incomplete, etc.) to the ideal exemplar representation. The transformation of a noisy binary image of characters to a clear letter is one vision-related application; binary image recognition examples can be found in [Kosko 91, Rogers and Kabrisky 91].

The Hopfield neural net always converges to a *local* minimum which may mean that the correct exemplar (the *global* minimum) is not found. Moreover, the number of local minima grows rapidly with the number of exemplars stored in the associative network. It can be shown that the minimum number of nodes N required is about seven times the number of memories M to be stored (this is known as the $0.15N \geq M$ rule) [McEliece et al. 87, Amit 89], causing a rapid increase in the number of necessary nodes.

This overview has shown only the main principles of neural nets and their connections to conventional statistical pattern recognition and we have not discussed many neural net techniques, methods, and implementations. The state of the art and many references may be found in a set of selected papers [Carpenter and Grossberg 91] and in [Amit 89, Hecht-Nielsen 90, Judd 90, Simpson 90, Mozer 91, Zhou 92], and various useful introductory texts [Wasserman 89, Beale and Jackson 90, Dayhoff 90, Eberhart and Dobbins 90, Zeidenberg 90].

7.4 Syntactic pattern recognition

Quantitative description of objects using numeric parameters (the feature vector) is used in statistical pattern recognition, while **qualitative** description of an object is a characteristic of syntactic pattern recognition. The object structure is contained in the syntactic description. Syntactic object description should be used whenever feature description is not able to represent the complexity of the described object and/or when the object can be represented as a hierarchical structure consisting of simpler parts. The elementary properties of the syntactically described objects are called **primitives** (Section 6.2.4 covered the syntactic description of object borders using border primitives, these border primitives representing parts of borders with a specific shape). Graphical or relational descriptions of objects where primitives represent subregions of specific shape is another example (see Sections 6.3.3 to 6.3.5). After each primitive has been assigned a symbol, relations between primitives in the object are described, and a **relational structure** results (Chapters 3 and 6). As in statistical recognition, the design of description primitives and their relation is not algorithmic. The design is based on the analysis of the problem, designer experience and abilities. However, there are some principles that are worth following:

1. The number of primitive types should be small.

2. The chosen primitives must be able to form an appropriate object representation.

3. Primitives should be easily segmentable from the image.

4. Primitives should be easily recognizable using some statistical pattern recognition method.

5. Primitives should correspond with significant natural elements of the described object (image) structure.

For example, if technical drawings are described, primitives are line and curve segments, binary relations describe relations such as *to be adjacent, to be left of, to be above,* etc. This description structure can be compared with the structure of a natural language. The text consists of sentences, sentences consist of words, words are constructed by concatenation of letters. Letters are considered primitives in this example; the set of all letters is called the **alphabet**. The set of all words in the alphabet that can be used to describe objects from one class (the set of all feasible descriptions) is named the **description language** which represents descriptions of all objects in the specific class. In addition, a **grammar** exists to represent a set of rules that must be followed when words of the specific language are constructed from letters (of the alphabet). Grammars can describe infinite languages as well. These definitions will be considered in more detail in Section 7.4.1.

Assume that the object is appropriately described by some primitives and their relations. Moreover, assume that the grammar is known for each class that generates descriptions of all objects of the specified class. Syntactic recognition decides whether the description word is or is not syntactically correct according to the particular class grammars, meaning that each class consists only of objects whose syntactic description can be generated by the particular grammar. Syntactic recognition is a process that looks for the grammar that can generate the syntactic word that describes an object.

We mentioned relational structure in the correspondence with the syntactic description of objects. Each relational structure with multiple relations can be transformed to a relational structure with at most binary relations; the image object is then represented by a **graph** which is **planar** if only relations with adjacent regions are considered. A graphical description is very natural, especially in the description of segmented images – examples were given in Section 6.3. Each planar graph can be represented either by a graph grammar or by a sequence of symbols (chain, word, etc.) over an alphabet. Sequential representation is not always advantageous in image object recognition because the valuable correspondence between the syntactic description and the object may be lost. Nevertheless, work with chain grammars is more straightforward and understandable and all the main features of more complex grammars are included in chain grammars. Therefore, we will mostly discuss sequential syntactic descriptions and chain grammars. More precise and detailed discussion of grammars, languages, and syntactic recognition methods can be found in [Fu 74, Fu 77, Chen 76, Pavlidis 77, Rosenfeld 79, Fu 80, Pavlidis 80].

The syntactic recognition process is described by the following algorithm.

Algorithm 7.8: Syntactic recognition

---

1. Learning: Based on the problem analysis, define the primitives and their possible relations.

2. Construct a description grammar for each class of objects using either hand analysis of syntactic descriptions or automated grammar inference

(see Section 7.4.3).

3. Recognition: For each object, extract its primitives first; recognize the primitives' classes and describe the relations between them. Construct a description word representing an object.

4. Based on the results of the syntactic analysis of the description word, classify an object into that class for which its grammar (constructed in step (2)) can generate the description word.

It can be seen that the main difference between statistical and syntactic recognition is in the learning process. Grammar construction can rarely be algorithmic using today's approaches, requiring significant human interaction. It is usually found that the more complex the primitives are, the simpler is the grammar, and the simpler and faster is the syntactic analysis. More complex description primitives on the other hand make step (3) of the algorithm more difficult and more time consuming; also, primitive extraction and evaluation of relations may not be simple.

7.4.1 Grammars and languages

Assuming that the primitives have been successfully extracted, all the inter-primitive relations can then be syntactically described as n-ary relations; these relations form structures (chains, trees, graphs) called **words** that represent the object or the pattern. Each pattern is therefore described by a word. Primitive classes can be understood as letters from the alphabet of symbols called **terminal symbols**. Let the alphabet of terminal symbols be V_t.

The set of patterns from a particular class corresponds to a set of words. This set of words is called the **formal language** which is described by a **grammar**. The grammar is a mathematical model of a generator of syntactically correct words (words from the particular language); it is a quadruple

$$G = [V_n, V_t, P, S] \tag{7.37}$$

where V_n and V_t are disjoint alphabets, elements of V_n are called **non-terminal symbols**, and elements of V_t are terminal symbols. Define V^* to be the set of all terminal and non-terminal symbols

$$V^* = V_n \cup V_t \tag{7.38}$$

The symbol S is the grammar axiom or the *start* symbol. The set P is a non-empty finite subset of the set $V^* \times V^*$; elements of P are called the substitution rules. The set of all words that can be generated by the grammar G is called the **language** $L(G)$. Grammars that generate the same language are called **equivalent**.

A simple example will illustrate this terminology. Let the words generated by the grammar be squares of arbitrary size with sides parallel to the coordinate axes, and let the squares be represented by the Freeman chain code of the border in 4-connectivity (see Section 6.2.1). There are four terminal symbols (primitives) of the grammar in this case, $V_t = \{0, 1, 2, 3\}$. Let the non-terminal symbols be $V_n = \{s, a, b, c, d\}$. Note that the terminal symbols correspond to natural primitives of the 4-connectivity Freeman code; the non-terminal symbols were chosen from an infinite set of feasible symbols. The set of substitution rules P demonstrates how the start symbol $S = s$ can be transformed to words corresponding to the Freeman chain code description of squares:

$$P: \begin{array}{lll} (1) & s & \rightarrow \quad abcd \\ (2) & aAbBcCdD & \rightarrow \quad a1Ab2Bc3Cd0D \\ (3) & aAbBcCdD & \rightarrow \quad ABCD \end{array} \qquad (7.39)$$

where A (B, C, D, respectively) is a variable representing any chain (including an empty one) consisting only of terminal symbols 1 ($2, 3, 0$). Rule (3) stops the word generating process. For example, a square with a side length $l = 2$ with the Freeman chain description 11223300 is generated by the following sequence of substitution rules (see Figure 7.16)

$$s \rightarrow^1 abcd \rightarrow^2 a1b2c3d0 \rightarrow^2 a11b22c33d00 \rightarrow^3 11223300$$

where the arrow superscript refers to the appropriate substitution rule. The simple analysis of generated words shows that the generated language consists only of Freeman chain code representations of squares with sides parallel to the plane co-ordinates.

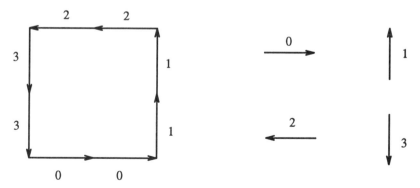

Figure 7.16 *Square shape description.*

Grammars can be divided into four main groups ordered from the general to the specific [Chomsky 66, Chomsky et al. 71]:

1. Type 0 – **General Grammars**
   There are no limitations for the substitution rules.

2. Type 1 – **Context-Sensitive Grammars**
   Substitution rules can be of the form

$$W_1 \alpha W_2 \rightarrow W_1 U W_2 \qquad (7.40)$$

that can contain the substitution rule $S \rightarrow e$ where e is an empty word; words W_1, W_2, U consist of elements of V^*, $U \neq e$, $\alpha \in V_n$. This means that the non-terminal symbols can be substituted by the word U in the context of words W_1 and W_2.

3. Type 2 – **Context-Free Grammars**
   Substitution rules have the form

$$\alpha \rightarrow U \qquad (7.41)$$

where $U \in V^*$, $U \neq e$, $\alpha \in V_n$. Grammars can contain the rule $S \rightarrow e$. This means that the non-terminal symbol can be substituted by a word U independently of the context of α.

4. Type 3 – **Regular Grammars**
   The substitution rules of regular grammars are of the form

$$\alpha \rightarrow x\beta \qquad or \qquad \alpha \rightarrow x \qquad (7.42)$$

where $\alpha, \beta \in V_n$, $x \in V_t$. The substitution rule $S \rightarrow e$ may be included.

All the grammars discussed so far have been **non-deterministic**. The same left hand side might appear in several substitution rules with different right hand sides, and no rule exists that specifies which rule should be chosen. A non-deterministic grammar generates a language in which no words are 'preferred'. If it is advantageous to generate some words (those more probable) more often than others, substitution rules can be accompanied by numbers (for instance by probabilities) that specify how often the substitution rule should be applied. If the substitution rules are accompanied by probabilities, the grammar is called **stochastic**. If the accompanying numbers do not satisfy the properties of probability (unit sum of probabilities for all rules with the same left hand side), the grammar is called **fuzzy** [Zimmermann et al. 84].

Note, that the evaluation of the frequency with which each substitution rule should be used can substantially increase the efficiency of syntactic analysis in the recognition stage [Fu 74].

7.4.2   *Syntactic analysis, syntactic classifier*

If appropriate grammars exist that can be used for representation of all patterns in their classes, the last step is to design a syntactic classifier which
assigns the pattern (the word) to an appropriate class. It is obvious that the
simplest way is to construct a separate grammar for each class; an unknown
pattern x enters a parallel structure of blocks that can decide if $x \in L(G_j)$
where $j = 1, 2, ...R$ and R is the number of classes; $L(G_j)$ is the language
generated by the jth grammar. If the jth block's decision is positive, the pattern is accepted as a pattern from the jth class and the classifier assigns the
pattern to the class j. Note that generally more than one grammar can accept
a pattern as belonging to its class.

The decision of whether or not the word can be generated by particular
grammar is made during **syntactic analysis**. Moreover, syntactic analysis
can construct the pattern derivation tree which can represent the structural
information about the pattern.

If a language is finite, the syntactic classifier can search for a match between the analysed word and all the words of the language. Another simple
syntactic classifier can be based on comparisons of the chain word descriptions
with typical representatives of classes comparing primitive type presence only.
This method is very fast and easily implemented, though it does not produce
reliable results since the syntactic information is not used at all. However, impossible classes can be rejected in this step which can speed up the syntactic
analysis process.

Syntactic analysis is based on efforts to construct the tested pattern by
the application of some appropriate sequence of substitution rules to the start
symbol. If the substitution process is successful, the analysis process stops
and the tested pattern can be generated by the grammar. The pattern can
be classified into the class represented by the grammar. If the substitution
process is unsuccessful, the pattern is not accepted as representing an object
of this class.

If the class description grammar is regular (type 3), syntactic analysis is
very simple. The grammar can be substituted with a finite non-deterministic
automaton and it is easy to decide if the pattern word is accepted or rejected
by the automaton [Fu 82]. If the grammar is context-free (type 2), the syntactic analysis is more difficult. Nevertheless, it can be designed using stack
automata.

Generally, which process of pattern word construction is chosen is not
important; the transformation process can be done in top-down or bottom-up
manner.

A top-down process begins with the start symbol and substitution rules are
applied in the appropriate way to obtain the same pattern word as that under
analysis. The final goal of syntactic analysis is to generate the same word as
the analysed word; every partial substitution creates a set of subgoals, just

as new branches are created in the generation tree. Effort is always devoted to fulfil the current subgoal. If the analysis is not successful in fulfilling the subgoal, it indicates an incorrect choice of the substitution rule somewhere in the previous substitutions, and backtracking is invoked to get back to the nearest higher tree level (closer to the root), and to pick another applicable rule. The process of rule applications and backtracking is repeated until the required pattern word results. If the whole generating process ends unsuccessfully, the grammar does not generate the word, and the analysed pattern does not belong to the class.

This top-down process is a series of expansions starting with the start symbol S. A bottom-up process starts with the analysed word, which is **reduced** by applying reverse substitutions, the final goal being to reduce the word to the start symbol S. The main principle of bottom-up analysis is to detect subwords in the analysed word that match the pattern on the right hand side of some substitution rule, then the reduction process substitutes the former right hand side with the left hand side of the rule in the analysed word. The bottom-up method follows no subgoals, all the effort is devoted to obtaining a reduced and simplified word pattern until the start symbol is obtained. Again, if the process is not successful, the grammar does not generate the analysed word.

The pure top-down approach is not very efficient since too many incorrect paths are generated. The number of misleading paths can be decreased by application of consistency tests. For example, if the word starts with a non-terminal symbol I, only rules with the right hand side starting with I should be considered. Many more consistency tests can be designed that take advantage of prior knowledge. This approach is also called **tree pruning** (See Figure 7.17) [Nilsson 71, Nilsson 82].

Tree pruning is often used if the complete search cannot be completed because the search effort would exceed any reasonable bounds. Note that pruning can mean that the final solution is not optimal or may not be found at all (especially if tree search is used to find the best path through the graph, Section 5.2.4). This depends on the quality of the a priori information that is applied during the pruning process.

There are two main principles for recovery from following a wrong path. The first one is represented by the backtracking mechanism already mentioned, meaning that the generation of words returns to the nearest point in the tree where another substitution rule can be applied which has not yet been applied. This approach requires the ability to reconstruct the former appearances of generated subwords and/or remove some branches of the derivation tree completely.

The second approach does not include backtracking. All possible combinations of the substitution rules are applied in parallel and several generation trees are constructed simultaneously. If any tree succeeds in generating the

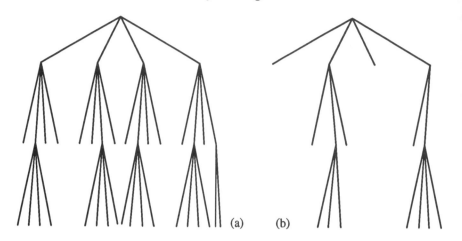

Figure 7.17 *Tree pruning: (a) Original tree, (b) pruning decreases size of the searched tree.*

analysed word, the generation process ends. If any tree generation ends with a non-successful word, this tree is abandoned. The latter approach uses more brute force, but the algorithm is simplified by avoiding backtracking.

It is difficult to compare the efficiency of these two. Bottom-up analysis is more efficient for some grammars, and top-down is more efficient for others. The majority of syntactic analysers which produce all generated words is based on the top-down principle. This approach is appropriate for most grammars but is usually less efficient.

Another approach to syntactic analysis uses example relational structures of classes. The syntactic analysis consists of matching the relational structure that represents the analysed object with the example relational structure. The main goal is to find an **isomorphism** of both relational structures. These methods can be applied to n-ary relational structures as well. Relational structure matching is a perspective approach to syntactic recognition, a perspective way of image understanding (see Section 7.5). A simple example of relational structure matching is shown in Figure 7.18. A detailed description of relational structure matching approaches can be found in [Barrow and Popplestone 71, Pavlidis 77, Baird 84, Ballard and Brown 82].

7.4.3 Syntactic classifier learning, grammar inference

To model a language of any class of patterns as closely as possible, the grammar rules should be extracted from a training set of example words. This process of grammar construction from examples is known as **grammar inference**, the essence of which can be seen in Figure 7.19.

The source of words generates finite example words consisting of the terminal symbols. Assume that these examples include structural features that

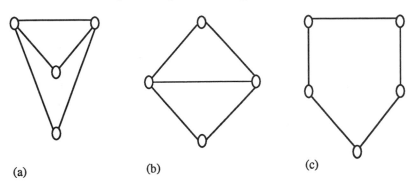

(a) (b) (c)

Figure 7.18 *Matching relational structures: (a) and (b) match assuming nodes and relations of the same type, (c) does not match either (a) or (b).*

should be represented by a grammar G which will serve as a model of this source. All the words that can be generated by the source are included in the language $L(G)$ and the words that cannot be generated by the source represent a residuum of this set $L^C(G)$. This information enters the inference algorithm whose goal is to find and describe the grammar G. Words that are included in the language $L(G)$ can be acquired simply from the source of examples. However, the elements of $L^C(G)$ must be presented by a teacher that has additional information about the grammar properties [Gonzalez and Thomason 74, Barrero 91].

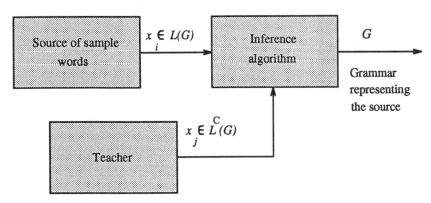

Figure 7.19 *Grammar inference.*

Note that the number of example words generated by the source is finite and it is therefore not sufficient to define the possibly infinite language $L(G)$ unambiguously. Any finite set of examples can be represented by an infinite set of languages, making it impossible to identify unambiguously the grammar that generated the examples. Grammar inference is expected to construct the grammar that describes the training set of examples, plus another set of words that in some sense have the same structure as the examples.

The inference methods can be divided into two groups, based on **enumeration** and **induction**. Enumeration detects the grammar G from the finite set M of grammars that can generate the entire training set of examples or its main part. The difficulty is in the definition of the set M of grammars and in the procedure to search for the grammar G. Induction based methods start with the analysis of words from the training set; the substitution rules are derived from these examples using patterns of similar words.

There is no general method for grammar inference that constructs a grammar from the presented training set. Existing methods can be used to infer regular and context-free grammars, and may furthermore be successful in some other special cases. Even if simple grammars are considered, the inferred grammar usually generates a language that is much larger than the minimum language that can be used for appropriate representation of the class. This property of grammar inference is extremely unsuitable for syntactic analysis because of the computational complexity. Therefore, the main role in syntactic analyser learning is still left to a human analyst, and the grammar construction is based on heuristics, intuition, experience, and prior information about the problem.

If the recognition is based on sample relational structures, the main problem is in its automated construction. The conventional method for the sample relational structure construction is described in [Winston 75] where the relational descriptions of objects from the training set are used. The training set consists of examples and counter-examples. The counter-examples should be chosen to have only one typical difference in comparison with a pattern that is a representative of the class.

7.5 Recognition as graph matching

The following section is devoted to recognition methods based on graph comparisons. Graphs with evaluated nodes and evaluated arcs will be considered as they appear in the image description using relational structures. The aim is to decide whether the reality represented by an image matches prior knowledge about the image incorporated into the graphical models. An example of a typical graph matching task is in Figure 7.20.

If this task is presented as an object recognition problem, the object graph must match the object model graph exactly. If the problem is to find an object (represented by a model graph) in the graphical representation of the image, the model must match a subgraph in the image graph exactly. An exact match of graphs is called graph **isomorphism** – for example, the graphs in Figure 7.20 are isomorphic.

Graph isomorphism and subgraph isomorphism evaluation is a classical problem in graph theory and is important from both practical and theoretical

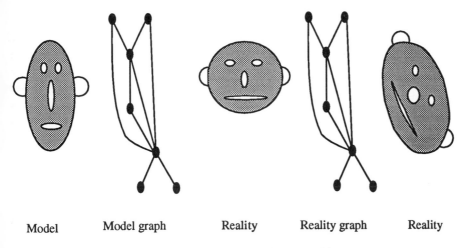

| Model | Model graph | Reality | Reality graph | Reality |

Figure 7.20 *Graph matching problem.*

points of view. Graph theory is covered in [Harary 69, Berge 76, Mohring 91, Nagl 90], and graph theoretical algorithms can be studied in [Even 79, Lau 89, McHugh 90]. The problem is actually more complex in reality, since the requirement of an exact match is very often too strict in recognition problems.

Because of imprecise object descriptions, image noise, overlapping objects, lighting conditions, etc., the object graph usually does not match the model graph exactly. Graph matching is a difficult problem and evaluation of graph **similarity** is not any easier. An important problem in graph similarity evaluation is to design a graph similarity metric which determines how similar two graphs are.

7.5.1 *Isomorphism of graphs and subgraphs*

Regardless of whether graph or subgraph isomorphism is required, the problems can be divided into three main classes [Harary 69, Berge 76, Ballard and Brown 82]

1. **Graph isomorphism.** Given two graphs $G_1 = (V_1, E_1)$ and $G_2 = (V_2, E_2)$, find a *one-to-one* and *onto* mapping (an isomorphism) f between V_1 and V_2 such that for each edge of E_1 connecting any pair of nodes $v, v' \in V_1$, there is an edge of E_2 connecting $f(v)$ and $f(v')$; further, if $f(v)$ and $f(v')$ are connected by an edge in G_2, v and v' are connected in G_1.

2. **Subgraph isomorphism.** Find an isomorphism between a graph G_1 and subgraphs of another graph G_2. This problem is more difficult than the previous one.

3. **Double subgraph isomorphism**. Find all isomorphisms between subgraphs of a graph G_1 and subgraphs of another graph G_2. This problem is of the same order of difficulty as number 2.

The subgraph isomorphism and the double subgraph isomorphism problems are NP-complete, meaning that the solution can only be found in time proportional to an exponential function of the length of the input. It is still not known whether the graph isomorphism problem is NP-complete (see [Even 79, Sedgewick 84, Blum and Rivest 88] for details and examples). Despite extensive effort, there is neither an algorithm that can test for graph isomorphism in polynomial time, nor is there a proof that such an algorithm cannot exist. However, non-deterministic algorithms for graph isomorphism that use heuristics and look for suboptimal solutions give a solution in polynomial time in both graph and subgraph isomorphism testing.

Isomorphism testing is computationally expensive for both non-evaluated and evaluated graphs. Evaluated graphs are more common in recognition and image understanding, where nodes are evaluated by properties of regions they represent, and graph arcs are evaluated by relations between nodes they connect (see Section 7.1).

The evaluations can simplify the isomorphism testing. More precisely, the evaluation may make disproof of isomorphism easier. Isomorphic evaluated graphs have the same number of nodes with the same evaluation, and the same number of arcs with the same evaluation. An isomorphism test of two evaluated graphs $G_1 = (V_1, E_1)$ and $G_2 = (V_2, E_2)$ can be based on partitioning the node sets V_1 and V_2 in a consistent manner looking for inconsistencies in the resulting set partitions. The goal of the partitioning is to achieve a one-to-one correspondence between nodes from sets V_1 and V_2 for all nodes of the graphs G_1 and G_2. The algorithm consists of repeated node set partitioning steps, and the necessary conditions of isomorphism are tested after each step (the same number of nodes of equivalent properties in corresponding sets of both graphs). The node set partitioning may, for example, be based on the following properties:

- Node attributes (evaluations)

- The number of adjacent nodes (connectivity)

- The number of edges of a node (node degree)

- Types of edges of a node

- The number of edges leading from a node back to itself (node order)

- The attributes of adjacent nodes

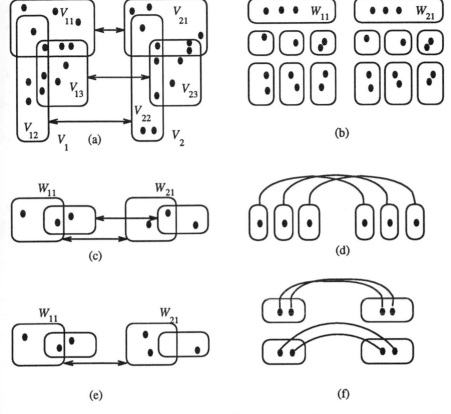

Figure 7.21 *Graph isomorphism: (a) Testing cardinality in corresponding subsets, (b) partitioning node subsets, (c) generating new subsets, (d) subset isomorphism found, (e) graph isomorphism disproof, (f) situation when arbitrary search is necessary.*

After the new subsets are generated based on one of the listed criteria, the cardinality of corresponding subsets of nodes in graphs G_1 and G_2 are tested, see Figure 7.21a. Obviously, if v_{1i} is in several subsets V_{1j} then the corresponding node v_{2i} must also be in the corresponding subsets V_{2j}, or the isomorphism is disproved

$$v_{2i} \in \bigcap_{j|v_{1i} \in V_{1j}} V_{2j} \tag{7.43}$$

If all the generated subsets satisfy the necessary conditions of isomorphism in step i, the subsets are split into new sets of nodes W_{1n}, W_{2n} (Figure 7.21b)

$$\begin{aligned} W_{1i} \cap W_{1j} &= \emptyset \quad \text{for } i \neq j \\ W_{2i} \cap W_{2j} &= \emptyset \quad \text{for } i \neq j \end{aligned} \tag{7.44}$$

Clearly, if $V_{1j} = V_{2j}$ and if $v_{1i} \notin V_{1k}$ then $v_{2i} \in V_{2k}^C$, where V^C is the set complement. Therefore, by equation (7.43), corresponding elements v_{1i}, v_{2i} of W_{1n}, W_{2n} must satisfy [Niemann 90]

$$v_{2i} \in \{ \bigcap_{\{j|v_{1i} \in W_{1j}\}} W_{2j} \} \bigcap \{ \bigcap_{\{k|v_{1i} \notin W_{1k} \wedge W_{1k} = W_{2k}\}} W_{2k}^C \} \qquad (7.45)$$

The cardinality of all the corresponding sets W_{1n}, W_{2n} is tested to disprove the graph isomorphism.

The same process is repeated in the following steps applying different criteria for graph node subset generation. Note that the new subsets are generated independently in W_{1i}, W_{2i} (Figure 7.21c).

The process is repeated unless one of three cases occurs:

1. The set partitioning reaches the stage when all the corresponding sets W_{1i}, W_{2i} contain one node each. The isomorphism is found (Figure 7.21d).

2. The cardinality condition is not satisfied in at least one of the corresponding subsets. The isomorphism is disproved (Figure 7.21e).

3. No more new subsets can be generated before one of the previous cases occurs. In that situation, either the node set partitioning criteria are not sufficient to establish an isomorphism, or more than one isomorphism is possible. If this is the case, the systematic arbitrary assignment of nodes that have more than one possible corresponding node and cardinality testing after each assignment may provide the solution (Figure 7.21f).

The last part of the process based on systematic assignment of possibly corresponding nodes and isomorphism testing after each assignment may be based on backtracking principles. Note that the backtracking approach can be used from the very beginning of the isomorphism testing, however it is more efficient to start the test using all the available prior information about the matched graphs. The backtracking process is applied if more than one potential correspondence between nodes is encountered. Backtracking tests for directed graph isomorphism and a recursive algorithm is given in [Ballard and Brown 82] together with accompanying hints for improving the efficiency of backtrack searches [Bittner and Reingold 75, Haralick and Elliott 79, Nilsson 82]. The process presented above, graph isomorphism testing, is summarized in the following algorithm

---

Algorithm 7.9: Graph isomorphism

---

1. Take two graphs $G_1 = (V_1, E_1), G_2 = (V_2, E_2)$.

2. Use a node property criterion to generate subsets V_{1i}, V_{2i} of the node sets V_1 and V_2. Test whether the cardinality conditions hold for corresponding subsets. If not, the isomorphism is disproved.

3. Partition the subsets V_{1i}, V_{2i} into subsets W_{1j}, W_{2j} satisfying the conditions given in equation (7.44) (no two subsets W_{1j} or W_{2j} contain the same node). Test whether the cardinality conditions hold for all the corresponding subsets W_{1j}, W_{2j}. If not, the isomorphism is disproved.

4. Repeat steps (2) and (3) using another node property criterion in all subsets W_{1j}, W_{2j} generated so far. Stop if one of the three above mentioned situations occurs.

5. Based on the situation that stopped the repetition process, the isomorphism either was proved, disproved, or some additional procedures (like backtracking) must be applied to complete the proof or disproof.

A classic approach to subgraph isomorphism can be found in [Ullmann 76]. A brute force enumeration process is described as a depth-first tree-search algorithm. As a way of improving the efficiency of the search, a refinement procedure is entered after each node is searched in the tree – the procedure reduces the number of node successors which yields a shorter execution time. An alternative approach testing isomorphism of graphs and subgraphs transforms the graph problem into a linear programming problem [Zdrahal 81].

The double subgraph isomorphism problem can be translated into a subgraph isomorphism problem using the **clique** (a complete (totally connected) subgraph) approach. A clique is said to be maximal if no other clique properly includes it. Note that a graph may have more than one maximal clique; however, it is often important to find the largest maximal clique (that with the largest number of elements). (Other definitions exist which consider a clique always to be maximal [Harary 69].)

The search for the maximal clique is a well-known problem in graph theory. An example algorithm for finding all cliques of an undirected graph can be found in [Bron and Kerbosch 73]. The maximal clique $G_{clique} = (V_{clique}, E_{clique})$ of the graph $G = (V, E)$ can be found as follows [Niemann 90];

Algorithm 7.10: Maximal clique location

1. Take an arbitrary node $v_j \in V$; construct a subset $V_{clique} = \{v_j\}$.

2. In the set V_{clique}^C search for a node v_k that is connected with all nodes in V_{clique}. Add the node v_k to a set V_{clique}.

3. Repeat step (2) as long as new nodes v_k can be found.

4. If no new node v_k can be found, V_{clique} represents the node set of the maximal clique subgraph G_{clique} (the maximal clique that contains the node v_j).

To find the largest maximal clique, an additional maximizing search is necessary. Other clique-finding algorithms are discussed in [Ballard and Brown 82, Yang et al. 89].

The search for isomorphism of two subgraphs (the double subgraph isomorphism) is transformed to a clique search using the **assignment graph** [Ambler 75]. A pair (v_1, v_2), $v_1 \in V_1$, $v_2 \in V_2$ is called an **assignment** if the nodes v_1 and v_2 have the same node property descriptions, and two assignments (v_1, v_2) and (v'_1, v'_2) are **compatible** if (in addition) all relations between v_1 and v'_1 also hold for v_2 and v'_2 (graph arcs between v_1, v'_1 and v_2, v'_2 must have the same evaluation, including the no-edge case). The set of assignments defines the set of nodes V_a of the assignment graph G_a. Two nodes in V_a (two assignments) are connected by an arc in the assignment graph G_a if these two nodes are compatible. The search for the maximum matching subgraphs of graphs G_1 and G_2 is a search for the maximum totally connected subgraph in G_a (the maximum totally compatible subset of assignments).

The maximum totally connected subgraph is a maximal clique and the maximal clique finding algorithm can be applied to solve this problem.

7.5.2 *Similarity of graphs*

All the approaches mentioned above tested for a perfect match between graphs and/or subgraphs. This cannot be anticipated in real applications, and these algorithms are not able to distinguish between a small mismatch of two very similar graphs and the case when the graphs are not similar at all. Moreover, if graph similarity is tested, the main stress is given to the ability to quantify the similarity. Having three graphs G_1, G_2, G_3 the question as to which two are the most similar is a natural one [Buckley 90].

The similarity of two strings (chains) can be based on the **Levenshtein distance** which is defined as the smallest number of deletions, insertions and substitutions necessary to convert one string into the other. Transformations of string elements can be assigned a specific transition cost to make the computed similarity (distance) more flexible and more sensitive. This principle can be applied to graph similarity as well. The set of feasible transformations of nodes and arcs (insertion, deletion, substitution, relabelling) is defined, and these transformations are accompanied by transition costs. Any sequence of transformations is assigned a combination of single step costs (like the sum of individual costs). The set of transformations that has the minimum cost and transforms one graph to another graph defines a distance between them [Niemann 90, Shapiro and Haralick 80].

Note that similarity can be searched for in hierarchical graph structures. The compared graphs consist of a number of subgraphs in which isomorphism (or similarity) has already been proved. The next step is to detect, describe and evaluate relations between these subgraphs (Figure 7.22, cf. Figure 7.20).

To explain the principles, a physical analogy of templates and springs

Fischler and Elschlager 73] is usually considered. The templates (subgraphs) are connected by springs (relations between subgraphs). The quality of the match of two graphs relates to the quality of the local fit (in corresponding templates) and to the amount of energy used to stretch the springs to match one graph onto the second (reference) graph. To make the graph similarity measure more flexible, extra costs may be added for missing parts of the graph as well as for some extra ones. The spring energy penalty may be made highly nonlinear better to reflect the descriptive character in particular applications.

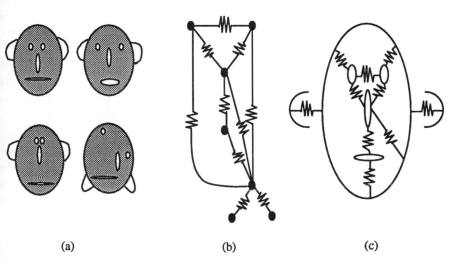

| (a) | (b) | (c) |

Figure 7.22 *Templates and springs principle: (a) Different objects having the same description graphs, (b),(c) nodes (templates) connected by springs, graph nodes may represent other graphs in finer resolution.*

7.6 Optimization techniques in recognition

Optimization itself is much more flexible than is usually recognized. Considering image recognition and understanding, the best image representation is sought (the best matching between the image and the model is required, the best image understanding is the goal). Whenever 'the best' is considered, some objective function of *goodness* must be available, implying that an optimization technique can be applied which looks for the evaluation function maximum ... for *the best*.

A function optimization problem may be defined as follows: given some finite domain D and a function $f : D \rightarrow R$, R being the set of real numbers, find the *best* value in D under f. Finding the *best* value in D is understood as finding a value $\mathbf{x} \in D$ yielding either the minimum (function minimization) or the maximum (function maximization) of the function f:

$$f_{min}(\mathbf{x}) = \min_{\mathbf{x} \in D} f(\mathbf{x}), \qquad f_{max}(\mathbf{x}) = \max_{\mathbf{x} \in D} f(\mathbf{x}) \qquad (7.46)$$

The function f is called the **objective** function. Maximization of the objective function will be considered here as it is typical in image interpretation applications, discussed in Chapter 8. However, optimization methods for seeking maxima and minima are logically equivalent, and optimization techniques can be equally useful if either an objective function maximum or function minimum is required.

It should be noted that no optimization algorithm can guarantee finding a good solution to the problem if the objective function does not reflect the *goodness* of the solution. Therefore, the design of the objective function is a key factor in the performance of any optimization algorithm (similarly, appropriate feature selection is necessary for the success of a classifier).

Conventional approaches to optimization use calculus based methods which can be compared to climbing a hill (in the case of maximization) – the gradient of the objective function gives the steepest direction to climb. The main limitation of calculus based methods is their local behaviour; the search can easily end in a local maximum and the global maximum can be missed (see Figure 7.23).

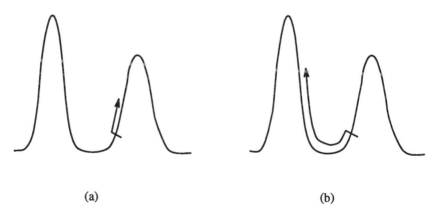

(a)   (b)

Figure 7.23 *Limitations of hill-climbing methods.*

There are several methods which improve the probability of finding the global maximum; to start the hill-climbing at several points in the search space, to apply enumerative searches like dynamic programming, to apply random searches, etc. One of these possibilities is to apply the genetic algorithm approach.

7.6.1 Genetic algorithms

Genetic algorithms (GA) represent a relatively new approach to optimization that uses natural evolution mechanisms to search for the maximum of an objective function. As with any optimization technique, they can be used in recognition and machine learning.

Genetic algorithms do not guarantee that the global optimum will be found. However, empirical results from many applications show that the final solution is usually very close to it. This is very important in image understanding applications as will be seen in the next chapter. There are almost always several consistent (feasible) solutions that are locally optimal in image understanding, or matching, and only one of those possible solutions is the best one represented by the global maximum. The opportunity to find the (near) global optimum is very valuable in these tasks.

Genetic algorithms differ substantially from other optimization methods in the following ways [Goldberg 89];

1. GAs work with a coding of the parameter set, not the parameters themselves. Genetic algorithms require the natural parameter set of the optimization problem to be coded as a finite length string over some finite alphabet. This implies that any optimization problem representation must be transformed to a string representation; binary strings are often used (the alphabet consisting of (0,1) symbols only). The design of the problem representation as a string is an important part of the GA method.

2. GAs search from a population of points, not a single point. The population of solutions that is processed in each step is large, meaning that the search for the optimum is driven from many places in the search space. This gives a better chance of finding the global optimum.

3. GAs use objective function information, not derivatives or other auxiliary knowledge. The search for new, better solutions depends on the values of the evaluation function only. Note that as in other recognition methods, the GAs find the (near) global optimum of the evaluation function but there is no guarantee at all that the evaluation function is relevant to the solved problem. The evaluation function describes the *goodness* of the particular string. The value of the evaluation function is called **fitness** in GAs.

4. GAs use probabilistic transition rules, not deterministic rules. Rules of transition from the current population of strings to a new and better population of strings are based on the natural idea of supporting good strings with higher fitness and removing poor strings with lower fitness. This is the key idea of genetic algorithms. The best strings representing

the best solutions are allowed to survive the evolution process with a higher probability.

The survival of the fittest and the death of the poor code strings is achieved by applying three basic operations: **reproduction, crossover and mutation**.

The population of strings represents all the strings that are being processed in the current step of the GA. The sequence of reproduction, crossover, and mutation generates a new population of strings from the previous population.

Reproduction

The reproduction operator is responsible for the survival of the fittest and for the death of others based on a probabilistic treatment.

The reproduction mechanism copies strings with highest fitness into the next generation of strings. The selection process is usually probabilistic, the probability that a string is reproduced into the new population being given by its relative fitness in the current population – this is their mechanism of survival. The lower the fitness of the string the lower the chances for survival. This process results in a set of strings where some strings of higher fitness may be copied more than once into the next population. The total number of strings in the population usually remains unchanged, and the average fitness of the new generation is higher than it was before.

Crossover

There are many variations on the crossover. The basic idea is to mate the newly reproduced strings at random, randomly choosing a position for the border of each pair of strings, and to produce new strings by swapping all characters between the beginning of the string pairs and the border position, see Figure 7.24.

Not all newly reproduced strings are subject to the crossover. There is a probability parameter representing the number of pairs which will be processed by crossover; also, it may be performed such that the best reproduced strings are kept in an unchanged form.

The crossover operation together with reproduction represent the main power of GAs. However, there is one more idea in the crossover operation; blocks of characters can be detected in the strings that have locally correct structure even if the string as a whole does not represent a good solution. These blocks of characters in strings are called **schemata**. Schemata are substrings that can represent building blocks of the string, and can be understood as the local pattern of characters. Clearly, if schemata can be manipulated as locally correct blocks, the optimal solution can be located faster than if all the characters are handled independently. In every generation of n strings, about n^3 schemata are processed. This is called the **implicit parallelism** of genetic algorithms [Goldberg 89].

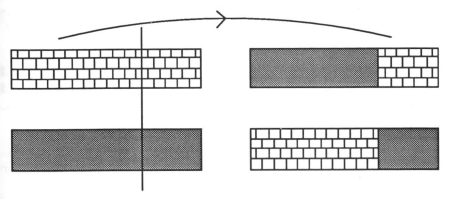

Figure 7.24 *Principle of crossover.*

Mutation

The mutation operator plays only a secondary role in GAs. Its principle is randomly to change one character of some string of the population from time to time – it might, for example, take place approximately once per thousand bit transfers (i.e. one bit mutation per one thousand bits transferred from generation to generation). The main reason for mutation is the fact that some local configuration of characters in strings of the population can be totally lost as a result of reproduction and crossover operations. Mutation protects GAs against such irrecoverable loss of good solution features.

Population convergence in GAs is a serious question. For practical purposes this question becomes one of when to stop generating the new string populations. A common and practically proven criterion recommends that the population generating process be stopped when the maximum achieved fitness in the population has not improved substantially through several previous generations.

We have not yet discussed how to create the starting population, which usually consists of a large number of strings, the number depending on the application. The starting population can be generated at random, assuming the alphabet of characters and the desired length of strings are known. Nevertheless, as always, if there is some prior knowledge about the solution available (i.e. the probable local patterns of characters, the probable percentages of characters in strings, etc.), then it is advantageous to use this information to make the starting population as fit as possible. The better the starting population, the easier and faster the search for the optimum.

The simplified version of the genetic algorithm is as follows:

Algorithm 7.11: Genetic algorithm

---

1. Create a starting population of code strings, and find the value of their objective functions.

2. Probabilistically reproduce high fitness strings in the new population, remove poor fitness strings (reproduction).

3. Construct new strings combining reproduced code strings from the previous population (crossover).

4. From time to time change one character of some string at random (mutation).

5. Order code strings of the current population according to the value of their objective function (fitness).

6. If the maximum achieved string fitness does not increase over several steps, stop. The desired optimum is represented by the current string of maximum fitness. Otherwise, repeat the sequence of steps starting at step 2.

See Section 8.5.2 for an example of the algorithm function. A more detailed and precise description of genetic algorithms can be found in [Goldberg 89, Rawlins 91]. Many examples and descriptions of related techniques are included there as well, such as knowledge implementation into mutation and crossover, GA learning systems, hybrid techniques that combine good properties of conventional hill-climbing searches and GAs, etc.

7.6.2 Simulated annealing

Simulated annealing [Kirkpatrick et al. 83, Cerny 85] represents another group of robust optimization methods. Similarly to genetic algorithms, simulated annealing searches for a minimum of an objective function (cost function) that represents the goodness of some complex system. Searching for minima is considered in this section because it simplifies energy-related correspondences with the natural behaviour of matter. Simulated annealing may be suitable for NP-complete optimization problems. If we require a fast solution, simulated annealing does not guarantee that the global optimum is found; the solution is usually near-optimal.

Cerny [Cerny 85] often uses the following example to explain the principle of simulated annealing optimization. Imagine a sugar bowl freshly filled with cube sugar. Usually, some cubes do not fit in the sugar bowl and the lid cannot be closed. From experience, everybody knows that shaking the sugar bowl will result in better placement of the cubes inside the bowl and the lid will close properly. In other words, considering the number of cubes that can be inside the bowl as an evaluation function, shaking the bowl results in a near-minimal solution (considering sugar space requirements). The degree of shaking is a parameter of this optimization process and corresponds to the heating and cooling process as described below.

Simulated annealing combines two basic optimization principles, **divide and conquer** and **iterative improvement** (hill-climbing). This combination avoids getting stuck in local optima. A strong connection between statistical mechanics or thermodynamics, and multivariate or combinatorial optimization is the basis for annealing optimization.

In statistical mechanics, only the most probable change of state of a system in thermal equilibrium at a given temperature is observed in experiments; each configuration (state) defined by the set of atomic positions $\{x_i\}$ of the system is weighted by its Boltzmann constant probability factor

$$\exp(\frac{-E(\{x_i\})}{k_B T}) \tag{7.47}$$

where $E(\{x_i\})$ is the energy of the state, k_B is the Boltzmann constant, and T is the temperature [Kirkpatrick et al. 83].

One of the main characteristics of the Boltzmann density is that at high temperature each state has an almost equal chance of becoming the new state, but at low temperature only states with low energies have a high probability of becoming current. The optimization can be compared with the ability of matter to form a crystalline structure that represents an energy minimum if the matter is melted and cooled down slowly. This minimum can be considered the optimization minimum for the energy function playing the role of the objective function. The crystalization process depends on the cooling speed of the molten liquid; if the cooling is too fast, the crystal includes many local defects and the global energy minimum is not reached.

Simulated annealing consists of downhill iteration steps combined with controlled uphill steps that make it possible to escape from local minima (see Figure 7.25).

The physical model of the process starts with heating the matter until it melts; then the resulting liquid is cooled down slowly to keep the quasi-equilibrium. The cooling algorithm [Metropolis et al. 53] consists of repeated random displacements (state changes) of atoms in the matter, and the energy change ΔE is evaluated after each state change. If $\Delta E \leq 0$ (lower energy), the state change is accepted, and the new state is used as the starting state of the next step. If $\Delta E > 0$, the state is accepted with probability

$$P(\Delta E) = \exp(\frac{-\Delta E}{k_B T}) \tag{7.48}$$

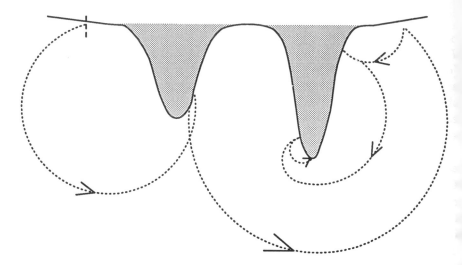

Figure 7.25 *Uphill steps make it possible to get out of local minima; the dotted line shows a possible convergence route.*

To apply this physical model to an optimization problem, the temperature parameter T must be decreased in a controlled manner during optimization. The random part of the algorithm can be implemented by generating random numbers uniformly distributed in the interval (0,1); one such random number is selected and compared with $P(\Delta E)$.

Algorithm 7.12: Simulated annealing optimization

1. Let $\mathbf{x}$ be a vector of optimization parameters; compute the value of the objective function $J(\mathbf{x})$. Repeat steps 2 to 4 for decreasing values of temperature T until *stop*.

2. Repeat steps 3 and 4 $n(T)$ times.

3. Perturb the parameter vector $\mathbf{x}$ slightly, creating the vector $\mathbf{x}_{new}$, and compute the new value of the optimization function $J(\mathbf{x}_{new})$.

4. Generate a random number $r \in (0,1)$, from a uniform distribution in the interval (0,1). If

$$r < \exp(\frac{-(J(\mathbf{x}_{new}) - J(\mathbf{x}))}{k_B T}) \qquad (7.49)$$

   then assign $\mathbf{x} = \mathbf{x}_{new}$ and $J(\mathbf{x}) = J(\mathbf{x}_{new})$.

5. The parameter vector $\mathbf{x}$ now represents the solution of the optimization problem.

Note that nothing is known beforehand about how many steps n, what perturbations to the parameter (state changes), what choice of temperatures T, and what speed of cooling down should be applied to achieve the best (or even good) results, although some general guidelines exist and appropriate parameters can be found for particular problems. It is only known that the annealing process must continue long enough to reach a steady state for each temperature. Remember the sugar bowl example, the shaking is much stronger at the beginning and gradually decreases for the best results.

The sequence of temperatures and the number n of steps necessary to achieve equilibrium in each temperature is called the **annealing schedule**. Large values of n and small decrements of T yield low final values of the optimization function (the solution is close to the global minimum) but require long computation time. A small number of repetitions n and large decrements in T proceed faster but the results may not be close to the global minimum. The values T and n must be chosen to give a solution close to the minimum without wasting too much computation time. There is no known practically applicable way to design an optimal annealing schedule.

The annealing algorithm is easy to implement. Annealing has been applied to many optimization problems including pattern recognition, graph partitioning, and many others and has been demonstrated to be of great value (although examples of optimization problems exist in which it performs worse that standard algorithms and other heuristics). In the computer vision area, recent applications include boundary detection [Geman et al. 90], texture segmentation [Bouman and Liu 91] and edge detection [Tan et al. 92]. Implementation details and annealing algorithm properties together with an extensive list of references can be found in [Aarts and van Laarhoven 86, van Laarhoven and Aarts 87, van Laarhoven 88, Otten and van Ginneken 89].

References

[Aarts and van Laarhoven 86] E H L Aarts and P J M van Laarhoven. Simulated annealing: a pedestrian review of the theory and some applications. In P A Devijver and J Kittler, editors, *Pattern Recognition Theory and Applications*, pages 179–192. Springer Verlag, Berlin-New York-Tokyo, 1986.

[Ambler 75] A P H Ambler. A versatile system for computer controlled assembly. *Artificial Intelligence*, 6(2):129–156, 1975.

[Amit 89] D J Amit. *Modeling Brain Function: The World of Attractor Neural Networks*. Cambridge University Press, Cambridge, England; New York, 1989.

[Baird 84] H S Baird. *Model-Based Image Matching using Location*. MIT Press, Cambridge, Ma, 1984.

[Ballard and Brown 82] D H Ballard and C M Brown. *Computer Vision* Prentice-Hall, Englewood Cliffs, NJ, 1982.

[Barrero 91] A Barrero. Inference of tree grammars using negative samples *Pattern Recognition*, 24(1):1–8, 1991.

[Barrow and Popplestone 71] H G Barrow and R J Popplestone. Relational descriptions in picture processing. *Machine Intelligence*, 6, 1971.

[Beale and Jackson 90] R Beale and T Jackson. *Neural Computing – An Introduction*. Adam Hilger, Bristol, 1990.

[Berge 76] C Berge. *Graphs and Hypergraphs*. American Elsevier, New York, 2nd edition, 1976.

[Bittner and Reingold 75] J R Bittner and E M Reingold. Backtrack programming techniques. *Communications of the ACM*, 18(11):651–656, 1975.

[Blum and Rivest 88] A Blum and R L Rivest. Training a three node neural network is np-complete. In *Proceedings of IEEE Conference on Neural Information Processing Systems*, page 494, 1988.

[Bouman and Liu 91] C Bouman and B Liu. Multiple resolution segmentation of textured images. *IEEE Transactions on Pattern Analysis and Machine Intelligence*, 13(2):99–113, 1991.

[Bron and Kerbosch 73] C Bron and J Kerbosch. Finding all cliques of an undirected graph. *Communications of the ACM*, 16(9):575–577, 1973.

[Buckley 90] F Buckley. *Distance in Graphs*. Addison-Wesley, Redwood City, Ca, 1990.

[Carpenter 89] G A Carpenter. Neural network models for pattern recognition. *Neural Networks*, 2:243–257, 1989.

[Carpenter 91] G A Carpenter. Neural network models for pattern recognition. In G A Carpenter and S Grossberg, editors, *Pattern Recognition by Self-Organizing Neural Networks*, pages 1–34. MIT Press, Cambridge, Ma, 1991.

[Carpenter and Grossberg 91] G A Carpenter and S Grossberg. *Pattern Recognition by Self-organizing Neural Networks*. MIT Press, Cambridge, Ma, 1991.

[Cerny 85] V Cerny. Thermodynamical approach to the travelling salesman problem: An efficient simulation algorithm. *Journal of Optimization Theory and Applications*, 45:41–51, 1985.

[Chen 76] C H Chen, editor. *Pattern Recognition and Artificial Intelligence*. Academic Press, New York, 1976.

[Chomsky 66] N Chomsky. *Syntactic Structures*. Mouton, Hague, 6th edition, 1966.

[Chomsky et al. 71] N Chomsky, J P B Allen, and P Van Buren. *Chomsky: Selected Readings*. Oxford University Press, London-New York, 1971.

[Clocksin and Mellish 81] W F Clocksin and C S Mellish. *Programming in Prolog*. Springer Verlag, Berlin-New-York-Tokyo, 1981.

[Dasarathy 91] B V Dasarathy. *Nearest Neighbor (NN) Norms: NN Pattern Classification Techniques*. IEEE Comp. Society Press, Los Alamitos, Ca, 1991.

[Dayhoff 90] J E Dayhoff. *Neural Network Architectures: An Introduction*. Van Nostrand Reinhold, New York, 1990.

[Devijver and Kittler 82] P A Devijver and J Kittler. *Pattern Recognition: A Statistical Approach*. Prentice-Hall, Englewood Cliffs, NJ, 1982.

[Devijver and Kittler 86] P A Devijver and J Kittler. *Pattern Recognition Theory and Applications*. Springer Verlag, Berlin-New York-Tokyo, 1986.

[Duda and Hart 73] R O Duda and P E Hart. *Pattern Classification and Scene Analysis*. John Wiley and Sons, New York, 1973.

[Eberhart and Dobbins 90] R C Eberhart and R W Dobbins. *Neural Network PC Tools: A Practical Guide*. Academic Press, San Diego, Ca, 1990.

[Even 79] S Even. *Graph Algorithms*. Computer Science Press, Rockville, Md, 1979.

[Fischler and Elschlager 73] M A Fischler and R A Elschlager. The representation and matching of pictorial structures. *IEEE Transactions on Computers*, C-22(1):67–92, 1973.

[Foley 72] D H Foley. Consideration of sample and feature size. *IEEE Transactions on Information Theory*, IT-18(5):618–626, 1972.

[Fu 68] K S Fu. *Sequential Methods in Pattern Recognition and Machine Learning*. Academic Press, New York, 1968.

[Fu 74]   K S Fu. *Syntactic Methods in Pattern Recognition*. Academic Press, New York, 1974.

[Fu 77]   K S Fu. *Syntactic Pattern Recognition – Applications*. Springer Verlag, Berlin, 1977.

[Fu 80]   K S Fu. Picture syntax. In S K Chang and K S Fu, editors, *Pictorial Information Systems*, pages 104–127. Springer Verlag, Berlin, 1980.

[Fu 82]   K S Fu. *Syntactic Pattern Recognition and Applications*. Prentice-Hall, Englewood Cliffs, NJ, 1982.

[Fukunaga 90]   K Fukunaga. *Introduction to Statistical Pattern Recognition*. Academic Press, Boston, 2nd edition, 1990.

[Geman et al. 90]   D Geman, S Geman, C Graffigne, and P Dong. Boundary detection by constrained optimisation. *IEEE Transactions on Pattern Analysis and Machine Intelligence*, 12(7), 1990.

[Goldberg 89]   D E Goldberg. *Genetic Algorithms in Search, Optimization, and Machine Learning*. Addison-Wesley, Reading, Ma, 1989.

[Gonzalez and Thomason 74]   R C Gonzalez and M G Thomason. On the inference of tree grammars for pattern recognition. In *Proceedings of the IEEE International Conference on System, Man and Cybernetics*, pages 2–4. IEEE, 1974.

[Grossberg 70]   S Grossberg. Neural pattern discrimination. *Journal of Theoretical Biology*, 27:291–337, 1970.

[Grossberg 91]   S Grossberg. Neural pattern discrimination. In G A Carpenter and S Grossberg, editors, *Pattern Recognition by Self-Organizing Neural Networks*, pages 111–156. MIT Press, Cambridge, Ma, 1991.

[Haralick and Elliott 79]   R M Haralick and G L Elliott. Increasing tree search efficiency for constraint satisfaction problems. In *Proceedings of 6th IJCAI-79*, pages 356–364, 1979.

[Harary 69]   F Harary. *Graph Theory*. Addison-Wesley, Reading, Ma, 1969.

[Hayes 77]   P J Hayes. In defense of logic. In *Proceedings of 5th IJCAI*, Cambridge, Ma, 1977.

[Hecht-Nielsen 90]   R Hecht-Nielsen. *Neurocomputing*. Addison-Wesley, Reading, Ma, 1990.

[Hopfield and Tank 85]   J J Hopfield and D W Tank. Neural computation of decisions in optimization problems. *Biological Cybernetics*, 52:141–152, 1985.

[Hopfield and Tank 86] J J Hopfield and D W Tank. Computing with neural circuits: A model. *Science*, 233:625–633, 1986.

[Johnson and Wichern 90] R A Johnson and D W Wichern. *Applied Multivariate Statistical Analysis*. Prentice-Hall, Englewood Cliffs, NJ, 2nd edition, 1990.

[Judd 90] J S Judd. *Neural Network Design and the Complexity of Learning*. MIT Press, Cambridge, Ma, 1990.

[Kaufman and Rousseeuw 90] L Kaufman and P J Rousseeuw. *Finding Groups in Data: An Introduction to Cluster Analysis*. John Wiley and Sons, New York, 1990.

[Kirkpatrick et al. 83] S Kirkpatrick, C D Gelatt, and M P Vecchi. Optimization by simulated annealing. *Science*, 220:671–680, 1983.

[Kohonen 89] T Kohonen. *Self-Organization and Associative Memory*. Springer Verlag, Berlin-New York-Tokyo, 3rd edition, 1989.

[Kosko 91] B Kosko. Adaptive bidirectional associative memories. In G A Carpenter and S Grossberg, editors, *Pattern Recognition by Self-Organizing Neural Networks*, pages 425–450. MIT Press, Cambridge, Ma, 1991.

[Kowalski 79] R Kowalski. *Logic for Problem Solving*. North Holland, Amsterdam, 1979.

[Lau 89] H T Lau. *Algorithms on Graphs*. TAB Professional and Reference Books, Blue Ridge Summit, Pa, 1989.

[MacQueen 67] J MacQueen. Some methods for classification and analysis of multivariate observations. In *Proceedings of the 5th Berkeley Symposium – 1*, pages 281–297, 1967.

[McEliece et al. 87] R J McEliece, E C Posner, E R Rodemich, and S S Venkatesh. The capacity of the Hopfield associative memory. *IEEE Transactions on Information Theory*, 33:461, 1987.

[McHugh 90] J A McHugh. *Algorithmic Graph Theory*. Prentice-Hall, Englewood Cliffs, NJ, 1990.

[McQuitty 87] L L McQuitty. *Pattern-Analytic Clustering: Theory, Method, Research, and Configural Findings*. University Press of America, Lanham, NY, 1987.

[Metropolis et al. 53] N Metropolis, A W Rosenbluth, M N Rosenbluth, A H Teller, and E Teller. Equation of state calculation by fast computing machines. *Journal of Chemical Physics*, 21:1087–1092, 1953.

[Michalski et al. 83] R S Michalski, J G Carbonell, and T M Mitchell. *Machine Learning I, II*. Morgan Kaufmann Publishers, Los Altos, Ca, 1983.

[Minsky 88] M L Minsky. *Perceptrons: An Introduction to Computational Geometry*. MIT Press, Cambridge, Ma, 2nd edition, 1988.

[Mohring 91] R H Mohring, editor. *Graph-Theoretic Concepts in Computer Science - 16th WG'90*, Berlin-New York-Tokyo, 1991. Springer Verlag.

[Mozer 91] M C Mozer. *The Perception of Multiple Objects: A Connectionist Approach*. MIT Press, Cambridge, Ma, 1991.

[Nagl 90] M Nagl, editor. *Graph-Theoretic Concepts in Computer Science - 15th WG'89*, Berlin-New York-Tokyo, 1990. Springer Verlag.

[Niemann 90] H Niemann. *Pattern Analysis and Understanding*. Springer Verlag, Berlin-New York-Tokyo, 2nd edition, 1990.

[Nilsson 71] N J Nilsson. *Problem Solving Methods in Artificial Intelligence*. McGraw Hill, New York, 1971.

[Nilsson 82] N J Nilsson. *Principles of Artificial Intelligence*. Springer Verlag, Berlin, 1982.

[Oja 83] E Oja. *Subspace Methods of Pattern Recognition*. Research Studies Press, Letchworth, England, 1983.

[Otten and van Ginneken 89] R H J M Otten and L P P P van Ginneken. *The Annealing Algorithm*. Kluwer Academic Publishers, Norwell, Ma, 1989.

[Patrick and Fattu 86] E A Patrick and J M Fattu. *Artificial Intelligence with Statistical Pattern Recognition*. Prentice-Hall, Englewood Cliffs, NJ, 1986.

[Pavel 89] M Pavel. *Fundamentals of Pattern Recognition*. M. Dekker, New York, 1989.

[Pavlidis 77] T Pavlidis. *Structural Pattern Recognition*. Springer Verlag, Berlin, 1977.

[Pavlidis 80] T Pavlidis. Structural descriptions and graph grammars. In S K Chang and K S Fu, editors, *Pictorial Information Systems*, pages 86–103, Springer Verlag, Berlin, 1980.

[Pospesel 76] H Pospesel. *Predicate Logic*. Prentice-Hall, Englewood Cliffs, NJ, 1976.

[Rao 65] C R Rao. *Linear Statistical Inference and its Application*. John Wiley and Sons, New York, 1965.

[Rawlins 91] G J E Rawlins. *Foundations of Genetic Algorithms*. Morgan Kaufmann, San Mateo, Ca, 1991.

[Reichgelt 91] H Reichgelt. *Knowledge Representation: An AI Perspective*. Ablex Publishing Corporation, Norwood, NJ, 1991.

[Rogers and Kabrisky 91] S K Rogers and M Kabrisky. *An Introduction to Biological and Artificial Neural Networks for Pattern Recognition*. SPIE, Bellingham, Wa, 1991.

[Romesburg 84] H C Romesburg. *Cluster Analysis for Researchers*. Lifetime Learning Publications, Belmont, Ca, 1984.

[Rosenblatt 62] R Rosenblatt. *Principles of Neurodynamics*. Spartan books, Washington, D.C., 1962.

[Rosenfeld 79] A Rosenfeld. *Picture Languages – Formal Models for Picture Recognition*. Academic Press, New York, 1979.

[Rumelhart and McClelland 86] D Rumelhart and J McClelland. *Parallel Distributed Processing*. MIT Press, Cambridge, Ma, 1986.

[Schutzer 87] D Schutzer. *Artificial Intelligence, An Application-Oriented Approach*. Van Nostrand Reinhold, New York, 1987.

[Sedgewick 84] R Sedgewick. *Algorithms*. Addison-Wesley, Reading, Ma, 2nd edition, 1984.

[Shapiro and Haralick 80] L G Shapiro and R M Haralick. Algorithms for inexact matching. In *Proceedings 5th International Conference on Pattern Recognition*, pages 202–207, IEEE Comp. Society Press, Los Alamitos, Ca, 1980.

[Sharples et al. 89] M Sharples, D Hogg, C Hutchinson, S Torrance, and D Young. *Computers and Thought, A Practical Introduction to Artificial Intelligence*. The MIT Press, Cambridge, Ma, 1989.

[Simons 84] G L Simons. *Introducing Artificial Intelligence*. NCC Publications, Manchester, 1984.

[Simpson 90] P K Simpson. *Artificial Neural Systems: Foundations, Paradigms, Applications, and Implementations*. Pergamon Press, New York, 1990.

[Sklansky 81] J Sklansky. *Pattern Classifiers and Trainable Machines*. Springer Verlag, New York, 1981.

[Sonka 86] M Sonka. A new texture recognition method. *Computers and Artificial Intelligence*, 5(4):357–364, 1986.

[Tan et al. 92] H K Tan, S B Gelfand, and E J Delp. A cost minimization approach to edge detection using simulated annealing. *IEEE Transactions on Pattern Analysis and Machine Intelligence*, 14(1), 1992.

[Ullmann 76] J R Ullmann. An algorithm for subgraph isomorphism. *Journal of the Association for Computing Machinery*, 23(1):31–42, 1976.

[van Laarhoven 88] P J M van Laarhoven. *Theoretical and Computational Aspects of Simulated Annealing*. Centrum voor Wiskunde en Informatik, Amsterdam, 1988.

[van Laarhoven and Aarts 87] P J M van Laarhoven and E H L Aarts. *Simulated Annealing: Theory and Applications*. Dordrecht and Kluwer Academic Publisher, Norwell, Ma, 1987.

[Wasserman 89] P D Wasserman. *Neural Computing – Theory and Practice*. Van Nostrand Rheinhold, New York, 1989.

[Wechsler 90] H Wechsler. *Computational Vision*. Academic Press, London – San Diego, 1990.

[Winston 75] P H Winston, editor. *The Psychology of Computer Vision*. McGraw Hill, New York, 1975.

[Winston 84] P H Winston. *Artificial Intelligence*. Addison-Wesley, Reading, Ma, 2nd edition, 1984.

[Yang et al. 89] B Yang, W E Snyder, and G L Bilbro. Matching oversegmented 3D images to models using association graphs. *Image and Vision Computing*, 7(2):135–143, 1989.

[Young and Calvert 74] T Y Young and T W Calvert. *Classification, Estimation, and Pattern Recognition*. American Elsevier, New York-London-Amsterdam, 1974.

[Zdrahal 81] Z Zdrahal. A structural method of scene analysis. In *Proceedings of IJCAI-81*, pages 680–682, Vancouver, BC, Canada, 1981.

[Zeidenberg 90] M Zeidenberg. *Neural Network Models in Artificial Intelligence*. E. Hoerwood, New York, 1990.

[Zhou 92] Y T Zhou. *Artificial Neural Networks for Computer Vision*. Springer Verlag, New York, 1992.

[Zimmermann et al. 84] H J Zimmermann, L A Zadeh, and B R Gaines. *Fuzzy Sets and Decision Analysis*. North Holland, Amsterdam-New York, 1984.

8

Image understanding

Image understanding requires mutual interaction of processing steps. The building blocks necessary for image understanding have been presented in earlier chapters – now an internal image model must be built that represents the machine vision system's concept about the processed image of the world.

Consider a typical human approach: A human being is well prepared to do image processing, analysis and understanding. Despite this fact, it may sometimes be difficult to recognize what is seen if what to expect is not known. If a microscopic image of some tissue is presented to an observer who has never had a chance to study tissue structure or morphology then the question of the location of diseased tissue may be unanswerable. A similar problem can result if an observer is required to understand an aerial or satellite image of some urban area, even if the data correspond to a city with which the observer is familiar. Further, we can require the observer to watch the scene on a 'per part' basis – like using a telescope; this is an approach similar to a machine vision system's abilities. If a human observer solves the problem of orientation in such a scene, probably a start is made by trying to locate some known object. The observer constructs an image model of the city starting with the object believed to be recognized. Consider an aerial city view (see the simplified map of Prague, Figure 8.1), and suppose our observer sees two Gothic towers. They may be the towers of Prague castle, of the Vysehrad castle, or towers of some other Gothic churches. Let our observer begin with a hypothesis that the towers belong to the Vysehrad castle; a model of Vysehrad consists of the adjacent park, closely located river, etc. The observer attempts to verify the hypothesis with the model – does the model match the reality? If it matches, the hypothesis is supported and if it does not, the hypothesis is weakened and finally rejected. The observer constructs a new hypothesis describing the scene, builds another model, and again tries to verify it. Two main forms of knowledge are used when the internal model is constructed – the general knowledge of placement of streets, houses, parks, etc. in cities, and specific knowledge of the order of specific houses, streets, rivers, etc. in the specific city.

The machine vision system can be asked to solve similar problems. The main difference between a human observer and an artificial vision system is in a lack of widely applicable, general, and modifiable knowledge of the real

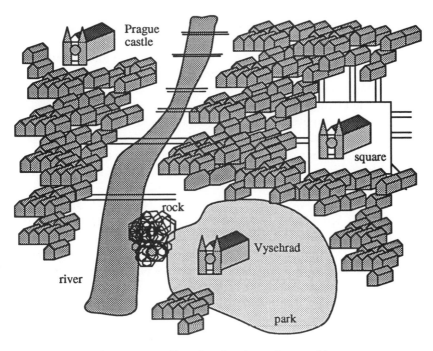

Figure 8.1 *Simulated orientation problem.*

world in the latter. Machine vision systems construct internal models of the processed scene, verify them, and update them, and an appropriate sequence of processing steps must be performed to fulfil the given task. If the constructed internal model matches the reality, image understanding is achieved. On the other hand, the example described above showed that existence of an image model is a prerequisite for perception; there is no inconsistency in this. The image representation has an incremental character; new data or perceptions are compared with an existing model, and are used for model modification. Image data interpretation is not explicitly dependent on image data alone. The variations in starting models, as well as differences in previous experience, cause the data to be interpreted differently, even if always consistently with the constructed model; any final interpretation can be considered correct if just a match between a model and image data is evaluated [Levine 78, Zucker 78, Rosenfeld 79, Tsosos 84, Li and Uhr 87, Basu 87, Mulder 88, Niemann 90].

We have said that machine vision consists of lower and upper processing levels, and image understanding is the highest processing level in this classification. The main task of this processing level is to define control strategies that ensure an appropriate sequence of processing steps. Moreover, a machine vision system must be able to deal with a large number of interpretations that are hypothetical and ambiguous. Generally viewed, the organization of the machine vision system consists of a weak hierarchical structure of image models.

Many important results have been achieved in image understanding in recent years. Despite that, the image understanding process remains an open area of computer vision and is under continued investigation. Image understanding is one of the most complex challenges of AI, and to cover this complicated area of computer vision in detail it would be necessary to discuss relatively independent branches of AI – knowledge representation, relational structures, semantic networks, general matching, inference, production systems, problem solving, planning, control, and learning from experience, a difficult and not fully understood area. These areas are used and described in various AI references [Bajcsy and Rosenthal 80, Nilsson 82, Michalski et al. 83, Winston 84, Simons 84, Devijver and Kittler 86, Wechsler 90, Reichgelt 91, Marik et al. 92] and their application to computer vision is an active area of research. Nevertheless, to cover these topics in detail exceeds the frame of this book; therefore, we present here an overview of basic image understanding control strategies and describe contextual and semantic methods of image understanding. Image understanding control is a crucial problem in machine vision, and the control strategies described give a better rationale for the application of various methods of image processing, object description, and recognition described earlier. At the same time, it explains why the specific AI methods are incorporated in image understanding processes.

8.1   Image understanding control strategies

Image understanding can be achieved only as a result of cooperation of complex information processing tasks and appropriate control of these tasks. Biological systems include a very complicated and complex control strategy incorporating parallel processing, dynamic sensing subsystem allocation, behaviour modifications, interrupt driven shifts of attention, etc. As in other AI problems, the main computer vision goal is to achieve machine behaviour similar to that of biological systems by applying technically available procedures.

8.1.1   Parallel and serial processing control

Both parallel and serial approaches can be applied to image processing, although sometimes it is not obvious which steps should be processed in parallel and which serially. Parallel processing makes several computations simultaneously (e.g. several image parts can be processed simultaneously) and an extremely important consideration is the synchronization of processing actions; that is, the decision of when, or if, the processing should wait for other processing steps to complete [Ghosh and Harrison 90, Prasanna Kumar 91].

Operations are always sequential in serial processing. A serial control strategy is natural for conventional von Neumann computer architectures, and the large numbers of operations that biological organisms process in parallel often cannot be done serially at the required speed. Pyramid image representations, and corresponding pyramid processor architectures, resulted from speed requirements (including implementation of cognitive processes in lower processing levels, etc.). Parallel computers have become generally available, and despite substantial difficulties with their programming, the parallel processing option is now a reality. The feasibility of parallel processing implementation of various approaches and algorithms has been mentioned throughout this book, and it has been made clear that almost all low-level image processing can be done in parallel. However, high-level processing using higher levels of abstraction is usually serial in essence. There is an obvious comparison with the human strategy of solving complex sensing problems: A human always concentrates on a single topic during later phases of vision even if the early steps are done in parallel.

8.1.2 Hierarchical control

Image information is stored in different representations during processing. There is one crucial question related to processing control: Should the processing be controlled by the image data information or by higher level knowledge? These different approaches can be described as follows:

1. **Control by the image data (bottom-up control)**: Processing proceeds from the raster image to segmented image, to region (object) description, and to their recognition.

2. **Model-based control (top-down control)**: A set of assumptions and expected properties is constructed from applicable knowledge. The satisfaction of those properties is tested in image representations at different processing levels in a top-down direction, down to the original image data. The image understanding is an internal model verification, and the model is either accepted or rejected.

The two basic control strategies do not differ in the types of operation applied, but do differ in the sequence of their application, in the application either to all image data or just to selected image data, etc. The chosen control mechanism is not only a route to the processing goal, it influences the whole control strategy. Neither top-down nor bottom-up control strategies can explain the vision process or solve complex vision sensing problems in their standard forms. However, their appropriate combination can yield a more flexible and powerful vision control strategy.

8.1.3 Bottom-up control strategies

A general bottom-up algorithm is;

Algorithm 8.1: Bottom-up control

---

1. Pre-processing: Transform the raster image data (pre-process the image) to highlight information that may be useful in further processing steps. Appropriate transformations are applied throughout the image.

2. Segmentation: Detect and segment image regions that can correspond to real objects or object parts.

3. Understanding: If region descriptions were not used in step (2), determine an appropriate description for regions found in the segmented image. Compare the detected objects with real objects that are present in the solution domain (i.e. using pattern recognition techniques).

It is obvious that the bottom-up control strategy is based on the construction of data structures for the following processing steps. Note that each algorithm step can consist of several substeps, however the image representation remains unchanged in the substeps. The bottom-up control strategy is advantageous if a simple and efficient processing method is available that is independent of the image data content. Bottom-up control yields good results if unambiguous data are processed and if the processing gives reliable and precise representations for later processing steps. The recognition of well illuminated objects in robotic applications may serve as an example – in this case, bottom-up control results in fast and reliable processing. If the input data are of low quality, bottom-up control can yield good results only if unreliability of the data causes just a limited number of insubstantial errors in each processing step. This implies that the main image understanding role must be played by a control strategy that is not only a concatenation of processing operations in the bottom-up direction, but that also uses an internal model goal specifications, planning, and complex cognitive processes.

A good example of a bottom-up control strategy is Marr's image understanding approach [Marr 82]. The processing begins with a two-dimensional intensity image and tries to achieve a three-dimensional image understanding through a sequence of intermediate image representations. Marr's understanding strategy is based on a pure bottom-up data flow using only very general assumptions about the objects to be identified – a more detailed description of this approach is given in Chapter 9.

8.1.4 Model-based control strategies

There is no specific version of top-down control as was presented in the bottom-up control algorithm. The main top-down control principle is the construction of an internal model and its verification, meaning that the main principle is **goal oriented processing**. Goals at higher processing levels are split into subgoals at lower processing levels, which are split again into subgoals etc., until the subgoals can either be accepted or rejected directly.

An example will illustrate this principle. Imagine that you are in a large hotel, and your spouse parked your white Ford Escort somewhere in the large car park in front of the hotel. You are trying to find your car, looking from the hotel room window. The first level goal is to find the car park. A subgoal may be to detect all white cars in the car park and to decide which of those white cars are Ford Escorts. All the given goals can be fulfilled by looking from the window and using general models (general knowledge) of cars, colours, and Escorts.

If all the former goals were fulfilled, the last goal is to decide if the detected white Ford Escort really is your car and not some other white Escort; to satisfy this goal, specific knowledge of your car is necessary. You have to know what makes your car special – the differences between your car and others. If the test of the specific properties of the detected car is successful, the car is accepted as yours; the model you built for your white Escort was accepted, the car was located, and the search is over. If the test of specific properties was not successful, you have to resume testing at some higher level, for instance to detect another as yet untested white Ford Escort.

The general mechanism of top-down control is hypothesis generation and its testing. The internal model generator predicts what a specific part of the model must look like in lower image representations. The image understanding process consists of sequential hypothesis generation and testing. The internal model is updated during the processing according to the results of the hypothesis tests. The hypothesis testing relies on a (relatively small) amount of information acquired from lower representation levels, and the processing control is based on the fact that just the necessary image processing is required to test each hypothesis. The model-based control strategy (top-down, hypothesize and verify) seems to be a way of solving computer vision tasks by avoiding brute force processing; at the same time, it does not mean that parallel processing should not be applied whenever possible.

Not surprisingly, real-world models play a substantial role in model vision. Many approaches presented throughout this book may be considered either models of a part of an image or object models. However, to represent a variety of real-world domains, to be able to model complex image objects, their physical properties must be included in the representation. This is especially true in modelling natural objects – human faces together with their mimics may serve as a good example. Physical modelling is a fast developing branch of computer vision and image understanding [Kanade and Ikeuchi 91] in which four main techniques appear; reflection models for vision, relations between shape and reflection, statistical and stochastic modelling, and modelling deformable shapes (**elastics in vision**). Clearly, all these techniques may significantly increase the knowledge available in the image understanding process. From the point of view of the context being discussed here, deformable models of non-rigid objects seem to widen substantially the rank of feasible applications.

Elastics in vision [Witkin et al. 87, Terzopoulos and Fleischer 88, Terzopoulos 91] represent deformable bodies mostly using **dynamically moving splines – snakes** [Kass et al. 87a] and **superquadrics** [Terzopoulos and Metaxas 91, Metaxas and Terzopoulos 91] to fit complex three-dimensional shapes, with a potential for sub-pixel accuracy [Zucker 88]. Snakes and balloons as active contour models are discussed later in Section 8.2.

8.1.5 Combined control strategies

A combined control mechanism that uses both data driven and model driven control strategies is widely used in today's computer vision applications. It usually gives better results than any of the previously discussed, separately applied, basic control strategies. All available higher level information is used to make the lower level processing easier, but is alone insufficient to solve the task. Looking for cars in aerial or satellite image data may be a good example; data driven control is necessary to find the cars but at the same time, higher level knowledge can be used to simplify the problem since cars appear as rectangular objects of specific size, and the highest probability of their appearance is on roads.

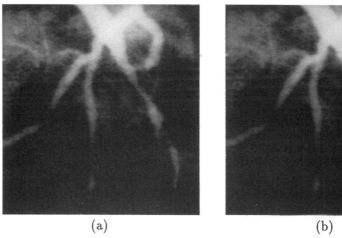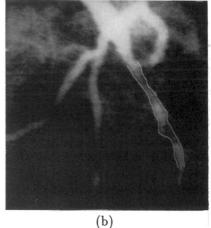

(a)   (b)

Figure 8.2 *Coronary angiograph: (a) Original X-ray image, (b) borders detected by a bottom-up graph search approach.*

An example of a robust approach to automated coronary border detection in angiographic images illustrates the combined control strategy [Collins et al.

91, Sonka et al. 92a, Sonka et al. 93, Sonka et al. 92b]. X-ray images are acquired after injecting a fluorescent opaque dye into the arteries of a human heart. An example of a successful bottom-up detection of coronary borders using a graph-search approach is given in Section 5.2.4, Figure 5.21.

Unfortunately, the bottom-up graph search often fails in more complicated images, in the presence of closely parallel, branching, or overlapping vessels, and in low quality images. Image data representing such a difficult case are shown in Figure 8.2 together with the result of the bottom-up graph search (the same method that worked so well in a single vessel case). To achieve a reliable border detection in difficult images, a hybrid control strategy was designed combining bottom-up and top-down control steps – the following principles are incorporated in the process

1. **Model-based approach:** The model favours symmetric left and right borders as those most typical in coronary imagery.

2. **Hypothesize and verify approach:** Based on multiresolution processing, the approximate vessel border is detected at low resolution and the precision is increased at full resolution (also, multiresolution speeds up the border detection process).

3. **A priori knowledge:** Knowledge about directions of edges forming the vessel border is used to modify a graph search cost function.

4. **Multi-stage approach:** Models of different strength are applied throughout the processing.

The method searches for left and right coronary borders simultaneously, performing a three-dimensional graph search and the border symmetry model is thus incorporated in the search process. The three-dimensional graph results from combining two conventional edge detection graphs of the left and the right coronary borders (see Section 5.2.4). The model guides the search in regions of poor data, and where the image data have an acceptable quality, the search is guided by the image data.

A frequent problem of model-based control strategies is that the model control necessary in some parts of the image is too strong in other parts (the symmetry requirements of the model have a larger influence on the final border than a non-symmetric reality) corrupting the border detection results. This is the rationale for a multi-stage approach where a strong model is applied at low resolution, and a weaker model leaves enough freedom for the search to be guided predominantly by data at full-resolution, thereby achieving higher accuracy overall. Nevertheless, the low-resolution coronary borders detected by cooperation with the model guarantee that the full-resolution search will not get lost – the low-resolution border is used as a model border in the full-resolution search.

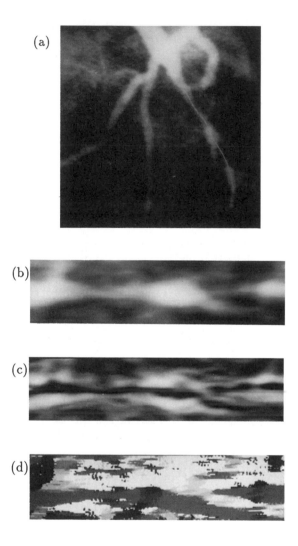

Figure 8.3 *Steps of the coronary border detection (1): (a) Centreline definition, (b) straightened image data, (c) edge detection, (d) edge direction detection.*

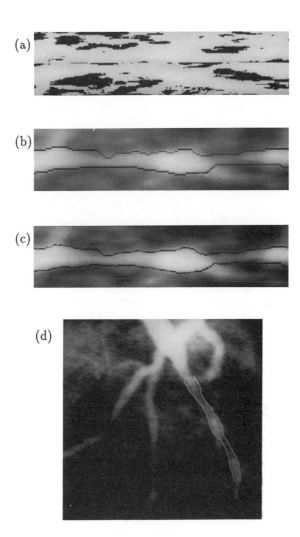

Figure 8.4 *Steps of the coronary border detection (II): (a) Modified cost function; note that the cost increases in non-probable border locations image areas (where the edge direction does not support location of the border), (b) approximate coronary borders acquired in low-resolution, (c) precise full-resolution border in straightened image, (d) full-resolution coronary borders in original image data.*

A block algorithm of the control steps is now given accompanied by a label showing whether the particular step is done in a bottom-up or top-down manner.

Algorithm 8.2: Coronary border detection – a combined control strategy

---

1. *(top-down)* Detect a vessel centreline in interaction with an operator (show which vessel is to be processed), and straighten the vessel image, Figure 8.3a,b.

2. *(bottom-up)* Detect image edges in full resolution, Figure 8.3c.

3. *(bottom-up)* Detect local edge directions in the straightened intensity image, Figure 8.3d.

4. *(top-down)* Modify the cost matrix using a priori knowledge about edge directions and the directional edge image, Figure 8.4a.

5. *(bottom-up)* Construct a low-resolution image and a low-resolution cost matrix.

6. *(top-down)* Search for the low-resolution pair of approximate borders using the vessel symmetry model Figure 8.4b.

7. *(top-down)* Find an accurate position of the full-resolution border using the low-resolution border as a model to guide the full-resolution search, Figure 8.4c. The symmetry model is much weaker than in the low-resolution search.

8. *(bottom-up)* Transform the results from the straightened image to the original image, Figure 8.4d.

9. *(top-down)* Evaluate the coronary disease severity.

Results of this strategy applied to coronary vessel data are given in Figure 8.5.

It is obvious that a combined control strategy can improve processing efficiency. Further, some of the presented steps are not sequential in principle (like edge image construction) and can be computed in parallel.

8.1.6 Non-hierarchical control

There is always an upper and a lower level in hierarchical control. Conversely, non-hierarchical control can be seen as a cooperation of competing experts at the same level.

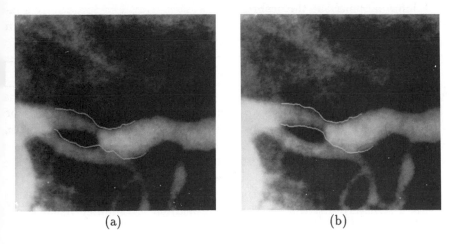

(a) (b)

Figure 8.5 *Coronary border detection. (a) Borders resulting from the pure bottom-up graph search approach follow borders of incorrect structures in the image, (b) results of the combined control graph search strategy follow the true coronary borders precisely.*

Non-hierarchical control can be applied to problems that can be separated into a number of subproblems, each of which require some expertise. The order in which the expertise should be deployed is not fixed. The basic idea of non-hierarchical control is to ask for assistance from the expert that can help most to obtain the final solution. The chosen expert may be known, for instance, for high reliability, high efficiency, or for the ability to provide the most information under given conditions, etc. Criteria for selection of an expert from the set may differ; one possibility is to let the experts calculate their own abilities to contribute to the solution in particular cases – the choice is based on these local and individual evaluations. Another option is to assign a fixed evaluation to each expert beforehand and help is then requested from the expert with the highest evaluation [Ambler 75]. The criterion for expert choice may be based on some appropriate combination of empirically detected evaluations computed by experts, and evaluations dependent on the actual state of the problem solution. Non-hierarchical control strategies can be illustrated by the following algorithm outline;

Algorithm 8.3: Non-hierarchical control

---

1. Based on the actual state and acquired information about the solved problem, decide on the best action, and execute it.

2. Use the results of the last action to increase the amount of acquired

information about the problem.

3. If the goals of the task are met, stop. Otherwise, return to step (1).

A system for analysis of complex aerial photographs [Nagao and Matsuyama 80] is an example of a successful application of non-hierarchical control – the blackboard principle was used for competing experts. To explain the main idea of the blackboard, imagine a classroom full of experts. If any of them wants to share knowledge or observations with others, a note is made on the blackboard. Therefore, all others can see the results and use them. A blackboard is a specific data structure that can be accessed by all the experts, and is a data structure first used in speech recognition – computer vision applications followed (e.g. VISIONS [Hanson and Riseman 78], COBIUS [Kuan et al. 89]). The blackboard usually includes a mechanism that retrieves specialized subsystems which can immediately affect the standard control. These subsystems are very powerful; because of their power they are usually called **daemons**. The blackboard must include a mechanism that synchronizes the daemon activity. Programming with daemons is not easy, and the design of daemon behaviour is based on general knowledge of the problem domain. Therefore, the programmer can never be absolutely sure if the daemon procedure based on some specific property will be activated or not; moreover, there is no guarantee that the daemon will be activated in the correct way. To limit the uncertainty of daemon behaviour, the following additional rules are usually added:

- The blackboard represents a continuously updated part of the internal model that corresponds to image data.

- The blackboard includes a set of rules that specify which daemon subsystem should be used in specific cases.

The blackboard is sometimes called the **short term memory** – it contains information about interpretation of the processed image. The **long term memory**, the knowledge base, consists of more general information that is valid for (almost) all representations of the problems to be solved [Hanson and Riseman 78].

In a system for the analysis of complex aerial photographs [Nagao and Matsuyama 80], all the information about a specific image is stored in the blackboard (segmented region properties and their relations). The blackboard can activate thirteen subsystems of region detection, all of which communicate with the blackboard in a standard way, and the only way the subsystems can communicate with each other is via the blackboard. The blackboard data structure depends on the application; in this particular case, the structure takes advantage of a priori global knowledge of the domain like the physical size of pixels, direction of the sun, etc. Additionally, the blackboard maintains a property table in which all the observations on image regions is stored, together with the information about the region class (resulting from recognition). An integral part of the blackboard is represented by the symbolic region image that provides information about relations between regions. The main aim of the blackboard system is to identify places of interest in the image that should be processed with higher accuracy, to locate places with a high probability of a target region being present. The approximate region borders are found first based on a fast computation of just a few basic characteristics, saving computational time and making the detailed analysis easier. The control process follows the **production system** principle [Nilsson 82], using the information that comes from the region detection subsystems via the blackboard. The blackboard serves as a place where all the conflicts between region labelling are solved (one region can be marked by two or more region detection subsystems at the same time and it is necessary to decide which label is the best one). Furthermore, the labelling errors are detected in the blackboard, and are corrected using backtracking principles.

The principal image understanding control strategies have been presented here – it was noted that a wide variety of knowledge representation techniques, object description methods, and processing strategies must co-exist in any image understanding system. The role of knowledge and control is reviewed in [Rao and Jain 88] within a frame of image and speech understanding systems such as ACRONYM [Brooks et al. 79], HEARSAY [Lesser et al. 75], and VISIONS [Hanson and Riseman 78].

8.2 Active contour models - snakes

The development of active contour models results from the work of Kass, Witkin, and Terzopoulos [Kass et al. 87a, Witkin et al. 87, Terzopoulos et al. 87], and they offer a solution to a variety of tasks in image analysis and machine vision. This section is based on the paper [Kass et al. 87b] in which the energy-minimization approach to achieve computer vision goals was first presented; the original notation is used.

Active contour models may be used in image segmentation and understanding, and are also suitable for analysis of dynamic image data or 3D image data. The active contour model, or **snake**, is defined as an energy minimizing spline – the snake's energy depends on its shape and location within the image. Local minima of this energy then correspond to desired image properties. Snakes may be understood as a special case of a more general technique of matching a deformable model to an image by means of energy minimization. Snakes do not solve the entire problem of finding contours in images but rather, they depend on other mechanisms like interaction with a user, interaction with some higher level image understanding process, or information from image data adjacent in time or space. This interaction must specify an approximate shape and starting position for the snake somewhere near the desired contour. A priori information is then used to push the snake toward an appropriate solution – see Figure 8.6. Unlike most other image models, the snake is *active*, always minimizing its energy functional, therefore exhibiting dynamic behaviour.

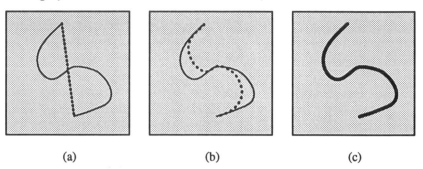

(a)   (b)   (c)

Figure 8.6 *Active contour model – snake: (a) Initial snake position interactively defined near the true contour, (b), (c) iteration steps of snake energy minimization; the snake is pulled toward the true contour.*

The energy functional which is minimized is a weighted combination of internal and external forces. The internal forces emanate from the shape of the snake, while the external forces come from the image and/or from higher level image understanding processes. The snake is parametrically defined as $\mathbf{v}(s) = (x(s), y(s))$ where $x(s), y(s)$ are x, y co-ordinates along the contour and $s \in [0, 1]$ (see Figure 6.11a). The energy functional to be minimized may be written as

$$
\begin{aligned}
E^*_{snake} &= \int_0^1 E_{snake}(\mathbf{v}(s)) ds \\
&= \int_0^1 E_{int}(\mathbf{v}(s)) + E_{image}(\mathbf{v}(s)) + E_{con}(\mathbf{v}(s)) ds \qquad (8.1)
\end{aligned}
$$

where E_{int} represents the internal energy of the spline due to bending, E_{image} denotes image forces, and E_{con} external constraint forces. Usually, $\mathbf{v}(s)$ is approximated as a spline to ensure desirable properties of continuity.

The internal spline energy can be written

$$
E_{int} = \alpha(s)\left|\frac{d\mathbf{v}}{ds}\right|^2 + \beta(s)\left|\frac{d^2\mathbf{v}}{ds^2}\right|^2 \qquad (8.2)
$$

where $\alpha(s), \beta(s)$ specify the *elasticity* and *stiffness* of the snake. Note that setting $\beta(s_k) = 0$ at a point s_k allows the snake to become second-order discontinuous at that point, and develop a corner.

The second term of the energy integral (8.1) is derived from the image data over which the snake lies. As an example, a weighted combination of three different functionals is presented which attracts the snake to lines, edges, and terminations

$$E_{image} = w_{line} E_{line} + w_{edge} E_{edge} + w_{term} E_{term} \tag{8.3}$$

The line-based functional may be very simple

$$E_{line} = f(x, y) \tag{8.4}$$

where $f(x, y)$ denotes image grey levels at image location (x, y). The sign of w_{line} specifies whether the snake is attracted to light or dark lines. The edge-based functional

$$E_{edge} = -|\text{grad} f(x, y)|^2 \tag{8.5}$$

attracts the snake to contours with large image gradients – that is, to locations of strong edges. Line terminations and corners may influence the snake using a weighted energy functional E_{term}: Let g be a slightly smoothed version of the image f, let $\psi(x, y)$ denote the gradient directions along the spline in the smoothed image g, and let

$$n(x, y) = (\cos \psi(x, y), \sin \psi(x, y)), \quad n_R(x, y) = (-\sin \psi(x, y), \cos \psi(x, y))$$

be unit vectors along and perpendicular to the gradient directions $\psi(x, y)$. Then the curvature of constant-grey level contours in the smoothed image can be written [Kass et al. 87a]

$$E_{term} = \frac{\partial \psi}{\partial n_R} = \frac{\partial^2 g / \partial n_R^2}{\partial g / \partial n} = \tag{8.6}$$

$$\frac{(\partial^2 g / \partial y^2)(\partial g / \partial x)^2 - 2(\partial^2 g / \partial x \partial y)(\partial g / \partial x)(\partial g / \partial y) + (\partial^2 g / \partial x^2)(\partial g / \partial y)^2}{((\partial g / \partial x)^2 + (\partial g / \partial y)^2)^{3/2}}$$

The snake behaviour may be controlled by adjusting the weights w_{line}, w_{edge}, w_{term}. A snake attracted to edges and terminations is shown in Figure 8.7.

The third term of the integral (8.1) comes from external constraints imposed either by a user or some other higher level process which may force the snake toward or away from particular features. If the snake is near to some desirable feature, the energy minimization will pull the snake the rest of the way. However, if the snake settles in a local energy minimum that a higher level process determines as incorrect, an area of energy peak may be made at this location to force the snake away to a different local minimum.

A contour is defined to lie in the position in which the snake reaches a local energy minimum. From equation (8.1), the functional to be minimized is

$$E_{snake}^* = \int_0^1 E(v(s)) ds$$

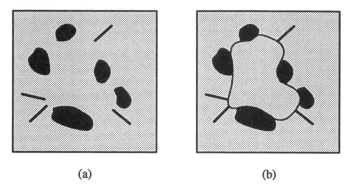

(a)   (b)

Figure 8.7 *A snake attracted to edges and terminations. (a) Contour illu-*
sion, (b) a snake attracted to the subjective contour. Adapted from [Kass et
al. 87b].

Then from the calculus of variations, the Euler-Lagrange condition states that
the spline $\mathbf{v}(s)$ which minimizes E^*_{snake} must satisfy

$$\frac{d}{ds}E_{\mathbf{v}_s} - E_{\mathbf{v}} = 0 \qquad (8.7)$$

where $E_{\mathbf{v}_s}$ is the partial derivative of E with respect to $d\mathbf{v}/ds$ and $E_{\mathbf{v}}$ is the
partial derivative of E with respect to $\mathbf{v}$. Using equation (8.2) and denoting
$E_{ext} = E_{image} + E_{con}$, the previous equation reduces to

$$-\frac{d}{ds}(\alpha(s)\frac{d\mathbf{v}}{ds}) + \frac{d^2}{ds^2}(\beta(s)\frac{d^2\mathbf{v}}{ds^2}) + \nabla E_{ext}(\mathbf{v}(s)) = 0 \qquad (8.8)$$

To solve the Euler-Lagrange equation, suppose an initial estimate of the solution is available. An evolution equation is formed

$$\frac{\partial \mathbf{v}(s,t)}{\partial t} - \frac{\partial}{\partial s}(\alpha(s)\frac{\partial \mathbf{v}(s,t)}{\partial s}) + \frac{\partial^2}{\partial s^2}(\beta(s)\frac{\partial^2 \mathbf{v}(s,t)}{\partial s^2}) + \nabla E_{ext}(\mathbf{v}(s,t)) = 0 \quad (8.9)$$

The solution is found if $\partial \mathbf{v}(s,t)/\partial t = 0$. Nevertheless, minimization of the
snake energy integral is still problematic; numerous parameters must be de-
signed (weighting factors, iteration steps, etc.), a reasonable initialization must
be available and, moreover, the solution of the Euler-Lagrange equation suffers
from numerical instability.

Originally [Kass et al. 87a], a resolution minimization method was proposed; partial derivatives in s and t were estimated by the finite differences
method. Later [Amini et al. 88, Amini et al. 90], a dynamic programming
approach was proposed which allows 'hard' constraints to be added to the
snake. Further, a requirement that the internal snake energy must be a continuous function may thus be eliminated and some snake configurations may

be prohibited (that is, have infinite energy) allowing more a priori knowledge to be incorporated.

Difficulties with the numerical instability of the original method were overcome by Berger [Berger and Mohr 90] by incorporating an idea of **snake growing**. In this method a single primary snake may begin which later divides itself into pieces. The pieces of very low energy are allowed to grow in directions of their tangents while higher energy pieces are eliminated. After each growing step, the energy of each snake piece is minimized (the ends are pulled to the true contour, see Figure 8.8) and the snake growing process is repeated. Further, the snake growing method may overcome the initialization problem. The primary snake may fall into an unlikely local minimum but parts of the snake may still lie on salient features. The very low energy parts (the probable pieces) of the primary snake are used to initialize the snake growing in later steps. This iterative snake growing always converges and the numerical solution is therefore stable – the robustness of the method is paid for by an increase in the processing cost of the algorithm.

Algorithm 8.4: Snake growing

---

1. Based on a priori knowledge, estimate the desired contour position and shape as a curve S^0.

2. Use this curve S^0 to initialize the conventional snake algorithm (equations 8.1 – 8.9). This yields a contour C^0.

3. Segment the contour C^0 to eliminate high-energy segments, resulting in a number of initial shorter low-energy contour segments C_i^0, where i is a segment identifier.

4. Repeat steps (5) and (6) while lengthening is needed.

5. Each contour segment C_i^k is allowed to grow in the direction of tangents (see Figure 8.8). This yields a new estimate S_i^{k+1} for each contour segment C_i^k.

6. For each contour segment C_i^k, run the conventional snake algorithm using S_i^{k+1} as an initial estimate to get a new (longer) contour segment C_i^{k+1}.

A different approach to the energy integral minimization that is based on a Galerkin solution of the finite element method was proposed in [Cohen 91b] and has the advantage of greater numerical stability and better efficiency. This approach is especially useful in the case of closed or nearly closed contours.

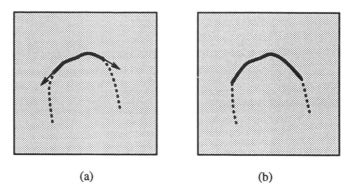

(a)   (b)

Figure 8.8 *Snake growing: (a) Lengthening in tangent direction, (b) energy minimization after a growing step.*

An additional pressure force is added to the contour interior by considering the curve as a **balloon** which is inflated. This allows the snake to overcome isolated energy valleys resulting from spurious edge points giving better results all over (see Figure 8.9). Another approach using a finite element method [Karaolani et al. 92] also significantly improves the solution's efficiency; forces are scaled by the size of an element, preventing very small contributions (which may be noise) from contributing as much as longer elements to the global solution.

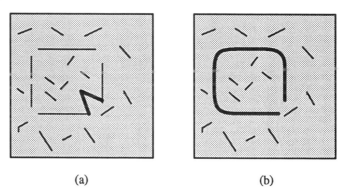

(a)   (b)

Figure 8.9 *Active contour model – balloon: (a) Initial contour, (b) final contour after inflation and energy minimization. Adapted from [Cohen and Cohen 92].*

Deformable models based on active contours were generalized to three dimensions by Terzopoulos [Terzopoulos et al. 87, Terzopoulos et al. 88, McInerney and Terzopoulos 93], and 3D balloons were introduced in [Cohen and Cohen 92]. Further, fast algorithms for active contour models are beginning to appear [Williams and Shah 92]. Applications can be found in many areas of machine vision, medical image analysis being a very promising field because living organisms and organs are naturally deformable and their shape varies considerably; for applications to magnetic resonance images of a human head and to coronary vessel detection see [Cohen and Cohen 92, Hyche et al. 92].

Active contour models represent a recent approach to contour detection and image interpretation. They differ substantially from classical approaches where features are extracted from an image and higher level processes try to interpolate sparse data to find a representation that matches the original data – active contour models start from an initial estimate based on higher level knowledge and an optimization method is used to refine the initial estimate. During the optimization, image data, an initial estimate, desired contour properties and knowledge-based constraints are considered. Feature extraction and knowledge-based constrained grouping of these features are integrated into a single process, which seems to be the biggest advantage. Active contour models search for local energy minima, which is another significant difference from most other image interpretation techniques which usually seek a global minimum of some objective function.

8.3 Pattern recognition methods in image understanding

Pattern recognition methods (Chapter 7) frequently appear in image understanding – classification-based segmentation of multispectral images (satellite images, magnetic resonance medical images, etc.) is a typical example.

The basic idea of classification-based segmentation is the same as that of statistical pattern recognition. Consider a magnetic resonance image (MRI) of the brain, and suppose the problem is to find areas of white matter, grey matter, and cerebro-spinal fluid (WM, GM, CSF). Let the image data be available in two image modalities of multi-spin-echo images as $T2$-weighted and PD-weighted images (see Figure 8.10). As can be seen, neither single image can be used to detect the required areas reliably.

Grey level values of pixels in particular image channels, their combinations, local texture features, etc. may be considered elements of a feature vector, one of which is assigned to each pixel. If an MR brain image is considered, four features $PD, T2, PD - T2, PD \times T2$ may be used to construct the vector; subsequent classification-based understanding may be supervised or unsupervised.

If supervised methods are used for classification, a priori knowledge is applied to form a training set (see Figure 8.11a) and classifier learning based on this training set was described in Section 7.2.3. In the image understanding stage, feature vectors derived from local multispectral image values of image pixels are presented to the classifier which assigns a label to each pixel of the image. Image understanding is then achieved by pixel labelling; labels assigned to the MR brain image pixels can be seen in Figure 8.11b. Thus the

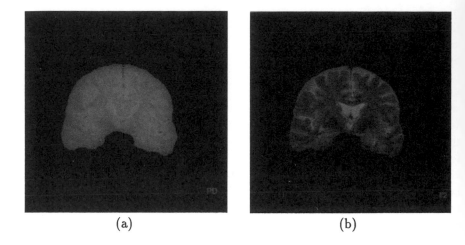

(a)   (b)

Figure 8.10 *Magnetic resonance multi-spin-echo images: (a) PD-weighted, (b) T2-weighted. Courtesy N. Andreasen, G. Cohen, University of Iowa.*

understanding process segments a multispectral image into regions of known labels, in this case areas of white matter, grey matter, and cerebro-spinal fluid are detected and labelled.

Training set construction, and therefore human interaction, is necessary for supervised classification methods, but if unsupervised classification is used, training set construction is avoided (see Section 7.2.4). As a result, the clusters and the pixel labels do not have a one-to-one correspondence with the class meaning. This implies the image is segmented, but labels are not available to support image understanding. Fortunately, a priori information can often be used to assign appropriate labels to the clusters without direct human inter-action. In the case of MR brain images, cerebro-spinal fluid is known always to form the brightest cluster, and grey matter to form the darkest cluster in $T2$ pixel values. Based on this information, clusters can be assigned appro-priate labels. Cluster formation in feature space, and results of unsupervised labelling are shown in Figure 8.12 [Parkkinen et al. 90, Parkkinen et al. 91].

In the supervised classification of MR brain images, the Bayes minimum error classification method was applied, and the ISODATA method of cluster analysis was used for unsupervised labelling. Validation of results proved a high accuracy of the method; further, the supervised and the unsupervised methods give almost identical results [Cohen 91a, Gerig et al. 92].

8.3.1 Contextual image classification

The method presented above works well in non-noisy data, and if the spectral properties determine classes sufficiently well. If noise or substantial variations

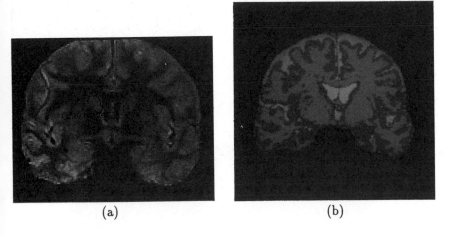

Figure 8.11 *MR brain image labelling: (a) Training set construction, (b) result of supervised classification labelling. Courtesy J. Parkkinen, University of Kuopio, G. Cohen, N. Andreasen, University of Iowa.*

n in-class pixel properties are present, the resulting image segmentation may have many small (often one-pixel) regions, which are misclassified. Several standard approaches can be applied to avoid this misclassification, which is very common in classification-based labelling. All of them use contextual information to some extent [Kittler and Foglein 84a].

- The first approach is to apply a post-processing filter to a labelled image, e.g. a median filter. Small or single-pixel regions then disappear as the most probable label from the local neighbourhood is assigned to them. This approach works well if the small regions are caused by noise. Unfortunately, the small regions can result from true regions with different properties in the original multispectral image, and in this case such filtering would worsen labelling results. Post-processing filters are widely used in remote sensing applications (see Figure 8.13).

- A slightly different post-processing classification improvement is introduced in [Wharton 82]. Pixel labels resulting from pixel classification in a given neighbourhood form a new feature vector for each pixel, and a second-stage classifier based on the new feature vectors assigns final pixel labels. The contextual information is incorporated in the labelling process of the second-stage classifier learning.

- Context may also be introduced in earlier stages, merging pixels into homogeneous regions and classifying these regions (see Chapter 5).

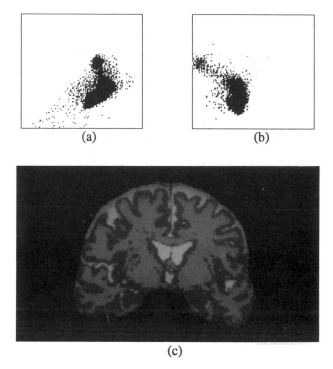

Figure 8.12 *MR brain image labelling: (a) Clusters in feature space,*
(PD, T2) plane (b) clusters in feature space, (PD, PD × T2) plane (c) result
of an unsupervised classification labelling. Courtesy J. Parkkinen, University
of Kuopio, G. Cohen, N. Andreasen, University of Iowa.

- Another contextual pre-processing approach is based on acquiring pixel
  feature descriptions from a pixel neighbourhood. Mean values, vari-
  ances, texture description, etc. may be added to (or may replace) original spectral data. This approach is very common in textured image
  recognition (see Chapter 13).

- The most interesting option is to combine spectral and spatial information in the same stage of the classification process [Kittler and Foglein
  84a, Kittler and Foglein 84b, Kittler and Pairman 85]. The label assigned to each image pixel depends not only on multispectral grey level
  properties of the particular pixel but also considers the context in the
  pixel neighbourhood.

This section will discuss the last approach.

Contextual classification of image data is based on the Bayes minimum
error classifier (Section 7.2.2, equation 7.16). For each pixel $\mathbf{x}_0$, a vector consisting of (possibly multispectral) values $f(\mathbf{x}_i)$ of pixels in a specified neigh-

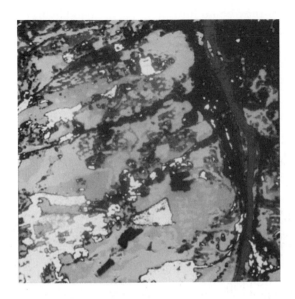

Figure 8.13 *Remotely sensed data of Prague, Landsat Thematic Mapper. Unsupervised classification, post-processing filter applied: White – no vegetation (note the sport stadium), green (varying hue) – vegetation types, red – urban areas. A colour version of this picture may be seen in the colour inset. Courtesy V. Cervenka, K. Charvat, Geodetic Institute Prague.*

bourhood $N(\mathbf{x}_0)$ is used as a feature representation of the pixel $\mathbf{x}_0$. Each pixel is represented by the vector

$$\boldsymbol{\xi} = (f(\mathbf{x}_0), f(\mathbf{x}_1), \ldots, f(\mathbf{x}_k)) \tag{8.10}$$

where

$$\mathbf{x}_i \in N(\mathbf{x}_0); \qquad i = 1, \ldots, k$$

Some more vectors are defined which will be used later. Let labels (classification) of pixels in the neighbourhood $N(\mathbf{x}_0)$ be represented by a vector (see Figure 8.14)

$$\boldsymbol{\eta} = (\theta_0, \theta_1, \ldots, \theta_k) \tag{8.11}$$

where

$$\theta_i \in \{\omega_1, \omega_2, \ldots, \omega_R\}$$

and ω_s denotes the assigned class. Further, let the labels in the neighbourhood excluding the pixel $\mathbf{x}_0$ be represented by a vector

$$\tilde{\boldsymbol{\eta}} = (\theta_1, \theta_2, \ldots, \theta_k) \tag{8.12}$$

Theoretically there may be no limitation on the neighbourhood size, but the majority of contextual information is believed to be present in a small neighbourhood of the pixel x_0. Therefore, a 3×3 neighbourhood in 4-connectivity or in 8-connectivity is usually considered appropriate (see Figure 8.14); also computational demands increase exponentially with growth of neighbourhood size.

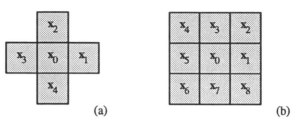

(a)   (b)

Figure 8.14 *Pixel neighbourhoods used in contextual image classification, pixel indexing scheme: (a) 4-neighbourhood, (b) 8-neighbourhood.*

A conventional minimum error classification method assigns a pixel x_0 to a class ω_r if the probability of x_0 being from the class ω_r is the highest of all possible classification probabilities (as given in equation (7.16))

$$\theta_0 = \omega_r \quad \text{if} \quad P(\omega_r | f(x_0)) = \max_{s=1,\ldots,R} P(\omega_s | f(x_0)) \tag{8.13}$$

A contextual classification scheme uses the feature vector ξ instead of x_0, and the decision rule remains similar

$$\theta_0 = \omega_r \quad \text{if} \quad P(\omega_r | \xi) = \max_{s=1,\ldots,R} P(\omega_s | \xi) \tag{8.14}$$

The a posteriori probability $P(\omega_s | \xi)$ can be computed using the Bayes formula

$$P(\omega_s | \xi) = \frac{p(\xi | \omega_s) P(\omega_s)}{p(\xi)} \tag{8.15}$$

Note that each image pixel is classified using a corresponding vector ξ from its neighbourhood, and so there are as many vectors ξ as there are pixels in the image. Many accompanying details, and a formal proof that contextual information increases classification reliability, are given in [Kittler and Foglein 84a]. The basic contextual classification algorithm can be summarized as;

Algorithm 8.5: Contextual image classification

1. For each image pixel, determine a feature vector ξ (equation 8.10).

2. From the training set, determine parameters of probability distributions $p(\xi | \omega_s)$ and $P(\omega_s)$.

3. Compute maximum a posteriori probabilities $P(\omega_r|\xi)$ and label (classify) all pixels in the image according to equation (8.14). An image classification results.

A substantial limitation in considering larger contextual neighbourhoods s exponential growth of computational demands with increasing neighbourhood size. A **recursive contextual classification** overcomes these difficulties [Kittler and Foglein 84a, Kittler and Foglein 84b, Kittler and Pairman 85]. The main trick of this method is in propagating contextual information through the image although the computation is still kept in small neighbourhoods. Spectral and neighbourhood pixel labelling information are both used in classification. Therefore, context from a distant neighbourhood can propagate to the labelling θ_0 of the pixel x_0; this is illustrated in Figure 8.15.

The vector $\tilde{\eta}$ of labels in the neighbourhood may further improve the contextual representation. Clearly, if the information contained in the spectral data in the neighbourhood is unreliable (e.g. based on spectral data, the pixel x_0 may be classified into a number of classes with similar probabilities) the information about labels in the neighbourhood may increase confidence in one of those classes. If a majority of surrounding pixels are labelled as members of a class ω_i, the confidence that the pixel x_0 should also be labelled ω_i increases.

More complex dependencies may be found in the training set – for instance imagine a thin striped noisy image. Considering labels in the neighbourhood of the pixel x_0, the decision rule becomes

$$\theta_0 = \omega_r \quad \text{if} \quad P(\omega_r|\xi, \tilde{\eta}) = \max_{s=1,\dots,R} P(\omega_s|\xi, \tilde{\eta}) \tag{8.16}$$

After several applications of the Bayes formula [Kittler and Pairman 85] the decision rule transforms into

$$\theta_0 = \omega_r \quad \text{if} \quad p(\xi|\eta_r)P(\omega_r|\tilde{\eta}) = \max_{s=1,\dots,R} p(\xi|\eta_s)P(\omega_s|\tilde{\eta}) \tag{8.17}$$

where η_r is a vector η with $\theta_0 = \omega_r$. Assuming all necessary probability distribution parameters were determined in the learning process, the recursive contextual classification algorithm follows:

Algorithm 8.6: Recursive contextual image classification

---

1. Determine an initial image pixel labelling using the non-contextual classification scheme, equation (8.13)

2. Update labels in each image pixel x_0, applying the current label vectors η, $\tilde{\eta}$, and local spectral vector ξ to the decision rule equation (8.17).

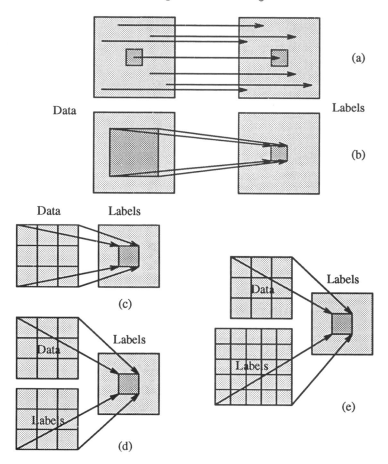

Figure 8.15 *Principles of contextual classification: (a) Conventional non-contextual method, (b) contextual method, (c) recursive contextual method – step 1, (d) step 2, (e) step 3.*

3. Terminate the algorithm if the labels of all pixels in the image are stable, repeat step (2) otherwise.

Only a general outline of the contextual classification methods has been given; for more details, discussion of convergence, other techniques, and specific algorithms see [Kittler and Foglein 84a, Kittler and Foglein 84b, Kittler and Pairman 85, Haralick et al. 88, Watanabe and Suzuki 89, Zhang et al. 90]. A comparison of contextual classifiers is given in [Mohn et al. 87, Watanabe and Suzuki 88], and a parallel implementation is described in [Tilton 87]. Applications are mostly related to remote sensing and medical images [Gonzalez and

Lopez 89, Moller-Jensen 90, Franklin 90, Wilkinson and Megier 90, Algorri et al. 91]. Contextual classification of textures based on the context of feature vectors is described in [Fung et al. 90] and the application of neural networks to contextual image segmentation is given in [Toulson and Boyce 92].

There is a crucial idea incorporated in the algorithm of recursive contextual image classification that will be seen several times throughout this chapter; this is the idea of information propagation from distant image locations without the necessity for expensive consideration of context in large neighbourhoods. This is a standard approach used in image understanding.

8.4 Scene labelling and constraint propagation

Context plays a significant role in image understanding; the previous section was devoted to context present in pixel data configurations, and this section deals with semantic labelling of regions and objects. Assume that regions have been detected in an image that correspond to objects or other image entities, and let the objects and their inter-relationships be described by a region adjacency graph and/or a semantic net (see Sections 3.2.3 and 7.1). Object properties are described by unary relations, and inter-relationships between objects are described by binary (or n-ary) relations. The goal of scene labelling is to assign a label (a meaning) to each image object to achieve an appropriate image interpretation.

The resulting interpretation should correspond with available scene knowledge. The labelling should be consistent, and should favour more probable interpretations if there is more than one option. Consistency means that no two objects of the image appear in an illegal configuration – e.g. an object labelled *house* in the middle of an object labelled *lake* will be considered inconsistent in most scenes. Conversely, an object labelled *house* surrounded by an object labelled *lawn* in the middle of a *lake* may be fully acceptable.

Two main approaches may be chosen to achieve this goal.

- **Discrete** labelling allows only one label to be assigned to each object in the final labelling. Effort is directed to achieving a consistent labelling all over the image.

- **Probabilistic** labelling allows multiple labels to co-exist in objects. Labels are probabilistically weighted, with a label confidence being assigned to each object label.

The main difference is in interpretation robustness. Discrete labelling always finds either a consistent labelling or detects the impossibility of assigning consistent labels to the scene. Often, as a result of imperfect segmentation, discrete labelling fails to find a consistent interpretation even if only a small number of local inconsistencies is detected. Probabilistic labelling always gives an interpretation result together with a measure of confidence in the interpretation. Even if the result may be locally inconsistent, it often gives a better scene interpretation than a consistent and possibly very unlikely interpretation resulting from a discrete labelling. Note that discrete labelling may be considered a special case of probabilistic labelling with one label probability always being 1 and all the others being 0 for each object.

The scene labelling problem is specified by

- A set of objects R_i, $i = 1, \ldots, N$

- A finite set of labels Ω_i for each object R_i (without loss of generality, the same set of labels will be considered for each object; $\Omega_i = \Omega_j$ for any i, j)

- A finite set of relations between objects

- The existence of a compatibility function (reflecting constraints) between interacting objects

To solve the labelling problem considering direct interaction of all objects in an image is computationally very expensive and approaches to solving labelling problems are usually based on **constraint propagation**. This means that local constraints result in local consistencies (local optima), and by applying an iterative scheme the local consistencies adjust to global consistencies (global optima) in the whole image.

Many types of relaxation exist, some of them being used in statistical physics, for example, simulated annealing (Section 7.6.2), and stochastic relaxation [Geman and Geman 84], etc. Others, such as **relaxation labelling**, are typical in image understanding. To provide a better understanding of the idea, the discrete relaxation approach is considered first.

8.4.1   *Discrete relaxation*

Consider the scene shown in Figure 8.16a. Six objects are present in the scene, including the background. Let the labels be *background (B), window (W), table (T), drawer (D), phone (P)*, and let the unary properties of object interpretations be (the example is meant to be illustrative only);

- A window is rectangular.

- A table is rectangular.

- A drawer is rectangular.

Let the binary constraints be

- A window is located above a table.

- A phone is above a table.

- A drawer is inside a table.

- Background is adjacent to the image border.

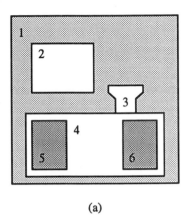
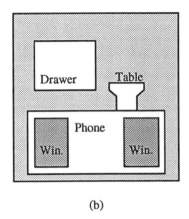

(a)   (b)

Figure 8.16 *Scene labelling: (a) Scene example, (b) inconsistent labelling.*

Given these constraints, the labelling in Figure 8.16b is inconsistent. Discrete relaxation assigns all existing labels to each object and iteratively removes all the labels which may not be assigned to an object without violating the constraints. A possible relaxation sequence is shown in Figure 8.17.

At the beginning, all labels are assigned to each object, and for each object all its labels are tested for consistency. Therefore, the label B can immediately be removed as inconsistent in objects 2, 3, 4, 5, and 6. Similarly, object 3 is not rectangular, therefore it violates the unary relation that must hold for T, W, D, etc.

The final consistent labelling is given in Figure 8.17c; note the mechanism of constraint propagation. The distant relations between objects may influence labelling in distant locations of the scene after several steps, making it possible to achieve a global labelling consistency of the scene interpretation although all the label removing operations are local.

Algorithm 8.7: Discrete relaxation

---

1. Assign all possible labels to each object, considering the unary constraints.

2. Repeat steps (2)-(5) until global consistency is achieved.

3. If any object has no label, stop – a consistent labelling was not found.

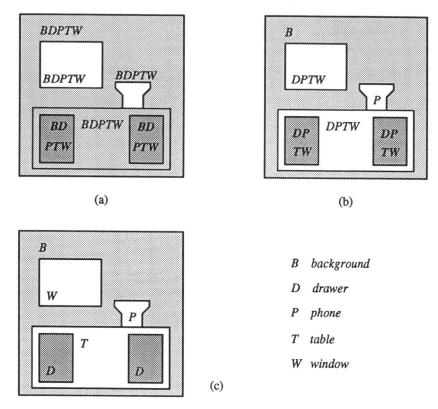

Figure 8.17 *Discrete relaxation: (a) All labels assigned to each object, (b) locally inconsistent labels are removed, (c) final consistent labelling.*

4. Choose one object to update its labels.

5. Modify (delete inconsistent) labels of the chosen object considering relations with other interacting objects.

The algorithm may be implemented in parallel with one difference; step (4) would disappear as all objects are treated in parallel.

For a more detailed survey of discrete relaxation techniques, their properties, and technical difficulties that limit their applicability see [Hancock and Kittler 90a]. Although discrete relaxation is naturally parallel, a study of the complexity of discrete relaxation given in [Kasif 90] shows that a parallel solution is unlikely to improve known sequential solutions much. An interesting discrete relaxation control strategy using asynchronous activation of object updating actions (**daemons**) was introduced in [Barrow and Tenenbaum 76].

8.4.2 Probabilistic relaxation

Constraints are a typical tool in image understanding. The classical problem of discrete relaxation labelling was first introduced in [Waltz 57] in understanding 3D line drawings, and this problem is briefly discussed in Chapter 9. Discrete relaxation results in an unambiguous labelling, however in a majority of real situations, it represents an oversimplified approach to image data understanding; it cannot cope with incomplete or imprecise segmentation. Using semantics and knowledge, image understanding is supposed to solve segmentation problems which cannot be solved by bottom-up interpretation approaches. Probabilistic relaxation may overcome the segmentation problems of missing objects or extra regions in the scene, however it results in an ambiguous image interpretation which is often inconsistent. It has been mentioned that a locally inconsistent but very probable (global) interpretation may be more valuable than a consistent but unlikely interpretation (e.g. a non-rectangular window located far above the table would be considered a phone in our example; this labelling would be consistent, even if very unlikely, see Figure 8.18).

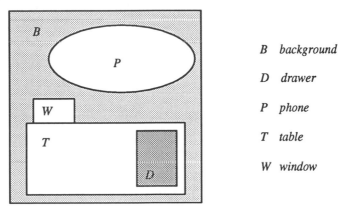

Figure 8.18 *Consistent but unlikely labelling.*

B	background
D	drawer
P	phone
T	table
W	window

Probabilistic relaxation was introduced in [Rosenfeld et al. 76] and has been used extensively in image understanding ever since. Consider the relaxation problem as specified above (regions R_i and sets of labels Ω_i) and in addition, let each object R_i be described by a set of unary properties X_i. Similarly to discrete relaxation, object labelling depends on the object properties and on a measure of compatibility of the potential object labels with the labelling of other directly interacting objects. All the image objects may be considered directly interacting and a general form of the algorithm will be given assuming this. Nevertheless, only adjacent objects are usually considered to interact directly to reduce computational demands of the relaxation. However, as before, more distant objects still interact with each other as a

result of the constraint propagation. A region adjacency graph is usually used
to store the adjacency information.

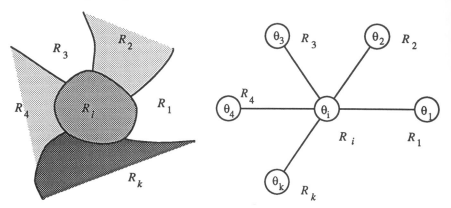

Figure 8.19 *Local configuration of objects in an image – part of a region
adjacency graph.*

Consider the local configuration of objects given in Figure 8.19; let the
objects R_j be labelled by labels θ_j; $\theta_j \in \Omega$; $\Omega = \{\omega_1, \omega_2, \ldots, \omega_R\}$. Confidence in the label θ_i of an object R_i depends on the configuration of labels
of directly interacting objects. Let $r(\theta_i = \omega_k, \theta_j = \omega_l)$ represent the value
of a compatibility function for two interacting objects R_i and R_j with labels
θ_i and θ_j (the probability that two objects with labels θ_i and θ_j appear in a
specific relation). The relaxation algorithm [Rosenfeld et al. 76] is iterative
and its goal is to achieve the locally best consistency in the entire image. The
support q_j^s for a label θ_i of the object R_i resulting from the binary relation
with the object R_j at the sth step of the iteration process is

$$q_j^s(\theta_i = \omega_k) = \sum_{l=1}^{R} r(\theta_i = \omega_k, \theta_j = \omega_l) P^s(\theta_j = \omega_l) \qquad (8.18)$$

where $P^s(\theta_j = \omega_l)$ is the probability that region R_j should be labelled ω_l. The
support Q^s for the same label θ_i of the same object R_i resulting from all N
directly interacting objects R_j and their labels θ_j at the sth step is

$$\begin{aligned}
Q^s(\theta_i = \omega_k) &= \sum_{j=1}^{N} c_{ij} q_j^s(\theta_i = \omega_k) \\
&= \sum_{j=1}^{N} c_{ij} \sum_{l=1}^{R} r(\theta_i = \omega_k, \theta_j = \omega_l) P^s(\theta_j = \omega_l) \qquad (8.19)
\end{aligned}$$

where c_{ij} are weights satisfying $\sum_{j=1}^{N} c_{ij} = 1$. The coefficients c_{ij} represent the
strength of interaction between objects R_i and R_j. Originally [Rosenfeld et

al. 76], an updating formula was given which specified the new probability of a label θ_i according to the previous probability $P^s(\theta_i = \omega_k)$ and probabilities of labels of interacting objects

$$P^{s+1}(\theta_i = \omega_k) = \frac{1}{K} P^s(\theta_i = \omega_k) Q^s(\theta_i = \omega_k) \tag{8.20}$$

where K is a normalizing constant

$$K = \sum_{l=1}^{R} P^s(\theta_i = \omega_l) Q^s(\theta_i = \omega_l) \tag{8.21}$$

This form of the algorithm is usually referred to as a **nonlinear relaxation scheme**. A **linear scheme** [Rosenfeld et al. 76] looks for probabilities such as

$$P(\theta_i = \omega_k) = Q(\theta_i = \omega_k) \quad \text{for all } i, k \tag{8.22}$$

with a non-contextual probability

$$P^0(\theta_i = \omega_k) = P(\theta_i = \omega_k | X_i) \tag{8.23}$$

being used only to start the relaxation process [Blake 82, Elfving and Eklundh 82].

A relaxation algorithm can also be treated as an optimization problem, the goal being maximization of the global confidence in the labelling [Berthod and Faugeras 80, Hummel and Zucker 83]. The global objective function is

$$F = \sum_{k=1}^{R} \sum_{i=1}^{N} P(\theta_i = \omega_k) \sum_{j=1}^{N} c_{ij} \sum_{l=1}^{R} r(\theta_i = \omega_k, \theta_j = \omega_l) P(\theta_j = \omega_l) \tag{8.24}$$

subject to the constraint that the solution satisfies

$$\sum_{k=1}^{R} P(\theta_i = \omega_k) = 1 \quad \text{for any } i, \quad P(\theta_i = \omega_k) > 0 \quad \text{for any } i, k \tag{8.25}$$

Optimization approaches to relaxation can be generalized to allow n-ary relations among objects. A projected gradient ascent method [Hummel and Zucker 83, Illingworth and Kittler 87] may be used to optimize equation (8.24), and an efficient version of this updating principle is introduced in [Parent and Zucker 89].

Convergence is an important property of iterative algorithms; as far as relaxation is concerned, convergence problems have not yet been satisfactorily solved. Although convergence of a discrete relaxation scheme can always be achieved by an appropriate design of label updating scheme (e.g. to remove the inconsistent labels), convergence of more complex schemes where labels may be added, or of probabilistic relaxation, often cannot be guaranteed mathematically. Despite this fact, the relaxation approach may still be quite useful.

Relaxation algorithms are one of the foundation stones of the high-level vision understanding processes, and applications can also be found outside the area of computer vision.

Relaxation algorithms are naturally parallel since the label updating may be done on all objects at the same time. Many parallel implementations exist and parallel relaxation does not differ in essence from the serial version. A general version is

---

Algorithm 8.8: Probabilistic relaxation

1. Define conditional probabilities of interpretations (labels) for all objects R_i in the image (e.g. using equation (8.23)).

2. Repeat steps (3), (4) until the best scene interpretation (a maximum of the objective function F) is reached.

3. Compute the objective function F (equation 8.24), which represents the quality of the scene labelling.

4. Update probabilities of object interpretations (labels) to increase the value of the objective function F.

Parallel implementations of relaxation algorithms can be found in [Kamada et al. 88, Millin and Ni 89, Dew et al. 89, Bhandarker and Suk 90, Zen et al. 90].

Relaxation algorithms are still being developed. One existing problem with their behaviour is that the labelling improves rapidly during early iterations followed by a degradation, which may be very severe. The reason is that the search for the global optimum over the image may cause highly non-optimal local labelling. A treatment that allows spatial consistency to be developed while avoiding labelling degradation is based on decreasing the neighbourhood influence with the iteration count [Lee et al. 89]. For a survey and an extensive list of references see [Kittler and Illingworth 85, Kittler and Foglein 86, Kittler and Hancock 89, Hancock and Kittler 90b]. A compact theoretical basis for probabilistic relaxation and close relations to the contextual classification schemes is given in [Kittler 87]. Application of the relaxation scheme to image segmentation is described in the next section.

8.4.3 Searching interpretation trees

Note that relaxation is not the only way to solve discrete labelling problems and classical methods of **interpretation tree** searching may be applied. The tree has as many levels as there are objects present in the scene. Tree nodes are assigned all possible labels, and a depth-first search based on backtracking is applied. Starting with a label assigned to the first object node (tree root), a consistent label is assigned to the second object node, to the third object node, etc. If a consistent label cannot be assigned, a backtracking mechanism changes the label of the closest node at the higher level. All the label changes are done in a systematic way. An interpretation tree search tests all possible labellings, and therefore computational inefficiency is common, especially if an appropriate tree pruning algorithm is not available. However, successful applications of the interpretation tree searching method exist [Grimson and Lozano-Perez 87].

8.5   Semantic image segmentation and understanding

This section presents a higher level extension of region growing methods which were discussed in Section 5.3. These ideas fall under the heading of this chapter, rather than simple segmentation, for a number of reasons; semantic approaches represent a significantly advanced field of image segmentation and as such require a well developed set of techniques not fully covered until this point, while from another viewpoint, semantic segmentation includes image region interpretation and may result in image understanding and therefore should be included in this chapter. Whichever, it is considered appropriate to present semantic segmentation methods at this point after the reader is comfortable with the necessary background material: Region growing, object description, minimum error classification, contextual classification, image understanding strategies, etc.

Algorithms already discussed in Section 5.3 merge regions on the basis of general heuristics using local properties of regions, and may be referred to as syntactic information based methods. Conversely, semantic information representing higher level knowledge was included in [Feldman and Yakimovsky 74] for the first time. It is intuitively clear that including more information, especially information about assumed region interpretation, can have a beneficial effect on the merging process, and it is also clear that context and criteria for global optimization of region interpretation consistency will also play an important role. Further, the approaches described in this section are meant to serve as examples of incorporating context, semantics, applying relaxation methods to propagate constraints, and to show how the global consistency function may be optimized – for applications see also [Roberto et al. 90, Cabello et al. 90, Strat and Fischler 91].

The first issue in semantic region growing is the representation of image regions and their inter-relationships. The concept of the region adjacency graph, in which nodes represent regions and arcs connect nodes of adjacent regions, was introduced in Section 3.2.3. Nodes of the region adjacency graph represent regions, arcs connect nodes of adjacent regions. An artificial region may surround the image in order to treat all regions consistently. A dual graph can be constructed from the region adjacency graph in which nodes correspond to intersecting points of boundary segments of different regions, and arcs correspond to boundary segments. An example of a region adjacency graph and its dual is shown in Figure 8.20. Each time two regions are merged, both graphs change – the following algorithm [Ballard and Brown 82]

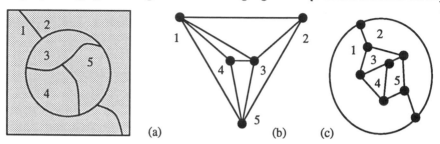

Figure 8.20 *Region adjacency graph: (a) Segmented image, (b) region adjacency graph, (c) dual graph.*

describes how to update the region adjacency graph and its dual after merging two regions R_i and R_j.

Algorithm 8.9: Updating the region adjacency graph and its dual to merge two regions

---

1. *Region Adjacency Graph*

   (a) Add all nonexisting arcs connecting region R_i and all regions adjacent to R_j.

   (b) Remove the node R_j and all its arcs from the graph.

2. *Dual Graph*

   (a) Remove all arcs corresponding to the boundaries between regions R_i and R_j from the graph.

   (b) For each node associated with these arcs:

      - If the number of arcs associated with the node is equal to 2, remove this node and combine the arcs into a single one.
      - If the number of arcs associated with the node is larger than 2, update the labels of arcs that corresponded to parts of borders of region R_j to reflect the new region label R_i.

The region adjacency graph is one in which costs are associated with both nodes and arcs, implying that an update of these costs must be included in the given algorithm as node costs change due to the connecting two regions R_i and R_j.

8.5.1   Semantic region growing

A classical method of semantic region growing is now presented [Feldman and Yakimovsky 74]. Consider remotely sensed photographs, in which regions can be defined with interpretations such as *field, road, forest, town*, etc. It then makes sense to merge adjacent regions with the same interpretation into a single region. The problem is that the interpretation of regions is not known and the region description may give unreliable interpretations. In such a situation, it is natural to incorporate context into the region merging using a priori knowledge about relations (unary, binary) among adjacent regions, and then to apply constraint propagation to achieve globally optimal segmentation and interpretation throughout the image.

A region merging segmentation scheme is now considered in which semantic information is used in later steps, with the early steps being controlled by general heuristics similar to those given in Section 5.3. Only after the preliminary heuristics have terminated are semantic properties of existing regions evaluated, and further region merging is either allowed or restricted; these are steps (4) and (6) of the next algorithm. The same notation is used as in the previous section; a region R_i has properties X_i, its possible labels are denoted $\theta_i \in \{\omega_1, \ldots, \omega_R\}$, and $P(\theta_i = \omega_k)$ represents the probability that the interpretation of the region R_i is ω_k.

Algorithm 8.10: Semantic region merging

---

1. Initialize a segmentation with many small regions.

2. Merge all adjacent regions that have at least one weak edge on their common boundary.

3. For preset constants c_1 and c_2, and threshold T_1, merge neighbouring regions R_i and R_j if $S_{ij} \leq T_1$, where

$$S_{ij} = \frac{c_1 + a_{ij}}{c_2 + a_{ij}}, \qquad a_{ij} = \frac{(area_i)^{\frac{1}{2}} + (area_j)^{\frac{1}{2}}}{perimeter_i \ perimeter_j} \qquad (8.26)$$

4. For all adjacent regions R_i and R_j, compute the conditional probability P that their mutual border B_{ij} separates them into two regions of the same interpretation ($\theta_i = \theta_j$), equation (8.29). Merge regions R_i and R_j if P is larger than a threshold T_2. If no two regions can be so merged continue with step (5).

5. For each region R_i, compute the initial conditional probabilities

$$P(\theta_i = \omega_k | X_i), \quad k = 1, \ldots, R \tag{8.27}$$

6. Repeat this step until all regions are labelled as *final*. Find a *non-final* region with the highest confidence C_i in its interpretation (equation 8.31); label the region with this interpretation and mark it as *final*. For each *non-final* region R_j and each of its possible interpretations $\omega_k, k = 1, \ldots, R$ update the probabilities of its interpretations according to equation (8.32).

The first three steps of the algorithm do not differ in essence from Algorithm 5.17 but the final two steps, where semantic information has been incorporated, are very different and represent a variation of a serial relaxation algorithm combined with a depth-first interpretation tree search. The goal is to maximize an objective function

$$F = \prod_{i,j=1,\ldots,R} P(B_{ij} \text{ is between } \theta_i, \theta_j | X(B_{ij})) \prod_{i=1,\ldots,R} P(\theta_i | X_i) \prod_{j=1,\ldots,R} P(\theta_j | X_j) \tag{8.28}$$

for a given image partition.

The probability that a border B_{ij} between two regions R_i and R_j is a false one must be found in step (4). This probability P can be found as a ratio of conditional probabilities; let P_t denote the probability that the boundary should remain, and P_f denote the probability that the boundary is false (i.e. should be removed and the regions should be merged), and $X(B_{ij})$ denote properties of the boundary B_{ij}: Then

$$P = \frac{P_f}{P_t + P_f} \tag{8.29}$$

where

$$P_f = \sum_{k=1}^{R} P(\theta_i = \theta_j | X(B_{ij})) \, P(\theta_i = \omega_k | X_i) \, P(\theta_j = \omega_k | X_j)$$

$$P_t = \sum_{k=1}^{R} \sum_{l=1; k \neq l}^{R} P(\theta_i = \omega_k \text{ and } \theta_j = \omega_l | X(B_{ij})) \, P(\theta_i = \omega_k | X_i) \, P(\theta_j = \omega_l | X_j) \tag{8.30}$$

The confidence C_i of interpretation of the region R_i (step (6)) can be found as follows. Let θ_i^1, θ_i^2 represent the two most probable interpretations of region R_i. Then

$$C_i = \frac{P(\theta_i^1 | X_i)}{P(\theta_i^2 | X_i)} \tag{8.31}$$

After assigning the final interpretation θ_f to a region R_f, interpretation probabilities of all its neighbours R_j (with *non-final* labels) are updated to maximize the objective function (8.28)

$$P_{new}(\theta_j) = P_{old}(\theta_j)\, P(B_{fj} \text{ is between regions labelled } \theta_f, \theta_j | X(B_{fj})) \quad (8.32)$$

The computation of these conditional probabilities is very expensive in terms of time and memory. It may be advantageous to precompute them beforehand and refer to table values during processing; this table must have been constructed with suitable sampling.

It should be understood that appropriate models of the inter-relationship between region interpretations, the collection of conditional probabilities, and methods of confidence evaluation must be specified to implement this approach.

8.5.2 Semantic genetic segmentation and interpretation

The previous section described the first historical semantic region growing method, which is still conceptually up to date. However, there is a fundamental problem in the region growing segmentation approach – the results are sensitive to the split/merge order (see Section 5.3). The conventional split-and-merge approach usually results in an undersegmented or an oversegmented image. It is practically impossible to stop the region growing process with a high confidence that there are neither too many nor too few regions in the image.

A method [Liow and Pavlidis 88, Pavlidis and Liow 90] was mentioned in Section 5.3.3 in which region growing always resulted in an oversegmented image and post-processing steps were used to remove false boundaries. Similar approach of removing false oversegmented regions can be found in a conceptually very different knowledge-based morphological region growing algorithm based on watersheds for graphs [Vincent and Soille 91]. Further, conventional region growing approaches are based on evaluation of homogeneity criteria and the goal is either to split a non-homogeneous region or to merge two regions, which may form a homogeneous region. Remember that the result is sensitive to the merging order; therefore, even if a merge results in a homogeneous region, the realized merge may not be optimal. In addition, there is no mechanism for seeking the optimal merges. Consequently, the semantic region growing approach to segmentation and interpretation starts with an oversegmented image in which some merges were not best possible. The semantic process is then trying to locate the maximum of some objective function by grouping regions which may already be incorrect and is therefore trying to obtain an optimal image interpretation from partially processed data where some significant information has already been lost. Further, conventional semantic region growing merges regions in an interpretation level only and does not evaluate properties of newly merged regions. It also very often ends in a local optimum of region labelling; the global optimum is not found because of the character of the optimization. Unreliability of image segmentation and interpretation of complex images results. The semantic genetic segmentation method solves these basic problems in the following manner:

- Both region merging and splitting is allowed; no merge or split is ever final, a better segmentation is looked for even if the current segmentation is already good.

- Semantics and higher level knowledge are incorporated into the main segmentation process, not applied as post-processing after the main segmentation steps are over.

- Semantics are included in an objective evaluation function (that is similar to conventional semantic-based segmentation).

- In contrast to conventional semantic region growing, any merged region is considered a contiguous region in the semantic objective function evaluation and all its properties are measured.

- The semantic genetic method does not look for local maxima; its search is likely to yield an image segmentation and interpretation specified by a (near) global maximum of an objective function.

The genetic semantic segmentation method is based on a **hypothesize and verify** principle. An objective function (similar to the objective functions used in previous sections) which evaluates the quality of a segmentation and interpretation is optimized by a genetic algorithm (the basics of which were presented in Section 7.6.1). The method is initialized with an oversegmented image called a **primary segmentation**, in which starting regions are called **primary regions**. Primary regions are repeatedly merged into current regions during the segmentation process. The genetic algorithm is responsible for generating new populations of feasible image segmentation and interpretation hypotheses.

An important property of genetic algorithms is that the whole population of segmentations is tested in a single processing step, in which better segmentations survive, and others die (see Section 7.6.1). If the objective function suggests that some merge of image regions was a good merge, it is allowed to survive into the next generation of image segmentation (the code string describing that particular segmentation survives), while bad region merges are removed (their description code strings die).

The **primary region adjacency graph** is the adjacency graph describing the primary image segmentation. The **specific region adjacency graph** represents an image after the merging of all adjacent regions of the same interpretation into a single region (collapsing the primary region adjacency graph).

The genetic algorithm requires any member of the processed population to be represented by a code string. Each primary region corresponds to one element in the code string; this correspondence is made once at the beginning of the segmentation/interpretation process. A region interpretation is given by the current code string in which each primary region of the image corresponds uniquely to some specific position. Each feasible image segmentation defined by a generated code string (segmentation hypothesis) corresponds to an unambiguous specific region adjacency graph. The specific region adjacency graphs serve as tools for evaluating objective segmentation functions. The specific region adjacency graph for each segmentation is constructed by collapsing a primary region adjacency graph.

Design of a segmentation optimization function (the fitness function in genetic algorithms), is crucial for a successful image segmentation. The genetic algorithm is responsible for finding an optimum of the objective function. Nevertheless, the optimization function must really represent segmentation optimality. To achieve this, the function must be based on properties of image regions and on relations between the regions – a priori knowledge about the desired segmentation must be included in the optimization criterion.

An applicable objective function may be similar to that given in equation (8.24) keeping in mind that the number of regions N is not constant since it depends on the segmentation hypothesis.

The conventional approach evaluates image segmentation and interpretation confidences of all possible region interpretations. Based on the region interpretations and their confidences, the confidences of neighbouring interpretations are updated, some being supported, and others becoming less probable. This conventional method can easily end at a consistent but sub-optimal image segmentation and interpretation. In the genetic approach, the algorithm is fully responsible for generating new and increasingly better hypotheses about image segmentation. Only these hypothetical segmentations are evaluated by the objective function (based on a corresponding specific region adjacency graph). Another significant difference is in the region property computation – as mentioned earlier, a region consisting of several primary regions is treated as a single region in the property computation process which gives a more appropriate region description.

Optimization criteria consist of three parts. Using the same notation as earlier, the objective function consists of;

- A confidence in the interpretation θ_i of the region R_i according to the region properties X_i

$$C(\theta_i|X_i) = P(\theta_i|X_i) \tag{8.33}$$

- A confidence in the interpretation θ_i of a region R_i according to the interpretations θ_j of its neighbours R_j

$$C(\theta_i) = \frac{C(\theta_i|X_i)\sum_{j=1}^{N_A}(r(\theta_i,\theta_j)C(\theta_j|X_j))}{N_A} \qquad (8.34)$$

where $r(\theta_i,\theta_j)$ represents the value of a compatibility function of two adjacent objects R_i and R_j with labels θ_i and θ_j, N_A is the number of regions adjacent to the region R_i, (confidences C replace the probabilities P used in previous sections because they do not satisfy necessary conditions which must hold for probabilities; however the intuitive meaning of interpretation confidences and interpretation probabilities remains unchanged).

- An evaluation of interpretation confidences in the whole image

$$C_{image} = \frac{\sum_{i=1}^{N_R} C(\theta_i)}{N_R} \qquad (8.35)$$

or

$$C'_{image} = \sum_{i=1}^{N_R}\left(\frac{C(\theta_i)}{N_R}\right)^2 \qquad (8.36)$$

where $C(\theta_i)$ is computed from equation (8.34) and N_R is the number of regions in the corresponding specific region adjacency graph.

The genetic algorithm attempts to optimize the objective function C_{image}, which represents the confidence in the current segmentation and interpretation hypothesis.

As presented, the segmentation optimization function is based on both unary properties of hypothesized regions and on binary relations between these regions and their interpretations. A priori knowledge about the characteristics of processed images is used in evaluation of the local region confidences $C(\theta_i|X_i)$, and the compatibility function $r(\theta_i,\theta_j)$ represents the confidence that two regions with their interpretations can be present in an image in the existing configuration.

The method is described by the following algorithm:

Algorithm 8.11: Semantic genetic image segmentation and interpretation

1. Initialize the segmentation into primary regions, and define a correspondence between each region and the related position of its label in the code strings generated by a genetic algorithm.

2. Construct a primary region adjacency graph.

3. Pick the starting population of code strings at random. If a priori information is available that can help to define the starting population, use it.

4. *Genetic Optimization.* Collapse a region adjacency graph for each code string of the current population (Algorithm 8.9). Using the current region adjacency graphs, compute the value of the optimization segmentation function for each code string from the population.

5. If the maximum of the optimization criterion does not increase significantly in several consecutive steps, go to step (7).

6. Let the genetic algorithm generate a new population of segmentation and interpretation hypotheses. Go to step (4).

7. The code string with the maximum confidence (the best segmentation hypothesis) represents the final image segmentation and interpretation.

A simple example

Consider an image of a ball on a lawn (see Figure 8.21). Let the interpretation labelling be B for *ball* and L for *lawn*, and let the following higher level knowledge be included: *There is a circular ball in the image* and *the ball is inside the green lawn region.* In reality, some more a priori knowledge would be added even in this simple example but this knowledge will be sufficient for our purposes. The knowledge must be stored in appropriate data structures.

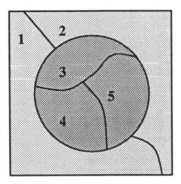

Figure 8.21 *A simulated scene 'ball on the lawn'.*

- Unary condition: Let the confidence that a region is a *ball* be based on its compactness (see Section 6.3.1);

$$C(\theta_i = B | X_i) = compactness(R_i) \tag{8.37}$$

and let the confidence that a region is *lawn* be based on its greenness.

$$C(\theta_i = L | X_i) = greenness(R_i) \tag{8.38}$$

Let the confidences for regions forming a perfect ball and perfect lawn be equal to one

$$C(B|circular) = 1 \qquad C(L|green) = 1$$

- Binary condition: Let the confidence that one region is positioned inside the other be given by a compatibility function

$$r(B \text{ is inside } L) = 1 \tag{8.39}$$

and let the confidences of all other positional combinations be equal to zero.

The unary condition says that the more compact a region is, the better its circularity, and the higher the confidence that its interpretation is a ball. The binary condition is very strict and claims that a ball can only be completely surrounded by a lawn.

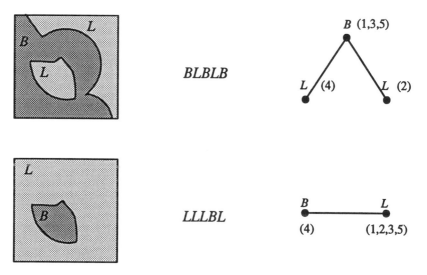

Figure 8.22 *Starting hypotheses about segmentation and interpretation: Interpretation, corresponding code strings and corresponding region adjacency graphs.*

Suppose the primary image segmentation consists of five primary regions $R_1, \ldots, R_5$ (see Figure 8.21); the primary region adjacency graph and its dual are in shown in Figure 8.20. Let the region numbers correspond to the position of region labels in code strings which are generated by the genetic algorithm as segmentation hypotheses and assume, for simplicity, that the starting population of segmentation hypotheses consists of just two strings (in any practical application the starting population would be significantly larger). Let the starting population be picked at random:

$$BLBLB$$
$$LLLBL$$

- this represents segmentation hypotheses as shown in Figure 8.22. After a random crossover between second and third positions, the population is as follows; assigned confidences reflect the circularity of the region labelled *ball* and the positioning of the region labelled *ball* inside the *lawn* region – the confidence computation is based on equation (8.35):

$$BL|BLB \quad C_{image} = 0.00$$
$$LL|LBL \quad C_{image} = 0.12$$
$$LLBLB \quad C_{image} = 0.20$$
$$BLLBL \quad C_{image} = 0.00$$

The second and the third segmentation hypotheses are the best ones, so they are reproduced and another crossover is applied; the first and the fourth code strings die (see Figure 8.23):

$$LLL|BL \quad C_{image} = 0.12$$
$$LLB|LB \quad C_{image} = 0.20$$
$$LLLLB \quad C_{image} = 0.14$$
$$LLBBL \quad C_{image} = 0.18$$

After one more crossover:

$$LLBL|B \quad C_{image} = 0.20$$
$$LLBB|L \quad C_{image} = 0.18$$
$$LLBLL \quad C_{image} = 0.10$$
$$LLBBB \quad C_{image} = 1.00$$

The code string (segmentation hypothesis) $LLBBB$ has a high (the highest achievable) confidence. If the genetic algorithm continues generating hypotheses, the confidence of the best hypothesis will not be any better and so it stops. The optimum segmentation/interpretation is shown in Figure 8.24.

This example only illustrates the basic principles of the method. Any practical application requires more complex a priori knowledge, the genetic algorithm would have to work with larger string populations, the primary image segmentation would have more regions, and the optimum solution would not be found in three steps. Nevertheless the principles remain the same.

Conventional semantic region growing methods start with a non-semantic phase and use semantic post processing to assign labels to regions. Based on the segmentation achieved in the region growing phases, the labelling process

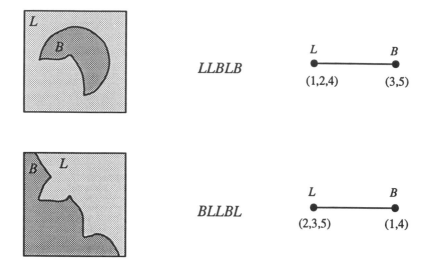

Figure 8.23 *Hypotheses about segmentation and interpretation: Interpretations, corresponding code strings and corresponding region adjacency graphs.*

Figure 8.24 *Optimal segmentation and interpretation: Interpretation, corresponding code string and region adjacency graph.*

is trying to find a consistent set of interpretations for regions. The semantic genetic approach functions in a quite different way.

Firstly, there are not separate phases. The semantics are incorporated into the segmentation/interpretation process. Secondly, segmentation hypotheses are generated first, and the optimization function is used only for evaluation of hypotheses. Thirdly, a genetic algorithm is responsible for generating segmentation hypotheses in an efficient way.

The method can be based on any properties of region description and on any relations between regions. The basic idea of generating segmentation hypotheses solves one of the problems of split-and-merge region growing – the sensitivity to the order of region growing. The only way to re-segment an image in a conventional region growing approach if the semantic post-processing does not provide a successful segmentation is to apply feedback control to change region growing parameters in a particular image part. There

s no guarantee that a global segmentation optimum will be obtained even after
everal feedback re-segmentation steps.

In the semantic genetic approach, no region merging is ever final. Natu-
al and constant feedback is contained in the semantic genetic segmentation
method because it is a part of the general genetic algorithm – this gives a
good chance that a (near) global optimum segmentation/interpretation will
be found in a single processing stage.

Note that throughout this chapter, the methods cannot and do not guarantee a correct segmentation – all the approaches try to achieve optimality
according to the chosen optimization function. Therefore, a priori knowledge
s essential to design a good optimization function. A priori knowledge is
often included into the optimization function in the form of heuristics, and
moreover, may affect the choice of the starting population of segmentation
hypotheses that can affect computational efficiency.

An important property of the discussed method is the possibility of parallel
mplementation. Similarly to the relaxation algorithm, this method is also
naturally parallel. Moreover, there is a straightforward generalization leading
to a semantic genetic segmentation and interpretation in three dimensions.
Considering a set of image planes forming a three-dimensional image (like
MRI or CT images), a primary segmentation can consist of regions in all
image planes and can be represented by a 3D primary relational graph. The
interesting possibility is to look for a global three-dimensional segmentation
and interpretation optimum using 3D properties of generated 3D regions
in a single complex processing stage. In such an application, the parallel
implementation would be a necessity.

References

[Algorri et al. 91] M E Algorri, D R Haynor, and Y Kim. Contextual classification of multiple anatomical tissues in tomographic images. In
*Proceedings of the Annual International Conference IEEE EMBS,
Vol.13, 1991, Orlando, Fl*, pages 106–107, IEEE, Piscataway, NJ,
1991.

[Ambler 75] A P H Ambler. A versatile system for computer controlled assembly. *Artificial Intelligence*, 6(2):129–156, 1975.

[Amini et al. 88] A Amini, S Tehrani, and T Weymouth. Using dynamic
programming for minimizing the energy of active contours in the
presence of hard constraints. In *Proceedings, Second International
Conference on Computer Vision, Tampa, Fl*, pages 95–99, IEEE,
Piscataway, NJ, 1988.

[Amini et al. 90] A Amini, T Weymouth, and R Jain. Using dynamic programming for solving variational problems in vision. *IEEE Transac-*

tions on Pattern Analysis and Machine Intelligence, 12(9):855–867 1990.

[Bajcsy and Rosenthal 80] R Bajcsy and D A Rosenthal. Visual and con ceptual focus of attention. In S Tanimoto and A Klinger, editors *Structured Computer Vision*, pages 133–154. Academic Press, Nev York, 1980.

[Ballard and Brown 82] D H Ballard and C M Brown. *Computer Vision* Prentice-Hall, Englewood Cliffs, NJ, 1982.

[Barrow and Tenenbaum 76] H G Barrow and I M Tenenbaum. MSYS: A system for reasoning about scenes. Technical Report Tech. Note 121 Stanford Research Institute, Menlo Park, Ca, 1976.

[Basu 87] S Basu. Image segmentation by semantic method. *Pattern Recog nition*, 20(5):497–511, 1987.

[Berger and Mohr 90] M O Berger and R Mohr. Towards autonomy in active contour models. In *Proceedings, 10th International Conference on Pattern Recognition, Atlantic City, NJ*, pages 847–851, IEEE, Pis cataway, NJ, 1990.

[Berthod and Faugeras 80] M Berthod and O D Faugeras. Using context in the global recognition of a set of objects: an optimisation approach. In *Proceedings of the 8th World Computing Congress (IFIP), Tokyo, Japan*, pages 695–698, 1980.

[Bhandarker and Suk 90] S Bhandarker and M Suk. Computer vision as a coupled system. In *Applications of Artificial Intelligence VIII, Or lando, Fl*, pages 43–54, SPIE, Bellingham, Wa, 1990.

[Blake 82] A Blake. A convergent edge relaxation algorithm. Technical Report MIP-R-135, Machine Intelligence Unit, University of Edin bourgh, 1982.

[Brooks et al. 79] R A Brooks, R Greiner, and T O Binford. The ACRONYM model-based vision system. In *Proceedings of the International Joint Conference on Artificial Intelligence, IJCAI-6, Tokyo*, pages 105– 113, 1979.

[Cabello et al. 90] D Cabello, A Delgado, M J Carreira, J Mira, R Moreno-Diaz, J. A. Munoz, and S. Candela. On knowledge-based medical im age understanding. *Cybernetics and Systems*, 21(2-3):277–289, 1990.

[Cohen 91a] G A Cohen. *Optimization of Radiologic Imaging Through Anatomic Classification: An Application to Magnetic Resonance Imaging*. PhD thesis, University of Iowa, 1991.

[Cohen 91b] L D Cohen. On active contour models and balloons. *CVGIP – Image Understanding*, 53(2):211–218, 1991.

[Cohen and Cohen 92] L D Cohen and I Cohen. Deformable models for 3D medical images using finite elements & balloons. In *Proceedings, IEEE Conference on Computer Vision and Pattern Recognition, Champaign, Il*, pages 592–598, IEEE, Los Alamitos, Ca, 1992.

[Collins et al. 91] S M Collins, C J Wilbricht, S R Fleagle, S. Tadikonda, and M D Winniford. An automated method for simultaneous detection of left and right coronary borders. In *Computers in Cardiology 1990, Chicago, Il*, page 7, IEEE, Los Alamitos, Ca, 1991.

[Devijver and Kittler 86] P A Devijver and J Kittler. *Pattern Recognition Theory and Applications*. Springer Verlag, Berlin-New York-Tokyo, 1986.

[Dew et al. 89] P M Dew, R A Earnshaw, and T R Heywood, editors. *Parallel Processing for Computer Vision and Display*. Addison-Wesley, Reading, Ma, 1989.

[Elfving and Eklundh 82] T Elfving and J O Eklundh. Some properties of stochastic labeling procedures. *Computer Graphics and Image Processing*, 20:158–170, 1982.

[Feldman and Yakimovsky 74] J A Feldman and Y Yakimovsky. Decision theory and artificial intelligence: A semantic–based region analyzer. *Artificial Intelligence*, 5:349–371, 1974.

[Franklin 90] S E Franklin. Topographic context of satellite spectral response. *Computers & Geosciences*, 16(7):1003–1010, 1990.

[Fung et al. 90] P W Fung, G Grebbin, and Y Attikiouzel. Contextual classification and segmentation of textured images. In *Proceedings of the 1990 International Conference on Acoustics, Speech, and Signal Processing - ICASSP 90, Albuquerque, NM*, pages 2329–2332, IEEE, Piscataway, NJ, 1990.

[Geman and Geman 84] S Geman and D Geman. Stochastic relaxation, Gibbs distributions, and the Bayesian restoration of images. *IEEE Transactions on Pattern Analysis and Machine Intelligence*, 6(6):721–741, 1984.

[Gerig et al. 92] G Gerig, J Martin, R Kikinis, O Kubler, M Shenton, and F A Jolesz. Unsupervised tissue type segmentation of 3D dual-echo MR head data. *Image and Vision Computing*, 10(6):349–360, 1992.

[Ghosh and Harrison 90] J Ghosh and C G Harrison, editors. *Parallel Architectures for Image Processing, Santa Clara, Ca*, Bellingham, Wa. 1990. SPIE.

[Gonzalez and Lopez 89] A F Gonzalez and S S Lopez. Classification of satellite images using contextual classifiers. *Digest - International Geoscience and Remote Sensing Symposium (IGARSS)*, 2:645–648, 1989.

[Grimson and Lozano-Perez 87] W E L Grimson and T Lozano-Perez. Localizing overlapping parts by searching the interpretation tree. *IEEE Transactions on Pattern Analysis and Machine Intelligence*, 9(4):469–482, 1987.

[Hancock and Kittler 90a] E R Hancock and J Kittler. Discrete relaxation. *Pattern Recognition*, 23(7):711–733, 1990.

[Hancock and Kittler 90b] E R Hancock and J Kittler. Edge-labeling using dictionary-based relaxation. *IEEE Transactions on Pattern Analysis and Machine Intelligence*, 12(2):165–181, 1990.

[Hanson and Riseman 78] A R Hanson and E M Riseman. VISIONS – a computer system for interpreting scenes. In A R Hanson and E M Riseman, editors, *Computer Vision Systems*, pages 303–333. Academic Press, New York, 1978.

[Haralick et al. 88] R M Haralick, M C Zhang, and R W Ehrich. Dynamic programming approach for context classification using the Markov random field. In *9th International Conference on Pattern Recognition, Rome, Italy*, pages 1169–1181, IEEE, New York, 1988.

[Hummel and Zucker 83] R A Hummel and S W Zucker. On the foundation of relaxation labeling proceses. *IEEE Transactions on Pattern Analysis and Machine Intelligence*, 5(3):259–288, 1983.

[Hyche et al. 92] M E Hyche, N F Ezquerra, and R Mullick. Spatiotemporal detection of arterial structure using active contours. In *Proceedngs of Visualization in Biomedical Computing '92 Proceedings, Chapel Hill, NC*, pages 52–62, 1992.

[Illingworth and Kittler 87] J Illingworth and J Kittler. Optimisation algorithms in probabilistic relaxation labelling. In *Pattern Recognition Theory and Applications*, pages 109–117. Springer Verlag, Berlin-New York-Tokyo, 1987.

[Kamada et al. 88] M Kamada, K Toraichi, R Mori, K Yamamoto, and H. Yamada. Parallel architecture for relaxation operations. *Pattern Recognition*, 21(2):175–181, 1988.

Kanade and Ikeuchi 91] T Kanade and K Ikeuchi. Special issue on physical modeling in computer vision. *IEEE Transactions on Pattern Analysis and Machine Intelligence*, 13:609–742, 1991.

Karaolani et al. 92] P Karaolani, G D Sullivan, and K D Baker. Active contours using finite elements to control local scale. In D C Hogg and R D Boyle, editors, *Proceedings of the 1992 British Machine Vision Conference, Leeds, UK*, pages 472–480. Springer Verlag, 1992.

Kasif 90] S Kasif. On the parallel complexity of discrete relaxation in constraint satisfaction networks. *Artificial Intelligence*, 45(3):275–286, 1990.

Kass et al. 87a] M Kass, A Witkin, and D Terzopoulos. Snakes: Active contour models. *International Journal of Computer Vision*, 1(4):133–144, 1987.

Kass et al. 87b] M Kass, A Witkin, and D Terzopoulos. Snakes: Active contour models. In *Proceedings, First International Conference on Computer Vision, London, England*, pages 259–268, IEEE, Piscataway, NJ, 1987.

Kittler 87] J Kittler. Relaxation labelling. In *Pattern Recognition Theory and Applications*, pages 99–108. Springer Verlag, Berlin-New York-Tokyo, 1987.

Kittler and Foglein 84a] J Kittler and J Foglein. Contextual classification of multispectral pixel data. *Image and Vision Computing*, 2(1):13–29, 1984.

Kittler and Foglein 84b] J Kittler and J Foglein. Contextual decision rules for objects in lattice configuration. In *Proceedings of 7th International Conference on Pattern Recognition, Montreal, Canada*, pages 270–272. IEEE, 1984.

Kittler and Foglein 86] J Kittler and J Foglein. On compatibility and support functions in probabilistic relaxation. *Computer Vision, Graphics, and Image Processing*, 34:257–267, 1986.

Kittler and Hancock 89] J Kittler and E R Hancock. Combining evidence in probabilistic relaxation. *International Journal on Pattern Recognition and Artificial Intelligence*, 3:29–52, 1989.

Kittler and Illingworth 85] J Kittler and J Illingworth. Relaxation labelling algorithms – a review. *Image and Vision Computing*, 3(4):206–216, 1985.

[Kittler and Pairman 85] J Kittler and D Pairman. Contextual pattern recognition applied to cloud detection and identification. *IEEE Transactions on Geoscience and Remote Sensing*, 23(6):855–863, 1985.

[Kuan et al. 89] D Kuan, H Shariat, and K Dutta. Constraint-based image understanding system for aerial imagery interpretation. In *Proceedings of the Annual AI Systems in Government Conference, Washington, DC*, pages 141–147, 1989.

[Lee et al. 89] D Lee, A Papageorgiou, and G W Wasilkowski. Computing optical flow. In *Proceedings, Workshop on Visual Motion*, pages 99–106, IEEE, Irvine, Ca, 1989.

[Lesser et al. 75] V R Lesser, R D Fennell, L D Erman, and D R Reddy. Organisation of the HEARSAY II speech understanding system. *IEEE Transactions on Acoustics, Speech and Signal Processing*, 23(1):11–24, 1975.

[Levine 78] M D Levine. A knowledge based computer vision system. In A R Hanson and E M Riseman, editors, *Computer Vision Systems*, pages 335–352. Academic Press, New York, 1978.

[Li and Uhr 87] Z Li and L Uhr. Pyramid vision using key features to integrate image–driven bottom–up and model–driven top–down processes. *IEEE Transactions on Systems, Man and Cybernetics*, 17(2):250–263, 1987.

[Liow and Pavlidis 88] Y Liow and T Pavlidis. Enhancements of the split-and-merge algorithm for image segmentation. In *1988 IEEE International Conference on Robotics and Automation, Philadelphia, Pa*, pages 1567–1572, Computer Society Press, Washington, DC, 1988.

[Marik et al. 92] V Marik, O Stepankova, and R Trappl, editors. *Advances Topics in Artificial Intelligence, LNAI No. 617*. Springer Verlag, Heidelberg, 1992.

[Marr 82] D Marr. *Vision – A Computational Investigation into the Human Representation and Processing of Visual Information*. W.H. Freeman and Co., San Francisco, 1982.

[McInerney and Terzopoulos 93] T McInerney and D Terzopoulos. A finite element based deformable model for 3D biomedical image segmentation. In *Proceedings SPIE, Vol. 1905, Biomedical Image Processing and Biomedical Visualization, San Jose, Ca*, SPIE, Bellingham, Wa, 1993.

Metaxas and Terzopoulos 91] D Metaxas and D Terzopoulos. Constrained deformable superquadrics and nonrigid motion tracking. In *Proceedings of the Computer Vision and Pattern Recognition Conference CVPR-91, Lahaina, Hi*, pages 337–343, 1991.

Michalski et al. 83] R S Michalski, J G Carbonell, and T M Mitchell. *Machine Learning I, II*. Morgan Kaufmann Publishers, Los Altos, Ca, 1983.

Millin and Ni 89] B M Millin and L M Ni. A reliable parallel algorithm for relaxation labeling. In P M Dew, R A Earnshaw, and T R Heywood, editors, *Parallel Processing for Computer Vision and Display*, pages 190–207. Addison-Wesley, Reading, Ma, 1989.

Mohn et al. 87] E Mohn, N L Hjort, and G O Storvik. Simulation study of some contextual classification methods for remotely sensed data. *IEEE Transactions on Geoscience and Remote Sensing*, 25(6):796–804, 1987.

Moller-Jensen 90] L Moller-Jensen. Knowledge-based classification of an urban area using texture and context information in Landsat-TM imagery. *Photogrammetric Engineering and Remote Sensing*, 56(6):899–904, 1990.

Mulder 88] J A Mulder. Discrimination vision. *Computer Vision, Graphics, and Image Processing*, 43:313–336, 1988.

Nagao and Matsuyama 80] M Nagao and T Matsuyama. *A Structural Analysis of Complex Aerial Photographs*. Plenum Press, New York, 1980.

Niemann 90] H Niemann. *Pattern Analysis and Understanding*. Springer Verlag, Berlin-New York-Tokyo, 2nd edition, 1990.

Nilsson 82] N J Nilsson. *Principles of Artificial Intelligence*. Springer Verlag, Berlin, 1982.

Parent and Zucker 89] P Parent and S W Zucker. Radial projection: an efficient update rule for relaxation labeling. *IEEE Transactions on Pattern Analysis and Machine Intelligence*, 11(8):886–889, 1989.

Parkkinen et al. 90] J Parkkinen, G Cohen, M Sonka, J C Ehrhardt, and N. Andreasen. Some problems of brain image analysis. In *Proceedings of Biosignal '90, Brno, Czechoslovakia*. Czech Technical Society, 1990.

[Parkkinen et al. 91] J Parkkinen, G Cohen, M Sonka, and N Andreasen. Seg mentation of MR brain images. In *Proceedings of the Annual Interna tional Conference of the IEEE Engineering in Medicine and Biolog Society, Volume 13, Orlando, Fl*, pages 71–72, IEEE, Piscataway NJ, 1991.

[Pavlidis and Liow 90] T Pavlidis and Y Liow. Integrating region growing and edge detection. *IEEE Transactions on Pattern Analysis an Machine Intelligence*, 12(3):225–233, 1990.

[Prasanna Kumar 91] V K Prasanna Kumar. *Parallel Architectures and Al gorithms for Image Understanding*. Academic Press, Boston, Ma 1991.

[Rao and Jain 88] A R Rao and R Jain. Knowledge representation and con trol in computer vision systems. *IEEE Expert*, 3(1):64–79, 1988.

[Reichgelt 91] H Reichgelt. *Knowledge Representation: An AI Perspective* Ablex Publishing Corporation, Norwood, NJ, 1991.

[Roberto et al. 90] V Roberto, L Gargiulo, A Peron, and C Chiaruttini. A knowledge-based system for geophysical interpretation. In *Proceed ings of the 1990 International Conference on Acoustics, Speech, anc Signal Processing - ICASSP 90, Albuquerque, NM*, pages 1945–1948, IEEE, Piscataway, NJ, 1990.

[Rosenfeld 79] A Rosenfeld. *Picture Languages – Formal Models for Picture Recognition*. Academic Press, New York, 1979.

[Rosenfeld et al. 76] A Rosenfeld, R A Hummel, and S W Zucker. Scene labelling by relaxation operations. *IEEE Transactions on Systems, Man and Cybernetics*, 6:420–433, 1976.

[Simons 84] G L Simons. *Introducing Artificial Intelligence*. NCC Publica tions, Manchester, 1984.

[Sonka et al. 92a] M Sonka, C J Wilbricht, M D Winniford, and S M Collins. Simultaneous detection of left and right coronary borders: A robust approach to automated angiographic analysis. *Circulation (*, 86(4):I-121, 1992.

[Sonka et al. 92b] M Sonka, M D Winniford, and S M. Collins. Reduction of failure rates in automated analysis of difficult images: Improved simultaneous detection of left and right coronary borders. In *Com puters in Cardiology, Durham, NC, 1992*, pages 111–114, IEEE, Los Alamitos, CA, 1992.

[Sonka et al. 93] M Sonka, C J Wilbricht, S R Fleagle, S K Tadikonda, M D Winniford, and S M Collins. Simultaneous detection of both coronary borders. *IEEE Transactions on Medical Imaging*, 12(3), 1993.

[Strat and Fischler 91] T M Strat and M A Fischler. Context-based vision: Recognizing objects using information from both 2D and 3D imagery. *IEEE Transactions on Pattern Analysis and Machine Intelligence*, 13(10):1050–1065, 1991.

[Terzopoulos 91] D Terzopoulos. Visual modeling. In *Proceedings of the British Machine Vision Conference, Glasgow, Scotland*, pages 9–11, Springer Verlag, London-Berlin-New York, 1991.

[Terzopoulos and Fleischer 88] D Terzopoulos and K Fleischer. Deformable models. *The Visual Computer*, 4(6):306–331, 1988.

[Terzopoulos and Metaxas 91] D Terzopoulos and D Metaxas. Dynamic 3D models with local and global deformations: Deformable superquadrics. *IEEE Transactions on Pattern Analysis and Machine Intelligence*, 13(7):703–714, 1991.

[Terzopoulos et al. 87] D Terzopoulos, A Witkin, and M Kass. Symmetry-seeking models for 3D object reconstruction. In *Proceedings, First International Conference on Computer Vision, London, England*, pages 269–276, IEEE, Piscataway, NJ, 1987.

[Terzopoulos et al. 88] D Terzopoulos, A Witkin, and M Kass. Constraints on deformable models: Recovering 3D shape and nonrigid motion. *Artificial Intelligence*, 36(1):91–123, 1988.

[Tilton 87] J C Tilton. Contextual classification on the massively parallel processor. In *Frontiers of Massively Parallel Scientific Computation, Greenbelt, Md*, pages 171–181, NASA, Washington, DC, 1987.

[Toulson and Boyce 92] D L Toulson and J F Boyce. Segmentation of MR images using neural nets. *Image and Vision Computing*, 10(5):324–328, 1992.

[Tsosos 84] J K Tsosos. Knowledge and the visual process. *Pattern Recognition*, 17(1):13–28, 1984.

[Vincent and Soille 91] L Vincent and P Soille. Watersheds in digital spaces: An efficient algorithm based on immersion simulations. *IEEEPAMI*, 13(6):583–598, 1991.

[Waltz 57] D L Waltz. Understanding line drawings of scenes with shadows. In *The Psychology of Computer Vision*. McGraw Hill, New York, 1957.

[Watanabe and Suzuki 88] T Watanabe and H Suzuki. An experimental evaluation of classifiers using spatial context for multispectral images.
Systems and Computers in Japan, 19(4):33–47, 1988.

[Watanabe and Suzuki 89] T Watanabe and H Suzuki. Compound decision
theory and adaptive classification for multispectral image data. *Systems and Computers in Japan*, 20(8):37–47, 1989.

[Wechsler 90] H Wechsler. *Computational Vision*. Academic Press, London –
San Diego, 1990.

[Wharton 82] S Wharton. A contextual classification method for recognising
land use patterns in high resolution remotely sensed data. *Pattern
Recognition*, 15:317–324, 1982.

[Wilkinson and Megier 90] G G Wilkinson and J Megier. Evidential reasoning in a pixel classification hierarchy. A potential method for integrating image classifiers and expert system rules based on geographic
context. *International Journal of Remote Sensing*, 11(10):1963–1968,
1990.

[Williams and Shah 92] D J Williams and M Shah. A fast algorithm for active
contours and curvature estimation. *CVGIP – Image Understanding*,
55(1):14–26, 1992.

[Winston 84] P H Winston. *Artificial Intelligence*. Addison-Wesley, Reading,
Ma, 2nd edition, 1984.

[Witkin et al. 87] A Witkin, D Terzopoulos, and M Kass. Signal matching through scale space. *International Journal of Computer Vision*,
1(2):133–144, 1987.

[Zen et al. 90] C Zen, S Y Lin, and Y Y Chen. Parallel architecture for
probabilistic relaxation operation on images. *Pattern Recognition*,
23(6):637–645, 1990.

[Zhang et al. 90] M C Zhang, R M Haralick, and J B Campbell. Multispectral
image context classification using stochastic relaxation. *IEEE Transactions on Systems, Man and Cybernetics*, 20(1):128–140, 1990.

[Zucker 78] S W Zucker. Vertical and horizontal processes in low level vision.
In A R Hanson and E M Riseman, editors, *Computer Vision Systems*,
pages 187–195, Academic Press, New York, 1978.

[Zucker 88] S W Zucker. Organization of curve detection: Coarse tangent
fields and fine spline coverings. *Neural Networks*, 1(1):534, 1988.

9

3D Vision

A number of techniques have been presented so far that perform a range of tasks of varying complexity; some are specific to raw images, such as edge detection or the more elaborate region splitting and merging algorithms. Others are more abstract (or general purpose), such as the studies of graphical representations and pattern recognition techniques. What has been overlooked hitherto, though, is the (perhaps obvious) observation that the best known vision system, our own, is geared specifically to dealing with the 3D world and as yet the gap between images and the real world of 3D objects, with all their problems of relative depth, occlusion etc. has not been seriously examined.

There are, of course, many different uses to which a vision system may be put; at simplest there would indeed be no 3D information present in the images presented, and consequently no need to extract it. Examples may be optical character recognition, which is intrinsically 2D in nature, or analysis of remotely sensed images, where the scene contents are 3D but the analysis required (land use classification, perhaps) does not (necessarily) need that information. Alternatively, the scene may be composed of 3D objects, but the analysis required permits their presentation to be contrived so that one strictly 2D view suffices; a good example is the wide range of industrial inspection applications in which a single view allows the necessary confirmation of the suitability of a product. Such applications well illustrate the principle of taking sufficient care over an experimental set-up in order later to reduce the computational analysis. Frequently in the industrial domain the designer of a vision system is at liberty to specify adequate lighting, camera angles etc., thereby obviating the need for complicated algorithms at a later stage. The most general problems of all, however, are 3D in nature and demand 3D analysis – obvious examples are robot **bin-picking**, in which a robot is required to identify the position and orientation of a 3D object and then pick it up, or robot navigation and obstacle avoidance where, despite the likely ability to be able to control the environment to some degree (lighting etc.), the position in space of 'objects' detected is of primary importance, or more generally 'real-world' vehicle guidance (automobiles, for example), in which there is likely to be little foreknowledge of the objects the scene is likely to contain, and little if any control over lighting.

The central problem of computer vision has been stated as [Aloimonos and

373

Shulman 89]

> ...from one of a sequence of images of a moving or stationary
> object or scene, taken by a monocular or polynocular moving or
> stationary observer, to understand the object or the scene and its
> three-dimensional properties.

Here, the word 'understand' may be interpreted in many ways; it may, for example, imply classification of the objects located in the scene(s) – a recognition task. Alternatively more precision may be implied; the robot bin-picker for example, needs to identify an object first, and then locate it precisely in space for manipulation. It requires to reconstruct the scene it sees, or at least some part thereof. Fundamental to this problem is the fact that a single image is a 2D projection of some part of the 3D world, and there is a consequent loss of information in the view presented to the machine. No matter how sophisticated the algorithms applied, the reduction in dimension of the information supply will make recapture of the full 3D information set impossible without some further clue. Even with full knowledge of camera geometry (the perspective of the projection), an inversion is impossible. Coupled to this observation is the fact that a simple image provides brightness information on a per-pixel basis, but *brightness* is generated by a combination of several independent factors. To predict the contents of a 2D image, at least knowledge of the illumination and object surface orientations would be necessary, together with the individual reflectance properties of those surfaces. Starting from the image, it is unlikely in general that reconstruction of these three properties will be possible.

The human visual system has at its disposal considerably more than a camera and a processor, and solutions to the 3D problem may be proposed based on this model. In particular, we make use of two eyes to provide depth clues, especially for objects that are close, and we are highly mobile, allowing slight or gross movements of the head to contribute parallax information about relative object distances. At a higher level of abstraction, the brain deploys foreknowledge of great complexity to assist in scene interpretation, ranging from global constraints such as *expect gravity to work downwards* to more domain-specific constraints such as *expect to find vehicles in road scenes*. Human scene misinterpretation can often be attributed to fooling the architecture (misleading the stereo or parallax systems), or presenting the totally unexpected (misleading the constraint mechanism).

Taking these observations into account, we might hope to perform some 3D vision tasks either by augmenting the information input (stereo cameras, perhaps, or a system providing image sequences), or by supplying the analysis system with constraining foreknowledge. The richness of human foreknowledge is beyond computer systems, but it may be possible to isolate limited domains in which 3D information may be elicited from 2D input – a specific example may be accurate geometric information about the objects whose projections are going to be seen. Alternatively, control of the lighting system may be available, together with knowledge of object surface reflectance properties, and consequently reconstruction of surface orientations may be viable. Formally, we are hoping to provide enough extra information to permit the 3D to 2D projection to be inverted unambiguously.

9.1 Strategy

Theoretically, the problem may be viewed as determining a route from an image based, 2D co-ordinate system to an object-based, 3D co-ordinate system. As already remarked, the human visual system achieves this by using a wealth of clues and highly sophisticated processing; current approaches to solving the computational problem may be classed roughly as **bottom-up** or **top-down** (see Chapter 8). Bottom-up techniques are (potentially) highly general inasmuch as they work solely from the given information (image(s), together with any other information such as camera geometry) toward a 3D interpretation. Top-down approaches assume the presence of particular objects, or families of objects and set about locating them in the 2D projection provided ... this may be thought of as an 'engineering' approach to the problem. The former approach is exemplified by the theory proposed by Marr [Marr 82] while the latter falls under the generic heading **model-based vision**.

9.1.1 Marr's theory

Marr was a pioneer in the study of computer vision whose influence has been, and continues to be, considerable despite his early death. Critical of earlier work that, while successful in limited domains or image classes, was either empirical or unduly restrictive of the images with which it could deal, Marr proposed a more abstract and theoretical approach that permitted work to be put into a larger context. Restricting himself to the 3D interpretation of single, static scenes, Marr proposed that a computer vision system was just an example of an information processing device, and that any such device could be understood at three levels;

1. Computational theory: The theory describes what the device is supposed to do; what information it provides from other information provided as input. It should also describe the logic of the strategy that performs this task.

2. Representation and algorithm: These address precisely how the computation may be carried out; in particular, information representations and algorithms to manipulate them.

3. Implementation: The physical realization of the algorithm; specifically, programs and hardware.

It is stressed that it is important to be clear about which level is being addressed in attempting to solve or understand a particular problem - Marr illustrates this by noting that the effect of an after-image (induced by staring at a light bulb) is a physical effect, while the mental confusion provoked by the well known Necker cube illusion (see Figure 9.1) would appear to be at a

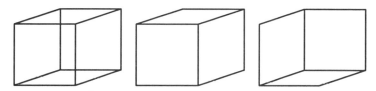

Figure 9.1 *The Necker cube, and two possible interpretations.*

different theoretical level entirely.

The point is then made that the lynch-pin of success is addressing the theory rather than algorithms or implementation – any number of edge detectors may be developed, each one specific to particular problems, but we would be no nearer any general understanding of how edge detection should or might be achieved. Marr remarks that the complexity of the vision task dictates a sequence of steps refining descriptions of the geometry of visible surfaces; having derived some such description, it is then necessary to remove the dependence on the vantage point then implicit, and transform the description into an **object centred** one. The requirement, then, is to move from pixels to surface delineation, then to surface characteristic description (orientation), then to a full 3D description. These transformations are effected by moving from the 2D image to a **primal sketch** then to a **2.5D sketch**, and thence to a full 3D representation.

The primal sketch

The primal sketch aims to capture, in as general a way as possible, the significant intensity changes in an image. Hitherto, such changes have been referred to as 'edges', but Marr makes the observation that this word implies a physical meaning that cannot at this stage be inferred. The first stage is to locate these changes at a range of scales (see Section 4.3.4) – informally, a range of blurring filters are passed across the image, after which second-order zero crossings (see Section 4.3.2) are located for each scale of blur [Marr and Hildreth 80]. The blurring recommended is a standard Gaussian filter (see equation (4.50)), while the zero crossings are located with a Laplacian operator (see equation (4.37)). The various blurring filters have the effect of isolating features of particular scales; then zero crossing evidence in the same locality at many scales provides strong evidence of a genuine physical feature in the scene.

To complete the primal sketch, these zero crossings are grouped, according to their location and orientations, to provide information about tokens in the image (edges, bars and blobs) that may help provide later information about (3D) orientation of scene surfaces. The grouping phase, paying attention to the evidence from various scales, extracts tokens that are likely to represent surfaces in the real world.

It is of interest to note that there is strong evidence for the existence of the various components used to build the primal sketch in the human visual system – we too engage in detection of features at various scales, the location of sharp intensity changes and their subsequent grouping into tokens.

The 2.5D sketch

The 2.5D sketch reconstructs the relative distances from the viewer of surfaces detected in the scene, and may be called a **depth map**. Observe that the output of this phase uses as input features detected in the preceding one, but that in itself it does not give us a 3D reconstruction – in this sense it is midway between 2D and 3D representations, and in particular, nothing can be said about the 'other side' of any objects in view. Instead, it may be the derivation of a surface normal associated with each likely surface detected in the primal sketch, and there may be an implicit improvement in the quality of this information.

There are various routes to the 2.5D sketch, but their common thread is the continuation of the bottom-up approach in that they do not exploit any knowledge about scene contents, but rather employ additional clues such as knowledge about the nature of lighting or motion effects, and are thus generally applicable and not domain-specific. The main approaches are known as **'Shape from X'** techniques, and are described in Section 9.3. At the conclusion of this phase, the representation is still in viewer-centred co-ordinates.

The 3D representation

At this stage the Marr paradigm of necessity overlaps with top-down, model-based approaches – it is required to take the evidence derived so far and identify objects within it. This can only be achieved with some knowledge about what 'objects' are, and, consequently, some means of describing them. The important point is that this is a transition to an object centred co-ordinate system, allowing object descriptions to be viewer independent.

This is the most difficult phase and successful implementation is remote, especially compared to the success seen with the derivation of the primal and 2.5D sketches – specifying what is required, however, has been very successful in guiding computer vision research since the theory was formulated. Unlike earlier stages, there is little physiological guidance that can be used to design algorithms since this level of human vision is not well understood. Marr observes that the target co-ordinate system(s) should be modular in the sense that each 'object' should be treated differently, rather than employing one global co-ordinate system – this prevents having to consider the orientation of model components with respect to the whole. It is further observed that a set of **volumetric** primitives is likely to be of value in representing models (in contrast to surface-based descriptions). Representations based on an object's 'natural' axes, derived from symmetries, or the orientation of stick features, are likely to be of greater use.

Various ways of modelling 3D objects are considered in the following section.

9.1.2   Modelling strategies

Identification of 3D objects requires, in addition to the recognition of appropriate features in the image (or images), some model of the objects to match with observations. Approaches to matching are discussed briefly later in this chapter, and general matching strategies are covered at length in other chapters. Here we present an overview of some of the more popular ways of constructing models of objects.

At this level of processing, object models will be **object centred** (as opposed to viewer centred). Their use is common in other areas, notably CAD and graphics where image synthesis is required – that is, an exact (2D) pictorial representation of some modelled 3D object. Use of an object representation which matches the representation generated by CAD systems has been an active research area for years, with substantial promise for industrial model-based vision. The latest progress in this area is presented in [Bowyer 92] with papers devoted to CAD-based models applied to pose estimation [Kriegman 92, Ponce et al. 92, Seales and Dyer 92], 3D specular object recognition [Sato et al. 92], and invariant feature extraction from range data [Flynn and Jain 92].

Various well known schemes exist, with different properties. A representation is called **complete** if two different objects cannot correspond to the same model, so a particular model is unambiguous. A representation is called **unique** if an object cannot correspond to two different models. Most 3D representation methods sacrifice either the completeness or uniqueness property. Commercial CAD systems frequently sacrifice uniqueness; different design methodologies may produce the same object. Some solid modellers maintain multiple representations of objects in order to offer flexibility in design.

The principal schemes are summarized below;

Wire-frames

A wire-frame may be used to represent edges of objects, and provides only (3D) vertex and edge information – normally the objects have planar faces and straight edges, simplifying the representation considerably. The representation is a simple list of vertices and edges joining those vertices. This is an attractive idea since it is simple, fast, and well suited to the polyhedral blocks world that is considered in Section 9.2 [Shapira 74]. The significant problem with them is that they are often ambiguous since they do not include any surface information – this is easily demonstrated in Figure 9.2.

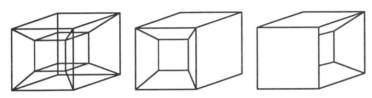

Figure 9.2 *A wire-frame model of an object, and two possible interpretations.*

Constructive Solid Geometry (CSG)

An idea which has found some success, notably with IBM's WINSOM [Quarendon 84], is to construct 3D bodies from a selection of solid primitives. Popularly, these primitives are a cuboid, a cylinder, a sphere, a cone and a 'half space' – the cylinder and cone are considered to be infinite. They are scaled, positioned and combined by union, intersection and difference; thus a finite cone is formed by intersecting an infinite cone with an appropriately positioned half space. A CSG model is stored as a tree, with leaf nodes representing the primitive solid, and edges enforcing precedence among the set theoretical operations. The versatility of such a simply stated scheme is surprising. In contrast to wire-frames, CSG models define properties such as object volume unambiguously, but suffer the drawback of being non-unique. For example, the solid illustrated in Figure 9.4 may be formed by the union of two different pairs of cuboids. Further, it is not easy to model 'natural' shapes (a head, for instance) with CSG. A more serious drawback is that it is not straightforward to recover surfaces given a CSG description; such a procedure is very computationally expensive.

Surface models

Surface or object **boundary representations (B-reps)** can be viewed conceptually as a triple:

- A set of surfaces of the object.

- A set of space curves representing intersections between the above surfaces.

- A graph describing the surface connectivity.

B-reps are an appealing and intuitively natural way of representing 3D bodies in that they consist of an explicit list of the bodies' faces. 'Faces' are usually taken to be planar, so bodies are always polyhedral, and we are dealing the whole time with piecewise planar surfaces. A useful side-effect of this scheme is that properties such as surface area and solid volume are well defined. The simplest B-rep scheme would model everything with the simplest possible 2D polygon, the triangle; triangularization is a well understood process – see, for example, [Preparata and Shamos 85]. By taking small enough primitives quite satisfactory representations of complex objects can be achieved, and it is an obvious generalization to consider polygons with more edges than three.

A drawback with these B-reps is that 'face' may not be well defined. We would hope that a face should have no 'dangling' edges, and that the union of a body's faces should be its boundary. Unfortunately the real world is not cooperative and many (simple) bodies exist in which face boundaries are not well defined. The next step in generality is the **quadric surface model**. In CAD systems rational B-spline surfaces are used; this permits much greater flexibility in the description, but it becomes important to restrict the number of possible face edges in order to limit the complexity of the computations involved.

Volumetric models

An object is placed in some reference co-ordinate system and its volume is subdivided into small volume primitives called **voxels** – cubes and parallelepipeds are the most common.

A more recently used set of volumetric primitives are superquadrical solids; the implicit equation for a superquadric is

$$\left(\left(\frac{x}{a_1}\right)^{2/\varepsilon_1} + \left(\frac{y}{a_2}\right)^{2/\varepsilon_1}\right)^{\varepsilon_2/\varepsilon_1} + \left(\frac{z}{a_3}\right)^{2/\varepsilon_1} = 1 \qquad (9.1)$$

where a_1, a_2, and a_3 define the superquadric size in x, y, and z directions respectively. ε_1 is the squareness parameter in the latitude plane and ε_2 is the squareness parameter in the longitude plane. Superquadric volumetric primitives can be deformed by bending, twisting and tapering and boolean combinations can be used to represent arbitrarily complicated shapes. Superquadric fitting is described in [Gupta 89].

Generalized cylinders

Generalized cylinders, or **generalized cones**, are often also called **sweep representations**. Recall that a cylinder may be defined as the surface swept out by a circle whose centre is travelling along a straight line (spine) normal to the circle's plane. We can generalize this idea in a number of ways – we may permit any closed curve to be 'pulled along' any line in three space. We may even permit the closed curve to adjust as it travels in accordance with some function, so a cone is defined by a circle whose radius changes linearly with distance travelled, moving along a straight line. Further, the closed curve section need not contain the spine. Usually it is assumed that the curve is perpendicular to the spine curve at each point. Figure 9.3 illustrates two simple generalized cylinders.

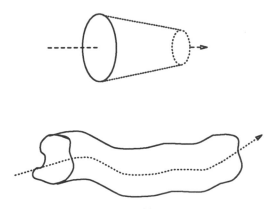

Figure 9.3 *Solids represented as generalized cylinders.*

These generalized cones turn out to be very good at representing some classes of solid body [Binford 71, Soroka and Bajcsy 78]. The advantage of symmetrical volumetric primitives, such as generalized cylinders and superquadrics, is their ability to capture common symmetries and represent certain shapes with few parameters. They are, however, ill-suited for modelling many natural objects that do not have the set of regularities incorporated into the primitives. A well known vision system called ACRONYM [Brooks et al. 79] used generalized cones as its modelling scheme.

There is a modification of the sweep representation called a **skeleton representation**, which stores only the spines of the objects [Besl and Jain 85].

Geons

This is a qualitative representation, while most solid representations are quantitative since solids are specified in terms of numerical parameters. For visual recognition tasks the quantitative description might contain redundant detail.

Examining some qualitative features of the segmented primitives can ease recognition. However qualitative representations cannot in general be used to synthesize an image of an object.

Biederman [Biederman 87] developed a catalogue of 36 geons (GEOmetrical iONs), each member of which has a unique set of four qualitative features:

- Edge: straight or curved.

- Symmetry: rotational, reflective, asymmetric.

- Size variation: constant, expanding, expanding/contracting.

- Axis: straight or curved.

3D objects would be composed of a number connected geons. Biederman proposes an edge-based procedure for segmenting images into their geon components – places where geons join are searched for using non-accidental alignments and concavities.

On the other hand the lack of quantitative information limits the use of geons. When one wants to distinguish qualitatively similar objects (say parts which differ in scale) it becomes difficult. The way out of the problem is to add some quantitative information.

In general one can recognize the type of an object using qualitative information but it would be much more difficult to find object position if no quantitative information were available.

Multiview representations and aspect graphs

A 3D object can be described by some set of its possible 2D projections – these projections are often called view-centred models. One possibility is to enclose a 3D model by a unit viewsphere whose surface can be densely discretized into view patches. An icosahedron with triangularized faces is an effective approximation of the viewsphere [Horn 86].

An object can be modelled as many 2D projections of the original 3D model. Separate views of the same object are stored separately, as if they were actually different objects. This approach was used by Goad [Goad 86], and is examined in detail in Section 9.4.1.

Other representation methods attempt to combine all the viewpoint specific models into a single data structure. An **aspect graph** (considered further in Section 9.4) is a possibility.

9.2 Line labelling

Early in the attempt to develop 3D vision systems, an approach was taken that attempted to reconstruct a full 3D representation from a single, fully segmented view of a scene. The step between the dimensions was made by assuming that all objects in the scene had planar faces (see Figure 9.4), and that three faces met at each vertex; a perfect segmentation then provides straight edged regions, and in general three of these will meet at a vertex. The idea was that this constraint was sufficient to permit a single 2D view to permit unambiguous reconstruction. For obvious reasons, this is sometimes called a **blocks world** approach.

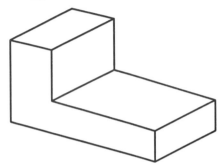

Figure 9.4 *An example blocks world object.*

The approach is clearly unrealistic for two reasons: Firstly the requirement for a perfect segmentation is unlikely to be met except in the most contrived situations; it is assumed that all edges are found, they are all linked into complete straight boundaries, and that spurious evidence is filtered out. Secondly, there is a very limited number of circumstances in which objects do consist strictly of planar faces. It is perhaps possible that industrial applications exist where both conditions might be met by constraining the objects, and providing lighting of a quality that permits full segmentation.

The idea was pioneered some time ago by Roberts [Roberts 65], who made significant progress, especially considering the time at which the work was done. Independently, two other researchers built on these ideas to develop what is now a very well known **line labelling** algorithm [Clowes 71, Huffman 71]. Mindful of the limitations of the blocks world approach, research into 3D vision has left these ideas behind and they are now largely of historical interest only. What follows is only an overview of how line labelling works, but it is instructive as firstly it illustrates how the 3D reconstruction task may be naively approached, and secondly it is good example of **constraint propagation** (see Chapter 8) in action. The algorithm rests on observing that, since each 3D vertex is a meeting of exactly three planar faces, there are only four types of junction that may appear in any 2D scene (see Figure 9.5). In the 3D world, an edge may be concave or convex, and in its 2D projection, the three faces meeting at a vertex may be visible or occluded. These finite possibilities permit an exhaustive listing of interpretations of a 2D vertex as a 3D vertex – there are in fact twenty-two of them [Clowes 71].

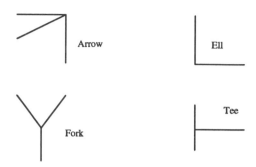

Figure 9.5 *The four possible 2D junctions.*

The problem now reduces to deriving a mutually consistent set of vertex labels; this may be done by employing constraints such as an edge interpretation (convex or concave) being the same at both ends, and that circumnavigating a region provides a coherent 3D surface interpretation. At a high level, the algorithm is;

Algorithm 9.1: Line labelling

1. Extract a complete and accurate segmentation of the 2D scene projection into polygons.

2. Determine the set of possible 3D interpretations for each 2D vertex from a pre-computed exhaustive list.

3. Determine 'edge-wise' coherent labellings of vertices by enforcing either concave or convex interpretations to each end of an edge.

4. Deduce an overall interpretation by requiring a circumnavigation of a region to have a coherent 3D interpretation.

Line labelling is able to detect as 'impossible' objects such as that shown in Figure 9.6a, since it would not pass the final stage of the informally described algorithm; it would not, however, register Figure 9.6b, which defies a 3D interpretation along its upper front horizontal edge, as impossible. It is also unable, in the simple form described, to cope with 'accidental' junctions which are the meeting of four or more lines (caused by chance occlusion), although these could be analysed as special cases.

This simple approach received a lot of attention, and was extended to consider solids whose vertices may have more than three faces meeting at a vertex (such as square-based pyramids), and scenes in which regions might

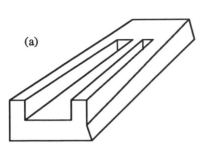 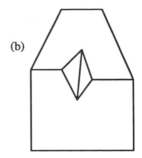

(a)

(b)

Figure 9.6 *Impossible blocks world figures.*

represent shadows of solids [Waltz 75]. Interestingly, while the number of possible junction interpretations increases enormously, the constraint satisfaction that is required for admissible candidate interpretations prevents the resulting algorithms becoming unworkable. In general, however, line labelling exists as an interesting historical idea – the way perhaps that one might approach the problem of 3D vision as a first attempt. It is clear though that its results are limited, and fraught with problems in overcoming 'special cases'.

9.3 Shape from X

The Marr paradigm prompted a number of attempts to derive the 2.5D sketch in a domain independent, bottom-up fashion. In the absence of prior (top-down) knowledge, this implies some constraints on the world from which the scene comes, or information supplementary to a single image. Remembering that the target of the exercise is an idea of 'shape' – that is, surfaces and their orientation in 3D – it should be clear why this family of techniques became called 'Shape from X', where X is one of a number of options. In the spirit of Marr's theory and its base on the human visual system, these options are those the human clearly uses to assist in determining depth from retinal images. We will study here four of the best developed and understood shape extraction approaches; the reader should be aware that others exist which we do not present, notably Shape from contour [Brady and Yuille 83, Brady 84], Shape from focus [Krotkov 89] and Shape from vergence [Krotkov et al. 90].

9.3.1 Shape from stereo

To the uneducated observer, the most obvious difference between the human visual system and most of the material presented thus far in this book is that we have two eyes and therefore (a priori, at any rate) twice as much input as a single image. From Victorian times, the use of two slightly different views to provide an illusion of 3D has been common, culminating in the '3D movies' of the 1950s. Conversely, we might hope that a 3D scene, if presenting two different views to two eyes, might permit the recapture of depth information when the information therein is combined with some knowledge of the sensor geometry (eye locations).

Stereo vision is not essential to the human visual system, as demonstrated by the number of successful one-eyed sportsmen and women, but its enormous importance to us has provoked a great deal of research into vision systems with two inputs that exploit the knowledge of their own relative geometry to derive depth information from the two views they receive. An early and successful algorithm was due to Marr and Poggio [Marr and Poggio 79, Marr et al. 78]; here a more recent alternative [Pollard et al. 85] is presented in detail.

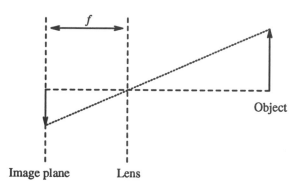

Figure 9.7 *A simple camera model.*

A simple camera model will be used to illustrate the operation of stereo vision. The world is focussed by a lens onto some sort of target – regarding the target as the image plane, we use the model shown in Figure 9.7; the obvious analogy is the eye focusing an image onto the retina. The distance from the image plane to the lens is f.

A simple diagram demonstrates how a two camera system might be used to determine the depth (distance from viewer(s)) of image points. In Figure 9.8, which is purely schematic, we have a bird's eye view of two cameras separated by a distance $2h$ and the images they provide, together with one point P with co-ordinates (x, y, z) in the scene, showing this point's projection onto left (P_l) and right (P_r) images. The co-ordinates in Figure 9.8 have the z axis representing distance from the cameras (at which $z = 0$) and the x axis representing 'horizontal' distance (the y co-ordinate, into the page, does not therefore appear). $x = 0$ will be the position midway between the cameras; each image will have a local co-ordinate system (x_l on the left, x_r on the right) which for the sake of convenience we measure from the centre of the respective images; that is, a simple translation from the global x co-ordinate. Without fear of confusion P_l will be used simultaneously to represent the position of the projection of P onto the left image, and its x_l co-ordinate – its distance from the centre of the left image (and similarly for P_r).

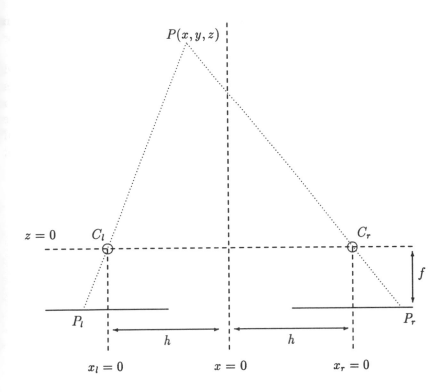

Figure 9.8 *Elementary stereo geometry.*

It is clear that there is a **disparity** between x_l and x_r as a result of the different camera positions (that is, $|P_l - P_r| > 0$); we can use elementary geometry to deduce the z co-ordinate of P.

Note that P_l, C_l and C_l, P are the hypotenuses of similar right-angled triangles. Noting further that h and f are (positive) numbers, z is a positive co-ordinate and x, P_l, P_r are co-ordinates that may be positive or negative, we can then write:

$$\frac{P_l}{f} = -\frac{h+x}{z} \tag{9.2}$$

and similarly from the right hand side of Figure 9.8

$$\frac{P_r}{f} = \frac{h-x}{z} \tag{9.3}$$

Eliminating x from these equations gives

$$z(P_r - P_l) = 2hf \tag{9.4}$$

and hence

$$z = \frac{2hf}{P_r - P_l} \tag{9.5}$$

Notice in this equation that $P_r - P_l$ is the detected disparity in the observations of P. If $P_r - P_l = 0$ then $z = \infty$ – quite correctly, no disparity indicates the point is (effectively) at an infinite distance from the viewer.

It all seems very easy: Find the points, match them and then an elementary calculation yields three-dimensional co-ordinates. In fact, of course, this begs some very serious questions. Which points are matched, and how? Given a set of 'features' from one image – probably edges or corners located by some standard edge detector or interest operator – how is the stereo correspondence derived when there is no guarantee even (without further information) that a point in one image appears at all in the other? This is the **stereo correspondence problem**, which has received a lot of attention, and to which there is a variety of solutions.

A particular solution to this problem is the **PMF algorithm**, named after its inventors [Pollard et al. 85]. It proceeds by assuming that a set of 'points to match' (for example, detected edges) has been extracted from each image, and its output is a correspondence between pairs of such points. In order to do this, three constraints are applied – one is geometric (the **epipolar** constraint), the second intuitive and the third, the **disparity gradient limit**, derived from psycho-physical observations of human vision.

1. The epipolar constraint is deployed to restrict to one dimension the possible matches of a point in one image to a point in the other. To illustrate this, consider two cameras side by side and pointing in parallel directions – it should be clear that a point on the image plane of the left camera must appear on a straight horizontal line on the plane of the right camera; in fact, this line corresponds to the raster on which the point appears on the left. In general, if the optical axes (directions) of the two cameras intersect at a point F (which is at infinity if the cameras are parallel), and the optical centres of the cameras are at O_l and O_r respectively, then the points F, O_l and O_r define a plane in 3D. This plane intersects the two image planes along a pair of **epipolar lines**. A point on one epipolar line can only ever match a point on the corresponding epipolar line in the other image.

   Using this observation, the search for matches is reduced in dimension from two to one.

2. It is further assumed that one point in the left image matches at most one point in the right (and vice versa). In almost all instances it is intuitively clear that this will be true, and only in rare cases of chance occlusion (or near occlusion) will one point match two in the other image.

3. The preceding two constraints are not peculiar to this algorithm (indeed they are also used by Marr [Marr and Poggio 79]) – the third, however, of stipulating a disparity gradient limit, is its novelty. The **disparity gradient** measures the relative disparity of two pairs of matching points. Suppose (Figure 9.9) that a point A (B) in 3D appears as $A_l = (a_{xl}, a_y)$

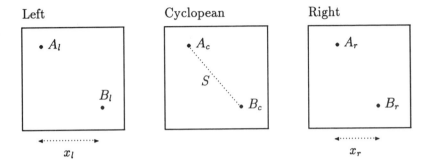

Left   Cyclopean   Right

Figure 9.9 *Definition of the disparity gradient.*

$(B_l = (b_{xl}, b_y))$ in the left image and $A_r = (a_{xr}, a_y)$ $(B_r = (b_{xr}, b_y))$ in the right (the epipolar constraint requires the y co-ordinates to be equal); the **cyclopean** image is defined as that given by their average co-ordinates;

$$A_c = (\frac{a_{xl} + a_{xr}}{2}, a_y) \qquad (9.6)$$

$$B_c = (\frac{b_{xl} + b_{xr}}{2}, b_y) \qquad (9.7)$$

and their **cyclopean separation** S is given by their distance apart in this image;

$$
\begin{aligned}
S(A, B) &= \sqrt{((\frac{a_{xl} + a_{xr}}{2}) - (\frac{b_{xl} + b_{xr}}{2}))^2 + (a_y - b_y)^2} \\
&= \sqrt{\frac{1}{4}((a_{xl} - b_{xl}) + (a_{xr} - b_{xr}))^2 + (a_y - b_y)^2} \\
&= \sqrt{\frac{1}{4}(x_l + x_r)^2 + (a_y - b_y)^2} \qquad (9.8)
\end{aligned}
$$

The difference in disparity between the matches of A and B is

$$
\begin{aligned}
D(A, B) &= (a_{xl} - a_{xr}) - (b_{xl} - b_{xr}) \\
&= (a_{xl} - b_{xl}) - (a_{xr} - b_{xr}) \\
&= x_l - x_r \qquad (9.9)
\end{aligned}
$$

The disparity gradient of the pair of matches is then given by the ratio of the disparity difference to the cyclopean separation;

$$\Gamma(A, B) = \frac{D(A, B)}{S(A, B)}$$

$$= \frac{x_l - x_r}{\sqrt{\frac{1}{4}(x_l + x_r)^2 + (a_y - b_y)^2}} \qquad (9.10)$$

Given these definitions, the constraint exploited is that, in practice, the disparity gradient Γ can be expected to be limited; in fact, it is unlikely to exceed 1. This means that very small differences in disparity are not acceptable if the corresponding points are extremely close to each other in 3D – this seems an intuitively reasonable observation, and it is supported by a good deal of physical evidence [Pollard et al. 85].

A solution to the correspondence problem is then extracted by a relaxation process in which all possible matches are scored according to whether they are supported by other (possible) matches that do not violate the stipulated disparity gradient limit. High scoring matches are regarded as correct, permitting firmer evidence to be extracted about subsequent matches.

Algorithm 9.2: PMF stereo correspondence

---

1. Extract features to match in left and right images. These may be, for example, edge pixels.

2. For each feature in the left (say) image, consider its possible matches in the right; these are defined by the appropriate epipolar line.

3. For each such match, increment its likelihood score according to the number of other possible matches found that do not violate the chosen disparity gradient limit.

4. Any match which is highest scoring for *both* the pixels composing it is now regarded as correct. Using the uniqueness constraint, these pixels are removed from all other considerations.

5. Return to (2) and re-compute the scores taking account of the definite match derived.

6. Terminate when all possible matches have been extracted

Note here that the epipolar constraint is used at point (2) to limit to one dimension the possible matches of a pixel, and the uniqueness constraint is used at (4) to ensure that a particular pixel is never used more than once in the calculation of a gradient.

The scoring mechanism has to take account of the fact that the more remote two (possible) matches are, the more likely they are to satisfy the disparity gradient limit. This is catered for by;

- Considering only matches that are 'close' to the one being scored. In practice it is typically adequate to consider only those inside a circle of radius seven, centred at the matching pixels (although this number depends on the precise geometry and scene in hand).

- Weighting the score by the reciprocal of its distance from the match being scored. Thus more remote pairs, which are more likely to satisfy the limit by chance, count for less.

The PMF algorithm has been demonstrated to work most successfully, in particular on scenes (artificial and natural) which could not be resolved by stereo matching algorithms which proceed using different constraints. It is attractive also because it lends itself to parallel implementation and could be extremely fast on suitably chosen hardware. It has a drawback (along with a number of similar algorithms) in that horizontal line segments are hard to match; they often move across adjacent rasters and, with parallel camera geometry, any point on one such line can match any point on the corresponding line in the other image.

The PMF algorithm is far from the only solution to the stereo correspondence problem; Marr and Poggio's alternative has already been mentioned, and the reader should also be aware of the approaches due to Barnard using a derivative of simulated annealing (see Chapter 7) [Barnard 86, Barnard 89].

Another approach worthy of mention is that of Nishihara [Nishihara 84], who observes that the given algorithm, along with those due to Marr, Barnard and others, in attempting to correlate individual pixels (by, e.g. matching zero crossings) is inclined toward poor performance when noise causes the detected location of such features to be unreliable. A secondary observation is that such pointwise correlators are very heavy on processing time in arriving at a correspondence. Nishihara notes that the *sign* (and magnitude) of an edge detector response is likely to be a much more stable property to match than the edge or feature locations, and devises an algorithm that simultaneously exploits a scale-space matching attack.

The approach is to match large patches at a large scale, and then refine the quality of the match by reducing the scale, using the coarser information to initialize the finer grained match. An edge response is generated at each pixel of both images at a large scale (see Section 4.3.4), and then a large area of the left (represented by, say, its central pixel) is correlated with a large area of the right. This can be done quickly and efficiently by using the fact that the correlation function peaks very sharply at the correct position of a match, and so a small number of tests permits an ascent to a maximum of a correlation measure. This coarse area match may then be refined to any desired resolution in an iterative manner, using the knowledge from the coarser scale as a clue to the correct disparity at a given position. At any stage of the algorithm, therefore, the surfaces in view are modelled as square prisms of varying height; the area of the squares may be reduced by performing the algorithm at a finer scale – for tasks such as obstacle avoidance it is possible that only coarse scale information is necessary, and there will be a consequent gain in efficiency.

This algorithm is enhanced by casting random dot light patterns on the scene to provide patterns to match even in areas of the scene that are texturally uniform. The resulting system has been demonstrated in use in robot guidance and bin-picking applications, and has been implemented robustly in real time.

9.3.2   Shape from shading

The human brain is able to make very good use of clues from shadows and shading in general. Not only do detected shadows give a clear indication of where occluding edges are, and the possible orientation of their neighbouring surfaces, but general shading properties are of great value in deducing depth. A fine example of this is a photograph of a face; from a straight-on, 2D representation, our brains make good guesses about the probable lighting model, and then deductions about the 3D nature of the face – for example, deep eye sockets and protuberant noses or lips are often recognizable without difficulty.

The problem in mimicking this activity in a computer based system is that the foreknowledge used in making this sort of deduction is considerable and complicated. The light intensity of a point (or pixel) in a 2D projection is dependent on;

- The lighting; this is an obvious observation – we are not surprised when a view changes with extra, reduced or changed illumination. The brain is very good at making plausible hypotheses about the lighting model.

- The **reflectance** properties of the surfaces in view. Again, we know 'automatically' how surfaces we see are going to reflect light – some reflect near perfectly. Such mirror-like surfaces are called **specular** and in fact the light they reflect depends solely on the angle of the incident light (see Figure 9.10). Alternatively, **matte** surfaces reflect light equally in all directions of an intensity that depends on the angle of incident light. Our knowledge of surface properties allows us to compensate for these very different behaviours, and we are often confused when surface reflectance properties are not what we expect.

- Surface orientation; again, it is an obvious observation that tilting a surface will (usually) alter the light reflected towards an observer.

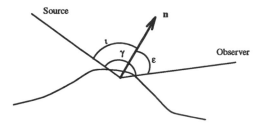

Figure 9.10 *Angles affecting reflectance.*

The aim is to extract information about the last of these on the basis of image information alone. One approach might therefore be to make assumptions about the lighting and reflectance properties, and hope that these constraints are sufficient to use a single 2D projection to reconstruct depth information. This is in fact possible, given suitable pre-conditions, and the resulting 'shape from shading' approach was first suggested by Horn in the 1970s [Horn 75]. An overview of the shape from shading algorithm is given here; which requires an understanding of two preliminary concepts.

The reflectance function

Given a particular light source, the quantity that reaches an observer at a particular position depends on the nature of the reflecting surface, and three angles: ι, the angle of incidence between the surface normal and the incident light; ϵ, the angle between the observer and the surface normal; and γ, the angle between incident and emitted rays (see Figure 9.10). The **reflectance function** $\Phi(\iota, \epsilon, \gamma)$ is a function of these three angles that characterizes the surface properties; formally, it provides the fraction of incident light reflected per unit surface area, per unit solid angle in the direction of the viewer. Two simple examples may illustrate this. A perfect mirror has the reflectance function

$$\begin{aligned} \Phi(\iota, \epsilon, \gamma) &= 1 \quad &if \quad \iota = \epsilon \ and \ \iota + \epsilon = \gamma \\ &= 0 \quad &otherwise \end{aligned} \qquad (9.11)$$

Thus reflection is perfect in one direction, and zero in all others. Conversely, a matte (**Lambertian**) surface reflects equally in all directions, with the amount of reflected light depending only on ι;

$$\Phi(\iota, \epsilon, \gamma) = \cos \iota \qquad (9.12)$$

Many surfaces with less simple behaviour can have their reflectance behaviour described analytically by a function Φ.

Gradient space

Gradient space is a way of describing surface orientations, and is a concept of general value that has also been used to help in the analysis of line labelling problems [Mackworth 73]. We proceed by noting that at nearly every point a surface has a unique normal, which may be described by a vector (n_x, n_y, n_z). Since only the orientation of the surface is of interest, only the direction of this vector need be considered, which, assuming $n_z \neq 0$, is given equally well by the vector

$$\left(\frac{n_x}{n_z}, \frac{n_y}{n_z}, 1\right)$$

or, without any loss of information,

$$\left(\frac{n_x}{n_z}, \frac{n_y}{n_z}\right) = (p, q)$$

This pair (p, q) is the two-dimensional gradient space representation of the orientation.

Gradient space has a number of attractive properties that allow elegant description of surface properties. Interpreting the image plane as $z = 0$, we see that the origin of gradient space corresponds to the vector $(0, 0, 1)$, normal to the image, implying a surface parallel to the image plane. The more remote a vector is from the origin of gradient space, the steeper its corresponding surface is inclined to the image plane.

Using these two concepts, we can begin to analyse the problem of extracting shape from shading information when the reflectance function and the lighting model are both known perfectly. Even given these constraints, it should be clear that the mapping 'surface orientation to brightness' is many-to-one – there are many orientations that can produce the same point intensity. Acknowledging this, a particular brightness can be produced by an infinite number of orientations that can be plotted as a (continuous) line in gradient space. An example for the simple case of a light source directly adjacent to the viewer, incident on a matte surface, is shown in Figure 9.11 – two points lying on the same curve (circles in this case) indicate two different orientations that will reflect light of the same intensity, thereby producing the same pixel grey level.

Now presented with an intensity image, a locus of possible orientations for each pixel can be located in gradient space, immediately reducing the number of possible interpretations of the scene. Of course, at this stage, a pixel may be part of any surface lying on the gradient space contour; to determine which, another constraint needs to be deployed. The key to deciding which point on the contour is correct is to note that 'almost everywhere' 3D surfaces are smooth, in the sense that neighbouring pixels are very likely to represent orientations whose gradient space positions are also very close. This additional

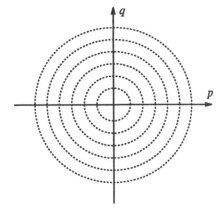

Figure 9.11 *Reflectance map for a matte surface – the light source is adjacent to the viewer.*

constraint allows a relaxation process to determine a best fit (minimum-cost) solution to the problem. The details of the procedure are very similar to those used to extract optical flow, and are discussed more fully in Section 14.2.1, but may be summarized as:

Algorithm 9.3: Extracting shape from shading

1. For each pixel (x, y), select an initial guess to orientation $p^0(x, y)$, $q^0(x, y)$.

2. Apply two constraints:

   (a) The observed intensity $f(x, y)$ should be close to that predicted by the reflectance map $R(p, q)$ derived from foreknowledge of the lighting and surface properties.

   (b) p and q vary smoothly – therefore their Laplacians $\nabla^2 p$ and $\nabla^2 q$ should be small.

3. Apply the method of Lagrange multipliers to minimize the quantity

$$\Sigma_{(x,y)} E(x, y) \tag{9.13}$$

where

$$E(x, y) = (f(x, y) - R(p, q))^2 + \lambda((\nabla^2 p)^2 + (\nabla^2 q)^2) \tag{9.14}$$

The first term of equation (9.14) is the intensity 'knowledge', while the second, in which λ is a Lagrange multiplier, represents the smoothness constraint. Deriving a suitable solution to this problem is a standard technique that iterates

p and q until E falls below some reasonable bound; a closely related problem
is inspected in more detail in Section 14.2.1, and the method of optimization
using Lagrange multipliers is described in many books [Horn 86, Strang 86].

The significant work in this area is due to Horn [Horn 75] and Ikeuch
[Ikeuchi and Horn 81] and predated the publication of Marr's theory, being
complete in the form presented here by 1980. Shape from shading, as implemented by machine vision systems, is often not as reliable as other 'Shape
from' techniques since it is so easy to confuse with reflections, or for it to
fail through poorly modelled reflectance functions. This observation serves to
reinforce the point that the human recognition system is very powerful since
in deploying elaborate knowledge, it does not suffer these drawbacks. A review of significant developments in the area since may be found in [Horn and
Brooks 89].

9.3.3 Shape from motion

Motion is another primary property exploited by human observers of the 3D
world. The real world we see is dynamic in many respects, and the relative
movement of objects in view, their translation and rotation relative to the
observer, the motion of the observer relative to other static and moving objects
all provide very strong clues to shape and depth – consider how just moving
your head from side to side provides rich information from parallax effects. It
should therefore come as no surprise to learn that attempts at shape extraction
are able to make use of motion. Motion, and particularly lower level algorithms
associated with its analysis, is considered in detail in Chapter 14, and in this
section study is restricted to shape extraction alone.

A study of human analysis of motion is instructive, and was conducted
comprehensively in a computational context by Ullman [Ullman 79]. Exactly
how we make deductions from moving scenes is far from clear, and several theories have come and gone in efforts to understand this matter – in particular,
Gestaltist theories (that groupings of observations are of primary importance)
were disproved, notably by an experiment of Ullman's that is now very fa-
mous. On a computer screen, he simulated two coaxial cylinders of different
radii rotating about their common axis in opposite directions. The view is
perpendicular to the common axis; the cylinders were not drawn, but only
randomly placed dots on their surfaces. Thus what is seen (on a per-point
basis), is a large number of dots moving from left to right or right to left,
at varying speeds. Exactly what speed and direction depends upon which
cylinder surface a dot belongs to, and at what point of rotation it is – in fact,
each individual dot executes simple harmonic motion about a point that is on
a line that is the projection onto the image of the axis. The striking conclusion is that the human observer is in no doubt about the nature of the scene,
despite the absence of surface clues and the complete absence of structure in
any single frame from the sequence.

What we exploit are particular constraints that assist in resolving the non-uniqueness of the interpretation of a sequence of frames as a moving 3D scene. In fact, motion may be presented to us as widely spaced (in time) discrete frames, or as (pseudo-) continuous – that is, so many frames that changes between a given pair are imperceptible. We shall examine each case separately, each using Ullman's observation that the extraction of 3D information from moving scenes can be done as a two phase process; preliminary processing (which is outlined below but explained in detail in Chapter 14) operates on pixel arrays to make correspondences, or calculate the nature of flow, while the shape extraction follows on as a separate, higher level process. It is worth noting that researchers are not unanimous in the view that these two phases should be held separate, and approaches exist that are different from those discussed here [Negahdaripour and Horn 85].

Rigidity, and the structure from motion theorem

One approach to the analysis of motion is superficially similar to that of stereo vision – images that are relatively widely separated in time are taken, and correspondences between visible features made. The solution to this correspondence problem is considered in detail in Chapter 14, but it is worth remarking here that resemblance to the stereo correspondence problem is deceptive since the scene may well contain any number of independently moving objects which could mean that correlations may be strictly local. Two images are not of the same scene, but (more probably) of the same objects in different relative positions.

For now, suppose that the correspondence problem has been solved, and that it remains to extract some shape information – that is, given that a collection of points has been identified in two different views, how might they be interpreted as 3D objects? As might be expected, the large number of possible interpretations is resolved by deploying a constraint; Ullman's success in this area was based on the psycho-physical observation that the human visual system seems to assume that objects are **rigid**. This rigidity constraint prompted the proof of an elegant theorem saying that *three orthographic projections of four non-coplanar points have a unique 3D interpretation as belonging to one rigid body.* We shall proceed to outline the proof of this theorem, which is constructive and therefore permits the extraction of the appropriate geometry, given point correspondences in three frames from a motion sequence. In use, the theorem allows samples of four points to be taken from an image sequence – *if* they belong to the same (rigid) body, an interpretation is generated, but if they do not, the probability of there being a chance rigid interpretation turns out to be negligibly small, meaning that the algorithm is self-verifying in the sense that it only ever generates answers that are 'correct'. Thus if there are N points in the correspondence, we might search for $N/4$ rigid interpretations, some of which will be invalid, and others of which will group according to the rigid object to which they belong.

The theorem proof involves a rephrasing of the problem to permit its definition as the solution of an equivalent problem in 3D geometry. Given three orthographic views (see Chapter 2) of four points that have a rigid interpretation, the correspondence allows them to be labelled as O, A, B and C in each image. First note that the body's motion may be decomposed into translational and rotational movement; the former gives the movement of a fixed point with respect to the observer, and the latter relative rotation of the body (for example, about the chosen fixed point). Translational movement, as far as it is recognizable, is easy to identify. All that can be resolved is movement perpendicular to the projection, and this is given by the translation (in 2D) of an arbitrarily chosen point, say O. Observe that motion parallel to the projection cannot be identified.

It remains to identify rotational motion; to do this we can assume that O is a fixed point, and seek to identify an interpretation of A, B and C as belonging to the same rigid body as O. Accordingly, we transform the problem to that of knowing three sets of (2D) co-ordinates for A, B and C with respect to a common origin O, each a different orthographic projection; what is now required is the (3D) directions of the projections.

Formally, suppose we have in 3D an origin O and three vectors $\mathbf{a}$, $\mathbf{b}$ and $\mathbf{c}$ corresponding to A, B and C; given projections of $\mathbf{a}$, $\mathbf{b}$ and $\mathbf{c}$ onto three planes Π_1, Π_2 and Π_3 of unknown orientation we require to reconstruct the 3D geometry of $\mathbf{a}$, $\mathbf{b}$ and $\mathbf{c}$. Now let the co-ordinate system of the plane Π_i be defined by vectors $\mathbf{x}_i$ and $\mathbf{y}_i$; that is, $\mathbf{x}_i$ and $\mathbf{y}_i$ are orthogonal 3D unit vectors lying in the plane Π_i. With respect to these systems, suppose that on plane Π_i the points' projections have co-ordinates (a_{xi}, a_{yi}), (b_{xi}, b_{yi}), (c_{xi}, c_{yi}) – these nine pairs are the input to the algorithm. Finally, let $\mathbf{u}_{ij}$ be a unit vector lying on the line defined by the intersection of planes Π_i and Π_j.

Elementary co-ordinate geometry gives

$$
\begin{aligned}
a_{xi} &= \mathbf{a} \cdot \mathbf{x}_i & a_{yi} &= \mathbf{a} \cdot \mathbf{y}_i \\
b_{xi} &= \mathbf{b} \cdot \mathbf{x}_i & b_{yi} &= \mathbf{b} \cdot \mathbf{y}_i \\
c_{xi} &= \mathbf{c} \cdot \mathbf{x}_i & c_{yi} &= \mathbf{c} \cdot \mathbf{y}_i
\end{aligned}
\tag{9.15}
$$

Further, since $\mathbf{u}_{ij}$ lies on both Π_i and Π_j, there must exist scalars $\alpha_{ij}, \beta_{ij}, \gamma_{ij}, \delta_{ij}$ such that

$$
\begin{aligned}
\alpha_{ij}^2 + \beta_{ij}^2 &= 1 \\
\gamma_{ij}^2 + \delta_{ij}^2 &= 1
\end{aligned}
\tag{9.16}
$$

and

$$
\begin{aligned}
\mathbf{u}_{ij} &= \alpha_{ij}\mathbf{x}_i + \beta_{ij}\mathbf{y}_i \\
\mathbf{u}_{ij} &= \gamma_{ij}\mathbf{x}_j + \delta_{ij}\mathbf{y}_j
\end{aligned}
\tag{9.17}
$$

nd hence

$$\alpha_{ij}\mathbf{x}_i + \beta_{ij}\mathbf{y}_i = \gamma_{ij}\mathbf{x}_j + \delta_{ij}\mathbf{y}_j \tag{9.18}$$

We can take the scalar product of this equation with each of **a**, **b** and **c**, and using equation (9.15) see that

$$\begin{aligned}
\alpha_{ij}a_{xi} + \beta_{ij}a_{yi} &= \gamma_{ij}a_{xj} + \delta_{ij}a_{yj} \\
\alpha_{ij}b_{xi} + \beta_{ij}b_{yi} &= \gamma_{ij}b_{xj} + \delta_{ij}b_{yj} \\
\alpha_{ij}c_{xi} + \beta_{ij}c_{yi} &= \gamma_{ij}c_{xj} + \delta_{ij}c_{yj}
\end{aligned} \tag{9.19}$$

- thus we have relations between unknowns $(\alpha, \beta, \gamma, \delta)$ in terms of known quantities $(a_x, a_y, \text{etc.})$.

It is easy to show that the equations (9.19) are linearly independent (this is where the fact that O, A, B and C are not coplanar is used). Therefore, using the constraint of equation (9.16), it is possible to solve for $\alpha_{ij}, \beta_{ij}, \gamma_{ij}, \delta_{ij}$ - in fact, there are two possible solutions that differ in sign only.

This (findable) solution is important as it means that we are able to express the vectors $\mathbf{u}_{ij}$ in terms of the co-ordinate basis vectors $\mathbf{x}_i$, $\mathbf{y}_i$, $\mathbf{x}_j$ and $\mathbf{y}_j$. To see why this is important, picture the three planes in 3D — they intersect at the common origin O and therefore define a tetrahedron; what interests us is the *relative* angles between the planes, and if the geometry of the tetrahedron can be recaptured, these angles are available. Note though that knowledge of $\mathbf{x}_{ij}, \beta_{ij}, \gamma_{ij}, \delta_{ij}$ allows calculation of the distances

$$\begin{aligned}
d_1 &= |\mathbf{u}_{12} - \mathbf{u}_{13}| \\
d_2 &= |\mathbf{u}_{12} - \mathbf{u}_{23}| \\
d_3 &= |\mathbf{u}_{13} - \mathbf{u}_{23}|
\end{aligned} \tag{9.20}$$

For example,

$$\begin{aligned}
\mathbf{u}_{12} - \mathbf{u}_{13} &= (\alpha_{12}\mathbf{x}_1 + \beta_{12}\mathbf{y}_1) - (\alpha_{13}\mathbf{x}_1 + \beta_{13}\mathbf{y}_1) \\
&= (\alpha_{12} - \alpha_{13})\mathbf{x}_1 + (\beta_{12} - \beta_{13})\mathbf{y}_1
\end{aligned} \tag{9.21}$$

and hence

$$d_1 = (\alpha_{12} - \alpha_{13})^2 + (\beta_{12} - \beta_{13})^2 \tag{9.22}$$

since $\mathbf{x}_1$ and $\mathbf{y}_1$ are orthogonal. Now the tetrahedron formed by the three intersecting planes is defined by the origin O and a triangular base – we might consider the base given by the three points at unit distance from the origin. By construction, this triangle has sides d_1, d_2, d_3, and we can thus reconstruct the required tetrahedron.

Determining the 3D structure is now possible by noting that a particular point lies at the intersection of the normals to any two of the planes drawn from the projections of the point concerned.

There is a complication in the proof not discussed here that occurs when one of the d_i is zero, and the tetrahedron is degenerate. It is possible to resolve this problem without difficulty – the full proof is given in [Ullman 79].

It is worth noting that Ullman's result is best possible in the sense that unique reconstruction of a rigid body cannot be guaranteed with fewer than three projections of four points, or with three projections of fewer than four points. It should also be remembered that the result refers to *orthographic* projection when in general image projections are *perspective* (of which, of course the orthographic projection is a special case). This turns out not to be a problem since a similar result is available for the perspective projection [Ullman 79]. In fact this is not necessary, since it is possible to approximate neighbourhoods within a perspective projection by a number of different orthographic projections; thus in such a neighbourhood, the theorem as outlined is valid. Interestingly, there seems to be evidence that the human visual system uses this sort of orthographic approximation in extracting shape information from motion.

This result is of particular value in **active** vision applications such as a robot arm having a camera mounted upon it; when such a system finds itself unable to 'see' particular objects of interest, the arm will move for a different view, that will then need reconciling with earlier ones.

Shape from optical flow

The motion presented to human observers is not that considered in the previous section, but rather is continuous – the scene in view varies smoothly. The approach of considering widely spaced (in time) views is therefore a simplification, and it is natural to ask how to treat the 'limiting case' of separate frames being temporally very close to each other – it is well known that, in fact, the human eye perceives continuous motion from relatively few frames per second (as illustrated by cinema film). Clearly the approach of making correspondences is no longer any use since corresponding points will be separated by infinitesimally small distances – it is the apparent velocity (direction and speed) of pixels that is of interest in the study of continuous motion. In a continuous sequence, we are therefore interested in the apparent movement of each pixel (x, y) which is given by the **optical flow field** $(\frac{dx}{dt}, \frac{dy}{dt})$. In Chapter 14, optical flow is considered at length, and an algorithm described for its extraction from observation of changes in the intensity function (grey levels); accordingly, in this section, it is assumed that the flow field is available, and we ask how it may be used to extract shape in the form of surface orientation (in fact optical flow is useful for deducing a number of motion properties, such as the nature of the translational or rotational movement – these points are considered in Chapter 14).

Determining shape from optical flow is mathematically non-trivial, and here a simplification of the subject is presented as an illustration [Clocksin

0]. The simplification is in two parts;

- Motion is due to the observer travelling in a straight line through a static landscape. Without loss of generality, suppose the motion is in the direction of the z axis of a viewer centred co-ordinate system (i.e. the observer is positioned at the origin).

- Rather than being projected onto a 2D plane, the image is seen on the surface of a unit sphere, centred at the observer (a 'spherical retina'). Points in 3D are represented in spherical polar rather than Cartesian co-ordinates – spherical polar co-ordinates (r, θ, ϕ) (see Figure 9.12) are

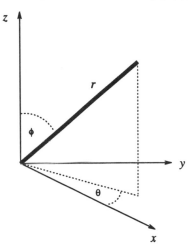

Figure 9.12 *Definition of spherical polar co-ordinates.*

related to (x, y, z) by the equations

$$r^2 = x^2 + y^2 + z^2 \qquad (9.23)$$
$$y = x \tan \theta \qquad (9.24)$$
$$z = r \cos \phi \qquad (9.25)$$

Since the image is spherical, we can specify co-ordinates as (θ, ϕ) pairs rather than (x, y) as usual, and the optical flow is then $(\frac{d\theta}{dt}, \frac{d\phi}{dt})$. Supposing the observer's speed to be v (in the direction of the z axis), the motion of points in 3D is given by

$$\frac{dx}{dt} = 0 , \quad \frac{dy}{dt} = 0 , \quad \frac{dz}{dt} = -v \qquad (9.26)$$

Differentiating equation (9.23) with respect to t gives

$$2r\frac{dr}{dt} = 2x\frac{dx}{dt} + 2y\frac{dy}{dt} + 2z\frac{dz}{dt}$$

$$= -2vz$$

$$\frac{dr}{dt} = -\frac{vz}{r}$$

$$= -v\cos\phi \qquad (9.27$$

Differentiating equation (9.24) with respect to t gives

$$\frac{dy}{dt} = \tan\theta\frac{dx}{dt} + x\sec^2\theta\frac{d\theta}{dt}$$

$$0 = 0 + x\sec^2\theta\frac{d\theta}{dt} \qquad (9.28$$

and hence

$$\frac{d\theta}{dt} = 0 \qquad (9.29$$

Differentiating equation (9.25) with respect to t gives

$$\frac{dz}{dt} = \cos\phi\frac{dr}{dt} - r\sin\phi\frac{d\phi}{dt} \qquad (9.30$$

and hence, by equations 9.26 and 9.27

$$-v = -v\cos^2\phi - r\sin\phi\frac{d\phi}{dt} \qquad (9.31$$

and so

$$\frac{d\phi}{dt} = \frac{v(1 - \cos^2\phi)}{r\sin\phi} = \frac{v\sin\phi}{r} \qquad (9.32$$

Equations (9.29) and (9.32) are important. The former says that, for this particular motion, the rate of change of θ is zero (θ is constant). More interestingly, the latter says that given the optical flow $\frac{d\phi}{dt}$, then the distance r of a 3D point from the observer can be recaptured up to a scale factor v – in particular, if v is known, then r, and a complete depth map, can be deduced from the optical flow. The depth map allows a reconstruction of the 3D scene and hence characteristics of surfaces (smoothly varying areas of r) and of edges (discontinuities in r) will be available.

In the case that v is not known, it turns out that surface information is still available directly from the flow. In particular, suppose a point P lies on a smooth surface, which at P may be specified by the direction of a normal vector $\mathbf{n}$. Such a direction may be specified by two angles α and β where α is the angle between $\mathbf{n}$ and a plane Π_1 defined by P and the z axis, and β is the angle between $\mathbf{n}$ and a plane Π_2 which passes through P and the origin, and is perpendicular to Π_1 (if the representation seems complicated, it does not matter – it is sufficient to understand that the angles α and β can be extracted). Intuitively, it is clear that the rate of change of r with respect to θ and ϕ provides information about the direction of **n**. Moderately straightforward co-ordinate geometry gives the relations

$$\tan \alpha = \frac{1}{r}\frac{\partial r}{\partial \phi} \qquad \tan \beta = \frac{1}{r}\frac{\partial r}{\partial \theta} \tag{9.33}$$

These equations depend upon a knowledge of r (the depth map), but it is possible to combine them with equation (9.32) to overcome this. For convenience, write $\frac{d\phi}{dt} = \dot\phi$; then, by equation (9.32)

$$r = \frac{v \sin \phi}{\dot\phi} \tag{9.34}$$

and so

$$\frac{\partial r}{\partial \phi} = v\frac{\dot\phi \cos \phi - \sin \phi \frac{\partial \dot\phi}{\partial \phi}}{\dot\phi^2}$$

$$\frac{\partial r}{\partial \theta} = -v\frac{\sin \phi \frac{\partial \dot\phi}{\partial \theta}}{\dot\phi^2} \tag{9.35}$$

Substituting (9.34) and (9.35) into equations (9.33) gives

$$\tan \alpha = \cot \phi - \frac{1}{\dot\phi}\frac{\partial \dot\phi}{\partial \phi}$$

$$\tan \beta = \frac{1}{\dot\phi}\frac{\partial \dot\phi}{\partial \theta} \tag{9.36}$$

Thus, given the flow $\dot\phi$ (which we assume), the angles α and β are immediately available, irrespective of S and without any need to determine the depth map given by r.

The original reference [Clocksin 80] provides full information on this derivation, and proceeds to describe how edge information may also be extracted from knowledge of the flow. It also includes some interesting discussion of psycho-physical considerations of human motion perception in the context of a computational theory.

9.3.4 Shape from texture

A further property of which there is clear psycho-physical evidence of human use to extract depth is texture [Marr 82]. To appreciate this, it is only necessary to consider a regularly patterned object viewed in 3D – two effects would be apparent; the angle at which the surface is seen would cause a (perspective) distortion of the **texture primitive (texel)**, and the relative size of the primitives would vary according to distance from the observer. A simple

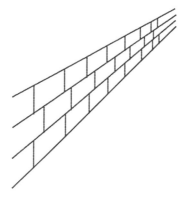

Figure 9.13 *A simple texture pattern in 3D.*

example, shown in Figure 9.13 is sufficient to illustrate this. Much use can be made of texture in computer vision at various levels of abstraction, and Chapter 13 examines them in some detail. Here we look briefly at the use of textural properties to assist in the extraction of shape.

Considering a textured surface, patterned with identical texels which have been recovered by lower level processing, note that with respect to a viewer it has three properties at any point projected onto a retinal image; distance from the observer, **slant**, the angle at which the surface is sloping away from the viewer (the angle between the surface normal and the line of sight), and **tilt**, the direction in which the slant takes place. Attempts to recapture some of this information is based on the **texture gradient** – that is, the direction of maximum rate of change of the perceived size of the texels, and a scalar measurement of this rate. There is evidence to suggest [Stevens 79] that the human viewer uses the texture gradient as a primary clue in the extraction of tilt and (relative) distance, but that slant is inferred by processing based on estimates of the other two parameters. Tilt is indicated by the direction of the texture gradient (see Figure 9.14), while the apparent size of objects decreases as the reciprocal of their distance from the viewer.

 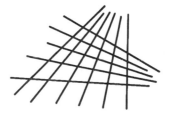

Figure 9.14 *Tilt affects the appearance of texture.*

If the texture is particularly simple, the shape of the perceived texels will

eveal surface orientation information. For example, if a plane is marked with
lentical circles they will be seen in an image as ellipses (see Figure 9.15).
'he eccentricity of the ellipses provides information about the slant, while
he orientation of the ellipse axes indicates the tilt [Stevens 79].

Figure 9.15 *Slant and tilt are revealed by texel properties.*

Large scale texture effects can provide information about large scale scene
eometry; in particular, strong linear effects will indicate 'vanishing points'
hat may be joined to give the scene horizon. Note that it is not necessary
n fact for the image to contain large numbers of long straight lines for this
onclusion to be available since often such lines can be inferred by a number
f segments whose co-linearity may be deduced by, for example, a Hough
ransform. Such co-linearity may well be a property of urban scenes in which
ectangular objects, some large, can predominate.

'Texture' has many interpretations and there is a correspondingly large
umber of attempts to exploit it in shape extraction – a useful grounding may
e found in [Witkin 81], and [Aliomonos and Swain 85] gives an interesting
pproach in which 'Shape from texture' is shown to be equivalent to 'Shape
rom shading', thereby allowing the use of established results in surface pa-
ameter extraction from shading. Texture is usually used as an additional or
omplementary feature, augmenting another, stronger clue in shape extrac-
ion.

.4 Approaches to the recognition of 3D objects

he final phase of the 3D vision task is the successful recognition of real-world
bjects – this is hard. A selection of lower level processing techniques will gen-
rate some selection of clues and features, and from some model base there
vill be a selection of objects which may or may not match the observations.
Earlier chapters have discussed several approaches to matching, such as hy-
othesize and verify, efficient pruning of interpretation trees, graph matching
tc. and in Section 9.2 the line labelling approach to the recapture of 3D was
utlined, and it was explained why in general this solution is inadequate. Here
ve shall make some general remarks about 3D object recognition, and present
n detail a well known algorithm that solves the problem for the simple case
f a well-understood object with planar, straight edged faces by replacing the
D problem by many 2D ones [Goad 86].

Among approaches is the **characteristic view technique** [Chakravart and Freeman 82] in which all possible 2D projections of the object are groupe into a finite number of topologically equivalent classes. Different views within an equivalence class are related via linear transformations. This general pur pose representation specifies the 3D structure of the object. A similar ap proach is based on **aspect** [Koenderink and van Doorn 79], which is define as the topological structure of singularities in a single view of an object - aspect has useful invariance properties. Most small changes in vantage poin will not affect aspect, and such vantage points (that is, most) are referred t as **stable**. Then the set of stable vantage points yielding a given aspect i contiguous in space, and the space surrounding an object may be partitione into subspaces from within which the same aspect is generated. Moving from one such subspace into another generates an **event** – a change in aspect; th event is said to connect the two aspects. It is now possible to construct a **aspect graph** with respect to this connectivity relationship in which node are aspects and edges are events. This aspect graph is sometimes referred t as the **visual potential** of the object, and paths through it represent orbit of an observer around the object.

If reliable region and boundary information can be extracted from an im age, there is much that may be done towards recognition using the technique of Chapter 6 by applying straightforward geometry [Brady 84]. In particu lar, if a planar surface has 'real' area A_R (area in the 'real world', and th angle between it and the image plane is θ, it is easy to see that the regior corresponding to it in the image will have area

$$A_I = A_R \cos \theta$$

Knowledge of this is useful, since a well-known measure of compactness o a region is the ratio of its area to the square of its perimeter. If the 'real perimeter is P_R, a useful 'shape from contour' approach is to find the plane which maximizes

$$\frac{A_R}{P_R^2}$$

given an observed A_I and P_I. Extracting perimeter information (estimating P_R from P_I) is less straightforward, but is possible and can lead to good results [Brady and Yuille 83]. In reality, this quality of information is rarely available.

9.4.1 Goad's algorithm

A particular model matching algorithm due to Goad [Goad 83] has received a lot of attention and been widely implemented. Goad's algorithm is interesting since it is simple enough in principle to show how the task may be done, but generates enough complexities in implementation to illustrate how difficult the task of model matching, even in a relatively simple case, can become. In this section, the algorithm is outlined in some detail.

Goad's algorithm aims to recover the 3D co-ordinates and orientation of a known object from a single intensity image; the object is 'known' in the sense that its edges, which are assumed to be straight, and their relative position to each other, are exhaustively listed in the object model with which the algorithm is provided. This contrasts with the easier problems of locating a known object of known orientation (a common aim in industrial vision systems), and the harder one of locating imprecisely defined objects of unknown orientation (a more widely applicable, and elusive, solution).

Following the terminology of the original reference, an object edge will refer to a straight line segment in 3D that forms part of the boundary of an object face. Projections of these into 2D (the image) are referred to as lines. The algorithm proceeds on a number of assumptions;

1. It is assumed that an edge and line detector has done its work and the lines (straight boundaries) in the image have been extracted. The algorithm permits these extracted lines to be imprecise within certain bounds, and, in its full form, is able to make allowances for spurious and missing evidence (that is, lines where there should be none and no lines where there ought to be).

2. The object to be located is either fully in the field of view, or not visible at all.

3. The distance to the object is known; this permits the further assumption that the camera lies at some point on a sphere centred at the origin of an object-based co-ordinate system. Without loss of generality, we assume this is a unit sphere.

4. The field of view is sufficiently narrow to permit the assumption that changing the *orientation* of the camera at a given position only causes the features in view to undergo a simple rotation and translation. While such a change in orientation may affect which features are visible, the lengths of lines in view will not alter, within a small tolerance.

The general strategy of the algorithm is intuitively simple. An edge of the object is taken and a likely match for it found in the image. This possible match will not constrain the position of the object completely - there will be a range (a locus) of camera positions that is consistent with what is observed. Now select another edge from the model; the restrictions provided by the (putatively) matched edge will limit the possible position of the projection of this new edge into the image; we may thus predict the position of this edge in the image, within bounds governed by the accuracy of measurements and line finders. If this projected edge cannot be located, the supposed match is false. If it can, it may be expected to restrict further the locus of possible camera positions that is consistent with all hitherto deduced possible camera positions

- the *observation* is used to *back project* and thereby reduce the possible locus. Another edge is now selected and the procedure repeated iteratively until either the match fails, or there is strong enough evidence (sufficient matched edges, and a restricted enough locus) to deduce that the match is correct and thereby specify the object's location and orientation. Early in the matching process, with few object edges matched, the bounds on the prediction may be very wide; as the match proceeds so the predictions will become more precise. When the match fails, we may backtrack to a point where more than one image edge was a possible match for an object edge and try again.

This 'Predict-Observe-Back Project' cycle is a simple instance of an elementary matching algorithm – sequential matching with backtracking [Hayes-Roth et al. 83], and is a typical example of a top-down, hypothesize and verify approach.

Some notation and definitions are necessary to proceed. Remember we are working in object-centred co-ordinates, so the object is regarded as fixed while the camera position and orientation are the unknowns to be determined. Throughout, an object edge will be regarded as an *oriented* line segment, given by an ordered pair of co-ordinates, while an image line may be unoriented. Thus an object edge is an *ordered* pair of (3D) co-ordinates, while an image line is given by a (perhaps unordered) pair of (2D) co-ordinates.

Let $\mathbf{p}$ be a 3D (camera) position, and $\mathbf{q}$ a 3D (camera) orientation. $\mathbf{p}$ is just a 3D co-ordinate, which we are constraining to lie on the unit sphere. If e is an object edge, let $P([\mathbf{p}, \mathbf{q}], e)$ denote the *oriented* image line which results from viewing e from $\mathbf{p}$ at orientation $\mathbf{q}$, using a perspective transformation. $P([\mathbf{p}, \mathbf{q}], e)$ may be undefined if e is occluded, or the projection is outside the field of view. If it is defined, it is an *ordered* pair of 2D co-ordinates.

The possible positions on the surface of the unit sphere are quantized – a set of such positions will be referred to as a **locus**. A given edge e will only be visible from some of these positions, which is referred to as the **visibility locus** of e.

An assignment between object edges and image lines will be called a **match** M. For an object edge e, $M(e)$ will denote the oriented image line assigned to it by M; for some e, $M(e)$ may be undefined, so a match need not be a complete assignment of object edges. Then a match M is **consistent** with a camera position and orientation $[\mathbf{p}, \mathbf{q}]$ if for each object edge e we have $P([\mathbf{p}, \mathbf{q}], e) = M(e)$ to within errors of measurement. A match M is consistent with a camera position $\mathbf{p}$ if there is some orientation $\mathbf{q}$ such that M is consistent with $[\mathbf{p}, \mathbf{q}]$. A match is consistent with a locus L if it is consistent with every position of that locus. L is initialized from the assumptions deduced from the match of the first edge.

In overview, the algorithm is then;

Algorithm 9.4: Goad's matching algorithm

1. Initialize by finding a plausible match in the image for one edge.

2. For the current match M and the current locus L, select an unmatched edge e.

3. By considering a matched edge e_0, compute bounds on the possible position of $P([\mathbf{p}, \mathbf{q}], e)$ relative to $P([\mathbf{p}, \mathbf{q}], e_0)$ as $\mathbf{p}$ ranges over L (this position depends only on $\mathbf{p}$ and not on $\mathbf{q}$ from assumption 4 above). Thus determine a range of possible positions for $M(e)$ in the image.

4. If a candidate for $M(e)$ is located, back project – that is restrict the locus L to L' by rejecting all points in L that are not consistent with the measured position of $M(e)$. L' is those points $\mathbf{p}$ in L from which the predicted position of $P([\mathbf{p}, \mathbf{q}], e)$ relative to $P([\mathbf{p}, \mathbf{q}], e_o)$ is the same as the position of $M(e)$ relative to $M(e_0)$ to within measurement error.

5. If more than one candidate for $M(e)$ is located, mark this as a choice point for future backtracking.

6. If no candidate for $M(e)$ is located, backtrack to the last choice point.

7. Iterate until the match is regarded as certain.

It is acknowledged that the image line detector is not going to be perfect. Some e, although expected to be in view, will not have a match $M(e)$ in the image. Two measures are maintained as the algorithm proceeds that gauge whether its oversights are 'reasonable', and whether it is likely to be 'complete'. These are:

1. Reliability: The probability that the edges making up the match to date arose by chance from background information is calculated and the inverse of this probability is called the reliability of the match. When the reliability exceeds a certain threshold, the match is regarded as correct and the algorithm terminated. These probabilities may best be computed on the basis of statistics gathered from images of the same class as that under examination.

2. Plausibility: Assuming the match is correct, and has missed some edges, the probability that those edges would indeed have been missed by the line detector in use is calculated – these probabilities assume knowledge of the performance of the line detector which once again are best accumulated from running it on sample images.

Now high reliability indicates that the match is correct, while low plausibility indicates it is probably incorrect (although we must beware – high plausibility does not imply a correct match and low reliability does not imply it is incorrect). Plausibility is introduced into the algorithm by requiring that if it falls below a certain threshold, then we must backtrack. In fact, this generates another possible choice point – if we assume e is visible, search for it and fail to find it, we may assume it should be visible but is absent from the image and proceed with reduced plausibility accordingly. Only if this assumption leads to no match do we backtrack, and consider whether the edge should be visible at all.

Edge **visibility** considers from which points of L an edge e may actually be seen – (that is, whether the visibility locus V of e intersects L). This provides another possible choice point for backtracking; first assume e is visible (that is, restrict L to its intersection with V) and proceed as described above. If a match is not found, and we require to backtrack, at this point we can now assume e is not visible and restrict L to its intersection with the complement of V. 'Visibility' needs to be defined with caution here – an edge is only regarded as visible if it is likely to be found by the line detector. Very short lines (object edges viewed nearly 'end on' for instance) would not meet this criterion.

A feature of the problem that this algorithm is designed to solve is that the object searched for is modelled precisely. This fact may be exploited to speed up what would otherwise be at best a ponderous execution by going through a 'set-up' phase during which the features of the object are coded into the algorithm to be exploited at run time. Goad refers to this as the 'compile-time' of the algorithm.

There are several ways we may exploit this compile-time;

1. From a given position $\mathbf{p}$, we require during the algorithm to determine bounds on the position of an edge e relative to a matched edge e_0. This relative position, $relpos(e, e_o, \mathbf{p})$ depends only on the object, which is fully characterized independent of the run. These relative position bounds may therefore be computed at compile-time and stored for lookup. A complete, reliable and plausible set of constraints on $relpos$ is proposed in [Bray and Hlavac 91].

   In fact we require $relpos(e, e_0, \mathbf{p})$ for all $\mathbf{p} \epsilon L$; this is easily done by taking the union of the bounds for each such $\mathbf{p}$. This table can also be used for the back projection; given a likely $M(e)$ we need only determine for which $\mathbf{p} \epsilon L$ this $M(e)$ is within the bounds predicted by $relpos(e, e_0, \mathbf{p})$.

2. When selecting the next edge to match, care should be taken to maximize the return on the effort put into trying to match it. This may be ensured by maximizing the likelihood of the selected edge being visible

(and findable by the line detector), and by requiring that the measurements of the image position of the observed edge should provide as much information as possible about the camera position (so the locus is reduced as much as possible by making a match).

These judgements may be made at compile-time. Supposing a uniform distribution of camera positions around the sphere (in fact, allowances can be made if this is an unreasonable assumption) then the probability of the visibility of a given edge over any locus can be pre-computed. Likewise, the 'value' of measuring the position of a given edge can be computed at compile-time. If we determine a way of combining these factors by appropriately weighting the values determined (and this is not necessarily straightforward), the 'best next edge' to match, given a particular partial match, can be determined at compile-time. Goad observes that this particular pre-computation may be very expensive.

3. The elemental contributions to the plausibility measurements can also be pre-computed.

There is no doubt that performing the compile-time operations outlined will be very expensive, but this should not worry us since the expected run-time efficiency gain will make the effort well worth the cost. It is a familiar idea to pay the price of lengthy compilation in order to generate efficient running code.

Goad's algorithm is in principle quite simple – there is a variety of things we may expect to see, and they are searched for in a 2D projection. Nevertheless, when examined with all its ramifications, it should be clear that the algorithm's implementation is not quite so simple.

When running, Goad managed to get respectable efficiency from his system. To deduce a complete match, it is really only necessary to make reliable matches for four object edges. He reports that on an 'average 1 MIPS machine' (remember this work is dated 1983), one matching step will take of the order of a few milliseconds, permitting several hundred attempts at matching every second. The run-time for a complete match is quoted at approximately one second, but this excludes edge and line detection. As has been remarked, much of this efficiency has been achieved at the expense of a very long 'compile-time'.

The algorithm has actually been applied to several problems – single occurrences of objects such as a connecting rod or universal joint have been located in cluttered scenes, and, more interesting, key caps (the plastic keys from a keyboard or typewriter) have been located in an image of a pile of caps. In industrial terms this problem, often referred to as bin-picking, is unreasonably difficult – multiple occurrences of the target object at multiple orientations, many partially occluded (remember the first assumption above, that the object is visible either fully or not at all). The algorithm succeeds despite the fact that the background consists of features very similar to those composing the target, and that the target has few distinguishing features.

Goad's algorithm turns out to be quite powerful. The idea of 'pre-compiling the object description (special purpose automatic programming) produces systems of acceptable efficiency. Various elaborations exist which are not explored here, such as exploiting recurring patterns or symmetries in the object, or variable camera-to-object distance. Remember this object location is done by two-dimensional matching; that it works despite unknown orientation is dependent on complete and thorough knowledge of the image and line detector properties, and the target object. Various elaborations on the ideas presented here have been developed [Grimson 89, Bray and Hlavac 91]

9.4.2 Features for model-based recognition of curved objects

Object models contain more object information than sensor data extracted from one view and therefore it is not possible to transform sensor data into a complete model data representation. Fortunately, sensor data can be matched with *partial* model data. It is useful to work with an intermediate representation scheme computable both from sensor and model data which permits the reduction of the large amount of sensor data. A matching between an object and the model is then carried out at this intermediate representation level. The best matching occurs when the hypothetical object model configuration represent the scene world as accurately as possible. Accuracy might then be measured quantitatively by **matching errors**. This difference might be used to control the whole recognition process by closing a feedback loop.

A very rich description is based on properties of object surfaces. The term **surface features** (or characteristics) refers to descriptive features of a general smooth surface; **surface characterization** refers to the process of partitioning a surface into regions with equivalent characteristics. A very similar process might be applied to an intensity image, and a function describing an intensity image has the same mathematical form as a surface, i.e. a function of two variables. What makes the problem difficult is the separation of illumination effects.

The symbolic scene description features should be invariant to translations and rotations of object surfaces. Differential geometry-based features are useful if they can be reliably computed from the sensor data, but this is not usually the case and surface (or curve) approximation should be adopted first.

One interesting possibility which might be useful for an intensity image is **topographic characterization** of the surface. At each pixel in an image, a local facet-model bicubic polynomial surface is fitted to estimate the first three partial derivatives. The magnitude of the gradient, eigenvalues of a 2×2 Hessian matrix (the matrix of second derivatives) and directions of its eigenvectors are computed; these five numbers are used to characterize the surface at the pixel. The following ten labels are used [Besl and Jain 85]; peak, pit, ridge, ravine (valley), saddle, flat (planar), slope, convex hill, concave hill, and saddle hill. This is called a **topographic primal sketch**. The main advantage of these labels is the invariance to monotonic grey level transformations such as change in brightness and contrast.

Another approach is called the **curvature primal sketch** [Brady 84] in which the differential geometry quantities are used with concentration on lines of curvature, asymptotes, bounding contours, surface intersections and planar surface patches. Principal curvatures and principal directions are computed. An ad hoc breadth-first method is used to link the principal direction at each point into the line of curvature. This approach is domain independent.

The representation of planar image curves is based on curvature, which is computed in different scales by smoothing. The smoothing coefficient appropriate to intrinsic properties is chosen for each significant part of the curve [Lowe 89].

Another possibility for obtaining robust approximation of curves in an image is Weiss' approximation to general curves (or curved surfaces) by conic sections (or quadric patches). The approximation comes from the observation that midpoints of chords across a conic lie on a straight line. Having a reliable approximation of the curve by conic sections, Weiss proposes to use as features differential and algebraic **invariants** to perspective projection [Weiss 88]. These invariants might be used as shape describing features for recognition purposes. Invariants are computed for the model and then searched for in the image. Weiss' invariants are based on derivatives up to the fourth order and are thus extremely noise dependent. Analytic curve approximation by conics enables the calculation of invariants' functions. Section 6.2.7 discusses invariants in more detail.

9.5   Depth map technologies

'Shape from X' ideas can be thought of as **passive** range finding techniques in the sense that nothing is actually projected onto the scene. Other such passive schemes exist – we may for instance 'sense' depth by determining the necessary focus of wide aperture lenses, whose depth of field is very small.

Alternatively, we may consider **active** depth-sensing where the detection of object distance from the sensor is a primary rather than secondary aim, and is achieved by projection (probably of some electromagnetic wave) onto the scene. Such schemes appear to the human observer as special purpose in the sense that we are not accustomed to doing this ourselves (other animals, such as bats, make heavy use of such ideas, of course). Active depth sensors will produce pixel arrays where the pixel values encode the depth from the sensor of that point of the scene – the price we may pay is the loss of all intensity information. It may be argued that this is a very heavy price; even in the complete absence of depth data the multitude of clues provided by intensity data gives a great deal of information.

The predominant technology for active depth-sensing is lasers. Sometimes called spot ranging, this technique involves beaming a laser spot at the scene and measuring the reflection; depth may actually be determined by timing the delay in the return or measuring the phase difference between the reflection and the original. Spot ranging can provide good quality data but requires electronics with a very fine resolution (of the order of 70 picoseconds to determine depth to a precision of 0.005m). It may also, for high quality results, demand a laser of such power as to be harmful to human beings. The latter technique is, in relative terms, slow, requiring perhaps minutes to capture one image of a scene [Jarvis 83].

We can remark in passing that spot range data is susceptible to many of the segmentation techniques we have developed for intensity images; Hough transforms, region growers and simple edge detectors will work as well on depth data as they do on grey level matrices.

An older active depth-sensing technique, which is intuitively more simple, is **light striping**, in which a camera is sited at a known co-ordinate, and a stripe of light is shone along a known plane. A single stripe of light is detected in the scene – this may actually be done by shining the light in a darkened room or by using a laser source that will be detectable anyway. Given that the plane and camera co-ordinates are known, provided the focal point of the camera does not lie in the plane of the light, simple co-ordinate geometry permits the depth of any object intersecting the light stripe to be determined – Figure 9.16 illustrates the principle of the idea. Comprehensive

(a)   (b)

Figure 9.16 *Light striping: (a) A light stripe, (b) the output presented.*

depth information is extracted by shining a (probably parallel) selection of stripes at the scene. This idea has defects in that, unless the stripe directions are carefully chosen, concavities in the scene will not appear at all, and that surfaces near parallel to the range of stripes will provide relatively little data since they will intersect few stripes. On the other hand, the continuous lines the stripes present on a given surface allow simple and accurate segmentation of light stripe data, in contrast to spot range data.

The whole issue of approaching vision from the point of view of range rather than intensity images has been addressed [Li 92], and shown to be susceptible to an optimization attack at low, intermediate and high levels. The range image approach may be expected to become more common as range finding technology matures.

9.6 Summary

The completion of the vision problem by finalizing 3D shape and recognition of 3D objects is not easy. This chapter has given an indication of some partial solutions to the problem, and an overview of some of the theoretical approaches to what is still a very active research topic.

Several 3D vision systems have been developed in recent years, some geared to highly specific tasks and others more general and consequently more elaborate. One of the best known is the complex **ACRONYM** [Brooks 81] system which is a useful practical illustration of several concepts. Originally demonstrated in the domain of recognizing aircraft from aerial views, it has been shown to be general enough to be applied to other domains as well. ACRONYM models objects as generalized cylinders, and each such object has its own co-ordinate system.

A central feature of ACRONYM is the way it reasons about the positions of objects in space – using **geometric reasoning** it constructs an 'object graph' whose nodes are objects, or parts thereof, and whose (directed) arcs define relationships between them. Using constraints (such as size, and number, of subparts of an object) it also constructs a companion 'restriction graph' describing how the objects may (or may not) co-exist. A constraint manipulation system proceeds to reason about possible occlusions to determine whether postulated parts of object may be visible.

A backward chaining production system then tests hypotheses about the scene by searching for particular features in the 2D projection provided by the image – these features are projections of the generalized cylinders that make up the model, and appear as 'ribbons'. A matcher attempts to make appropriate correspondences between predictions of what should appear in the projection, and features actually found. In the case of aircraft scenes, the ribbons would be aircraft bodies and wings, and larger features such as runways.

3D computer vision represents an enormous challenge, and as such it is an area in which human performance is of particular interest as a demonstration that some of these difficult problems have a solution at all. In this respect, the approach of **perceptual organization** [Lowe 85] is especially interesting since it follows psychological principles rather than attempting to build explicit depth maps in the bottom-up manner advocated by Marr. Lowe argues that a constraint deployed by the human visual system in trying to overcome the non-uniqueness of the inversion of the 3D to 2D projection is one of 'non-accidentalness'. This is a more abstract notion than the constraints such as gradient disparity limits and knowledge of reflectance properties considered hitherto, and hinges on the observation that, given a strange scene, we will concentrate on features that are unlikely to occur by chance. Biederman [Biederman 87] too uses this idea in the 'geon' approach to 3D vision. This is likely to mean long, straight lines, co-linearity or co-termination of straight line segments and, more particularly, long parallel pairs of lines, which may reasonably be expected to correspond to objects of interest – they are most unlikely to occur by chance. A pass through an image locating such clues then allows 'perceptual organization' to appeal to a model base and ask which objects, from which points of view, might generate that which is seen. This permits hypotheses to be generated that may be tested by referring back to the image; ultimately a hypothesis is sufficiently reinforced to be accepted as object recognition. This approach has been extended beyond line based features using a type of neural network [Sha'ashua and Ullman 88], and has also been used to reduce the search space in solving the correspondence problem [Quan and Mohr 88]. The vision system CANC2 [Mohan and Nevatia 92] uses perceptual organization to provide high quality input to high-level shape extraction (for example, from stereo). Using indoor scenes, and pictures of manufactured objects, it proceeds from a simple edge detection to group co-linear and close elements into lines and curves which are then extended to determine co-termination points. Thereafter, symmetries are sought between pairs of curves that permit the reconstruction of ribbons, after which a segmentation of the scene into surfaces becomes apparent.

References

[Aliomonos and Swain 85] J Aliomonos and M J Swain. Shape from texture. In *Proceedings of the Ninth Joint Conference on Artificial Intelligence IJCAI*, volume 2, pages 926–931, 1985.

[Aloimonos and Shulman 89] Y Aloimonos and D Shulman. *Integration of Visual Modules - An Extension of the Marr Paradigm*. Academic Press, New York, 1989.

[Barnard 86] S T Barnard. A stochastic approach to stereo vision. In *Proceedings of the Fifth National Conference on AI (Philadelphia)*, volume 1, pages 676–680, AAAI, Menlo Park, Ca, 1986.

[Barnard 89] S T Barnard. Stochastic stereo matching over scale. *International Journal of Computer Vision*, 3:17–32, 1989.

[Besl and Jain 85] P J Besl and R C Jain. Three-dimensional object recognition. *ACM Computing Surveys*, 17(1):75–145, March 1985.

[Biederman 87] I Biederman. Recognition by components: A theory of human image understanding. *Psychological Review*, 94(2):115–147, 1987.

[Binford 71] T O Binford. Visual perception by computer. In *Proceedings of the IEEE Conference on Systems, Science and Cybernetics*, IEEE, Miami, Fl, December 1971.

[Bowyer 92] K W Bowyer, editor. *Special issue on directions in CAD-based vision*, volume 55, 1992.

[Brady 84] M Brady. Representing shape. In M Brady, L A Gerhardt, and H F Davidson, editors, *Robotics and Artificial Intelligence*, pages 279–300. Springer + NATO, Berlin, 1984.

[Brady and Yuille 83] M Brady and A Yuille. An extremum principle for shape from contour. Technical Report MIT-AIM 711, MIT, AI Laboratory, 1983.

[Bray and Hlavac 91] A J Bray and V Hlavac. Properties of local geometric constraints. In *Proceedings of the British Machine Vision Conference*, pages 95–103, Glasgow, U.K., September 1991.

[Brooks 81] R A Brooks. Symbolic reasoning among 3D models and 2D images. *Artificial Intelligence*, 17:285–348, 1981.

[Brooks et al. 79] R A Brooks, R Greiner, and T O Binford. The ACRONYM model-based vision system. In *Proceedings of the International Joint Conference on Artificial Intelligence, IJCAI-6, Tokyo*, pages 105–113, 1979.

[Chakravarty and Freeman 82] I Chakravarty and H Freeman. Characteristic views as a basis for three-dimensional object recognition. *Proceedings of The Society for Photo-Optical Instrumentation Engineers Conference on Robot Vision*, 336:37–45, 1982.

[Clocksin 80] W F Clocksin. Perception of surface slant and edge labels from optical flow – a computational approach. *Perception*, 9:253–269, 1980.

[Clowes 71] M B Clowes. On seeing things. *Artificial Intelligence*, 2(1):79–116, 1971.

[Flynn and Jain 92] P J Flynn and A K Jain. 3D object recognition using invariant feature indexing of interpretation tables. *CVGIP – Image Understanding*, 55(2):119–129, 1992.

[Goad 83] C Goad. Special purpose automatic programming for 3D model-based vision. In *Proceedings of the Image Understanding Workshop*, pages 94–104, McLean, Va, 1983.

[Goad 86] C Goad. Fast 3D model-based vision. In A P Pentland, editor, *From Pixels to Predicates*, pages 371–374. Ablex Publishing Corporation, Norwood, NJ, 1986.

[Grimson 89] W E L Grimson. On the recognition of curved objects. *IEEE Transactions on Pattern Analysis and Machine Intelligence*, 11(6), 1989.

[Gupta 89] A Gupta. Part description and segmentation using contour, surface and volumetric primitives. Technical Report MS-CIS-89-33, University of Pennsylvania, Grasp Laboratory, Department of Computer and Information Science, Philadelphia, May 1989.

[Hayes-Roth et al. 83] F Hayes-Roth, D A Waterman, and D B Lenat. *Building Expert Systems*. Addison-Wesley, Reading, Ma, 1983.

[Horn 75] B K P Horn. Shape from shading. In P H Winston, editor, *The Psychology of Computer Vision*. McGraw Hill, New York, 1975.

[Horn 86] B K P Horn. *Robot Vision*. MIT Press, Cambridge, Ma, 1986.

[Horn and Brooks 89] B K P Horn and M J Brooks, editors. *Shape from Shading*. MIT Press, Cambridge, Ma, 1989.

[Huffman 71] D A Huffman. Impossible objects as nonsense sentences. In B Metzler and D M Michie, editors, *Machine Intelligence*, volume 6, pages 295–323. Edinburgh University Press, 1971.

[Ikeuchi and Horn 81] K Ikeuchi and B K P Horn. Numerical shape from shading and occluding boundaries. *Artificial Intelligence*, 17:141–184, 1981.

[Jarvis 83] R A Jarvis. A perspective on range finding technologies for computer vision. *IEEE Transactions on Pattern Analysis and Machine Intelligence*, PAMI-5(2):122–139, 1983.

[Koenderink and van Doorn 79] J J Koenderink and A J van Doorn. Internal representation of solid shape with respect to vision. *Biological Cybernetics*, 32(4):211–216, 1979.

[Kriegman 92] D J Kriegman. Computing stable poses of piecewise smooth objects. *CVGIP – Image Understanding*, 55(2):109–118, 1992.

[Krotkov 89] E Krotkov. *Active Computer Vision by Cooperative Focus and Stereo*. Springer Verlag, Berlin, 1989.

[Krotkov et al. 90] E Krotkov, K Henriksen, and R Kories. Stereo ranging with verging cameras. *IEEE Transactions on Pattern Analysis and Machine Intelligence*, 12(12):1200–1205, December 1990.

[Li 92] S Z Li. Toward 3D vision from range images: An optimization framework and parallel networks. *CVGIP – Image Understanding*, 55(3):231–260, 1992.

[Lowe 85] D G Lowe. *Perceptual Organisation and Visual Recognition*. Kluwer Nijhoff, Norwell Ma, 1985.

[Lowe 89] D G Lowe. Organization of smooth image curves at multiple scales. *International Journal of Computer Vision*, 1:119–130, 1989.

[Mackworth 73] A K Mackworth. Interpreting pictures of polyhedral scenes. *Artificial Intelligence*, 4(2):121–137, 1973.

[Marr 82] D Marr. *Vision – A Computational Investigation into the Human Representation and Processing of Visual Information*. W.H. Freeman and Co., San Francisco, 1982.

[Marr and Hildreth 80] D Marr and E Hildreth. Theory of edge detection. *Proceedings of the Royal Society*, B 207:187–217, 1980.

[Marr and Poggio 79] D Marr and T A Poggio. A computational theory of human stereo vision. *Proceedings of the Royal Society*, B 207:301–328, 1979.

[Marr et al. 78] D Marr, G Palm, and T A Poggio. Analysis of a co-operative stereo algorithm. *Biological Cybernetics*, 28:223–229, 1978.

[Mohan and Nevatia 92] R Mohan and R Nevatia. Perceptual organization for scene segmentation and description. *IEEE Transactions on Pattern Analysis and Machine Intelligence*, 14(6):616–635, 1992.

[Negahdaripour and Horn 85] S Negahdaripour and B K P Horn. Determining 3D motion of planar objects from image brightness measurements. In *Proceedings of the Ninth Joint Conference on Artificial Intelligence IJCAI*, volume 2, pages 898–901, 1985.

[Nishihara 84] H K Nishihara. Practical real-time imaging stereo matcher. *Optical Engineering*, 23(5):536–545, 1984.

[Pollard et al. 85] S B Pollard, J E W Mayhew, and J P Frisby. PMF: A stereo correspondence algorithm using a disparity gradient limit. *Perception*, 14:449–470, 1985.

[Ponce et al. 92] J Ponce, A Hoogs, and D J Kriegman. On using CAD models
    to compute the pose of curved 3d objects. *CVGIP – Image Under-
    standing*, 55(2):184–197, 1992.

[Preparata and Shamos 85] F P Preparata and M I Shamos. *Computational
    Geometry - An Introduction*. Springer Verlag, Berlin, 1985.

[Quan and Mohr 88] L Quan and R Mohr. Matching perspective images using
    geometric constraints and perceptual grouping. In *Proceedings of
    the Second International Conference on Computer Vision, Tarpon
    Springs, Fl*, pages 679–684, IEEE, Piscataway, NJ, 1988.

[Quarendon 84] P Quarendon. *WINSOM User's Guide*. IBM, IBM UK Sci-
    entific Centre, August 1984.

[Roberts 65] L G Roberts. Machine perception of three-dimensional solids.
    In J T Tippett, editor, *Optical and Electro-Optical Information Pro-
    cessing*, pages 159–197. MIT Press, Cambridge, Ma, 1965.

[Sato et al. 92] K Sato, K Ikeuchi, and T Kanade. Model based recognition of
    specular objects using sensor models. *CVGIP – Image Understand-
    ing*, 55(2):155–169, 1992.

[Seales and Dyer 92] W B Seales and C R Dyer. Viewpoints from occluding
    contour. *CVGIP – Image Understanding*, 55(2):198–211, 1992.

[Sha'ashua and Ullman 88] A Sha'ashua and S Ullman. Structural saliency:
    the detection of globally salient structures using a locally connected
    network. In *Proceedings of the Second International Conference on
    Computer Vision, Tarpon Springs, Fl*, pages 321–327, IEEE, Piscat-
    away, NJ, 1988.

[Shapira 74] R Shapira. A technique for the reconstruction of a straight edge,
    wire-frame object from two or more central projections. *Computer
    Graphics and Image Processing*, 4(3):318–326, 1974.

[Soroka and Bajcsy 78] B I Soroka and R K Bajcsy. A program for describ-
    ing complex three dimensional objects using generalised cylinders. In
    *Proceedings of the Pattern Recognition and Image Processing Confer-
    ence (Chicago)*, pages 331–339, IEEE, New York, 1978.

[Stevens 79] K A Stevens. Representing and analyzing surface orientation.
    In P A Winston and R H Brown, editors, *Artificial Intelligence: An
    MIT Persepctive*, volume 2. MIT Press, Cambridge, Ma, 1979.

[Strang 86] G Strang. *Introduction to Applied Mathematics*, Chapter 2.
    Wellesley Cambridge Press, Wellesley Ma, 1986.

[Ullman 79] S Ullman. *The Interpretation of Visual Motion.* MIT Press, Cambridge, Ma, 1979.

[Waltz 75] D L Waltz. Understanding line drawings of scenes with shadows. In P H Winston, editor, *The Psychology of Computer Vision*, pages 19–91. McGraw Hill, New York, 1975.

[Weiss 88] I Weiss. Projective invariants of shapes. In *Proceedings of Image Understanding Workshop*, volume 2, pages 1125–1134, Cambridge, Ma, 1988.

[Witkin 81] A P Witkin. Recovering surface shape and orientation from texture. *Artificial Intelligence*, 17:17–45, 1981.

10

Mathematical morphology

Mathematical morphology, which started to develop in the late Sixties, stands as a relatively separate part of image analysis. Its main protagonists were Matheron [Matheron 67] and Serra [Serra 82], whose monographs are highly mathematical books. Here, we shall present a simple explanation of this topic.

The non-morphological approach to image processing is close to the calculus, being based on the point spread function concept (e.g. Dirac impulse) and linear transformations such as convolution. We have discussed image processing from this point of view in Chapter 4. Mathematical morphology is based on geometry and shape; morphological operations simplify images, and preserve the main shape characteristics of objects.

We shall tackle basic mathematical morphology techniques from the point of view of the user; if the reader prefers an exact mathematical explanation, a classic monograph [Serra 82] or more recent book [Giardina and Dougherty 88] might be preferred. The tutorial paper [Haralick et al. 87] covers basic morphological transformations. Concepts introduced in this chapter may be generalized into higher dimensions; grey scale morphology adds the third dimension – the brightness of the point in the image. Grey scale morphology is explained in [Serra 82] or [Giardina and Dougherty 88]. For the sake of simplicity we shall constrain ourselves to binary images. Other significant references are [Maragos and Schafer 87a, Maragos and Schafer 87b, Serra 87, Roerdink and Heijmans 88].

Morphological transformations, if used, usually constitute an intermediate part of the image processing sequence. In the first phase the image is digitized and pre-processed using local convolution operators and segmented to obtain a binary image with objects separated from the background. Morphological operations may constitute the second phase which operates on the shape of these objects. The last processing step evaluates results of morphology using different numerical descriptors or a syntactic approach.

Morphological operations are predominantly used for the following purposes:

- Image pre-processing (noise filtering, shape simplification).

- Enhancing object structure (skeletonizing, thinning, thickening, convex hull, object marking).

- Quantitative description of objects (area, perimeter, projections, Euler-Poincaré characteristic).

10.1 Basic principles and morphological transformations

10.1.1 *Morphological transformations*

Mathematical morphology exploits point set properties, results of integral geometry, and topology. The initial assumption states that real images can be modelled using **point sets** of any dimension (e.g. N-dimensional Euclidean space); the Euclidean 2D space E^2 and its system of subsets is a natural domain for planar shape description. Understanding of inclusion ($\subset$ or $\supset$), intersection ($\cap$), union ($\cup$), the empty set $\emptyset$ and set complement (^{c}) is assumed. Set **difference** is defined by

$$X \setminus Y = X \cap Y^c \tag{10.1}$$

Computer vision uses the digital equivalent of Euclidean space – sets of integer pairs for binary image morphology or sets of integer triples for grey scale morphology.

In this chapter we consider binary images that can be viewed as subsets of the 2D space of all integers. A point is represented by a pair of integers that give co-ordinates with respect to the two co-ordinate axes of the digital grid; the unit length of the grid equals the sampling period in each direction. This representation is suitable for both rectangular or hexagonal grids, but a rectangular grid is assumed hereafter.

A binary image can be treated as a 2D point set. Points belonging to objects in the image represent a set X – these points are pixels with value equal to one. Points of the complement set X^c correspond to the background with pixel values equal to zero. The origin (marked as a diagonal cross in our examples) has co-ordinates $(0,0)$ and co-ordinates of any point are interpreted as $(row, column)$. Figure 10.1 shows an example of such a set – points belonging to the object are denoted by small black squares. Any point $\mathbf{x}$ from a discrete image X can be treated as a vector with respect to the origin $(0,0)$.

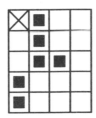

Figure 10.1 *A point set example.*

A morphological transformation ϕ is given by the relation of the image (point set X) with another small point set B called a **structuring element**. B is expressed with respect to a local origin $\mathcal{O}$ (called representative point). Some typical structuring elements are shown in Figure 10.2 in which the representative point is marked by a cross. Figure 10.2c illustrates the possibility of the point $\mathcal{O}$ not being a member of the structuring element B.

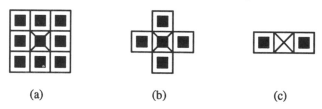

(a)   (b)   (c)

Figure 10.2 *Typical structuring elements.*

The morphological transformation $\phi(X)$ applied to the image X means that the structuring element B is moved systematically across the entire image. Assume that B is positioned at some point in the image; the pixel in the image corresponding to the representative point $\mathcal{O}$ of the structuring element is called the **current** pixel. The result of the relation (that can be either zero or one) between the image X and the structuring element B in the current position is stored in the current image pixel.

The **duality** of morphological operations is deduced from the existence of the set complement; for each morphological transformation $\phi(X)$ there exists a dual transformation $\phi^*(X)$

$$\phi(X) = (\phi^*(X^c))^c \tag{10.2}$$

The **translation** of the point set X by the vector $\mathbf{h}$ is denoted by X_h; it is defined by

$$X_h = \left\{ \mathbf{d} \in E^2, \ \mathbf{d} = \mathbf{x} + \mathbf{h} \text{ for some } \mathbf{x} \in X \right\} \tag{10.3}$$

This is illustrated in Figure 10.3.

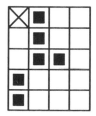   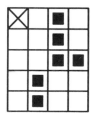

Figure 10.3 *Translation by a vector.*

It is appropriate to restrict the set of possible morphological transformations in image analysis by imposing several constraints on it; we shall briefly present here four morphological principles that express such constraints. These concepts may be found difficult to understand, but an understanding of them is not essential to a comprehension of what follows, and they may be taken for granted. A detailed explanation of these matters may be found in [Serra 82].

A morphological transformation is called **quantitative** if and only if it satisfies four basic morphological principles [Serra 82]:

- Compatibility with translation: Let the transformation ϕ depend on the position of the origin $\mathcal{O}$ of the co-ordinate system, and denote such a transformation by $\phi_{\mathcal{O}}$. If all points are translated by the vector $-\mathbf{h}$ it is expressed as $\phi_{-\mathbf{h}}$. The **compatibility with translation** principle is given by

$$\phi_{\mathcal{O}}(X_{\mathbf{h}}) = (\phi_{-\mathbf{h}}(X))_{\mathbf{h}} \qquad (10.4)$$

If ϕ does not depend on the position of the origin $\mathcal{O}$ then the compatibility with translation principle reduces to invariance under translation

$$\phi(X_{\mathbf{h}}) = (\phi(X))_{\mathbf{h}} \qquad (10.5)$$

- Compatibility with change of scale: Let λX represent the homothetic of a point set X (i.e. the co-ordinates of each point of the set are multiplied by some positive constant λ). This is equivalent to change of scale with respect to some origin. Let ϕ_{λ} denote a transformation that depends on the positive parameter λ (change of scale). **Compatibility with change of scale** is given by

$$\phi_{\lambda}(X) = \lambda \, \phi(\frac{1}{\lambda} X) \qquad (10.6)$$

If ϕ does not depend on the scale λ, then compatibility with change of scale reduces to invariance to change of scale

$$\phi(\lambda X) = \lambda \, \phi(X) \qquad (10.7)$$

- Local knowledge: The local knowledge principle considers the situation in which only a part of a larger structure can be examined – this is always the case in reality due to the restricted size of the digital grid. The morphological transformation ϕ has the **local knowledge principle** if for any restricted point set Z' in the transformation $\phi(X)$ there exists a restricted set Z, knowledge of which is sufficient to provide ϕ. The local knowledge principle may be written symbolically as

$$(\phi(X \cap Z)) \cap Z' = \phi(X) \cap Z' \qquad (10.8)$$

- Upper-semi-continuity: The upper-semi-continuity principle says that the morphological transformation does not exhibit any abrupt changes. A precise explanation needs many concepts from topology and is given in [Serra 82].

The simplest set of quantitative morphological transformations is dilation, erosion, opening, and closing.

10.1.2 Dilation

The morphological transformation **dilation** $\oplus$ combines two sets using vector addition (or Minkowski set addition). The dilation $X \oplus B$ is the point set of all possible vector additions of pairs of elements, one from each of the sets X and B.

$$X \oplus B = \left\{ \mathbf{d} \in E^2 \,:\, \mathbf{d} = \mathbf{x} + \mathbf{b} \text{ for every } \mathbf{x} \in X \text{ and } \mathbf{b} \in B \right\} \qquad (10.9)$$

Figure 10.4 illustrates an example of dilation.

$$
\begin{aligned}
X &= \{(0,1),(1,1),(2,1),(2,2),(3,0),(4,0)\} \\
B &= \{(0,0),(0,1)\} \\
X \oplus B &= \{(0,1),(1,1),(2,1),(2,2),(3,0),(4,0), \\
&\qquad (0,2),(1,2),(2,2),(2,3),(3,1),(4,1)\}
\end{aligned}
$$

Figure 10.4 *Dilation.*

Figure 10.5 shows a 256 × 256 original image (the emblem of the Czech Technical University) on the left, and its dilation by a 3×3 structuring element on the right (Figure 10.2a). This dilation is an **isotropic** (behaves the same way in all directions) expansion of the object by one pixel. This operation is also sometimes called **fill** or **grow**.

Dilation with an isotropic 3×3 structuring element might be explained as a transformation which changes all background pixels neighbouring the object.

Dilation has several interesting properties that may ease its hardware or software implementation; we present some here without proof. The interested reader may consult [Serra 82] or the tutorial paper [Haralick et al. 87].

Figure 10.5 *Dilation as isotropic expansion.*

The dilation operation is commutative

$$X \oplus B = B \oplus X \tag{10.10}$$

and is also associative

$$X \oplus (B \oplus D) = (X \oplus B) \oplus D \tag{10.11}$$

Dilation may be also expressed as a union of shifted point sets

$$X \oplus B = \bigcup_{b \in B} X_{\mathbf{b}} \tag{10.12}$$

and is invariant to translation

$$X_{\mathbf{h}} \oplus B = (X \oplus B)_{\mathbf{h}} \tag{10.13}$$

Equations (10.12) and (10.13) show the importance of shifts in speeding up implementation of dilation, and this holds for implementations of binary morphology on serial computers in general. One processor word represents several pixels (e.g. 32 for a 32 bit processor), and shift or addition corresponds to a single instruction. Shifts may also be easily implemented as delays in a pipeline parallel processor.

Dilation is an **increasing** transformation;

$$\text{If } X \subseteq Y \text{ then } X \oplus B \subseteq Y \oplus B \tag{10.14}$$

Figure 10.6 illustrates the result of dilation if the representative point is not a member of the structuring element B; if this structuring element is used, the dilation result is substantially different from the input set.

Dilation is used to fill small holes and fill narrow gulfs in objects. It increases the object size – if the original size needs to be preserved, then the dilation is combined with erosion, described in the next section.

Figure 10.6 *Dilation where the representative point is not a member of the structuring element.*

10.1.3 Erosion

Erosion $\ominus$ combines two sets using vector subtraction of set elements and is the dual of dilation. Neither erosion nor dilation are invertible transformations

$$X \ominus B = \{ \mathbf{d} \in E^2 : \mathbf{d} + \mathbf{b} \in X \text{ for every } \mathbf{b} \in B \} \qquad (10.15)$$

This formula says that every point d from the set X (image) is tested; the result of the erosion is given by those points d for which all possible $d + b$ are in X. Figure 10.7 shows an example of the point set X eroded by the structuring element B

$$
\begin{aligned}
X &= \{(0,1),(1,1),(2,1),(3,0),(3,1),(3,2),(3,3),(4,1)\} \\
B &= \{(0,0),(0,1)\} \\
X \ominus B &= \{(3,0),(3,1),(3,2)\}
\end{aligned}
$$

Figure 10.7 *Erosion.*

Figure 10.8 shows the erosion by a 3×3 element (Figure 10.2a) of the same original as in Figure 10.5. Notice that lines of one pixel width disappear. Erosion (such as Figure 10.8) with an isotropic structuring element is called **shrink** or **reduce** by some authors.

Basic morphological transformations can be used to find the contours of objects in an image very quickly. This can for instance be achieved by the subtraction from the original picture of its eroded version – see Figure 10.9.

Figure 10.8 *Erosion as isotropic shrink.*

Figure 10.9 *Contours obtained by the subtraction of an eroded image from an original (left).*

Erosion is used to simplify the structure of an object – objects or their parts with width equal to one will disappear. It might thus decompose complicated objects into several simpler ones.

There is an equivalent definition of erosion [Matheron 75] that may better express its properties

$$X \ominus B = \{ \mathbf{d} \in E^2 : B_d \subseteq X \} \qquad (10.16)$$

The structuring element B might be interpreted as a probe sliding across the image X; then if B translated by the vector $\mathbf{d}$ is contained in the image X the point corresponding to the representative point of B belongs to the erosion $X \ominus B$.

An implementation of erosion might be simplified by noting that an image X eroded by the structuring element B can be expressed as an intersection of all translations of the image X by the vector[1] $-\mathbf{b} \in B$

$$X \ominus B = \bigcap_{b \in B} X_{-b} \qquad (10.17)$$

---

[1]This definition of erosion $\ominus$ differs from that used in [Serra 82]. There $\ominus$ denotes Minkowski subtraction that is an intersection of all translations of the image by the vector $b \in B$. In our case the minus sign has been added.

If the representative point is a member of the structuring element the erosion is an anti-extensive transformation; that is, if $(0,0) \in B$ then $X \ominus B \subseteq X$ Erosion is also translation invariant

$$X_h \ominus B = (X \ominus B)_h \qquad (10.18)$$

$$X \ominus B_h = (X \ominus B)_{-h} \qquad (10.19)$$

and, like dilation, is an increasing transformation

$$\text{If } X \subseteq Y \text{ then } X \ominus B \subseteq Y \ominus B \qquad (10.20)$$

If B, D are structuring elements, and D is contained in B, then erosion by B is more aggressive than by D; that is, if $D \subseteq B$ then $X \ominus B \subseteq X \ominus D$. This property enables the ordering of erosions according to structuring elements of similar shape but different size.

Denote by $\check{B}$ the **symmetrical set** to B (The symmetrical set is called the **transpose** [Serra 82] or **rational set** [Haralick et al. 87] by some authors) with respect to the representative point $\mathcal{O}$

$$\check{B} = \{-b : b \in B\} \qquad (10.21)$$

For example

$$\begin{aligned} B &= \{(1,2),(2,3)\} \\ \check{B} &= \{(-1,-2)(-2,-3)\} \end{aligned} \qquad (10.22)$$

We have already mentioned that erosion and dilation are dual transformations. Formally

$$(X \ominus Y)^C = X^C \oplus \check{Y} \qquad (10.23)$$

The differences between erosion and dilation are illustrated by the following properties. Erosion (in contrast to dilation) is not commutative

$$X \ominus B \neq B \ominus X \qquad (10.24)$$

The properties of erosion and intersection combined together are

$$\begin{aligned} (X \cap Y) \ominus B &= (X \ominus B) \cap (Y \ominus B) \\ B \ominus (X \cap Y) &\supseteq (B \ominus X) \cup (B \ominus Y) \end{aligned} \qquad (10.25)$$

On the other hand image intersection and dilation cannot be interchanged; the dilation of the intersection of two images is contained in the intersection of their dilations

$$\begin{aligned} (X \cap Y) \oplus B &\subseteq (X \oplus B) \cap (Y \oplus B) \\ B \oplus (X \cap Y) &\subseteq (X \oplus B) \cap (Y \oplus B) \end{aligned} \qquad (10.26)$$

The order of erosion (respectively, dilation) may be interchanged with set union. This fact enables the structuring element to be decomposed into a union of simpler structuring elements;

$$B \oplus (X \cup Y) = (X \cup Y) \oplus B = (X \oplus B) \cup (Y \oplus B)$$

$$
\begin{aligned}
(X \cup Y) \ominus B &\supseteq (X \ominus B) \cup (Y \ominus B) \\
B \ominus (X \cup Y) &= (X \ominus B) \cup (Y \ominus B)
\end{aligned}
\tag{10.27}
$$

Successive dilation (respectively, erosion) of the image X first by the structuring element B and then by the structuring element D is equivalent to the dilation (erosion) of the image X by $B \oplus D$

$$
\begin{aligned}
(X \oplus B) \oplus D &= X \oplus (B \oplus D) \\
(X \ominus B) \ominus D &= X \ominus (B \oplus D)
\end{aligned}
\tag{10.28}
$$

10.1.4 Opening and closing

Erosion and dilation are not invertible transformations – if an image is eroded and then dilated the original image is not re-obtained. Instead, the result is a simplified and less detailed version of the original image.

Erosion followed by dilation creates an important morphological transformation called **opening**. The opening of an image X by the structuring element B is denoted by $X \circ B$ and is defined as

$$X \circ B = (X \ominus B) \oplus B \tag{10.29}$$

Dilation followed by erosion is called **closing**. The closing of an image X by the structuring element B is denoted by $X \bullet B$ and is defined as

$$X \bullet B = (X \oplus B) \ominus B \tag{10.30}$$

If an image X is unchanged by opening with the structuring element B it is called **open with respect to** B. Similarly, if an image X is unchanged by closing with B it is called **closed with respect to** B.

Opening and closing with an isotropic structuring element is used to eliminate specific image details smaller than the structuring element – the global shape of the objects is not distorted. Closing connects objects that are close to each other, fills up small holes, and smooths the object outline by filling up narrow gulfs. Meanings of 'near', 'small', and 'narrow' are related to the size and the shape of the structuring element. Opening is illustrated in Figure 10.10, and closing in Figure 10.11.

Figure 10.10 *Opening (original on the left).*

Figure 10.11 *Closing (original on the left).*

Unlike dilation and erosion, opening and closing are invariant to translation of the structuring element. Equations (10.14) and (10.20) imply that both opening and closing are increasing transformations. Opening is anti-extensive $(X \circ B \subseteq X)$ and closing is extensive $(X \subseteq X \bullet B)$.

Opening and closing, like dilation and erosion, are dual transformations

$$(X \bullet B)^C = X^C \circ \check{B} \tag{10.31}$$

Another significant fact is that iteratively-used openings and closings are **idempotent**, meaning that reapplication of these transformations does not change the previous result. Formally

$$X \circ B = (X \circ B) \circ B \tag{10.32}$$

$$X \bullet B = (X \bullet B) \bullet B \tag{10.33}$$

10.2 Skeleton and other topological processing

10.2.1 Homotopic transformations

Topological properties are associated with contiguity (Section 2.3.1) and mathematical morphology can be used to study such properties of objects in images.

There is an interesting group among morphological transformations called **homotopic transformations** [Serra 82].

A transformation is homotopic if it does not change the contiguity relation between regions and holes in the image. This relation is expressed by the homotopic tree; its root corresponds to the background of the image, first level branches correspond to the objects (regions), and second level branches match holes within objects, etc.

Figure 10.12 shows an example of a homotopic tree in which there are two different images with the homotopic tree below them. On the left side are some biological cells and on the right a house and a pine tree; both images correspond to the same tree. Its root b corresponds to the background, node r_1 matches the larger cell (the outline of the house), and node r_2 matches the smaller cell (the pine tree). The node h_1 corresponds to the empty hole in the cell r_1 (the hole inside the roof of the house) – the other correspondences to nodes should now be clear. A transformation is homotopic if it does not

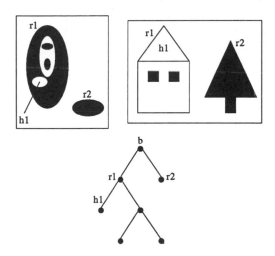

Figure 10.12 *The same homotopic tree for two different images.*

change the homotopic tree.

10.2.2 Skeleton

It is sometimes advantageous to convert an object to an archetypical stick figure called the **skeleton** [Giardina and Dougherty 88, Serra 82] (also considered in Section 6.3.4). We shall explain this in the context of 2D Euclidean space, which is more illustrative than on the digital grid[2].

---

[2]The **medial axis** (see Section 6.3.4) is another concept similar to the skeleton. The difference between them is described in [Serra 82].

The skeleton[3] $S(Y)$ of a set Y has the following property;

- Let $D(\mathbf{x})$ be the largest disk centred at the point $\mathbf{x}$ that is contained in the set Y. If $\mathbf{x}$ is a point of the skeleton $S(Y)$, there is no larger disk D_1 (not necessarily centred at $\mathbf{x}$) which contains disk $D(\mathbf{x})$ and is at the same time contained in the set Y.

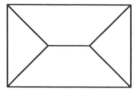 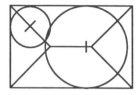

Figure 10.13 *Skeleton of the rectangle.*

Figure 10.13 illustrates the skeleton of a rectangle, and Figure 6.32 shows several objects together with their skeletons. The properties of the (Euclidean) skeleton can be seen here – in particular, Figure 6.32 shows that the skeleton of two adjacent circles consists of two distinct points. We deduce that the skeleton need not be a contiguous point set.

From the point of view of morphological algorithms it is important that the skeleton $S(Y)$ can be created using erosion and opening transformations [Serra 82]. Such a skeleton has two unfortunate properties in practical applications; first, it need not be homotopic, and second, it consists of lines that may be wider than one pixel.

We shall see later that the skeleton is often substituted by sequential homotopic thinning that does not have the two properties mentioned above. On the other hand, the computation of the homotopic skeleton substitute is slower (typically ten times) than computation of the skeleton from the definition [Serra 82].

10.2.3 Thinning and thickening

Operations described hitherto used a structuring element B, and we have tested points for their membership of X; we can also test whether some points do not belong to X. An operation may be denoted by a pair of disjoint sets $B = (B_1, B_2)$, called a **composite structuring element**. The **hit or miss** transformation $\otimes$ is defined as

$$X \otimes B = \{\mathbf{x} : \ B_1 \subset X \text{ and } B_2 \subset X^c\} \tag{10.34}$$

This means that for a point $\mathbf{x}$ to be in the resulting set, two conditions should be fulfilled simultaneously. Firstly the part B_1 of the composite structuring

---

[3]It can be said informally that the skeleton $S(Y)$ of the set Y is the union of the centres x of circles $D(x)$ included in Y that touch its boundary in at least two distinct points.

element that has its representative point at $\mathbf{x}$ should be contained in X, and secondly, the part B_2 of the composite structuring element should be contained in X^c.

The hit or miss transformation operates as a binary matching between an image X and the structuring element (B_1, B_2). It may be expressed using erosions and dilations as well

$$X \otimes B = (X \ominus B_1) \cap (X^c \ominus B_2) = (X \ominus B_1) \,|\, (X \oplus B_2) \qquad (10.35)$$

One application of the hit or miss transformation is **thinning** and **thickening** of point sets. For an image X and a composite structuring element $B = (B_1, B_2)$, **thinning** is defined as

$$X \oslash B = X \,|\, (X \otimes B) \qquad (10.36)$$

and **thickening** is defined as

$$X \odot B = X \cup (X \otimes B) \qquad (10.37)$$

When thinning, a part of the boundary of the object is subtracted from it by the set difference operation. When thickening, a part of the boundary of the background is added to the object. Thinning and thickening are dual transformations

$$(X \odot B)^c = X^c \oslash B^* \,, \quad B^* = (B_2, B_1) \qquad (10.38)$$

Thinning and thickening transformations are very often used sequentially. Let $\{B_{(1)}, B_{(2)}, B_{(3)}, \ldots\}$ denote a sequence of composite structuring elements $B_{(i)} = (B_{i_1}, B_{i_2})$. **Sequential thinning** can then be expressed as

$$X \oslash \{B_{(i)}\} = ((((X \oslash B_{(1)}) \oslash B_{(2)}) \ldots \oslash B_{(i)}) \ldots) \qquad (10.39)$$

and **sequential thickening** as

$$X \odot \{B_{(i)}\} = ((((X \odot B_{(1)}) \odot B_{(2)}) \ldots \odot B_{(i)}) \ldots) \qquad (10.40)$$

There are several sequences of structuring elements $\{B_{(i)}\}$ that are useful in practice. Many of them are given by a permissible rotation of a structuring element in the appropriate digital raster (e.g. hexagonal, square or octagonal). These sequences, sometimes called the **Golay alphabet** [Golay 69], are summarized for the hexagonal raster in [Serra 82]. We shall present structuring elements of the Golay alphabet for square and octagonal rasters; the index 4 denotes an element on the square raster and the index 8 denotes an element on the octagonal raster. The 3×3 matrices will be shown in the first two rotations, from which the other rotations can easily be derived.

The composite structuring element will be expressed by one matrix only. A value of one in it means that this element belongs to B_1 (it is a subset of objects in the hit or miss transformation), and a value zero belongs to B_2 and is a subset of the background. An asterisk $*$ in the matrix denotes an element that is not used in the matching process, i.e. its value is not significant.

Thinning and thickening sequential transformations converge to some image – the number of iterations needed depends on the objects in the image and the structuring element used. If two successive images in the sequence are identical the thinning (or thickening) can be stopped.

Sequential thinning by structuring element L

This sequential thinning is quite important as it serves as the homotopic substitute of the skeleton; the final thinned image consists only of lines of width one and isolated points.

The structuring element L is given by

$$L_1^{(4)} = \begin{bmatrix} 0 & 0 & 0 \\ * & 1 & * \\ 1 & 1 & 1 \end{bmatrix}, \ L_2^{(4)} = \begin{bmatrix} * & 0 & * \\ 1 & 1 & 0 \\ 1 & 1 & * \end{bmatrix} \dots \qquad (10.41)$$

$$L_1^{(8)} = \begin{bmatrix} 0 & 0 & 0 \\ * & 1 & * \\ 1 & 1 & 1 \end{bmatrix}, \ L_2^{(8)} = \begin{bmatrix} * & 0 & 0 \\ 1 & 1 & 0 \\ * & 1 & * \end{bmatrix} \dots \qquad (10.42)$$

Figure 10.14 shows the result of thinning with the structuring element $L^{(4)}$, after 5 iterations, and Figure 10.15 shows the homotopic substitute of the skeleton (in both cases, the original is shown on the left).

Figure 10.14 *Sequential thinning using element L after 5 iterations.*

Sequential thinning by structuring element E

Assume that the homotopic substitute of the skeleton by element $L^{(4)}$ has been found. The skeleton is usually jagged due to sharp points on the outline of the object, but it is possible to 'smooth' the skeleton by sequential thinning by structuring element E. Using n iterations, several points (whose number

Figure 10.15 *Homotopic substitute of the skeleton (element L).*

depends on n) from the lines of width one (and isolated points as well) are removed from free ends. If thinning by element E is performed until the image does not change, then only closed contours remain.

The structuring element E is given by

$$E_1^{(4)} = \begin{bmatrix} * & * & * \\ 0 & 1 & 0 \\ * & 0 & * \end{bmatrix}, \quad E_2^{(4)} = \begin{bmatrix} * & 0 & * \\ 0 & 1 & * \\ * & 0 & * \end{bmatrix} \dots \qquad (10.43)$$

$$E_1^{(8)} = \begin{bmatrix} * & 1 & * \\ 0 & 1 & 0 \\ 0 & 0 & 0 \end{bmatrix}, \quad E_2^{(8)} = \begin{bmatrix} 0 & * & * \\ 0 & 1 & 0 \\ 0 & 0 & 0 \end{bmatrix} \dots \qquad (10.44)$$

Figure 10.16 shows sequential thinning (five iterations) by the element $E^{(4)}$ of the skeleton from Figure 10.15. Notice that lines were shortened from their free ends.

Figure 10.16 *5 iterations of sequential thinning by element E.*

Sequential thinning by structuring element M

Sequential thinning by the structuring element M is infrequently used to find the homotopic substitute of the skeleton. The resulting skeleton is too jagged and therefore the structuring element L is more often used for this purpose. The only case when element M behaves better is if the background contains isolated points.

The structuring element M is given by

$$M_1^{(4)} = \begin{bmatrix} * & 0 & * \\ * & 1 & * \\ 1 & 1 & 1 \end{bmatrix} , \quad M_2^{(4)} = \begin{bmatrix} * & 0 & * \\ 1 & 1 & 0 \\ 1 & 1 & * \end{bmatrix} \dots \qquad (10.45)$$

$$M_1^{(8)} = \begin{bmatrix} * & 0 & * \\ 1 & 1 & 1 \\ * & 1 & * \end{bmatrix} , \quad M_1^{(8)} = \begin{bmatrix} * & 0 & 0 \\ 1 & 1 & 0 \\ * & 1 & * \end{bmatrix} \dots \qquad (10.46)$$

Sequential thinning and thickening by element D

Possible applications of the element D are twofold:

- Thinning by an element D replaces all objects without holes by one isolated point. Only the closed contours are unchanged. This operation is sometimes called **homotopic marking**.

- Thickening by the element D^* (see equation (10.38)) creates a pseudo-convex hull of the set X. The prefix pseudo is used because if the homotopic tree should be changed, the process stops and the set X is not convex.

The structuring element D is given by

$$D_1^{(4)} = \begin{bmatrix} * & 0 & * \\ 0 & 1 & 1 \\ * & 0 & * \end{bmatrix} , \quad D_2^{(4)} = \begin{bmatrix} 0 & 0 & * \\ 0 & 1 & 1 \\ * & 1 & 1 \end{bmatrix} \dots \qquad (10.47)$$

$$D_1^{(8)} = \begin{bmatrix} 0 & * & * \\ 0 & 1 & 1 \\ 0 & * & * \end{bmatrix} , \quad D_2^{(8)} = \begin{bmatrix} 0 & 0 & 0 \\ 0 & 1 & * \\ 0 & * & 1 \end{bmatrix} \dots \qquad (10.48)$$

Note that thinning of the set X by the structuring element D is equivalent to thickening of the set X^c by the structuring element D^*.

Sequential thickening by the element C

Sequential thickening by the element C creates the convex hull of the set X. This operation does not preserve homotopy.

The structuring element C is given by

$$C_1^{(4)} = \begin{bmatrix} 1 & 1 & * \\ 1 & 0 & * \\ * & * & * \end{bmatrix} , \quad C_2^{(4)} = \begin{bmatrix} * & 1 & 1 \\ * & 0 & 1 \\ * & * & * \end{bmatrix} \dots \qquad (10.49)$$

$$C_1^{(8)} = \begin{bmatrix} * & 1 & * \\ 1 & 0 & * \\ * & 1 & * \end{bmatrix}, \quad C_2^{(8)} = \begin{bmatrix} * & 1 & * \\ 1 & 0 & * \\ 1 & * & * \end{bmatrix} \ldots \qquad (10.50)$$

10.2.4 Conditional dilation and ultimate erosion

Define the isotropic structural element (called the regular octagon) nQ of size n on the octagonal raster. An elementary regular octagon approximates the smallest isotropic structuring element in the octagonal raster and n expresses its size – note that nQ corresponds to a circle of radius n in a continuous image.

$1Q$ is the elementary regular octagon (9 points in a 3×3 matrix). The regular octagon nQ is obtained by $n-1$ successive dilations of the elementary regular octagon using a structuring element given by an 8-neighbourhood

$$nQ = \underbrace{Q \oplus \ldots \oplus Q}_{n \ times} \qquad (10.51)$$

We can now describe another morphological operation. The **conditional dilation** of the set Y under the condition given by the set X is denoted by[4]

$$Z = Y \oplus nQ; \ X \qquad (10.52)$$

(where the condition is expressed by the semicolon). Conditional dilation is defined by

$$\begin{aligned} Y_0 &= Y \\ Y_i &= (Y_{i-1} \oplus Q) \cap X, \quad \text{for } i = 1, \ldots, n \\ Z &= Y_n \end{aligned} \qquad (10.53)$$

Conditional dilation is used for two purposes:

- We might want to exclude objects in the set of objects (image) X that touch the limits R of the raster (image). These objects are given by the conditional dilation

$$Z = R \oplus nQ; \ X \qquad (10.54)$$

---

[4] We use Serra's notation [Serra 82] for a conditional operation. It may be understood as

conditional dilation	$X \oplus Q; Y = (X \oplus Q) \cap Y$
conditional erosion	$X \ominus Q; Y = (X \ominus Q) \cup Y$
conditional thinning	$X \oslash Q; Y = (X \oslash Q) \cup Y$
conditional thickening	$X \odot Q; Y = (X \odot Q) \cap Y$

- If the holes Y in the image X are to be found (and maybe filled) the following equation can be used

$$Y = (R \oplus nQ ; X^c)^c \qquad (10.55)$$

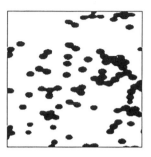

Figure 10.17 *Original latex particles.*

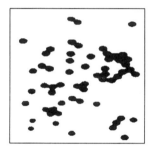

Figure 10.18 *Particles touching the image border are eliminated.*

Another important morphological transformation is called **ultimate erosion**. The ultimate erosion Y of the point set X is given by

$$
\begin{aligned}
X_i &= X \ominus iQ,\ i = 1, 2, \ldots \\
Y_i &= X_i \,|\, (X_{i+1} \oplus Q ; X_i) \\
m &= \max\{i :\ X_i \neq \emptyset\} \\
Y &= \bigcup_{i=1}^{m} Y_i \qquad (10.56)
\end{aligned}
$$

The sets Y_i are often empty for the initial steps of the ultimate erosion; the reason for this is that the set difference is empty if the subtracted set covers the set from which it is subtracted. Later iterations give Y_i that match to the expected points in the centres of objects. The aggregation of these points is then done by set union.

If an image X (or its part) consists of two overlapping convex objects then the result of the ultimate erosion is two disjoint 'centres of objects'. The ultimate erosion is neither a continuous, nor an increasing transformation.

Figure 10.17 shows latex particles under a microscope after thresholding – the aim is to count them. Individual particles have rounded (convex) shapes, but unfortunately some of them touch each other and constitute one object. Methods of mathematical morphology can explore knowledge about particle roundness and separate them.

Figure 10.19 *Ultimate erosion gives the particle centres.*

Particles touching the border of the image (limits of the raster R) are eliminated using conditional dilation as described in equation (10.54). This means that the point set corresponding to the image constitutes the condition X. An image without particles touching the image border is shown in Figure 10.18.

Ultimate erosion Y of the image X, equation (10.56), gives the approximate centres of the rounded particles (see Figure 10.19). Some of them are not individual points due to noise in the image and the distorted shape of the particles.

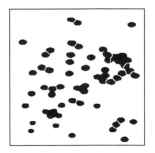

Figure 10.20 *Particles found. Figures 10.17 – 10.20 reproduced courtesy M. Svoboda, Laboratory Imaging Ltd., Praha.*

The last step is the homotopic thickening of particles from the centres found in the last step for which the structuring element D is used; homotopic

thickening ensures that individual particles do not join together. The result
is in Figure 10.20 – notice that not every particle was separated. The reason
for this is that these joined particles did not meet the shape criteria that are
embedded in the structuring element used (in our case 3×3 squares).

References

[Giardina and Dougherty 88] C R Giardina and E R Dougherty. *Morpholog-
        ical Methods in Image and Signal Processing*. Prentice-Hall, Engle-
        wood Cliffs, NJ, 1988.

[Golay 69] M J E Golay. Hexagonal parallel pattern transformation. *IEEE
        Transactions on Computers*, C–18:733–740, 1969.

[Haralick et al. 87] R M Haralick, S R Stenberg, and X Zhuang. Image anal-
        ysis using mathematical morphology. *IEEE Transactions on Pattern
        Analysis and Machine Intelligence*, 9(4):532–550, 1987.

[Maragos and Schafer 87a] P Maragos and R W Schafer. Morphological filters
        – part I: Their set-theoretic analysis and relations to linear shift-
        invariant filters. *IEEE Transactions on Acoustics, Speech and Signal
        Processing*, 35(8):1153–1169, August 1987.

[Maragos and Schafer 87b] P Maragos and R W Schafer. Morphological fil-
        ters – part II: Their relation to median, order-statistic, and stack
        filters. *IEEE Transactions on Acoustics, Speech and Signal Process-
        ing*, 35(8):1170–1184, August 1987.

[Matheron 67] G Matheron. *Elements pour une Theorie del Milieux Poreux
        (in French)*. Masson, Paris, 1967.

[Matheron 75] G Matheron. *Random Sets and Integral Geometry*. John Wiley
        and Sons, New York, 1975.

[Roerdink and Heijmans 88] J B T M Roerdink and H J A M Heijmans.
        Mathematical morphology for structures without translation sym-
        metry. *Signal Processing*, 15(3):271–277, October 1988.

[Serra 82] J Serra. *Image Analysis and Mathematical Morphology*. Academic
        Press, London, 1982.

[Serra 87] J Serra. Morphological optics. *Journal of Microscopy*, 145(1):1–22,
        1987.

11

Linear discrete image transforms

Image processing and analysis based on continuous or discrete image transforms is a classic processing technique. Image transforms are widely used in image filtering, image data compression, image description, etc.; they were actively studied at the end of the Sixties and in the beginning of the Seventies. This research was highly motivated by space flight achievements; first, an efficient method of image data transmission was needed, and second, transmitted images were often received locally or globally corrupted. Both analogue and discrete methods were investigated – analogue optical methods suffered from a lack of suitable high-resolution storage material, and the rapid development of digital computer technology slowed analogue research in the middle of the Seventies. However, much research is now being devoted to optical methods again, especially with new technological achievements in developing high-resolution optical storage materials. The main focus is in possible real-time image processing.

Image transform theory is a well known area characterized by a precise mathematical background and image transforms must be mentioned as a powerful and unified area of image processing. Nevertheless, this chapter is only included to introduce the basic concepts and essential references, because a number of excellent books can be be found. There are many monographs devoted just to two-dimensional image transforms [Andrews 70, Shulman 70, Ahmed and Rao 75, Andrews and Hunt 77, Huang 81, Nussbaumer 82, Dudgeon and Mersereau 84, Yaroslavskii 85, Wolberg 90, Rao and Yip 90], and many image processing books with extensive coverage of image transforms [Hall 79, Rosenfeld and Kak 82, Gonzalez and Wintz 87, Lim 90, Pratt 91], not to mention an endless list of signal processing or purely mathematical references. Only general theory is discussed in this chapter, with an image processing application outline. Familiarity with the one-dimensional Fourier transform, basic operations in the frequency domain, and convolution in the frequency domain, is assumed. All of the mathematical proofs, more complicated mathematical connections, and all implementation aspects are omitted.

11.1 Basic theory

Let an image f be represented as a matrix of integer numbers. An image transform can generally either process the whole image, or some (usually rectangular) subimage. We will assume that the image size is $M \times N$.

$$
\mathbf{f} = \begin{bmatrix} f(0,0) & f(0,1) & \dots & f(0,N-1) \\ & \dots & & \dots \\ f(M-1,0) & f(M-1,1) & \dots & f(M-1,N-1) \end{bmatrix} \quad (11.1)
$$

Transform matrices $\mathbf{P}$ and $\mathbf{Q}$ of dimension $M \times M$ and $N \times N$ respectively are used to transform $\mathbf{f}$ into a matrix $\mathbf{F}$ ($M \times N$ matrix) of the same size

$$
\mathbf{F} = \mathbf{P} \, \mathbf{f} \, \mathbf{Q} \quad (11.2)
$$

which we may write as

$$
F(u,v) = \sum_{m=0}^{M-1} \sum_{n=0}^{N-1} P(u,m) f(m,n) Q(n,v) \quad (11.3)
$$

$$
u = 0, 1, ..., M-1; \quad v = 0, 1, ..., N-1
$$

If $\mathbf{P}$ and $\mathbf{Q}$ are non-singular (i.e. have non-zero determinants), inverse matrices $\mathbf{P}^{-1}$ and $\mathbf{Q}^{-1}$ exist and the inverse transform can be computed as follows

$$
\mathbf{f} = \mathbf{P}^{-1} \mathbf{F} \, \mathbf{Q}^{-1} \quad (11.4)
$$

Let us establish a few terms and formulae. Let $\mathbf{M}^T$ represent the transpose of matrix $\mathbf{M}$;

- $\mathbf{M}$ is **symmetric** if $\mathbf{M} = \mathbf{M}^T$.

- $\mathbf{M}$ is **orthogonal** if $\mathbf{M}^T \mathbf{M} = \mathbf{I}$, where $\mathbf{I}$ is the identity matrix.

- For any symmetric, real, and orthogonal matrix: $\mathbf{M}^{-1} = \mathbf{M}$.

- A complex matrix $\mathbf{C}$ is **Hermitian** if $\mathbf{C}^{*T} = \mathbf{C}$, where $\mathbf{C}^*$ results from $\mathbf{C}$ by taking a complex conjugate of every element.

- A complex matrix $\mathbf{C}$ is **unitary** if $\mathbf{C}^{*T} \mathbf{C} = \mathbf{I}$.

- For any square, complex, Hermitian, and unitary matrix: $\mathbf{C}^{-1} = \mathbf{C}$.

If $\mathbf{P}$ and $\mathbf{Q}$ are both symmetric, real, and orthogonal, then

$$
\mathbf{F} = \mathbf{P} \, \mathbf{f} \, \mathbf{Q}, \qquad \mathbf{f} = \mathbf{P} \, \mathbf{F} \, \mathbf{Q} \quad (11.5)
$$

and the transform is an **orthogonal transform**. If $\mathbf{P}, \mathbf{Q}$ are complex matrices, equation (11.5) still holds provided they are Hermitian and unitary.

11.2 The Fourier transform

The basics of the one-dimensional continuous Fourier transform were briefly discussed in Section 2.1.3. The discrete Fourier transform is analogous to the continuous one and may be efficiently computed using the fast Fourier transform algorithm. The properties of linearity, shift of position, modulation, convolution, multiplication, and correlation are analogous to the continuous case, with the difference of the discrete periodic nature of the image and its transform. Let Φ_{JJ} be a transform matrix of size $J \times J$:

$$\Phi_{JJ}(k,l) = \frac{1}{J}\exp(-i\frac{2\pi}{J}kl) \qquad\qquad k,l = 0,1,...,J-1 \qquad (11.6)$$

The discrete Fourier transform can be defined according to equation (11.2):
$$\mathbf{P} = \Phi_{MM}, \mathbf{Q} = \Phi_{NN}$$

$$\mathbf{F} = \Phi_{MM}\ \mathbf{f}\ \Phi_{NN} \qquad (11.7)$$

and

$$F(u,v) = \frac{1}{MN}\sum_{m=0}^{M-1}\sum_{n=0}^{N-1} f(m,n)\exp[-2\pi i(\frac{mu}{M}+\frac{nv}{N})] \qquad (11.8)$$

$$u = 0,1,...,M-1 \qquad v = 0,1,...,N-1$$

The inverse transform matrix Φ_{JJ}^{-1} is

$$\Phi_{JJ}^{-1}(k,l) = \exp(\frac{2\pi i}{J}kl) \qquad (11.9)$$

and the inverse Fourier transform is given by

$$f(m,n) = \sum_{u=0}^{M-1}\sum_{v=0}^{N-1} F(u,v)\exp[2\pi i(\frac{mu}{M}+\frac{nv}{N})] \qquad (11.10)$$

$$m = 0,1,...,M-1; \qquad n = 0,1,...,N-1$$

The kernel function of the discrete transform (11.8) is

$$\exp[-2\pi i(\frac{mu}{M}+\frac{nv}{N})] \qquad (11.11)$$

Consider how the discrete Fourier transform may be implemented. Equation (11.8) can be modified to

$$F(u,v) = \frac{1}{M}\sum_{m=0}^{M-1}[\frac{1}{N}\sum_{n=0}^{N-1}\exp(\frac{-2\pi inv}{N})f(m,n)]\exp(\frac{-2\pi imu}{M}) \qquad (11.12)$$

$$u = 0,1,...,M-1 \qquad v = 0,1,...,N-1$$

The term in square brackets corresponds to the one-dimensional Fourier transform of the mth line and can be computed using standard fast Fourier transform (FFT) procedures (usually assuming $N = 2^k$). Each line is substituted with its Fourier transform, and the one-dimensional discrete Fourier transform of each column is computed. Algorithms for FFT computation can be found in [Nussbaumer 82, Pavlidis 82, Gonzalez and Wintz 87].

Periodicity is an important property of the discrete Fourier transform. We have defined the transform as a matrix with elements $F(u, v)$ for $u = 0, 1, ..., M - 1$; $v = 0, 1, ..., N - 1$. In arrays where other values of u, v are allowed, a periodic transform F (equation 11.8) is derived and a periodic image f defined

$$
\begin{array}{ll}
F(u, -v) = F(u, N - v), & f(-m, n) = f(M - m, n) \\
F(-u, v) = F(M - u, v), & f(m, -n) = f(m, N - n)
\end{array}
\tag{11.13}
$$

and

$$
F(aM + u, bN + v) = F(u, v), \quad f(aM + m, bN + n) = f(m, n) \tag{11.14}
$$

where a and b are integers.

In image processing, image Fourier spectra play an important role. Considering equation (11.10), image values $f(m, n)$ can be seen as a linear combination of periodic patterns $\exp[2\pi i((mu/M) + (nv/N))]$ and $F(u, v)$ may be considered a weighting function. The Fourier transform of a real function is a complex function, that is

$$
F(u, v) = R(u, v) + iI(u, v) \tag{11.15}
$$

where $R(u, v)$ and $I(u, v)$ are, respectively, the real and imaginary components of $F(u, v)$. The magnitude function $|F(u, v)|$ is called the **frequency spectrum** of image $f(m, n)$; in addition, the **phase spectrum** $\phi(u, v)$ and **power spectrum** $P(u, v)$ are used. The frequency spectrum is defined by

$$
|F(u, v)| = \sqrt{R^2(u, v) + I^2(u, v)} \tag{11.16}
$$

the phase spectrum by

$$
\phi(u, v) = \tan^{-1}\left[\frac{I(u, v)}{R(u, v)}\right] \tag{11.17}
$$

(note that care must be taken over interpretation of the signs of these quantities since *tan* is π periodic, and ϕ ranges from 0 to 2π) and the power spectrum (also called **spectral density**) as

$$
P(u, v) = |F(u, v)|^2 = R^2(u, v) + I^2(u, v) \tag{11.18}
$$

An example of an image and its spectrum is given in Figure 11.1.

 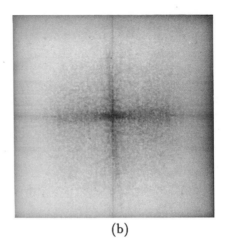

(a)   (b)

Figure 11.1 *Fourier spectrum: (a) Image, (b) frequency spectrum as an intensity function.*

The Fourier transform is of great use in the calculation of image convolutions (see Sections 2.1.2, 4.3). If a convolution of two (periodic) images f and h of the same size $M \times N$ is computed, a (periodic) image g results

$$g(a, b) = \frac{1}{MN} \sum_{m=0}^{M-1} \sum_{n=0}^{N-1} f(m, n) h(a - m, b - n) \qquad (11.19)$$

Note that h is periodic, or the index calculation in $h(a - m, b - r)$ must be done modulo M, N respectively. The **convolution theorem** states that f, g and h, and their transforms F, G and H, are related by the equation

$$G(u, v) = F(u, v) H(u, v) \qquad (11.20)$$

that is, element-by-element multiplication. Thus we may write

$$g(a, b) = \sum_{u=0}^{M-1} \sum_{v=0}^{N-1} F(u, v) H(u, v) \exp[2\pi i (\frac{au}{M} + \frac{bv}{N})] \qquad (11.21)$$

Use of this relationship can reduce the computational load of calculating convolutions very significantly.

11.3 Hadamard transforms

If in equation (11.2) matrices **P** and **Q** are **Hadamard** matrices, then **F** is a Hadamard transform of an image **f**. As shown in the previous section, the Fourier transform may be represented using a set of orthogonal sinusoidal waveforms; the coefficients of Fourier representation are called frequency components and the waveforms are ordered by frequency. If the set of orthogonal functions used to represent an orthogonal transform is chosen to consist of square waves (namely Walsh functions), analogous spectral analysis may be performed with a simple computation. The Walsh functions are ordered by the number of their zero crossings and the coefficients are called **sequency components** [Ahmed and Rao 75]. The Walsh functions are real (not complex) and only take on the values ±1. A Hadamard matrix $\mathbf{H}_{JJ}$ is a symmetric matrix $J \times J$, with elements all ±1; the Hadamard matrix of the second order $\mathbf{H}_{22}$ is

$$\mathbf{H}_{22} = \begin{vmatrix} 1 & 1 \\ 1 & -1 \end{vmatrix} \tag{11.22}$$

Any Hadamard matrix of order 2^k can be written as

$$\mathbf{H}_{2J2J} = \begin{vmatrix} \mathbf{H}_{JJ} & \mathbf{H}_{JJ} \\ \mathbf{H}_{JJ} & -\mathbf{H}_{JJ} \end{vmatrix} \tag{11.23}$$

Hadamard matrices of orders other than 2^k exist but they are not widely used in image processing. Inverse Hadamard matrices can be easily computed

$$\mathbf{H}_{JJ}^{-1} = \frac{1}{J}\mathbf{H}_{JJ} \tag{11.24}$$

and the Hadamard transform can therefore be represented by

$$\mathbf{F} = \mathbf{H}_{MM}\mathbf{f}\ \mathbf{H}_{NN}, \quad \mathbf{f} = \frac{1}{MN}\mathbf{H}_{MM}\mathbf{F}\ \mathbf{H}_{NN} \tag{11.25}$$

It can be seen that only matrix multiplication is necessary to compute a Hadamard transform, and further, only additions are computed during the matrix multiplication. The Hadamard transform is sometimes called a Walsh-Hadamard transform, since the base of the transform consists of Walsh functions. This transform has been found useful in image coding and pattern recognition [Hall 79].

11.4 Discrete cosine transform

There are four definitions of the discrete cosine transform, sometimes denoted DCT-I, DCT-II, DCT-III, and DCT-IV [Rao and Yip 90]. The most commonly used discrete cosine transform in image processing and compression is DCT-II – it can be defined using equation (11.2) and considering a set of basis vectors that are sampled cosine functions. Assuming a square $N \times N$ image, the discrete transform matrix (equation 11.2) can be expressed as [Hall 79]

$$C_{NN}(k,l) \ \begin{aligned} &= \frac{1}{\sqrt{N}} && \text{for } l = 0 \\ &= (\tfrac{2}{N})^{1/2}\cos[\tfrac{(2k+1)l\pi}{2N}] && \text{all other } k,l \end{aligned} \tag{11.26}$$

and

$$\mathbf{F} = \mathbf{C}_{NN} \, \mathbf{f} \, \mathbf{C}_{NN}^T, \qquad\qquad \mathbf{f} = \mathbf{C}_{NN}^T \mathbf{F} \, \mathbf{C}_{NN} \qquad (11.27)$$

In the two-dimensional case, the formula for a normalized version of the discrete cosine transform (forward cosine transform DCT-II) may be written [Rao and Yip 90]

$$F(u,v) = \frac{2c(u)c(v)}{N} \sum_{m=0}^{N-1} \sum_{n=0}^{N-1} f(m,n) \cos\left(\frac{2m+1}{2N}u\pi\right) \cos\left(\frac{2n+1}{2N}v\pi\right)$$

$$(11.28)$$

$$u = 0, 1, ..., N-1 \qquad v = 0, 1, ..., N-1$$

where

$$c(k) \begin{array}{ll} = \frac{1}{\sqrt{2}} & \text{for} \quad k = 0 \\ = 1 & \text{otherwise} \end{array}$$

and the inverse cosine transform is

$$f(m,n) = \frac{2}{N} \sum_{u=0}^{N-1} \sum_{v=0}^{N-1} c(u)c(v)F(u,v) \cos\left(\frac{2m+1}{2N}u\pi\right) \cos\left(\frac{2n+1}{2N}v\pi\right)$$

$$(11.29)$$

$$m = 0, 1, ..., N-1 \qquad n = 0, 1, ..., N-1$$

Note that the discrete cosine transform computation can be based on the Fourier transform, all N coefficients of the discrete cosine transform may be computed using a $2N$-point fast Fourier transform [Ahmed and Rao 75, Rosenfeld and Kak 82, Rao and Yip 90].

11.5 Other discrete image transforms

Many other discrete image transforms exist. **Paley** and **Walsh** transforms are both very similar to the Hadamard transform, using transformation matrices consisting of ±1 elements only. Details can be found in [Gonzalez and Wintz 87].

The **Haar** transform is based on non-symmetric Haar matrices whose elements are either 1, –1, or 0, multiplied by powers of $\sqrt{2}$, and may also be computed in an efficient way. The **Hadamard-Haar** transform results from a combination of the Haar and Hadamard transforms, and a modified Hadamard-Haar transform is similar. The **Slant** transform and its modification the **Slant-Haar** transform represents another transform containing sawtooth waveforms or **slant** basic vectors; a fast computational algorithm is also available. The **discrete sine transform** is very similar to the discrete cosine transform. All transforms mentioned here are discussed in detail in [Hall 79, Dougherty and Giardina 87, Gonzalez and Wintz 87, Pratt 91], where references for computational algorithms can also be found.

The significance of image reconstruction from projections can be seen in computer tomography (CT), magnetic resonance imaging (MRI), positron emission tomography (PET), astronomy, holography, etc., where image formation is based on the **Radon** transform [Dougherty and Giardina 87, Sanz et al. 88, Kak and Slaney 88, Jain 89]. In image reconstruction, projections are acquired by sensors and the two-dimensional image must be reconstructed; therefore, the inverse Radon transform is of particular interest. The main Radon inverse transform techniques are based on Fourier transforms, convolution, or algebraic formulations. Note that the Hough transform (see Section 5.2.6) has been shown to be an adaptation of the more general Radon transform.

The **Karhunen-Loeve** transform plays a slightly different role. Its transform matrices consist of eigenvectors of the correlation matrix of the original image, or of a class of original images. The power of the Karhunen-Loeve transform is in the search for non-correlated transform coefficients, which makes it very useful in data compression (see Chapter 12). The Karhunen-Loeve transform is used to order features according to their information content in statistical recognition methods (see Chapter 13). A detailed description of the Karhunen-Loeve transform can be found in [Andrews 70, Rosenfeld and Kak 82].

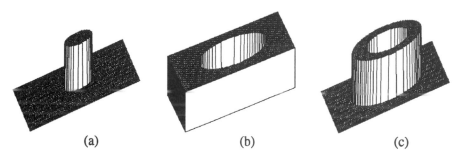

Figure 11.2 *Frequency filters displayed in 3D: (a) Low-pass filter, (b) high-pass filter, (c) band-pass filter.*

11.6 Applications of discrete image transforms

Section 11.2 noted that the Fourier transform makes convolution of two images in the frequency domain very easy. In Chapter 4 many filters used in image pre-processing were presented – the convolution masks in most cases were used for image filtering or image gradient computation. It is natural to think about processing these (and many other) convolutions in the frequency domain. Such operations are usually called spatial filtering.

Assume that f is an input image, and F its Fourier transform. A convolution filter h can be represented by its Fourier transform H; h may be called the unit pulse response of the filter and H the frequency transfer function, and either of the representations h or H can be used to describe the filter. The Fourier transform of the filter output after an image f has been convolved with the filter h can be computed in the frequency domain (equations 11.19–11.21)

$$G(u,v) = F(u,v)H(u,v) \qquad (11.30)$$

Note that equation (11.30) represents a term-by-term multiplication, not a matrix multiplication. The filtered image g can be obtained by applying the inverse Fourier transform to **G** – equation 11.4.

Some basic examples of spatial filtering are linear **low-pass** and **high-pass** frequency filters. A low-pass filter is defined by a frequency transfer function $H(u,v)$ with small values at points (u,v) located far from the co-ordinate origin in the frequency domain (that is, small transfer values for high spatial frequencies) and large values at points close to the frequency space co-ordinate origin (large transfer values for low spatial frequencies) – see Figure 11.2a. In other words, this filter highlights low spatial frequencies and suppresses high spatial frequencies. Such a filter has behaviour similar to smoothing by standard averaging – it blurs sharp edges. A high-pass filter, on the other hand, is defined by small transfer function values located around the frequency co-ordinate system origin, and larger values outside this area – larger transfer coefficients for higher frequencies (Figure 11.2b). **Band-pass** filters, which select frequencies in a certain range for enhancement, can be constructed in a similar way, and also filters with directional response, etc. (Figure 11.2c).

The most common image enhancement problems include noise suppression, edge enhancement, and structured noise removal. Noise represents a high-frequency image component, and to suppress it, the magnitudes of image frequencies of the noise must be decreased. This can be achieved by applying a low-pass filter as shown in Figure 11.3, which demonstrates the principles of frequency filtering on Fourier image spectra; the original image spectrum is multiplied by the filter spectrum and a low-frequency image spectrum results. Unfortunately, as a result of noise suppression, all high-frequency phenomena are suppressed including high frequencies that are not related to noise (sharp edges, lines, etc.). Low-pass filtering results in a blurred image.

Again, edges represent a high-frequency image phenomenon. Therefore, to enhance the edges, low-frequency components of image spectrum must be suppressed and to achieve this, a high-frequency filter must be applied.

To remove structured noise, the filter design must include a priori knowledge about the noise properties. This knowledge may be acquired either from the image data, or from the corrupted image Fourier spectrum where the structured noise usually causes notable peaks.

(a)   (b)

(c)   (d)

Figure 11.3 *Low-pass frequency domain filtering; for the original image and its spectrum see Figure 11.1: (a) Spectrum of a low-pass filtered image, all higher frequencies were filtered out, (b) image resulting from the inverse Fourier transform applied to spectrum a, (c) spectrum of a low-pass filtered image, only very high frequencies were filtered out, (d) inverse Fourier transform applied to spectrum c.*

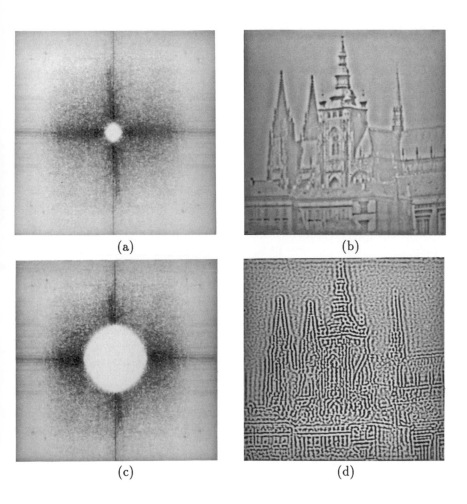

Figure 11.4 *High-pass frequency domain filtering: (a) Spectrum of a high-pass filtered image, only very low frequencies were filtered out, (b) image resulting from the inverse Fourier transform applied to spectrum a, (c) spectrum of a high-pass filtered image, all lower frequencies were filtered out, (d) inverse Fourier transform applied to spectrum c.*

Some examples of frequency domain image filtering are shown in Figures 11.3 – 11.6. The original image and its frequency spectrum are given in Figure 11.1. Figure 11.4 shows results after application of a high-pass filter followed by an inverse Fourier transform. It can be seen that edges represent high-frequency phenomena in the image. Results of band-pass filtering can be seen in Figure 11.5. Figure 11.6 gives an even more powerful example of

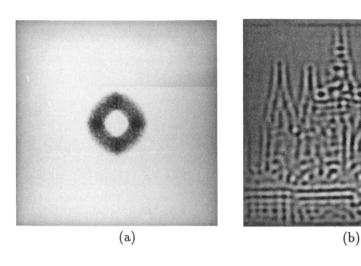

(a)   (b)

Figure 11.5 *Band-pass frequency domain filtering: (a) Spectrum of a band-pass filtered image, low and high frequencies were filtered out, (b) image resulting from the inverse Fourier transform applied to spectrum a.*

frequency filtering – removal of periodic noise that was present in the image. The vertical periodic noise lines in the original image are transformed into frequency spectrum peaks after the transform. To remove these frequencies from an image, a filter was designed which suppresses the periodic noise in the image, which are visible as white circular areas of the spectrum. Discrete image transforms are computationally very expensive, but note that the Fourier transform can be obtained in real time using optical processing methods (for example, a convex lens may produce the Fourier transform) [Shulman 70, Francon 79, Stark 82].

The most substantial progress in discrete image transforms was probably motivated by image transmission and image data storage requirements. The main goal was to decrease the amount of data necessary for image representation and to decrease the amount of transferred or stored data, and the next chapter is devoted to this application area.

Another large application area can be found in image description, especially in texture description and recognition (see Section 13.1.1). Reconstruction of images corrupted by camera motion, defocusing, etc. in the image acquisition stage can also be achieved using discrete image transforms [Andrews and Hunt 77, Bates and McDonnell 86].

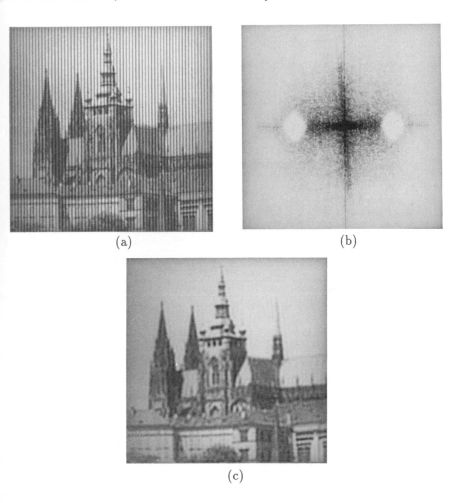

(a)

(b)

(c)

Figure 11.6 *Periodic noise removal: (a) Noisy image, (b) image spectrum used for image reconstruction, note that the areas of frequencies corresponding with periodic vertical lines are filtered out, (c) filtered image.*

References

[Ahmed and Rao 75] N Ahmed and K R Rao. *Orthogonal Transforms for Digital Signal Processing.* Springer Verlag, Berlin, 1975.

[Andrews 70] H C Andrews. *Computer Techniques in Image Processing.* Academic Press, New York, 1970.

[Andrews and Hunt 77] H C Andrews and B R Hunt. *Digital Image Restoration.* Prentice-Hall, Englewood Cliffs, NJ, 1977.

[Bates and McDonnell 86] R H T Bates and M J McDonnell. *Image Restoration and Reconstruction.* Clarendon Press, Oxford, England, 1986.

[Dougherty and Giardina 87] E R Dougherty and C R Giardina. *Image Processing - Continuous to Discrete, Vol.1.* Prentice-Hall, Englewood Cliffs, NJ, 1987.

[Dudgeon and Mersereau 84] D F Dudgeon and R M Mersereau. *Multidimensional Digital Signal Processing.* Prentice-Hall, Englewood Cliffs, NJ, 1984.

[Francon 79] M Francon. *Optical Image Formation and Processing.* Academic Press, New York, 1979.

[Gonzalez and Wintz 87] R C Gonzalez and P Wintz. *Digital Image Processing.* Addison-Wesley, Reading, Ma, 2nd edition, 1987.

[Hall 79] E L Hall. *Computer Image Processing and Recognition.* Academic Press, San Diego-New York, 1979.

[Huang 81] T S Huang. *Two-Dimensional Digital Signal Processing II: Transform and Median Filters.* Springer Verlag, Berlin-New York, 1981.

[Jain 89] A K Jain. *Fundamentals of Digital Image Processing.* Prentice-Hall, Englewood Cliffs, NJ, 1989.

[Kak and Slaney 88] A.C. Kak and M. Slaney. *Principles of Computerized Tomographic Imaging.* IEEE, Piscataway, NJ, 1988.

[Lim 90] J S Lim. *Two-Dimensional Signal and Image Processing.* Prentice-Hall, Englewood Cliffs, NJ, 1990.

[Nussbaumer 82] H J Nussbaumer. *Fast Fourier Transform and Convolution Algorithms.* Springer Verlag, Berlin, 2nd edition, 1982.

[Pavlidis 82] T Pavlidis. *Algorithms for Graphics and Image Processing.* Computer Science Press, New York, 1982.

[Pratt 91] W K Pratt. *Digital Image Processing.* John Wiley and Sons, New York, 2nd edition, 1991.

[Rao and Yip 90] K R Rao and P Yip. *Discrete Cosine Transform, Algorithms, Advantages, Applications.* Academic Press, Boston, Ma, 1990.

[Rosenfeld and Kak 82] A Rosenfeld and A C Kak. *Digital Picture Processing.* Academic Press, New York, 2nd edition, 1982.

[Sanz et al. 88] J L C Sanz, E B Hinkle, and A K Jain. *Radon and Projection Transform-Based Computer Vision.* Springer Verlag, Berlin-New York, 1988.

[Shulman 70] A R Shulman. *Optical Data Processing.* John Wiley and Sons, New York, 1970.

[Stark 82] H Stark. *Applications of Optical Fourier Transforms.* Academic Press, New York, 1982.

[Wolberg 90] G Wolberg. *Digital Image Warping.* IEEE, Los Alamitos, Ca, 1990.

[Yaroslavskii 85] L P Yaroslavskii. *Digital Picture Processing: An Introduction.* Springer Verlag, Berlin-New York, 1985.

12

Image data compression

Image processing is often very difficult due to the large amounts of data used to represent an image. Technology permits ever-increasing image resolution (spatially and in grey levels), and increasing numbers of spectral bands, and there is a consequent need to limit the resulting data volume. Consider an example from the remote sensing domain where image data compression is a very serious problem. A Landsat D satellite broadcasts 85×10^6 bits of data every second and a typical image from one pass consists of 6100×6100 pixels in 7 spectral bands – in other words 260 megabytes of image data. A Japanese Advanced Earth Observing Satellite (ADEOS) will be launched in 1994 with the capability of observing the Earth's surface with a spatial resolution of 8 metres for the polychromatic band and 16 metres for the multispectral bands. The transmitted data rate is expected to be 120 Mbps [Arai 90]. Thus the amount of storage media needed for archiving of such remotely sensed data is enormous. One possible way how to decrease the necessary amount of storage is to work with compressed image data.

We have seen that segmentation techniques have the side effect of image compression; by removing all areas and features that are not of interest, and leaving only boundaries or region descriptors, the reduction in data quantity is considerable. However, from this sort of representation no image reconstruction to the original, uncompressed, image (or only a very limited reconstruction) is possible. Conversely, image compression algorithms aim to remove redundancy present in data in a way which makes image reconstruction possible; this is sometimes called information preserving compression. Here, compression is the main goal of the algorithm – we aim to represent an image using a lower number of bits per pixel, without losing the ability to reconstruct the image. It is necessary to find statistical properties of the image to design an appropriate compression transformation of the image; the more correlated the image data are, the more data items can be removed. In this chapter, we will discuss this group of methods – the methods which do not change image entropy and do not change image information content. More detailed surveys of image compression techniques may be found in [Rosenfeld and Kak 82, Clarke 85, Lovewell and Basart 88, Netravali 88, Jain 89, Rabbani 91].

A general algorithm for data compression and image reconstruction is

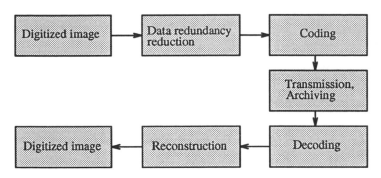

Figure 12.1 *Data compression and image reconstruction.*

shown in a block diagram in Figure 12.1. The first step removes information redundancy caused by high correlation of image data – transform compressions, predictive compressions, and hybrid approaches are used. The second step is coding of transformed data using a code of fixed or variable length. An advantage of variable length codes is the possibility of coding more frequent data by shorter codes and therefore increasing compression efficiency, while an advantage of fixed length coding is a standard codeword length that offers easy handling. Compressed data are decoded after transmission or archiving and reconstructed. Note that no non-redundant image data may be lost in the data compression process, otherwise error-free reconstruction is impossible.

Data compression methods can be divided into two principal groups: **information preserving** compressions permit error free data reconstruction, while compression methods **with loss of information** do not preserve the information completely. In image processing, a faithful reconstruction is often not necessary in practice and then the requirements are weaker – the image data compression must not cause significant changes in an image. Data compression success is usually measured in the reconstructed image by the mean quadratic error, signal to noise ratio etc.

Image data compression design consists of two parts. Image data properties must be determined first; grey level histogram, image entropy, various correlation functions, etc. often serve this purpose. The second part yields an appropriate compression technique design with respect to measured image properties.

Data compression methods with loss of information are typical in image processing and therefore this group of methods is described in some detail. Although lossy compression techniques can give substantial image compression with very good quality reconstruction, there are considerations that may prohibit their use. For example, diagnosis in medical imaging is often based on visual image inspection, and no loss of information can be tolerated and information preserving techniques must be applied. Information preserving compression methods are mentioned briefly at the end of the chapter.

12.1 Image data properties

Information content of an image is an important image property of which
entropy is a measure. If an image has G grey levels, and the probability
of grey level k is $P(k)$ (see Section 2.1.4), then entropy H_e, not considering
correlation of grey levels, is defined as

$$H_e = - \sum_{k=0}^{G-1} P(k) \log_2(P(k)) \tag{12.1}$$

Information **redundancy** r is defined as

$$r = b - H_e \tag{12.2}$$

where b is the smallest number of bits with which the image quantization levels
can be represented. This definition of image information redundancy can be
evaluated only if a good estimate of entropy is available, which is usually not
so because the necessary statistical properties of the image are not known.
Image data entropy can however be estimated from a grey level histogram
[Moik 80, Pratt 91]. Let $h(k)$ be the frequency of grey level k in an image f,
$0 \leq k < 2^{b-1}$, and let the image size be $M \times N$. The probability of occurrence
of grey level k can be estimated as

$$\tilde{P}(k) = \frac{h(k)}{MN} \tag{12.3}$$

and the entropy can be estimated as

$$\tilde{H}_e = - \sum_{k=0}^{2^{b-1}-1} \tilde{P}(k) \log_2(\tilde{P}(k)) \tag{12.4}$$

The information redundancy estimate is $\tilde{r} = b - \tilde{H}_e$. The definition of the
compression ratio K is then

$$K = \frac{b}{\tilde{H}_e} \tag{12.5}$$

Note that a grey level histogram gives an inaccurate estimate of entropy due
to grey level correlation. A more accurate estimate can be obtained from a
histogram of the first grey level differences.

Theoretical limits of possible image compression can be found using the
given formulae. For example, the entropy of satellite remote sensing data may
be $\tilde{H}_e \in [4,5]$, where image data are quantized into 256 grey levels, or 8 bits
per pixel. We can easily compute the information redundancy as $\tilde{r} \in [3,4]$ bits.
This implies that these data can be represented by an average data volume
of 4 to 5 bits per pixel with no loss of information, and the compression ratio
would be $K \in [1.6, 2]$.

12.2 Discrete image transforms in image data compression

Image data representation by coefficients of discrete image transforms (see Chapter 11) is the basic idea of this approach. The transform coefficients are ordered according to their importance, i.e. according to their contribution to the image information contents, and the less important (low contribution) coefficients omitted. Coefficient importance can be judged, for instance, in correspondence to spatial or grey level visualization abilities of the display; image correlation can then be avoided and data compression may result.

To remove correlated image data, the **Karhunen-Loeve** transform is the most important. This transform builds a set of non-correlated variables with decreasing variance. The variance of a variable is a measure of its information content; therefore, a compression strategy is based on considering only transform variables with high variance, thus representing an image by only the first k coefficients of the transform. More details about the Karhunen-Loeve transform can be found in [Rosenfeld and Kak 82, Savoji and Burge 85, Netravali 88, Jain 89, Pratt 91]. The Karhunen-Loeve transform is computationally expensive with a two-dimensional transform of an $M \times N$ image having computational complexity $\mathcal{O}(M^2 N^2)$. It is the only transform that guarantees non-correlated compressed data, and the resulting data compression is optimal in the statistical sense. This makes the transform basis vectors image-dependent which also makes this transform difficult to apply for routine image compression. Therefore, the Karhunen-Loeve transform is mainly used as a benchmark to evaluate other transforms. For example, one reason for the popularity of the discrete cosine transform DCT-II is that its performance approaches the Karhunen-Loeve transform better than others.

Other discrete image transforms discussed in the previous chapter are computationally less demanding – fast computation algorithms of these transforms have computational complexity $\mathcal{O}(MN \log_2(MN))$. Cosine, Fourier, Hadamard, Walsh, or binary transforms are all suitable for image data compression. If an image is compressed using discrete transforms, it is usually divided into subimages of 8×8 or 16×16 pixels, and then each subimage is transformed and processed separately. The same is true for image reconstruction, with each subimage being reconstructed and placed into the appropriate image position [Anderson and Huang 71, Wintz 72]. This image segmentation into a grid of subimages does not consider any possible data redundancy caused by subimage correlation even if this correlation is the most serious source of redundancy. **Recursive block** coding [Farelle 90] is an important novel approach to reducing interblock redundancy and tiling effects (blockiness). The most popular image transform used for image compression seems to be the discrete cosine transform with many modifications [Chen and Bovik 89, Azadegan 90, Chitprasert and Rao 90] and variations of wavelet transforms [Ebrahimi et al. 90, Zettler et al. 90].

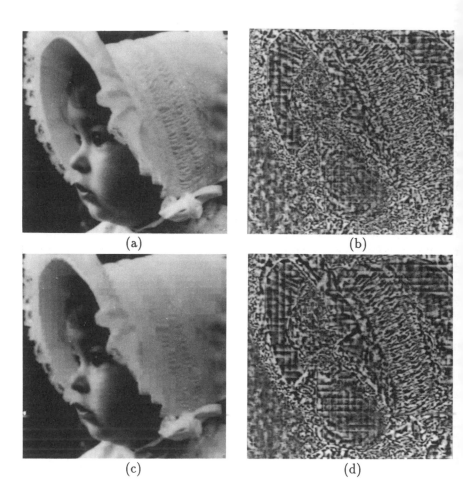

(a)   (b)

(c)   (d)

Figure 12.2 *Discrete cosine image compression: (a) Reconstructed image, compression ratio $K = 4.2$, (b) difference image – differences between pixel values in the original and the reconstructed image ($K = 4.2$); the maximum difference is 78 grey levels (image is histogram equalized for visualization purposes), (c) reconstructed image, compression ratio $K = 5.6$, (d) difference image – differences between pixel values in the original and the reconstructed image ($K = 5.6$); the maximum difference is 125 grey levels (image is histogram equalized for visualization purposes). Courtesy A. Kruger, University of Iowa.*

Image compression possibilities are shown in Figure 12.2. The discrete cosine transform DCT-II applied here provides good compression and low computational demands, the compression ratio in the presented images being $K = 4.2$ and $K = 5.6$. Note that square blocks resulting from DCT compression and reconstruction decrease the image quality for larger compression ratios.

12.3 Predictive compression methods

Predictive compressions use image information redundancy (correlation of data) to construct an estimate $\tilde{f}(i,j)$ of the grey level value of an image element (i,j) from values of grey levels in the neighbourhood of (i,j). In image parts where data are not correlated, the estimate $\tilde{f}$ will not match the original value. The differences between estimates and reality, which may be expected to be relatively small in absolute terms, are coded and transmitted (stored) together with prediction model parameters – the whole set now represents compressed image data. Image reconstruction in location (i,j) results from a computed estimate $\tilde{f}(i,j)$ and the stored difference $d(i,j)$

$$d(i,j) = \tilde{f}(i,j) - f(i,j) \tag{12.6}$$

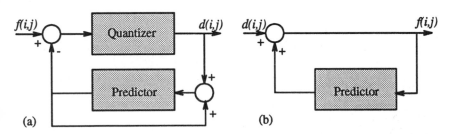

(a)   (b)

Figure 12.3 *Differential pulse code modulation: (a) Compression, (b) reconstruction.*

This method is called Differential Pulse Code Modulation (DPCM) – its block diagram is presented in Figure 12.3. Experiments show that a linear predictor of the third order is sufficient for estimation in a wide variety of images [Habibi 71]. If the image is processed line by line, the estimate $\tilde{f}$ can be computed as

$$\tilde{f}(i,j) = a_1 f(i,j-1) + a_2 f(i-1,j-1) + a_3 f(i-1,j) \tag{12.7}$$

where a_1, a_2, a_3 are image prediction model parameters. These parameters are set to minimize the mean quadratic estimation error e,

$$e = \mathcal{E}([\tilde{f}(i,j) - f(i,j)]^2) \tag{12.8}$$

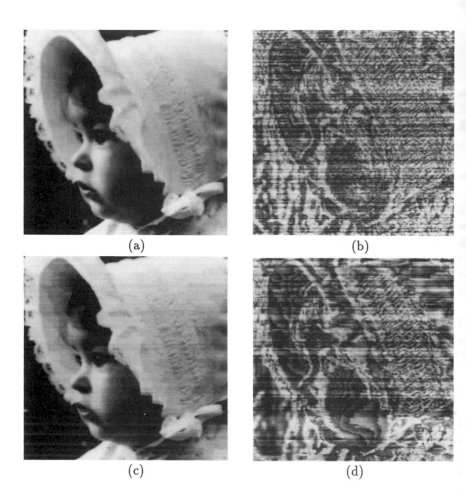

Figure 12.4 *Predictive compression: (a) Reconstructed image, compression ratio K = 3.8, (b) difference image – differences between pixel values in the original and the reconstructed image (K = 3.8); the maximum difference is 6 grey levels (image is histogram equalized for visualization purposes), (c) reconstructed image, compression ratio K = 6.2, (d) difference image – differences between pixel values in the original and the reconstructed image (K = 6.2); the maximum difference is 140 grey levels (image is histogram equalized for visualization purposes). Courtesy A. Kruger, University of Iowa.*

and the solution, assuming f is a stationary random process with a zero mean, using a predictor of the third order, is

$$a_1 R(0,0) + a_2 R(0,1) + a_3 R(1,1) = R(1,0)$$
$$a_1 R(0,1) + a_2 R(0,0) + a_3 R(1,0) = R(1,1)$$
$$a_1 R(1,1) + a_2 R(1,0) + a_3 R(0,0) = R(0,1) \qquad (12.9)$$

where $R(m,n)$ is the autocorrelation function of the random process f (see Chapter 2). The image data autocorrelation function is usually of exponential form and the variance of differences $d(i,j)$ is usually smaller than the variance of the original values $f(i,j)$, since the differences $d(i,j)$ are not correlated. The (probable) relatively small magnitude of the differences $d(i,j)$ makes data compression possible.

Predictive compression algorithms are described in detail in [Rosenfeld and Kak 82, Netravali 88]. A predictive method of the second order with variable code length coding of the differences $d(i,j)$ was used to obtain the compressed images shown in Figure 12.4; data compression ratios $K = 3.8$ and $K = 6.2$ were achieved. Note that horizontal lines and false contours resulting from the predictive compression and reconstruction decrease the image quality for larger compression ratios.

Many modifications of predictive compression methods can be found in the literature, some of them combining predictive compression with other coding schemes [Guha et al. 88, Daut and Zhao 90, Gonzalez et al. 90, Zailu and Taxiao 90].

12.4   Vector quantization

Dividing an image into small blocks and representing these blocks as vectors is another option [Gray 84, Chang et al. 88, Netravali 88, Gersho and Gray 92]. The basic idea for this approach comes from information theory (Shannon's rate-distortion theory), which states that a better compression performance can always be achieved by coding vectors instead of scalars. Input data vectors are coded using unique codewords from a codeword dictionary, and instead of vectors, the vector codes are stored or transmitted. The codeword choice is based on the best similarity between the image block represented by a coded vector and the image blocks represented by codewords from the dictionary. The code dictionary (code book) is transmitted together with the coded data. The advantage of vector quantization is a simple receiver structure consisting of a look-up table, but a disadvantage is a complex coder. The coder complexity is not caused directly by the vector quantization principle; the method can be implemented in a reasonably simple way, however the coding would be very slow. To increase the processing speed, special data structures (K-D trees) and other tricks are needed which increases the coder complexity. Further, the necessary statistical properties of images are usually not available. Therefore, the compression parameters must be based on an image training set and the appropriate code book may vary from image to image. As a result, images with statistical properties dissimilar from images in the training set may not be well represented by the code vectors in the look-up table. Furthermore, edge degradation may be more severe than in other techniques. To decrease the coder complexity, the coding process may be divided into several levels, two being typical. The coding process is hierarchical using two or more code books according to the number of coding levels.

A modification that allows blocks of variable size is described in [Boxerman and Lee 90] where a segmentation algorithm is responsible for detecting appropriate image blocks. The block vector quantization approach may also be applied to compression of image sequences. Identifying and processing only blocks of the image that change noticeably between consecutive frames using vector quantization and DPCM is described in [Thyagarajan and Sanchez 89]. Hybrid DPCM combined with vector quantization of coloured prediction errors is presented in [De Lameillieure and Bruyland 90].

12.5 Pyramid compression methods

Multiresolution pyramids have been mentioned many times throughout the book and may also be used for efficient image compression. **Run length** codes were introduced in Section 3.2.2, Figure 3.2; run length coding identifies long runs of the same value word (or byte), and stores them as this value together with a word count. If the file (or image) is characterized by such long runs (or areas of equal intensity) this will significantly reduce storage requirements. A similar approach may be applied to image pyramids. Recently, it was shown that a substantial reduction in bit volume can be obtained by merely representing a source as a pyramid [Rao and Pearlman 91], and even more significant reduction can be achieved for images with large areas of the same grey level if a quadtree coding scheme is applied (see Section 3.3.2). An example is given in Figure 12.5, where the principle of quadtree image compression is presented. Large image areas of the same grey level can be represented in higher level quadtree nodes without the necessity of including lower level nodes in the image representation [White 87]. Clearly, the compression ratio achieved is image dependent and, for instance, a fine checkerboard image will not be represented efficiently using quadtrees. Modifications of the basic method exist, some of them successfully applied to motion image compression [Strobach 90] or incorporating hybrid schemes [Park and Lee 91].

Nevertheless, there may be an even more important aspect connected with this compression approach – the feasibility of progressive image transmission and the idea of **smart** compression.

Progressive image transmission is based on the fact that transmitting all image data may not be necessary under some circumstances. Imagine a

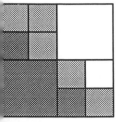 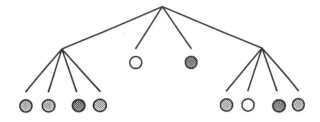

Figure 12.5 *Principle of quadtree image compression; original image and the corresponding quadtree.*

situation in which an operator is searching an image database looking for a particular image. If the transmission is based on a raster-scanning order, all the data must be transmitted to view the whole image but often it is not necessary to have the highest possible image quality to find the image for which the operator is looking. Images do not have to be displayed with the highest available resolution, and lower resolution may be sufficient to reject an image and to begin displaying another one. Therefore, in progressive transmission, the images are represented in a pyramid structure, the higher pyramid levels (lower resolution) being transmitted first. The number of pixels representing a lower resolution image is substantially smaller and thus the user can decide from lower resolution images whether further image refinement is needed. A standard M-pyramid (mean or matrix pyramid) consists of about 1/3 more nodes than the number of image pixels. Several pyramid encoding schemes were designed to decrease the necessary number of nodes in pyramid representation; reduced sum pyramids, difference pyramids and reduced difference pyramids [Wang and Goldberg 89, Wang and Goldberg 90]. The reduced difference pyramid has the number of nodes exactly equal to the number of image pixels and can be used for a lossless progressive image transmission with some degree of compression. It is shown in [Wang and Goldberg 90] that using an appropriate interpolation method in the image reconstruction stage, reasonable image quality can be achieved at a bit rate of less than 0.1 bit/pixel and excellent quality at a bit rate of about 1.2 bits/pixel. Progressive image transmission stages can be seen in Figure 12.6, where two different image resolutions are presented.

The concept of smart compression is based on the sensing properties of human visual sensors [Burt 89]. The spatial resolution of the human eye decreases significantly with increasing distance from the optical axis. Therefore, the human eye can only see in high resolution in a very small area close to the point where the eye is focused. Similarly as with image displays, where it does not make sense to display an image in higher resolution than that of the display device, it is not necessary to display an image in full resolution in image areas where the user's eyes are not focused. This is the principle of **smart**

image compression. The main difficulty remains in determining the interest areas of the image which the user will focus on when viewing the image. When considering a smart progressive image transmission, the image should be transmitted in higher resolution in areas of interest first – this improves a subjective rating of transmission speed as sensed by a human user. The interest areas may be obtained in a feedback control manner from tracking the user's eyes (assuming the communication channel is fast enough). The image point the user is focused on may be used to increase the resolution in that particular image area so that the most important data are transmitted first. This smart image transmission and compression may be extremely useful if applied to dynamic image generators in driving or flight simulators, or to high definition television [Abdel-Malek and Bloomer 90]. These ideas are shown in Figure 12.7; the typical foci of attention on a human face image are the areas around eyes, nose, and mouth. Therefore, these areas are displayed at the highest available resolution while the rest of the image is displayed at much lower resolution (Gaussian post-processing interpolation was applied here).

12.6 Comparison of compression methods

The main goal of image compression is to minimize image data volume with no significant loss of information, and all basic image compression groups have advantages and disadvantages. Transform-based methods better preserve subjective image quality, and are less sensitive to statistical image property changes both inside a single image and between images. Prediction methods, on the other hand, can achieve larger compression ratios in a much less expensive way, tend to be much faster than transform-based or vector quantization compression schemes, and can easily be realized in hardware. If compressed images are transmitted, an important property is insensitivity to transmission channel noise. Transform-based techniques are significantly less sensitive to the channel noise – if a transform coefficient is corrupted during transmission, the resulting image distortion is homogeneously spread through the image or image part and is not too disturbing. Erroneous transmission of a difference value in prediction compressions causes not only an error in a particular pixel, it influences values in the neighbourhood because the predictor involved has a considerable visual effect in a reconstructed image. Vector quantization methods require a complex coder, their parameters are very sensitive to image data, and blur image edges. The advantage is in a simple decoding scheme consisting of a look-up table only. Pyramid compression techniques represent a natural compression ability and show a potential for further improvement of compression ratios. They are suitable for dynamic image compression and for progressive and smart transmission approaches.

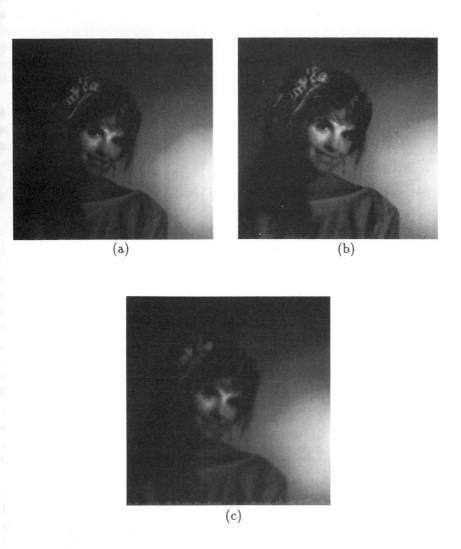

Figure 12.6 *Progressive image transmission: (a) Original image, (b) 1/2
resolution, (c) 1/4 resolution. Courtesy A. Abdel-Malek, General Electric
Corporate Research and Development, Schenectady, NY.*

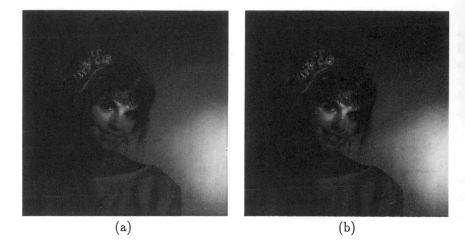

(a)   (b)

Figure 12.7 *Smart image compression: (a) Original uncompressed image, (b) compressed image displayed in full resolution in interest areas only, interest areas being determined around eyes, nose, and mouth; three levels of image resolution used. Courtesy A. Abdel-Malek, General Electric Corporate Research and Development, Schenectady, NY.*

Hybrid compression methods combine good properties of the presented groups [Habibi 74, Habibi and Robinson 74]. A hybrid compression of three-dimensional image data (two spatial dimensions plus one spectral dimension) is a good example. A two-dimensional discrete transform (cosine, Hadamard, ...) is applied to each monospectral image followed by a predictive compression in the third dimension of spectral components. Hybrid methods combine the different dimensionalities of transform compressions and predictive compressions. As a general rule, at least a one-dimensional transform compression precedes predictive compression steps. In addition to combinations of transform and predictive approaches, predictive approaches are often combined with vector quantization. A discrete cosine transform combined with vector quantization in a pyramid structure is described in [Park and Lee 91].

For more detailed comparison of some image compression techniques refer to [Chang et al. 88, Lovewell and Basart 88, Jaisimha et al. 89, DiMento and Berkovich 90, Hccr and Reinfelder 90].

12.7 Other techniques

Various other image data compression methods exist. If an image is quantized into a small number of grey levels and if it has a small number of regions of the same grey level, an effective compression method may be based on **coding region borders** [Wilkins and Wintz 71]. Image representation by

ts **low and high frequencies** is another method – image reconstruction is
. superposition of inverse transforms of low and high frequency components.
The low-frequency image can be represented by a significantly smaller volume
of data than the original image. The high-frequency image has significant
image edges only and can be efficiently represented [Graham 67, Giunta et al.
90]. The **region growing process** compression method stores an algorithm
or region growing from region seed points, each region being represented by
ts seed point. If an image can be represented only by region seed points,
significant data compression is achieved.

A technique that is gaining popularity is **block truncation** coding [Delp
and Mitchell 79, Rosenfeld and Kak 82, Kruger 92], in which an image is
divided into small square blocks of pixels, and each pixel value in a block
s truncated to one bit by thresholding and moment preserving selection of
binary levels. One-bit value per pixel has to be transmitted, together with
information describing how to recreate the moment preserving binary levels
during reconstruction. This method is fast and easy to implement. **Visual
pattern image** coding is capable of high quality compression with very good
compression ratios (30:1) and is exceptionally fast [Silsbee et al. 91].

In addition to techniques designed explicitly to cope with 2D (or higher
dimension) data, there is a wide range of well known algorithms designed with
serial data (e.g. simple text files) in mind. These algorithms see wide use in
the compression of ordinary computer files to reduce disk consumption. Very
well known is **Huffman encoding** which can provide optimal compression
and error-free decompression [Rosenfeld and Kak 82, Benelli 86]. The main
idea of Huffman coding is to represent data by codes of variable length, with
more frequent data being represented by shorter codes. Many modifications
of the original algorithm [Huffman 52] exist, with recent adaptive Huffman
coding algorithms requiring only one pass over the data [Knuth 85, Vitter 87].
More recently, the **Lempel-Ziv** algorithm of **dictionary-based** coding [Ziv
and Lempel 78, Welch 84] has found wide favour as a standard compression
algorithm. In this approach, data are represented by pointers pointing to a
dictionary of symbols.

These, and a number of similar techniques, are often used as part of de-
facto standard image representations, for example the TIFF format, and the
Sun rasterfile format both have *compressed* options designed in to their image
representations.

There is an increasing effort to achieve a standardization in image compression. The Joint Photographic Experts Group (JPEG) has developed an
international standard for general purpose, continuous tone, still-image compression. The JPEG compression system has three main parts [Aravind et
al. 89, Wallace 90]; the Baseline System offers a simple compression method
suitable for many needs (discrete cosine transform compression followed by
Huffman coding), the Extended System capabilities satisfy a wider range of

applications (DCT followed by arithmetic coding), and an independent Loss-less method (based on differential and run length coding) is also included, which guarantees lossless compression if needed.

References

[Abdel-Malek and Bloomer 90] A Abdel-Malek and J Bloomer. Visually op-timized image reconstruction. In *Proceedings of the SPIE Conference on Human Vision and Electronic Imaging, Santa Clara, Ca*, pages 330–335, SPIE, Bellingham, Wa, 1990.

[Anderson and Huang 71] G B Anderson and T S Huang. Piecewise Fourier transformation for picture bandwidth compression. *IEEE Transactions on Communications Technology*, 19:133–140, 1971.

[Arai 90] K Arai. Preliminary study on information lossy and loss-less coding data compression for the archiving of ADEOS data. *IEEE Transactions on Geoscience and Remote Sensing*, 28(4):732–734, 1990.

[Aravind et al. 89] R Aravind, G L Cash, and J P Worth. On implement-ing the JPEG still-picture compression algorithm. In *Proceedings of SPIE Conference Visual Communications and Image Processing IV, Philadelphia, Pa*, pages 799–808, SPIE, Bellingham, Wa, 1989.

[Azadegan 90] F Azadegan. Discrete cosine transform encoding of two-dimensional processes. In *Proceedings of the 1990 International Conference on Acoustics, Speech, and Signal Processing - ICASSP 90, Abuquerque, NM*, pages 2237–2240, IEEE, Piscataway, NJ, 1990.

[Benelli 86] G Benelli. Image data compression by using the Laplacian pyra-mid technique with adaptive Huffman codes. In V Cappellini and R Marconi, editors, *Advances in Image Processing and Pattern Recognition*, pages 229–233. North Holland, Amsterdam, 1986.

[Boxerman and Lee 90] J L Boxerman and H J Lee. Variable block-sized vec-tor quantization of grayscale images with unconstrained tiling. In *Visual Communications and Image Processing '90, Lausanne, Switzerland*, pages 847–858, SPIE, Bellingham, Wa, 1990.

[Burt 89] P J Burt. Multiresolution techniques for image representation, anal-ysis, and 'smart' transmission. In *Visual Communications and Image Processing IV, Philadelphia, Pa*, pages 2–15, SPIE, Bellingham, Wa, 1989.

[Chang et al. 88] C Y Chang, R Kwok, and J C Curlander. Spatial compres-sion of Seasat SAR images. *IEEE Transactions on Geoscience and Remote Sensing*, 26(5):673–685, 1988.

[Chen and Bovik 89] D Chen and A C Bovik. Fast image coding using simple image patterns. In *Visual Communications and Image Processing IV, Philadelphia, Pa*, pages 1461–1471, SPIE, Bellingham, Wa, 1989.

[Chitprasert and Rao 90] B Chitprasert and K R Rao. Discrete cosine transform filtering. *Signal Processing*, 19(3):233–245, 1990.

[Clarke 85] R J Clarke. *Transform Coding of Images*. Academic Press, London, 1985.

[Daut and Zhao 90] D G Daut and D Zhao. Improved DPCM algorithm for image data compression. In *Image Processing Algorithms and Techniques, Santa Clara, Ca*, pages 199–210, SPIE, Bellingham, Wa, 1990.

[De Lameillieure and Bruyland 90] J De Lameillieure and I Bruyland. Single stage 280 Mbps coding of HDTV using HDPCM with a vector quantizer based on masking functions. *Signal Processing: Image Communication*, 2(3):279–289, 1990.

[Delp and Mitchell 79] E J Delp and O R Mitchell. Image truncation using block truncation coding. *IEEE Transactions on Communications*, 27:1335–1342, 1979.

[DiMento and Berkovich 90] L J DiMento and S Y Berkovich. The compression effects of the binary tree overlapping method on digital imagery. *IEEE Transactions on Communications*, 38(8):1260–1265, 1990.

[Ebrahimi et al. 90] T Ebrahimi, T R Reed, and M Kunt. Video coding using a pyramidal Gabor expansion. In *Visual Communications and Image Processing '90, Lausanne, Switzerland*, pages 489–502, SPIE, Bellingham, Wa, 1990.

[Farelle 90] P M Farelle. *Recursive Block Coding for Image Data Compression*. Springer Verlag, New York, 1990.

[Gersho and Gray 92] A Gersho and R M Gray. *Vector Quantization and Signal Compression*. Kluwer Academic Publishers, Norwell, Ma, 1992.

[Giunta et al. 90] G Giunta, T R Reed, and M Kunt. Image sequence coding using oriented edges. *Signal Processing: Image Communication*, 2(4):429–439, 1990.

[Gonzalez et al. 90] C A Gonzalez, K L Anderson, and W B Pennebaker. DCT based video compression using arithmetic coding. In *Image Processing Algorithms and Techniques, Santa Clara, Ca*, pages 305–311, SPIE, Bellingham, Wa, 1990.

[Graham 67] D N Graham. Image transmission by two–dimensional contour coding. *Proceedings IEEE*, 55:336–346, 1967.

[Gray 84] R M Gray. Vector quantization. *IEEE ASSP Magazine*, 1(2):4–29, 1984.

[Guha et al. 88] R K Guha, A F Dickinson, and G Ray. Non-transform methods of picture compression applied to medical images. In *Proceedings - Twelfth Annual Symposium on Computer Applications in Medical Care, Washington, DC*, pages 483–487, IEEE, Piscataway, NJ, 1988.

[Habibi 71] A Habibi. Comparison of nth order DPCM encoder with linear transformations and block quantization techniques. *IEEE Transactions on Communications Technology*, 19(6):948–956, 1971.

[Habibi 74] A Habibi. Hybrid coding of pictorial data. *IEEE Transactions on Communications Technology*, 22(4):614–623, 1974.

[Habibi and Robinson 74] A Habibi and G S Robinson. A survey of digital picture coding. *Computer*, 7(5):22–34, 1974.

[Heer and Reinfelder 90] V K Heer and H E Reinfelder. Comparison of reversible methods for data compression. In *Medical Imaging IV: Image Processing, Newport Beach, Ca*, pages 354–365, SPIE, Bellingham, Wa, 1990.

[Huffman 52] D A Huffman. A method for the construction of minimum-redundancy codes. *Proceedings of IRE*, 40(9):1098–1101, 1952.

[Jain 89] A K Jain. *Fundamentals of Digital Image Processing*. Prentice-Hall, Englewood Cliffs, NJ, 1989.

[Jaisimha et al. 89] M Y Jaisimha, H Potlapalli, H Barad, and A B Martinez. Data compression techniques for maps. In *Energy and Information Technologies in the Southeast, Columbia, SC*, pages 878–883, IEEE, Piscataway, NJ, 1989.

[Knuth 85] D E Knuth. Dynamic Huffman coding. *Journal of Algorithms*, 6:163–180, 1985.

[Kruger 92] A Kruger. Block truncation compression. *Dr Dobb's J Software Tools*, 17(4):48–55, 1992.

[Lovewell and Basart 88] B K Lovewell and J P Basart. Survey of image compression techniques. *Review of Progress in Quantitative Nondestructive Evaluation*, 7A:731–738, 1988.

[Moik 80] J G Moik. *Digital Processing of Remotely Sensed Images.* NASA SP–431, Washington DC, 1980.

[Netravali 88] A N Netravali. *Digital Pictures: Representation and Compression.* Plenum Press, New York, 1988.

[Park and Lee 91] S H Park and S U Lee. Pyramid image coder using classified transform vector quantization. *Signal Processing*, 22(1):25–42, 1991.

[Pratt 91] W K Pratt. *Digital Image Processing.* John Wiley and Sons, New York, 2nd edition, 1991.

[Rabbani 91] M Rabbani. *Digital Image Compression.* SPIE Optical Engineering Press, Bellingham, Wa, 1991.

[Rao and Pearlman 91] R P Rao and W A Pearlman. On entropy of pyramid structures. *IEEE Transactions on Information Theory*, 37(2):407–413, 1991.

[Rosenfeld and Kak 82] A Rosenfeld and A C Kak. *Digital Picture Processing.* Academic Press, New York, 2nd edition, 1982.

[Savoji and Burge 85] M H Savoji and R E Burge. On different methods based on the Karhunen–Loeve expansion and used in image analysis. *Computer Vision, Graphics, and Image Processing*, 29:259–269, 1985.

[Silsbee et al. 91] P Silsbee, A C Bovik, and D Chen. Visual pattern image sequencing coding. In *Visual Communications and Image Processing '90, Lausanne, Switzerland*, pages 532–543, SPIE, Bellingham, Wa, 1991.

[Strobach 90] F Strobach. Tree-structured scene adaptive coder. *IEEE Transactions on Communications*, 38(4):477–486, 1990.

[Thyagarajan and Sanchez 89] K S Thyagarajan and H Sanchez. Image sequence coding using interframe VDPCM and motion compensation. In *International Conference on Acoustics, Speech, and Signal Processing - 1989, Glasgow, Scotland*, pages 1858–1861, IEEE, Piscataway, NJ, 1989.

[Vitter 87] J S Vitter. Design and analysis of dynamic Huffman codes. *Journal of the ACM*, 34(4):825–845, 1987.

[Wallace 90] G K Wallace. Overview of the JPEG (ISO/CCITT) still image compression standard. In *Proceedings of SPIE Conference Image Processing Algorithms and Techniques, Santa Clara, Ca*, pages 220–233, SPIE, Bellingham, Wa, 1990.

[Wang and Goldberg 89] L Wang and M Goldberg. Reduced-difference pyramid: a data structure for progressive image transmission. *Optical Engineering*, 28(7):708–716, 1989.

[Wang and Goldberg 90] L Wang and M Goldberg. Reduced-difference pyramid. A data structure for progressive image transmission. In *Image Processing Algorithms and Techniques, Santa Clara, Ca*, pages 171–181, SPIE, Bellingham, Wa, 1990.

[Welch 84] T A Welch. A technique for high performance data compression. *Computer*, 17(6):8–19, 1984.

[White 87] R G White. Compressing image data with quadtrees. *Dr Dobb's J Software Tools*, 12(3):16–45, 1987.

[Wilkins and Wintz 71] L C Wilkins and P A Wintz. Bibliography on data compression, picture properties and picture coding. *IEEE Transactions on Information Theory*, 17:180–199, 1971.

[Wintz 72] P A Wintz. Transform picture coding. *Proceedings IEEE*, 60:809–820, 1972.

[Zailu and Taxiao 90] H Zailu and W Taxiao. MDPCM picture coding. In *1990 IEEE International Symposium on Circuits and Systems, New Orleans, LA*, pages 3253–3255, IEEE, Piscataway, NJ, 1990.

[Zettler et al. 90] W R Zettler, J Huffman, and D C P Linden. Application of compactly supported wavelets to image compression. In *Image Processing Algorithms and Techniques, Santa Clara, Ca*, pages 150–160, SPIE, Bellingham, Wa, 1990.

[Ziv and Lempel 78] J Ziv and A Lempel. Compression of individual sequences via variable-rate coding. *IEEE Transactions on Information Theory*, 24(5):530–536, 1978.

13

Texture

Texture is a term that refers to properties that represent the surface of an object; it is widely used, and perhaps intuitively obvious, but has no precise definition due to its wide variability. We might define texture as *something consisting of mutually related elements*; therefore we are considering a group of pixels (a **texture primitive** or **texture element**) and the texture described is highly dependent on the number considered (the texture scale) [Haralick 79]. Examples are shown in Figure 13.1; dog fur, grass, river pebbles, cork, chequered textile, and knitted fabric. Many other examples can be found in [Brodatz 66].

Texture consists of texture **primitives** or texture **elements**, sometimes called **texels**. Primitives in grass and dog fur are represented by several pixels and correspond to a stalk or a pile; cork is built from primitives comparable in size with pixels. It is difficult, however, to define primitives for the chequered textile or fabric which can be defined in at least two hierarchical levels. The first level of primitives corresponds to textile checks or knitted stripes, and the second the finer texture of the fabric or individual stitches. As we have seen in many other areas, this is a problem of **scale**; texture description is **scale-dependent**.

The main aim of texture analysis is texture recognition and texture-based shape analysis. Textured properties of regions are referred to many times while considering image segmentation (Chapter 5), and derivation of shape from texture is discussed in Chapter 9. People usually describe texture as **fine**, **coarse**, **grained**, **smooth**, etc., implying that some more precise features must be defined to make machine recognition possible. Such features can be found in the **tone** and **structure** of a texture [Haralick 79]. Tone is mostly based on pixel intensity properties in the primitive, while structure is the spatial relationship between primitives.

Each pixel can be characterized by its location and tonal properties. A texture primitive is a contiguous set of pixels with some tonal and/or regional property, and can be described by its average intensity, maximum or minimum intensity, size, shape, etc.

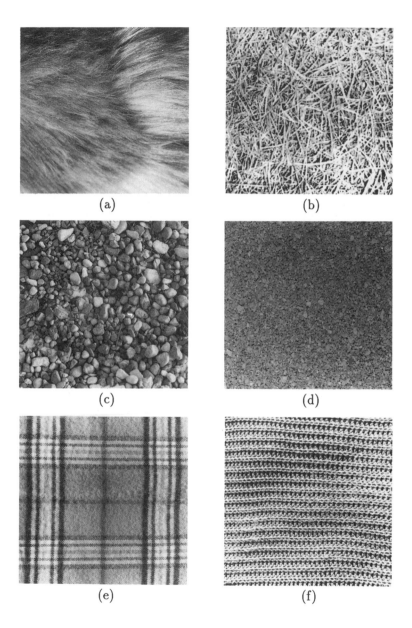

Figure 13.1 *Textures: (a) Dog fur, (b) grass, (c) river pebbles, (d) cork, (e) chequered textile, (f) knitted fabric.*

The spatial relationship of primitives can be random, or they may be pairwise dependent, or some number of primitives can be mutually dependent. Image texture is then described by the number and types of primitives and by their spatial relationship. Figures 13.1a and b and 13.2a and b show that the same number and the same type of primitives does not necessarily give the same texture. Similarly, Figure 13.2a and c show that the same spatial

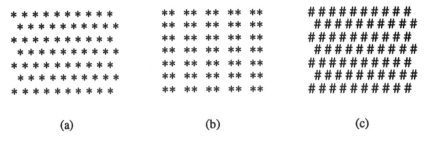

(a)   (b)   (c)

Figure 13.2 *Artificial textures.*

relationship of primitives does not guarantee texture uniqueness, and therefore is not sufficient for texture description. Texture tone and structure are not independent; textures always display both tone and structure even though one or the other usually dominates, and we usually speak about one or the other only. Tone can be understood as tonal properties of primitives, taking primitive spatial relationships into consideration. Structure refers to spatial relationships of primitives considering their tonal properties as well.

If the texture primitives in the image are small and if the tonal differences between neighbouring primitives are large, a **fine** texture results (Figure 13.1a, b and d). If the texture primitives are larger and consist of several pixels, a **coarse** texture results (Figure 13.1c and e). Again, this is a reason for using both tonal and structural properties in texture description. Note that the fine/coarse texture characteristic depends on scale.

Further, textures can be classified according to their strength – texture strength then influences the choice of texture description method. **Weak** textures have small spatial interactions between primitives, and can be adequately described by frequencies of primitive types appearing in some neighbourhood. Because of this, many statistical texture properties are evaluated in the description of weak textures. In **strong** textures, the spatial interactions between primitives are somewhat regular. To describe strong textures, the frequency of occurrence of primitive pairs in some spatial relationship may be sufficient. Strong texture recognition is usually accompanied by an exact definition of texture primitives and their spatial relationships [Chetverikov 82, Rao 90].

It remains to define a constant texture. One existing definition [Sklansky 78] claims that '*an image region has a constant texture if a set of its local properties in that region is constant, slowly changing, or approximately*

periodic'. The set of local properties can be understood as primitive types
and their spatial relationships. An important part of the definition is that
the properties must be repeated inside the constant texture area. How many
times must the properties be repeated? Assume that a large area of constant
texture is available, and consider smaller and smaller parts of that texture,
digitizing it at constant resolution as long as the texture character remains
unchanged. Alternatively, consider larger and larger parts of the texture, digitizing it at constant raster, until details become blurred and the primitives
finally disappear. We see that image resolution (scale) must be a consistent
part of the texture description; if the image resolution is appropriate, the
texture character does not change for any position in our window.

Two main texture description approaches exist – **statistical** and **syntactic** [Haralick 79]. Statistical methods compute different properties and are
suitable if texture primitive sizes are comparable with the pixel sizes. Syntactic and **hybrid** methods (combination of statistical and syntactic) are more
suitable for textures where primitives can be assigned a label – the primitive
type – meaning that primitives can be described using a larger variety of properties than just tonal properties; for example, shape description. Instead of
tone, brightness will be used more often in the following sections because it
better corresponds to grey level images.

Recent research on pre-attentive (early) vision [Julesz 81, Julesz and Bergen
87] shows that human ability to recognize texture quickly is mostly based on
textons, which are elongated blobs (rectangles, ellipses, line segments, line-
ends, crossings, corners) that can be detected by pre-attentive vision, while
the positional relationship between neighbouring textons must be done slowly
by an attentive vision subsystem. As a result of these investigations, another
group of methods has begun to appear, based on texton detection and on
texton density computation [Voorhees and Poggio 87, Ando 88].

13.1   Statistical texture description

Statistical texture description methods describe textures in a form suitable for
statistical pattern recognition. As a result of the description, each texture is
described by a feature vector of properties which represents a point in a multi-
dimensional feature space. The aim is to find a deterministic or probabilistic
decision rule assigning a texture to some specific class (see Chapter 7).

13.1.1   Methods based on spatial frequencies

Measuring spatial frequencies is the basis of a large group of texture recognition methods. Textural character is in direct relation to the spatial size of
the texture primitives; coarse textures are built from larger primitives, fine
textures from smaller primitives. Fine textures are characterized by higher
spatial frequencies, coarse textures by lower spatial frequencies.

One of many related spatial frequency methods evaluates the **autocorrelation function of a texture**. In an autocorrelation model, a single pixel is considered a texture primitive, and primitive tone property is the grey level. Texture spatial organization is described by the correlation coefficient that evaluates linear spatial relationships between primitives. If the texture primitives are relatively large, the autocorrelation function value decreases slowly with increasing distance, while it decreases rapidly if texture consists of small primitives. If primitives are placed periodically in a texture, the autocorrelation increases and decreases periodically with distance.

Texture can be described using the following algorithm;

Algorithm 13.1: Autocorrelation texture description

1. Evaluate autocorrelation coefficients for several different values of parameters p, q.

$$C_{ff}(p,q) = \frac{MN}{(M-p)(N-q)} \frac{\sum_{i=1}^{M-p} \sum_{j=1}^{N-q} f(i,j)f(i+p,j+q)}{\sum_{i=1}^{M} \sum_{j=1}^{N} f^2(i,j)} \quad (13.1)$$

where p, q is the position difference in the i, j direction, and M, N are the image dimensions.

If the textures described are circularly symmetric, the autocorrelation texture description can be computed as a function of the absolute position difference not considering direction; that is, a function of one variable.

Spatial frequencies can be determined from an **optical image transform** (e.g. the Fourier transform – see Chapter 11) as well [Shulman 70], a big advantage of which is that it may be computed in real time. The Fourier transform describes spatial frequencies extremely well; average values of energy in specific wedges and rings of the Fourier spectrum can be used as textural description features (see Figure 13.3). Features evaluated from rings reflect coarseness of the texture – high energy in large radius rings is characteristic of fine textures (high frequencies), while high energy in small radii is characteristic of coarse textures (with lower spatial frequencies). Features evaluated from wedge slices of the Fourier transform image depend on directional properties of textures – if a texture has many edges or lines in a direction ϕ, high energy will be present in a wedge in direction $\phi + \pi/2$.

Similarly, a **discrete image transform** may be used for texture description. A textured image is usually divided into small square non-overlapping subimages. If the subimage size is $n \times n$, the grey levels of its pixels may be interpreted as a n^2-dimensional vector, and an image can be represented as a set of vectors. These vectors are transformed applying a Fourier, Hadamard,

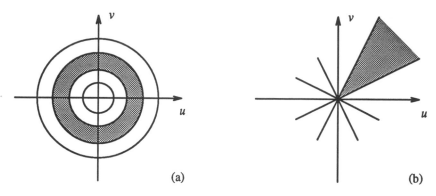

Figure 13.3 *Partitioning of Fourier power spectrum: (a) Ring filter, (b) wedge filter.*

or other discrete image transform (Chapter 11). The new co-ordinate system's basis vectors are related to the spatial frequencies of the original texture image and can be used for texture description [Rosenfeld 76]. When description of noisy texture becomes necessary, the problem becomes more difficult. From a set of 28 spatial-frequency domain features a subset of features insensitive to additive noise was extracted (dominant peak energy, power spectrum shape, entropy) in [Liu and Jernigan 90].

Spatial frequency texture description methods are based on a well-known approach. Despite that, many problems remain – the resulting description is not invariant even to monotonic image grey level transforms; further, it can be shown that [Weszka et al. 76] the frequency-based approach is less efficient than others. A joint spatial/spatial-frequency approach is recommended, the Wigner distribution giving the best results [Reed et al. 90].

13.1.2 Co-occurrence matrices

This method of texture description is based on the repeated occurrence of some grey level configuration in the texture; this configuration varies rapidly with distance in fine textures, slowly in coarse textures [Haralick et al. 73]. Let the analysed part of a textured image be a rectangular window $M \times N$. An occurrence of some grey level configuration may be described by a matrix of relative frequencies $P_{\phi,d}(a, b)$, describing how frequently two pixels with the grey levels a, b appear in the window separated by a distance d in direction ϕ. These matrices are symmetric if defined as given below. However, an asymmetric definition may be used where matrix values are also dependent on the direction of co-occurrence. A co-occurrence matrix computation scheme was given in Algorithm 3.1.

Non-normalized frequencies of co-occurrence as functions of angle and distance can be represented formally as

$$\begin{aligned}
P_{0^o,d}(a,b) &= |\{((k,l),(m,n)) \in (M \times N) \times (M \times N) : \\
&\quad k-m=0, |l-n|=d,\ \ f(k,l)=a, f(m,n)=b\}| \\
P_{45^o,d}(a,b) &= |\{((k,l),(m,n)) \in (M \times N) \times (M \times N) : \\
&\quad (k-m=d, l-n=-d)\ OR\ (k-m=-d, l-n=d), \\
&\quad f(k,l)=a, f(m,n)=b\}| \\
P_{90^o,d}(a,b) &= |\{((k,l),(m,n)) \in (M \times N) \times (M \times N) : \\
&\quad |k-m|=d, l-n=0,\ \ f(k,l)=a, f(m,n)=b\}| \\
P_{135^o,d}(a,b) &= |\{((k,l),(m,n)) \in (M \times N) \times (M \times N) : \\
&\quad (k-m=d, l-n=d)\ OR\ (k-m=-d, l-n=-d), \\
&\quad f(k,l)=a, f(m,n)=b\}|
\end{aligned} \tag{13.2}$$

(where $|\{\ldots\}|$ refers to set cardinality).

An example will illustrate co-occurrence matrix computations for the distance $d = 1$. A 4×4 image with four grey levels is presented in Figure 13.4. The matrix $P_{0^o,1}$ is constructed as follows: The element $P_{0^o,1}(0,0)$ represents

0	0	1	1
0	0	1	1
0	2	2	2
2	2	3	3

Figure 13.4 *Grey level image.*

the number of times the two pixels with grey levels 0 and 0 appeared separated by distance 1 in direction 0°; $P_{0^o,1}(0,0) = 4$ in this case. The element $P_{0^o,1}(3,2)$ represents the number of times two pixels with grey levels 3 and 2 appeared separated by distance 1 in direction 0°; $P_{0^o,1}(3,2) = 1$. Note that $P_{0^o,1}(2,3) = 1$ due to matrix symmetry

$$P_{0^o,1} = \begin{vmatrix} 4 & 2 & 1 & 0 \\ 2 & 4 & 0 & 0 \\ 1 & 0 & 6 & 1 \\ 0 & 0 & 1 & 2 \end{vmatrix} \qquad P_{135^o,1} = \begin{vmatrix} 2 & 1 & 3 & 0 \\ 1 & 2 & 1 & 0 \\ 3 & 1 & 0 & 2 \\ 0 & 0 & 2 & 0 \end{vmatrix}$$

The construction of matrices $P_{\phi,d}$ for other directions ϕ and distance values d is similar.

Texture classification can be based on criteria derived from these co-occurrence matrices:

- **Energy:** or angular second moment (an image homogeneity measure – the more homogeneous the image, the larger the value)

$$\sum_{a,b} P^2_{\phi,d}(a,b) \tag{13.3}$$

- **Entropy:**

$$\sum_{a,b} P_{\phi,d}(a,b) \log P_{\phi,d}(a,b) \tag{13.4}$$

- **Maximum probability:**

$$\max_{a,b} P_{\phi,d}(a,b) \tag{13.5}$$

- **Contrast:** (a measure of local image variations; typically $\kappa = 2, \lambda = 1$)

$$\sum_{a,b} |a - b|^\kappa P_{\phi,d}^\lambda(a,b) \tag{13.6}$$

- **Inverse difference moment:**

$$\sum_{a,b;a\neq b} \frac{P_{\phi,d}^\lambda(a,b)}{|a - b|^\kappa} \tag{13.7}$$

- **Correlation:** (a measure of image linearity; linear directional structures in direction ϕ result in large correlation values in this direction)

$$\frac{\sum_{a,b}[(ab)P_{\phi,d}(a,b)] - \mu_x \mu_y}{\sigma_x \sigma_y} \tag{13.8}$$

where μ_x, μ_y are means and σ_x, σ_y standard deviations

$$\mu_x = \sum_a a \sum_b P_{\phi,d}(a,b)$$

$$\mu_y = \sum_b b \sum_a P_{\phi,d}(a,b)$$

$$\sigma_x = \sum_a (a - \mu_x)^2 \sum_b P_{\phi,d}(a,b)$$

$$\sigma_y = \sum_b (b - \mu_x)^2 \sum_a P_{\phi,d}(a,b)$$

A general algorithm for texture description based on co-occurrence matrices is;

Algorithm 13.2: Co-occurrence method of texture description

---

1. Construct co-occurrence matrices for given directions and given distances.

2. Compute texture feature vectors for four directions ϕ, different values of d, and the six characteristics. This results in many correlated features.

The co-occurrence method describes second-order image statistics and works well for a large variety of textures (see [Gotlieb and Kreyszig 90] for a survey of texture descriptors based on co-occurrence matrices). Good properties of the co-occurrence method are the description of spatial relations between tonal pixels, and invariance to monotonic grey level transformations. On the other hand, it does not consider primitive shapes, and therefore cannot be recommended if the texture consists of large primitives. Memory requirements represent another big disadvantage, although this is definitely not as limiting as it was few years ago. The number of grey levels may be set to 32 or 64 which decreases the co-occurrence matrix sizes, but loss of grey level accuracy is a resulting negative effect (although this loss is usually insignificant in practice).

Although co-occurrence matrices give very good results in discrimination between textures, the method is computationally expensive. A fast algorithm for co-occurrence matrix computation is given in [Argenti et al. 90], and a modification of the method efficiently applicable to texture description of detected regions is proposed in [Carlson and Ebel 88], in which a co-occurrence array size varies with the region size.

13.1.3 Edge frequency

Methods discussed so far describe texture by its spatial frequencies, but comparison of edge frequencies in texture can be used as well. Edges can be detected either as microedges using small edge operator masks, or as macroedges using large masks [Davis and Mitiche 80]. The simplest operator that can serve this purpose is Robert's gradient, but virtually any other edge detector can be used (see Section 4.3.2). Using a gradient as a function of distance between pixels is another option [Sutton and Hall 72]. The distance-dependent texture description function $g(d)$ can be computed for any subimage f defined in a neighbourhood N for variable distance d

$$g(d) = \begin{aligned} &|f(i,j) - f(i+d,j)| + |f(i,j) - f(i-d,j)| + \\ &|f(i,j) - f(i,j+d)| + |f(i,j) - f(i,j-d)| \end{aligned} \qquad (13.9)$$

The function $g(d)$ is similar to the negative autocorrelation function; its minimum corresponds to the maximum of the autocorrelation function, and its maximum corresponds to the autocorrelation minimum.

Algorithm 13.3: Edge-frequency texture description

---

1. Compute a gradient $g(d)$ for all pixels of the texture.

2. Evaluate texture features as average values of gradient in specified distances d.

Dimensionality of the texture description feature space is given by the number of distance values d used to compute the edge gradient.

Several other texture properties may be derived from first-order and second-order statistics of edge distributions [Tomita and Tsuji 90]:

- **Coarseness:** Edge density is a measure of coarseness. The finer the texture, the higher the number of edges present in the texture edge image.

- **Contrast:** High contrast textures are characterized by large edge magnitudes.

- **Randomness:** Randomness may be measured as entropy of the edge magnitude histogram.

- **Directivity:** An approximate measure of directivity may be determined as entropy of the edge-direction histogram. Directional textures have an even number of significant histogram peaks, direction-less textures have a uniform edge-direction histogram.

- **Linearity:** Texture linearity is indicated by co-occurrences of edge pairs with the same edge direction at constant distances, and edges are positioned in the edge direction (see Figure 13.5, edges a and b).

- **Periodicity:** Texture periodicity can be measured by co-occurrences of edge pairs of the same direction at constant distances in directions perpendicular to the edge direction (see Figure 13.5, edges a and c).

- **Size:** Texture size measure may be based on co-occurrences of edge pairs with opposite edge directions at constant distance in a direction perpendicular to the edge directions (see Figure 13.5, edges a and d).

Note that the first three measures are derived from first-order statistics, the last three measures from second-order statistics.

Many existing texture recognition methods are based on texture detection. The concepts of pre-attentive vision and textons have been mentioned, which are also based mostly on edge-related information. A zero crossing operator was applied to edge-based texture description in [Perry and Lowe 89]; the method determines image regions of a constant texture, assuming no a priori knowledge about the image, texture types, or scale. Feature analysis is performed across multiple window sizes.

A slightly different approach to texture recognition may require detection of borders between homogeneous textured regions. A hierarchical algorithm for textured image segmentation is described in [Fan 89], and a two-stage contextual classification and segmentation of textures based on a coarse-to-fine principle of edge detection is given in [Fung et al. 90]. Texture description

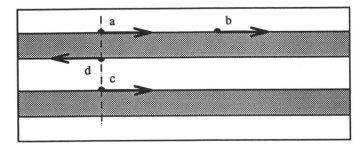

Figure 13.5 *Texture linearity, periodicity, and size measures may be based on image edges. Adapted from [Tomita and Tsuji 90].*

and recognition in the presence of noise represents a difficult problem. A noise-tolerant texture classification approach based on a Canny-type edge detector is discussed in [Kjell and Wang 91] where texture is described using periodicity measures derived from noise-insensitive edge detection.

13.1.4 Primitive length (run length)

A large number of neighbouring pixels of the same grey level represents a coarse texture, a small number of these pixels represents a fine texture and the lengths of texture primitives in different directions can serve as a texture description [Galloway 75]. A primitive is a maximum contiguous set of constant grey level pixels located in a line; these can then be described by grey level, length, and direction. The texture description features can be based on computation of continuous probabilities of the length and the grey level of primitives in the texture [Gisolfi et al. 86].

Let $B(a,r)$ be the number of primitives of the length r and grey level a, M, N the image dimensions, and L the number of image grey levels. Let N_r be the maximum primitive length in the image. The texture description features can be determined as follows; let K be the total number of runs

$$K = \sum_{a=1}^{L} \sum_{r=1}^{N_r} B(a,r) \tag{13.10}$$

Then

short primitives emphasis:

$$\frac{1}{K} \sum_{a=1}^{L} \sum_{r=1}^{N_r} \frac{B(a,r)}{r^2} \tag{13.11}$$

long primitives emphasis:

$$\frac{1}{K} \sum_{a=1}^{L} \sum_{r=1}^{N_r} B(a,r)r^2 \tag{13.12}$$

grey level uniformity:

$$\frac{1}{K}\sum_{a=1}^{L}(\sum_{r=1}^{N_r} B(a,r))^2 \tag{13.13}$$

primitive length uniformity:

$$\frac{1}{K}\sum_{r=1}^{N_r}(\sum_{a=1}^{L} B(a,r))^2 \tag{13.14}$$

primitive percentage:

$$\frac{K}{\sum_{a=1}^{L}\sum_{r=1}^{N_r} r\ B(a,r)} = \frac{K}{MN} \tag{13.15}$$

A general algorithm might then be;

Algorithm 13.4: Primitive length texture description

1. Find primitives of all grey levels, all lengths, and all directions in the texture image.

2. Compute texture description features as given in (13.11 – 13.15). These features then provide a description vector.

13.1.5 Other statistical methods of texture description

A brief overview of some other texture description techniques will illustrate the variety of published methods; we present here only the basic principles of some additional approaches [Haralick 79, Ahuja and Rosenfeld 81, Davis et al. 83, Derin and Elliot 87, Tomita and Tsuji 90].

The **mathematical morphology** approach looks for spatial repetitiveness of shapes in a binary image using structure primitives (see Chapter 10). If the structuring elements consist of a single pixel only, the resulting description is an autocorrelation function of the binary image. Using larger and more complex structuring elements, general correlation can be evaluated. The structuring element usually represents some simple shape, such as a square, a line, etc. When a binary textured image is eroded by this structuring element, texture properties are present in the eroded image [Serra and Verchery 73]. One possibility for feature vector construction is to apply different structuring elements to the textured image and to count the number of pixels with unit value in the eroded images, each number forming one element of the feature vector. The mathematical morphology approach stresses the shape properties of texture primitives, however its applicability is limited due to the assumption of a binary textured image. Methods of grey level mathematical morphology may help to solve this problem. The mathematical morphology approach to texture description is often successful in granulated materials, which can be segmented by thresholding. Using a sequence of openings and counting the number of pixels after each step, a texture measure was derived in [Dougherty et al. 89].

The **texture transform** represents another approach. Each texture type present in an image is transformed into a unique grey level; the general idea is to construct an image g where the pixels $g(i,j)$ describe a texture in some neighbourhood of the pixel $f(i,j)$ in the original textured image f. If microtextures are analysed, a small neighbourhood of $f(i,j)$ must be used, and an appropriately larger neighbourhood should be used for description of macrotextures. In addition, a priori knowledge can be used to guide the transformation and subsequent texture recognition and segmentation [Simaan 90]. In [Linnett and Richardson 90], local texture orientation is used to transform a texture image into a feature image, after which supervised classification is applied to recognize textures.

Linear estimates of grey levels in texture pixels can also be used for texture description. Pixel grey levels are estimated from grey levels in their neighbourhood – this method is based on the **autoregression texture model** where linear estimation parameters are used [Deguchi and Morishita 78]. The model parameters vary substantially in fine textures, but remain mostly unchanged if coarse texture is described. The autoregression model has been compared with an approach based on second-order spatial statistics [Gagalowicz et al. 88]; it was found that even if the results are almost the same, spatial statistics performed much more quickly and reliably.

The **peak and valley** method [Mitchell et al. 77, Ehrick and Foith 78] is based on detection of local extrema of the brightness function in vertical and horizontal scans of a texture image. Fine textures have a large number of small-sized local extrema, coarse textures are represented by a smaller number of larger-sized local extrema – higher peaks and deeper valleys.

The sequence of pixel grey levels can be considered a **Markov chain** in which the transition probabilities of an mth order chain represent $m+1^{th}$ order statistics of textures [Pratt and Faugeras 78]. This approach may also be used for texture generation [Gagalowicz 79].

Texture description is highly scale-dependent. To decrease scale sensitivity, a texture may be described in multiple resolutions and an appropriate scale may be chosen to achieve the maximum texture discrimination [Unser and Eden 89]. A coarse-to-fine multiresolution strategy is often used if texture segmentation is a goal [Gagalowicz and Graffigne 88, Bouman and Liu 91], approximate position of borders between texture regions being detected first in a low-resolution image, and accuracy being improved in higher resolutions using the low-level segmentation as a priori information.

Many of the texture description features presented so far are interrelated; the Fourier power spectrum, the autoregression model, and autocorrelation functions represent the same subset of second-order statistics. The mathematical relationships between texture description methods are summarized in [Tomita and Tsuji 90], an experimental comparison of performance between several methods can be found in [Du Buf et al. 90], and criteria for comparison are discussed in [Soh and Huntsberger 91].

It has been shown that higher than second-order statistics contain little information that can be used for texture discrimination [Julesz and Caelli 79]. Nevertheless, identical second-order statistics do not guarantee identical textures; examples can be found in [Julesz and Bergen 87] together with a study of human texture perception. Texture-related research of the human visual system seems to bring useful results and a texture analysis method based on studies of it was designed to emulate the process of texture-feature extraction in each individual channel in the multichannel spatial filtering model of perception. Results of the texture recognition process were compared with co-occurrence matrix recognition, and the model-based approach gave superior results in many respects [Tan and Constantinides 90].

13.2 Syntactic texture description methods

Syntactic and hybrid texture description methods are not as widely used as statistical approaches [Tomita et al. 82]. **Syntactic** texture description is based on an analogy between the texture primitive spatial relations and the structure of a formal language. Descriptions of textures from one class form a language that can be represented by its grammar which is inferred from a training set of words of the language (from descriptions of textures in a training set) – during a learning phase, one grammar is constructed for each texture class present in the training set. The recognition process is then a syntactic analysis of the texture description word. The grammar that can be used to complete the syntactic analysis of the description word determines the texture class (see Section 7.4).

Purely syntactic texture description models are based on the idea that textures consist of primitives located in almost regular relationships. Primitive descriptions and rules of primitive placement must be determined to describe a texture [Tsuji and Tomita 73, Lu and Fu 78]. Primitive spatial relation description methods were discussed at the beginning of this chapter. One of the most efficient ways to describe the structure of primitive relationships is using a grammar which represents a rule for building a texture from primitives applying transformation rules to a limited set of symbols. Symbols represent the texture primitive types and transformation rules represent the spatial relations between primitives. In Chapter 7 it was noted that any gram-

mar is a very strict formula. On the other hand, textures of the real world
are usually irregular in which structural errors, distortions, or even structural
variations are frequent. This means that no strict rule can be used to describe
a texture in reality. To make syntactic description of real textures possible,
variable rules must be incorporated into the description grammars, and non-
deterministic or stochastic grammars must be used (see Section 7.4 and [Fu
74]). Further, there is usually no single description grammar for a texture
class, which might be described by an infinite number of different grammars
using different symbols and different transformation rules, and different grammar types as well. We will discuss chain grammars and graph grammars in
the next sections [Pavlidis 80], and other grammars suitable for texture description (tree, matrix) can be found in [Fu 80, Ballard and Brown 82, Fu
82, Vafaie and Bourbakis 88]. Another approach to texture description using
generative principles is to use **fractals** [Mandelbrot 83, Barnsley 88]. Fractal-
based texture analysis was introduced in [Pentland 84] where a correlation
between texture coarseness and fractal dimension of a texture was demonstrated. Nevertheless, the fractal dimension is not sufficient for description of
natural textures. A class of texture measures based on lacunarity and fractal
dimension is introduced in [Keller et al. 89].

13.2.1 Shape chain grammars

Shape chain grammars, whose definition matches that given in Section 7.4,
are the simplest grammars that can be used for texture description. They
generate textures beginning with a start symbol followed by application of
transform rules, called **shape rules**. The generating process is over if no
further transform rule can be applied. Texture generation consists of several
steps: First, the transform rule is found. Second, the rule must be geometrically adjusted to match the generated texture exactly (rules are more general,
they may not include size, orientation, etc.)

Algorithm 13.5: Shape chain grammar texture generation

---

1. Start a texture generation process by applying some transform rule to
   the start symbol.

2. Find a part of a previously generated texture that matches the left side
   of some transform rule. This match must be an unambiguous correspondence between terminal and non-terminal symbols of the left hand side
   of the chosen transform rule with terminal and non-terminal symbols of
   the part of the texture to which the rule is applied. If no such part of
   the texture can be found, stop.

3. Find an appropriate geometric transform that can be applied to the left hand side of the chosen rule to match it to the considered texture part exactly.

4. Apply this geometric transform to the right hand side of the transform rule.

5. Substitute the specified part of the texture (the part that matches a geometrically transformed left hand side of the chosen rule) with the geometrically transformed right hand side of the chosen transform rule.

6. Continue with step (2).

We can demonstrate this algorithm on an example of hexagonal texture generation. Let V_n be a set of non-terminal symbols, V_t a set of terminal symbols, R a set of rules, S the start symbol (as in Section 7.4). The grammar [Ballard and Brown 82] is illustrated in Figure 13.6, which can then be

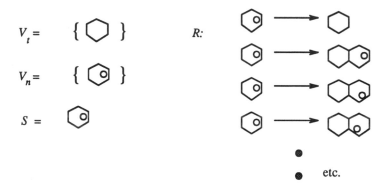

Figure 13.6 *Grammar generating hexagonal textures.*

used to generate hexagonal texture following Algorithm 13.5 – note that the nonterminal symbol may appear in different rotations. Rotation of primitives here is represented by a small circle attached to one side of the primitive hexagon in Figure 13.6. Recognition of hexagonal textures is the proof that the texture can be generated by this grammar; the texture recognition uses syntactic analysis as described in Section 7.4. Note that the texture shown in Figure 13.7a will be accepted by the grammar (Figure 13.6), and recognized as a hexagonal texture. Figure 13.7b will be rejected – it is not a hexagonal texture according to the definition of Figure 13.6.

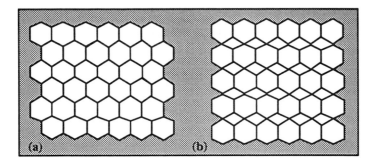

Figure 13.7 *Hexagonal textures: (a) Accepted, (b) rejected.*

13.2.2 Graph grammars

Texture analysis is more common than texture synthesis in machine vision tasks (even if texture synthesis is probably more common in general, i.e. in computer graphics and computer games). The natural approach to texture recognition is to construct a planar graph of primitive layout and to use it in the recognition process. Primitive classes and primitive spatial relations must be known to construct such a graph; spatial relationships between texture primitives will then be reflected in the graph structure. Texture primitive classes will be coded in graph nodes, each primitive having a corresponding node in the graph and two nodes will be connected by an arc if there is no other primitive in some specified neighbourhood of these two primitives. The size of this neighbourhood is the main influence on the complexity of the resulting planar graph – the larger the size of the neighbourhood, the smaller the number of graph arcs. Note that choosing the neighbourhood too large may result in no arcs for some nodes (the same may be true for the neighbourhood being too small). Characteristic properties of some graphs used practically (relative neighbourhood graphs, Gabriel graphs, Voronoi diagrams) are described in [Urquhart 82, Ahuja 82, Tuceryan and Jain 90]. These graphs are undirected since the spatial neighbourhood relation is symmetric, with evaluated arcs and nodes. Each node is labelled with a primitive class to which it corresponds, and arcs are evaluated by their length and direction.

The texture classification problem is then transformed into a graph recognition problem for which the following approaches may be used;

1. Simplify the texture description by decomposition of the planar graph into a set of chains, and apply the algorithms discussed in the previous section. The chain descriptions of textures can represent border primitives of closed regions, different graph paths, primitive neighbourhood, etc. A training set is constructed from the decomposition of several texture description planar graphs for each texture class. Appropriate grammars are inferred which represent textures in the training sets. The

presence of information noise is highly probable, so stochastic grammars should be used. Texture classification consists of the following steps:

- A classified texture is represented by a planar graph.
- The graph is decomposed into chains.
- The description chains are presented for syntactic analysis.
- A texture is classified into the class whose grammar accepts all the chains of the decomposed planar graph. If more than one grammar accepts the chains, the texture can be classified into the class whose grammar accepted the chains with the highest probability.

The main advantage of this approach is its simplicity. The impossibility of reconstructing the original planar graph from the chain decomposition is a disadvantage; it means that some portion of the syntactic information is lost during decomposition.

2. Another class of planar graph description may be represented by a stochastic graph grammar or by an extended graph grammar for description of distorted textures. This approach is very difficult from both the implementational and algorithmic points of view; the main problem is in grammar inference.

3. The planar graphs can be compared directly using graph matching approaches. It is necessary to define a 'distance' between two graphs as a measure of their similarity; if such a distance is defined, standard methods used in statistical classifier learning can be used – exemplar computation, cluster analysis, etc.

The syntactic approach is valued for its ability to describe a texture character at several hierarchical levels. It permits a qualitative analysis of textures, for decomposition into descriptive substructures (primitive grouping), to incorporate texture descriptions into the whole description of image, scene, etc. From this point of view, it significantly exceeds the complexity of simple object classification. Not considering the implementation difficulties, the second approach from the list above is recommended; if a descriptive graph grammar is chosen appropriately, it can generate a class of graphs independently of their size. It can be used if a pattern is searched for in an image at any hierarchical level. An example of a planar graph describing a texture is shown in Figure 13.8.

13.2.3 *Primitive grouping in hierarchical textures*

Several levels of primitives can be detected in hierarchical textures – lower level primitives form some specific pattern which can be considered a primitive at a

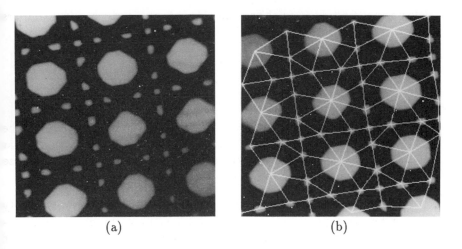

(a) (b)

Figure 13.8 *Planar graph describing a texture: (a) Texture primitives, (b) planar graph overlaid.*

higher description level (Figure 13.9). The process of detecting these primitive patterns (units) in a texture is called **primitive grouping**. Note that these units may form new patterns at an even higher description level. Therefore, the grouping process must be repeated until no new units can be formed.

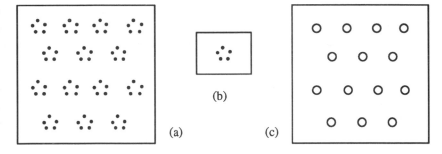

(a) (b) (c)

Figure 13.9 *Hierarchical texture: (a) Texture, (b) a pattern formed from low-level primitives, this pattern can be considered a primitive in the higher level, (c) higher level texture.*

Grouping makes a syntactic approach to texture segmentation possible. It plays the same role as local computation of texture features in statistical texture recognition. It has been claimed several times that different primitives and/or different spatial relationships represent different textures. Consider an example (Figure 13.10a) in which all the primitives at the lowest level are the same (small circles) and the two textures differ in the spatial relations between primitives. If a higher hierarchical level is considered, different primitives can be detected in both textures – the textures do not consist of the same primitive types any more, see Figure 13.10b.

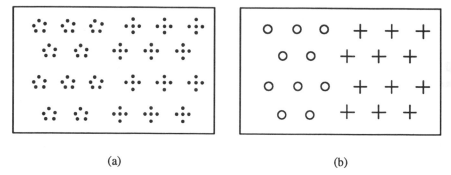

(a)   (b)

Figure 13.10 *Primitive grouping: (a) Two textures, same primitives in the lowest description level, (b) the same two textures, different primitives in the higher description level.*

A primitive grouping algorithm is described in [Tomita and Tsuji 90];

Algorithm 13.6: Texture primitive grouping

1. Determine texture primitive properties and classify primitives into classes

2. Find the nearest and the second nearest neighbour for each texture primitive. Using the primitive class and distances to the nearest two neighbouring primitives d_1, d_2, classify low-level primitives into **new** classes, see Figure 13.11.

3. Primitives with the same **new** classification which are connected (close to each other), are linked together and form higher level primitives, see Figure 13.11.

4. If any two resulting homogeneous regions of linked primitives overlap, let the overlapped part form a separate region, see Figure 13.12.

    Regions formed from primitives of the lower level may be considered primitives in the higher level and the grouping process may be repeated for these new primitives. Nevertheless, sophisticated control of the grouping process is necessary to achieve meaningful results – it must be controlled from a high-level vision texture understanding subsystem. A recursive primitive grouping, which uses histograms of primitive properties and primitive spatial relations is presented in [Tomita and Tsuji 90] together with examples of syntactic-based texture segmentation results.

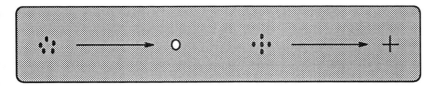

Figure 13.11 *Primitive grouping – low-level primitive patterns are grouped into single primitives at a higher level.*

o	o	o	x	o	x	o	x	x	x

Figure 13.12 *Overlap of homogeneous regions results in their splitting.*

13.3 Hybrid texture description methods

Purely syntactic methods of texture description are accompanied by many difficulties with syntactic analyser learning and with graph grammar (or other complex grammar) inference. This is the main reason why purely syntactic methods are not widely used. On the other hand, a precise definition of primitives brings many advantages and it is not wise to avoid it completely. Hybrid methods of texture description combine the statistical and syntactic approach. The technique is partly syntactic because the primitives are exactly defined, and partly statistical because spatial relations between primitives are based on probabilities [Conners and Harlow 80b].

The hybrid approach to texture description distinguishes between weak and strong textures. The syntactic part of weak texture description divides an image into regions based on a tonal image property (e.g. constant grey level regions) which are considered texture primitives. Primitives can be described by their shape, size, etc. The next step constructs histograms of sizes and shapes of all the texture primitives contained in the image. If the image can be segmented into two or more sets of homogeneous texture regions, the histogram is bimodal and each primitive is typical of one texture pattern. This can be used for texture segmentation.

If the starting histogram does not have significant peaks, a complete segmentation cannot be achieved. The histogram-based segmentation can be repeated in each so-far segmented homogeneous texture region. If any texture region consists of more than one primitive type, the method cannot be used and spatial relations between primitives must be computed. Some methods are discussed in [Haralick 79].

Description of strong textures is based on the spatial relations of texture primitives and two-directional interactions between primitives seem to carry most of the information. The simplest texture primitive is a pixel and its grey level property, while the maximum contiguous set of pixels of constant grey level is a more complicated texture primitive [Wang and Rosenfeld 81]. Such a primitive can be described by its size, elongatedness, orientation, average grey level, etc. The texture description includes spatial relations between primitives based on distance and adjacency relations. Using more complex texture primitives brings more textural information. On the other hand, all the properties of single pixel primitives are immediately available without the necessity of being involved in extensive primitive property computations.

The hybrid multi-level texture description and classification method [Sonka 86] is based on primitive definition and spatial description of inter-primitive relations. The method considers both tone and structural properties and consists of several consequent steps. Texture primitives must be extracted first, and then described and classified. As a result of this processing stage, a classifier knows how to classify texture primitives. Known textures are presented to the texture recognition system in the second stage of learning. Texture primitives are extracted from the image and the first level classifier recognizes their classes. Based on recognized texture primitives, spatial relations between primitive classes are evaluated for each texture from the training set. Spatial relations between texture primitives are described by a feature vector used to adjust a second level classifier. If the second level classifier is set, the two-level learning process is over, and unknown textures can be presented to the texture recognition system. The primitives are classified by the first level classifier, spatial primitive properties are computed and the second level classifier assigns the texture to one of the texture classes. Another hybrid method [Bruno 87] uses Fourier descriptors for shape coding and a texture is modelled by a reduced set of joint probability distributions obtained by vector quantization.

13.4 Texture recognition method applications

The estimated yield of crops or localization of diseased forests from remotely sensed data, automatic diagnosis of lung diseases from X-ray images, recognition of cloud types from meteorological satellite data, etc. are examples of texture recognition applications. Textures are very common in our world, and application possibilities are almost unlimited. The effectiveness of various texture recognition methods is discussed in [Conners and Harlow 80a].

Texture recognition of roads, road crossings, buildings, agricultural regions, and natural objects, or classification of trees into five classes, belong to classical applications of spatial frequency-based texture description methods. An interesting proof of the role of textural information in outdoor object recognition was done by comparison of classification correctness if textural information was and was not used; spectral information based classification achieved 74% correctly classified objects. Adding the textural information, accuracy increased to 99% [Haralick 79]. Real industrial applications of texture description and recognition are becoming more and more common. Examples can be found in almost all branches of industrial and biomedical activities – quality inspection in the motor or textile industries [Roning and Hall 87, Chen and Jain 88, Wood 90], workpiece surface monitoring [Adam and Nickolay 89], road surface skidding estimation [Heaton et al. 90, Kennedy et al. 90], microelectronics [Rao and Jain 90], remote sensing [IGARSS-89 90, Monjoux and Rudant 91], mammography [Miller and Astley 92], MR brain imaging [Toulson and Boyce 92], etc.

References

[Adam and Nickolay 89] W Adam and B Nickolay. Texture analysis for the evaluation of surface characteristics in quality monitoring. *SME Technical Paper (Series)*, MS, 1989.

[Ahuja 82] N Ahuja. Dot pattern processing using Voronoi neighborhood. *IEEE Transactions on Pattern Analysis and Machine Intelligence*, 4:336–343, 1982.

[Ahuja and Rosenfeld 81] N Ahuja and A Rosenfeld. Mosaic models for textures. *IEEE Transactions on Pattern Analysis and Machine Intelligence*, 3(1):1–11, 1981.

[Ando 88] S Ando. Texton finders based on Gaussian curvature of correlation with an application to rapid texture classification. In *Proceedings of the 1988 IEEE International Conference on Systems, Man, and Cybernetics,*, pages 25–28, IEEE, Beijing/Shenyang, China, 1988.

[Argenti et al. 90] F Argenti, L Alparone, and G Benelli. Fast algorithms for texture analysis using co-occurrence matrices. *IEE Proceedings, Part F: Radar and Signal Processing*, 137(6):443–448, 1990.

[Ballard and Brown 82] D H Ballard and C M Brown. *Computer Vision*. Prentice-Hall, Englewood Cliffs, NJ, 1982.

[Barnsley 88] M F Barnsley. *Fractals Everywhere*. Academic Press, Boston, Ma, 1988.

[Bouman and Liu 91] C Bouman and B Liu. Multiple resolution segmentation of textured images. *IEEE Transactions on Pattern Analysis and Machine Intelligence*, 13(2):99–113, 1991.

[Brodatz 66] P Brodatz. *Textures: A Photographic Album for Artists and Designers.* Dover Publishing Co., Toronto, 1966.

[Bruno 87] A Bruno. Hybrid model for the description of structured textures. In *Optical and Digital Pattern Recognition, Los Angeles, Ca,* pages 20–23, SPIE, Bellingham, Wa, 1987.

[Carlson and Ebel 88] G E Carlson and W J Ebel. Co-occurrence matrix modification for small region texture measurement and comparison. In *IGARSS'88 - Remote Sensing: Moving towards the 21st Century, Edinburgh, Scotland,* pages 519–520, IEEE, Piscataway, NJ, 1988.

[Chen and Jain 88] J Chen and A K Jain. Structural approach to identify defects in textured images. In *Proceedings of the 1988 IEEE International Conference on Systems, Man, and Cybernetics,* pages 29–32, IEEE, Beijing/Shenyang, China, 1988.

[Chetverikov 82] D Chetverikov. Experiments in the rotation-invariant texture discrimination using anisotropy features. In *Proceedings of the 6th IEEE Congress on Pattern Recognition,* pages 1071–1073, Munich, 1982.

[Conners and Harlow 80a] R W Conners and C A Harlow. A theoretical comparison of texture algorithms. *IEEE Transactions on Pattern Analysis and Machine Intelligence,* 2(3):204–222, 1980.

[Conners and Harlow 80b] R W Conners and C A Harlow. Toward a structural textural analyser based on statistical methods. *Computer Graphics and Image Processing,* 12:224–256, 1980.

[Davis and Mitiche 80] L S Davis and A Mitiche. Edge detection in textures. *Computer Graphics and Image Processing,* 12:25–39, 1980.

[Davis et al. 83] L S Davis, L Janos, and S M Dunn. Efficient recovery of shape from texture. *IEEE Transactions on Pattern Analysis and Machine Intelligence,* 5(5):485–492, 1983.

[Deguchi and Morishita 78] K Deguchi and I Morishita. Texture characterization and texture-based partitioning using two-dimensional linear estimation. *IEEE Transactions on Computers,* 27:739–745, 1978.

[Derin and Elliot 87] H Derin and H Elliot. Modelling and segmentation of noisy and textured images using Gibbs random fields. *IEEE Transactions on Pattern Analysis and Machine Intelligence,* 9(1):39–55, 1987.

[Dougherty et al. 89] E R Dougherty, E J Kraus, and J B Pelz. Image segmentation by local morphological granulometries. In *IGARSS'89 -
Twelfth Canadian Symposium on Remote Sensing, Vancouver, BC*,
pages 1220–1223, IEEE, Piscataway, NJ, 1989.

[Du Buf et al. 90] J M H Du Buf, M Kardan, and M Spann. Texture feature performance for image segmentation. *Pattern Recognition*, 23(3–
4):291–309, 1990.

[Ehrick and Foith 78] R W Ehrick and J P Foith. A view of texture topology
and texture description. *Computer Graphics and Image Processing*,
8:174–202, 1978.

[Fan 89] Z Fan. Edge-based hierarchical algorithm for textured image segmentation. In *International Conference on Acoustics, Speech, and
Signal Processing, Glasgow, Scotland*, pages 1679–1682, IEEE, Piscataway, NJ, 1989.

[Fu 74] K S Fu. *Syntactic Methods in Pattern Recognition*. Academic Press,
New York, 1974.

[Fu 80] K S Fu. Picture syntax. In S K Chang and K S Fu, editors, *Pictorial
Information Systems*, pages 104–127. Springer Verlag, Berlin, 1980.

[Fu 82] K S Fu. *Syntactic Pattern Recognition and Applications*. Prentice-
Hall, Englewood Cliffs, NJ, 1982.

[Fung et al. 90] P W Fung, G Grebbin, and Y Attikiouzel. Contextual classification and segmentation of textured images. In *Proceedings of
the 1990 International Conference on Acoustics, Speech, and Signal
Processing - ICASSP 90, Albuquerque, NM*, pages 2329–2332, IEEE,
Piscataway, NJ, 1990.

[Gagalowicz 79] A Gagalowicz. Stochatic texture fields synthesis from a priori
given second order statistics. In *Proceedings, Pattern Recognition and
Image Processing, Chicago, Il*, pages 376–381. IEEE, 1979.

[Gagalowicz and Graffigne 88] A Gagalowicz and C Graffigne. Blind texture
segmentation. In *9th International Conference on Pattern Recognition, Rome, Italy*, pages 46–50, IEEE, Piscataway, NJ, 1988.

[Gagalowicz et al. 88] A Gagalowicz, C Graffigne, and D Picard. Texture
boundary positioning. In *Proceedings of the 1988 IEEE International
Conference on Systems, Man, and Cybernetics*, pages 16–19, IEEE,
Beijing/Shenyang, China, 1988.

[Galloway 75] M M Galloway. Texture classification using gray level run length. *Computer Graphics and Image Processing*, 4:172–179, 1975.

[Gisolfi et al. 86] A Gisolfi, S Vitulano, and A Cacace. Texture and structure. In V Cappelini and R Marconi, editors, *Advances in Image Processing and Pattern Recognition*, pages 179–183. North Holland, Amsterdam, 1986.

[Gotlieb and Kreyszig 90] C C Gotlieb and H E Kreyszig. Texture descriptors based on co-occurrence matrices. *Computer Vision, Graphics, and Image Processing*, 51(1):70–86, 1990.

[Haralick 79] R M Haralick. Statistical and structural approaches to texture. *Proceedings IEEE*, 67(5):786–804, 1979.

[Haralick et al. 73] R M Haralick, K Shanmugam, and I Dinstein. Textural features for image classification. *IEEE Transactions on Systems, Man and Cybernetics*, 3:610–621, 1973.

[Heaton et al. 90] B S Heaton, J J Henry, and J C Wambold. Texture measuring equipment vs skid testing equipment. In *Proceedings of the 15th ARRB Conference, Darwin, Australia*, pages 53–64, Australian Road Research Board, Nunawading, 1990.

[IGARSS-89 90] *Quantitative Remote Sensing: An Economic Tool for the Nineties, IGARSS'89*, Canada, 1990. IEEE.

[Julesz 81] B Julesz. Textons, the elements of texture perception, and their interactions. *Nature*, 290:91–97, 1981.

[Julesz and Bergen 87] B Julesz and J R Bergen. Textons, the fundamental elements in preattentive vision and perception of textures. In *Readings in Computer Vision*, pages 243–256. Morgan Kaufmann Publishers, Los Altos, Ca, 1987.

[Julesz and Caelli 79] B Julesz and T Caelli. On the limits of Fourier decompositions in visual texture perception. *Perception*, 8:69–73, 1979.

[Keller et al. 89] J M Keller, S Chen, and R M Crownover. Texture description and segmentation through fractal geometry. *Computer Vision, Graphics, and Image Processing*, 45(2):150–166, 1989.

[Kennedy et al. 90] C K Kennedy, A E Young, and I C Butler. Measurement of skidding resistance and surface texture and the use of results in the UK. In *First International Symposium on Surface Characteristics, State College, Pa*, pages 87–102, ASTM, Philadelphia, Pa, 1990.

[Kjell and Wang 91] B P Kjell and P Y Wang. Noise-tolerant texture classification and image segmentation. In *Intelligent Robots and Computer Vision IX: Algorithms and Techniques, Boston, Ma*, pages 553–560, SPIE, Bellingham, Wa, 1991.

[Linnett and Richardson 90] L M Linnett and A J Richardson. Texture segmentation using directional operators. In *Proceedings of the 1990 International Conference on Acoustics, Speech, and Signal Processing - ICASSP 90, Albuquerque, NM*, pages 2309–2312, IEEE, Piscataway, NJ, 1990.

[Liu and Jernigan 90] S S Liu and M E Jernigan. Texture analysis and discrimination in additive noise. *Computer Vision, Graphics, and Image Processing*, 49:52–67, 1990.

[Lu and Fu 78] S Y Lu and K S Fu. A syntactic approach to texture analysis. *Computer Graphics and Image Processing*, 7:303–330, 1978.

[Mandelbrot 83] B B Mandelbrot. *The Fractal Geometry of Nature*. Freeman, New York, 1983.

[Miller and Astley 92] P Miller and S Astley. Classification of breast tissue by texture analysis. *Image and Vision Computing*, 10(5):277–282, 1992.

[Mitchell et al. 77] O R Mitchell, C R Myer, and W Boyne. A max-min measure for image texture analysis. *IEEE Transactions on Computers*, 26:408–414, 1977.

[Monjoux and Rudant 91] E Monjoux and J P Rudant. Texture segmentation in aerial images. In *Image Processing Algorithms and Techniques II, San Jose, Ca*, pages 310–318, SPIE, Bellingham, Wa, 1991.

[Pavlidis 80] T Pavlidis. Structural descriptions and graph grammars. In S K Chang and K S Fu, editors, *Pictorial Information Systems*, pages 86–103, Springer Verlag, Berlin, 1980.

[Pentland 84] A P Pentland. Fractal-based description of natural scenes. *IEEE Transactions on Pattern Analysis and Machine Intelligence*, 6:661–674, 1984.

[Perry and Lowe 89] A Perry and D G Lowe. Segmentation of non-random textures using zero-crossings. In *1989 IEEE International Conference on Systems, Man, and Cybernetics, Cambridge, Ma*, pages 1051–1054, IEEE, Piscataway, NJ, 1989.

[Pratt and Faugeras 78] W K Pratt and O C Faugeras. Development and evaluation of stochastic-based visual texture features. *IEEE Transactions on Systems, Man and Cybernetics*, 8:796–804, 1978.

[Rao 90] A R Rao. *A Taxonomy for Texture Description and Identification.* Springer Verlag, New York, 1990.

[Rao and Jain 90] A R Rao and R Jain. Quantitative measures for surface texture description in semiconductor wafer inspection. In *Integrated Circuit Metrology, Inspection, and Process Control IV, San Jose, Ca*, pages 164–172, SPIE, Bellingham, Wa, 1990.

[Reed et al. 90] T R Reed, H Wechsler, and M Werman. Texture segmentation using a diffusion region growing technique. *Pattern Recognition*, 23(9):953–960, 1990.

[Roning and Hall 87] J Roning and E L Hall. Shape, form, and texture recognition for automotive brake pad inspection. In *Automated Inspection and Measurement, Cambridge, Ma*, pages 82–90, SPIE, Bellingham, Wa, 1987.

[Rosenfeld 76] A Rosenfeld, editor. *Digital Picture Analysis.* Springer Verlag, Berlin, 1976.

[Serra and Verchery 73] J Serra and G Verchery. Mathematical morphology applied to fibre composite materials. *Film Sci. Tech.*, 6:141–158, 1973.

[Shulman 70] A R Shulman. *Optical Data Processing.* John Wiley and Sons, New York, 1970.

[Simaan 90] M Simaan. Knowledge-guided segmentation of texture images. In *Proceedings of the 1990 IEEE International Conference on Systems Engineering, Pittsburgh, Pa*, pages 539–542, IEEE, Piscataway, 1990.

[Sklansky 78] J Sklansky. Image segmentation and feature extraction. *IEEE Transactions on Systems, Man and Cybernetics*, 8(4):337–347, 1978.

[Soh and Huntsberger 91] S N J Soh, Y Murthy and T L Huntsberger. Development of criteria to compare model-based texture analysis methods. In *Intelligent Robots and Computer Vision IX: Algorithms and Techniques, Boston, Ma*, pages 561–573, SPIE, Bellingham, Wa, 1991.

[Sonka 86] M Sonka. A new texture recognition method. *Computers and Artificial Intelligence*, 5(4):357–364, 1986.

[Sutton and Hall 72] R Sutton and E Hall. Texture measures for automatic classification of pulmonary diseases. *IEEE Transactions on Computers*, C–21(1):667–678, 1972.

[Tan and Constantinides 90] T N Tan and A G Constantinides. Texture analysis based on a human visual model. In *Proceedings of the 1990 International Conference on Acoustics, Speech, and Signal Processing - ICASSP 90, Albuquerque, NM*, pages 2137–2140, IEEE, Piscataway, NJ, 1990.

[Tomita and Tsuji 90] F Tomita and S Tsuji. *Computer Analysis of Visual Textures*. Kluwer Academic Publishers, Norwell, Ma, 1990.

[Tomita et al. 82] F Tomita, Y Shirai, and S Tsuji. Description of textures by a structural analysis. *IEEE Transactions on Pattern Analysis and Machine Intelligence*, 4(2):183–191, 1982.

[Toulson and Boyce 92] D L Toulson and J F Boyce. Segmentation of MR images using neural nets. *Image and Vision Computing*, 10(5):324–328, 1992.

[Tsuji and Tomita 73] S Tsuji and F Tomita. A structural analyser for a class of textures. *Computer Graphics and Image Processing*, 2:216–231, 1973.

[Tuceryan and Jain 90] M Tuceryan and A K Jain. Texture segmentation using Voronoi polygons. *IEEE Transactions on Pattern Analysis and Machine Intelligence*, 12(2):211–216, 1990.

[Unser and Eden 89] M Unser and M Eden. Multiresolution feature extraction and selection for texture segmentation. *IEEE Transactions on Pattern Analysis and Machine Intelligence*, 11(7):717–728, 1989.

[Urquhart 82] R Urquhart. Graph theoretical clustering based on limited neighbourhood sets. *Pattern Recognition*, 15(3):173–187, 1982.

[Vafaie and Bourbakis 88] H Vafaie and N G Bourbakis. Tree grammar scheme for generation and recognition of simple texture paths in pictures. In *Third International Symposium on Intelligent Control 1988, Arlington, Va*, pages 201–206, IEEE, Piscataway, NJ, 1988.

[Voorhees and Poggio 87] H Voorhees and T A Poggio. Detecting textons and texture boundaries in natural images. In *Proceedings - First International Conference on Computer Vision, London, England*, pages 250–258, IEEE, Piscataway, NJ, 1987.

[Wang and Rosenfeld 81] S Wang and A Rosenfeld. A relative effectiveness of selected texture primitive. *IEEE Transactions on Systems, Man and Cybernetics*, 11:360–370, 1981.

[Weszka et al. 76] J S Weszka, C Dyer, and A Rosenfeld. A comparative study of texture measures for terrain classification. *IEEE Transactions on Systems, Man and Cybernetics*, 6(4):269–285, 1976.

[Wood 90] E J Wood. Applying Fourier and associated transforms to pattern characterization in textiles. *Textile Research Journal*, 60(4):212–220, 1990.

14

Motion analysis

In recent years, interest in motion processing has increased with advances in motion analysis methodology and processing capabilities. The usual input to a motion analysis system is an image sequence, with a corresponding increase in the amount of processed data. Motion analysis is often connected with real-time analysis, for example, for robot navigation. Another common motion analysis problem is to obtain comprehensive information about objects present in the scene, including moving and static objects. Detecting 3D shape and relative depth from motion are also fast-developing fields – these issues are considered in Chapter 9.

A set of assumptions can help to solve motion analysis problems – as always, prior knowledge helps to decrease the complexity of analysis. Prior knowledge includes information about the camera motion – mobile or static – and information about the time interval between consecutive images, especially if this interval was short enough for the sequence to represent continuous motion. This prior information about data helps in the choice of an appropriate motion analysis technique. As in other areas of machine vision, there is no foolproof technique in motion analysis, no general algorithm and furthermore, the techniques presented in this chapter work only if certain conditions are met. A very interesting aspect of motion analysis is research into visual sensing of living organisms that are extremely well adapted to motion analysis. The psychological aspects of motion sensing can be studied in [Koenderink and Doorn 75, Ullman 79, Clocksin 80, Thompson and Barnard 81, Marr 82, Koenderink 86].

There are three main groups of motion-related problems from the practical point of view [Yachida et al. 80, Radig 84, Kanatani 85, Horn 86, Schalkoff 87, Vesecky 88, Anandan 88, Aggarwal and Nandhakumar 88, Vega-Riveros and Jabbour 89, Murray and Buxton 89, Thompson and Pong 90, Fleet 92]

1. Motion detection is the simplest problem. This registers any detected motion and is often used for security purposes. This group usually uses a single static camera.

2. Moving object detection and location represent another set of problems. A camera is usually in a static location and objects are moving in the scene, or the camera moves and objects are static. These problems are

considerably more difficult in comparison with the first group. If only moving object detection is required (note the difference between motion detection and moving object detection), the solution can be based on motion-based segmentation methods. Other more complex problems include the detection of a moving object, the detection of the trajectory of its motion and the prediction of its future trajectory [Webb and Aggarwal 82, Sethi and Jain 87]. Image object-matching techniques are often used to solve this task; typically, direct matching in image data, matching of object features, matching of specific representative object points (corners, etc.) in an image sequence, or representing moving objects as graphs and consequent matching of these graphs. Practical examples of methods from this group include cloud tracing from a sequence of satellite meteorological data, including cloud character and motion prediction, automatic satellite location by detecting specific points of interest on the Earth's surface, city traffic analysis, and many military applications. The most complex methods of this group work even if both camera and objects are moving.

3. The third group is related to the derivation of 3D object properties from a set of 2D projections acquired at different time instants of object motion. Three-dimensional object description is covered in Chapter 9, and more information on this topic can be found in [Ullman 79, Tsai and Huang 81, Tsai and Huang 82, Webb and Aggarwal 82, Dreschler and Nagel 82, Huang 83, Costabile et al. 85, Mutch and Thomson 85, Jain et al. 87, WVM 89, Weng et al. 89, Adiv 89, Murray and Buxton 90, Zheng and Tsuji 90, Heel 90] and the references to Chapter 9.

Even though motion analysis is often called **dynamic image analysis**, it is frequently based on a small number of consecutive images, sometimes just two or three in a sequence. This case is similar to an analysis of static images, and the motion is actually analysed at a higher level looking for **correspondence** between pairs of points of interest in sequential images. This is the main rationale for the extensive application of matching in motion analysis. A two-dimensional representation of a (generally) three-dimensional motion is called a **motion field** in which each point is assigned a **velocity vector** corresponding to the motion direction, velocity, and distance from an observer at an appropriate image location. A different approach analyses motion from an **optical flow** computation (Section 14.2), where a very small time distance between consecutive images is required, and no significant change occurs between two consecutive images. Optical flow computation results in motion direction and motion velocity determination at (possibly all) image points. The immediate aim of optical-flow based image analysis is to determine a motion field. As will be discussed later, optical flow does not always correspond with the true motion field because illumination changes are reflected in the optical flow. Object motion parameters can be derived from computed optical flow vectors. In reality, estimates of optical flow or point correspondence are noisy, but, unfortunately, three-dimensional interpretation of motion is ill-conditioned and requires high precision of optical flow or point correspondence. To overcome these difficulties, approaches that are not based on optical flow or point correspondence have begun to appear, since if the intermediate step (optical flow, point correspondence) does not have to be computed, possible errors can be avoided. Estimates of general motion of multiple moving objects in an image sequence based on grey level and image gradient without using any higher level information such as corners or borders is introduced in [Wu and Kittler 90].

Motion field or **velocity field** computations represent a compromise technique; information similar to the optical flow is determined but it is based on images acquired at intervals that are not short enough to ensure small changes due to motion. The velocity field can also be acquired if the number of images in a sequence is small.

Motion evaluation may or may not depend on object detection. An example of object-independent analysis is optical flow computation, whereas velocity field computation or differential methods search for points of interest or points of motion and represent object-dependent analysis. Object-dependent methods are usually based on searching for a correspondence between points of interest or between regions. A recent approach to motion analysis uses active contour models called snakes which were discussed in Section 8.2. In motion analysis, the initial estimate necessary to start the snake energy minimization process is obtained from the detected position of the contour in the previous frame. For details, see Section 8.2.

If motion analysis is based on moving object detection, the following object motion assumptions can help to localize moving objects (Figure 14.1).

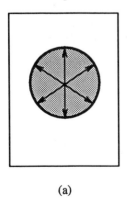 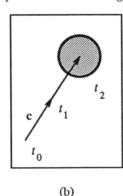 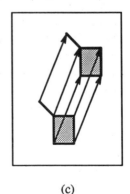

| (a) | (b) | (c) |

Figure 14.1 *Object motion assumptions: (a) Maximum velocity, (b) small acceleration, (c) common motion and mutual correspondence (rigid objects).*

- **Maximum velocity**: Assume that a moving object is scanned at time intervals of dt. A possible position of a specific object point in a subsequent image is inside a circle with its centre at the original object point position and its radius $c_{max}dt$, where c_{max} is the assumed maximum velocity of the moving object.

- **Small acceleration**: The change of velocity in time dt is bounded by some constant.

- **Common motion** (similarity in motion): All the object points move in a similar way.

- **Mutual correspondence**: Rigid objects exhibit stable pattern points. Each point of an object corresponds to exactly one point in the next image in sequence and vice versa, although there are exceptions due to occlusion and object rotation.

14.1 Differential motion analysis methods

Simple subtraction of images acquired at different instants in time makes motion detection possible, assuming a stationary camera position and constant illumination. A **difference image** $d(i,j)$ is a binary image where non-zero values represent image areas with motion, that is, areas where there was a substantial difference between grey levels in consecutive images f_1 and f_2;

$$d(i,j) = 0 \quad \text{if } |f_1(i,j) - f_2(i,j)| \le \varepsilon$$
$$= 1 \quad \text{otherwise} \tag{14.1}$$

where ε is a small positive number. The difference image can be based on more complex image features like average grey level in some neighbourhood, local texture features, etc. It is clear that the motion of any object distinct from its background can be detected (considering motion detection represents motion registration only).

Let f_1 and f_2 be two consecutive images separated by a time interval. An element $d(i,j)$ of the difference image between images f_1 and f_2 may have a value 1 due to any one of the following reasons

1. $f_1(i,j)$ is a pixel on a moving object
   $f_2(i,j)$ is a pixel on the static background
   (or vice versa)

2. $f_1(i,j)$ is a pixel on a moving object
   $f_2(i,j)$ is a pixel on another moving object

3. $f_1(i,j)$ is a pixel on a moving object
   $f_2(i,j)$ is a pixel on a different part of the same moving object

4. Noise, inaccuracies of stationary camera positioning, etc.

The system errors mentioned in the last item must be suppressed. The simplest solution is not to consider any regions of the difference image that are smaller than a specified threshold, although this may cause slow motion and small object motions not to be detected. Further, results of this approach are highly dependent on an object-background contrast. On the other hand, we can be sure that all the resulting regions in the difference images result from motion.

The trajectories detected using differential image motion analysis do not reveal what the direction of the motion was. If direction is needed, construction of a **cumulative difference image** can solve this problem. Cumulative difference images contain information about motion direction and other time-related motion properties, and about slow motion and small object motion as well. The cumulative difference image d_{cum} is constructed from a sequence of n images, with the first image (f_1) being considered a reference image. Values of the cumulative difference image reflect how often the image grey level was different from the grey level of the reference image (if we do not include weight coefficients a_k)

$$d_{cum}(i,j) = \sum_{k=1}^{n} a_k |f_1(i,j) - f_k(i,j)| \qquad (14.2)$$

a_k gives the **significance** of images in the sequence of n images; more recent images may be given larger weights to reflect the importance of current motion and to specify current object location.

Assume that an image of a static scene is available, and only stationary objects are present in the scene. If this image is used for reference, the difference image suppresses all motionless areas, and any motion in the scene can be detected as areas corresponding to the actual positions of the moving objects in the scene. Motion analysis can then be based on a sequence of difference images. The only problem with this approach may be the impossibility of getting an image of a static reference scene if the motion never ends; then a learning stage must construct the reference image. The most straightforward method is to superimpose moving image objects on non-moving image backgrounds from other images taken in a different phase of the motion. Which image parts should be superimposed can be judged from difference images, or the reference image can be constructed interactively (which can be allowed in the learning stage).

Subsequent analysis usually determines motion trajectories; often only the centre of gravity trajectory is needed. The task may be considerably simplified if objects can be segmented out of the first image of the sequence. A practical problem is the prediction of the motion trajectory if the object position in several previous images is known. There are many methods [Jain 81, Jain 84] that find other motion parameters from difference images – whether the object is approaching or receding, which object overlaps which, etc. Note that difference motion analysis methods give good examples of motion analysis principles and present a good introduction to the problem; unfortunately, the difference images do not carry enough information to work reliably in reality. Some problems are common for most motion field detection approaches – consider just a simple example of a rectangular object moving parallel to the object boundary; differential motion analysis can only detect the motion of two sides of the rectangle (see Figure 14.2a and b). Similarly, an aperture problem may cause ambiguity of contained motion information – in the situation shown in Figure 14.2c, only part of an object boundary is visible and it is impossible to determine the motion completely. The arrows indicate three possibilities of motion all yielding the same final position of the object boundary in the image. Differential motion analysis is often used in digital subtraction angiography where a vessel motion is estimated [Rong et al. 89, Abdel-Malek et al. 90].

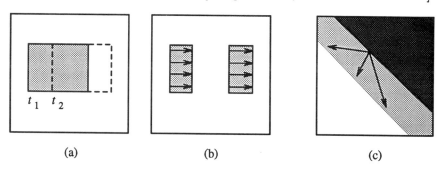

(a)   (b)   (c)

Figure 14.2 *Problems of motion field construction: (a) Object position at times t_1 and t_2, (b) motion field, (c) aperture problem – ambiguous motion.*

14.2 Optical flow

Optical flow reflects the image changes due to motion during a time interval dt, and the optical flow field is the velocity field that represents the three-dimensional motion of object points across a two-dimensional image [Kearney and Thompson 88]. Optical flow is an abstraction typical of the kind that computational methods are trying to achieve. Therefore, it should represent only those motion-related intensity changes in the image that are desired in further processing, and all other image changes reflected in the optical flow should be considered errors of flow detection. For example, optical flow should not be sensitive to illumination changes and motion of unimportant objects (e.g. shadows). However, a non-zero optical flow is detected if a fixed sphere is illuminated by a moving source. Similarly, considering a smooth sphere rotating under constant illumination, no optical flow is sensed despite the rotational motion and the true non-zero motion field [Horn 86]. Of course, the aim is to determine an optical flow that corresponds closely with the true motion field. Optical flow computation is a necessary precondition of subsequent higher level processing that can solve motion-related problems if a camera is stationary or moving; it provides tools to determine parameters of motion, relative distances of objects in the image, etc. A simulated example of two consecutive images and a corresponding optical flow image are shown in Figure 14.3.

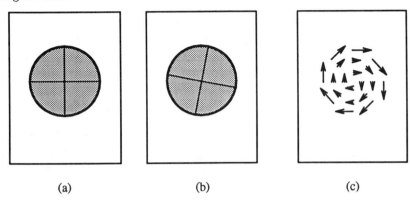

(a)   (b)   (c)

Figure 14.3 *Optical flow: (a) Time t_1, (b) time t_2, (c) optical flow.*

14.2.1 Optical flow computation

Optical flow computation is based on two assumptions:

1. The observed brightness of any object point is constant over time.

2. Nearby points in the image plane move in a similar manner (the **velocity smoothness** constraint).

Suppose we have a continuous image; $f(x, y, t)$ refers to the grey level of (x, y) at time t. Representing a dynamic image as a function of position and time permits it to be expressed as a Taylor series;

$$f(x + dx, y + dy, t + dt) = f(x, y, t) + \frac{\partial f}{\partial x}dx + \frac{\partial f}{\partial y}dy + \frac{\partial f}{\partial t}dt + O(\partial^2)$$
$$= f(x, y, t) + f_x dx + f_y dy + f_t dt + O(\partial^2)$$
$$(14.3)$$

We can assume that the immediate neighbourhood of (x, y) is translated some small distance (dx, dy) during the interval dt; that is, we can find dx, dy, dt such that

$$f(x + dx, y + dy, t + dt) = f(x, y, t) \qquad (14.4)$$

If dx, dy, dt are very small, the higher order terms in equation (14.3) vanish and

$$-f_t = f_x \frac{dx}{dt} + f_y \frac{dy}{dt} \qquad (14.5)$$

The goal is to compute the velocity

$$\mathbf{c} = (\frac{dx}{dt}, \frac{dy}{dt}) = (u, v)$$

f_x, f_y, f_t can be computed or, at least, approximated, from $f(x, y, t)$. The motion velocity can then be estimated as

$$-f_t = f_x u + f_y v = grad(f)\mathbf{c} \tag{14.6}$$

where $grad(f)$ is a two-dimensional image gradient. It can be seen from equation (14.6) that the grey level difference f_t at the same location of the image at times t and $t + dt$ is a product of spatial grey level difference and velocity in this location according to the observer.

Equation (14.6) does not specify the velocity vector completely; rather, it only provides the component in the direction of the brightest gradient (see Figure 14.2c). To solve the problem completely, a smoothness constraint is introduced; that is, the velocity vector field changes slowly in a given neighbourhood. Full details of this approach may be found in [Horn and Schunk 81], but the approach reduces to minimizing the squared error quantity

$$E^2(x, y) = (f_x u + f_y v + f_t)^2 + \lambda(u_x^2 + u_y^2 + v_x^2 + v_y^2) \tag{14.7}$$

where $u_x^2, u_y^2, v_x^2, v_y^2$ denote partial derivatives squared as error terms. The first term represents a solution to equation (14.6), the second term is the smoothness criterion and λ is a Lagrange multiplier. Using standard techniques [Horn and Schunk 81], this reduces to solving the differential equations

$$(\lambda^2 + f_x^2)u + f_x f_y v = \lambda^2 \overline{u} - f_x f_t \tag{14.8}$$

$$f_x f_y u + (\lambda^2 + f_y^2)v = \lambda^2 \overline{v} - f_y f_t$$

where $\overline{u}, \overline{v}$ are mean values of the velocity in directions x and y in some neighbourhood of (x, y). It can be shown that a solution to these equations is

$$u = \overline{u} - f_x \frac{P}{D} \tag{14.9}$$

$$v = \overline{v} - f_y \frac{P}{D} \tag{14.10}$$

where

$$P = f_x \overline{u} + f_y \overline{v}, \qquad D = \lambda^2 + f_x^2 + f_y^2 \tag{14.11}$$

Determination of the optical flow is then based on a Gauss-Seidel iteration method using pairs of (consecutive) dynamic images [Horn 86].

Algorithm 14.1: Relaxation computation of optical flow from a pair of dynamic images

1. Initialize velocity vectors $c(i, j) = 0$ for all (i, j).

2. Let k denote the iteration number. Compute values u^k, v^k for all pixels (i, j)

$$
\begin{aligned}
u^k(i, j) &= \bar{u}^{k-1}(i, j) - f_x(i, j)\frac{P(i, j)}{D(i, j)} \\
v^k(i, j) &= \bar{v}^{k-1}(i, j) - f_y(i, j)\frac{P(i, j)}{D(i, j)}
\end{aligned}
\tag{14.12}
$$

The partial derivatives f_x, f_y, f_t can be estimated from the pair of consecutive images.

3. Stop if

$$
\sum_i \sum_j E^2(i, j) < \varepsilon
$$

where ε is the maximum permitted error; return to step (2) otherwise.

If more than two images are to be processed, computational efficiency may be increased by using the results of one iteration to initialize the current image pair in sequence.

Algorithm 14.2: Optical flow computation from an image sequence

1. Evaluate starting values of the optical flow $c(i, j)$ for all points (i, j).

2. Let k be the sequence number of the currently processed image. For all pixels of the next image evaluate

$$
\begin{aligned}
u^{k+1}(i, j) &= \bar{u}^k(i, j) - f_x(i, j)\frac{P(i, j)}{D(i, j)} \\
v^{k+1}(i, j) &= \bar{v}^k(i, j) - f_y(i, j)\frac{P(i, j)}{D(i, j)}
\end{aligned}
\tag{14.13}
$$

3. Repeat step (2) to process all images in the sequence.

Both these algorithms are naturally parallel. The iterations may be very slow, with a computational complexity $\mathcal{O}(n^p)$ where p is the order of the partial differential equation set (14.8). Experimentally, it is found that thousands of iterations are needed until convergence if a second-order smoothness criterion is applied [Glazer 84]. On the other hand, the first 10-20 iterations usually leave an error smaller than the required accuracy, and the rest of the iterative process is then very gradual.

If the differences dx, dy, dt are very small, all the higher order terms vanish in the continuous derivative of equation (14.3). Unfortunately, in reality, this is often not the case if subsequent images are not taken frequently enough. As a result, the higher order terms do not vanish and an estimation error results if they are neglected. To decrease this error, the second-order terms may be considered in the Taylor series, and the problem becomes a minimization of an integral over a local neighbourhood N [Nagel 83, Nagel 86, Nagel 87]

$$\int\int_N [\ f(x,y,t) - f(x_0,y_0,t_0) - f_x[x-u] - f_y[y-v] - \tfrac{1}{2}f_{xx}[x-u]^2 -$$
$$f_{xy}[x-u][y-v] - \tfrac{1}{2}f_{yy}[y-v]^2]^2 \ dx \ dy \qquad (14.14)$$

This minimization is rather complex and may be simplified for image points that correspond to corners (Section 4.3.7). Let the co-ordinate system be aligned with the main curvature direction at (x_0, y_0); then $f_{xy} = 0$ and the only non-zero second-order derivatives are f_{xx} and f_{yy}. However, at least one of them must cross zero at (x_0, y_0) to get a maximum gradient: If, say, $f_{xx} = 0$, then $f_x \rightarrow$ max and $f_y = 0$. With these assumptions, equation (14.14) simplifies, and the following formula is minimized [Nagel 83, Vega-Riveros and Jabbour 89]

$$\sum_{x,y \in N} [f(x,y,t) - f(x_0,y_0,t_0) - f_x[x-u] - \frac{1}{2}f_{yy}[y-v]^2]^2 \qquad (14.15)$$

A conventional minimization approach of differentiating equation (14.15) with respect to u and v and equating to zero results in two equations in the two velocity components u, v.

14.2.2 Global and local optical flow estimation

Optical flow computation will be in error to the extent that the constant brightness and velocity smoothness assumptions are violated. Unfortunately, in real imagery, their violation is quite common. Typically, the optical flow changes dramatically in highly textured regions, around moving boundaries, depth discontinuities, etc. [Kearney and Thompson 88]. A significant advantage of global relaxation methods of optical flow computation is to find the smoothest velocity field consistent with the image data; as discussed in Section 8.4, an important property of relaxation methods is their ability to propagate local constraints globally. As a result, not only constraint information but also all optical flow estimation errors propagate across the solution. Therefore, even a small number of problem areas in the optical flow field may cause widespread errors and poor optical flow estimates.

Since global error propagation is the biggest problem of the global optical flow computation scheme, local optical flow estimation appears a natural solution to the difficulties. The local estimate is based on the same brightness and smoothness assumptions, and the idea is to divide the image into small regions where the assumptions hold. This solves the error propagation problem but another problem arises – in regions where the spatial gradients change slowly, the optical flow estimation gets ill-conditioned because of lack of motion information, and it cannot be detected correctly. If a global method is applied to the same region, the information from neighbouring image parts propagates and represents a basis for optical flow computation even if the local information was not sufficient by itself. The conclusion of this comparison is that global sharing of information is beneficial in constraint sharing and detrimental with respect to error propagation [Kearney and Thompson 88].

One way to cope with the smoothness violation problem is to detect regions in which the smoothness constraints hold. Two heuristics for identifying neighbouring constraint equations, that differ substantially in their flow value were introduced in [Horn and Schunk 81]. The main problem is in selecting a threshold to decide which flow value difference should be considered substantial – if the threshold is set too low, many points are considered positioned along flow discontinuities, while if the threshold is too high, some points violating smoothness remain part of the computational net. The boundary between smooth subnets is not closed; paths between them remain, and the error propagation problem is not solved.

An approach of continuous adaptation to errors was introduced in [Kearney et al. 87]. As with the basic global relaxation method, optical flow is determined iteratively by combining the local average flow vector with the gradient constraint equation. However, a confidence is assigned to each flow vector based on heuristic judgements of correctness and the local average flow is computed as a weighted average by confidence. Thus, the propagation of error-free estimates is inhibited. Details of confidence estimation, smoothness violation detection, combining partial estimates, implementation details, and discussion of results are given in [Kearney et al. 87, Kearney and Thompson 88].

Performance of the method is illustrated in Figures 14.4 and 14.5. The first image pair is shown in Figure 14.4a and b and contains a collection of toys and the second pair of images (Figure 14.5a and b) simulates a view from an aircraft flying over a city. Optical flow resulting from a simple local optimization is shown in Figures 14.4c and 14.5c, and results of the global method of continuous adaptation to errors are given in Figures 14.4d and 14.5d. The optical flow improvement achieved by the latter method is clearly visible.

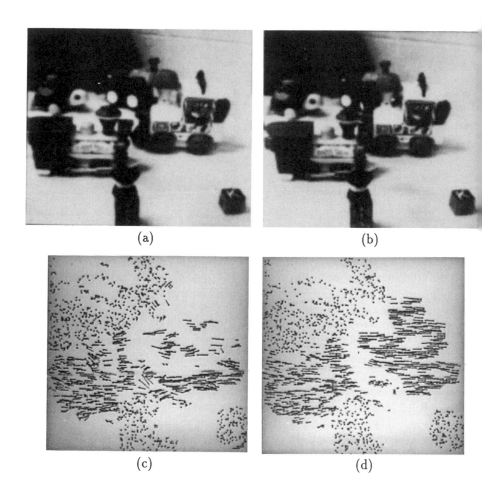

Figure 14.4 *Moving trains image sequence: (a) First frame, (b) last frame, (c) optical flow detection – local optimization method, (d) optical flow-detection – method of continuous adaptation to errors. (Only 20% of vectors with moderate and high confidence shown.) Courtesy J. Kearney, University of Iowa.*

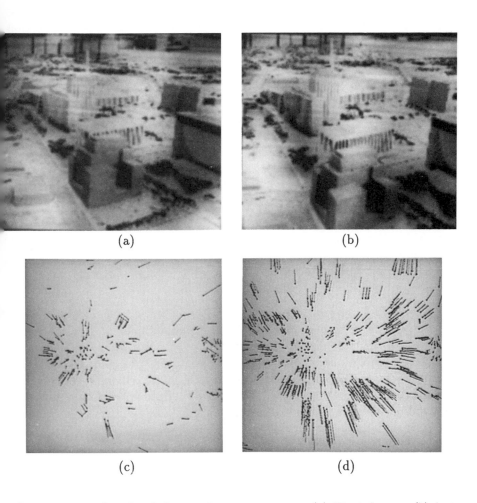

(a)   (b)

(c)   (d)

Figure 14.5 *Simulated flyover image sequence: (a) First frame, (b) last frame, (c) optical flow detection – local optimization method, (d) optical flow detection – method of continuous adaptation to errors. (Only 20% of vectors with moderate and high confidence shown.) Courtesy J. Kearney, University of Iowa.*

Optical flow – its computation and use, and the many variations thereon, has generated an enormous literature, and continues so to do.

Optical flow constraints are discussed in detail in several other papers [Snyder 89, Girosi et al. 89, Verri et al. 89], and computational aspects are considered in [Lee et al. 89]. Several approaches to optical flow computation have been investigated which are not based on velocity smoothness; a spatio-temporal gradient method is described in [Paquin and Dubois 83], and motion of planar surfaces is considered in [Waxman and Wohn 85, Waxman et al. 87]. Smoothing the flow only along one-dimensional curves corresponding to zero crossings was introduced in [Hildreth 83], and selective application of smoothness requirements also can be found in [Davis et al. 83, Nagel and Enkelmann 84, Fogel 88, Fogel 89]. A robust algorithm for computing image flow from object boundary information is presented in [Schunck 89]. Minimization of a penalty function as a weighted sum of the two constraining terms and the smoothness term (using a divergence-free and an incompressibility constraint) is proposed in [Song and Leahy 91], where results were tested on cine CT image sequences of a beating heart. Another approach is to compute the flow at certain locations in the image at seed points [Brady 87]; this approach has a direct link to the parallel computation of optical flow. A detailed description of local optical flow computation necessary for fully parallel implementation is discussed in [Burt et al. 83, Gong 87, Anandan 87, Gong 88, Enkelmann 88, Gong 89].

Many other approaches to computation of constrained optical flow equations can be found. A linear combination of the optical flow estimate in adjacent windows is used in [Cafforio and Rocca 83]. A vector field smoothness constrained only in the direction perpendicular to the grey value gradient is considered in [Nagel and Enkelmann 84]. Optical flow computation in pyramid image representation is described in [Glazer 84]; iterations converge significantly faster in lower resolution pyramid levels, and the computed values can be used as starting values in lower pyramid levels with higher resolution. This hierarchical approach is claimed to give better results than conventional single-resolution methods because the optical flow computation assumptions can be satisfied more easily especially if the optical flow is relatively large and the accompanying grey level changes are small. Several other approaches are mentioned in [Vega-Riveros and Jabbour 89].

Comparison of the performance of many optical flow techniques is given in [Barron et al. 92a] – local differential approaches [Lucas and Kanade 81, Fleet and Jepson 90] were found to be most accurate and robust. Techniques using global smoothness constraints were found to produce visually attractive motion fields, but give an accuracy suitable only for qualitative use, insufficient for egomotion computation and 3D structure from motion detection; see [Barron et al. 92a, Barron et al. 92b] for details.

14.2.3 Optical flow in motion analysis

Optical flow gives a description of motion and can be a valuable contribution to image interpretation even if no quantitative parameters are obtained from motion analysis. Optical flow can be used to study a large variety of motions – moving observer and static objects, static observer and moving objects, or both moving. Optical flow analysis does not result in motion trajectories as described in Section 14.1; instead, more general motion properties are detected that can significantly increase the reliability of complex dynamic image analysis [Thompson et al. 85, Sandini and Tistarelli 86, Kearney et al. 87, Aggarwal and Martin 88].

Motion, as it appears in dynamic images, is usually some combination of four basic elements:

- Translation at constant distance from observer.

- Translation in depth relative to observer.

- Rotation at constant distance about the view axis.

- Rotation of a planar object perpendicular to the view axis.

Optical-flow based motion analysis can recognize these basic elements by applying a few relatively simple operators to the flow [Thompson et al. 83, Mutch and Thompson 84]. Motion form recognition is based on the following facts (Figure 14.6):

- Translation at constant distance is represented as a set of parallel motion vectors.

- Translation in depth forms a set of vectors having a common focus of expansion.

- Rotation at constant distance results in a set of concentric motion vectors.

- Rotation perpendicular to the view axis forms one or more sets of vectors starting from straight line segments.

Exact determination of rotation axes and translation trajectories can be computed, but with a significant increase in difficulty of analysis.

Consider translational motion: If the translation is not at constant depth, then optical flow vectors are not parallel, and their directions have a single focus of expansion (FOE). If the translation is at constant depth, the FOE is at infinity. If several independently moving objects are present in the image, each motion has its own FOE – this is illustrated in Figure 14.7, where an observer moves in a car towards other approaching cars on the road.

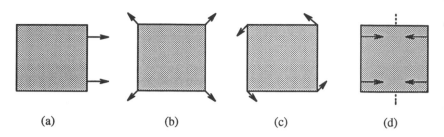

(a) (b) (c) (d)

Figure 14.6 *Motion form recognition: (a) Translation at constant distance, (b) translation in depth, (c) rotation at constant distance, (d) planar object rotation perpendicular to the view axis.*

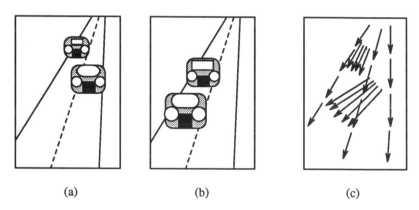

(a) (b) (c)

Figure 14.7 *Focus of expansion: (a) Time t_1, (b) time t_2, (c) optical flow.*

The mutual velocity **c** of an observer and an object represented by an image point can be found in an optical flow representation. Let the mutual velocities in directions x, y, z be $c_x = u, c_y = v, c_z = w$, where z gives information about the depth (note that $z > 0$ for points in front of the image plane). To distinguish image co-ordinates from real-world co-ordinates in the following, let the image co-ordinates be x', y'. From perspective considerations, if (x_0, y_0, z_0) is the position of some point at time $t_0 = 0$ then the position of the same point at time t can, assuming unit focal distance of the optical system and constant velocity, be determined as follows

$$(x', y') = (\frac{x_0 + ut}{z_0 + wt}, \frac{y_0 + vt}{z_0 + wt})$$ (14.16)

The FOE in a two-dimensional image can be determined from this equation. Let us assume motion directed toward an observer; as $t \to -\infty$, the motion can be traced back to the originating point at infinite distance from the observer. The motion toward an observer continues along straight lines and the originating point in the image plane is

$$\mathbf{x}'_{FOE} = (\frac{u}{w}, \frac{v}{w}) \tag{14.17}$$

Note, that the same equation can be used for $t \to \infty$ and motion in the opposite direction. Clearly any change of motion direction results in changes of velocities u, v, w, and the FOE changes its location in the image [Jain 83].

Because of the presence of a z co-ordinate in equation (14.16), optical flow can be used to determine the current distance of a moving object from the observer's position. The distance information is contained indirectly in equation (14.16). Assuming points of the same rigid object and translational motion, at least one actual distance value must be known to evaluate the distance exactly. Let $D(t)$ be the distance of a point from the FOE, measured in a two-dimensional image, and let V(t) be its velocity dD/dt. The relationship between these quantities and the optical flow parameters is then

$$\frac{D(t)}{V(t)} = \frac{z(t)}{w(t)} \tag{14.18}$$

This formula is a basis for determination of distances between moving objects. Assuming an object moving towards the observer, the ratio z/w specifies the time at which an object moving at a constant velocity w crosses the image plane. Based on the knowledge of the distance of any single point in an image which is moving with a velocity w along the z axis, it is possible to compute the distances of any other point in the image that is moving with the same velocity w

$$z_2(t) = \frac{z_1(t)V_1(t)D_2(t)}{D_1(t)V_2(t)} \tag{14.19}$$

where $z_1(t)$ is the known distance and $z_2(t)$ is the unknown distance. Using the given formulae, relations between real-world co-ordinates x, y and image co-ordinates x', y' can be found related to the observer position and velocity;

$$
\begin{aligned}
x(t) &= \frac{x'(t)w(t)D(t)}{V(t)} \\
y(t) &= \frac{y'(t)w(t)D(t)}{V(t)} \\
z(t) &= \frac{w(t)D(t)}{V(t)}
\end{aligned}
\tag{14.20}
$$

A very practical application is analysis of the motion of a robot in the real world where the optical flow approach is able to detect potential collisions with scene objects. Observer motion – as seen from optical flow representation – aims into the FOE of this motion; co-ordinates of this FOE are $(u/w, v/w)$. The origin of image co-ordinates (the imaging system focal point) proceeds in the direction $s = (u/w, v/w, 1)$ and follows a path in real-world co-ordinates at each time instant defined as a straight line

$$(x, y, z) = ts = t(\frac{u}{w}, \frac{v}{w}, 1) \qquad (14.21)$$

where the parameter t represents time. The position of an observer x_{obs} when at its closest point of approach to some x in the real world is then

$$x_{obs} = \frac{s(s \cdot x)}{s \cdot s} \qquad (14.22)$$

(where scalar product of vectors is implied). The smallest distance d_{min} between a point x and an observer during observer motion is

$$d_{min} = \sqrt{(x \cdot x) - \frac{(x \cdot s)^2}{s \cdot s}} \qquad (14.23)$$

Thus, a circular-shaped observer with radius r will collide with objects if their smallest distance of approach $d_{min} < r$.

The analysis of motion, computation of FOE, depth, possible collisions, time to collision, etc. are all very practical problems. Interpretation of motion is discussed in [Subbarao 88], and motion analysis and computing range from an optical flow map is described in [Albus and Hong 90]. A robust method for extracting dense depth-maps from a sequence of noisy intensity images is described in [Shahraray and Brown 88] and a method of unique determination of rigid body motion from optical flow and depth is given in [Zhuang et al. 88]. Obstacle detection by evaluation of optical flow is presented in [Enkelmann 91]. Time to collision computation from first-order derivatives of image flow is described in [Subbarao 90], where it is shown that higher order derivatives, which are unreliable and computationally expensive, are not necessary. Computation of FOE does not have to be based on optical flow; the spatial gradient approach and a natural constraint that an object must be in front of the camera to be imaged are used in a direct method of locating FOE in [Negahdaripour and Horn 89, Negahdaripour and Ganesan 92].

14.3 Motion analysis based on detection of interest points

The optical flow analysis method can be applied only if the intervals between image acquisitions are very short. Motion detection based on **interest points** works even for time intervals that cannot be considered small enough. Detection of corresponding object points in subsequent images is a fundamental part of this method – if this correspondence is known, velocity fields can easily be constructed (this does not consider the hard problem of constructing a dense velocity field from a sparse correspondence point velocity field).

The first step of the method is to find significant points in all images of the sequence – points least similar to their surrounding, representing object corners or borders, etc. Point detection is followed by a matching procedure, which looks for correspondences between these points. The process results in a sparse velocity field construction.

14.3.1 Detection of interest points

The Moravec operator described in Section 4.3.7 can serve as an interest point detector which evaluates a point significance from a small neighbourhood. Corners play a significant role in detection of interest points; the Kitchen-Rosenfeld and Zuniga-Haralick operators look for object vertices in images (Section 4.3.7, equation (4.72)). The operators are almost equivalent, even if it is possible to get slightly better results applying the Zuniga-Haralick operator where a located vertex must be positioned at an edge pixel. This is represented by a term

$$\frac{1}{\sqrt{c_2^2 + c_3^2}}$$

in the facet model [Haralick and Watson 81]. This assumption has computationally important consequences; significant edges in an edge image can be located first and a vertex function then evaluated at significant edge pixels only, a vertex being defined as a significant edge pixel with a vertex measuring function registering above some threshold.

An optimal detector of corners, which are defined as the junction points of two or more straight line edges, is described in [Rangarajan et al. 89]. The approach detects corners of arbitrary angles and performs well even in noisy images. Another definition of a corner as an intersection of two half-edges oriented in two different directions, which are not 180° apart, is introduced in [Mehrotra and Nichani 90]. In addition to the location of corner points, information about the corner angle and orientation is determined.

These methods detect significant image points whose location changes due to motion, and motion analysis works with these points only. To detect points of interest that are connected with the motion, a difference motion analysis method can be applied to two or more images of a sequence.

14.3.2 Correspondence of interest points

Assuming that interest points have been located in all images of a sequence, a correspondence between points in consecutive images is sought [Ullman 79, Shah and Jain 83].

Many approaches may be applied to seek the optimal correspondence between sets of interest points, and several possible solutions have been presented earlier (Chapters 7 and 9). The graph matching problem, stereo matching, and 'Shape from X' problems treat essentially the same problem.

One method [Barnard 79, Thompson and Barnard 81] is a very good example of the main ideas of this approach: The correspondence search process is iterative and begins with the detection of all potential correspondence pairs in consecutive images. A maximum velocity assumption can be used for potential correspondence detection which decreases the number of possible correspondences, especially in large images. Each pair of corresponding points is assigned a number representing the probability of their correspondence. These probabilities are then iteratively recomputed to get a globally optimum set of pairwise correspondences (the maximum probability of pairs in the whole image, equation 14.29) using another motion assumption – the common motion principle. The process ends if each point of interest in a previous image corresponds with precisely one point of interest in the following image **and**

- The global probability of correspondences between image point pairs is significantly higher than other potential correspondences.

- Or the global probability of correspondences of points is higher than a preselected threshold.

- Or the global probability of correspondences gives a maximum probability (optimum) of all possible correspondences.

Let $A_1 = \{x_m\}$ be the set of all interest points in the first image, and $A_2 = \{y_n\}$ the interest points of the second image. Let c_{mn} be a vector connecting points x_m and y_n (c_{mn} is thus a velocity vector; $y_n = x_m + c_{mn}$). Let the probability of correspondence of two points x_m and y_n be P_{mn}. Two points x_m and y_n can be considered potentially corresponding if their distance satisfies the assumption of maximum velocity

$$|x_m - y_n| \leq c_{max} \qquad (14.24)$$

where c_{max} is the maximum distance a point may move in the time interval between two consecutive images. Two correspondences of points $x_m y_n$ and $x_k y_l$ are termed consistent if

$$|c_{mn} - c_{kl}| \leq c_{dif} \qquad (14.25)$$

where c_{dif} is a preset constant derived from prior knowledge. Clearly, consistency of corresponding point pairs increases the probability that a correspondence pair is correct. This principle is applied in Algorithm 14.3 [Barnard and Thompson 80].

Algorithm 14.3: Velocity field computation from two consecutive images

1. Determine the sets of interest points A_1 and A_2 in images f_1, f_2, and detect all potential correspondences between point pairs $\mathbf{x}_m \in A_1$ and $\mathbf{y}_n \in A_2$.

2. Construct a data structure in which potential correspondence information of all points $\mathbf{x}_m \in A_1$ with points $\mathbf{y}_n \in A_2$ will be stored, as follows

$$[\mathbf{x}_m, (\mathbf{c}_{m1}, P_{m1}), (\mathbf{c}_{m2}, P_{m2}), \ldots, (V^*, P^*)] \qquad (14.26)$$

P_{mn} is the probability of correspondence of points $\mathbf{x}_m$ and $\mathbf{y}_n$, and V^* and P^* are special symbols indicating that no potential correspondence was found.

3. Initialize the probabilities P^0_{mn} of correspondence based on the local similarity – if two points correspond, their neighbourhood should correspond as well;

$$P^0_{mn} = \frac{1}{(1 + kw_{mn})} \qquad (14.27)$$

where k is a constant and

$$w_{mn} = \sum_{\Delta\mathbf{x}}[f_1(\mathbf{x}_m \mid \Delta\mathbf{x}) - f_2(\mathbf{y}_n + \Delta\mathbf{x})]^2 \qquad (14.28)$$

$\Delta\mathbf{x}$ defines a neighbourhood for image match testing – a neighbourhood consists of all points $(\mathbf{x} + \Delta\mathbf{x})$, where $\Delta\mathbf{x}$ may be positive or negative and usually defines a symmetric neighbourhood around $\mathbf{x}$.

4. Iteratively determine the probability of correspondence of a point $\mathbf{x}_m$ with all potential points $\mathbf{y}_n$ as a weighted sum of probabilities of correspondence of all consistent pairs $\mathbf{x}_k\mathbf{y}_l$, where $\mathbf{x}_k$ are neighbours of $\mathbf{x}_m$ and the consistency of $\mathbf{x}_k\mathbf{y}_l$ is evaluated according to $\mathbf{x}_m, \mathbf{y}_n$. A quality q_{mn} of the correspondence pair is

$$q^{(s-1)}_{mn} = \sum_k \sum_l P^{(s-1)}_{kl} \qquad (14.29)$$

where s denotes an iteration step, k refers to all points $\mathbf{x}_k$ that are neighbours of $\mathbf{x}_m$, and l refers to all points $\mathbf{y}_l \in A_2$ that form pairs $\mathbf{x}_k\mathbf{y}_l$ consistent with the pair $\mathbf{x}_m\mathbf{y}_n$.

5. Update the probabilities of correspondence for each two points $\mathbf{x}_m$ and $\mathbf{y}_n$

$$\hat{P}^{(s)}_{mn} = P^{(s-1)}_{mn}\left(a + bq^{(s-1)}_{mn}\right) \qquad (14.30)$$

where a and b are preset constants. Normalize

$$P^{(s)}_{mn} = \frac{\hat{P}^{(s)}_{mn}}{\sum_j \hat{P}^{(s)}_{mj}} \qquad (14.31)$$

6. Iterate (4) and (5) until the best correspondence $\mathbf{x}_m\mathbf{y}_n$ is found for all points $\mathbf{x}_m \in A_1$

7. Vectors $\mathbf{c}_{ij}$ of the correspondence form a velocity field of the analysed motion.

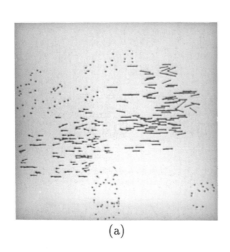
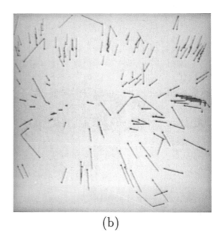

(a)   (b)

Figure 14.8 *Velocity fields: (a) Train sequence, (b) flyover. Courtesy J. Kearney, University of Iowa.*

The velocity field resulting from this algorithm applied to the image pairs given in Figures 14.4a and b and 14.5a and b are shown in Figure 14.8. Note that the results are much better for the train sequence; compare the flyover velocity field with the optical flow results given in Figure 14.5d.

Velocity fields can be applied in position prediction tasks as well as optical flow. A good example of interpretation of motion derived from detecting interest points is given in [Scott 88].

A different method of interest point correspondence detection has been used in the analysis of cardiac wall motion from magnetic resonance images [Fisher 90, Fisher et al. 91], where rigid body motion assumptions could not be used since the human heart is not rigid. Interest points were magnetically applied to the heart using a special magnetic resonance pulse sequence known as SPAMM (spatial modulation of magnetisation). This results in an image with a rectangular grid of markers, see Figure 14.9; heart motion is clearly visible on images if markers are applied. The first step of the motion analysis algorithm is a precise automatic detection of markers. Using a correlation technique (Section 5.4), the exact position of markers is determined (possibly at subpixel resolution), see Figure 14.10.

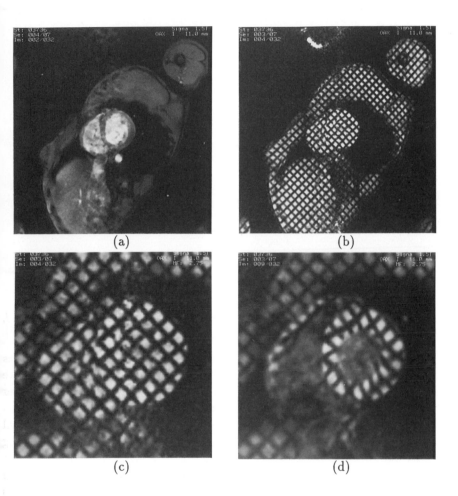

Figure 14.9 *Magnetic resonance image of the heart: (a) Original chest image, diastole, (b) chest image with magnetic resonance markers, diastole, (c) image of the heart with markers, diastole, (d) image with markers, systole. Courtesy D. Fisher, S. Collins, University of Iowa.*

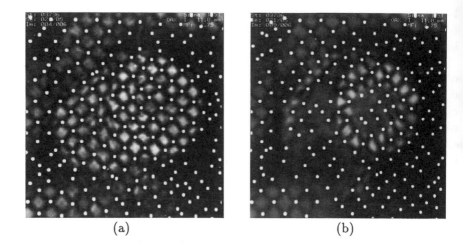

Figure 14.10 *Detected position of markers: (a) Diastole, (b) systole. Courtesy D. Fisher, S. Collins, University of Iowa.*

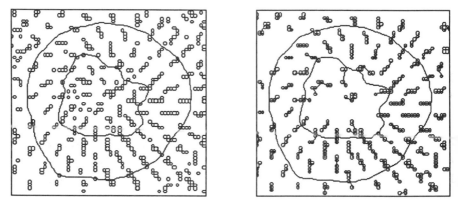

Figure 14.11 *Velocity field: Identified markers (left) and tracked markers (right). Note that the dynamic programming has removed most of the spurious nodes that occur in the centre of the cavity).*

To track the marker locations, specific knowledge about small relative motion of marker positions in consecutive frames is used. Markers are considered as nodes of a two-dimensional graph and dynamic programming is used to determine optimal trajectories (see Section 5.2.5). The optimality criterion is based on distance between markers in consecutive images, on the quality of marker detection, and on consistency of motion direction in consecutive images. Marker quality evaluation results from the marker detection correlation process. Successor nodes are determined by requiring that the trajectory length between successors be less than some specified constant. Identified and tracked markers are illustrated in Figure 14.11, and a resulting velocity field is shown in Figure 14.12.

Another approach to motion analysis of tagged MRI heart images based on left ventricle boundary detection and matching tag templates in expected directions can be found in [Guttmann and Prince 90]. Deformable models can also be applied to analyse 3D motion using tagged MRI heart images as described in [Young and Axel 92]. In [Kambhamettu and Goldgof 92], estimation of point correspondences on a surface undergoing non-rigid motion is based on changes in Gaussian curvature.

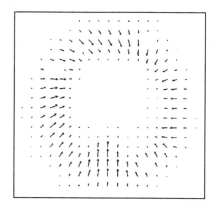

Figure 14.12 *Velocity field derived from the information in Figure 14.11. Courtesy D. Fisher, S. Collins, University of Iowa.*

Many motion-related applications can be found in remote sensing, especially in meteorological satellite data analysis. An example of a **meteotrend** analysis of the cloud motion in both horizontal and vertical directions, and prediction of cloud motion and cloud types is given in Figures 14.13 and 14.14.

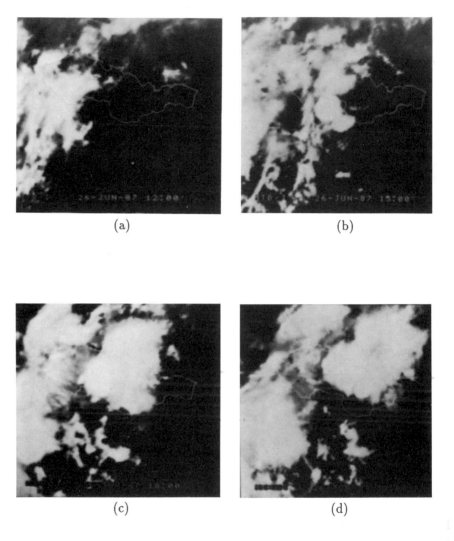

Figure 14.13 *Meteosat image sequence. Courtesy L. Vlcak, D. Podhorsky, Slovak Hydrometeorological Institute, Bratislava.*

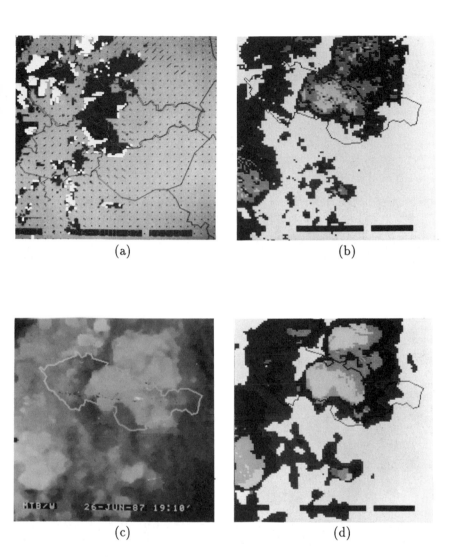

(a) (b)

(c) (d)

Figure 14.14 *Meteotrend: (a) Cloud motion analysis in horizontal and vertical directions, vertical speed coded in colour, (b) cloud type classification, (c) cloud cover (motion) prediction, (d) cloud type prediction. A colour version of a, b and d may be seen in the colour inset. Courtesy L. Vlcak, D. Podhorsky, Slovak Hydrometeorological Institute Bratislava.*

References

[Abdel-Malek et al. 90] A Abdel-Malek, O Hasekioglu, and J Bloomer. Image segmentation via motion vector estimates. In *Medical Imaging IV: Image Processing, Newport Beach, Ca*, pages 366–371, SPIE, Bellingham, Wa, 1990.

[Adiv 89] G Adiv. Inherent ambiguities in recovering 3D motion and structure from a noisy flow field. *IEEE Transactions on Pattern Analysis and Machine Intelligence*, 11(5):477–489, 1989.

[Aggarwal and Martin 88] J K Aggarwal and W Martin. *Motion Understanding*. Kluwer Academic Publishers, Boston, Ma, 1988.

[Aggarwal and Nandhakumar 88] J K Aggarwal and N Nandhakumar. On the computation of motion from sequences of images - a review. *Proceedings of the IEEE*, 76(8):917–935, 1988.

[Albus and Hong 90] J S Albus and T H Hong. Motion, depth, and image flow. In *Proceedings of the 1990 IEEE International Conference on Robotics and Automation, Cincinnati, Oh*, pages 1161–1170, IEEE, Los Alamitos, Ca, 1990.

[Anandan 87] P Anandan. A unified perspective on computational techniques for the measurement of visual motion. In *Proceedings, First International Conference on Computer Vision*, pages 219–230, London, England, 1987.

[Anandan 88] P Anandan. Motion detection and analysis. State of the art and some requirements from robotics. In *Robot Control 1988 (SYROCO '88) - Selected Papers from the 2nd IFAC Symposium*, pages 347–352, Pergamon Press Inc, Karlsruhe, FRG, 1988.

[Barnard 79] S T Barnard. *The Image Correspondence Problem*. PhD thesis, University of Minnesota, 1979.

[Barnard and Thompson 80] S T Barnard and W B Thompson. Disparity analysis of images. *IEEE Transactions on Pattern Analysis and Machine Intelligence*, 2(4):333–340, 1980.

[Barron et al. 92a] J L Barron, D J Fleet, S S Beauchemin, and T A Burkitt. Performance of optical flow techniques. In *Proceedings, 1992 Computer Vision and Pattern Recognition, Champaign, Il*, pages 236–242, IEEE, Los Alamitos, Ca, 1992.

[Barron et al. 92b] J L Barron, D J Fleet, S S Beauchemin, and T A Burkitt. Performance of optical flow techniques. Technical Report TR 299,

Dept. of Computer Science, University of Western Ontario, Canada, 1992.

[Brady 87] J M Brady. Seeds of perception. In *Proceedings of the Third Alvey Vision Conference*, pages 259–267, University of Cambridge, Cambridge, England, 1987.

[Burt et al. 83] P J Burt, C Yen, and X Xu. Multi-resolution flow through motion analysis. In *Proceedings of IEEE CVPR Conference*, pages 246–252, IEEE, Washington, DC, 1983.

[Cafforio and Rocca 83] C Cafforio and F Rocca. The differential method for image motion estimation. In T S Huang, editor, *Image Sequence Processing and Dynamic Scene Analysis*, pages 104–124, Springer Verlag, Berlin, 1983.

[Clocksin 80] W F Clocksin. Perception of surface slant and edge labels from optical flow – a computational approach. *Perception*, 9:253–269, 1980.

[Costabile et al. 85] M F Costabile, C Guerra, and G G Pieroni. Matching shapes: A case study in time–varying images. *Computer Vision, Graphics, and Image Processing*, 29:296–310, 1985.

[Davis et al. 83] L S Davis, Z Wu, and H Sun. Contour based motion estimation. *Computer Vision, Graphics, and Image Processing*, 23:246–252, 1983.

[Dreschler and Nagel 82] L S Dreschler and H H Nagel. Volumetric model and 3D trajectory of a moving car derived from monocular TV frame sequences. *Computer Graphics and Image Processing*, 20:199–228, 1982.

[Enkelmann 88] W Enkelmann. Investigations of multigrid algorithms for the estimation of optical flow fields in image sequences. *Computer Vision, Graphics, and Image Processing*, 43:150–177, 1988.

[Enkelmann 91] W Enkelmann. Obstacle detection by evaluation of optical flow fields from image sequences. *Image and Vision Computing*, 9(3):160–168, 1991.

[Fisher 90] D J Fisher. *Automatic Tracking of Cardiac Wall Motion Using Magnetic Resonance Markers*. PhD thesis, University of Iowa, Iowa City, IA, 1990.

[Fisher et al. 91] D J Fisher, J C Ehrhardt, and S M Collins. Automated detection of noninvasive magnetic resonance markers. In *Computers in Cardiology, Chicago, Il*, pages 493–496, IEEE, Los Alamitos, Ca, 1991.

[Fleet 92] D J Fleet. *Measurement of Image Velocity.* Kluwer Academic Publishers, Norwell, Ma, 1992.

[Fleet and Jepson 90] D J Fleet and A D Jepson. Computation of component image velocity from local phase information. *International Journal of Computer Vision*, 5:77–105, 1990.

[Fogel 88] S V Fogel. A nonlinear approach to the motion correspondence problem. In *Proceedings of the Second International Conference on Computer Vision, Tarpon Springs, Fl*, pages 619–628, IEEE, Piscataway, NJ, 1988.

[Fogel 89] S V Fogel. Implementation of a nonlinear approach to the motion correspondence problem. In *Proceedings, Workshop on Visual Motion*, pages 87–98, IEEE, Irvine, Ca, 1989.

[Girosi et al. 89] F Girosi, A Verri, and V Torre. Constraints for the computation of optical flow. In *Proceedings: Workshop on Visual Motion, Washington, DC*, pages 116–124. IEEE, 1989.

[Glazer 84] F Glazer. Multilevel relaxation in low level computer vision. In Rosenfeld A, editor, *Multiresolution Image Processing and Analysis*, pages 312–330. Springer Verlag, Berlin, 1984.

[Gong 87] S G Gong. *Parallel Computation of Visual Motion.* Master's thesis, Oxford University, England, 1987.

[Gong 88] S G Gong. Improved local flow. In *Proceedings of the Fourth Alvey Vision Conference*, pages 129–134, University of Manchester, Manchester, England, 1988.

[Gong 89] S G Gong. Curve motion constraint equation and its application. In *Proceedings, Workshop on Visual Motion*, pages 73–80, IEEE, Irvine, Ca, 1989.

[Guttmann and Prince 90] M A Guttmann and J L Prince. Image analysis methods for tagged MRI cardiac studies. In *Medical Imaging IV: Image Processing, Newport Beach, Ca*, pages 168–175, SPIE, Bellingham, Wa, 1990.

[Haralick and Watson 81] R M Haralick and L Watson. A facet model for image data. *Computer Graphics and Image Processing*, 15:113–129, 1981.

[Heel 90] J Heel. Dynamic motion vision. *Robotics*, 6(3):297–314, 1990.

[Hildreth 83] E C Hildreth. Computations underlining the measurement of visual motion. *Artificial Intelligence*, 23(3):309–354, 1983.

[Horn 86] B K P Horn. *Robot Vision*. MIT Press, Cambridge, Ma, 1986.

[Horn and Schunk 81] B K P Horn and B Schunk. Determining optical flow. *Artificial Intelligence*, 17:185–204, 1981.

[Huang 83] T S Huang, editor. *Image Sequence Processing and Dynamic Scene Analysis*. Springer Verlag, Berlin, 1983.

[Jain 81] R Jain. Dynamic scene analysis using pixel–based processes. *Computer*, 14(8):12–18, 1981.

[Jain 83] R Jain. Direct computation of the focus of expansion. *IEEE Transactions on Pattern Analysis and Machine Intelligence*, 5(1):58–64, 1983.

[Jain 84] R Jain. Difference and accumulative difference pictures in dynamic scene analysis. *Image and Vision Computing*, 2(2):99–108, 1984.

[Jain et al. 87] R Jain, S L Bartlett, and N O'Brien. Motion stereo using ego–motion complex logarithmic mapping. *IEEE Transactions on Pattern Analysis and Machine Intelligence*, 9(3):356–369, 1987.

[Kambhamettu and Goldgof 92] C Kambhamettu and D B Goldgof. Point correspondence recovery in non-rigid motion. In *Proceedings, IEEE Conference on Computer Vision and Pattern Recognition, Champaign, Il*, pages 222–227, IEEE, Los Alamitos, Ca, 1992.

[Kanatani 85] K I Kanatani. Detecting the motion of a planar surface by line and surface integrals. *Computer Vision, Graphics, and Image Processing*, 29:13–22, 1985.

[Kearney and Thompson 88] J K Kearney and W B Thompson. Bounding constraint propagation for optical flow estimation. In J K Aggarwal and W Martin, editors, *Motion Understanding*. Kluwer Academic Publishers, Boston, Ma, 1988.

[Kearney et al. 87] J K Kearney, W B Thompson, and D L Boley. Optical flow estimation – an error analysis of gradient based methods with local optimization. *IEEE Transactions on Pattern Analysis and Machine Intelligence*, 9(2):229–244, 1987.

[Koenderink 86] J J Koenderink. Optic flow. *Vision Research*, 26(1):161–180, 1986.

[Koenderink and Doorn 75] J J Koenderink and A J Doorn. Invariant properties of the motion parallax field due to the movement of rigid bodies relative to an observer. *Optica Acta*, 22(9):773–791, 1975.

[Lee et al. 89] D Lee, A Papageorgiou, and G W Wasilkowski. Computing optical flow. In *Proceedings, Workshop on Visual Motion*, pages 99–106, IEEE, Irvine, Ca, 1989.

[Lucas and Kanade 81] B Lucas and T Kanade. An iterative image registration technique with an application to stereo vision. In *Proceedings, DARPA Image Understanding Workshop, Washington, D.C.*, pages 121–130, 1981.

[Marr 82] D Marr. *Vision – A Computational Investigation into the Human Representation and Processing of Visual Information*. W.H. Freeman and Co., San Francisco, 1982.

[Mehrotra and Nichani 90] R Mehrotra and S Nichani. Corner detection. *Pattern Recognition Letters*, 23(11):1223–1233, 1990.

[Murray and Buxton 89] D W Murray and B F Buxton. Scene segmentation from visual motion using global optimization. *IEEE Transactions on Pattern Analysis and Machine Intelligence*, 9(2):200–228, 1989.

[Murray and Buxton 90] D W Murray and B F Buxton. *Experiments in the Machine Interpretation of Visual Motion*. MIT Press, Cambridge, Ma, 1990.

[Mutch and Thompson 84] K M Mutch and W B Thompson. Hierarchical estimation of spatial properties from motion. In A Rosenfeld, editor, *Multiresolution Image Processing and Analysis*, pages 343–354, Springer Verlag, Berlin, 1984.

[Mutch and Thomson 85] K M Mutch and W B Thomson. Analysis of accretion and deletion at boundaries in dynamic scenes. *IEEE Transactions on Pattern Analysis and Machine Intelligence*, 7(2):133–137, 1985.

[Nagel 83] H H Nagel. Displacement vectors derived from second order intensity variations. *Computer Vision, Graphics, and Image Processing*, 21:85–117, 1983.

[Nagel 86] H H Nagel. An investigation of smoothness constraints for the estimation of displacement vector fields from image sequences. *IEEE Transactions on Pattern Analysis and Machine Intelligence*, 8(5):565–593, 1986.

[Nagel 87] H H Nagel. On the estimation of optical flow: relations between different approaches and some new results. *Artificial Intelligence*, 33:299–324, 1987.

[Nagel and Enkelmann 84] H H Nagel and W Enkelmann. Towards the estimation of displacement vector fields by oriented smoothness constraint. In *Proceedings of the 7th International Conference on Pattern Recognition*, pages 6–8, Montreal, Canada, 1984.

[Negahdaripour and Ganesan 92] S Negahdaripour and V Ganesan. Simple direct computation of the FOE with confidence measures. In *Proceedings, 1992 Computer Vision and Pattern Recognition, Champaign, Il*, pages 228–233, IEEE, Los Alamitos, Ca, 1992.

[Negahdaripour and Horn 89] S Negahdaripour and B K P Horn. Direct method for locating the focus of expansion. *Computer Vision, Graphics, and Image Processing*, 46(3):303–326, 1989.

[Paquin and Dubois 83] R Paquin and E Dubois. A spatio-temporal gradient method for estimating the displacement field in time-varying imagery. *Computer Vision, Graphics, and Image Processing*, 21:205–221, 1983.

[Radig 84] B Radig. Image sequence analysis using relational structure. *Pattern Recognition*, 17(1):161–168, 1984.

[Rangarajan et al. 89] K Rangarajan, M Shah, and D van Brackle. Optimal corner detector. *Computer Vision, Graphics, and Image Processing*, 48(2):230–245, 1989.

[Rong et al. 89] J H Rong, J L Coatrieux, and R Collorec. Combining motion estimation and segmentation in digital subtracted angiograms analysis. In *Sixth Multidimensional Signal Processing Workshop, Pacific Grove, Ca*, page 44, IEEE, Piscataway, NJ, 1989.

[Sandini and Tistarelli 86] G Sandini and M Tistarelli. Analysis of camera motion through image sequences. In V Cappelini and R Marconi, editors, *Advances in Image Processing and Pattern Recognition*, pages 100–106. North Holland, Amsterdam, 1986.

[Schalkoff 87] R J Schalkoff. Dynamic imagery modelling and motion estimation using weak formulations. *IEEE Transactions on Pattern Analysis and Machine Intelligence*, 9(4):578–584, 1987.

[Schunck 89] B G Schunck. Robust estimation of image flow. In *Sensor Fusion II: Human and Machine Strategies, Philadelphia, Pa*, pages 116–127, SPIE, Bellingham, Wa, 1989.

[Scott 88] G L Scott. *Local and Global Interpretation of Moving Images.* Pitman; Morgan Kaufmann, London; San Mateo, Ca, 1988.

[Sethi and Jain 87] I K Sethi and R Jain. Finding trajectories of feature points in a monocular image sequence. *IEEE Transactions on Pattern Analysis and Machine Intelligence*, 9(1):56–73, 1987.

[Shah and Jain 83] M A Shah and R Jain. Detecting time–varying corners. In *Proceedings of the 7th International Conference on Pattern Recognition*, pages 42–48, Canada, 1983.

[Shahraray and Brown 88] B Shahraray and M K Brown. Robust depth estimation from optical flow. In *Proceedings of the Second International Conference on Computer Vision, Tarpon Springs, Fl*, pages 641–650, IEEE, Piscataway, NJ, 1988.

[Snyder 89] M A Snyder. The precision of 3D parameters in correspondence-based techniques: the case of uniform translational motion in a rigid environment. *IEEE Transactions on Pattern Analysis and Machine Intelligence*, 11(5):523–528, 1989.

[Song and Leahy 91] S M Song and R Leahy. Computation of 3D velocity fields from 3D cine CT images of a human heart. *IEEE Transactions on Medical Imaging*, 10(3):295–306, 1991.

[Subbarao 88] M Subbarao. *Interpretation of Visual Motion: A Computational Study.* Pitman; Morgan Kaufmann, London; San Mateo, Ca, 1988.

[Subbarao 90] M Subbarao. Bounds on time-to-collision and rotational component from first-order derivatives of image flow. *Computer Vision, Graphics, and Image Processing*, 50(3):329–341, 1990.

[Thompson and Barnard 81] W B Thompson and S T Barnard. Lower level estimation and interpretation of visual motion. *Computer*, 14(8):20–28, 1981.

[Thompson and Pong 90] W B Thompson and T C Pong. Detecting moving objects. *International Journal of Computer Vision*, 4(1):39–57, 1990.

[Thompson et al. 83] W B Thompson, K M Mutch, and V A Berzins. Analyzing object motion based on optical flow. In *Proceedings of the 7th International IEEE Conference on Pattern Recognition*, pages 791–194, Canada, 1983.

[Thompson et al. 85] W B Thompson, K M Mutch, and V A Berzins. Dynamic occlusion analysis in optical flow fields. *IEEE Transactions on Pattern Analysis and Machine Intelligence*, 7(4):374–383, 1985.

[Tsai and Huang 81] R Y Tsai and T S Huang. Estimating three-dimensional motion parameters of a rigid planar patch. In *Proceedings of PRIP Conference*, pages 94–97. IEEE, 1981.

[Tsai and Huang 82] R Y Tsai and T S Huang. Uniqueness and estimation of three-dimensional motion parameters of rigid objects with curved surfaces. In *Proceedings of PRIP Conference*, pages 112–118. IEEE, 1982.

[Ullman 79] S Ullman. *The Interpretation of Visual Motion.* MIT Press, Cambridge, Ma, 1979.

[Vega-Riveros and Jabbour 89] J F Vega-Riveros and K Jabbour. Review of motion analysis techniques. *IEE Proceedings, Part I: Communications, Speech and Vision*, 136(6):397–404, 1989.

[Verri et al. 89] A Verri, F Girosi, and V Torre. Mathematical properties of the 2D motion field: From singular points to motion parameters. In *Proceedings: Workshop on Visual Motion, Washington, DC*, pages 190–200. IEEE, 1989.

[Vesecky 88] J F Vesecky. Observation of sea–ice dynamics using synthetic aperture radar images automated analysis. *IEEE Transactions on Geoscience and Remote Sensing*, 26(1):38–48, 1988.

[Waxman and Wohn 85] A M Waxman and K Wohn. Contour evolution, neighbourhood deformation, and global image flow. *The International Journal of Robotics Research*, 4(3):95–108, 1985.

[Waxman et al. 87] A M Waxman, K Behrooz, and S Muralidhara. Closed-form solutions to image flow equations for 3D structure and motion. *International Journal of Computer Vision*, 1:239–258, 1987.

[Webb and Aggarwal 82] J A Webb and J K Aggarwal. Structure from motion of rigid and jointed objects. *Artificial Intelligence*, 19:107–130, 1982.

[Weng et al. 89] J Weng, T S Huang, and N Ahuja. Motion and structure from two perspective views: algorithms, error analysis, and error estimation. *IEEE Transactions on Pattern Analysis and Machine Intelligence*, 11(5):451–476, 1989.

[Wu and Kittler 90] S F Wu and J Kittler. General motion estimation and segmentation. In *Visual Communications and Image Processing '90, Lausanne, Switzerland*, pages 1198–1209, SPIE, Bellingham, Wa, 1990.

[WVM 89] *Proceedings, Workshop on Visual Motion*, Irvine, Ca, 1989. IEEE.

[Yachida et al. 80] M Yachida, M Ikeda, and S Tsuji. A plan guided analysis of cineangiograms for measurment of dynamic behavior of heart wall. *IEEE Transactions on Pattern Analysis and Machine Intelligence*, 2(6):537–543, 1980.

[Young and Axel 92] A Young and L Axel. Non-rigid heart wall motion using MR tagging. In *Proceedings, 1992 Computer Vision and Pattern Recognition, Champaign, Il*, pages 399–404, IEEE, Los Alamitos, Ca, 1992.

[Zheng and Tsuji 90] J Y Zheng and S Tsuji. From anorthoscope perception to dynamic vision. In *Proceedings of the 1990 IEEE International Conference on Robotics and Automation, Cincinnati, Oh*, pages 1154–1160, IEEE, Los Alamitos, Ca, 1990.

[Zhuang et al. 88] X Zhuang, R M Haralick, and Y Zhao. From depth and optical flow to rigid body motion. In *Proceedings - CVPR '88: Computer Society Conference on Computer Vision and Pattern Recognition, Ann Arbor, Mi*, pages 393–397, IEEE, Los Alamitos, Ca, 1988.

Index